VISUAL HISTORY
of the TWENTIETH CENTURY

Text and design copyright © 1999 Carlton Books Limited

CLD 21522

This edition published in 1999 for Colour Library Direct Ltd

Godalming Business Centre

Woolsack Way

Godalming

Surrey

GU7 1XW

A CIP catalogue for this book is available from the British Library

ISBN 1 85868 878 7

EXECUTIVE EDITOR: Sarah Larter
EDITOR: Janice Anderson
MANAGING ART EDITOR: Zoë Mercer
DESIGN: Pauline Hoyle, Jessica Barr
PICTURE RESEARCH: Lorna Ainger, Richard Philpot
PRODUCTION: Alexia Turner

Printed and bound in Italy

VISUAL HISTORY
of the TWENTIETH
CENTURY

FOREWORD BY THE RT. HON. SIR EDWARD HEATH, K.G., M.B.E., M.P.
GENERAL EDITOR: TERRY BURROWS

Colour
Library
Direct

CONTENTS

FOREWORD

"Fellow citizens," said Abraham Lincoln, "we cannot escape history". He was right, but he might have added that we all do ourselves the greatest of favours by acquainting ourselves with as much of it as possible.

Whatever the niceties of the school curriculum may or may not have been during the postwar era, I am repeatedly shocked and disappointed by how little people these days know even of recent history. Often they are acquainted with only the barest bones of their own nation's extraordinary past, and even less of what has occurred beyond these shores. A book such as this is capable of filling an enormous deficit in this respect.

In considering the history of our own century, we have a number of advantages. There is a wealth of documentary evidence; enough to satisfy even the most determined sceptic. We have a tremendous selection of subjective reflections from wise analysts and commentators that we may weigh up alongside the objective evidence. We also have photographs and films.

If a picture is indeed worth a thousand words – or even more – then a book such as this can be of the most enormous benefit. We can see for ourselves the human significance of what might otherwise seem to be abstruse or remote developments, and we can draw our own conclusions by seeing despair or elation, triumph or disaster, etched in the faces of our fellow citizens or made manifest in the world around us. All of this brings home to us why we live as we do, and what opportunities our parents and grandparents had or lacked, took or missed.

We end this century far more advanced across the board compared with the year 1900. Yet there are so many lessons which history can give which are widely ignored. As I write, the century seems destined to end more or less as it began, with bloodshed and turmoil in the Balkans. It is said that a people which ignores the lessons of history is doomed to repeat it. I hope that this book will enable more lessons to be learned, more catastrophes to be avoided – and more people to enjoy lively and informed debates about the many choices that face humanity as we steer our course through life. As a result, we may all have the opportunity of living better lives.

Edward Heath

Rt Hon Sir Edward Heath K.G., M.B.E., M.P.

INTRODUCTION

In 1895 H.G.Wells published his first novel. An immediate success, *The Time Machine* tapped into the fascination that always accompanies the ending of the century milestone, as we look back on how our world has changed, and speculate on our hopes and fears for the century to follow.

Now, over a hundred years later, we are able to see that the most apocalyptic of Wells's predictions did not come to pass – at least in the manner he described them. But imagine for a moment that an ordinary member of the public had been able to use H.G.Wells's magical invention to skip forward to the present day. What would they have made of the changing face of the world that surrounded them? It's no exaggeration to say that the course of the twentieth century has seen radical developments in every imaginable area of human life. But can it be true that the world really has changed almost beyond recognition?

First consider the way that we travel. At the dawn of the twentieth century the most effective form of domestic transport came from the mighty steam locomotives that tore smoke-filled paths between the major cities of the developed world. For international travel, luxury ocean-going liners pandered to the whims of the wealthy, making a journey across the Atlantic as arduous as a week at the Savoy. For most others who sought a globe-trotting way of life there were few opportunities outside of joining the army or navy.

The inventors of the new internal combustion engine were still struggling to make the automobile a practical form of transport. Noisy, unreliable and not much faster than travelling by horse-drawn carriage, our time traveller would have found it hard to imagine that within the course of a century the automobile would move on from an amusing curiosity to become a necessity for most modern-day Westerners.

Most dramatically, it is perhaps hardest to imagine that air travel which we now take for granted was then still one of humankind's last great unconquered milestones. Although hot-air balloons had taken to the skies over a century earlier, mechanical flight was in the earliest throes of experimentation. Indeed, there were still scientists and engineers who declared that the very idea of "heavier-than-air" flight was simply not possible. As we now know, the Wright Brothers proved them wrong during their experiments at Kitty Hawk in 1903. But even the Wrights' most ardent supporters would not have even dared dream that within the space of a few decades, there would be total conquest of the skies and that a man would land on the surface of the Moon and return safely to earth.

Our methods of communication have also leapt forward in the past 100 years. The telephone – patented by Alexander Graham Bell in 1876 – was still something of a novelty at the turn of the century. It wasn't until the 1950s that the ordinary working man could even consider the possibility of such a luxury – if you wanted to communicate with another person you had to do it face-to-face or with pen and paper. If you wanted to know what was going on in the world, the newspaper told you all about it. This process was revolutionized in the 1920s with the advent of wireless radio. But the most influential communication innovation of the century came about from the experiments of a Scottish engineer named John Logie Baird – television. The impact of Baird's discovery on the dynamics of society is incalculable. It now provides viewers with the vast majority of its news and entertainment. While doubters across the decades have scorned "the box" for everything from corrupting family life to turning us away from religion, the "small screen" and its relatives like home computers, the Internet and the worldwide web are now firmly established at the heart of all of our lives.

But for all this technical magnificence, many age-old attitudes have remained in place. The twentieth century continues to prove that when it comes to resolving disputes among ourselves, our proclivity towards taking up arms seems as strong as ever. On two occasions during the course of the last hundred years, devastating war engulfed much of the world. World War One, fought between 1914 and 1918, saw over ten million young men lose their lives in a conflict that had little purpose or ideological meaning. The casualties piled up as outmoded military strategies showed themselves to be willfully inept in the face of increasingly powerful weaponry. Twenty-one years after the "War To End All Wars", Europe geared itself up for a repeat performance. Between 1939 and 1945 the combined Allied forces stood firm against the aggressive expansionism of Germany under the Nazis. World War Two was a pivotal period of the modern age. For six years much of the world was turned upside down. When on August 6, 1945 America detonated an atom bomb on the Japanese city of Hiroshima, instantaneously killing over a quarter-of-a-million people, it was clear that the world could ever be quite the same.

The threat of nuclear annihilation cast a giant shadow over the next 45 years as the two ideologically irreconcilable "Superpowers" – America and the Soviet Union – engaged in a rapid build-up of nuclear arms as a part of an ongoing "Cold War". It was only after the collapse of communism in 1990 that the fear of nuclear nightmare began to subside.

As we enter a new millennium, technological advancement continues at an almost baffling pace. Cable and satellite television lets us watch hundreds of channels at the push of a button. The Internet offers us everyday access to information that even ten years ago would have seemed impossible. Our understanding of the way the human body works continues to grow. The mysteries of the universe slowly unravel, telling us more and more about how life on Earth came to exist. But, as Alfred Lord Tennyson mused, "Knowledge comes but wisdom lingers". In spite of a hundred years of staggering scientific progress, we ought to find it shocking that we have greater faith in the likelihood of one of us walking on the surface of a distant planet over the coming century than in his ability to create a lasting peace in the Middle East, solve the eternal struggles of Northern Ireland, ease the debt-ridden famines of the Third World or bring harmony to the Balkan states. Sadly, it seems tragically inevitable that many of the key historical events of the twenty-first century seem are likely to stem from these perennial conflicts.

1900–09

At the start of the twentieth century, national boundaries and balances of power between the nations of the world looked very different to the present day. Europe was still largely dominated by the two mighty empires of Britain and the recently unified Germany. Although not quite the superpower it had been at peak of its world influence during the previous century – a time when the British Empire spanned almost a third of the globe – the "pink bits on the map" still showed dominance over the Indian sub-continent, Canada and Australasia, as well as extensive interests in the African continent.

In other parts of Europe, the once mighty Hapsburg Empire that had expanded to unify Austria, Hungary as well as much of Poland and the Balkan region was now experiencing decline. The unpredictable "Russian Bear" was on the cusp of drifting into revolution as the harsh, autocratic rule of the Romanov dynasty began to falter. Not for the first time – or last – the sheer physical scale of the Russian Empire would not only provide a natural defence against invaders, but also proved to be its greatest impediment to the foundation of a strong central government.

On the other side of the Atlantic Ocean the United States – by the end of World War One the richest and most powerful nation on Earth – was in the midst of a period of extraordinarily rapid industrial growth. Only forty years earlier the USA had undergone a bitterly divisive civil war that had threatened the very existence of the Union. Now it was poised to take its position at the centre of the world stage.

In the Far East, Japan, only an economic superpower since the 1960s, was still an inward-looking feudal society. It was only toward the end of the nineteenth century that Japan emerged from hundreds of years of self-imposed isolation from much of the outside world. Now war was periodically waged with Russia over influence in China - perhaps the first outward signs of the expansionism that would dominate much of Southeast Asia during World War Two.

In the Middle East, the oil-rich nations of the past forty years were at this time largely undeveloped tribal states. It was during this period that the first signs of Arab nationalism emerged, along with a growing tension between the Arab populations and the Jewish immigrants who had moved to the new Zionist colonies. Conflict arose between Arabs who sought the creation of a permanent Palestinian state, and those who sought the foundation of a permanent Jewish state.

For Great Britain, the twentieth century started with the death of Queen Victoria: a fundamental symbolic change that heralded a gradual progression away from the bleak austerity that characterized her reign. It also saw the British army still engaged in a savage and costly war against the Boers of South Africa. Although ultimately victorious, the war, along with brief skirmishes in Somaliland and India served as distraction from events taking place within Europe – notably the widescale build-up of armaments ordered by Kaiser Wilhelm II of Germany. Throughout the decade, relations between the two mighty states remained fraught, even though few would have predicted that they would wage war on such a devastating scale during the decade that followed.

As far as technological achievement was concerned, the first decade of the century was dominated by the Wright Brothers – first tentative steps toward a mastery of the skies. Although their pioneering manned flight in 1903 lasted only 12 seconds and measured 120 feet from start to finish, it would soon revolutionize transportation. Another innovation that would impact greatly on life throughout the twentieth century was made by an Italian inventor named Gugliemo Marconi. In 1901, Marconi made the first successful transatlantic wireless communication. His work would later form the basis of radio broadcasting and ultimately television, which would become perhaps the most radical development in human communication.

BIRTH OF BRITAIN'S LABOUR MOVEMENT

▲ **Ramsay MacDonald, the first secretary of the Labour Representation Committee.**

The British labour movement took a major step forward in its aim of achieving parliamentary success on February 28, 1900. The Labour Representation Committee (LRC) was established following co–operation between the Independent Labour Party (founded in 1893) and the Trades Union Council (founded in 1868). The first secretary of this body was the Scotsman James Ramsay MacDonald, who had already stood unsuccessfully as a parliamentary candidate in 1894.

The work of social reformers such as Robert Owen and the Chartists during the mid–nineteenth century had already done much to improve the plight of the British worker, but in the 30 years since they had won the right to vote, the movement had been too fragmented to offer a viable alternative to successive governments formed by the Tories (Conservatives) and Whigs (Liberals). The LRC sought to unite the disparate elements that made up the labour movement and to end the widespread antipathy that the working class showed toward a system of government which had largely ignored their interests.

On the far left was the hardline Social Democratic Federation, led by Henry Hyndman. A prominent Marxist, Hyndman in 1881 had published *England For All*, the first socialist document to be produced in Britain since the Chartist era. Although a major influence on other British socialists, Hyndman was disliked by Karl Marx who felt that Hyndman had taken too much credit for his own ideas. Also vocal were the more moderate Fabian Society, a group of intellectuals whose aim was to establish a democratic socialist state through social reform within the law rather than through Marxist revolution.

The LRC formally changed its name to the Labour Party in 1906, but would have to wait a further 18 years for a first brief glimpse of parliamentary power.

THE BOXER REBELLION

May 1900 saw an officially sanctioned uprising among the peasants of northern China. The initiators were a sect known as the *I–ho ch'uan* – literally "fists of righteous harmony". The sect were practitioners of boxing and other physical rituals that they believed gave them extraordinary powers.

The Boxers, as they became known to westerners, had been active since the eighteenth century and their avowed aim was to drive all foreign influence from China. With an increase in foreign aggression in northeast China during the late 1890s, the Boxers came under the influence of Cixi, the ruling Empress Dowager, who encouraged their use as a private militia.

First among the Boxer targets were the Christian missionaries who sought to implement Western values. By May 1900 Boxer armies had massed

► **A group of British officers "inspect" the gates of Peking.**

around Peking and the northern port of Tientsin.

The following month, Cixi ordered that all foreigners be put to death. In Peking, churches and other foreign buildings were razed, Chinese Christians were massacred and the German ambassador, Baron von Ketteler, was slain. Foreign legations faced a siege that lasted until August 14, when a powerful international relief force progressed through Tientsin and onward to the capital where the Boxer armies were overpowered. Although they significantly outnumbered the invading force, with their poor provisions and a lack of armaments, the motley assortment of Boxers and peasants were always doomed to failure.

In spite of the Empress Dowager's decree, the Boxer rebellion was largely confined to northeast China. Imperial governors in southern and central China believed that maintaining a relationship with the rest of the world was crucial to China's development and ignored Peking's anti-foreign stance. They promoted the view among their people that the unrest was not supported by the government, but was merely a localized rebellion.

Hostilities were brought to an end in September 1901 when a treaty was signed in Peking between China and a dozen foreign powers.

◀ **Cavalry from Britain and Germany occupy the "Forbidden City" of Peking following the collapse of the Boxer rebellion.**

A NEW CIVILIZATION

▲ **The throne room of the palace of Knossos, the centrepiece of Sir Arthur Evans's remarkable discovery on the island of Crete.**

On March 19, 1900, the excavations of British archeologist Sir Arthur Evans uncovered one of the most remarkable finds of the ancient world. On the Aegean island of Crete, Evans discovered the ruins of the city of Knossos.

The curator of Oxford University's Ashmolean Museum, Evans had already suggested that the Mycenaean civilization of mainland Greece had originated on Crete. In 1886 he purchased a tract of land near Crete's modern–day capital of Heraklion, which included the site of Knossos. His findings astonished the archeological world, providing clear evidence that a highly developed Bronze Age civilization had thrived on the island between 3000 and 1100BC.

At the heart of the discovery were the ruins of an extraordinary palace with complex winding corridors: according to Greek mythology, this was the home of King Minos, son of Zeus. Indeed, the palace was purported to have contained a labyrinth inhabited by a minotaur – a fabulous monster with the body of a man and the head of a bull.

Knossos, like much of Cretan culture, was decimated around 1450BC following earthquakes linked to the massive eruption of the volcanic island of Thera, an event that may have given birth to the legend of the lost city of Atlantis.

In honour of the mythical king, Evans named this new civilization Minoan. He continued to excavate the site for the next 25 years, the numerous artefacts he unearthed providing crucial new data on the development of civilization. His later work concentrated on attempting to interpret the "Linear B" Minoan script found on over 3,000 clay tablets unearthed at the site. Although unsuccessful at the time of his death in 1941, he laid the groundwork for its eventual encryption by Michael Ventris 11 years later.

THE END OF A MAGNIFICENT ERA

▲ **Queen Victoria, who ascended the throne when she was just 18, photographed at the age of 80, two years before her death.**

January 22, 1901 saw the death of Britain's longest-reigning monarch, Queen Victoria. She was 82 years old.

Victoria acceded to the throne in 1837, following the death of her uncle, King William IV. Although William had fathered a number of illegitimate children, the two daughters of his marriage had died in infancy.

Born on May 24, 1819, at Kensington Palace, London, Alexandrina Victoria was the only child of Edward, Duke of Kent. Her father died a year after her birth and a dominant figure of her early life was her uncle Leopold, later King of the Belgians.

Early in her reign Victoria enjoyed a close relationship with the Whig Prime Minister, Lord Melbourne. He remained her principal political influence until she married her cousin, Prince Albert of Saxe-Coburg-Gotha, in 1840. At a time when the sovereign still played a decisive role in everyday affairs of state, Albert emerged as one of the key figures of nineteenth–century British politics. Stricken with grief at Albert's premature death in 1861, the Queen never fully recovered from her loss and the years that followed were marked by a personal austerity.

Victoria's reign was contradictory in that although she always sought an active role in running the country and its empire, hers was an era that saw a gradual shift towards an increasingly neutered "figurehead" monarch. Popular among her subjects, Victoria's greatest legacy may well have been that, following the tainted reigns of George IV and William IV, she brought a level of dignity and respectability to the monarchy that would allow this somewhat anachronistic establishment to thrive in the democratic twentieth century.

A passionate and strong-willed woman to the very end, Victoria's death was accompanied by an unprecedented level of public mourning.

▲ **Thousands of mourners pay their final respects to Queen Victoria as the funeral cortege passes along The Mall.**

DAWN OF THE RADIO AGE

The first ever transatlantic telegraphic transmission was successfully made on December 12, 1901, by the physicist Guglielmo Marconi.

Marconi had begun his experiments in his native Bologna, Italy in 1894 where he successfully transmitted signals to a receiver 3 km (2 miles) away. After failing to interest the Italian Government in his work he moved to England where he won the support of Sir William Peace, the Postmaster General. By the end of the century

▲ **Guglielmo Marconi gives a demonstration of his pioneering wireless telegraphy apparatus.**

Marconi had patented his idea and successfully managed a 50-km (30-mile) transmission across the English Channel.

Marconi still had his doubters, some scientists believing that the curvature of the Earth would limit the distance over which transmissions could be made. Marconi proved them wrong when a signal sent from a 50-metre (164-ft) transmitter in Poldhu, Cornwall was received across the Atlantic Ocean in St Johns, Newfoundland – a distance of 3,500 km (2,232 miles).

Marconi's work played a crucial role in the development of radio communications over the next 50 years.

DEATH OF A PRESIDENT

William McKinley, the 25th president of the United States, died on September 14, 1901, following an attempt on his life eight days earlier. McKinley had been visiting the Pan-American Exposition in Buffalo, New York when he was shot by Leon Czolgosz, a Polish-born anarchist. McKinley was the third US president to be assassinated.

After serving under Colonel Rutherford B Hayes during the Civil War, McKinley enjoyed a distinguished legal career before entering Congress in 1877. A staunch Republican, McKinley made his mark nationally in 1890 following the introduction of the "McKinley Tariff", a policy that sought to protect US industry and commerce from overseas competition by increasing import duties to an unprecedented level.

Winning the Republican

▲ President William McKinley led the United States during a period of unprecedented economic growth and prosperity.

nomination in 1896, McKinley became president after defeating Democrat–Populist candidate William Jennings Bryan. During his first term in the White House, McKinley was the guiding hand behind the first major wave of US global imperialism, a period which saw the acquisition of territories such as Hawaii and, following the Spanish–American War in 1898, the Philippines and Puerto Rico.

The general level of prosperity enjoyed by most Americans in the last years of the nineteenth century made McKinley very popular. It came as little surprise when the 1900 election saw him voted in for a second term of office with a huge majority. Inaugurated in March 1901, McKinley had been in office only six months. He was succeeded by his vice president, the young progressive, Theodore "Teddy" Roosevelt.

INTELLECTUAL GIANTS AWARDED

During his lifetime, the Swede Alfred Bernhard Nobel (1833–1896) had found wealth and fame as a chemist, engineer and industrialist, his fortune founded on the invention of the explosive dynamite. However, it is for an extraordinary legacy that he will ultimately be remembered. Nobel's will outlined the creation of a trust fund to finance a series of annual awards given to those who, in his own words, "during the preceding year, shall have conferred the greatest benefit on mankind."

In all, five awards were to be made in the categories of physics, chemistry, physiology or medicine, literature and peace (a sixth, economics, was added in

1969). The first Nobel Prizes were awarded on December 10, 1901. Among the noted recipients were Wilhelm Röntgen, the physicist who discovered X–rays, Jean Henri Dunant, the founder of the Red Cross movement, and author Sully Prudhomme.

The Nobel prizes are now the most highly regarded of all intellectual awards and recipients have included eminent scientists Pierre and Marie Curie, Max Planck, Albert Einstein and Linus Pauling. Literary giants similarly honoured have been Rudyard Kipling, William Butler Yeats, Ernest Hemingway and Albert Camus. It is, however, the annual award for peace for which the name Nobel has become the most widely recognized.

▲ Swedish industrialist Alfred Bernhard Nobel, the founder of the most prestigious awards for human achievement.

END OF AN EMPIRE BUILDER

On March 26, 1902, Cecil Rhodes, the towering figure of the British imperial presence in Africa, died.

Rhodes was born in 1853 in Bishop's Stortford, Hertfordshire. His early ambitions had shown a leaning towards law or the clergy, but his early education was seriously impeded by a lung condition. At the age of 17 he joined his brother in South Africa. Together, they gravitated towards Kimberley, the world's diamond mining capital. Over the next decade Rhodes accrued considerable wealth in South Africa while intermittently returning to England to complete his studies at Oxford. Rhodes continually expanded his claims, and by 1890 the company he founded, De Beers Consolidated Mines, was believed to own over 90 per cent of the world's diamond deposits.

Above all, however, Rhodes was a man of the Empire. His dream was to see an African continent unified under British rule. During the 1880s he became actively engaged in the politics of the

▲ **Cecil Rhodes, the relentless imperialist who sought an African continent under British rule.**

region. At his behest the British South Africa Company was formed with a government charter to create a new territory and extend British control to the north, encourage trade and colonization and to secure mineral deposits. In 1890 his "Pioneers" marched

northwards through Matabeleland, establishing a base they named Salisbury, after the current British prime minister. Five years later this territory was formally renamed Rhodesia.

In 1890 Rhodes became Prime Minister of the Cape Colony. A dictatorial figure, his rule was dominated by a fierce personal rivalry with Paul Kruger, president of the Transvaal. His political downfall came in December 1995 when he tacitly authorized the disastrous Jameson Raid, an attempt to invade the Transvaal that did much to damage the already fractious relationship between the two states.

Cecil Rhodes died with a considerable fortune to his name. Much of this was channelled into setting up Rhodes Scholarships, which continue to offer gifted students from outside Great Britain the opportunity to study at Oxford University. Among the recipients of this award have been US President Bill Clinton.

THE SOUTH AFRICAN WAR

The signing of the Peace of Vereening in Pretoria on May 31, 1902, brought an end to the costly hostilities between Britain and the two independent Boer states of Southern Africa. The outcome saw both the Transvaal (South African Republic) and the Orange Free State placed under British administration.

Conflict began on October 11, 1899, ostensibly a result of the Transvaal President Paul Kruger's refusal to grant full citizenship

◄ **Thousands gather around London's Mansion House to celebrate Britain's victory over the Boers in South Africa.**

rights to Uitlanders – the non-Afrikaner (largely British) immigrants, many of whom had come to the region to prospect for gold. Matters were made worse by the aggressive and uncompromising stance of Alfred Milner, the British governor of the Cape Colony. Although the region was widely viewed as one of the less significant parts of the British Empire, the Transvaal's gold mines made it an attractive proposition for take-over.

Following a declaration of war, the Boer forces quickly capitalized on an undermanned British army's fallibility in hostile terrain. Attacking from their own territories, advances were made from the Transvaal into Natal and into the Northern Cape from Orange Free State – the latter aided by an anti-British rebellion in the region. The Boer successes peaked in December 1899 with "black week", during which British forces sustained major defeats in the towns of Ladysmith, Mafeking and Kimberley.

British fortunes gradually turned as reinforcements arrived and by the start of 1900 almost half a million troops could be called upon to engage barely 80,000 Boers. Under the ruthless leadership of Earl Kitchener the Boer armies were beaten back and by June 1900 the British had taken Johannesburg and Pretoria. For almost 18 months depleted Boer forces continued to carry out bold, destructive commando raids on British bases, but Kitchener's brutal war of attrition eventually forced them into submission.

Ultimately, the war proved to be a costly distraction for the British; while they were waging war in South Africa, a wide-spread military build-up was taking place in Germany and Central Europe.

THE TAMING OF THE NILE

▲ **The 1.6-km (1-mile) long Aswan Dam crossing the River Nile revolutionized agriculture and the production of energy in Egypt.**

As long as there has been civilization in Egypt, the lifeblood of the nation has been the River Nile. Stretching a total length of 6,741 km (4,187 miles), it rises in the heart of the African continent and flows to the north-east before draining into the Mediterranean Sea. Each year, the Nile waters begin to rise in May, reaching their maximum height in the late summer floods. This irregular supply of water always posed a major problem for Egyptian farmers, who, at the start of the twentieth century, still largely used traditional irrigation techniques developed during the time of the pharaohs.

A partial solution to this problem was the development of a dam 1.6-km (1-mile) long at Aswan, 965 km (600 miles) south of Cairo. As the Nile flooded, water passed through 180 sluices which, when shut off, trapped the water behind the 40-metre (130-ft) walls of the dam. When the flood subsided there would remain a massive artificial lake covering an area of almost 320 km (200 miles). The water impounded could be slowly released throughout the year, providing irrigation for arid land that would otherwise be impossible to cultivate.

Completed on December 10, 1902, the first Aswan dam was a major feat of engineering for its time, taking a workforce of 11,000 almost four years to complete. The dam helped to take Egypt's economy far in advance of other African states, revolutionizing agriculture and later being used to generate hydro-electric power.

THE NEW AMERICANS

▲ **The national registry hall on Ellis Island saw a mix of cultures from around the globe all hoping for a new life in the United States.**

The United States had traditionally been seen as the immigrant's friend. But by the early 1900s, the flood of new citizens through the major ports, such as Ellis Island in Upper New York Bay, was beginning to cause tensions with the established communities there.

Called "the new immigration", this new wave of people came from Italy and Greece, from what had once been the Austro-Hungarian empire and from the grim ghettos of Poland. As the US became more of a melting pot, it wasn't just the sheer volume of new arrivals – almost a million a year by 1903 – that was the problem. The situation was made much more serious by a clash of beliefs. Americans were predominantly Protestant, while many of the new wave of immigrants were

▲ **A young German family arrive at Ellis Island. The majority of the "new immigrants" hailed from Central Europe.**

Catholics and Jews, who came from ever-widening areas of Europe. Eventually, the foreign-language publications with the biggest circulations in America were in Yiddish, out-numbering even those in German.

As the numbers of immigrant workers grew, the conditions they lived in worsened. Many were illiterate and were crowded into tenements in the largest cities. As a consequence, the relationship between the wealthier inhabitants of the cities and these new Americans became more and more strained.

In early March 1903, Congress signalled its determination to resolve the dilemma when it passed a bill taxing each new immigrant $2 on arrival. The same law also refused admission entirely to certain groups: the new European immigrants often came from a tradition of anti-governmental feeling. Anarchists were singled out for exclusion from entry – indeed it was an anarchist who assassinated President McKinley in 1901 – as were criminals, those judged insane and polygamists. It was a major policy change for a nation that had been famed for accepting all who had applied for residency up until this point.

BULGARIAN MASSACRE

Revolt and unrest characterized 1903 in the Balkans. By the autumn the response to demands for freedom from Turkish rule in the Macedonian area had ended in vengeance.

The twentieth century was to be scattered with the bloody results of ancient feuds in the Slavic nations. In 1903, it was the Internal Macedonian Revolutionary Organization (IMRO,) whose claim that the people of Macedonia were neither Bulgars nor Serbs but a distinct nation, which led to a series of revolts in the area.

A small village near Monastir was the subject of a savage Bulgarian attack in April, followed by a bombing raid on official Turkish buildings in Salonika. The following month, Italian and Austrian warships were sent to Salonika to help the Turks put down the uprising and in September an Hungarian steamer was blown up by the rebels, killing 29 passengers and crew.

The IMRO, whose slogan was "Macedonia for the Macedonians", had planned to throw off what they saw as their oppressors in a revolt at the beginning of August that was to be called "The St Elijah's Day Uprising". A Turkish army sent to quell the disturbance was more than adequate for the task, but as the weeks went by it became clear that the real aim of the army was retaliation. Many outrages against humanity were committed over the course of the year, culminating in a massacre of thousands of Bulgars in the area of Monastir in September. The Turkish troops destroyed the town of Kastoria, killing 10,000. That same month the great European powers were urged to intervene in the situation. The response to the rebellion had been a brutal one, as no village in the area was left untouched in a sweeping attack against ordinary people.

▶ **Revolutionary Macedonian troops organize themselves in their fight against the oppression of Turkish rule.**

DEATH OF AN IMPRESSIONIST

Although he was a resident in the Marquesas Islands in the South Pacific when he died on May 8, 1903, the artist Paul Gauguin was French, born in Paris on June 7, 1848.

He had no formal artistic training, learning about art through the collection of his guardian, who also helped Gauguin obtain a job as a stockbroker. Gauguin was introduced to the Impressionists, the school of artists which strived to capture life as an experience, rather than an emotional or imaginative response, by the artist Camille Pissarro and eventually exhibited with them.

Gauguin developed his style of Impressionism throughout the 1880s, while at the same time enduring a troubled personal life. He lost his job in a stock market crash, his marriage broke up and eventually he moved to the French countryside with his son.

By 1888, Gauguin had reached stylistic maturity, breaking with Impressionism with the powerful *Vision After the Sermon: Jacob Wrestling with the Angel*, depicting Jacob – unusually – on the same plane as the real people in the painting. Later that year, Gauguin

▲ **Paul Gauguin as seen through the eyes of the artist. This self-portrait, which Gauguin called** *Golgotha,* **was painted in 1896.**

stayed with van Gogh in Arles, exchanging ideas. But van Gogh's mental health was deteriorating and on December 23 he threatened his guest with a razor blade before cutting off his own left ear.

Restless, Gauguin returned to Paris. His art was moving toward a symbolism imbued with spiritual resonance and a contrast between savage innocence and knowledge. In 1891, he went to Tahiti, of which he declared, "After the disease of civilization, life in this new world is a return to health."

Gauguin returned to Paris to find his popularity had waned and he departed for Tahiti again in 1895. Just two years later, he learned of the death of his daughter, part of the inspiration for his painting *Where Do We Come From? What Are We? Where Are We Going?* Shortly after, he attempted suicide.

He moved to Hua Oa in 1901, where he found inspiration in the primitive world. His influence was to spread through a wide range of artists in the twentieth century.

'03

NEWS IN BRIEF

June
- King Alexander I and Queen Draga of Serbia murdered
- Ford Motor Company formed

July
- Discussions between France and Britain leading to the Entente Cordiale
- Pope Leo XIII dies; Patriarch of Venice, Giuseppe Sarto, chosen to succeed him, as Pius X
- Japan protests at Russian failure to leave Manchuria
- Death of US painter James McNeill Whistler

August
- Details of atrocities in the Balkans begin to emerge
- Colombian government refuses to ratify the Panama Canal agreement
- Death of former British Prime Minister, Lord Salisbury

September
- More than 50,00 Bulgarians massacred by Turks in Macedonia
- US state of Massachusetts issues the first car licence plates
- King Peter I of Serbia elected
- Major cabinet reshuffle in Britain provoked by disagreements over foreign trade policy
- Alfred Deakin becomes second Prime Minister of Australia

CHURCH AND STATE CLASH IN FRANCE

Over the course of the year, the Roman Catholic church in France watched as its power steadily eroded. Together with the army, it was curbed by a centre-left government that was suspicious of these influential bodies.

The clash had its roots partly in the controversy over a trial of one man, an officer named Dreyfus. Ten years previously he had been charged with selling secrets to Germany and was sent to Devil's Island. There was doubt about his guilt and a suggestion that, as a Jew, he was being singled out for religious reasons. On retrial in 1899, while he was again found guilty, he was this time pardoned. Army documents against him were found to have been forged, but it was not just the military's image that suffered. The affair had dragged on for many bitter years and the Roman Catholic church's reputation was also damaged, as

▲ **Alfred Dreyfus, court-martialled and convicted as a German spy but pardoned by President Loubet of France in 1901.**

its fight to keep him imprisoned fuelled the talk of anti-Semitism.

It seemed clear to many that those in positions of power in the old institutions would have been happy for a wronged man to stay imprisoned in order to maintain the *status quo*. But a new administration signalled a change of emphasis. A coalition which would become known as "Socialist Radicals" came to power in 1899 and within four years were dismantling the instruments of church authority. In March 1903, religious groups found that their requests for teaching positions were turned down, a move welcomed by teachers at a congress in Marseilles on August 5. The Catholic orders themselves were dissolved by the government.

The Roman Catholic church expressed its outrage, in certain cases through non-cooperation or even violence. But change was inevitable: within two years, most religious orders were dissolved and exiled, with new laws separating church and state.

THE FIRST LADY OF SCIENCE

In December 1903 Marie Curie became the first woman to win a Nobel prize. The award was given jointly to Curie and two fellow scientists, her husband Pierre, and Henri Becquerel.

Although she worked for most of her life in France and her husband was French, Curie's roots were in Poland, where she was born Maria Słodowska in Warsaw on July 11, 1867. Even

▶ **Marie Curie, the first woman to be awarded a Nobel Prize. She later became the first female professor at the Sorbonne.**

as a child she had a phenomenal memory and began her career as a teacher. She moved to France in 1891, working hard while subsisting on bread and butter.

In 1895 she married Pierre Curie. Together with Becquerel, they worked on the phenomenon in which Marie Curie would have particular interest and which she named "radioactivity". The couple's pioneering work in the field included the discovery of polonium, an element she named after her native country, and, most important of all, the highly radioactive element, radium.

Marie Curie had a huge influence on the scientists who followed her in the twentieth century, including her own daughter, Irene, who would, with her own husband, win a Nobel Prize for her work with radioactivity in 1935. And although Curie would herself go on, in what would be another first for a woman, to take the professor's chair at the Sorbonne in Paris following the death of Pierre Curie in 1906, her popular fame stretched far further than the fields of science. Perhaps it was due to the applications her work had in the search for a cure for cancer, or perhaps it was the way she proved that a woman could scale academic heights just as well as any man. In 1911, Curie was awarded an unprecedented second Nobel prize for her work.

TOUR DE FRANCE BEGINS

In order to promote and attract readers from a rival publication, the proprietor of the French newspaper *L'Auto,* Henri Desgrange, announced a new cycle race in January 1903, the *Tour de France*.

The rival paper, *Le Velo,* sponsored what were then the biggest cycle races in France: the Bordeaux–Paris and the Paris–Brest. Desgrange, himself a cyclist who had set records in the sport, devised a race that featured 60 riders over 2,500 kilometres (1,500 miles). The race began on July 1, took 19 days and comprised six stages, travelling from Paris via Lyon, Bordeaux and Nantes, for a total prize fund of 20,000 francs. It was an arduous race, the basic format of which has changed little since its inception, and was even then only for those with a fanatical dedication to finishing the testing course. Only 21 riders made it to the end of this first race.

The super-fit, pioneer riders were identified by armbands and red badges. They had heavy cycles equipped with just one front brake which worked by

▲ **Riders in the 1907 Tour de France brings life in a French town to a standstill as they sweep through.**

pressing directly against the front tyre. In the early days of the race, the riders had no support crew and the longer stages were raced by night. Of the tough enthusiasts, a former chimney-sweep named Maurice Garin was the winner, almost three hours ahead of the second-placed rider. Aside from the honour, Garin also won 3,000 francs.

There was no guarantee for the original promoters that the venture would be a success until the race was over. Yet even though this was the same year that the first Harley-Davidson motorcycle purred on to the road, the *Tour de France* was to find a permanent place in the hearts of sports fans all over the world. And, although not without its fair share of controversy, occasional doubts about its future, and even drug-taking allegations against some competitors, the *Tour de France* has certainly retained its place as the twentieth century's greatest cycling event.

October
- Demarcation of the Alaskan frontier between USA and UK
- Austria and Russia agree on reform in Macedonia

November
- Russian Social Democratic Party splits into Mensheviks and Bolsheviks
- British War Office begins reorganization of the armed forces
- Panama secedes from Colombia
- China moves more than 10,000 troops into Manchuria
- Death of French painter Camille Pissarro

December
- USA-Panama treaty is signed, giving USA control over Panama Canal Zone
- French Congo divided into four districts – Gabon, Chad, Ubangi-Shanti and Middle Congo
- More than six hundred die in theatre fire in Chicago
- Wilbur and Orville Wright's *Flyer* makes first heavier-than-air flight
- Marie and Pierre Curie and Henri Becquerel win the Nobel Prize for Physics.

THE BIRTH OF THE AIR AGE

Epic adventures of men, animals and gods and their quest for flight have played a role in the mythology, art and religions of numerous civilizations. The legendary Chinese prince, Ki Kung-shi flew in a chariot; the Persian king Kai Ka'us, on a throne. In Roman mythology Mercury was the winged messenger of the gods. Most famous of all, perhaps, is the Greek legend of Icarus who fashioned a pair of wings from wax but perished when they melted as he soared too close to the sun. Since earliest times the desire to fly has been within us.

Many of man's early flight fantasies revolved around attempts to simulate mechanically the actions of birds and other creatures of flight. Thus it may have seemed surprising that man first left *terra firma* via the means of "lighter-than-air" transport, pioneered by the Frenchmen Joseph-Michel and Jacques-Étienne Montgolfier, who launched the first ever manned hot-air balloon in October 1783. Magnificent achievement as this was, although altitude could be controlled, for direction the pilot largely remained at the mercy of the winds. Man may have taken to the skies, but he could not lay claim to being their conqueror.

It was over a century later that the first "heavier-than-air" design made its first flight. The greatest of the early aeronautical pioneers was the German engineer Otto Lilienthal. The inventor of the glider, Lilienthal made over 2000

▲ **Wilbur Wright in the air at Kitty Hawk in 1902. His brother, Orville, piloted the first flight.**

successful flights in his aircraft. Both his work and writing – in particular the book *Der Vogelflug als Grundlage der Fliegekunst* (*The Flight of the Bird as a Basis for the Art of Flying*) – were major inspirations for the next generation of pioneers. Among them, two American bicycle makers based in Dayton, Ohio, Orville and Wilbur Wright, had been intrigued to read about his exploits. It was the news of Lilienthal's death in a glider accident in August 1896 that provided the impetus for the brothers to make their own groundbreaking experiments.

The Wright Brothers aimed to produce the first powered and totally controllable means of air transport. Initial work began in October 1900 when they built their own biplane glider. The design was based largely on Lilienthal's calculations on the wing surface area required to lift the overall weight of the glider and the "warping" of the wing.

Following advice from the US Weather Bureau, they relocated from Dayton to Kitty Hawk in North Carolina, where there were hills from which their aircraft could be launched, high stable winds and soft sand dunes on which a landing could be made. The initial flight was a disappointment, the glider failing to lift as high as their calculations had led them to believe. A second glider

was built and flown a year later, this time with an increased wing span and overall surface area. Although the improvement was not as marked as they had hoped, Wilbur Wright nonetheless was able to pilot the glider over a 122-metre (400-ft) flight.

It was perhaps the reaction to failure that mark the Wright Brothers out as visionary pioneers. Instead of continuing

▲ **The triumph at Kitty Hawk brought the Wright brothers worldwide fame. Here, with tuxedos and top hats, they receive medals in the USA.**

with unsatisfactory full-scale experiments, they chose instead to construct a large wind tunnel that enabled them to measure carefully the forces acting on different types of wing construction. In all, almost 200 different models were created, and data was collated on a wide variety of designs. Although this interrupted their practical experimentation for almost a year, when they built their third glider in October 1902 the test flight performed precisely as the model in the wind tunnel had done six months earlier. As well as mastering the aerodynamic issues, their latest glider also featured a significant mechanical innovation – a vertical rudder linked to wing mechanism. This gave the pilot a greater degree of control. The brothers made an estimated 800 test flights using this glider, gradually fine-tuning its performance.

The Wright Brothers were now ready to make the final step on their journey towards developing the first powered aircraft. Together with Charles Taylor, an engineer they had earlier employed in their bicycle workshop, they developed a lightweight 25-horsepower engine. This would be used to rotate a propeller which would power the aircraft.

Meanwhile, Wilbur Wright had been invited by US aeronaut Octave Chanute – himself a significant influence on the brothers' work – to address the Western Society of Engineers. Gradually the US scientific establishment began to take an interest in the goings-on at Kitty Hawk. However, controversy still raged on the matter of man taking to the skies. Indeed, noted

mathematician Professor Simon Newcomb of John Hopkins University published his own proof that powered heavier-than-air flight was an impossibility.

Undeterred, after two months in Kitty Hawk engaged in preparation and testing, on December 14, 1903, Wilbur Wright made the first attempt at powered flight. Unfortunately, the machine stalled while attempting to take off and the damage sustained took three days to repair.

The great breakthrough came at 10:35 a.m. on December 17, 1903, when after powering up the engine, Orville Wright took the aircraft a distance of approximately 40 metres (120 ft) in a flight lasting 12 seconds. During the course of the day the brothers made three further flights, concluding when Wilbur Wright sustained a flight for

59 seconds, covering a distance of 260 metres (850 ft).

As modest as these first successes may now seem, the extraordinary achievements of the

Wright brothers signalled the true beginning of the air age. It would prove to be one of the greatest of the many scientific revolutions of the twentieth century.

▶ An undated photograph of Orville Wright (left) and his brother Wilbur (right).

RUSSIA AND JAPAN AT WAR

The dispute between Russia and Korea over their imperial ambitions in Manchuria and Korea spilled over into fighting in 1904. The conflict had been brewing for some time, with its roots dating back to the nineteenth century.

In 1896, an alliance with China had won Russia the right to extend the Trans–Siberian railway across Chinese Manchuria to Vladivostock. Two years later, Russia pressurized China to grant a lease for Port Arthur in southern Manchuria. Japan was unhappy about this expansion of Russia's powers and negotiations over Manchuria and Korea broke down when Japan ceased its diplomatic contact with Russia in February 1904.

The attitude of Russia through-out diplomatic discussions had made it clear that the power felt secure about the outcome of any conflict, and the fall of one of the Tsar's few responsible men, the finance minister Sergei Witte, only exacerbated an already volatile situation. Tsar Nicholas II and many of his ministers felt that a successful war would focus attention away from the many internal problems Russia was suffering.

On the night of February 8, Japan showed that it was a more powerful force than the Russians believed, when a large part of the Japanese fleet made a surprise attack on Russian forces in Port Arthur. With no formal declaration of war, the Russians – showing the lack of good communication, strong leadership and will for a lengthy conflict that would charac-terize their war – reacted in confusion and Japan made deci-sive use of the turmoil and quickly landed troops in Korea. Within three weeks the Japanese

▲ Japanese troops of the 30th Regiment prepare to rebel the advancing Russian forces near Liao Yang.

were at the Yalu river, close to the border of Manchuria. Russia received no aid from other powers; indeed, earlier in the month, the governments of both Britain and the USA expressed their neutrality in the conflict. Korea's sovereignty was guaran-teed by Japan, in return for military help against Russia, whose gains in the country were effectively neutralized.

On February 10, the two countries made official declarations of war. At the time, no Asian power had beaten a European power in a modern conflict; this situation was to change within a year.

As February progressed, Russia's naval forces failed to

make any impact on the Japanese. Throughout February, repeated attacks were made on Port Arthur, the Japanese scuttling ships to block the harbour mouth as the Russian forces continued to weaken. It was May before Japan suf-fered any losses to its fleet with the mining of a torpedo boat off Kerr Bay and the loss of a battleship.

It was a pattern that was repeated over the course of the war; Russia was able to play something of a waiting game and make some gains over its enemy, but the Japanese action was cer-tainly superior. By early March, Vladivostock itself would be the subject of Japanese bombs.

BRITISH MILITARY ACTION IN TIBET

Tibet, a mountainous landscape between India and China was virtually independent by 1900. In July 1903, British forces sent a

military expedition to the region in order to investigate reports of a Russian presence there. The action took advantage of Russia's involvement in conflict with Japan and was intended to curb their ambitions in the area.

The British force set out from India under the command of Sir Francis Younghusband (1836–1942) with the intention of reaching the sacred capital of Tibet, Lhasa. Once there, they forced Tibet's spiritual leader, the Dalai Lama, to grant Britain trading posts in the country and not to concede territory to other foreign powers.

In March 1904, British troops under Brigadier General Macdonald encountered over two thousand Tibetan soldiers on the Guru road. Although the defenders put up a strong battle, they were no match for the superior arms of the enemy and soon found themselves outflanked and outmanoeuvred. Tibetan losses reached 300, including one of their generals and the road to Guru was cleared.

Within six months, the British forces reached the Lhasa and Tibetan leaders acceded to their demands. Despite Britain's declared aim of preventing Russian incursions into Tibet, no Russian forces were actually encountered during this campaign.

▲ **Brigadier General MacDonald of the British expedition forces the Tibetan lamas to provide grain for his troops.**

AGREEMENT BETWEEN FRANCE AND BRITAIN

▲ **Pierre Paul Cambon, the French ambassador to Great Britain and one of the signatories of the "entente cordiale".**

The phrase *"entente cordiale"*. came into common use with the agreement signed by France and Britain on April 8, 1904 that resolved the differences between the two nations, bringing them closer together.

The term was actually first used in the 1840s to describe a friendly period between the two powers but the 1904 agreement was also indicated Britain's move away from isolation following the Boer War. The agreement was a great progression from the atmosphere of autumn 1898, when a colonial dispute in Africa brought France and Great Britain to the brink of war at Fashoda in the Sudan.

The 1904 agreement changed much between the two nations: fishing rights in Newfoundland were settled as were ongoing territorial disputes – Britain relinquished parts of West Africa, and maintained control of Egypt; while France was given access to the Suez Canal and a free hand in Morocco, effectively ending

▲ **Lord Landsdowne, Henry Charles Keith Petty-Fitzmaurice, Britain's Foreign Secretary during the negotiations with France.**

that country's independence. Some of these issues dated back centuries and the negotiations had taken months. It was signed by Paul Cambon on behalf of the French Minister for Foreign Affairs and Lord Lansdowne, the British Foreign Secretary.

The initiative for the move was attributed by some to the British monarch, King Edward VII, who had visited Paris the previous year. Others were more cynical, suggesting that his role was limited to a willingness not to take affront at the Republican attitude he had discovered during his stay.

But beyond the physical agreements of the entente cordiale was the division of the major European powers into rival systems: France establishing closer ties with Britain – and both nations moving away from Germany.

RUSSIA'S BLOODY SUNDAY

The failure of the war with Japan had dealt a humiliating blow to the once-mighty Russian Empire. The defeat served as a catalyst for growing discontent at the autocracy of Tsar Nicholas II and his advisers and the way Russia was being ruled.

The earliest protests began at the end of 1904 with demonstrations centred around St Petersburg. The conflict reached a flashpoint on January 22, 1905 when a priest name Georgy Gapon organized a legitimate demonstration of the Assembly of Russian Working Men outside the Tsar's Winter Palace in St Petersburg. Gapon's aim was to present a petition of grievances and requests for reforms to the Tsar in person; however, he was unaware that the Tsar was away from the palace. Under the control of Grand Duke Vladimir, the Tsar's uncle, the security police were summoned to disperse the thousands of protesters. Imperial troops fired indiscriminately into the crowd, killing 105 marchers and injuring several hundred more.

Following this outrage the protests, which up to then had been peaceful, took a violent turn, spreading throughout the Russian empire. Nicholas was not always able to rely on the loyalty of his armed forces. Rebel troops took control of the Trans-Siberian railway and in the Black Sea port of Odessa, sailors on the battleship *Potemkin* mutinied to fire on the counter-revolutionary Black Hundreds, anti-Semitic volunteer groups that were loyal to the Tsar.

Throughout September 1906, the first workers councils – soviets – began to emerge under the influence of the Menshevik socialists. In October a general strike was called, bringing Russia's economy to a halt.

▲ The growing protests against the harsh rule of Tsar Nicholas II were centred around the city of St Petersburg.

On October 30, on the advice of his councillor Sergei Yulevich Witte, Nicholas II issued what became known as his October Manifesto, a document granting basic civil liberties such as freedom of speech and the press, the enfranchisement of all Russians and the adoption of an elected legislative body that would have the power to curtail some of the Tsar's autocratic rule. The Manifesto was accepted by the moderate factions for whom it constituted a victor, but was viewed with suspicion by revolutionaries. With the opposition seriously weakened, the Tsar was once again able to assume control by the end of 1906.

The 1905 revolution had failed to oust Tsar Nicholas II, create a new republic or even pave the way for democracy. The revolutionary leaders of the soviets were arrested or, like Bolshevik leader

▲ The mutineers of the Russian battleship *Potemkin* surrender to the authorities. They were later hailed as heroes by the Bolsheviks.

Lenin, returned to European exile. The Tsar's reforms were enacted in the Fundamental Laws of 1906. The result was a watered-down version of the October Manifesto which yielded little of his power. The most significant development was the creation of the Duma, a partially elected legislative body. Literally meaning "deliberation", the Duma had the theoretical power to overturn new legislation presented by the Tsar. The Duma was not in permanent session: the first session sat between May 10 and July 21, 1906; the second between March and June 1907. Outside of the these sessions, the Tsar's rule remained absolute.

Nicholas attempted to distil the revolutionary potential of the Duma by gearing the elective system in favour of conservative elements. Nonetheless it eventually evolved into the cradle of liberal and social-ist opposition within Russia. Resistance grew significantly during the fourth and final Duma which ran from November 1912 until the Tsar's enforced abdication in March 1917. It was the Duma that formed the basis of the first provisional government which held power briefly before the Bolsheviks seized power six months later.

▲ **Troops loyal to the Tsar were merciless in their repression of the Bloody Sunday revolt in which 105 protesters were killed.**

A NEW APPROACH TO TIME AND SPACE

The year 1905 was significant for the scientific community. It was the year in which physicist Albert Einstein first published his "Special Theory of Relativity", a theory that would change the way in which man thought about time, space and the universe. It would make Einstein the most famous scientist in history.

Born in Ulm, Germany in 1879, Einstein's early life was perhaps only remarkable in that his scholastic achievements were so mediocre. Einstein found school a dull chore, seeing no value in the rote learning that consigned facts to the memory but sought little in the way of understanding.

Failing to complete his diploma, Einstein left school at the age of 15 and moved to Milan with his family. As a child, Einstein had developed an interest in solving mathematical puzzles. So it was that a general fascination for science led him to take the entrance examination for the Federal Polytechnic Academy in Zürich. Failing the first time, he reapplied the following year and this time was successful. Nonetheless, he still found the formality of education stifling and although he graduated in 1900 it was not with high grades.

After a brief period as a maths teacher, Einstein, who was now a Swiss citizen, decided upon a career in the civil service, taking a position as an examiner in the Berne patent office in 1902. It was during this time that he formulated the basis for some of his most notable scientific achievements.

1905 turned out to be a water-shed for Einstein. He submitted a

▲ **One of the greatest minds of the twentieth century, Albert Einstein achieved worldwide celebrity.**

thesis "A New Determination of Molecular Dimension" which won him his doctorate from the University of Zürich. Four other papers followed the same year, including his "Special Theory of Relativity" in which he postulated that if the speed of light is constant and all natural laws are the same then both time and motion are relative to the observer. The mathematical progression that backed up his theory and tied together mass and energy is perhaps the best-known mathematical formula ever created: $E=mc^2$.

Much of Einstein's later life was devoted to the cause of pacifism. It was a tragic irony that his greatest scientific achievement – perhaps the most important scientific thesis since Isaac Newton discovered the effects of gravity – gave man the power to create the atomic bomb.

April
- Earthquake kills more than 10,000 in Lahore, India

May
- Riots in Poland leave many dead
- Japan decimates the Russian Baltic Fleet in the Battle of the Tsushima Straits

June
- Officers mutiny on the Russian battleship *Potemkin*
- Greek premier Delyannis is assassinated

July
- Alliance between Russia and Germany
- France agrees to international conference on Morocco

August
- Maji Maji uprising in German East Africa
- British-Japanese alliance renewed
- Tsar Nicholas II creates a limited parliament (Duma)

September
- War between Russia and Japan ends with the US-mediated Treaty of Portsmouth
- Death of Irish-born doctor and philanthropist Thomas John Barnardo

October
- Treaty of Separation between Norway and Sweden
- General strike in Russia, Tsar Nicholas II issues October Manifesto
- Death of actor Sir Henry Irving

November
- Prince Charles of Denmark elected Haakon VII of Norway
- Japan forces treaty on Korea allowing Japanese control over Korean foreign policy

December
- Revolution in Persia
- British Prime Minister Balfour resigns; new government formed by Liberals
- Korea declared a Japanese protectorate

'06

THE LIBERAL PARTY TAKES POWER

It was the resignation of the Conservative Prime Minister Arthur Balfour in December 1905 that made Henry Campbell-Bannerman, leader of the Liberal Party, Britain's Premier. The general election that followed on January 13, 1906, brought about a massive majority for the Liberals.

Long established as the principle opposition to the Tories, the Liberals had thrived in the nineteenth century, establishing a reputation as the party of reform under the dominant figure of William Gladstone. Towards the end of the Gladstone era the party was weakened by the defection of the unionist element who opposed his ideas for giving Ireland home rule.

After a lengthy period in the political doldrums, the Liberals, at the 1906 election, were able to take advantage of the Conservative Party's divisions on the matter of tariff reform. The scale of the Liberal victory was massive – a parliamentary majority of over 100 seats. The newly formed cabinet included two future prime ministers, Herbert Asquith and David Lloyd George.

The election was also notable for the promising showing of the Labour Representation Committee who, following a pre-election pact with the Liberals, secured 54 seats. Adopting Keir Hardie as their leader, five days after the election they re-christened themselves the Labour Party.

The Liberal Party remained in government for the next 11 years, a period of reform that saw the first seeds of Britain's welfare system being sown. It would be the last time that a Liberal government ruled outside of a coalition.

▶ **A future Prime Minister, David Lloyd George held a cabinet post in the 1906 government.**

A CITY IN RUINS

▲ **The remains of San Francisco after the earthquake of 1906. The few buildings that survived the tremors were destroyed by fire.**

Flourishing with the gold rush of the 1850s, the city of San Francisco has always lived a precarious existence, situated between two major earthquake fault lines. The San Andreas fault starts north of San Francisco Bay at Cape Mendocino, passing beneath the harbour and onwards for 1,000 km (600 miles) into the Colorado Desert. To the east of the city lies the smaller Hayward fault. Consequently, San Francisco's 450,000 inhabitants were largely blasé about the periodic tremors that had very little impact on life in the city. They could never have imagined the events of April 18, 1906.

Shortly after five o'clock in the morning, the San Andreas fault underwent a massive shift. The earthquake resulted in mayhem: within the space of barely a minute, much of San Francisco was reduced to rubble. By the time the tremors had subsided fires broke out in isolated parts of the city. However, as the pipes of the city's water supply had been laid across the San Andreas fault they had simply snapped. An already inadequate fire-fighting force were rendered helpless: by midday San Francisco was uncontrollably ablaze. The city burned for three more days before the fires were extinguished by a light rainstorm.

Given the severity of the disaster, the speed with which basic amenities were reintroduced was incredible. Within two weeks the electric supply and tram system was running again. A surprisingly small proportion of the population abandoned the area.

Although it was estimated that up to 700 people died as a result of the earthquake and its aftermath, San Francisco could consider itself fortunate in that the first tremors took place in the middle of the night when most people were safely in their homes, protected from debris which would have sent the death toll soaring.

The earthquake and its aftermath taught the San Francisco authorities a number of valuable lessons. New buildings were erected from concrete with steel reinforcements: they may not have been indestructible, but they were safer than the wood and brick constructions that had crumbled so easily.

As long as San Francisco exists it will be vulnerable to earthquakes, although thankfully none has so far approached the 8.25 that was registered on the Richter Scale on April 18, 1906.

US OCCUPATION OF CUBA

▲ **The USA helped Cuba win independence from Spain, but widespread poverty resulted from US occupation.**

The relationship between the USA and the island of Cuba, 145 km (90 miles) south of the tip of Florida, has always been a difficult one. Under Spanish rule since Christopher Columbus landed during his first American voyage in 1492, by the middle of the nineteenth century Cuba had become a close trading partner of the USA. 1868 saw the outbreak of a 10-year war which failed to secure Cuban independence from Spain. In 1898, the USA became embroiled in Cuba's second war with Spain following the sinking of the USS *Maine* in Havana harbour.

Cuba won the status of republic in 1902, albeit under US occupation. Tomás Estrada Palma, elected Cuba's first president in 1902, signed an agreement allowing the US to oversee the running of the government as a condition for the withdrawal of troops that eventually took place in 1904.

Palma was widely viewed as allowing the US too much involvement in Cuban affairs. Increasingly his leadership came under threat, primarily from the popular anti-American liberal José Miguel Gómez. Following Palma's re-election in February 1906, heavy fighting broke out on the island between government forces and rebels loyal to Gómez. Under threat, Palmer resigned. The US responded on September 28 by placing War Secretary William Taft in control. A week later, 6,000 US troops were sent in to restore order.

The US continued to govern the island until 1909 when Gómez was finally elected president. The widespread corruption that quickly became endemic in Cuban politics was quietly tolerated by successive US governments.

THE WOMEN'S PARLIAMENT

The evening of February 13, 1907 saw the women's suffrage movement take a violent turn as a large crowd of suffragettes attempted to storm the Houses of Parliament to hand in a petition to the British government.

The women had declared their own self-styled "parliament" earlier in the day, after which over 100 members of the Women's Social and Political Union (WSPU), the most prominent campaigners for women's suffrage in Great Britain, marched through the streets of Westminster to the House of Commons. Emmeline Pankhurst, the founder and leader of the WSPU, had already been jailed for issuing a pamphlet inciting women to "rush the House of Commons".

It took a battalion of mounted policemen five hours to quell the demonstration. In all, 57 women were arrested, although 15 suffragettes did manage to break into the Commons building. In Holloway prison the following day, one of the captives, Pankhurst's daughter Christabel, showed no remorse and described the event as a "great day for our movement".

The main target of WSPU activity had been the Liberal Party, which they saw as actively impeding the progress of women's suffrage. Until the storming of Parliament, protests had largely been non-violent, a situation that now looked certain to change.

▲ **Emmeline Pankhurst and her daughter Christabel, pioneers of the women's suffrage movement in Great Britain, in prison garb.**

THE GREAT RACE

Almost as soon as the internal combustion engine had been invented in the 1880s, man's competitive instincts saw the birth of the first automobile races. The earliest events took the form of town-to-town races, the first major competition taking place between Paris and Bordeaux in 1895. Thereafter the idea spread quickly throughout Europe and across to the United States where James Gordon Bennett, owner of the *New York Herald,* offered a trophy to be competed for annually by national automobile clubs.

June 1907 saw the birth of a new form of competition – an endurance rally that took place over a series checkpoints. This race, billed as the greatest ever staged, took place between Peking and Paris – a journey of over 12,500 km (8,000 miles).

Six drivers took part in the race, which passed the Great Wall of China and crossed the Ural Mountains and the Gobi Desert. During the course of the race, the drivers faced widely differing terrains and climates, not to mention the threats of attacks by bandits.

The eventual winner was Prince Borghese of Italy who completed the journey in 62 days.

▶ **The automobile driven by Prince Borghese arrives in Paris, having completed the 12,500-km (8,000-mile) journey from Peking.**

RIVALRY ON THE HIGH SEAS

At the end of 1907, the two new sister ships of the British Cunard line, the *Lusitania* and the *Mauretania,* began a series of record-breaking transatlantic voyages, with each new journey seemingly creating a new benchmark for ocean-going speed.

The *Lusitania* made her maiden voyage on September 6, 1907. Sailing from Queenstown on the Irish coast, she arrived in Sandy Hook, New Jersey, having made the fastest-ever crossing in just 5 days and 54 minutes. This achievement wrested the Blue Riband, awarded for speed of transatlantic travel, from the German liner *Deutschland.* Carrying a crew of 650 and 1200 paying passengers, the *Lusitania* averaged a speed of 24 knots. The record was shattered the following month on her return

▲ The *Lusitania,* winner of the Blue Riband in 1907, was later sunk by a German U-boat during World War One.

journey which took just 4 days and 20 hours.

On November 16, Cunard launched the *Mauretania.*

With improved turbines, she was capable of even greater speeds than her sister ship. During her maiden voyage to New York she achieved 635 knots in a single day – almost 20 knots faster than the *Lusitania.*

During a long life, the *Mauretania* became known as the "Grand Old Lady of the Atlantic", retaining the Blue Riband for speed until 1929. Interrupted only by World War One, during which she was decommissioned as a hospital ship, the *Mauretania* made 269 two-way transatlantic crossings until her farewell in 1934. She was broken up for scrap a year later.

The fate of the *Lusitania* was more dramatic. Her sinking by a German submarine on May 7, 1915, was one of a string of events that drew the United States into World War One.

LUMIÈRE BROTHERS INVENT COLOUR PHOTOGRAPHY

In 1907, the Parisian brothers Auguste and Louis Lumière, whose pioneering work at the end of the nineteenth century had created the first motion pictures, once again took photography to another stage of evolution, creating the first practical system for creating colour photographs.

Although colour photographs had been possible as far back as the 1860s, the techniques were complex and prohibitively expensive. Nonetheless, the desire for colour imagery was great and during the late nineteenth century the hand-tinting of black and white images became a highly skilled art form.

The Lumière brothers' colour process, which they called Autochrome, was based around

taking three separate photographs of the same image. Each screen comprised a glass plate covered with grains of starch which had been dyed to act as a primary colour filter. Thus they were able to create three separate plates, each filtered so that only red, green and blue could be seen in the respective plates. When the three plates were superimposed and light shone through, the result was a full-colour image.

Although still expensive by the standards of black and white photography, variants on the Autochrome process remained dominant until 1935 when US Kodak researchers Leopold Godowsky and Leopold Manne created the Kodachrome process,

the forerunner of the Kodacolor system which forms the basis of modern-day photography.

▲ Inventions by the Lumière brothers greatly influenced the development of both still and motion photography.

THE YOUNG TURKS REVOLUTION

On July 24, 1908, Sultan Abdülhamid II, ruler of the Ottoman Empire, was forced to initiate widespread reforms following pressure from the revolutionary Young Turks (*Jöntürkler*) movement. This included the reinstatement of the constitution of 1876 and the recall of parliament, both of which the Sultan's autocratic regime had previously outlawed.

The Young Turks were a coalition of disparate revolutionary groups, the most influential of which were the Committee of Union and Progress (CUP). The movement had begun in 1889 when a group of medical students at the Istanbul Academy initiated a campaign to overthrow the Sultan. The secret movement, which spread to other important colleges, was quickly suppressed by the authorities. The leaders were punished and many were exiled to Paris, where they planned a strategy for a future revolution.

The CUP was led by the intellectual Ahmed Riza who perpetuated his ideas as editor of the Parisian newspaper *Mesveret* (*Consultation*). The moderates of the Young Turk movement, the CUP, proposed the orderly institution of a centralized government. Like other factions, a major concern was not only the Sultan's

▲ **Mustafa Kemal, leader of the revolutionary Young Turks. He would later be known as Ataturk, "Father of the Turks".**

harsh authoritarian rule, but the growing influence of foreign powers that threatened the future of the Ottoman Empire.

The revolution only became possible when armed forces loyal to the Sultan joined the movement. The final impetus came when a discontented group of young officers of the 3rd Army Corps formed a secret revolutionary group which they allied to the CUP. On July 3, 1908, Major Ahmed Niyazi revolted against the provincial authorities. The insurrection quickly spread to other army divisions, leaving the Sultan with no choice but to capitulate.

Initially divisions within the CUP impaired its role in the new parliament, although by 1912 they were the principle power in Ottoman politics. Although their liberal reforms were popular, the disastrous foreign policy they pursued in World War One as allies of Germany was directly responsible for the eventual dissolution of the empire by the nationalist Mustafa Kemal, the father of modern Turkey.

CONTROVERSY AT THE LONDON OLYMPICS

▲ **Marathon runner Pietri Donado of Italy is aided across the finishing line by an official. This helping hand led to his later disqualification.**

The 1908 Olympic Games, the fourth such event of the modern era, had originally been scheduled to take place in Rome. Financial difficulties, including the cost of a spectacular eruption of Mount Vesuvius in 1906, caused Italy to pull out, and the venue was hastily moved to the newly built Shepherd's Bush stadium in London.

The 1908 Olympics were the first to begin with a formal opening ceremony. Not for the last time this became a forum for symbolic political protest. The athletes from Finland, protesting at Russian rule, refused to carry the Russian flag. Prevented by the Olympic Committee from carrying their own standard, the Finns pointedly marched flagless. It was also the first Olympics in which the Anglo-Irish problems reached a world stage, a number of Irish athletes with republican sympathies refused to take part in the games rather than compete under the British team flag.

The Games were also unfortunately noteworthy for the continual squabbling between Great Britain and the US. The controversy started at the opening ceremony when the US flag bearer, shot-putter Ralph Rose, refused to dip his flag in salute as he passed King Edward VII. Thereafter, British officials and US athletes clashed a number of times. Events reached a climax with the final of the 400 metres race, in which the American winner John Carpenter was disqualified for unfairly blocking the path of Britain's Wyndham Halswelle. Officials ordered the final to be re-run, the other qualifiers refused to take part, and Halswelle got the gold medal by a walkover – the only time this has happened in Olympic history.

Featuring over 2000 athletes from 22 nations, the 1908 Olympics were the biggest and most successful to date. As in the previous games, American athletes dominated most of the disciplines, although their successes also brought about charges of "professionalism". One of the stars of the 1908 Olympic Games was US athlete Ray Ewry who took gold medals in all three standing jump categories, giving him a total of 10 gold medals in three Olympic Games.

BALKANS ON THE BRINK OF WAR

October 1908 saw the delicate balance of power in the Balkans disturbed as the expansionist policies of the Hapsburg Empire took Europe to the brink of war.

Earlier in the year, the Young Turk revolution had caused much instability within the Ottoman

threatened to fight for the freedom of the many Serbs living in Bosnia and Herzegovina. An explosive war dragging in the whole of Central Europe seemed imminent as Great Britain and France voiced their support for Serbia in the event of a conflict, while Germany strongly backed the Austrian position.

▲ An early satirical cartoon illustrates the precarious balance of European leaders as they struggle to avert outright war in the Balkans.

Empire. The Hapsburgs saw this as an opportunity to extend their influence in the Balkans. The Hapsburg ambassador to Russia, Count Lexa von Aehrenthal, forged an agreement with Russia's Foreign Minister, Count Ivolsky, by which Austria's annexation of the Ottoman-ruled states of Bosnia and Herzegovina would not be opposed. In exchange, Austria would support the opening of the strategically valuable Balkan Straits to Russian war ships.

Announced on October 6, 1908, the annexation brought a violent reaction from Serbia, who

Relationships between the powers remained tense over the months that followed, the situation resolving unsatisfactorily when the newly appointed Turkish government agreed to sell Bosnia and Herzegovina to the Hapsburgs. While war was narrowly averted, Serbian-backed hostility towards the Hapsburgs grew in Bosnia and Herzegovina. Ultimately, the crisis of 1908 illustrated how little it took to disturb the volatile politics of the Balkans, and that, should this ever happen, there would be grave repercussions for all of Europe.

'08

FORD INTRODUCES MASS PRODUCTION

The first of Henry Ford's mould-breaking Model T cars emerged from his Detroit factory on August 12, 1908. Until then, automobiles had been much too expensive for all but the wealthiest citizens. Although at $850 the Model T – popularly known as the "Tin Lizzy" or the "Flivver" – was vastly cheaper than its competitors, it was still far out of the reach of the working man. Even so, it played a important role in popularizing and, as Henry Ford himself would have put it, "democratizing" the automobile.

Ford's new design was an immediate success, demand soon outstripped supply, and Ford was forced to look for an alternative means of production. His eventual solution – the moving assembly line – would revolutionize the manufacturing world and make possible mass production. The idea was simple: each man performed one set of tasks on every car; once his work was done, the car was moved along a conveyor belt for the next worker to perform a different set of

▲ The pioneering Ford Model T – also known as "Tin Lizzie" – created a transport revolution in the United States.

tasks. Using this method from 1913, Ford was able to bring down the manufacturing time, from components to finished car, from 14 hours to two. To further boost productivity his assembly line workers' wages were increased from $2.34 for a 9-hour day to $5 for an 8-hour day. With improved productivity Ford was able gradually to lower the price of the Model T until it reached a more affordable $300.

With more than 15 million cars built and sold, the Model T established the Ford Motor Company as the most successful automobile manufacturer in the world, and Henry Ford as one of America's wealthiest industrialists.

By the time production of the Model T ceased in 1927 it was estimated that half of the automobiles in the United States were Fords.

AN END TO BRUTALITY IN THE CONGO

On August 19, 1908, Leopold II, King of the Belgians, succumbed to pressure from the rest of Europe and handed over the Congo Free State to the Belgian government. He had ruled the region autocratically for almost 30 years.

The Congo Free State – later known as Zaire, and more recently the Democratic Republic of Congo – was established following the explorer Henry Morton Stanley's famed travels along the Congo river. A European consortium, headed by Leopold II who had financed Stanley's work, was formed to take advantage of the rich agricultural and mineral pickings, including rubber, ivory and palm oil, that had been discovered. Trade agreements were organized with the major tribal leaders to develop the region, and by 1884 Leopold had asserted his right to govern these separate territories as an independent nation, which was named the Congo Free State. The major powers of Europe recognized Leopold's sovereign claim.

Difficulties emerged during the 1890s when it had become clear that Leopold felt able to treat the indigenous inhabitants in any way he saw fit; among other things, he introduced slavery to gather crops and mine the region. Unspeakable brutalities became commonplace and during his rule the population of the region was reduced to 8 million – a fall of at least 70 per cent, according to one estimate.

When the reports of Leopold's regime reached Europe, opinion was outraged and the Belgian government felt compelled to take action. In Brussels, the national legislature voted to pay

the king 120 million francs for the territory, after which it would become a Belgian colony. Thereafter, the territory was known as the Belgian Congo until independence in 1960.

◄ **Leopold II, King of the Belgians, overseer of a brutal regime in the Congo Free State – his own personal empire.**

JACK JOHNSON THE FIRST BLACK SPORTING SUPERSTAR

On December 26, 1908, Jack Johnson became the first black heavyweight boxing champion of the world. The fight for the championship, which took place in Sydney, Australia, ended after police stepped into the ring during the fourteenth round, following fears for the safety of reigning champion, Canadian Tommy Burns.

Before his groundbreaking victory, Johnson, who hailed from Galveston, Texas, had faced perpetual discrimination at the hands of the US boxing establishment – indeed, Johnson had already fought professionally for 11 years before being given the opportunity of a world title fight.

As a boxing champion, Johnson became a heroic figure to the black community in America. At the same time, he found himself a hate figure among white supremacists, his two marriages to white women causing widespread outrage.

The boxing authorities searched long and hard for a suitable white contender to take the title from Johnson – hence the origination of the phrase "great white hope". Former champion James J Jeffries was lured out of retirement in the hope that he would put Johnson

in his place. He failed.

Johnson was, however, trapped by dubious morality legislation. In 1912, while driving with his future wife, he was arrested for violating the Mann Act, a law which forbade the transporting of women across state lines for "immoral purposes". Johnson was sentenced to a year in prison. While on bail awaiting his appeal he fled to Europe.

Johnson successfully defended his title three times while a fugitive in France, but in 1915 he was

forced into a match against Jess Willard in Cuba. Johnson was so easily beaten that it was suggested that he had thrown the fight in the belief that handing over his title to a white man would result in his conviction being quashed. He was wrong: five years later he surrendered to the US authorities and served his prison sentence.

▼ **Jack Johnson (right) was long past his peak by the time of his defeat at the hands of Jess Willard in 1915.**

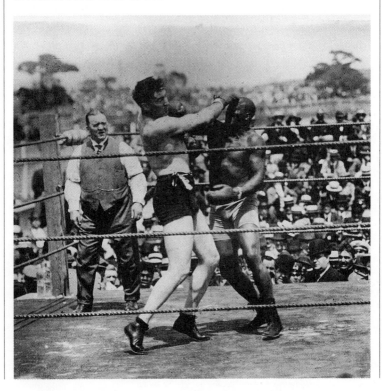

09

THE FUTURE OF ART?

▲ **Fillipo Tommaso Marinetti (centre), in Paris with fellow futurists Luigi Russolo, Carlo Carra, Umberto Boccioni and Gino Severini.**

Readers of the Paris newspaper *Le Figaro* were somewhat baffled to discover in the issue for February 20, 1909, the declaration of a *Manifesto de Futurism* (*Futurist Manifesto*) made by the French-Italian writer and editor Fillipo Tommaso Marinetti. The term "Futurism" was coined as a call-to-arms for artists of all disciplines to revolt. In the eyes of Marinetti, the art and culture of the past was static and irrelevant, and artists must be encouraged to embrace innovation and change. Furthermore, he called for the destruction of existing cultural institutions, including libraries and museums.

Although the manifesto provoked the intended strong reaction within the art establishment, some of the finest artists of the early twentieth century found themselves drawn to Marinetti's call. Painters like Boccioni, Balla and Carrá began to integrate all things modern into their work. Although the earliest Futurist paintings show the influence of Cubism, such as showing different surfaces of an object simultaneously, a new emphasis on the portrayal of speed and motion gradually gave birth to a recognizable Futurist style.

In other art forms, the Futurists decried the likes Beethoven, Chopin and Bach and called for the replacement of orchestras by great atonal noise-making machines: a number of Futurist concerts were performed in Europe, some attracting sizable audiences, if mostly for their curiosity value.

As a leading figure of the first artistic movement to embrace Bolshevism, Marinetti, visiting Russia, was a major influence on Velemir Khlebnikov and Vladimir Mayakovsky, the fathers of the later, more politically motivated and literary-based Russian Futurist movement.

Unusually for an artistic movement, Marinetti's manifesto also glorified militarism, violence, death and anarchy. Five years later, the Futurists actively embraced the outbreak of World War One; indeed, many of their finest artists, including Boccioni and the architectural visionary Sant'Elia, were killed in action.

PEARY AT THE NORTH POLE

◄ **Robert Peary, conqueror of the Arctic. Later evidence suggested that he may have mistakenly stopped short of his goal.**

After two failed attempts, naval commander Robert Peary finally achieved a dream when he planted the US flag at the North Pole on April 6, 1909.

Preparations for Peary's achievement had begun as early as 1886 when he and his colleague Matthew Hansen journeyed 160 km (100 miles) over uncharted ice sheet into Greenland. Five years later, they progressed by sledge more than 1,600 km (1,000 miles) into Greenland, providing the first real evidence that Greenland was an island in its own right.

His first attempt on the North Pole came in 1902 after almost a decade of studying the region for suitable routes, but it was thwarted by his ship's inability to travel through the frozen seas. A second attempt followed in 1905 after the US Navy had provided him with the *Roosevelt*, an ice-breaking ship built to Peary's own specifications. Although the craft enabled him to set up a base at Cape Sheridan, Ellesmere Island, his bid failed as weather conditions made sledging impossible.

Peary's triumphant journey began as he sailed from the US in July 1908. Fully prepared, Peary and his team left Cape Sheridan on March 1, 1909, for a final trek which saw the commander accompanied by Hansen, four Eskimos and 40 dogs.

Controversy marred what should have been a triumphant return to the US, when Peary discovered that one of his former colleagues, Frederick Cook, was claiming that his own expedition had already been successful 11 months earlier. In spite of what seemed like photographic evidence, Cook's claim was publicly discredited when the Eskimos who had accompanied him on that trip showed that he had stopped well over 160 km (100 miles) short of the Pole.

A final ironic twist came in the 1980s when a study of Peary's expedition journals suggested that, although he may have genuinely believed that he had reached the North Pole, a series of navigational errors may have meant that he was at least 50 km (30 miles) adrift of his goal.

BLÉRIOT CROSSES THE CHANNEL

▲ **Aviation pioneer Louis Blériot, the first man to fly an aircraft across the English Channel. Engine failure prevented his rival, Count de Lambert, taking his place in the record books.**

On July 25, 1909, Frenchman Louis Blériot made aviation history as he became the first man to pilot an aircraft the 34 km (21 miles) across the English Channel. Taking off from Calais, France at 5 a.m., Blériot made a clumsy but successful landing 37 minutes later in a field outside Dover. His achievement won him the prize of £1,000 awarded by the London *Daily Mail* newspaper.

Blériot, a wealthy man who had made his fortune as an inventor of car lights, had been one of France's best-known aviators, winning the French Aero Club Medal the previous year. Some of his early aircraft designs had been somewhat bizarre, including a model which flew tail first and another that closely resembled a box kite. By the time he had built the historic Bleriot XI in 1909 he had settled for more conventional features: a small monoplane with a three-cylinder, 28-horsepower engine driving a two-blade propeller.

In spite of the fact that greater distances had already been flown, the highly publicized prize money associated with the Channel crossing attracted a number of other noted aviators. Indeed, Blériot could count himself lucky in that only six days earlier an attempt by the Count de Lambert looked set to succeed until engine failure brought him down half way across the Channel. Thus it was left to Blériot to take not only the prize money but a place in the history books.

1910–19

T hroughout the history of humankind, waging war for territorial gain had always been a tragic but seemingly inevitable fact of life. But as weaponry grew in sophistication so did the potential to inflict the most appalling casualties on the enemy. It was during the second decade of the twentieth century that the perils of modern armed conflict were revealed to the fullest extent in a war that would dwarf all other events of the decade.

By 1910, the nations of Western and Central Europe had forged numerous inter-alliances seemingly able to cater for every possible act of aggression. Even though Europe was a cauldron of unrest, these treaties, along with an unprecedented build-up of armaments by Germany, France, Austria-Hungary and Russia seemed set to keep the rival empires apart. And yet it took a single brutal act – the assassination by a Serbian nationalist of Archduke Franz Ferdinand, heir to the Austro-Hungarian Empire – to send Europe stumbling into the biggest and bloodiest war the world had ever seen.

As the twentieth century draws to a close and we find the Balkans at the centre of the world's most brutal conflict. It was similar tensions in the region that created the spark that sent Europe to war. In 1912 rival Balkan states had joined forces to drive the Ottoman Empire out of the region. After succeeding they fought amongst themselves for territorial gain, Serbia, as ever, emerging the strongest state. Following the assassination of the Archduke, Austria-Hungary declared war on Serbia. Kaiser Wilhelm II of Germany declared his support for Austria; Russia and France allied with Serbia. When Germany invaded Belgium in an attempt to outflank France, Britain declared war on Germany.

Brutal trench warfare took place on the Eastern and Western Fronts. As ever, the military had been quick to see the potential of new technological advances. Demands for technical superiority drove progress forward at a rapid rate. During the four years of the war, armaments became increasingly more powerful delivering deadlier explosives at greater speeds. Armoured tanks showed themselves impenetrable to most infantry fire, creating a need for even more powerful weapons. The future dominance of air warfare became clear as the role of the early aircraft shifted from simple reconnaissance to evolve into sophisticated armed fighting machines capable of powerful gunfire and dropping bombs over enemy lines. At the same time the war in the sea found a deadly new threat in the submarine, the German navy exacting heavy tolls on Allied shipping in the Atlantic.

Failing to accompany this advanced technology, however, was a new type of military tactic. Commanders on both sides planned their strategies in much the same way as they had done since the seventeenth century. Opposing forces "dug in", fought skirmishes with the victors able to move their trench lines forwards. But in the era of the machine gun, the level of casualties was unforgivable. During the conflict that would until 1939 be known as The Great War, a generation wiped out. The rulers of Europe drafted over 60 million young men into their military forces. Over ten million never returned, having given their lives in a farcical war that had real little purpose or ideological meaning.

The Great War would also have grave repercussions on the future of Europe. The once powerful German Empire was brought to its knees by the victorious Allies. Punitive war reparations bankrupted the German economy creating an environment that would later bring about the rise of the Nazis. The Austria-Hungarian Empire was annihilated and splintered into its component states. In Russia, the Bolsheviks seized on a growing anti-war feeling that forced Russia out of the war and eventually brought about a Communist revolution. Britain and France were economically ravaged by the conflict as well as being indebted to the Americans who provided arms and troops during the final year.

The world shocked itself at the criminal barbarity of its greatest ever conflict. referred to as "The War To End All Wars", twenty years later, a different story would emerge.

10

PARIS SUFFERS WORST FLOODING SINCE 1746

▲ **The streets of Paris see an unusual new form of transport as heavy rains cause the River Seine to burst its banks.**

During the second half of January, unprecedented rains fell on central France, swelling the River Seine and flooding the streets and houses of Paris, until by January 26 half the city was under water. Although there was enough drinking water, there was not enough to run the factories, and 50,000 refugees were sheltered in public buildings where society ladies provided soup cooked in improvised kitchens.

As the Seine reached record heights, it hurtled through a city renowned for its culture and sophistication, carrying cattle from the fields to the south and furniture from the working-class suburbs. The Metro was inoperable and the trams and many railway lines ceased to run. Pedestrians made their way down the main streets as best they could by means of plank bridges. Sewers rose in the cellars and burst in the streets, so that by January 28, when the waters reached their highest point, the area around the Gare Saint-Lazare was an enormous repugnant lake.

AMERICA MOURNS THE DEATH OF MARK TWAIN

"The report of my death was an exaggeration," stated the cable that Mark Twain sent from Europe to the Associated Press several years ago in response to a newspaper article announcing his demise. This time – April 21, 1910 – the popular novelist and humorist really was dead.

Best remembered for his three Tom Sawyer books (published in 1876, 1894 and 1896) and the classic masterpiece *The Adventures of Huckleberry Finn* (1885), Mark Twain had a gift for presenting boyish rascality and innocence through the ironic adult eyes of one who had spent an idyllic childhood in Hannibal by the great Mississippi river, and experienced at first hand the great social changes brought about by the Civil War.

Born Samuel Langhorne Clemens on November 30, 1835, he achieved his boyhood ambition to be a river-boat pilot in 1857, a profession he loved "better than any I have followed since" (*Life on the Mississippi,* 1883). And when he began his writing career he used the pen name Mark Twain, which was the cry of the river-boat pilot, meaning two fathoms deep, the shallowest water that could be navigated by the Mississippi steamers.

In the 1890s, Twain became bankrupt due to failed literary speculations, and suffered the tragic death of his daughter in 1896. His later writings reflect his increasing sense of irony and bitterness. Pudd'nhead Wilson

▲ **Mark Twain relaxes in his home shortly before his death. He remains one of America's most revered literary figures.**

probably spoke for him when he said: "All say, 'How hard it is to die' – a strange complaint to come from the mouths of people who have had to live."

DR CRIPPEN OUTWITTED BY MARCONI WIRELESS SYSTEM

On July 31, US-born dentist, Dr Hawley Harvey Crippen, and his mistress, Ethel Le Neve, were arrested on board the SS *Montrose* by Inspector Walter Dew of Scotland Yard for the murder, some months previously, of his wife, the music-hall singer, Belle Elmore. It was a triumph for the Marconi wireless installed on the ship and ended a life on the run for Crippen.

Returning from a party on January 31, Dr Crippen gave his wife a dose of hyoscin hydrobromide. It was enough to kill her. Once his wife was dead, Crippen carved up her body, and buried the remains in the cellar. He told anyone who asked that his wife had gone to the United States.

Shortly afterwards he brought to his house, as secretary, 27-year-old Ethel Le Neve, and told the increasingly suspicious friends of Belle Elmore that his wife had died while in America. By July, when Inspector Dew came to investigate

▲ **Dr Crippen (far right) is escorted from SS *Megantis*, the ship that returned him to England, where he was tried and hanged.**

her disappearance, Dr Crippen and Ethel Le Neve were deeply in love. A few days after his first visit, Inspector Dew returned with a search warrant and found that the couple had vanished. The remains of Belle Elmore were found in the cellar and a warrant was issued for Dr Crippen's arrest.

The couple had fled to Belgium, disguised as Mr Robinson and his son: Crippen had shaved off his moustache and discarded his glasses, and Ethel Le Neve had dressed herself as a boy. At

Antwerp they boarded the SS *Montrose,* sailing to Quebec, Canada. The ship's captain, Henry Kendall, was immediately suspicious of the pair. He observed them closely over the next two days, then sent a radio message to Liverpool: "Have strong suspicions that Crippen London cellar murderer and accomplice are among saloon passengers."

Alerted, Inspector Dew boarded the faster White Star liner, *Laurentic;* off Canada, he radioed that he would board the *Montrose* from the St Lawrence, disguised as a river pilot. Once he was on board Captain Kendall invited "Mr Robinson" to his cabin to meet the "river pilot". As the two shook hands, Inspector Dew revealed himself and made the arrest.

On October 22, Dr Crippen was found guilty of poisoning his wife and sentenced to death; his mistress was acquitted. Crippen was hanged, protesting his innocence, on November 23 at Pentonville.

EDISON DEVELOPS NEW TECHNIQUE FOR TALKING PICTURES

The US inventor, Thomas Alva Edison, demonstrated the "kinetophone" to a select audience at his laboratory in West Orange, New Jersey, on August 27. The machine, part phonograph and part camera, marked a significant breakthrough in the development of talking motion pictures as it allowed both sound and image to be recorded at the same time.

Attempts to record sound simultaneously with image before

▲ **Thomas Alva Edison modestly described his successes as "one percent inspiration and ninety-nine percent perspiration".**

Edison's invention were less than satisfactory as they involved hiding a microphone somewhere on the set, towards which the actors had to direct their speech while continuing to act. This resulted either in rather static acting or the actors' voices fading in and out as they moved in and out of the range of the microphone. Edison hoped to have a talking picture made with the kinetophone in the theatres within two years.

'11

NEWS IN BRIEF

....

- Official Secrets Act passed in Britain
- Copyright Act in Britain
- Aeroplanes first use in combat (by Italy against Turkey in Libya)
- Cosmic radiation and super-conduction discovered
- Rutherford develops theory of the nuclear atom
- Greenwich Mean Time becomes international standard
- Last horse-drawn bus in London is retired
- First film studio established in Hollywood
- First Indianapolis 500 motor race held
- First Five Nations rugby contest held

January
- Attempted assassination of the French Prime Minister, Aristide Briand

February
- Ramsay MacDonald appointed head of Labour Party in Britain
- Canadian Parliament chooses to maintain union with Britain

March
- Fire at New York factory kills 146

April
- British House of Commons rejects referendum on Parliament Bill

May
- Tension increases between Russia and Turkey over Montenegro
- National Insurance Bill proposed in Britain

CORONATION OF KING GEORGE V

On June 22, 1911 at the beginning of an exceptionally hot summer, George V was crowned "King of the United Kingdom of Great Britain and Ireland and of the British Dominions beyond the seas, Defender of the Faith, Emperor of India" at Westminster Abbey in a ceremony that lasted seven hours.

Heads of state from throughout the Empire attended the moving

◀ **King George V photographed with his wife, Queen Mary, at Westminster Abbey on the day of his coronation.**

service, while thousands less elevated subjects stood outside the Abbey and lined the streets to watch the procession following King George V and Queen Mary.

The death of the expansive, worldly, sociable and charming King Edward VII had also marked the end of an extravagant, optimistic and glamorous era. His shy, modest and anxious son was crowned in the middle of a constitutional crisis amid growing unrest at home and abroad. The down-to-earth George V was to preside over far more complex and difficult times than his much-loved father and he would earn respect and popularity by the manner in which he handled them.

RACE TO THE SOUTH POLE ENDS IN TRAGEDY

On December 14, 1911, Norwegian explorer Roald Amundsen and his party became the first men to reach the South Pole, dashing the hopes of Captain Robert Falcon Scott and his team who would take another five weeks to achieve the same goal, and who tragically would not survive the journey back to the British base camp in Antarctica.

On June 1, 1910, Captain Scott and his party set out from London for Port Lyttleton in New Zealand in the *Terra Nova*, cheered on by crowds lining the quay of the East India Dock. Roald Amundsen had intended an expedition to the North Pole, but on his way to the Arctic he heard that US Commander Robert E Peary had already reached it, so he turned around and made the South Pole his goal.

For his Antarctic expedition Amundsen and his four companions used skis and relied on 52 dogs to pull the sledges on the

▲ **The flag planted by Norwegian explorer Roald Amundsen flies over the South Pole.**

way out and provide supplementary food to be left at each depot on the way back. He plotted his route carefully across 3,220 km (2,000 miles) of ice-covered mountain ranges and was able to report after his triumph that "everything went like a dance".

Scott chose to rely on motor sledges and ponies, taking only a few dog teams when he set out with 11 men from Cape Evans on October 24, 1911. The sledge motors soon broke down, and the ponies had to be shot when it got too cold. Consequently, the worst part of the journey, from the final depot 240 km (150 miles) from the Pole and back, had to be done on foot with barely a month's provisions for the five men attempting the journey. Exhausted, Captain Scott, Captain Oates, Edward Wilson and Petty Officer Edgar Evans reached the South Pole on January 18, 1912 only to find that Amundsen had got there first.

On the way back to the final depot, the five men encountered blizzards and increasingly low temperatures, forcing them to travel more slowly and to survive on less and less food.

The entry in Scott's diary dated March 19 makes agonizing reading: "Today we started in the usual dragging manner. Sledge dreadfully heavy. We are 15½ miles from the depot and ought to get there in three days. What progress! We have two days' food but barely a day's fuel. All our feet are getting bad … Amputation is the least I can hope for now … The weather doesn't give us a chance."

His last entry is dated March 29, but not until February 1913 did Scott's ship, the *Terra Nova,* reach New Zealand with the dreadful news of their demise.

▲ **The final entries of Captain Scott's diary tell the desperate story of a heroic but doomed struggle for survival.**

REBELLION IN MEXICO

▲ **Pancho Villa leads his band of rebels into battle. Villa's army fought a long guerrilla war in the rural mountain areas of northern Mexico.**

By 1911, 81-year-old General Porfirio Diaz had been ruler of Mexico for 35 years. The president had given Mexico peace and had modernized the economy. But he had also presided over a brutal regime in the countryside, where native peasants had seen their land stolen by large landowners and their efforts at resistance ruthlessly crushed. And he had created a totally corrupt political system, in which elections were rigged and the press was gagged.

In the election year of 1910, Francisco Madero, the US-educated son of a wealthy landowner, led a challenge to Diaz's automatic re-election. The regime responded by arresting Madero and many of his followers. He escaped to the United States, however, disguised as a railway worker, and called on Mexicans to rise against their ruler.

Madero won the support of effective rural guerrilla fighters, especially Emiliano Zapata in southern Mexico and the former bandit chief Pancho Villa in the north, and Diaz's army and police could not cope with the scale of the uprising. In May 1911, the ageing president agreed to resign in return for safe passage to Europe, where he later died in poverty.

Free elections confirmed the victorious Madero in power, but his triumph was to prove shortlived. A vegetarian and spiritualist, he was an unlikely ruler of a tough and troubled country. The idealistic liberal regime he established failed to satisfy conservative businessmen, landowners and army officers, who wanted protection against social revolution.

It also failed to satisfy the rural poor, who wanted immediate radical reforms – Zapata soon resumed his armed campaign for social justice. The press, given total freedom, used it to denounce the liberal government's every word and deed.

Madero's rule was destined to last only until February 1913, when he would be killed as a new military strongman seized power.

▲ **The southern "Zapatistas", rebels led by Emiliano Zapata, embark on the long march to victory at Xochamilco.**

'12

NEWS IN BRIEF

- Royal Flying Corps formed in Britain
- First seaplane built
- Stainless steel invented
- X-ray crystallography developed
- Vitamins discovered
- Piltdown Man hoax in Britain
- Wassily Kandinsky publishes theory on abstraction in painting
- *Pierrot Lunaire* by Arnold Schoenberg premieres
- Craze for ragtime songs sweeps Britain
- "SOS" adopted as universal distress signal
- Commercial airship service begins in Germany
- *Pravda* starts publication in Russia
- England regains cricket Ashes in Australia
- Warner Brothers, Fox and Universal film studios established in Hollywood

January
- Socialists dominate Reichstag in German elections
- New Mexico becomes 47th state of the USA

February
- France ratifies agreement with Germany over Morocco
- Manchus abdicate throne in China; republic declared
- Arizona becomes 48th state of the USA
- Minimum wage rejected by British parliament
- Coal miners strike in Britain

BIRTH OF THE CHINESE REPUBLIC

The last emperor of China, six-year-old Pu-yi, gave up his throne on February 12, 1912. His abdication marked the end of the Manchu Dynasty which had ruled China for 300 years.

Two months earlier, the leader of the Revolutionary Alliance, Sun Yat-sen (1866–1925), had been elected "provisional president" of the Chinese Republic by delegates from 16 provincial assemblies. In Nanjing on January 1, 1912, he inaugurated the new republic, instigating China's adherence, for the first time, to the Western solar calendar rather than the traditional Chinese lunar one. On the same day, acknowledging the weakness of his own military power base, he sent the powerful warlord, Yuan Shikai, a telegram stating that in due course he would offer him the presidency.

After the killing by bomb later in the month of the head of the

Imperial Guards Corps, senior commanders of the Beiyang army urged the Peking cabinet to form a republic. In exchange for the emperor's abdication, Yuan Shikai and the provisional government in Nanjing agreed to allow Pu-yi and his family the right to continue living in the imperial

▲ Students from the "Forbidden City" of Peking are recruited to join the forces of Sun Yat-sen's Revolutionary Alliance.

Forbidden City of Peking and to own its imperial treasures. It also granted them a stipend of $US4 million a year.

WOODROW WILSON ELECTED PRESIDENT

Previously a reformist Princeton president and successful Democrat governor of New Jersey, Woodrow Wilson became the first Democratic president of the United States to be elected for 20 years on November 5, 1912. A moral crusader by temperament, he proved an effective campaigner, taking hold of the mainstream of Progressivism in an approach he called the "New Freedom". He was critical of excessive wealth and power, and called for a pragmatic, approach, maintaining that government should change in response to the times. He called for the destruction of "evil" trusts to allow for greater competition and broader democracy. Because the Republican vote was split between Roosevelt and Taft, Wilson won the election with only 42 per cent of the total vote.

▲ The first Democrat president of the twentieth century, Woodrow Wilson was elected on a platform of social reform.

DISASTER STRIKES THE "UNSINKABLE" TITANIC

Twenty minutes before midnight on April 14, 1912, the *Titanic*, the largest liner in the world, pride of the White Star line, struck an iceberg in the freezing waters of the Atlantic off Newfoundland. Just two hours, forty minutes later the 270-metre (885-ft), 47,070-ton luxury steam ship – proclaimed by its owners to be virtually unsinkable – foundered with the loss of 1,523 passengers and crew. Only 705 people survived the disaster.

It had taken 11,000 men at the Belfast shipyards of Harland and Wolff a year to build the splendid

that occurred could be contained within the compartment affected. The ship was designed to continue to float if damage to the hull affected two separate compartments, or if as many as the first four compartments were flooded.

A record number of icebergs had been sighted in the north Atlantic during 1912, and Captain Edward J Smith was well aware of the high possibility of encountering icebergs. In the early afternoon of April 14, the *Titanic*'s Marconi wireless operators received an ice warning from the White Star liner

bridge. The ship was moving too fast to turn away quickly enough and at 11.40 p.m. the *Titanic* collided with the iceberg. Five compartments at the front were damaged – more than the ship could stand. As the *Titanic* dipped into the ocean, water flowed over the top of each of the bulkheads in turn, flooding one compartment after another. The ship was lost.

Uncovering, loading and launching the lifeboats was a chaotic affair – the crew were unfamiliar with the equipment and the planned lifeboat drill had been cancelled just a few days before. Only 18 of the 20 lifeboats were launched and most of them were only partially filled (mainly with wealthy first- and second-class passengers), resulting in the unnecessary loss of 500 lives.

At 2.20 a.m. the ship plunged to the bottom of the ocean, leaving hundreds of passengers and crew floundering in the icy waters. Most of them died within minutes, although a handful were picked up by two of the lifeboats that returned to the scene.

At 4.10 a.m. the Cunard liner *Carpathia* picked up the first of the lifeboats. It took four hours to complete the rescue operation of the 705 survivors of this terrible tragedy – a testament to human pride and complacency.

▲ The *Titanic* heads away from the port of Belfast for a final sea-going trial before her fateful maiden voyage.

SS *Titanic,* which was the second of three luxurious ocean giants planned by White Star to operate the route between Southampton and New York in competition with the – slightly less impressive – Cunard transatlantic ships. The massive liner boasted a restaurant with French walnut panelling, sumptuous ballroom, swimming pool, gymnasium, Turkish bath, Parisian-style café and indoor gardens. It also featured a double bottom for extra protection and a hull comprised of 16 watertight compartments, each transversed by a bulkhead. Doors in the bulkheads could be closed by a flick of a switch on the bridge of the ship. So, in theory, if the hull was damaged in one place any flooding

Baltic, which they passed to Captain Smith. That night there was no moon, although the skies were clear, and the two lookouts posted in the crow's nest would have found it difficult to discern icebergs in the smooth, inky ocean, especially as they had no binoculars. Despite this, Captain Smith gave no order to reduce speed from 22 knots. Later that evening another ice warning – of heavy pack ice and large icebergs – was received in the wireless room from the Atlantic Transport Line steamer *Mesaba*. Tragically, this message was never passed to the bridge.

The *Titanic* was almost upon the iceberg when the lookout rang the bell to alert the officers on the

▲ The disaster made headline news all over the world. There were 1,523 lives lost as the "unsinkable" liner went down.

March
- First parachute jump from a moving aircraft made
- Morocco becomes French protectorate

May
- Fifth Olympic Games start in Stockholm
- Strikes and riots in Hungary
- Deaths of Swedish dramatist August Strindberg and US aviation pioneer Wilbur Wright

June
- Frederick VIII of Denmark dies; Christian X succeeds

July
- Reform Party wins New Zealand general election
- Death of Japanese emperor Meiji Tenno; Yoshihito succeeds

September
- Demonstrations and unrest in Ulster over Irish Home Rule
- Revolution in Santo Domingo (Dominican Republic)

October
- International powers come to agreement to avert Balkan conflict
- Montenegro declares war on Turkey
- Turkey declares war on Bulgaria and Serbia
- War between Italy and Turkey ended with Treaty of Lausanne

November
- Turkey requests international intervention in Balkans
- Democrat candidate Woodrow Wilson wins US presidential election

December
- Armistice between Turkey and the Balkan allies

YOUNG TURKS STAGE A COUP IN TURKEY

By the end of 1912, the combined armies of the Balkan states of Bulgaria, Serbia, Montenegro and Greece stood just a few kilometres outside Istanbul, and the Turkish government was preparing to cede Edirne, second city of the Empire, to Bulgaria.

Humiliated and enraged by the decline of the Ottoman Empire, Enver Pasha, leader of the Young Turks, determined "to try to overturn everything". On January 23, accompanied by Talat and Kemal, key members of the Committee of Union and Progress, Enver led a small band of followers into the principal council chamber of the Sublime Porte, crying "Death to Kamil Pasha!" They forced the Grand Vizier's resignation at gunpoint and shot dead the Minister of War, General Nazim. Enver then forced the Sultan to appoint his ally, Shevket, Grand Vizier.

Although the British ensured that Kamil was given safe conduct out of Turkey, he was never reinstated as Grand Vizier, and the Young Turk triumvirate, Enver, Talat and Kemal, went on to establish a military junta, promoting nationalism and modernization in Turkey.

► **Enver Pasha, leader of the Young Turks, who was one of the architects of modern Turkey.**

THE BIRTH OF HOLLYWOOD

▲ **The set of *The Squaw Man*, Cecil B de Mille's first motion picture.**

When an ambitious young director named Cecil B De Mille arrived in the Los Angeles suburb of Hollywood in 1913, he found ideal conditions for the making of his first motion picture, *The Squaw Man*. The climate was temperate, allowing pictures to be made all year round without the need for electric lighting, and the scenery was varied. In addition, Los Angeles was a non-union town, so labour costs were half what they were in New York, and Mexican and Oriental workers were in good supply. Extras were extremely cheap, with some local people willing to work for nothing.

Crucially, California was a considerable distance from the reach of the Motion Picture Patents Company, dubbed "Edison's Trust", which required every film company to recognize Edison's Kinetoscope patents and submit royalties for each film it made.

The Centaur Film Company of Bayonne, New Jersey, was the first to establish a studio in Hollywood. In 1911 it leased the Blondeau roadhouse on Sunset Boulevard, and named it the Nestor studio. Other independent film companies followed suit, and on March 15, 1915, Carl Laemmle's Universal Film Manufacturing Company opened the new Universal studios on the north side of the Hollywood Hills amid a blaze of publicity.

The same year, after a long legal battle, the Edison Trust bit the dust; a new era in movie-making was born. Universal City produced 250 films in its first year and people began to seek to be in films, hoping for fame and fortune as the power of the stars grew apace.

THE DEATH OF A SUFFRAGETTE

▲ **Epsom race-goers look on in horror as women's suffrage campaigner Emily Davison throws herself under the king's horse.**

When Emily Wilding Davison threw herself in front of the king's horse at Epsom on Derby Day (June 4) 1913, she epitomized the courage and desperation of an increasingly militant suffragette movement. Often heard to say that one should be prepared to die for the cause, this 40-year-old Oxford graduate died four days later from the terrible injuries she had received. She was buried on June 14 in the family vault at Morpeth, Northumberland, at the end of a day which had begun with an impressive funeral procession – thousands of women marched across London from Victoria to King's Cross station in a display of suffragette colours, carrying banners and distributing leaflets.

The suffragette movement had been growing in militancy ever since the Liberals won the election in 1906. Many Liberal MPs sympathized with the suffragettes who were hopeful of gaining a limited suffrage for women after the Liberal win. However, the government was split on the issue, and nothing happened to progress the women's cause.

Angry and disappointed, leaders of the suffragette movement (embodied in the Women's Social and Political Union formed by Mrs Emmeline Pankhurst) pursued an increasingly militant policy. They organized demonstrations in places where demonstrations were forbidden in order to invite arrest. Then, given the option of paying a fine or going to prison, they chose prison in order to maximize the amount of publicity for their cause.

They also harassed government ministers, interrupting meetings and picketing their houses. When imprisoned, they immediately went on hunger strike, gaining much publicity and some public sympathy when prison doctors began to force-feed them via tubes inserted into their mouths and nostrils.

In 1910, the government passed the Conciliation Bill, and, once again, the suffragettes became hopeful. However, the Bill was soon shuffled into parliamentary oblivion, and in March 1912 Mrs Pankhurst stepped up the militancy of the campaign.

Groups of suffragettes smashed shop windows with hammers in the West End; they threw stones through the windows of the House of Commons, Downing Street and in Kensington; they dropped flaming rags through ministers' letter boxes and planted bombs in their houses when they were away. In short, the suffragettes waged war on the establishment and the prisons filled with suffragettes on hunger strikes.

To avoid the practice of force-feeding, which had attracted a great deal of negative publicity for the government, Home Secretary Reginald McKenna introduced the Prisoners (Temporary Discharge for Ill-Health) Act, dubbed the "Cat and Mouse Act". Instead of force-feeding prisoners, they were released, then, after a few days, were arrested again – that is if they could be found. It was under this Act that Mrs Pankhurst was arrested just as she was about to get into her carriage behind Emily Davison's hearse.

Although, the suffragettes continued their militant campaign until the outbreak of World War One, they had not then achieved their goal. The Representation of the People Act of 1918 gave married women over 30 the vote. It was the first step on the road to votes for all women.

▲ **Attended by thousands of fellow suffragettes, the funeral of Emily Davison became a rallying point for the suffrage movement.**

THE BALKANS AT WAR

NEWS IN BRIEF

April
- Parliament of China meets for the first time
- Suffragette Emmeline Pankhurst jailed
- US president Woodrow Wilson delivers first State of the Union address in Congress
- Armistice between Turkey and Bulgaria

May
- British House of Commons rejects female suffrage bill
- End of the first Balkan war with peace treaty between Turkey and Balkan allies

June
- Germany begins large expansion of army
- Military pact between Bulgaria and Austro-Hungary
- Second Balkan war begins with Bulgaria against Serbia and Greece
- Death of British Poet Laureate, Alfred Austin

July
- Irish Home Rule Bill passed by the House of Commons
- Russia declares war on Bulgaria
- Irish Home Rule Bill rejected by the House of Lords
- Turkey joins second Balkan war, recaptures Adrianople from Bulgaria
- Rebellion in Yangtze Valley in China
- Armistice in the second Balkan war

▲ **Macedonian rebels take control of the main highway passing from the north into Salonika. Once again, war in the Balkans came close to escalating into a wider conflict.**

By 1913 the Balkans had become the fighting ground of Europe, where ambitious young states competed for territory among themselves, and against the old empires of Ottoman Turkey and Hapsburg Austria.

The first Balkan war had begun in 1912, pitting the Balkan League – Serbia, Bulgaria, Greece and Montenegro – against the Turks. A peace deal brokered in London in May 1913 robbed Turkey of almost all its remaining territory in Europe, creating the new Muslim state of Albania and dividing up the rest of the spoils among the Balkan victors.

The habit of war was by now well established. The ink on the new treaty was barely dry when Bulgaria, feeling it had received less than its fair share of the plunder, declared war on Serbia and Greece.

The second Balkan war was a catastrophe for the Bulgarians, who had bitten off far more than they could chew. Both Romania and Turkey seized the opportunity to attack Bulgaria, claiming land in the north and south. The fighting was ended by the Peace of Bucharest in August, which subtracted from Bulgaria almost all the territory it had gained from the first Balkan conflict.

Serbia emerged from the wars of 1912–13 as a powerful regional state, its population increased by a million and a half. It did not, however, have access to the sea, which was blocked by Austrian-ruled Croatia and the newly formed Albanian state.

The Serbs planned to round off a victorious 1913 by swallowing up Albania, but were forced to back down when Austria declared its intransigent opposition.

The most significant point about the Peace of Bucharest was that it was made between the Balkan states without any great power involvement.

The Balkans was a region that had grown beyond the control of the great powers, yet it was one where Austria and Russia, at least, felt vital interests were at stake. In the last resort, Russia would have to back its Slav cousins in Serbia against Austria, yet Russia had no control over Serbian nationalist ambitions. The Balkans had become a predictable flashpoint for a wider war.

▲ **Over the years that followed the Balkan wars, the tools of modern warfare would become progressively more powerful and deadly.**

THE CREATION OF THE ASSEMBLY LINE

On October 7, 1913, Henry Ford pressed the button that activated the 76 m (250ft) long assembly line recently installed in his car manufacturing plant at Highland Park, Michigan. For the first time, instead of workers moving to cars situated on wooden "horses" all over the factory floor to carry out a number of different jobs on each, they stood in one place while the moving belt carried the car chassis past them, allowing each worker to perform a specific job on each chassis before it moved on. This innovative way of working greatly increased the speed at which Ford cars could be constructed. Where before a Model T

▲ Devised by automobile pioneer Henry Ford, Highland Park, Michigan was the the world's first mass-production assembly line.

Ford had taken 12½ hours to complete, after the installation of the assembly line the same car took just 93 minutes to construct from start to finish.

When Henry Ford had designed

the simple, light Model T using standardized parts and available only in black, his aim had been to create a cheap car for the mass market, and by 1913 the Model T was already an extremely popular car, selling for half the price of most other cars.

With the introduction of the assembly line, he was able to reduce the price further still with the result that by 1915 there were over one million Model T cars on the road in the US. This, despite the fact that he had to increase wages dramatically – to $5 a day – and reduce the working day to eight hours in order to attract and keep enough workers willing to endure the relentless pace and monotony of the work.

PANAMA CANAL COMPLETED

The Atlantic and Pacific Oceans were linked across the Isthmus of Panama on October 10, 1913. In a meticulously stage-managed demonstration of American technological prowess, President Woodrow Wilson pressed a button in the White House to detonate an explosion 6,435 km (4,000 miles) away, clearing the last obstacle in the path of the Panama Canal.

The attraction of building a canal across Central America had long been obvious. It would cut the sea journey from the east to the west coast of the United States by 12,870 km (8,000 miles). A French company set up by Ferdinand de Lesseps, builder of the Suez Canal, was awarded the original concession for an Atlantic-Pacific link in the 1880s, but the company foundered in

bankruptcy. The United States came up with its own plan for a canal across Nicaragua, but this, too, came to nothing.

By the early twentieth century, the US was determined to get a canal built and to have control over it. At this time, Panama was a part of Colombia. When the Colombian government hesitated to agree to US demands for sovereign control over a future Canal Zone, the United States promoted a Panamanian independence movement.

In November 1903, the US recognized an independent Panama under its protection, and the new Panamanian government duly granted the United States sovereignty over a 16 km (10 mile)-wide Panama Canal Zone, in return for a payment of $US10 million.

The building of the 82-km (51-mile) canal began in 1904. It was an extraordinary technological feat, overseen by US army engineer George W Goethals. Coping with tropical diseases such as malaria and yellow fever was almost as remarkable as the creation of canals, locks and artificial lakes in inhospitable terrain. The canal finally opened to traffic on August 15, 1914.

▲ The two great oceans of the Atlantic and Pacific are joined for the first time as the Panama Canal is formally opened.

August
- Compulsory military service introduced in France
- Peace treaty signed between Balkan states

September
- Japan engages in gunboat diplomacy with China
- Bulgaria and Turkey settle conflict by treaty

October
- Yuan Shikai elected president of the Republic of China
- Serbia invades Albania
- Royalist insurrection put down in Portugal

November
- Kuomintang Party outlawed in China
- Greater military cooperation between Germany and Turkey
- USA refuses to recognize Huerta as President of Mexico
- Russia and China recognize the autonomy of Mongolia
- Mohandas Gandhi arrested in South Africa
- Peace treaty between Greece and Turkey settles territorial disputes
- First ship travels through the Panama Canal
- Tensions increase between Germany and France over "Zabern" incident in Alsace-Lorraine

December
- Greece annexes Crete

THE ULSTER CONFLICT

If war had not broken out in Europe in August 1914, Britain might well have descended into some form of civil war over Ulster. The Conservative Party had made it clear that it would support an armed rebellion by Protestant Ulstermen to resist Irish Home Rule.

During the nineteenth century, Liberal governments had made two efforts to pass a Home Rule bill, which would have given the Irish limited self-government, but on each occasion the Conservative-dominated House of Lords had thrown the legislation out. In 1911, a Liberal government ended the power of the House of Lords to veto legislation permanently; henceforth, the Upper House could only block bills for three years. At a stroke, the road to Home Rule was open.

The Conservatives responded to the very mild Home Rule bill introduced in the House of Commons in 1912 with extraordinary vehemence. Their leader Andrew Bonar Law stated: "I can imagine no length of resistance to which Ulster can go in which I would not be prepared to support them." In April, 80,000 members of the Ulster Volunteer Force (UVF), an armed militia formed by Ulster Protestants, were reviewed by senior Tories, including the lawyer Sir Edward Carson, who became the UVF's chief spokesman.

The Home Rule bill was duly twice passed by the House of Commons and twice rejected by the Lords. In 1914, the Lords' veto would run out. However, many senior British army officers were strongly pro-Unionist and openly opined that the army could not be expected to force Ulster Protestants to accept rule by Irish Papists.

▲ **Ulster Unionists meet in an effort to encourage the House of Lords to continue their opposition to the Home Rule bill.**

Through 1914 the crisis deepened. Winston Churchill, the Liberal First Lord of the Admiralty, raised the temperature in March by publicizing the movement of a Battle Squadron to the west coast of Scotland. At the same time, the government decided to strengthen defences at armaments depots in Ireland. Ulster Protestants feared that a military crackdown was on its way.

Doubts about the reliability of the British army in Ireland now came to a head. Many officers were Ulstermen or had Ulster connections. The Third Cavalry Brigade, stationed at the Curragh outside Dublin, was commanded by General Sir Hubert Gough, a fervent Ulsterman.

On March 21, the general and 70 of his 90 officers announced they would rather be dismissed

than fight the UVF. Emboldened by this "Curragh mutiny", the UVF took temporary control of the Ulster port of Larne in April, and unloaded an estimated 30,000 rifles and 3 million rounds of ammunition from two steamers. The British authorities made no attempt to intervene. Meanwhile, Nationalists in southern Ireland flocked to join their own militia, the Irish Volunteers.

In the third week of July, an all-party conference on Home Rule was held at Buckingham Palace. For the first time, the Liberal prime minister, Herbert Asquith, proposed that six of the nine counties of Ulster might be excluded from Home Rule altogether. But the Conservatives found even this unacceptable.

On July 26, the Irish Volunteers smuggled in a quantity of arms through Howth. The incident was followed by a confrontation between British soldiers and local people in Dublin. Three civilians were shot dead and many more wounded. Civil war in Ireland seemed imminent.

Then came war with Germany, dwarfing all other concerns. The Home Rule bill was passed, but its implementation was postponed until after the end of the war. The Ulster Volunteers were, at their request, integrated into the British Army. Most of the Catholic Irish Volunteers also joined up, but thousands stayed in Ireland, vowing to continue the fight for Home Rule. Asquith promised the Ulster Protestants they would never be made to accept Home Rule against their will. The stage was set for the next act of the Irish tragedy.

◄ **Nationalists in the south flock to join the Irish Volunteers in response to the loyalist Ulster Volunteer Force (UVF).**

SCANDAL AND VENGEANCE IN PARIS

▲ Controversial French politician Joseph Caillaux felt he was being blackmailed by *Le Figaro*. His wife took the law into her own hands.

In March 1914, sex and politics came together in a Parisian scandal that was extreme even by the standards of the French Third Republic. It concerned the Radical politician Joseph Caillaux, a recurring figure in the Third Republic's ministerial merry-go-round, who was at this time Minister of Finance.

Caillaux was a hate figure for right-wing nationalists, who mounted a scurrilous campaign against him in the Paris press. Gustave Calmette, the editor of *Le Figaro*, got hold of torrid love letters that Caillaux had written to his second wife before their marriage, when she was his mistress. He then threatened to publish them. On March 16, Mme Caillaux went to the offices of *Le Figaro*, pulled out a revolver, and shot the editor dead.

Right-wing anti-Caillaux riots broke out on the Paris streets, and Caillaux's political career was ruined. His wife, however, was acquitted by a court that presumably agreed that she had the right to defend her honour.

ROCKEFELLER: NOT A POPULAR MAN

Billionaire John D Rockefeller Jr was one of the most hated men in the United States in 1914. The reason: the Rockefeller family's holdings included coal mines in southern Colorado.

When intolerable conditions in the mines provoked a strike, state militia and company guards were unleashed on the strikers.

On April 20, the militia overran a strikers' camp at Ludlow and burned it to the ground. The following day, the charred bodies of two women and 11 children were found in the camp.

Hostile crowds picketed the Rockefeller offices on Broadway. One of the speakers called for Rockefeller to be "shot down like a dog". In a tenement building on Lexington Avenue, four members of the Industrial Workers of the World movement built a time-bomb that they intended to deliver to Rockefeller's house. The bomb exploded prematurely, killing the four "Wobblies".

By the end of the year, the Colorado miners had returned to work, despite the fact that none of the grievances which caused the strike had been satisfied.

John D Rockefeller Jr lived on to be remembered as a great American philanthropist.

▶ John D Rockefeller Jr, patriarch of a dynasty that had created an almost unimaginable level of wealth.

ORIGINS OF THE GREAT WAR

Few wars had been as long-expected as was the Great War of 1914.

The cheering crowds that packed the streets of every European capital when war broke out were expressing, as much as anything, a relief that the awaited conflict had arrived at last.

Europe had long been divided into two armed camps engaged in a frantic arms race. The pivot of the great power confrontation was the hostility between France and Germany.

France had been defeated by the Prussian-led German army in 1871. The French had lost the provinces of Alsace-Lorraine to the new German Empire and had been forced to pay heavy war reparations. More than forty years later, France was still intent on revenge.

▲ **Archduke Franz Ferdinand of Austria talks to representatives of the Roman Catholic church in Sarajevo only hours before the assassination that plunged Europe headlong into war.**

▲ **Archduke Franz Ferdinand, heir to the throne of the Austro-Hungarian Empire: his killing sparked the "war to end all wars".**

Another focus of hostility was in the war-torn Balkans, where the Russian and Austro-Hungarian Empires were at loggerheads. Russia backed its fellow Slavs in the Balkan state of Serbia, while Austria's Hapsburg rulers, struggling to keep control of a multinational empire, were hostile to Serb nationalism.

Under the strain of these confrontations, France and Russia formed a defensive alliance against Germany and Austro-Hungary. Although Great Britain traditionally stood aside from European entanglements, the growing industrial and military might of Germany alarmed British statesmen. When the Germans embarked on rapid naval expansion in the first decade of the twentieth century, Britain responded in kind. The British

were also driven into an "Entente" with their traditional enemies, France and Russia, although this fell far short of a full military alliance.

Germany's ruler, Kaiser Wilhelm II, was an unstable, neurotic individual. He was born with a withered arm, a defect which provoked an overwhelming need to assert himself.

His gesture politics were the most obvious sign of instability in the early part of the century. He talked of Germany's need for a "place in the sun", causing the British to fear he had designs on their empire. He indulged in the kind of brinkmanship, then known as "sabre-rattling", culminating in the Agadir incident in 1911 when a German battleship was sent to oppose a French military presence in Morocco, and Europe for

a while teetered on the brink of war. By 1914, Germany's military elite had become convinced that the balance of power was shifting against them. Regarding a war as inevitable, they believed it would be better if it happened sooner rather than later.

Although Germany was the most militaristic state in Europe, all the major powers had schooled their populations in jingoistic attitudes and the military virtues of courage and self-sacrifice for the homeland.

By 1911, the major powers had not fought a war for forty years. Many men longed for a chance to show their metal. In principle, militarism was opposed by powerful socialist movements in all countries. But in practice, international socialism was to prove no match for militant patriotism.

Compared with 1911, the summer of 1914 seemed lacking in international tension. But on June 28, 1914, the Archduke Francis-Ferdinand, the heir to the Austro-Hungarian throne, began an official visit to the Bosnian capital, Sarajevo, accompanied by his wife, Sophie.

From a Serbian point of view, the visit was a provocation. Bosnia had been annexed by Austria-Hungary in 1908. Serb nationalists were campaigning to "liberate" the province, with its partially Serb population, from Hapsburg rule.

A Serb secret society known as the Black Hand decided to assassinate the Archduke. As the archducal car drove toward Sarajevo's town hall, a bomb was thrown. It exploded, but the royal couple were unharmed. Driving back after lunch, however, the car took a wrong turning and came to a halt exactly opposite 19-year-old Gavril Princip, one of the Black Hand assassination squad who was making his way back to the railway station. The startled young man drew his gun and shot both the Archduke and his wife.

The assassination gave Austria-Hungary a pretext for humiliating Serbia and its backers, the Russians. With the full support of Germany, the Hapsburg government demanded that the Serbs allow Austria to track down terrorists inside Serbia. Every Serb concession was brushed aside, and on July 28 Austria-Hungary declared war on Serbia.

All the major powers had war plans that involved the rapid mobilization of masses of conscripts, followed by swift offensive action. Each side feared that the other might deliver a decisive attack before a response could be organized. When Russia mobilized in support of Serbia, it tried to make it clear that it did not want a war with Germany. But the German government and military chiefs were nervous and, in the case of some individuals, eager for war. They set in motion the Schlieffen plan – a rapid blow in the West to destroy France, followed by a concentration of forces against Russia in the East.

On August 1, after the Tsar refused to stop mobilization, Germany declared war on Russia. The Germans then staged a fake French air raid on Nuremberg to justify declaring war on France.

The Germans did not, however, intend a war with Britain. The British Liberal government was anti-war by tradition and did not see itself as bound to aid France. But on August 3, as dictated by the Schlieffen plan, German forces entered neutral Belgium. As a guarantor of Belgian neutrality, the British felt they could not honourably stand by.

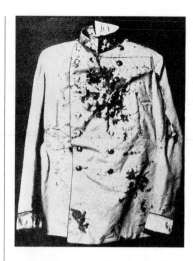

▲ The blood-stained tunic worn by Archduke Franz Ferdinand of Austria-Hungary at the time of his assassination.

The government issued an ultimatum to Germany.

British Foreign Secretary, Sir Edward Grey, stood at a window in Whitehall as dusk fell and said: "The lamps are going out all over Europe. We shall not see them lit again in our lifetime."

▲ Police prevent a public lynching with the arrest of the assassin, the Serbian anarchist Gavril Princip.

THE WESTERN FRONT

▲ **Trench warfare showed the folly of outmoded battle strategies in the age of modern armoury. The result was a massive loss of human life.**

The French, German and British soldiers who embarked for the front at the beginning of August 1914, amid scenes of patriotic enthusiasm, were instantly thrown into a series of battles more bloody than any previously seen in European warfare.

Both France and Germany planned to take the offensive. The French concentrated the bulk of their forces along their eastern frontier with Alsace-Lorraine, ready to strike directly into the heart of Germany.

The small British Expeditionary Force (BEF) was to hold the left of their line, but still leave a wide gap undefended along the Belgian frontier up to the Channel coast.

The Germans adopted a modified version of the Schlieffen plan, originally proposed in 1895. The main German force was to advance rapidly through Belgium and across northern France towards Paris.

France was to be knocked out of the war in six weeks, a move that would then allow Germany to turn its forces eastward against Russia.

The German invasion of neutral Belgium did not go smoothly. The Belgian army fought desperately, and bridges and railways were blown up to hamper the Germans' progress. German troops, outraged by Belgian resistance, burned villages and shot large numbers of civilians – atrocities no less real for being exaggerated by Allied propaganda.

As the Germans swung through Belgium, the French launched their Lorraine offensive. It was a catastrophe. Scorning drab camouflage gear in favour of traditional bright uniforms with red trousers, the French put their faith in the *élan* of cavalry charges and massed infantry advancing in close formation with bayonets fixed. The attackers were mown down in their thousands by German firepower.

The six divisions of the BEF, arriving somewhat belatedly on the Continent, were positioned in the path of the massive German force coming through Belgium.

At the Mons Canal, on August 23, the British performed creditably, their rapid and accurate rifle fire taking a heavy toll of the German attackers. Heavily outnumbered, however, the BEF was soon in retreat, as were the French on their right.

It seemed that nothing could prevent the Germans taking Paris, but they made the crucial mistake of withdrawing two corps to the Eastern Front. Also, the pace of the advance, over hundreds of kilometres on foot, exhausted the German infantry.

Commanded by General Joseph Joffre, the French counter-attacked at the Battle of the Marne. It was a masterpiece of

▲ **A woman presents flowers to German soldiers on the way to the Western Front. Few imagined the casualties that would result.**

improvization – some *poilus* were famously carried from Paris to the front in a fleet of 600 taxis. The BEF, whose demoralized commander, Sir John French, had been contemplating evacuating his forces to Britain, joined in the counter-offensive, and the Germans were forced to retreat.

The fighting shifted back towards the Belgian border. At the month-long Battle of Ypres (October 12–November 11), the BEF held the line against a desperate counter-attack by the Germans. Then, with winter coming on, the armies dug in. Two parallel lines of trenches stretched without a break from the Channel to Switzerland. With no more flanking movements possible, the only way forward for either side was a frontal assault in the face of overwhelming firepower. The armies would barely move for the next three years.

The human cost of the first five months of the war was astounding. About 90 per cent of the original BEF were casualties by the end of the year, 10 per cent of them having been killed. The French had lost over half a million troops. The German gamble on a swift victory in the West had failed and a long war of attrition was bound to follow.

▼ German troops on the Eastern Front take control of Lodz in Poland, enabling them to march on Warsaw.

LOOKING EAST

▲ **A battalion of French infantrymen prepare to open fire as German troops advance across the River Marne.**

On the Eastern Front, Germany and Austro-Hungary faced Russia's 3.4 million men – numerically the largest army in the world. But it was reckoned that Russia would be slow to mobilize. The Germans envisaged the Eastern Front as a holding operation, while they won their six-week war in the west.

It was soon clear that Germany would have to depend on its own efforts, rather than its Austro-Hungarian allies. The first offensive of the war, Austro-Hungary's assault on Serbia, was a disaster. This setback was followed by a defeat at the hands of the Russians, at Lemberg, which cost the Hapsburg armies about 250,000 casualties.

German calculations were thrown out not just by the weakness of the Austrians, but by the speed of Russian mobilization, which surprised everyone. By mid-August, two Russian armies were advancing into East Prussia from the east and the south, with a single German army facing them. The Russians were, however, poorly equipped and supplied. Food and ammunition were short. Some of the men even lacked boots. Crucially, ill-trained Russian radio operators failed to use code, allowing the Germans to intercept their messages and anticipate the Russian armies' every move.

To face the Russian challenge, General Paul von Hindenburg was appointed commander on the Eastern Front, with Erich von Ludendorff as his chief of staff. Leaving only a small covering force in front of the Russian army in the east, they turned the full weight of the German Eighth Army against the Russian Second Army in the south. The Battle of Tannenberg, fought in the last week of August, was a triumph for the German commanders, who achieved total victory, taking over 125,000 Russian prisoners.

Although the Austro-Hungarian armies continued to perform poorly, after Tannenberg there was no chance that Germany would be overrun. A further victory in September at the Masurian Lakes in East Prussia drove back the Russian army in the east. The triumphs on the Eastern Front made Hindenburg and Ludendorff national heroes, destined to play a major role in the direction of the rest of the war and in postwar German politics.

DEATH FROM THE SKY

Britain suffered the first air raid in its history on the night of January 19–20, 1915. Although the damage caused was relatively small, the attack was the prelude to a three-year air offensive that eventually killed more than 1,000 British civilians.

The air strike was delivered by Zeppelin airships of the German Navy. Three Zeppelins took off from Hamburg, intending to attack targets around the Humber. One got into difficulties, however, and had to turn back, while the other two, bearing the designations *L3* and *L4*, drifted off course.

At 8.20 pm, *L3* reached the English coast at Great Yarmouth, and dropped its load of six high-explosive bombs and seven incendiaries. *L4*, hopelessly lost, ranged over the Norfolk country-side terrorizing various small villages before flying over King's Lynn, which it bombed.

The raid of January 19–20 killed four people and injured 16 others. Many thousands more were terrified by this new experience of total war.

▲ Houses in the East Anglian town of King's Lynn are destroyed by an unexpected new threat from the skies: the Zeppelin.

CONTROVERSY STIRRED BY THE BIRTH OF A NATION

▲ Henry B Walthall and Lillian Gish, two of the stars of D W Griffith's controversial cinema epic *The Birth of a Nation*.

The release on March 3 in New York of D W Griffith's powerful epic silent movie *The Birth of a Nation* sparked both admiration for his technical achievement and horror at its racist content.

The film, based on Thomas Dixon's novel and play *The Clansman*, tells the story of the Civil War and the Reconstruction from the point of view of a white Southern family.

The story-line focuses on the rape of a Southern white woman (Lillian Gish) by a crazed black. All the black roles in the cast were played by blacked-up white actors. The heroes of the film are the Ku Klux Klan, who, led by the woman's brother, avenge her death and defeat the blacks who besiege her family.

Technically the film was a masterpiece: "Never before has such a combination of spectacle and tense drama been seen," wrote the *New York Sun*. People flocked to see the film even at $2 a head. The film also caused an outcry from blacks and white liberals against its offensive portrayal of blacks. The National Association for the Advancement of Colored People (NAACP) called on people to boycott the film and organized pickets at cinemas showing it.

SINKING OF THE LUSITANIA

On May 7, a Cunard ocean liner, the *Lusitania*, bound for Liverpool from New York, was sunk by a German U-boat 13 km (8 miles) off the south coast of Ireland. A total of 1,198 people drowned, 128 of them US citizens.

The *Lusitania* was one of the elite transatlantic liners that in prewar years vied for the Blue Riband, awarded to the vessel making the fastest Atlantic crossing. Its passengers included many figures from the highest circles of society, including US millionaire Alfred Vanderbilt.

The barbarism of the sinking of a passenger ship without warning brought widespread condemnation. It was not generally known at the time that, as well as passengers, the *Lusitania* was carrying munitions, making it arguably a valid military target.

A week before the liner sailed from New York, the German embassy had included it in a published list of vessels on which

US citizens should avoid travelling.

When the news of the sinking broke in Britain, rioters took to the streets, attacking German-owned shops – or shops with German-sounding names – in Liverpool, Manchester, London's East End, and other cities.

Once the mob was loosed, other "aliens" soon came under attack, including Jews and Chinese. In Liverpool, troops had to be sent in to restore order. A government promise to intern enemy aliens

▲ Paintings such as this enabled newspapers to portray the sinking of the *Lusitania* as "a crime that staggered humanity".

eventually managed to calm the "*Lusitania* riots". Although there was no comparable violent popular response in the United States, the sinking of the *Lusitania* played a huge part in turning US public opinion against Germany, preparing the way for the United States' eventual entry into the war.

WAR IN AFRICA

In the years before the Great War, Germany had acquired a scattering of colonies in Africa. When war broke out, they came under attack from British, French and Belgian colonial forces. In west Africa, Togo was easily captured and Cameroon succumbed to invasion after a desultory campaign.

German South West Africa (now Namibia) adjoined the Union of South Africa, a British colony in which the Afrikaner (Boer) population had fought for independence little over a decade earlier.

Although South Africa's prime minister, Jan Smuts, was a Boer, this did not stop several Boer generals from rebelling the moment Britain was distracted by war in Europe. Fortunately for the

British, while around 11,000 Afrikaners in the South African Defence Force joined the rebels, almost three times that number remained loyal.

Once the rebellion had been put down, the Defence Force, commanded by General Louis Botha, was able to turn its attention to the Germans. Invading the vast wastes of South West Africa in January, they took seven months to bring the German colonial forces to unconditional surrender.

Germany's most valuable colony was German East Africa (now Tanzania) There a spirited German officer, Colonel Paul von Lettow-Vorbeck, organized a force of about 2,500 African soldiers and 200 white officers, and took the

offensive, invading Kenya and Uganda. He routed an amphibious landing by troops from British India at Tanga in November 1914, capturing enough arms and ammunition to keep him supplied for several years.

Living off the land and avoiding pitched battles, von Lettow-Vorbeck sustained a guerrilla campaign against expanding British forces. In 1917, the German High Command sent a Zeppelin with a cargo of arms south from Europe to supply its East African force – but the flight was stopped at the Sudan after the Germans formed the mistaken belief that von Lettow-Vorbeck had been defeated. In fact, he fought on to the end of the war and was never beaten.

'15

NEWS IN BRIEF
........·...................

World World One Chronology

January
- Germans first use poison gas
- German cruiser *Blucher* sunk in the Battle of the Dogger Bank

February
- British troops begins offensive in Mesopotamia
- Germany and Austria begin Battle of Masuria against Russia
- Memel in Lithuania captured from Russia by German troops
- British and French navies shell Turkish positions in the Dardanelles

March
- Battle of Nueve Chappel in France begins
- Attempted Allied naval passage through the Dardanelles fails
- German airship raid on Paris
- Russian forces take Przemysl in Poland

April
- Second Battle of Ypres in Belgium begins
- Allied landings in Gallipoli
- Secret alliance treaty between France, Britain and Italy
- German offensive on the Eastern Front begins

May
- German submarines sink American ship *Gulflight*
- Russian line breaks under Austro-German offensive in Galicia
- Italy renounces Triple-Alliance pact with Germany
- Second Battle of Artois in France begins

GERMAN U-BOATS ON THE OFFENSIVE

The Allied blockade against Germany and the Central Powers was countered by Germany's declaration of a submarine blockade of British waters on February 18, 1915.

The declaration specified that all Allied shipping sighted in the approaches to the British Isles could be torpedoed on sight without warning. Not only was this a highly controversial undertaking, which would inevitably lead to loss of life among non-combatants and neutrals,it was also a highly ambitious strategy, not least because at the start of the campaign Germany had only 21 U-boats in the North Sea.

During the course of 1915, however, the numbers of U-boats increased as did the operational efficiency of their crews.

The first U-boat campaign lasted a little over a year and led to the sinking of over a million tonnes of Allied shipping. In the Mediterranean, U-boats operated out of Austrian and Turkish ports, where climatic conditions and laxity amongst merchant-ship crews made this a happy hunting ground for the Germans.

The British were forced to re-route vessels from Australia, India and the Far East around the Cape of Good Hope rather than risk these dangerous waters. In due course, Britain diverted as many as 500 naval vessels to combat the Mediterranean U-boats.

In the end, however, it was in the more difficult waters around Britain that the success of the U-boat campaign would be decided. Among the ships sunk close to the British Isles were an American tanker and two British liners – the *Lusitania* and *Arabic*

– both of which carried substantial numbers of US passengers. The resultant loss of lives caused an outcry and brought US opinion behind the Allied cause.

The international pressure which followed the sinking of the *Arabic* on August 19 compelled the German High Command to moderate its strategy, so that on September 1, 1915, unrestricted submarine warfare was temporarily ended. The Germans accepted that in future no passenger ships would be attacked without warning, although the sinking of merchant vessels continued.

Pressure from the United States on the Germans to further moderate their U-boat campaign was led by President Wilson. In the spring of 1916, he managed to extract an undertaking that German submarines would not torpedo or shell merchant vessels without warning, and would do their best to confine operations to the fighting forces of the belligerents. This promise effectively ended the first U-boat campaign; the second began early in 1917 when the need to cripple Britain's economic base became ever more pressing.

◄ **The hidden terror of the seas, the German U-boat campaign of 1915 created havoc amid Allied shipping.**

US EXPELS GERMAN SPIES

In December 1915, Captain Franz von Papen and Captain Karl Boy-Ed, military attachés at the German embassy in Washington, DC, were expelled for organizing espionage and sab-

otage in the neutral United States. Allied propagandists had worked hard through the first year of the war to convince the US that every explosion at a munitions plant was an act of

sabotage by German agents.

However, it was not until the summer of 1915 that there was any solid evidence of illegal activity by the German embassy. It occurred when a German official, Dr Albert, carelessly left his dispatch case on a subway train. Detective Frank Burke, who was tailing him, picked up the case and discovered among its contents plans for a sabotage campaign.

To avoid a diplomatic confrontation, the US did not acknowledge possession of the documents.

Instead they were leaked to the *New York World* for publication. The resulting scandal provided the pretext for throwing the military attachés out.

▶ **Franz von Papen, one of the two military attachés at the German embassy in Washington expelled from the United States.**

GALLIPOLI

In January 1915, the British government tried to get the war moving by a bold attack against Germany's ally, Turkey. Chiefly at the instigation of the First Lord of the Admiralty, Winston Churchill, the British planned to send a naval force through the Dardanelles, the narrow waterway that leads from the Mediterranean to the Turkish capital, Istanbul.

With the grudging support of France, a fleet of mostly outdated warships was assembled. But a full-scale attempt to break through the Dardanelles on March 18 failed after three battleships were sunk by mines.

The British decided that the navy could only get through after a landing force had captured the shores of the waterway.

The troops available in the eastern Mediterranean included volunteers of the Australia and New Zealand Army Corps (ANZAC), who had reached Egypt on their way to the Western Front. The site chosen for the landings was the Gallipoli peninsula. At dawn on April 25, British, French and ANZAC troops arrived off the Turkish shore aboard some 200 merchant vessels. Lacking specialist landing craft, most of the men went ashore in lines of rowing boats. Their officers had no idea of the terrain they were to face, nor of Turkish troop dispositions.

▲ **Troops from the Australian and New Zealand Army Corps make an unsuccessful landing during the Gallipoli campaign.**

The Australians and New Zealanders missed their designated landing beach, instead coming ashore at a small cove backed by steep ridges. The troops were soon stuck a mile inland, precariously hanging on to positions dominated by Turkish fire. The British and French landings had no more success.

By early May, the stalemate of the Western Front had been reproduced at Gallipoli, with Allied troops holding on to their small enclaves, blocked by Turkish trenches. The British attempted another landing at Suvla Bay in

August, but it too bogged down.

Although the Allied troops fought with great courage and endurance, by Christmas their commanders had decided to cut their losses. Over the following weeks, the survivors slipped away to sea – by far the most successful operation in the whole fiasco.

The Allies suffered 265,000 casualties at Gallipoli. For Australia and New Zealand, it was an experience never to be forgotten – one that encouraged a nascent national pride, and bred an enduring suspicion of the British authorities.

PANCHO VILLA WAGES WAR ON UNCLE SAM

▲ **American border guards camped at Naminquipa capture troops from Pancho Villa's rebel army.**

Raging discontent among Mexico's impoverished rural population was the basis for armed campaigns waged almost continuously through the 1910s by the renowned guerrilla chiefs Emiliano Zapata and Pancho Villa.

By 1916, Mexico was ruled by a liberal landowner, Venustiano Carranza, who had come to power after the overthrow of his brutal predecessor, General Huerta – a move engineered by the United States. Zapata and Villa had origi-nally backed Carranza, but now the guerrilla chiefs were almost immediately back at war with him.

Villa, who operated in northern Mexico, was especially outraged by US support for Carranza. In January 1916, he decided to take his revenge.

His men ambushed a train carrying a group of US mining engineers, and 15 of the *gringos* were shot. In March, Villa went a step further, sending a raiding party, almost 500 strong, across the border into New Mexico. At dawn on March 9, they attacked the small, dusty desert township of Columbus. Shouting: "*Muerte a los gringos*" and "*Viva Villa*", the Mexicans went on the rampage, burning and looting buildings and firing on their inhabitants, killing 18. They were eventually driven off by the US cavalry.

The attack led to an outcry in the United States. Senator Albert Bacon Fall called on the govern-ment to send an army of half a million men to occupy Mexico. Instead, President Woodrow Wilson organized a 6,000-strong punitive expedition commanded by General John Pershing.

Crossing into Mexico, Pershing hunted for Villa's men, but in vain. Taunted by hostile Mexican peasants and baffled in its pur-suit, the expedition pressed ever further south, until even Carranza himself became anxious about its intentions.

The Mexican army was ordered to confront Pershing's men and there was a brief clash before the US finally pulled out in January 1917. The futile expedition had cost the US $130 million.

BATTLE OF JUTLAND

Dreadnought battleships were the most advanced fighting machines of the early twentieth century. To the British public, an encounter between the German High Seas Fleet and the British Grand Fleet was anticipated as the climactic moment of the Great War. But when that battle came, at Jutland on May 31, 1916, it proved disappointingly indecisive.

Commanded by the aggressive Admiral Reinhard Scheer, the German fleet had begun to make sorties into the North Sea, hoping to inflict damage before the Royal Navy's main force of Dread-noughts could arrive, steaming south from Scapa Flow. Due to the cracking of German naval codes, however, the British had immediate warning when the High Seas Fleet set out to sea at the end of May. The British comman-der, Admiral Sir John Jellicoe, steamed to meet them.

In all, more than 250 warships headed for a showdown in grey, squally weather. With 28 Dreadnoughts and nine battle-cruisers to the Germans' 16 Dreadnoughts and five battle-cruisers, the Royal Navy had every expectation of victory.

When the British battlecruisers made contact with the enemy, they soon turned north, drawing the Germans after them toward the British Dreadnoughts. The ploy worked, and for five minutes the world's top battleships slugged it out. Then the Germans turned away and escaped the British pursuit in failing light.

Both sides claimed a victory. The Germans had lost only 11 ships and 2,551 men, compared with the Royal Navy's 15 ships and 6,094 men. On the other hand, the German High Seas Fleet was once more forced back into port, and had little effect on the further course of the war.

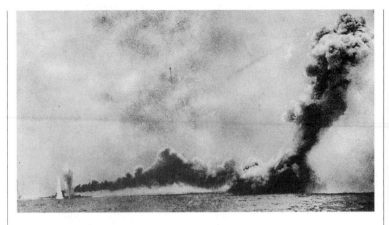

▲ HMS *Queen Mary* perishes during the Battle of Jutland in which over seven-and-a-half thousand British and German sailors lost their lives.

"A TERRIBLE BEAUTY IS BORN"

Although about 100,000 southern Irish enlisted to fight for Britain in the Great War, a minority of Irish Nationalists were determined to act on the saying: "England's extremity is Ireland's opportunity." The Irish Republican Brotherhood, led by Padraic Pearse and James Connolly's Citizen Army, planned an armed uprising for Easter 1916. The Nationalists established contact with Germany, which agreed to supply arms.

On Good Friday, a merchant vessel, the *Aud*, flying the Norwegian flag, arrived off the Irish coast carrying 20,000 German rifles. Due to a misunderstanding, however, no rebels turned up to take the weapons ashore, and the ship was scuttled.

Despite the incident, on Easter Monday, April 24, the planned uprising went ahead. About 1,800 rebels, armed with a mix of rifles, shotguns, pickaxes and sledge-hammers, took over key buildings in Dublin. One of them, the General Post Office, became the headquarters of the rebellion.

Pearse read out a proclamation setting up a "Provisional Government of the Irish Republic" and declaring that "Ireland, through us,

▲ British infantrymen snipe from behind a barricade of empty beer casks during the 1916 Easter Rising in Dublin.

summons her children to her flag and strikes for her freedom."

The rebels had, in fact, very little popular support in Ireland. The British response was severe and heavy-handed. Artillery was used extensively to dislodge the rebels, causing large-scale damage to property and considerable civilian casualties. In all about 500 people died and more than 2,000 were wounded during a week of intense fighting. Finally, with the General Post Office gutted by fire, the insurgents surrendered.

The British commander, General Sir John Maxwell, used his powers under martial law to send over 2,000 people to prison camps in Britain. At secret courts martial,

90 rebels were sentenced to death; fifteen were actually executed, including Pearse and Connolly. Among those spared – because he held a US passport – was future Irish president Eamon de Valera.

The executions, carried out over a 10-day period, completely altered public sentiment in Ireland. The unpopular rebels were transformed into national heroes by their blood sacrifice – a metamorphosis captured by the Irish poet W B Yeats's *Easter 1916,* in which the leaders of the uprising are said to have been "changed, changed utterly: /A terrible beauty is born."

▲ Dublin's General Post Office, destroyed by a bombardment of British shells that put an end to the rebellion.

LORD KITCHENER LOST AT SEA

Secretary for War, Lord Kitchener, was drowned when the ship on which he was sailing, HMS *Hampshire*, struck a mine in the North Sea within two hours of leaving Scapa Flow on June 5, 1916. Kitchener had been on his way to visit the Czar to ascertain the true state of affairs in Russia. Lloyd George, who was to have accompanied him, was called to Ireland at the last moment: the Irish negotiations saved his life.

Veteran of the Boer War, Lord Kitchener was idolized by the public who had rallied to his first recruiting appeal for 10,000 volunteers to join the army – a plea immortalized by the poster in

▲ The eternal image of Britain's great war veteran Lord Kitchener appealing for volunteers to enlist with the army.

which the words: "Your country needs you" were accompanied by a picture of him pointing his finger at the reader.

At the outbreak of the war Kitchener had fiercely opposed the common view that the conflict would be over by Christmas, believing that it would be long and difficult. Unfortunately, his effectiveness as Secretary for War was diminished by politicians who gave him little room for manoeuvre. Winston Churchill wrote of his death: "The sudden onrush of the night, the deep waters of the North, were destined to preserve him and his renown from the shallows."

THE ARAB REVOLT IN TURKEY

▲ The call to arms by Sherif Hussein Ibn Ali to the Moslem world that signalled the start of the Arab revolt in Mecca.

On June 5, 1916, Sherif Hussein Ibn Ali fired a rifle shot at the Ottoman barracks in Mecca, denouncing the rule of the Ottoman Empire by the Young

Turks. Within days there were no Turks in Mecca, and a week later the port of Jeddah and the town of Taif were also in Arab hands. The Arab rebellion in Hejaz had begun.

The Arabs in Turkey had become increasingly angered by the Turkish government, who since the coup in 1913, had pursued a Turkish-nationalist and secular policy.

In November 1914, the pro-German Young Turk government had officially declared war on the Allies and thereafter ruthlessly stamped out any possible rebellions within the Empire.

In the summer of 1915, Cemal determined to liquidate Arab secret societies and other dissident groups in Syria. He ordered the hanging of 11 Arabs in Beirut on August 28, 1915, and carried out arrests, deportations and executions in the Lebanon for the next 18 months.

Captain T E Lawrence, who later headed the British mission in Hejaz, wrote that Cemal had "united all classes, conditions and creeds in Syria, under pressure of a common misery and peril, and so made a concerted revolt possible".

The Allies seized on Arab hostility towards the Young Turks. During 1915, the British authorities in Egypt assured Sherif Hussein that they would "recognize and support the independence of the Arabs", although they were vague as to the exact extent of the territory of a Hashemite kingdom.

The British Foreign Secretary, Sir Edward Grey, also relayed to Sherif Hussein that he favoured "Arab independence of Turkish domination". Sherif Hussein of Mecca needed no further encouragement.

NEWS IN BRIEF

....

World World One Chronology

January
- Austria-Hungary attack Montenegro
- Russia begins offensive against Turkey

February
- Fifth Battle of the Isonzo between Italy and Austria
- Erzurum, Turkey captured by Russian troops
- Last German troops in Cameroon surrender
- Battle of Verdun, France begins
- Russians capture Bitlis, Turkey

March
- Germany declares war on Portugal
- Allied air attack on German submarine base in Zeebrugge, Belgium

April
- Trebizond in Turkey captured by Russian forces
- Kut-al-Imara in Mesopotamia recaptured by Turkish forces

May
- ANZAC troops arrive in France
- Austro-Hungary begins new offensive in Italy
- Naval battle of Jutland in the North Sea

June
- Russians begin new offensive on the Eastern Front
- Greece blockaded by Allies
- Wilhelmsthal in German East Africa falls to Allied forces
- Czernowitz in Ukraine falls to Russian troops

MARGARET SANGER OPENS BIRTH CONTROL CLINIC

"Mothers! Can you afford to have a large family? Do you want any more children? If not, why do you have them?" So began each of the 5,000 leaflets printed by Margaret Sanger to publicize the opening of her first birth control clinic in Brooklyn, New York, on October 16, 1916.

Keen to receive advice from Mrs Sanger and her two assistants and to view the various birth control devices displayed inside, 150 women queued outside the clinic on the first morning, waiting for the doors to open.

▶ **It would take more than sticky tape to silence Margaret Sanger, the birth-control pioneer and mother of feminism.**

Two years earlier, trained nurse Margaret Sanger had created a storm of controversy with the publication of a radical feminist magazine *The Woman Rebel*, in which she gave advice on contraception, asserting that "no

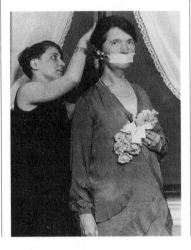

woman can call herself free who does not own and control her own body". When the post office confiscated the magazine she produced a pamphlet entitled *Family Limitation*, describing the use of birth control devices such as the sponge and diaphragm. She was indicted for distributing birth control literature and sentenced to one month in jail. She spent the next year travelling Europe where she learnt of the use of condoms and pessaries.

In Britain in July 1918, Dr Marie Stopes took up the cry for the use of birth control with the publication of her book *Married Love*. She went on to open the first birth control clinic in London in March 1921.

LLOYD GEORGE BECOMES PRIME MINISTER

On December 7, 1916 David Lloyd George became Prime Minister of Britain. His appointment followed a series of articles hostile to the Prime Minister, Asquith, that appeared in the press, including *The Times*, owned by Lord Northcliffe, and the *Daily Express* and *Daily Chronicle*, both greatly influenced by Lord Beaverbrook.

The papers increasingly favoured Lloyd George, Secretary of State for War, who, for a month, had battled with Asquith over the formation of a streamlined War Committee. Lloyd George proposed to run the committee, from which the Prime Minister would be excluded.

On the evening of December 5, Asquith went to Buckingham Palace to tender his resignation.

The King recorded in his diary that he accepted his resignation with "great regret". He then summoned colonial secretary Bonar Law, asking him to form a government.

The next day a conference was held at Buckingham Palace between the King, Asquith, Balfour, Lloyd George, Henderson and Bonar Law. The latter stated that he would lead a government only if Asquith agreed to join the government under him. It was agreed that Asquith should consider this proposal and should he decline, the commission would be passed to Lloyd George.

After several hours' thought Asquith declined a subordinate position, and so Bonar Law refused the King's commission, which was immediately passed to Lloyd George. Within 24 hours

▲ **David Lloyd George became Prime Minister after Herbert Asquith refused to serve under Bonar Law.**

Lloyd George informed the King that he was able to form an administration, and he was duly appointed Prime Minister and First Lord of the Treasury.

'16

1916: VERDUN AND THE SOMME

Since their limited attack at Ypres in April 1915, the Germans had adopted a defensive role on the Western Front. But in February 1916, the German High Command went over to the offensive. The German Chief-of-Staff, General Erich von Falkenhayn, decided to strike a mortal blow against the French Army, which had already been weakened by almost two million casualties since the outbreak of war. Instead of attempting a breakthrough, Falkenhayn planned to "bleed France to death" by attacking a section of the line the French felt compelled to defend, regardless of casualties. Verdun marked the beginning of planned attritional warfare on the Western Front.

The salient around the fortress of Verdun was chosen as the killing ground; not only was it of strong emotional value to the French, it also allowed the Germans to bring the maximum amount of artillery to bear on the defenders. Artillery would act as the cornerstone of the German plan: limited attacks by infantry would seize key points in order to suck in French reserves for the "grinding mill" of the German guns.

On February 21, 1916 the 1,200 guns (over half of heavy calibre) of the German Fifth Army opened their bombardment, the most devastating yet experienced in warfare. Later in the day, assault groups of German infantry advanced into the shattered French trenches. Over the

▲ **A British machine gun unit in action during the Battle of the Somme. Over a million lives were lost in the 142-day offensive.**

next few days the Germans advanced steadily, and captured the stronghold of Fort Douamont on February 25.

The French High Command had been caught by surprise, but on February 25, General Pétain was appointed to command the Second Army defending Verdun. Pétain was an excellent tactician, with a reputation for caring about his men, and he immediately set about organizing the supply, reinforcement and relief of his hard-pressed troops. The only route into Verdun was under constant artillery fire – along *La Voie Sacrée* ("the sacred way") – but 300 lorries a day brought the men and munitions to defend Verdun.

Throughout March, April and May the battle raged with undiminished intensity. And to the consternation of the Germans, they too found that their troops were going through the "grinding mill". On July 1, 1916, the Allied offensive on the Somme forced

the Germans to close down their operations at Verdun, while, at the end of the month, the French went over to the offensive and in a series of ferocious counterattacks won back most of the territory lost to the Germans earlier in the year. Total casualties were over a third of a million men on each side, and

while a battered French Army hung on to Verdun, the instigator of the German plan, General Falkenhayn, was sacked and replaced by the successful team of Hindenburg and Ludendorff.

Although the German attack on Verdun drew away much French support from the Allied summer offensive on the Somme, it still went ahead.

The British would now take the leading role. The main attack would be made by the eleven divisions of the British Fourth Army, commanded by General Rawlinson, supported by five French divisions south of the River Somme.

The British relied heavily on their enormously expanded artillery arm, which included just over 2,000 artillery pieces, and substantial supplies of ammunition. In an eight-day preliminary bombardment, 1,732,873 shells

▼ **French troops under attack at the strategically important fortress of Verdun, overlooking the River Meuse.**

were fired, sufficient, the British High Command thought, to destroy the German defences. But the British did not have enough heavy-calibre guns; nearly a third of the shells fired were defective, and the German dug-outs proved more shell-proof than anticipated.

Confident that the guns had done their work, however, the British infantry went "over the top" in perfect order on the morning of July 1, 1916, only to be cut down in their waves from well-directed German artillery and machine-gun fire.

Out of an attacking force of about 100,000 men, over 57,000 became casualties in the first day's fighting, with nearly 20,000 men killed outright.

The British attack was virtually stopped in its tracks, although over on the right flank the tactically more sophisticated French did manage to make some gains.

Although a terrible setback for the British, July 1 was only the first day of the great summer offensive, which was to continue until November. Lessons were learned and more flexible approaches adopted.

A successful dawn attack on July 14 demonstrated what the "New Armies" were capable of doing and represented a marked improvement in British staff work. But every attack soon became bogged down in desperate trench warfare, especially as the Germans operated a policy of vigorous counter-attacks; the commander of the German Second Army, General von Below, instructed his men: "to hold our present positions at any cost. The enemy should have to carve his way over heaps of corpses."

On September 15, tanks were thrown into the battle, but after some small local gains the hopes invested in them were also

dashed. The last phase of the battle ended with the capture of Beaumont Hamel on November 13, when cold and rain had turned the battlefield into a sea of freezing mud, making effective operations impossible.

The first great British offensive of the war ended in disappointment, although the British Army had proved itself a valiant and capable fighting force. The 142-day offensive of the Somme produced 415,000 British casualties; the French lost over 200,000. German casualties ranged from between 400,000 and 600,000 men. For great loss of life and scant territorial gains, Verdun and the Somme personified the horror of trench warfare on the Western Front.

▲ A deserted French dug-out following the end of the Somme offensive. Little territorial gain had been achieved at immense human cost.

▼ A helmet and rifle act as a gravestone for an unknown French soldier, killed on the battlefield of Verdun.

'17

THE USA ENTERS THE WAR

On April 2, 1917, US President Woodrow Wilson went before Congress to ask them to declare war on Germany. "The world must be made safe for democracy", he said during an eloquent speech in which he equated victory for the Allies with the upholding of democracy in the world. Four days later he gained the approval of Congress, and two months after that the first US troops set sail for Europe.

For the previous three years President Wilson had pursued a policy of neutrality despite provocation. In May 1915, Cunard's passenger liner, the *Lusitania,* was torpedoed by German submarines, Germany contending that the ship was carrying munitions intended for Britain. Although 128 Americans died, Wilson was not to be drawn, maintaining that "there is such a thing as a nation being so right

that it does not need to convince others by force that it is right". Elected in 1916 on a peace platform, as late as January 1917 he delivered his famous "Peace without Victory" speech to Congress. However, at the end of that month Germany declared that it would no longer show any restraint towards "neutral shipping", officially making any US merchant ship a target for German torpedoes.

The following month, British spies passed to the US an intercepted message – known as the Zimmermann note – from Germany to Mexico. In it Germany offered to back Mexico in the reconquest of the US south-west if Mexico would support Germany.

Finally, in March, three US cargo ships were sunk by German submarines, and, reluctantly, President Wilson was forced to abandon his neutral stance.

◀ **Hundreds of young Americans queue up in response to the government's call for volunteers to enlist with the US marines.**

BRITAIN PROPOSES JEWISH STATE

On November 2, 1917, Britain's Foreign Secretary Arthur Balfour declared: "His Majesty's government views with favour the establishment in Palestine of a national home for the Jewish people, and will use their best endeavours to facilitate the achievement of this object, it being clearly understood that nothing shall be done which may prejudice the civil and religious rights of existing non-Jewish communities in Palestine." In doing so he hoped to secure Zionist support for the Allies.

The Balfour Declaration shocked the Arab world. Only the previous year, with the help of Hussein Ibn Ali, ruler of the Hejaz and guardian of Mecca, the Allies had defeated the Turks, securing Palestine for Britain.

In return, Britain had pledged to help realize the independence of most of the Arab world. In addition, Muslims in Palestine outnumbered Jews by ten to one, and Arabs could conceive of no grant of rights that did not include self-determination for this majority.

▲ **Arthur Balfour (left), architect of the "Jewish State". His proposal caused consternation throughout the Arab world.**

THE ROLE OF WOMEN IN WORLD WAR ONE

▲ **With eligible young men on active war service in France, women took on increasingly significant roles at home.**

During 1914 and 1915, as more and more men answered Lord Kitchener's recruitment appeals labour came to be in short supply, especially in the engineering trades. By June 1915, one fifth of the men working in engineering had enlisted, at a time when the army desperately needed supplies. Wages rose dramatically – a shipyard riveter, for example, saw his wage double between 1914 and 1919 – and conditions at work improved not least in the introduction to the factories of canteens that provided workers with nutritious meals at low prices. Still, demand for workers in almost every field, especially munitions, was greater than supply.

Many women were eager to enter the workforce, suffragette Mrs Dacre Fox voicing the opinion of many when she said: "We believe women can be employed in almost any capacity of intellectual or physical work." In July 1915, 30,000 women marched down Whitehall behind suffragette Christabel Pankhurst, carrying banners bearing the words: "We demand the right to serve." Their demand was granted, as was their demand for "equal pay". And with the beginning of conscription on March 2, 1916, the government itself instigated a drive to recruit women to fill the places of those who had been conscripted.

Women flooded the market, taking on traditional male work roles, such as carrying sacks of coal, working on the land or making shells in the armaments factories, as well as joining other women in more traditional women's fields, such as nursing and teaching. Between 1915 and 1918 more than a million women embarked on some form of paid work for the first time in their lives. Nearly 800,000 women were recruited to the engineering and munitions industries; 100,000 became bus and tram drivers and conductors, railway porters, guards and inspectors. Government departments gained almost 200,000 women, and women employed in clerical work rose in numbers from 33,000 to 102,000. The female shorthand typist had taken the place of the male clerk with his quill pen for-

ever. More than 150,000 women joined the auxiliary branches of the armed forces.

This new-found independence increased women's confidence and changed their habits. It became usual to see women dine without a male chaperone, to buy their own drinks in pubs and to smoke cigarettes. Women took to dressing with a growing fashion confidence and a greater deference to practicality: they favoured shorter skirts that finished above the ankle, some wore trousers, even out of work, and hat styles were less flamboyant. Hair styles changed, too, with women preferring short neat cuts.

After the war, women's worthy contribution to the nation was recognized; the passing of the Fourth Reform Act in July 1918 gave those over the age of 30 the vote. Although many women had to give back their jobs to the returning men, many continued to work, and wider employment opportunities remained open to women. In 1919 the Sex Disqualification (Removal) Act provided that no person should be disqualified from any job because of sex or marriage. The status of women in society had changed for good.

▲ **"Land Girls"** engage in tough agricultural work. Female labour was vital to the economy during the war years.

In March 1917, a revolution overthrew the Tsar of Russia, Nicholas II, ending 300 years of Romanov rule. After two and half years of total war, the event did not come as a surprise. The tsarist regime had narrowly survived a revolutionary uprising in 1905. Despite economic progress and reforms in the years up to 1914, Russians of almost all classes had continued to regard the regime as outdated and autocratic. It was inevitable that as losses of Russian troops mounted and food supplies in the major cities dwindled, the tsar would be blamed.

The end came when a wave of strikes and demonstrations swept the capital, Petrograd, in early March. After troops sent to suppress the demonstrations fraternized with the crowd, moderate parliamentarians set up a Provisional Government and Tsar Nicholas abdicated. The throne was offered to his brother, Michael, but the Grand Duke turned it down. The Provisional Government began the slow task of organizing democratic elections to a Constituent Assembly, which would decide the future form of government.

The self-appointed Provisional Government was far from capable of exercising full control of Russia. A Petrograd soviet (council), elected by workers and soldiers, issued its own orders. Other soviets sprang up across the country in factories and military units, challenging the authority of officers and factory

▲ **Bolshevik supporters drive through the streets of Petrograd (St Petersburg) canvassing support for their own demands of the new Constituent Assembly.**

owners. However, Russia's three major left-wing parties, the Marxist Bolsheviks and Mensheviks, and the peasant-based Social Revolutionaries, generally assumed that the next step for Russia would be the establishment of a parliamentary liberal democracy.

This was not the view of the Bolshevik leader Vladimir Ilyich Lenin. In exile in Switzerland, Lenin saw the overthrow of the tsar as the first step towards a world revolution that would over-throw capitalism. Eager to destabilize their Russian enemies, the German authorities laid on a sealed train to carry Lenin and other revolutionaries back home.

Arriving at the Finland Station, Lenin shocked the Bolsheviks who had come to greet him by calling for immediate action to create a workers' state. The new Bolshevik slogan was: "All power to the Soviets".

As the Provisional Government dithered, conditions in the cities and the countryside deteriorated. Lenin adopted another slogan: "Bread, Peace, and Land". It offered most Russians exactly what they wanted, and Bolshevik support in major cities and among the rank-and-file of the armed forces grew rapidly.

In June, the Provisional Government launched a new military offensive in Galicia. It was a catastrophe. The Russian Army began to disintegrate. In the countryside, peasants had started to divide up landowners' estates to satisfy their age-old hunger for land. Peasant soldiers, already disillusioned by repeated

▲ **Crowds of protesters demonstrate outside of the Winter Palace in Petrograd prior to the abdication of Tsar Nicholas II.**

▶ Troops open fire as Bolsheviks besiege the Duma; July 1917 saw general disorder reign throughout many of Russia's cities.

defeats and heavy casualties, deserted the front in their millions, not wanting to be left out as the land was shared out.

Disorder also ruled in the cities. In July, soldiers, sailors and workers took to the streets of Petrograd, many chanting Bolshevik slogans. The Provisional Government put down the uprising, and many Bolshevik leaders were arrested, along with Leon Trotsky, a prominent revolutionary who was soon to join the Bolshevik party. Lenin fled to Finland.

But the Provisional Government's existence remained precarious. In response to popular pressure, Alexander Kerensky, a mild socialist, became prime minister. But in September he was faced with an attempted military coup by his commander-in-chief, General Kornilov. To repel the coup, Kerensky had to rely on the support of the militant Petrograd workers. The arrested Bolshevik leaders were released and arms were distributed to factory soviets.

From his exile in Finland, Lenin urged immediate action: "History will not forgive us if we do not seize control now!" His line was backed by Trotsky, now head of the Petrograd soviet. On November 4, Lenin returned to Petrograd in disguise. Trotsky set up a Revolutionary Military Committee of the Petrograd soviet to organize a seizure of power. It was timed to coincide with the meeting of the second All-Russian Soviet Congress, which would assemble delegates from soviets all over the country.

On the night of November 6, armed workers, soldiers and sailors – the Red Guards –

occupied key points in the city, such as bridges and power stations. Most people in Petrograd were completely unaware of what was happening. Cinemas were open and cafés full. The battleship *Aurora* was anchored opposite the Winter Palace, the seat of the Provisional Government, while Red Guards surrounded the building. The siege continued through the following day until, after minimal fighting, the Bolsheviks broke into the Palace. Kerensky fled by a side door.

When the Bolsheviks announced the news of the insurrection to the Soviet Congress, a large group of more moderate Menshevik and Socialist Revolutionary delegates walked out – consigning themselves, Trotsky contemptuously said, "to the dustbin of history". There was more disquiet when Lenin announced that the new government would be an exclusively Bolshevik Council of People's

Commissars. Railway workers immediately went on strike in protest at the exclusion of other revolutionary parties.

The Bolshevik coup was followed by a desperate struggle to assert the new government's authority, in which Lenin made ruthless use of the secret police to suppress opposition. He sought an immediate end to the war with Germany at almost any price,

and placated the peasants by legalizing the break-up of the large estates. When the elections for a Constituent Assembly were finally carried out, they showed that the Bolsheviks had the support of about 25 per cent of the Russian people. The Assembly met in January 1918, but was dismissed after a single day. Russia entered a long night of civil war, economic collapse and famine.

▲ Soldiers wait in ambush as Bolshevik troops prepare for a final assault on the Winter Palace.

TECHNOLOGY IN WORLD WAR ONE

▲ **The British Bristol Scout biplane. World War One was the first conflict in which aircraft played a role.**

For the first time since the Napoleonic wars, the great powers of Europe found themselves locked into a bitter war of survival, and the many industrial and technological advances that had taken place during the intervening century were used to full effect for the first time. After the mass slaughter that took place in the battles of 1914–15, the generals eventually realized that the combination of barbed-wire, machine guns and artillery placed a premium on defensive tactics, making advances against well-defended positions all but impossible. Accordingly, they began to turn to new technology to break the trench deadlock.

The use of chemical weapons to neutralize enemy front-line defences was pioneered by the Germans, who used chlorine gas to spearhead their attack against Ypres in 1915 (after some suc-

cess the German advance was halted, however). Initially, gas caused terror among the defending troops, but with better training and the use of effective masks, gas proved not to be the war-winner it had been hoped. And, because all the major nations began to use gas, its effect was largely cancelled out, although, of course, it caused terrible distress to those unfortunate troops who suffered from its effects.

Another chemically based weapon, which, like gas, relied on its tendency to cause panic, especially among poorly trained troops, was the man-portable flame-thrower, which could project a powerful jet of flame at short ranges. These were used by both the Germans and the French, and although they had some limited tactical uses in close-fighting they did little to affect the overall balance of the war.

The next major development intended to transform the strategic outlook in favour of mobility and the offensive was the armoured fighting vehicle. This was powered by the newly invented internal combustion engine and used caterpillar tracks to negotiate the broken ground of the Western Front. The British (soon followed by the French) were the first to produce such a vehicle, which, for security reasons during transit to France, was designated a "water tank" – and the name "tank" stuck.

The tanks were slow, with a top cross-country speed of 5 km/ph (3 mph) and vulnerable to enemy fire, and, worse still, they were unreliable. Nonetheless, they offered the chance to break through the German lines, and were used for the first time on September 15, 1916, during one of the many offensives that made up the Battle of the Somme.

The great lumbering monsters caused some disarray among

▶ **American officers inspect one of the first tanks used in a war situation. The earliest models were slow and unreliable, although major advances had been made by the end of World War One.**

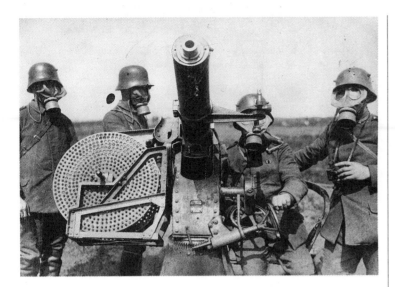

▲ **With a proliferation of the war in the air, heavy artillery was developed specifically to counter this new threat.**

the German defenders, and the limited British offensive around Flers-Courcelette was generally a success. But the following day, few tanks were capable of resuming operations.

During 1917, improvements were made and both British and French high commands placed great faith in their tank arms. The British massed their tanks together for the first time at the Battle of Cambrai in November 1917 and achieved a notable success, cutting a gap in the German lines. But, as on the Somme, after their initial push few tanks were still serviceable to resume the offensive, allowing the Germans to plug the gap and retake most of the ground lost to them in the initial attack.

In 1918, new lighter types of tank came into service, but again reliability and vulnerability to German anti-tank guns limited their effectiveness. During the Battle of Amiens, which began on August 8, 1918, tanks played a valuable role in opening up the German line, but of the 414 fighting tanks that took part on the first day, only six were still opera-

tional on August 12. Precision artillery tactics remained the best method of breaking the enemy lines; the tank would only become a decisive weapon in the next world war.

As the internal combustion engine powered the tank, so it made possible the aeroplane. The first aircraft flew in 1903, and by the outbreak of war in 1914 the great powers each had their own aviation branches to act as airborne reconnaissance troops. Throughout the war, reconnaissance was the key motive behind the expansion of military aviation; the glamorous fighter pilots who achieved such personal prominence during the conflict were merely the escorts for the two-seater reconnaissance aircraft which monitored enemy troop movements and the fall of shot from the ever-present artillery.

By 1916, however, the introduction of more powerful aircraft made possible new roles for the fledgling air forces. The first was to support advancing infantry by direct ground attack using machine guns and bombs. Although this was hazardous and unpopular work among the pilots, it became increasingly important, so that by 1918 all major offensives would be conducted in

conjunction with aviation units employed en masse.

The other new role for military aviation was very different: the long-range bombing of targets deep behind enemy lines. Although the bomber aircraft of World War One were slow and could carry only relatively small bomb loads, the pace of techno-logical change during the four years of war was sufficiently swift to allow Britain's Royal Air Force to develop a four-engined bomber with the capability of attacking Berlin.

Despite the success of military aviation, the hopes that the commanders on both sides placed in technology to solve the impasse of trench warfare were rarely fulfilled. The close relation-ship that would exist between the military and the scientist in World War Two was in its infancy during 1914–18, and the resulting hard-ware was generally insufficient to meet the harsh demands of military use. But the link had been made and was a portent for the future.

▲ **The submarine played an important role in Germany's war in the North Sea and Atlantic Ocean.**

MASSACRE OF THE TSAR AND HIS FAMILY

Early in the morning of July 17, 1918 the former Tsar Nicholas II and his wife and children and their retinue were taken downstairs to the cellar of Ipatev House in Ekaterinburg and shot in cold blood by the local Cheka (secret police) boss, Yakov Yurovsky, and his execution squad of six Hungarians and five Russians. It was the end of the Romanov dynasty.

Immediately after his abdication in March 1917, the former Tsar, his family and large retinue had been kept under house arrest in some considerable comfort at the palace of Tsarskoe Selo. However, in August, amid growing unrest, the Prime Minister of the provisional government, Alexander Kerensky, anxious for their safety, decided to evacuate the family to the Siberian town of Tobolsk, where they were held under guard in a former governor's house.

▲ Tsar Nicholas II and his family surrounded by armed guards in Tobolsk before they were slain.

On November 7, 1917, the Bolsheviks overthrew the provisional government and Kerensky could protect the imperial family no longer. Fearing that anti-communist forces in the area might help them escape or use them for their own ends, the Bolshevik government agreed in April 1918 to let Fillip Goloshchekin, leader of a Bolshevik presidium in the Urals Region, take sole control of the ex-Tsar and his family, allowing him to move them to the nearby city of Ekaterinburg. There they were imprisoned in Ipatev House, for the most part confined to their rooms by a hostile guard. On July 16, Goloshchekin informed Lenin that "military circumstances" demanded that they be executed. Later the same day Moscow confirmed that the execution should go ahead.

THE "FINAL PUSH": THE GREAT ALLIED OFFENSIVE

▲ The Great War draws to its inevitable close as thousands of German soldiers are left with no choice but surrender.

After the failure of the Germans to break through in the spring of 1918, the Allies went over to the offensive. The British Army spearheaded the attack, which began on August 8, a date Ludendorff would call "the black day of the German Army". General Rawlison's Fourth Army, comprising British, Australian and Canadian troops, opened the Battle of Amiens. The initial success was gained by a devastating bombardment by British artillery (using the advanced techniques of "predicted shooting") and supported by the advance of more than 400 tanks, whose presence had been masked by dense fog.

By August 11, the British had taken 30,000 prisoners and a great hole had been punched into the German line. The importance of the victory at Amiens lay in the effect it had on German morale. For the first time since the war began, whole German divisions had fallen back without a fight, while thousands of men were captured with little or no resistance.

ARMISTICE

The decline in morale was also felt at the top, so that at a conference with his generals held at Avesnes on August 11, the Kaiser was forced to concede: "I see that we must strike a balance. We have nearly reached the limit of our power of resistance. The war must be ended."

The British Fourth Army now began to approach the shattered landscapes of the Somme battle-fields of 1916 – a formidable obstacle – and Field Marshal Haig was determined that the advance should not become bogged down in this area. Consequently, the axis of attack was progressively extended northwards. General Byng's Third Army was brought into the attack on August 21 (Battle of Albert), and General Horne's First Army on August 26 (Battle of the Scarpe). To the south, the French attacked at Noyen, and on September 12, the Americans fought and won their first great battle at St Miheil.

The climax of the Allied offensive came in late September: the British began their assault on the Hindenburg Line; the French and Americans pushed forward in the Argonne; and a combined Belgian-British-French force attacked in Flanders.

On September 29, the British broke through the formidable Hindenburg Line, a magnificent feat of arms which brought them 35,000 prisoners and 380 guns. This marked the beginning of the end, for on this day the German High Command concluded that they must make an immediate approach to President Woodrow Wilson to ask for an armistice.

▲ Celebrations take place all over Europe and America as Armistice Day signals the official end of the war.

The inability of the German Army to stem the tide of the Allied advance on the Western Front during August and September of 1918, reluctantly forced the Kaiser and the German High Command to sue for peace. On October 4, Germany and Austria-Hungary contacted the US President, Woodrow Wilson, to call for an armistice, in the hope of gaining more favourable terms than they thought could be acquired directly from France and Britain. Wilson's reply – based on his famous "Fourteen Points" speech to Congress of January 8, 1918 – did not please the Germans, however, as it involved withdrawal from all foreign territories.

As the German High Command argued over whether to accept the Allied terms, the German military

and social system began to collapse. Against a backdrop of mutinies within the High Seas Fleet and rioting on the streets of Berlin, the new socialist Chancellor, Frederich Ebert, instructed the German armistice commission to ask for immediate terms. On November 7, two German members of the commission crossed the lines and met General Foch at his headquarters at Rethondes in the forest of Compiègne.

The Allied armistice terms reflected the bitterness resulting from four years of warfare. Germany would have to surrender Alsace-Lorraine; the Rhineland would be occupied; all U-boats were to be surrendered and the High Seas Fleet was to be interned; the treaties with Russia and Romania were to be annulled; and large quantities of war stocks were to be transferred to the Allies. After further discussion, the Germans returned to the conference, and at 5 a.m. on November 11, 1918, in a railway carriage in a siding at Compiègne, the armistice was signed to come into effect six hours later – at the eleventh hour, of the eleventh day of the eleventh month. World War One was over.

▶ **Jubilant Britons celebrate victory outside Buckingham Palace in London. They were later greeted by King George V.**

1918: AFTERMATH OF THE GREAT WAR

Great wars do not end in a day. The armistice of November 1918 left much of Europe in turmoil, with unresolved conflicts raging from Dublin to Moscow and Istanbul. Around 20 million people lost their lives in the war. In its aftermath, a flu epidemic swept the world and, according to some estimates, took an even heavier toll than the war itself. Much of Europe experienced hunger and hardship. The American Relief Association staved off mass starvation in Europe by providing 1.5 billion US dollars worth of food supplies. The great empires of the Romanovs, Ottomans, Hapsburgs and Prussian Hohenzollerns had all tumbled into the dustbin of history, crumpled by the pressures of modern war.

In January 1919, amid this chaos and devastation, the victorious Allies staged a conference in the glittering setting of Versailles. Although delegations arrived from as far afield as China, Japan and Siam, all the key decisions at the conference were taken by three men: Georges Clemenceau of France, Britain's Prime Minister David Lloyd George, and US President Woodrow Wilson. It turned into an almost clichéd confrontation between Old World cynicism and New World idealism. Wilson championed his famous 14 Points, trying to build a new Europe based on democracy and national self-determination. Clemenceau, and to a lesser extent, Lloyd George, mainly wanted to ensure that Germany, temporarily down, stayed down.

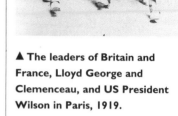

▲ The leaders of Britain and France, Lloyd George and Clemenceau, and US President Wilson in Paris, 1919.

The Germans and other defeated powers were not invited to negotiate – terms were decided between the victors and then imposed on the losers.

The attempt to draw a new map of Europe soon revealed how impossible it was to apply Wilson's principle of national self-determination – the idea that state borders should correspond to borders between nations – to the complex ethnic mix that characterized much of Europe. The new states of Czechoslovakia and the Kingdom of Serbs, Croats and Slovenes (later renamed Yugoslavia) that emerged from the collapse of the Austro-Hungarian Empire were ethnically diverse. The principle of national self-determination was not applied to Germany, since if all German speakers had been united in a single country, it would have handed the Germans the dominance of Europe for which they had fought the war.

The scope for resentment created by the new face of Europe was truly remarkable. Germany resented the fact that newly independent Poland had been given access to the sea via the "Polish corridor" to Danzig (Gdansk) – a primarily German port. Bolshevik

---

▼ No man's land: abandoned trenches in a destroyed forest in Alsace Lorraine after World War One

▲ Precautions against the devastating influenza epidemic which hit the postwar world included anti-flu spray for London omnibuses.

Russia also resented Poland after the war left Poland in control of much of the Ukraine. Hungary, much diminished by the peace settlement, resented all its neighbours, especially Romania. Italy, although one of the victors, was bitter for having received little in return for its war effort.

But nothing could equal the resentment and bitterness felt by the Germans. They could not accept either that they had been fighting an unjust war of conquest, or that they had lost the war on the battlefield. They only accepted peace terms imposed by the Allies because the armistice had rendered them defenceless and incapable of resuming the conflict.

Whether the terms Germany had to accept were excessively onerous has been a matter of dispute ever since the event. They included the return of Alsace-Lorraine to France, the occupation of the west bank of the Rhine by Allied forces, severe restrictions on the size and nature of German armed forces, the loss of some other territories,

▶ President Woodrow Wilson (centre, front) sees war damage for himself in Nieuport, Belgium, in June, 1919

and, most controversially of all, economic reparations.

There was nothing new about reparations – France had been forced to pay a massive sum to Germany, for example, after the war of 1870–71. Since both France and Britain had run up huge debts fighting World War One, it seemed natural to them both that Germany should have to pay the costs of a war they believed Germany had caused. But some intellectuals, notably the British economist John Maynard Keynes, argued that they were unpayable and a fatal block to postwar economic recovery in Europe. The Germans certainly had no intention of paying up, and proved ready to virtually destroy their economy

through hyperinflation rather than hand over the sums the Allies demanded. Reparations proved to be a running sore in postwar international relations.

The League of Nations, the centrepiece of President Wilson's plans for a lawful, just and peaceful postwar world, could never have coped with the problems left behind by the war – even if the United States had joined that worthy organization, which it did not.

The impact of the war went far deeper than redrawn borders and embittered relationships. It profoundly altered men and the societies they lived in. Former soldiers were an important element in all the combatant nations after the war, most leaning to the extreme right in politics. It was no accident that the two leading right-wing dictators of Europe between the wars, Adolf Hitler and Benito Mussolini, were both ex-servicemen shaped by their war experience – as was Britain's blackshirt leader Oswald Mosley.

People had grown used to the state exercising extraordinary powers over their lives. They had also become accustomed to killing on a scale unimaginable before 1914. Hitler's Holocaust and Stalin's Gulag would have been inconceivable without the example of mass slaughter set by the trenches.

August
- Soissons re-taken by French

September
- Peronne re-taken by British troops
- German army withdraws to the Siegfried Line
- US forces defeat Germans in the Battle of St Mihiel on Western Front
- Allied breakthrough in Bulgaria
- Turkish resistance collapses in Palestine
- Dixmude in Belgium captured by Belgian forces
- Armistice between Bulgaria and allies

October
- Allied forces take Damascus in Syria
- French forces take St. Quentin
- French forces occupy Beirut
- British forces take Cambrai
- Lille in France captured by British forces
- Belgians recapture Bruges and Zeebrugge
- Battle of Vittorio Veneto between Italy and Austria begins
- Armistice between Turkey and Allies

November
- Allied troops occupy Constantinople in Turkey
- Armistice between Austro-Hungary and Allies
- US troops occupy Sedan on the Western Front
- Armistice between Germany and Allies ends World War One
- German troops in Rhodesia surrender
- German troops leave France

19

THE SPARTACIST UPRISING

In January 1919, revolutionaries led by Rosa Luxemburg and Karl Liebknecht tried to build on the Bolshevik triumph in Russia by creating a workers' state in Germany. Had they succeeded, it would have changed the course of history.

At the end of World War One, Kaiser Wilhelm II had been forced to abdicate when soldiers, sailors and workers seized control of Berlin. A government dominated by Social Democrats took power and organized elections to a constituent assembly. But the political situation in Berlin remained volatile. The most influential extreme left party in the city was the Spartacist League, led by Luxemburg and Liebknecht. In December 1918, the Spartacists joined with other extreme left groups to found the German Communist Party. Many of their members were armed,

and they effectively controlled large parts of Berlin.

The government had the support of its own social-democrat militia, but it could not rely on the regular army to defend it against the Communists, because too many soldiers and sailors had left-wing sympathies. It turned instead to the Freikorps, irregular forces of volunteers under former army officers, dedicated to the defence of the Fatherland and the crushing of Bolshevik revolution.

On January 6, 1919, the Spartacists launched their uprising, seizing a number of key buildings across Berlin. Their lack of mass support among German workers, however, left them exposed to a counter-attack. Freikorps (Free Corps) units poured into the city and, after days of bloody street fighting, the uprising was crushed. On January 15, Luxemburg and Liebknecht

were arrested, then murdered in cold blood while on their way to prison.

▲ **Rosa Luxemburg, the co-leader of the extreme left-wing Spartacist organization that attempted a revolt in Berlin.**

A LEAGUE TO END WARS

On February 14, 1919, President Woodrow Wilson laid the articles of the League of Nations Covenant before the Paris Peace Conference. The League was a project of high idealism, intended to end the era of warring sovereign states and begin a new age of cooperation and the rule of law in international affairs.

Article 8 of the League's Covenant called for the reduction of armaments to "the lowest point consistent with national safety and the enforcement by common action of international obligations". Member states of the League would agree to renounce the use of force in international affairs. They would be obliged to submit disputes to arbitration, rather than resort to war. Any

▲ **Onlookers view an important historic moment, the signing of the Treaty of Versailles.**

state that broke the Covenant – for example, by committing an act of aggression – was to face joint action by the member states.

The proposal for the League was received with general acclaim,

and it was incorporated into the various peace treaties.

By the end of 1919, the new international organization was taking shape. Although dominated by Europe and based in Geneva, it was genuinely worldwide – Brazil and Japan were on its ruling Council, and its members included Ethiopia.

But the United States did not take part. When Wilson returned from Paris to Washington, he was ill and exhausted. The US Congress found the commitment to foreign entanglements implied in the Covenant too much to stomach. The treaty was never ratified and the world's most powerful country distanced itself from the first attempt at a form of world government.

ALCOCK AND BROWN

At 1.58 pm on June 14, 1919, two former RAF pilots, Captain John Alcock and Arthur Whitten-Brown, took off from St John's, Newfoundland, in a bid to fly non-stop across the Atlantic. The newspaper baron Lord Northcliffe had put up a £10,000 prize for the first person to achieve the feat.

The aircraft the pilots used was a World War One Vickers Vimy bomber with two Rolls Royce engines. Apart from a radio, the aircraft's equipment was primitive. The cockpit was open, giving the pilots no protection at all against the elements and exposing them to the full noise of the engines, which made any conversation impossible.

▲ Captain John Alcock and Arthur Whitten-Brown (centre), the first men to fly the Atlantic Ocean.

After 16 hours in the air, Alcock and Brown were cold, hungry, exhausted and rapidly losing hope. Then through the grey mist, they saw the darker hue of land. The aircraft flew in over the Galway coast and landed in a marshy bog which tipped the plane over on its nose. They had flown 2,735 km (1,700 miles) in 16 hours and 28 minutes.

Both men were knighted for their exploit, but Alcock had little chance to enjoy his triumph; he died in an air crash in France later that year.

MALE MONOPOLY OF PARLIAMENT ENDS

The 1918 Representation of the People Act at last gave British women the vote, although not on an equal basis with men – only women over 30 were judged rational enough to go to the polls. The general election that followed in November 1918 showed that female suffrage would not necessarily give women a share of political power.

One woman was elected to the House of Commons – Countess Markiewicz (Constance Gore-Booth), who represented a Dublin constituency. But she was a member of Sinn Fein, whose MPs did not take their seats in Westminster, instead proclaiming themselves the parliament of an Irish Republic.

It was not until 1919 that the House of Commons saw its first female MP. The honour fell to an American-born Conservative, Nancy Astor. She was the daughter of a Virginia tobacco auctioneer, and the wife of William Waldorf Astor, MP for Plymouth. After his father's death in 1919, Astor became Viscount Astor and was elevated to the House of Lords.

Lady Astor inherited his position as Plymouth Tory candidate and duly won a by-election, taking her seat in the Commons.

Despite coming to Parliament through her husband's influence, Lady Astor was to prove a vigorous and effective MP, with an active interest in women's rights and social problems.

▲ American-born Lady Nancy Astor, the first woman to be take her seat in the British parliament.

1920–29

After the ravages of the previous decade, the governments of the world, of whom even the Allied victors of the Great War had paid a heavy price, turned their attentions to minimizing the risk of a future grand-scale conflict through the initiation of the League of Nations. A body that aimed to represent every government of the world, the League would offer diplomatic solutions to international disagreements. Furthermore, acts of military aggression would be met by a combined force from within the League. Although clearly a reasonable principle, the idea foundered on a lack of real authority and was weakened by America's refusal to join. It did, however, signal that the rulers of the world seemed now only likely to wage war as a final desperate option.

The 1920s saw notable political upheavals in Europe. After a bitter civil war that followed the downfall of the Tsar, victory for the Bolsheviks saw Russia transformed into the Union of Soviet Socialist Republics (USSR). It was the beginning of the Communist revolution in which Lenin sought to unite the workers of the world against the imperialism that he believed caused all wars, not only the one for which Russia had just paid such a heavy price. Lenin's noble aims were subverted following his death in 1924 when under the brutal reign of Stalin, the Soviet Union was transformed from an agricultural state to an industrialized "superpower". Untold millions of political opponents were ruthlessly "purged" as Stalin consolidated a dictatorial position that would make him the single most powerful world leader of the twentieth century.

At the other political extreme, Italy saw the birth of Fascism when a former newspaper editor Benito Mussolini seized power. As the decade moved along, "Il Duce", abandoned more and more of the constitution until he was able to rule Italy with an authority that went beyond question. It would take total military defeat in 1943 to end Mussolini's dictatorship.

On the other side of the Atlantic, America was undergoing its "Jazz Age", an era of unprecedented wealth and development. Less affected than Europe by the Great War, America now asserted its authority on the world stage. The new wealth could be seen in its emerging cities. New York saw the birth of a new kind of urban panorama as the classic architectural models of the historic European capitals were eschewed in favour of mushrooming multi-storey skyscrapers. Just as the rulers of the ancient world had sought immortality by erecting great monuments, their modern-day counterparts, America's fabulously wealthy industrialists spent small fortunes commissioning ever taller and more spectacular shrines to their own business interests. Appropriately, by 1925, New York's Wall Street had established itself as the world's most important stock market. At the same time, another side of America was shown when the government took the unusual step of banning the sale of alcohol. With so much wealth concentrated in America's cities, the result of Prohibition was a huge wave of organized crime in which gangsters were happy to meet a continued demand for liquor. In this environment, Mafia "Dons" and other underground figures like Al Capone were said to have netted fortunes to rival the richest men in the country.

The 1920s also saw some of the most important scientific developments filtering down to the ordinary man. Since Henry Ford had created the first production lines, the cost of manufacturing automobiles had fallen sharply. While still too costly for most, their numbers proliferated rapidly. With greater mobility, communities became more elastic.

The nature of popular entertainment also began to change as singers and comedians were able to reach millions of listeners through the medium of the "wireless" radio. Similarly, by the end of the decade cinema audiences were able to hear their idols talk on screen for the first time.

But if the 1920s has often been painted as the frivolous decade where the world let its hair down after the hell of World War One, it all came tumbling down in 1929 when the stock markets of New York and London crashed sending the world's economies spiralling out of control. The result was the "Great Depression" that overshadowed the industrial world through much of the decade that followed.

THE FIRST RED SCARE

Although America's shores had not been touched by the fighting of World War One, a great many Americans had lost their lives. But soldiers returning home were not only greeted with a heroic welcome, but with economic uncertainty, too. This ushered in a period of industrial unrest and rioting, that peaked with the two-month mining strike at the end of 1919.

During the same period, the 1917 Bolshevik revolution in Russia had created widespread fears that a similar workers' uprising could take place anywhere. While there was little genuine evidence to suggest that the protests were the work of agitators, politicians took the "Red Scare" seriously: to them the Communist threat was knocking at the door of capitalism's greatest bastion. Their responses were swift and draconian.

January 2, 1920, saw raids take place in over 30 cities throughout the US. Almost 3,000 Communists, anarchists and other radicals were arrested. The campaign was the brainchild of Attorney General A Mitchell Palmer, who used the 1917 Espionage Act and the 1918 Sedition Act as a legitimate basis for his actions.

The "Palmer Raids" divided the political landscape. Some members of Congress pushed for the death sentence for many of those arrested, but the basic disregard for civil liberties with which the raids were executed caused widespread protests. Palmer, a high-ranking Democrat, paid the price for his zeal when he lost the presidential nomination later in the year, although he continued to maintain that he had foiled what amounted to a Bolshevik conspiracy to overthrow the government.

▲ Boston police officers display their haul of "subversive" Bolshevik literature. Authorities in the United States were quick to respond to the earliest signs of the spread of Communism.

THE PROHIBITION ERA

▲ Prohibition officers provide a quick and effective way to dispose of wines and spirits. The banning of alcohol was directly responsible for a wave of criminal activity that swept through the United States.

On January 16, 1920, the US government introduced the Eighteenth Amendment to the constitution, prohibiting the sale of all alcohol.

This idea was by no means new: religious revivalism in the nineteenth century had seen a number of states experiment temporarily with prohibition laws. However, by the beginning of the twentieth century, the temperance movement – led largely by the Anti-Saloon League – had become an influential force in America. Taking advantage of a temporary halt on liquor sales during World War One, ostensibly so that grain used in the making of liquor was available for use as food, their campaign grew to the point that by the time prohibition became law, a majority of states had already passed such legislation. The prohibition issue was sometimes viewed as a divide between rural and urban dwellers: the campaign played on a growing disapproval of the rapid growth of cities and their alien lifestyles, calling for a restoration of traditional rural values.

Prohibition may now have been legal, but demand for alcohol remained steady. Since it was still used legitimately as an anaesthetic, unscrupulous doctors were able to supplement their incomes by signing spurious prescriptions, on such a scale that government stocks were under threat.

In most of the big cities where, unlike in rural America, prohibition was deeply unpopular, there was insufficient manpower to enforce the law effectively. This created a booming black market for "bootleg" liquor, to which most of the notorious criminals of the period were in some way connected. To illustrate the lucrative nature of this market: during the mid-1920s, the annual earnings of Al Capone, Chicago's most infamous bootlegger, were estimated to be as high as $50 million – over 10 times more than the salary paid to Hollywood's biggest star, Douglas Fairbanks.

Prohibition had lost much of its widespread support by 1930. The temperance movement was in the hands of Fundamentalists, alienating the moderate majority, many of whom now viewed it as an infringement of civil liberty, and the cause of America's worst ever wave of crime. Prohibition was finally repealed in 1933.

FIRST MEETING OF THE LEAGUE OF NATIONS

After a protocol meeting in Paris the previous month, on February 11, 1920, the first session of the Council of the new League of Nations took place at St James's Palace, London. Overseeing proceedings was Britain's Prime Minister, Arthur Balfour. During the session, plans were drawn up for an international court of justice.

The League was formed as a part of the Treaty of Versailles to prevent further world conflict and maintain the status quo created by the various postwar territorial agreements. Its Council was made up of delegates from eight nations: Britain, Italy, France, Japan, Belgium, Spain, Brazil and Greece. The main purpose of the League was collective security – military aggression would be met by a joint force of League members.

Internal politics kept the US from ratifying the Treaty of Versailles, and hence joining the League, which did a great deal to harm to its credibility and effectiveness. This was especially ironic in that it was the tireless efforts of the ailing US President, Woodrow Wilson, that had given life to the idea. The principle US reservation was the clause in the Treaty that obliged all members to provide military assistance to defend any other member.

Throughout the decade, the League, initially comprising war allies, sought the membership of neutral and enemy nations. Ultimately, the League was only successful when its authority was not in question. Although it successfully mediated in minor national disputes, the inability to act collectively against, among other things, Germany's refusals to continue its war reparations in the 1930s, eroded the League's credibility. Although it theoretically still existed throughout World War Two it was by then wholly inactive and ineffective. Nonetheless, the League of Nations created a blueprint, however flawed, for the United Nations.

Delegates from eight nations meet for the inauguration of the League of Nations. The purpose of its existence was to prevent a recurrence of the horrors of World War One. ▼

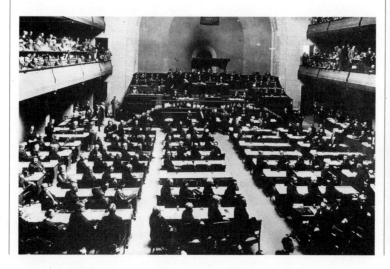

'20

▶ **Berliners responded to the new Kapp government with a general strike. Without their support the "Putsch" was doomed to fail.**

The turmoil within Germany following its defeat in World War One continued unabated into the 1920s. The political instability was heightened by divisions between the Communists of the extreme left and the nationalists of the far right. This rivalry frequently escalated into violence but it was on March 13, 1920 that the newly formed Weimar Republic received its first significant challenge. A bureaucrat and former Riechstag politician named Dr Wolfgang Kapp unsuccessfully attempted a military coup, aiming to restore the monarchy.

The immediate cause of the coup – known as the "Kapp Putsch" – was the imminent abolition of the nationalist *Freikorps* (Free Corps), a group of unofficial right-wing armies led by wartime officers and containing former soldiers and unemployed volunteers. Their self-appointed role was to fight against what were seen as Bolshevik-inspired uprisings that took place in some of Germany's major cities. Indeed, it was the *Freikorps* who were responsible for putting down the abortive Spartacist Revolt in Berlin in 1919 and murdering the ringleaders Karl Leibknecht and Rosa Luxemburg.

Although these roving armies had received semi-official support in the past they were now widely regarded as having grown out of control. Consequently, the new Weimar government took steps to demobilize each platoon. With the cooperation of military leader Baron von Luttwitz, on March 13, the *Freikorps* marched triumphantly into Berlin. Dr Kapp declared himself Chancellor of Germany, with the blessing of former military Chief of Staff Erich Ludendorff. Without the full support of the army on whom his position was dependent, President Ebert, the Social Democratic leader of the legitimate Weimar government, was unable to take preventative action and fled south.

The Kapp Putsch only lasted four days. Supported by the workers and trades unions, Ebert was able to call for a general strike. Communist agitators took advantage of the chaos and engaged in demonstrations and skirmishes on the streets of Berlin. On March 17, Kapp was forced to accept defeat, having failed to secure the cooperation of civil servants loyal to the Ebert government.

Kapp was never punished for his role in the coup. Having fled to Sweden, he returned home in 1922 but died before his trial could be heard. As far as the Weimar Republic was concerned, the Putsch was but one of many crises it would face over the coming decade.

SCANDAL BLACKENS THE CHICAGO WHITE SOX

The world of professional baseball was rocked on September 28, 1920, when eight stars of the Chicago White Sox were charged by a Grand Jury with conspiring with a gambling consortium to throw the 1919 World Series against the Cincinnati Reds.

The players in the dock were Eddie Cicotte, Oscar Felsch, Charlie Risberg, Buck Weaver, Chick Gandil, Claude "Lefty" Williams, Fred McMullin and star hitter, "Shoeless" Joe Jackson. The players were believed to have taken bribes worth up to $100,000 in exchange for losing the series by five games to three.

▼ "Say it ain't so, Joe!" America was shocked by the revelation that star hitter Joe "Shoeless" Jackson had taken a bribe.

The White Sox were strong favourites to take the title, but the manner of their defeat caused a number of sportswriters to voice their suspicions. It wasn't until the following season that an inquiry into gambling in professional sport resulted in admissions from three of the players. White Sox owner Charles Komiskey immediately suspended his team.

The brains behind the gambling scheme was thought to be notorious New York bootlegger and racketeer Arnold Rothstein. However, as an influence peddler, Rothstein could name high-ranking politicians and city officials among his social circle. He was never brought to trial.

Not surprisingly, witnesses from the illegal gambling fraternity were in short supply and on August 3, 1921 all eight players were acquitted. Nonetheless, the following day they were all banned from the game for life by baseball commissioner Judge Landis.

The "Black Sox" case, as it became known, is also remembered for the famous phrase "Say it ain't so, Joe", uttered by a distraught young fan waiting for his idol "Shoeless" Joe Jackson outside the court.

OXFORD GRANTS EQUAL STATUS TO FEMALE STUDENTS

The University of Oxford, Britain's oldest body of higher learning, began to align itself with the prevailing wind of change in the early twentieth century when on October 7, 1920, the first 100 female students were admitted as full members of the university.

Oxford University has a history that can be traced back to the twelfth century when it came in to being as result of English students being barred from the University of Paris in 1167. Since then, it has schooled many of the world's most noted scientists and political leaders.

Like its counterpart at Cambridge, Oxford has always operated on the collegiate system under which the university as a whole comprises a series of semi-autonomous colleges. The first women's college, Lady Margaret Hall, was established in 1878, but it was not until 1920 that it was considered appropriate to accept women on an equal par with male students. This had previously meant that although women may have received the tuition from one of the most reputable universities in the world, they would not be rewarded with a degree for their efforts.

Although this may not have had a great deal of impact on women as a whole – a university education at this time was only realistically available to the privileged – it was another indication that the British establishment was beginning to recognize the demands for a new role for women in the twentieth century.

▼ Female students at Oxford University gather in preparation for a visit from the Queen. Women had not been allowed full membership of the university before 1920.

August
- "Little Entente" between Czechoslovakia, Yugoslavia and Romania
- Negotiations between Egypt and Britain over Egyptian independence
- Russia recognizes state of Latvia
- Russia defeated at Warsaw by Poland
- Polish forces capture Brest-Litovsk
- The Olympic Games begin in Antwerp, Belgium

September
- Industrial unrest in Italy
- Alvaro Obregón elected President of Mexico
- Bomb kills at least 30 in New York's financial district; a Russian, Alexander Brailovsky, is arrested for the crime
- Alexandre Millerand elected President of France
- An earthquake in Italy kills 500

October
- Austria adopts new constitution
- Poland annexes Vilnia in Lithuania
- Peace treaty ends war between Russia and Poland
- Death of King Alexander of Greece
- League of Nations moves to Geneva

November
- Republican candidate Warren Harding wins US presidential election
- Red Army takes Sebastopol
- Russian civil war ends with Communist victory
- IRA murder 15 army cadets

December
- Turkey forces Armenia to sign treaty ceding territory
- Martial Law declared in Cork, Ireland
- King Constantine returns to Greece
- Government of Ireland Act passed by British parliament
- Gandhi warns of a "sea of blood" if Britain continues to rule India

'21

NEWS IN BRIEF

....

- Government control of food, rail and coal industries ends in Britain
- Britain gets its first female barrister
- British Legion founded
- The first flight in a helicopter is achieved by a French engineer
- Neolithic remains found in Yangshao, China
- Lenin announces New Economic Policy
- Survey reveals nearly 500,000 Berlin children are diseased.
- Communist Party is founded in China
- Films released this year include *The Kid*, Charlie Chaplin's first full-length film
- Books published this year include *Women in Love* by D H Lawrence, *Crome Yellow* by Aldous Huxley and *The Mysterious Affair at Styles* by Agatha Christie
- Babe Ruth makes record number of home runs (59) in US baseball season

January
- Greece initiates war with Turkey by invading Anatolia
- War crimes trials begin in Germany
- Aristide Briand forms government in France
- First Indian parliament

February
- Riots in Italy between Communists and Fascists
- Negotiations in London between Greek and Turkish governments

ALLIES INVADE THE RUHR

▲ **French troops march into the Rhineland following the refusal of the German government to pay war reparations.**

The Ruhr region in the south-west of Germany is one of the largest industrial areas in the world. It was during the late nineteenth century that its economic significance emerged as the Krupps and Thyssen companies made it one of Europe's major centres for coal mining and the production of steel.

The Ruhr was crucial in the Kaiser's military build up at the start of the twentieth century, and in the aftermath of World War One the Allies sought to neutralize the region to prevent a similar recurrence. Production capability was immediately cut back when the German-occupied region of Alsace-Lorraine was returned to France. Additionally, Allied forces were given leave to occupy the Rhineland region.

However, the specific issue of how the Allies should be compensated for the ravages of the war could not be agreed upon. On February 5 1921 the Reparations Commission agreed on a figure and presented the German government with a demand for 56 billion dollars which would be paid over a period of 42 years. Of this figure, 52 per cent would be paid to France.

This figure caused outrage in Germany, politicians viewing it as little more than enslavement of the German economy; on March 22, they defaulted on their first payment. Under pressure from the US to reduce the payments, the Allies offered a revised figure of 33 billion marks, warning that if no payment was made by May 1, they would invade the Ruhr. Four days later, when no payment was forthcoming, French and Belgian troops marched unopposed into the cities of Düsseldorf, Duisberg and Ruhrort. The Allies went further, declaring an additional 50 per cent duty to be paid on exports.

On May 15, 1921, faced with economic destruction, the German government capitulated, agreeing to an unconditional acceptance of the Allied reparation demands. At the end of September, French troops evacuated the Ruhr. Although this particular crisis was over, the humiliation dealt out to Germany resulted in the collapse of the German economy that would soon provide fertile ground for the rise of a new threat: the National Socialists.

THE EVIL RISE OF THE KLAN

The early 1920s saw a major revival in the activities of the American white supremacy movement as membership of the new Ku Klux Klan hit a peak of over four million.

The Klan first emerged in 1866 after the American Civil War and was formed by disaffected Confederate veterans. Although its aims were initially little more than social it soon became a forum for opposition to the reconstruction programme that saw the erosion of white supremacy in the Southern states. Intimidation and violence were the hallmarks of Klan activity and, although it was outlawed by the 1870 Force Act, it was a powerful political force during this era.

The Klan was given a second wind in 1915, aided by its glorification in D W Griffith's cinema epic *Birth of a Nation*. This time, the Klan became something of a patriotic front for the fading values of old south. Their targets, while still primarily blacks, now also included unions, Communists, Jews and other immigrants.

The widely attended Ku Klux Klan rituals made for a dramatic sight: thousands of members dressed identically in white robes and hoods marching behind their newly adopted symbol of a burning cross. On September 11, 1921, the Klan took control of a university faculty in Atlanta, Georgia. Their aim was to establish the teaching of a new subject: "Americanism". However, the lynchings and shootings of "undesirables" once again emerged, and on May 18, 1922, a black teenager was tortured and burned at the stake because he was a suspect in the murder of a white woman.

The Ku Klux Klan were at the very least regarded as something of an embarrassment by the rest of America, and even within its own society much of the violence was deplored. Consequently, during the 1930s and the Great Depression, membership dwindled and although it enjoyed a minor resurgence during the civil rights struggle of the 1960s, its popularity has never matched the peak of the 1920s.

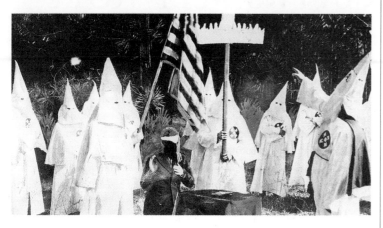

▲ **Another new recruit is initiated into the ranks of the Ku Klux Klan. Membership of the Klan reached record levels during the 1920s.**

IRELAND DIVIDED

▲ **The Dublin Customs House goes up in flames during the violent protest that preceded the first Anglo-Irish Treaty.**

On December 6, 1921, Britain attempted to solve centuries of political conflict in Ireland with the creation of the Irish Free State. Under the terms of the Anglo-Irish Treaty, the island would be divided into two self-governing areas, with territory allocated along sectarian lines. The predominantly Roman Catholic Irish Free State, which contained 26 of Ireland's 32 counties, would be accorded the same constitutional status as other British Empire members, while the Protestant majorities in the remaining six counties of the north would remain under "Home Rule".

The treaty angered many republicans. In 1919, 25 elected Sinn Fein members of the British Parliament had refused to take their seats, instead proclaiming their own illegal republican parliament in Dublin – the Dáil Eireann. The violent repression of the Easter Uprising had generated widespread anti-British feeling among the Catholic majority of the south, thus the Dáil, under the leadership of US-born Eamon de Valera, had a good deal of popular support. However, de Valera's aim was that Ireland as a whole should become an independent republic. While the British government's act went some way towards this end, republicans saw it as an unsatisfactory compromise.

Following the Anglo-Irish Treaty, a newly legitimate Dáil was set up, and military leader Michael Collins headed the cabinet until elections took place. When the Dáil itself ratified the Anglo-Irish Treaty, de Valera resigned in disgust, vowing to continue his fight for republicanism.

The division of Ireland was yet another chapter in one of the longest-running violent conflicts of the twentieth century, one for which, in spite of a recent and fragile cessation of violence, a satisfactory conclusion seems as far away as ever.

▼ **The Anglo-Irish Treaty split the Republican community, although it received the backing of Sinn Fein supporters.**

GANDHI REJECTS VIOLENCE AS INDIA SEEKS SELF RULE

On March 10, 1922, Mohandas Gandhi, the figure-head of Indian nationalism was arrested and imprisoned by the ruling British authorities. The key figure in a two-year campaign of non-cooperation, Gandhi was charged with sedition and given a six-year jail sentence.

India had been under formal British rule since the days of Clive of India in the mid-eighteenth century. Although a nationalist heritage existed during the century that followed, it was with the formation of the Indian National Congress in 1885 that a forum for independence first emerged. For its first 35 years, the Congress had largely contained well-meaning intellectuals. However, from 1920 Gandhi, a British-educated lawyer, dominated the organization.

Under Gandhi's leadership the struggle for independence moved from the wealthy upper-class of India's cities to the poorest of peasant villagers. His message was simple: British rule would best be ended through non-cooperation rather than through violent conflict. His example captured the imagination of millions throughout the country. He ordered a boycott of all British goods and furthermore declared the invalidity of all British-run institutions, including courts and schools. His aim was not to run the British out of India but to make India impossible to rule.

The campaign created chaos among the British authorities; however, it was Gandhi himself who brought it to an end after violence had flared up on the east coast of India. Gandhi wanted no part of such a rebellion. It was a stance that would establish his reputation as one of the greatest men of the twentieth century, but at the same time create frustration among militant nationalists who saw in him an immensely powerful symbol whose own scruples too often impeded their aims.

▼ **A symbol of peaceful resistance, Mohondas Gandhi took the struggle for independence to India's peasant villagers.**

IRISH LEADER ASSASSINATED

On August 22, 1922, Irish nationalist leader Michael Collins, one of the architects of the new Free State of Ireland, was killed in an ambush. His death was a direct result of a

◄ **Draped with the flag of the Irish Republic, the coffin of assassinated nationalist leader Michael Collins is paraded through the streets of Dublin.**

NEWS IN BRIEF

- Reform of Russian legal system
- Austin Seven becomes first mass-produced car in Britain
- Budget cuts passed by British government
- Marie Stopes campaigns for birth control
- Insulin isolated
- British Broadcasting Corporation (BBC) founded
- Britain signs a Treaty of Alliance with Iraq
- Films released during the year include Fritz Lang's *Doctor Mabuse*
- Books published this year include *The Wasteland* by T S Eliot, *Ulysses* by James Joyce and *The Garden Party* by Katherine Mansfield

January
- Gold miners strike in South Africa
- French Prime Minister Aristide Briand resigns; succeeded by Raymond Poincaré
- Michael Collins forms provisional government in the Irish Free State
- Pope Benedict XV dies; succeeded by Pope Pius XI
- Death of Sir Ernest Shackleton in South Georgia en route to a fourth expedition to Antarctica

February
- International conference in Washington limits use of poison gas and submarines in war
- Japan agrees to return Shantung province to China
- Crisis in Italy caused by resignation of Prime Minister, Bonomi

split in the ranks of republicanism that followed the signing of the Anglo-Irish Treaty in 1921.

Collins, along with former President Arthur Griffith, had been sent to London by Eamon de Valera to negotiate a peaceful settlement to the Irish crisis. The resulting treaty brought about the split between north and south. Although Collins con-sidered the treaty the best that could be achieved at that time, de Valera and many other hard-line republicans saw it as an unacceptable compromise.

The disagreements ultimately resulted in a state of civil war, sparked off by the seizure by republican rebels of the Four Courts building in Dublin on June 29, 1922. Collins, in spite of his relative youth – he was 31 years old – was a notable military strategist and took control of the Irish National Army. Following the death of Arthur Griffith earlier in August, Collins also became head of the government. It was while on his way to a troop inspection that his assassins – presumed to be a republican group – shot him dead.

HOLLYWOOD EXPOSED

▲ **A picture of innocence, Roscoe "Fattie" Arbuckle was one of the greatest stars of the silent movie era. Scandal ended his career and brought censorship to Hollywood.**

The early 1920s saw Hollywood branded as a latter-day Babylon. A new breed of influential tabloid newspaper owned by William Randolph Hearst quickly discovered that if one thing sold more papers than the lives of the rich and famous it was sex and scandal; when the two came together the results could be explosive.

The first major star to fall foul of trial by the press was Roscoe "Fattie" Arbuckle, one of the most popular comedians of the silent era. On September 5, 1921, Arbuckle hosted a party at the St Francis Hotel in San Francisco. Like most other opulent Hollywood events of the period, neither drunkenness nor sex were in short supply. Arbuckle's problems started when it was revealed that one of his guests, a young starlet named Virginia Rappe, had been taken to hospital after the party where she later died from a ruptured bladder.

Rumours were quick to circulate and, following the dubious evidence of a mysterious woman named Maude Delmont, Arbuckle was arrested and charged with murder. Delmont claimed that at the height of the party Arbuckle had dragged the screaming starlet into his bedroom where she was raped. Hearst's newspapers were quick to judge and within days every salacious detail of Arbuckle's eventful life – most of them untrue – was emblazoned across the front pages. Overnight, the baby-faced Arbuckle became the most reviled man in America; Rappe was painted as a paragon of virginal purity.

Arbuckle underwent three trials before, his innocence was finally established on April 12, 1922. Medical evidence previously with-held proved that Rappe had a history of abortions as well as a stomach condition made worse by her heavy drinking. It would seem that she had died as a result of a failed abortion and that Maude Delmont had tried to capitalize on the tragedy.

In spite of an unprecedented apology from the court, the tragedy destroyed Arbuckle. His once-popular films were no longer shown and his acting career came to an abrupt end. Many years later he was able to resume work as a director, but only by assuming the pseudonym William B Goodrich.

The scandal also had wider implications, having brought the hedonism of Hollywood into the public eye. A direct consequence of the Arbuckle fiasco was the creation of the Hays Office, a body that took it upon itself to censor films shown in America for the next 40 years.

- Treaty of Washington guarantees Chinese independence
- First session of the Court of International Justice

March
- Peace negotiations take place in Paris over Greek-Turkish war
- USA bans arms shipments to China
- Martial law declared in Johannesburg, South Africa
- Fuad I becomes King of Egypt with British approval
- Britain and Egypt assume joint control of Sudan
- Mohandas Gandhi jailed in India

April
- Coal miners strike in USA
- Irish rebels seize the Four Courts in Dublin
- Russia and Germany sign Treaty of Rapallo
- Six people die when a plane crashes en route to Paris from London
- On the orders of Lenin, Joseph Stalin is appointed General Secretary of the Communist Party

May
- Upper Silesia ceded to Poland by Germany
- Lenin suffers a stroke
- Vatican opposes British rule in Palestine
- Sinn Fein is outlawed in six counties in the Irish Free State
- Chinese rebel army is defeated by General Wu Peifu, bringing to an end the bloody civil war between south and north China

June
- Emergency economic measures taken in Germany
- An expedition to Everest, led by British mountaineer George Mallory, reaches over 8,000 metres (27,000 ft)
- Pro-British majority in Irish Free State elections
- Field Marshal Sir Henry Wilson killed by Irish patriots
- Anti-Semitic murder of German foreign secretary Rathenau

THE BIRTH OF FASCISM

◀ Benito Mussolini, the founding father of European fascism. Within five years of coming to power, *Il Duce* had virtually assumed dictatorial powers over the government of Italy.

On October 30, 1922, Italian nationalist Benito Mussolini marched on Rome with his army of 40,000, establishing the first European totalitarian state of the twentieth century.

Born in 1883, Mussolini began life as a school teacher. A voracious reader, he immersed himself in the works of the great philosophers and socialist political thinkers of the day. Entering politics in his early twenties, he quickly forged a reputation as a brilliant and charismatic orator and propagandist. His rhetoric was more often than not inflammatory and he often fell foul of the law — by 1910 his extreme socialist views had already earned him five prison sentences. After establishing a reputation as a powerful writer, he was made editor of *Avanti!*, Italy's best-selling socialist magazine, in 1912.

When Europe went to war in 1914, Mussolini's editorials took a strong line in opposition to Italian intervention; however, his views rapidly changed, losing him his job and earning him expulsion from the Socialist Party. Under the circumstances, he felt the only option open to him was to enlist in the Italian army.

After the war Mussolini turned his attention to politics. A well-attended meeting held in Milan in March 1919 heard him call for a dictatorship and the creation of a new force in Italian politics. Thus was born the *Fasci di Combattimento*, a league of fighters dedicated to the destruction of socialism and communism. It derived its name from the *fasces*, the insignia of authority in the Roman Empire. Mussolini urged his people to restore Italy to the greatness of an earlier age. To emphasize his authority, Mussolini assumed the title *Il Duce* ("the leader").

Fascist groups were quickly formed all over northern and central Italy and by 1920 they saw frequent strike-breaking action. Support for Mussolini was now widespread and when an election took place in May 1921, 35 fascists were elected to the Italian Parliament. Even then, however, they were not a true political party. Mussolini made them so when he founded the National Fascist Party in July 1921.

Mussolini was now a powerful force in Italy and his fascists had all but crushed the poorly organized Communist opposition. By August 1922 he felt ready to assume power.

So it was that on October 30, 40,000 black-shirted fascists marched triumphantly into Rome. King Victor Emmanuel III was urged to declare martial rule, but refused, fearing that it would result in all-out civil war. In his view, the safest place for Mussolini was in government, working within the confines of the constitution. The following day Mussolini received a telegram from the King asking him to form a new government.

Although for 18 months Mussolini ruled in a more or less constitutional manner; thereafter he gradually assumed increasingly great individual powers. Free speech was curbed and by 1927 all political opposition had been dissolved, making Mussolini Europe's first fascist dictator.

▼ Some of the 40,000 "black-shirts" who marched into Rome in a display of strength that brought Mussolini to power.

TUTANKHAMEN'S TREASURES REVEALED

▲ **Carefully wrapped and carried in a cardboard box, a life-size effigy of Tutankhamen's queen is carried from the pharaoh's tomb.**

On November 4, 1922 the great Egyptologist Howard Carter made one of the most amazing archeological finds of the age when after years of persistent research he discovered the tomb of the Pharaoh Tutankhamen in the Valley of the Kings in Luxor. The King ruled Egypt between 1333-23 BC and is thought to have died aged between 15 and 18 years.

The pharaohs of Ancient Egypt were well-known for the opulence of their burial grounds – it was seen as critical that they were interred with the necessary accoutrements to secure their safe passage to the afterlife. The great riches that accompanied the most powerful pharaohs had already been looted at the end of the twentieth dynasty (around 1000BC), but since then, the remaining tombs had lain untroubled and untouched.

During the course of the decade, Carter and his team meticulously unearthed an unimaginable parade of priceless treasures that would create an enduring popular interest in the world of ancient Egypt. The first room of the tomb contained gold statues and likenesses of the pharaoh, reliefs and papyri, as well as four exquisitely hand-carved chariots, each one inlaid with precious jewels. In one of the sealed rooms surrounding the main burial chamber, Carter discovered the mummified remains of the young king within a nest of three coffins, the inner coffin, containing the sarcophagus of Tutankhamen, was cast from solid gold. Covering the dead king's face was a magnificent gold mask.

The discovery unleashed an unprecedented level of interest in archeology and Egyptology. The idea of a mummified ancient king especially captured the imagination of Hollywood film makers, fuelled no doubt by the speculation that a number of mysterious deaths relating to those involved with the excavation were the result of an ancient curse.

Over 1,700 items were eventually taken from the tomb where they were displayed at the Egyptian Museum in Cairo. During the 1970s, some of these items were allowed to leave the museum as part of a hugely successful tour of Europe and America. In every city, massive crowds queued to get a glimpse of some of the most magnificent specimens of Egyptian antiquity ever seen.

Perhaps the greatest irony surrounding the enduring fascination with Tutankhamen is that, while he remains by far the best known of all the Egyptian pharaohs – indeed, he is one of the most famous figures of the ancient world – his celebrity is entirely due to the magnificent treasures discovered in his tomb. His reign began at such an early age – possibly as young as five – that Egypt was effectively run by his regent, the vizier Ay. In fact, King Tutankhamen was arguably the least historically significant of all the pharaohs.

▼ **Howard Carter kneels in front of the doors of the fourth shrine in the tomb; here, Tutankhamen's sarcophagus was found.**

DEATH OF A BANDIT

◀ One of the leading lights of the Mexican Revolution, notorious bandit General Francisco "Pancho" Villa was offered a formal pardon in exchange for his agreement to retire.

Francisco Villa, best known by his nickname "Pancho", the revolutionary leader and Mexico's most notorious bandit, was shot dead on July 10, 1923.

Born in 1878, Villa, the son of a farm worker, began his fugitive life in his adolescence, killing an employer in revenge for the rape of his sister. Villa found popular fame with his 2,000-strong vigilantes – *El Division del Norte* – who helped initiate the revolt against the dictatorship of President Victoriano Huerta. He joined with Emiliano Zapata under the leadership of Venustiano Carranza to overthrow Huerta in 1914. However, Carranza's refusal to grant social reforms caused a split among the revolutionaries. Carranza became President and waged a series of battles against the forces of Villa and Zapata, finally securing victory in April 1915. Villa and his men fled to the mountains in the north of the country where they gained a reputation as ruthless bandits, even managing to avoid an American attempt to kill him.

Following the violent overthrow of Carranza in 1920, Villa was offered a full pardon if he surrendered to the government. He accepted and retired from politics. His freedom lasted barely three years before he was shot dead by members of the Herrera family, four of whom Villa had executed during the revolution.

COLLAPSE OF THE GERMAN ECONOMY

November 15, 1924 saw Germany's situation deteriorate as crippling inflation finally brought about the complete collapse of the German economy. At the height of this hyper-inflation crisis, the cost of a loaf of bread was known to have increased two hundred-fold during the course of a single day.

Although the German economy was already struggling with the harsh terms of the Treaty of Versailles, the inflation was attributable to the government's refusal to pay the reparations demanded by the Allies. The German government encouraged the factory workers of Rhineland to strike, which resulted in the French and Belgian occupation the Ruhr. During this time, the Government paid their workers even though industrial output had ceased. Furthermore, the money supply was increased by printing more bank notes which started the inflationary spiral that would soon make the mark worth – quite literally – less than the paper it was printed on.

From the beginning of 1923,

▶ With the mark crashing by the hour, a cash register is of no use to this Berlin shopkeeper who is forced to use a tea chest to store bank notes.

the story of Germany's currency was one of a dramatic downward spiral. Before World War One, a US dollar had been worth just over four marks; by August 1923, that same dollar could buy nearly five million marks. When the final collapse came in November it would have taken 4.2 trillion marks to buy one US dollar. To a German, 4.2 trillion marks would have bought little more than a pound of beef and a loaf of bread.

Had it not resulted in starvation for so many, the situation would have been comically absurd. Workers had to be paid twice a day and required a wheelbarrow to take home their earnings. The Reichsbank responded by producing a new banknote, on which a new mark was worth a trillion of the old devalued currency.

Although the crisis created poverty and strife among Germany's workers, it was perhaps the middle class who bore the greatest suffering. In the space of a few days a lifetime's worth of savings were suddenly worth no more than the cost of a postage stamp.

Germany's economic woes were eased from 1924 under the guiding hand of foreign minister Gustav Streseman. Realizing that resistance to the reparations demanded would do Germany more damage, he carried out a policy of appeasement. The political landscape was also calmed when 77-year-old Paul von Hindenburg, the former field marshal, became President after the death of Friedrich Ebert.

Nonetheless, throughout what became known as "the era of fulfilment", there remained widespread discontent which the extremist political parties were more than happy to fuel.

TOKYO IN RUINS

Throughout history, Tokyo, formerly the great imperial city of Edo, has had more than its share of disaster. In 1657, the city's bicentennial year, fire destroyed well over half of the city and took the lives of over 100,000 people. On the morning of September 1, 1923, Japan suffered its most devastating natural disaster, as an earthquake all but eradicated Tokyo and the neighbouring port of Yokohama.

The sequence of events began at 11:58 when three violent tremors were felt in quick succession. The impact was immediate: every major building in Tokyo was flattened, including the imperial palace, over 600 Buddhist temples, 150 Shinto shrines and 200 churches. Almost all domestic housing collapsed. Although many thousands died immediately, the consequential peril facing the survivors was the old enemy – "the flower of Edo" – fire. As it swept through the debris, violent winds further spread the devastation. With all of the water pipes broken and no electricity supply

working, nothing could be done to save the city.

There was more to come. The shock of the tremors also set off a *tsunami* (tidal wave). Almost 12 metres (40 ft) high at its peak, a giant wave leapt out of the Sagami Gulf and washed away entire coastal villages to the west of Tokyo.

The city was cut off for almost two days before food was eventually flown in for the starving refugees, 13,000 of whom were gathered on the grounds of the ruined imperial palace. The military erected temporary barracks and tents. Within a week an international aid campaign had begun, the Red Cross coordinating over $10 million worth of donations from the US alone.

It was estimated that 150,000 died as a result of the Tokyo earthquake, killed by the tremors, *tsunami*, fire, cholera, dysentery and typhoid. Almost all of the domestic wooden buildings were destroyed; over half of the brick buildings met with a similar fate. In all, 2.5 million people were made homeless.

▼ **A picture of destruction: only a day earlier this had been one of the busiest streets in the centre of Tokyo.**

KEMAL BRINGS TURKEY IN TO THE WESTERN WORLD

On October 29, 1923, under the leadership of the charismatic Mustafa Kemal, Turkey proclaimed itself a republic. This was the first stage of a process that would usher in an era of quite extraordinary reform.

Allied to Germany during World War One, the mighty Ottoman Empire ended the hostilities defeated and humbled. Postwar treaties agreed among the Allies maintained territorial gains made during the war. French troops occupied Istanbul and Cilecia; Italy now occupied large parts of the Western empire; Armenia was to be an independent state; Greece occupied Anatolia and was advancing further.

Mustafa Kemal was a powerful military leader, and was now strongly opposed to the conciliatory tone of Sultan Mehmed VI's government in Istanbul. In March 1920, Kemal, having fled south to Ankara with many other nationalists, proclaimed a new government dedicated to the recovery of Turkey's prewar territories. Elections were held and Kemal was named President.

Kemal's first move was to reclaim Armenia, whose weak forces proved no match for the nationalist army. There followed a bitter campaign against Greece which was only concluded in September 1922 when Kemal personally took control of Turkey's war strategy. By now, Kemal was a national hero. The Ankara government proclaimed the abolition of the sultanate and the illegitimacy of the Istanbul regime. The nationalists reclaimed the former capital on October 2 and Sultan Mehmed was exiled. On October 29, Turkey was proclaimed a republic.

Heading the Republican People's Party, Kemal set about an unprecedented reign of reform with the aim of creating a modern, self-sufficient industrialized state to rival any European power.

Symbols associated with the sultanate era were banished: religious schools and organizations were abolished, as was the wearing of traditional costume, such as the fez. Islamic law was discarded, replaced directly by models from the West. Women were allowed not only to vote but

▲ A symbol of the new, modern Turkey, a fleet of American-built Model T Fords parades through the streets of Constantinople, proclaiming victory for Kemal's Republican People's Party.

to stand for government - impossible under the Islamic regime. Kemal also brought about the adoption of the European tradition of using first names and family names. The most radical move of all was his decision to replace Arabic script with the Latin alphabet used in the West. This set off an unprecedented growth in education and literacy. Kemal also proved to be a fine diplomat, creating treaties of reconciliation with most of Turkey's former enemies.

Kemal's reforms were not uniformly popular. Indeed, a number of Islamic revolts – most notably by the Kurds of Anatolia – were ruthlessly suppressed. Similarly, a failed plot to assassinate Kemal resulted in the execution of all suspected ringleaders. Although he never fully enjoyed dictatorial powers, his towering role in the modernization of Turkey was such that in 1934 Kemal was officially renamed Ataturk, meaning "Father of the Turks".

▼ The man who brought Turkey into twentieth century, Mustafa Kemal initiated unprecedented reform in the new republic.

POLITICAL INSTABILITY IN UK

▲ **Andrew Bonar Law makes his final exit from No. 10 Downing Street, the traditional home of the Prime Ministers of Great Britain. Terminal illness caused his resignation.**

By the middle of 1922, the coalition government in Britain, led by David Lloyd George since the end of the war, finally seemed to be running out of steam. A combination of the continuing Irish problem, a scandal regarding the sale of honours and a political incident which brought Britain and Turkey to the brink of war had raised doubts among the Conservative back-benchers. When Lloyd George, a Liberal, proposed that a further election be called to approve a continued coalition, a Conservative revolt ensued. Andrew Bonar Law, a former Conservative member of the war cabinet who had retired from politics a year earlier through ill health, called for a party vote. A majority of 2:1 came out against continuing the coalition. Instead, the rebel majority pledged to fight an election independently under Bonar Law and Stanley Baldwin.

On October 20, 1922, Lloyd George had no choice but to tender his resignation: the Conservatives in the cabinet followed suit. The general election, which took place in November,

resulted in a comfortable majority for the Tories.

During 1923, the relationship between Law and his Chancellor, Baldwin, was uneasy, and he came close to resignation over a number of disagreements with his party. However, it was ill health that forced his final resignation. Suffering from an incurable cancer of the throat, on May 20, 1923 he handed over leadership to Baldwin: Andrew Bonar Law died six months later.

Although Stanley Baldwin had been a member of parliament for 15 years, he was a relatively unknown quantity. His avowed aim was to bring stability to government, but his task was not an easy one. Most of the senior influential Tories of the coalition government were now in the political wilderness (Churchill had described the Law cabinet as the "second team"). Additionally, Britain's economy was stagnant and unemployment was rising.

Seeking, somewhat controversially, the reintroduction of import duties abandoned in favour of "free trade" by his predecessor, Baldwin appealed for a mandate. This turned out to be an error of judgement: it was refused, bringing about a second general

election within a year. This time the Conservative majority was reduced significantly. There was an additional sting for Baldwin, however. Herbert Asquith's Liberal Party, now with little hope of achieving office on its own, had agreed to support a minority Labour government if they polled sufficient seats. Together, they managed a 92-seat majority over the Conservatives; thus, on January 24, 1924, 58-year-old Scotsman Ramsay MacDonald became Britain's first-ever Labour Prime Minister.

The MacDonald reign was little longer than Law's. He stemmed the growing violence in Ireland by cancelling the debt owed by the Irish Free State in exchange for abandoning their demands for the six counties of Northern Ireland. However, after losing a vote of censure following a scandal regarding the prosecution of a Communist newspaper editor, the MacDonald government began to show signs of weakness. Following the formation of new alliances within the government his leadership became untenable and he resigned on November 4, 1924. It was Stanley Baldwin who, once again, took the centre stage of British politics.

An unknown quantity, Stanley Baldwin had had a largely undistinguished political career before he came to the fore in 1922.

November
- Separatist riots in the German Rhineland
- Adolf Hitler attempts coup in Munich
- German Chancellor Streseman loses vote of confidence and resigns

December
- Adolfo de la Huerta rebels against Mexican government
- New coalition government in Germany under Wilhelm Brandt
- Conservatives suffer losses in British general elections
- King George II of Greece exiled; Greek Army later deposes him
- The Japanese regent, Hirohito, escapes an assassination attempt

LENIN LAID TO REST

On January 21, 1924 Vladimir Ilyich Lenin, the architect of the Russian Revolution and the Soviet Union, died. His influence on the course of twentieth-century history was immense.

Born on April 22, 1870, Vladimir Ilyich Ulyanov (he adopted the pseudonym "Lenin" in 1901) enjoyed a cultured, middle-class upbringing during which he excelled as a young scholar. Lenin's first brush with revolution came in 1887 when his influential elder brother was hanged after an attempt to depose Tsar Alexander III. That same year, Lenin began studying law at the imperial Kazan University. Within three months he had been expelled for organizing an illegal assembly. Over the next two years Lenin immersed himself in revolutionary works; it was here he came into contact with *Das Kapital*, Karl Marx's defining work that gave birth to Communism.

Finally allowed to take his university law examinations in 1891, Lenin graduated with the highest honours. After his admission to the bar he devoted his efforts to defending the poor. During this time he began his life as an active Marxist. It was a pamphleteering campaign explaining Marxism to un-educated workers that led to his arrest and exile to Siberia in 1894.

Completing his sentence in 1900, Lenin and his wife Nadezhda moved to Munich where he joined with other Russian Marxist exiles to produce

▼ Lenin addresses a crowd from the back of a lorry in 1917. While he attempted to apply the philosophies of Karl Marx to his native Russia, Lenin was also a skilled practical revolutionary organizer.

the revolutionary news pamphlet *Iskra* ("The Spark"). It was from this base that Lenin and his allies attempted to forge Marxism into a system that could be applied to Russia. It has been argued that Marxism was meaningless to Russia's peasant majority and that revolution by an industrially developed proletariat, as described in *Das Kapital*, could never happen, because within Russia it was too small a group. Through his editorials, Lenin argued that capitalism had brought about the evolution of a recognizable class system among the peasantry, the poor majority of which constituted a "semi-proletariat". All sides, however agreed that a proletarian revolution could only take place after a bourgeois revolution had deposed the autocracy of the ruling Tsar.

In 1902, Lenin produced *What Is to Be Done?,* a document in which he outlined his idea of a centralized party led by a hierar-

chy of professional revolutionaries that would act as the "vanguard of the proletariat". Four years earlier, the first congress of what later become the Russian Social Democratic Worker's Party (and later still the Communist Party) had taken place in Minsk, resulting in the arrest of their leaders. A second congress was held in exile in 1903, first in Brussels and then in London. Here, Lenin's document was heavily debated, causing a split in the ranks: those in agreement became known as Bolsheviks; opponents who favoured greater democracy were known as Mensheviks. These factions continued to argue until after the Bolshevik Revolution of 1917.

Lenin returned to Russia to play a small role in the 1905 uprising, but following its failure, he once again found himself exiled to Europe where, in 1912, he established the

Bolshevik Party as an entirely separate entity from the increasingly popular Mensheviks.

During the early years of World War One, Lenin unsuccessfully campaigned at socialist conferences throughout Europe to "transform the imperialist war into civil war". In his influential document *Imperialism, the Highest Stage of Capitalism*, published in 1917, he argued that imperialists were by definition expansionists and as long as they existed there would always be wars.

Lenin's time came in March 1917 when, with Russia starving, the Tsar was forced to abdicate. Lenin was allowed to return to Russia, the German authorities allowing him access through the Eastern Front because they believed he would be a destabilizing presence in Russia. At the first congress of Russian workers councils (Soviets) in June, Lenin clashed with moderate socialist

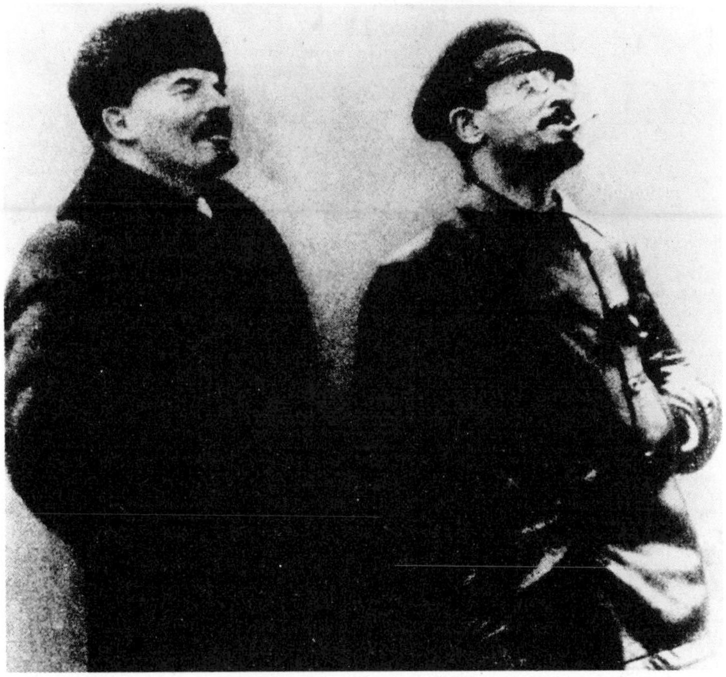

◀ **The two great intellectuals of Communism. Although Leon Trotsky (right) was Lenin's chosen successor, he lost out to Stalin.**

Aleksandr Kerensky, leader of the provisional government. Initially with little support, the Bolsheviks gained popularity as Kerensky failed to appease the starving workers, troops and peasants.

On November 7, Bolshevik Red Guards organized by Lenin and his ally Leon Trotsky staged a bloodless coup, proclaiming that all power was now in the hands of the Russian Soviets. At the second congress of Soviets Lenin was voted chairman.

Lenin's attentions thereafter were concentrated on ending Russia's involvement in the war and consolidating the revolution. He achieved the former at the Treaty of Brest-Litovsk in March 1918. Although the terms were harsh, Lenin needed the support of German finance to combat political opponents at home.

While Lenin began a programme of nationalization of land and industry, the south-west of Russia was thrown into turmoil as anti-Bolshevik parties, supported by Allied forces, came together to fight the new government. The so-called "White" armies made advances throughout 1919, but by 1921 the Red Army had fought back to occupy all the independent republics of the former Russian Empire. In 1922 Lenin proclaimed the founding of the Union of Soviet Socialist Republics (USSR).

During his final years, Lenin fought against the corruption he saw growing in the Soviet system. In his "testament", dictated to his secretary a year before his death following a series of strokes, he spelled out his fears for the future of the revolution, and was especially concerned by the power-mongering of the newly-elected General Secretary Joseph Stalin.

Under the ruthless leadership of Stalin, the USSR became a powerful dictatorship. Many of the attitudes and suspicions that prevailed throughout the latter half of the century during the Cold War era were fostered during his reign. Lenin died on January 21, 1924 at the age of 54 years. Had he lived to a greater age the course of the twentieth century might well have been very different.

▼ **The greatest revolutionary lies in state. Lenin's death brought Stalin to power, in whose hands the Communist revolution would take a very different direction.**

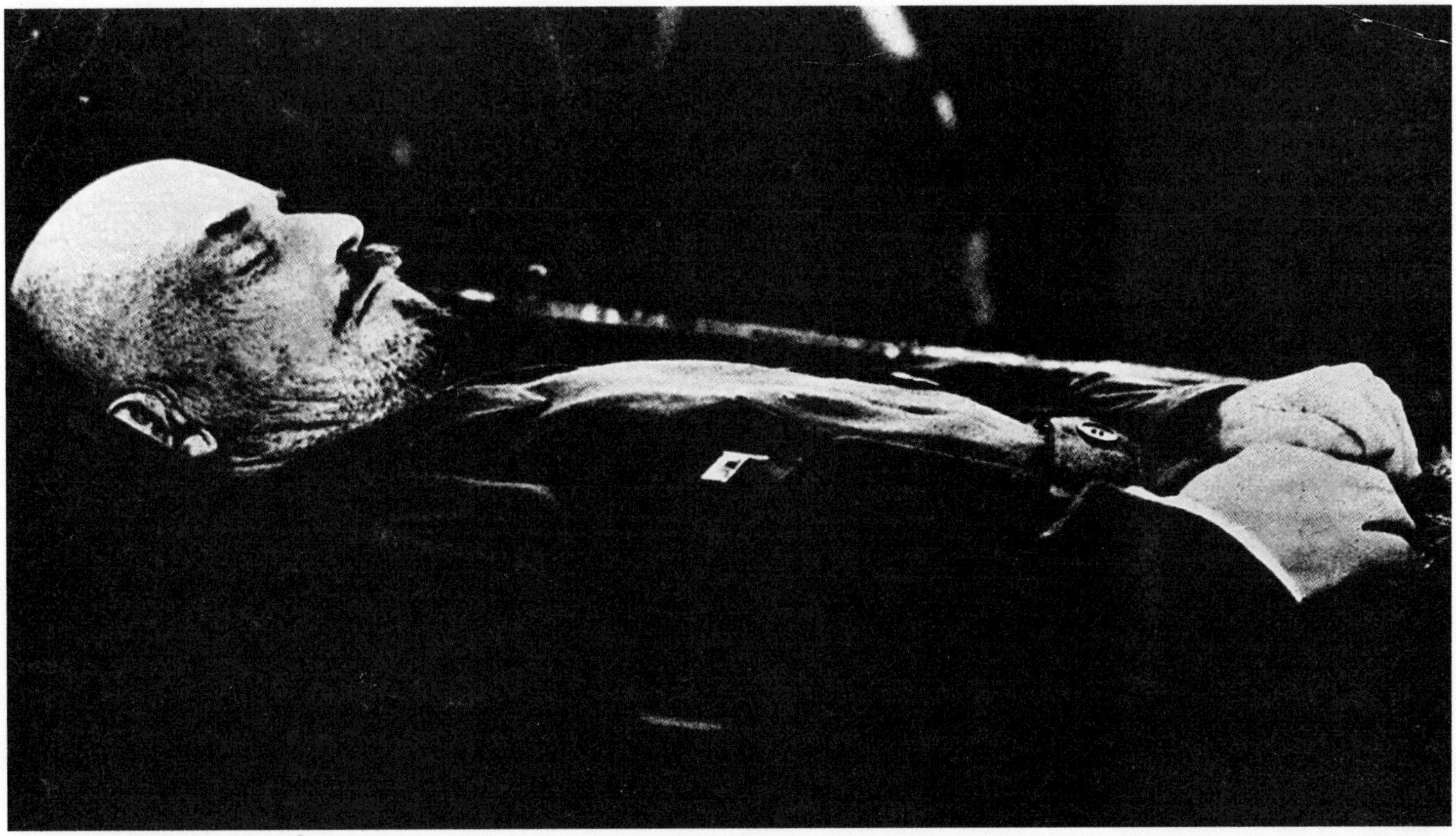

THE STRANGE CASE OF LEOPOLD AND LOEB

August 20, 1924 saw the conclusion of one of the most extraordinary murder cases of the century, as Nathan Leopold and Richard A. Loeb, two brilliant young American men who had both graduated from university before reaching the age of 18, were given life sentences for the random murder of 14-year-old Bobbie Franks.

On May 21, 1924 Leopold and Loeb, whose father was Vice-President of Sears Roebuck, had brought to fruition a long-held plan to execute a "perfect" undetectable murder. Their victim, the son of a Chicago millionaire, was kidnapped and taken to a plot of land outside the city. Bobbie Franks died quickly as Loeb struck at his head with a chisel. Before the body was discovered a typed ransom note demanding $10,000 and signed in the name of "George Johnson", was sent to the boy's father.

Although the plan seemed to have left nothing to chance, Leopold had unwittingly dropped

Born into wealth and privilege, Leopold (left) and Loeb should have had a bright future. Instead, they spent it behind bars. ▶

his glasses near the scene of the crime. Traced back through his optician, Leopold remained cool when questioned by the police: "If I were not positive that my glasses were at home I'd say these were mine." He was unable to produce them. A full confession followed after the discovery that the type on the ransom note was identical to that produced by Leopold's own Underwood typewriter.

Many had expected – and demanded – that Leopold and Loeb be put to death; however, it was the intervention of the celebrated lawyer Clarence

Darrow, with a passionate humanist argument against capital punishment, that spared their lives. The judge accepted Darrow's claim of diminished responsibility, and they each received a sentence of life for murder and 99 years for kidnapping. It was a verdict that fuelled a common belief that a different system of justice operated in the halls of privileged society.

Although Loeb was murdered while in prison, Leopold was paroled in 1958, whereupon he wrote the book *Life Plus Ninety-Nine Years*. He died of a heart attack in 1971.

THE ZINOVIEV LETTER

◀ Grigory Zinoviev: did he write the Zinoviev Letter? Timed to coincide with a general election, the Zinoviev scandal contributed to the downfall of Ramsay MacDonald's government.

Following the election of Ramsay MacDonald's socialist government, on February 1, 1924 Britain became the first major power to recognize the validity of the Soviet government. By the end of the year, however, Anglo-Soviet relations were in shreds and a second general election saw a massive swing back towards the Conservatives. These events were a consequence of the publication of the infamous "Zinoviev Letter".

MacDonald headed a tenuous minority government and it came as no surprise when on October 9, having lost a vote of censure, he had no choice but to call the second general election of the year. The campaign trail was rudely interrupted on October 24, 1924, when Foreign Secretary Sir Alexander Crowe released what purported to be a letter from Grigory Zinoviev, chairman of Comintern, a Soviet government committee, that sought to coordinate the efforts of Communist parties throughout the world. Addressed to the British Communist Party, the letter advised in practical terms how a workers' revolution could be achieved in Britain, including the infiltration of the armed forces.

The Zinoviev Letter dominated the press during the final week of the election campaign. In what amounted to Britain's very own Red Scare, the electorate came to associate the Labour Party with Communism and restored Stanley Baldwin's Conservatives to power with a large majority. Official relations with the Soviet Union were immediately suspended.

Controversy continued to surround the validity of the letter, and although the spreading of Communism as an ideology was always a part of the early Soviet agenda, the Zinoviev Letter is now generally acknowledged to have been a fake designed to discredit Britain's first Socialist government.

DEATH OF A LITERARY MASTER

▲ One of the great exponents of the English language, Polish-born Joseph Conrad (Jozef Teodor Konrad Korzeniowski) could speak little English until he reached his twenties.

Joseph Conrad, one of the greatest authors of the period, died on August 3, 1924.

Born Jozef Teodor Konrad Korzeniowski in Poland in 1857, Conrad moved with his family to the north of Russia when his father, the poet Apollo Korzeniowski, was exiled for leading an insurrection against Russian rule. Sent to school in Switzerland following the death of his father, Conrad was unable to adapt to his education and left to join the French merchant navy. His transfer to the British ship *Palestine* in 1881 changed his life and, later, provided the inspiration for many of his greatest novels, such as *Lord Jim*, which he wrote in 1900.

Conrad spent a further 16 years as a merchant sailor, a time that included his greatest adventure – his command of a steamboat sailing up the River Congo into the heart of Africa. The trauma he experienced during four years in the Congo – at the time a private colony of Leopold II, King of the Belgians – where greedy European traders brutally exploited the native tribes, was conveyed in the most troubled of his works, the story *Heart Of Darkness*. It was a title that not only symbolized the journey into "the dark continent", but also the evil and darkness within man.

Settling in England, Conrad found the life of an author difficult; not only did he and his young family live in near poverty, but the gout he had contracted in the Congo plagued him intermittently for the rest of his life. It was only in his last decade that he achieved widespread literary recognition.

Conrad is still widely viewed as one of the greatest writers of the English language. This is impressive in that English was not his native tongue, but astounding when we learn that at the age of 21 his vocabulary barely stretched to a dozen words.

'25

STALIN OUSTS TROTSKY

▲ One of the greatest minds of the Russian Revolution, Leon Trotsky was Lenin's preferred choice as successor.

January 1925 effectively saw the end of the power struggle to fill the vacuum left in the Soviet Union by the death of Lenin. Leon Trotsky, the greatest intellect of the Bolshevik revolution and Lenin's favoured successor, was ousted from a position of influence by the supporters of Joseph Stalin.

Although Trotsky was one of Lenin's fellow revolutionary exiles, his role in the Bolshevik Revolution of 1917 was considerably more active. By the time Lenin arrived in Russia during November 1917, Trotsky, as head of the Petrograd Soviet, had already paved the way for the fall of the Kerensky government.

Trotsky played an active role in the Brest-Litovsk peace negotiations and was also responsible for the formation of the Red Army, without which the Civil War that followed the revolution could not have been won.

When Lenin fell ill in May 1922 it was assumed that Trotsky would take over. However, as head of the Politburo and with involvement in numerous bureaucratic committees, Joseph Stalin was able to take advantage of circumstances to manoeuvre himself into power.

Much of Stalin's early life was obscured by Soviet revisionist propaganda. We do know, however, that as an unschooled man, Stalin was widely underestimated by Communist Party intellectuals. Allying himself with other influential Bolsheviks, Stalin began a succession of public attacks on Trotsky, portraying him as a factionist. With critically unfortunate timing, Trotsky himself fell ill and was unable to lead a campaign in his defence. While Trotsky was incapacitated, Lenin died, leaving Stalin to present himself to the Soviet people as Lenin's natural successor.

Following his recovery, Trotsky outlined his theory of permanent revolution in his paper *The Lessons of October 1917* which

was quickly denounced by Stalin as heresy. In January 1925, Stalin orchestrated Trotsky's removal from his post and eventual expulsion from the Central Committee of the Communist Party. In January 1929, after a year of exile, Trotsky was permanently banished from the Soviet Union. A decade later, living in Mexico, he was the victim of a notorious ice-axe murder, carried out by Soviet agents thought to have been acting for Stalin.

Having consolidated immense personal power within the world's largest national boundary, Stalin began a ruthless rule that lasted until his death in 1953. During that time, he became unquestionably one of the most powerful leaders of the twentieth century.

▲ A ruthless dictator, Joseph Stalin dominated the world's largest state for much of the twentieth century.

NEWS IN BRIEF

- France begins construction of fortifications on border with Germany
- US state of Tennessee bans the teaching of evolution
- Turkish government begins modernization program
- Peru suffers catastrophic rains
- Afrikaans recognized as an official language of South Africa
- Tornado in the USA kills nearly 1,000 people
- First Exposition des Arts Decoratifs opens in Paris
- Vitamins B and B2 isolated
- First BBC long-wave transmitter goes on-line
- Electrical methods of sound recording developed
- Films released this year include Sergei Eisenstein's *The Battleship Potemkin*, Charles Chaplin's *The Gold Rush* and Fred Niblo's *Ben-Hur*
- Books published this year include *Mrs Dalloway* by Virginia Woolf, *The Great Gatsby* by F Scott Fitzgerald, *The Trial* by Franz Kafka and *Mein Kampf* by Adolf Hitler

January
- The capital city of Norway, Christiania, is renamed Oslo
- First female US State Governor is appointed in Wyoming
- Mussolini becomes dictator of Italy
- New coalition government formed in Germany
- Leon Trotsky deposed from chairmanship of Russian Revolutionary Military Council
- Britain and China sign the Treaty of Peking

CHINESE COMMUNISTS GAIN FROM CIVIL UNREST

During 1925 China saw an outburst of anti-foreign sentiment of a kind that had not been seen since the Boxer rebellion at the turn of the century. Much of this unrest took place in and around the coastal city of Shanghai.

The crisis began in April 1925 when Chinese workers at a Japanese-run cotton mill went on strike, protesting at their very poor working conditions. Representatives were sent to meet the Japanese management, but the negotiations ended in an

affray that resulted in the death of one of the employees. The situation was exacerbated when the non-Chinese council governing Shanghai's international settlement not only refused to prosecute the killer, but arrested the workers for creating a disturbance.

This atmosphere of hostility towards what was widely viewed as foreign imperialism was exploited by the fledgling Chinese Communist Party. Active in politicizing both the work force and students, the Communist Party were behind the organization of a massive political protest on May 30, 1925. However, the demonstrators were met by members of the British Municipal Police who mercilessly opened fire, killing 13 demonstrators and wounding dozens of others.

The "Thirtieth of May" Incident as it became known, had two immediate repercussions. The people of China were outraged and, urged on by the communists, organized boycotts of British and Japanese merchandise. Foreign-owned factories soon found themselves under siege as demonstrations and riots broke out all over the country. Unrest continued into early 1926, until the British government agreed to punish the police officials and pay damages to those affected by the Incident.

Throughout the events of 1925, it was the Communist Party that made the biggest gains, their membership rising from virtually nothing to over 20,000 during the course of the year.

▼ Officers of the British Municipal Police stand guard outside the station in which rioting Chinese students were killed.

THE BITTER STRUGGLE FOR THE SOUL OF CHINA

▲ Dr Sun Yat-sen, the father of Chinese nationalism. His work helped bring an end to centuries of feudalism in China.

March 12, 1925, saw the passing of Sun Yat-sen, the father of modern China. He had been one of the architects who had brought an end to the Manchu dynasty in the revolution of 1911 and was leader of the Kuomintang – China's Nationalist Party – from its formation in 1912. The party was founded on what he termed the "Three principles of the People": nationalism, democracy and the improvement of their livelihoods. Initially, the Kuomintang was modelled on the traditional Chinese secret societies, but later Sun used the example of the Bolsheviks in the Soviet Union. Towards the end of his life, he devoted his energies to developing a professional army capable of unifying China and marginalizing the remaining regional warlords. By the time of his death it numbered some 40,000 troops, including a growing number of China's Communist Party.

Sun was succeeded by General Chiang Kai-shek, the military leader of the Kuomintang. In the early part of his leadership tensions between the Communists

▶ A former Bolshevik, General Chiang Kai-shek (left) fought in vain to purge China of the influence of Communism.

and the conservative nationalists began to emerge. At first Chiang was able to control these elements – a necessity for the continued support of the Soviet Union – but in 1927, fearing an attempted overthrow, he carried out a bloody purge of Communists from the Party. He vowed that China could never be whole until the Communists had been destroyed, and thus set the scene for twenty-two years of periodic armed struggle that would culminate in victory for the Communists in 1949.

'25 DARWINISM UNDER ATTACK

◄ **John T Scopes, the school teacher who fell foul of Tennessee's anti-evolution laws. Not until 1967 would it be legal to teach the theories of Charles Darwin in the state.**

NEWS IN BRIEF
....

June
- Coup in Greece; General Theodoros Pangalos takes power
- Coal mine dispute over productivity in Britain
- General strike breaks out in Hong Kong; continuing unrest in China
- MPs in South Africa pass a bill excluding blacks from holding any skilled job

July
- French and Belgian troops withdraw from the Ruhr
- First elected parliament of Iraq convenes
- Druse rebellion in Syria
- Italy and Yugoslavia settle Dalmatian dispute by treaty
- Suzanne Lenglen wins her sixth successive Wimbledon title
- A patient at a London hospital has the first successful treatment for diabetes

August
- Island of Spitzbergen officially annexed by Norway
- Amnesty in Germany for leaders of Kapp Putsch
- Seven men convicted of murdering the Governor-General of Sudan are hanged
- French World War One hero Marshal Pétain takes command of French soldiers fighting in Morocco
- Huge Ku Klux Klan parade in Washington DC

Perhaps one of the most significant characteristics of life in the West during the twentieth century has been changing attitudes to religion.

Throughout the ages, scientists had come into conflict with the teachings of the Bible. It was the work of the nineteenth-century British biologist, Charles Darwin, that resulted in some of the greatest controversy since Galileo Galilei was tried by the Roman Catholic church for promoting his view that the Earth revolved around the Sun and was not the centre of God's universe. Essentially, Darwin informed the world that the story of mankind did not begin with Adam and Eve

It was during the course of a 5-year expedition to the islands of the Pacific Ocean that Darwin conceived the view that life on Earth passed along a series of evolutionary chains. His belief was that God did not create fully formed man, but that he evolved from a lower order of mammals. Furthermore, other primates such as chimpanzees and monkeys

The books of anti-evolutionary author William Jennings-Bryan sold in record numbers during the so-called "Monkeyville" trial. ▶

were distant relatives to humans.

Initially controversial, by the end of the nineteenth century Darwin's "Theory of Evolution", which he laid out in his book *On the Origin of Species*, was widely accepted by the scientific fraternity. The non-scientific world, however, took a long time to catch up.

The issue of evolution burst into the American public eye in 1925. Early in that year the Tennessee Legislature had passed a law declaring that anyone denying the divine creation of man would be liable to prosecution. Then, in July, a young high-school teacher named John T Scopes, working in the small mountain community of Dayton, was charged with teaching Darwinism to a group of 13–15 year-olds.

The case, which opened on July 10, 1925, was further publicized by the celebrity lawyers involved. The prosecution was led by former presidential candidate William Jennings Bryan; his opponent was Clarence Darrow, famed for his defence of socialite murderers Leopold and Loeb. Darrow saw the case as the most important of its kind "since we stopped trying people for witchcraft".

Although some had viewed it as a rare public opportunity for scientific rationality to take on the beliefs of Christian fundamentalism, in his opening, Judge John . Ralston ordered that neither the validity of the law nor Darwinism was relevant to the case. Scopes admitted that he had taught Darwin's theories and was convicted. He received a fine of $100.

Although the teaching of Darwin's "Theory of Evolution" is now universal in the West, the Tennessee law under which Scopes was prosecuted was not repealed for another 42 years.

THE REALM OF THE UNCONSCIOUS

Paris became the home for one of the most significant artistic movements of the twentieth century when in November, 1925 the Pierre Loeb Gallery exhibited the first group show of surrealist art.

The term "Surrealism" had been coined a year earlier when the poet André Breton published his essay *"Manifeste du surréalisme" (The Surrealist Manifesto)*. He defined the word as "pure psychic automatism". Influenced by the work of Sigmund Freud, Breton's was an art that sought to defy logic, operating at an unconscious level, blurring the boundaries of the dream world and reality. Surrealist poetry was somewhat inaccessible, taking the form of "automatic writing", and it was the work of the painters within the movement that would make a lasting impression on twentieth-century art. Although Breton sought to lead the Surrealists on the basis of

his prescribed doctrine, the breadth of the work of the artists involved made this an impossility.

Many of the artists either evolved from or were influenced by the earlier Dada movement, a conceptual "anti-art" which had flourished largely in Germany during the previous decade. Among the Dadaist's best-known works were Kurt Schwitters' *Merz* collages, made from rubbish, the abstract paintings of Max Ernst, and the ready-made sculptures of Marcel Duchamp. However, rather than the destruction of the concept of art, the Surrealists sought to create a new form in reaction against the accepted "rational" world which was still recovering from the mind-numbing horror of World War One and appalling casualty figures.

On show at the Pierre Loeb Gallery were works by Max Ernst, Joan Miró, Georgio de Chirico, Yves Tanguy, cubist Pablo Picasso

and the American surrealist photographer Man Ray. Also drawn to the movement were Salvador Dalí and René Magritte, two of the most popular artists of the twentieth century.

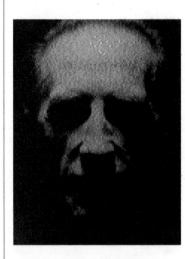

▲ **Clever lighting turns Marcel Duchamp's face into a shadowy skull. French-born Duchamp was a leading Dadaist and an influence on the Surrealists.**

NOBEL PEACE PRIZE FOR THE "DAWES PLAN" DUO

On December 10, 1925, the Nobel Committee presented its annual Peace Prize to US Vice President Charles Gates Dawes and British foreign Secretary Sir Austen Chamberlain, two of the architects of the war reparations agreement.

Former financier Dawes had been appointed head of the Reparations Commission in 1923, charged with the task of finding a solution to the inability of Germany to pay the Allies punitive damages for losses incurred during World War One. Published in August 1924, the solution

Dawes and Chamberlain reached was to reorganize the Reichsbank, making it independent from Germany's central government, and to help rebuild the German economy with the assistance of US investment worth 800 million

marks. This, it was proposed, would enable the German Government to begin making payments of one billion marks in the first year, rising to 2.5 billion marks in 1928.

The Dawes Plan, as it became known, can justly be said to have helped save Europe from short-term economic collapse.

◄ **US Vice President Charles Gates Dawes, the architect of the war reparations agreement. He argued that only by helping to rebuild Germany's economy would repayments be possible.**

JOHN LOGIE BAIRD INVENTS THE TELEVISION

On January 27, 1926, members of London's Royal Institution were given the first successful demonstration of the transmission of a moving image by wireless. The inventor of the system was a 38-year-old Scottish engineer named John Logie Baird, who coined the phrase "television" to describe the process. It was the first stage in the development of a communication system which was to revolutionize life in the second half of the twentieth century.

The scientific principle on which television works is based around the workings of the human eye.

Every image we see is retained momentarily after it hits the retina. If sections of a picture are shown fast enough on a screen, the brain is able to interpret a fully assembled image. In the same way as cinema projection or animated film works, continuously changing the picture at a speed of up to 30 images per second creates the effect of movement.

For his groundbreaking demonstration, Baird built an electric camera that was able to convert the moving image of the inventor holding a pair of ventriloquist's dummies into electrical signals.

These were transmitted in the same way as a radio signal and picked up and displayed independently by mechanically scanning a narrow beam of electrons in a series of lines on to the back of the cathode-ray picture tube. Baird's prototype scanned 240 horizontal lines, which produced a relatively crude, but nonetheless recognizable image.

Baird's mechanical system was updated by subsequent work by Isaac Shoenberg, who pioneered electrical scanning, and suggested that picture quality would be improved by increasing the number of lines that made up the picture: his 405-line standard became the norm in Europe until the 1970s when the use of ultra high frequency (UHF) transmissions allowed for improvements to 625 lines.

The impact of television on modern society has been incalculable, altering every aspect of human communication from the dissemination of news and popular culture to the dynamics of the family.

◀ **A "transmitting disc" sends the image of a human face which is then scanned by a beam of electrons. John Logie Baird called his invention "wireless vision".**

BRITAIN'S GENERAL STRIKE

Following the end of World War One, the great British coal mines of Wales and Yorkshire – crucial to Britain's economy – were in decline. The revival of the mining industry in Germany following the destruction of the war had brought about a collapse in the price of British coal. The situation was exacerbated when

Winston Churchill, the newly appointed Chancellor of the Exchequer, restored Britain to the gold standard, causing deflation and further unemployment. The government attempted to support the coal industry with a series of subsidies. However, when Prime Minister, Stanley Baldwin, announced that these were to be

withdrawn in early 1926, the mine owners took measures to prevent a further slump in profits: they reduced the wages of their employees. The Miners Federation, the trade union that represented mine workers, unsuccessfully lobbied the government to intervene. The outcome was inevitable: on May 1, 1926 over a

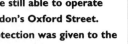

◀ In spite of the General Strike, buses were still able to operate along London's Oxford Street. Police protection was given to the volunteer strike-breakers who helped maintain public services.

million of Britain's coal miners went on strike.

The miners took their case to the Trades Union Congress (TUC), an association governing all of Britain's trades unions. The TUC had created a General Council in 1921 as a way of offering resistance to employers who sought to drive down wages in the uncertain economic climate. With a significant national membership of over five million, the Trade Union movement was now a powerful force in Britain. It was also one that made the British establishment uneasy: the birth of the TUC was hardly shrouded in bloody revolution, but many on the political right considered it part of a wider Red threat.

At the request of the Miners Federation, the TUC voted to back the miners' dispute and called for a general strike. It was, perhaps,

the first opportunity for Britain's Trade Union movement to flex its muscles.

So it was that on May 3, 1926, 3 million workers went on strike. In addition to the coal mines, Britain's railway and tram systems, docks, and iron and steel works were all immediately paralyzed.

Under the influence of Winston Churchill, the government took a firm line against the strike, resisting any form of negotiation while it was in progress. With all of the national newspapers frozen, Churchill – well-known as a writer outside of politics – edited an emergency newspaper, the *British Gazette*. His zeal for bombastic propaganda that would be so valuable to his country 20 years later helped to fuel public opinion against the strike. Calls for volunteers to keep Britain moving were met with enthusiasm. Creating a

wartime atmosphere, Churchill was able to draft servicemen and university students in to man crucial positions.

A week into the conflict the TUC, realizing that the strike was failing, attempted to negotiate a compromise. This was rejected by the miners. On May 12, 1926, with no hope of victory, the TUC instructed their members to return to work. Out on a limb, the miners continued their strike for a further seven months, but by winter the strike funds had run out. They were forced to return to the mines on lower wages and longer hours. The Union movement had been firmly defeated.

For all the drama surrounding the nine days of the general strike, it had no long-term impact on the economy. It was to be Britain's first and only general strike and one that set back the workers' movement in Britain. It would be another 40 years before the trades union movement would feel able to take on the might of the British government.

▼ A convoy of armoured cars assembles at Hyde Park Corner in London as troops are called in to maintain Britain's food supply.

'26

THE WORLD'S WOMEN MOURN VALENTINO

NEWS IN BRIEF

July
- Britain and Portugal define borders of South West Africa
- Anti-clerical legislation passed in Mexico
- Ruler of Portugal, General da Costa, overthrown by General de Fragoso
- Financial crisis in France causes resignation of government of Aristide Briand; Raymond Poincaré heads a new coalition government
- Alliance between USA and Panama assures protection of the Panama Canal
- Financial crisis in Belgium causes devaluation of Belgian franc
- Treaty between Albania, Yugoslavia and Greece defines Albanian border

August
- French franc devalued
- General Georgios Kondylis deposes Greek dictator Theodorus Pangalos
- Gertrude Ederle becomes the first woman to swim the Channel, setting a new record time for either sex of 14 hours and 31 minutes
- Riots break out among coalminers in Britain
- Germany's National Socialist Party holds a rally in Nuremburg
- Death of film actor Rudolph Valentino

◄ **Rudolph Valentino, the first great idol of the Silver Screen, continues to symbolize the romantic escapism of the movies. His death was marked by unprecedented hysteria.**

August 23, 1926 saw scenes of mass hysteria among the women of the world when it was announced that the greatest screen idol of them all, Rudolph Valentino, was dead.

Handsome, suave and sleek, Valentino was born in 1895 in Castellaneta, Italy, the son of a farmer. In 1913 he decided that fame and fortune were waiting for him in New York City. For the next four years, however, he worked as a gardener, dish-washer and later a gigolo before his talents as a dancer brought him work in vaudeville. A police investigation in a suspected blackmail offence caused him to flee New York for the West coast, where he settled in Hollywood. It was here he would make his mark as the greatest of all screen lovers.

After a number of small, undistinguished roles, he found overnight fame in 1921 playing the role of Julio in *The Four Horsemen of the Apocalypse*. Greater successes followed with other romantic dramas such as *The Sheik* and *Blood and Sand*.

Hollywood press agents were also keen to project Valentino's screen image into his real life image, and he enjoyed numerous well-publicized affairs, including a passionate tryst with Pola Negri, one of the greatest female stars of the silent era.

Valentino's sudden death at the age of 31 from a ruptured ulcer caused grieving on an unprecedented scale. At his funeral in New York City, Valentino was laid out in state where a crowd of thousands of sobbing women queued 11 blocks to see his body. It was reported that at least a dozen fans in America and Europe had taken their own lives, such was their distress.

Some have speculated that, like many other great romantic leads, he would have fallen foul of the birth of sound. However, even now the name Valentino remains synonymous with sweeping sex appeal.

▼ **Two distraught fans kneel at the steps of the New York hospital in which their idol, Rudolph Valentino, died.**

NO ESCAPE FROM DEATH

Throughout an incredible career he escaped from locks and chains, sealed chests and prison cells, but on October 31, 1926, death finally caught up with Harry Houdini, the world's greatest escapologist.

The son of a rabbi, Houdini was born Erik Weisz in 1874. As a teenager he migrated from his native Budapest, finally settling in New York City. His early life was spent performing as a trapeze artist in circuses and vaudeville.

It was during the early years of the twentieth century that Houdini gained his reputation for feats of remarkable daring. One of his most amazing stunts, which was widely exhibited on quaysides throughout America, saw Houdini chained, locked in a box bound with rope which

► **The greatest escapologist of the twentieth century, Harry Houdini was confined neither by ropes, chains nor straitjackets.**

was then dropped from a boat into the water. He always emerged unscathed.

Unlike other conjurers of the era, Houdini never sought to claim that his act was anything other that the skilful creation of illusion. In his later years he strove to unmask spiritualists and mediums, claiming their

supernatural powers could easily be emulated by natural means.

His demise was somehow banal for a man whose reputation was forged on the ability to cheat death. While addressing a group of students in Montreal he explained how it was possible for his stomach to withstand a heavy punch. Before he had the

chance to flex his abdominal muscles – the key to the trick – one of the audience punched him twice in quick succession. The following day Houdini collapsed in pain. Surgeons removed his appendix, but by that time peritonitis had set in, poisoning his system beyond treatment.

WHITE SUPREMACY TAKES HOLD IN SOUTH AFRICA

The idea of racial segregation can be said to have evolved naturally with the birth of the Union of South Africa in 1910. In an attempt to consolidate and protect the advantages already established by Afrikaaners and other white settlers, the rule of the South African Party between 1910 and 1924 saw the steady passing of statutes aimed at drawing racial distinctions within both industry and territory. This status quo was encapsulated in the Afrikaaner word "apartheid" – which literally translates as "apartness" – though the term was not officially used until 1948.

The mining industry dominated South Africa's economy by the 1920s. During this time, divisions of labour were already well established along racial lines: Afrikaaner and white settlers performed the skilled tasks; blacks, coloureds (mixed race) and Indians – all carefully defined by law – provided the unskilled labour. This division was first legally enshrined in the 1911 Mines and Works Act which placed a "colour bar" legally prohibiting certain mining jobs from being carried out by non-whites.

Organized Afrikaaner nationalism grew out of a number of

disputes with the mine owners and the government. The protests started when the Chamber of Mines announced in 1919 that amid falling gold prices and increasing costs it intended to replace semi-skilled Afrikaaners with black labourers – who were paid an average of ten times less than their white counterparts. In 1922 industrial unrest turned into a violent general strike. On March 12, hostilities reached a peak with an armed uprising that saw white nationalists seize control of the Rand. The rebellion was suppressed when Prime Minister Jan Smuts sent in artillery and aircraft to restore order. Over 200 died in what became known as the Rand Revolt.

As the white nationalists assumed an increasing influence, the Mines and Works Acts was amended in 1926, barring non-whites from all skilled and most semi-skilled occupations.

Laws such as these effectively consolidated the white hold over South Africa's economic and political landscape: it was a hold that would last until the 1990s.

◄ **South African Prime Minister Jan Smuts who suppressed the Rand Revolt and reinforced white supremacy in the country.**

LINDBERGH FLIES INTO HISTORY WITH SOLO FLIGHT

By the time American Charles Augustus Lindbergh landed his plane, *Spirit of St Louis*, at Le Bourget Airport on the outskirts of Paris, on May 21, 1927, he was an international celebrity. Aviation history was rewritten as he became the first man to have flown solo, non-stop across the Atlantic Ocean. In doing so, he also claimed a much-vaunted $25,000 prize.

The son of a midwest congressman, Lindbergh abandoned college to enroll at a flying school. After a brief period as a stunt pilot, he flew the St Louis-to-Chicago mail route in 1926. It was the announcement of the highly publicized prize that prompted him to seek the backing of a group of businessmen to provide him with a modified aircraft to make the 5790-km (3,600-mile) journey.

The 25-year-old aviator took a single-engine Ryan NYP monoplane and increased the engine size and fuel capacity. The extended cowling, required to cover the larger engine, obscured the cockpit window, meaning that a periscope was needed in order to see directly ahead.

His perilous flight was completed in 33½ hours, and the mild-mannered Lindbergh was somewhat perplexed by the crowd of almost 100,000 that awaited his arrival. *Spirit of St Louis* was returned to the US by sea, but Lindbergh, thereafter one of the most famous men in America, flew it extensively in exhibitions. It now holds pride of place in the Smithsonian Institute.

▼ **Charles Lindbergh and *Spirit of St Louis*. His pioneering feat captured the imagination of the American public.**

MURDERERS OR MARTYRS ?

▲ **Whether they were punished for a crime or for their political beliefs, most now agree that the the hapless anarchists Nicola Sacco and Bartolomeo Vanzetti failed to receive a fair trial.**

On August 23, 1927, one of America's longest-running criminal cases came to an end when Italian-born anarchists Nicola Sacco and Bartolomeo Vanzetti were executed. Their case became an international *cause célèbre*, provoking widespread condemnation.

The story began on April 15, 1920 when the paymaster and guard at a shoe factory in Braintree, Massachusetts were murdered during an attempt to steal the payroll.

Known anarchists Sacco and Vanzetti were tried the following month, and a jury found little difficulty in convicting them.

Many believed that the men's case had been poorly handled and Socialists and other radicals campaigned for their release, claiming that they had been convicted on the basis of their political beliefs. To others it was further evidence of the continuing prejudice against immigrants and other minorities. Even the admission in 1925 by a convicted criminal that he had taken part in the robbery failed to bring about a retrial. When the death sentence was finally announced on April 9, 1927 demonstrations spread outside of the state – and even the nation. US embassies were lobbied in Europe and riots took place in Philadelphia and New York.

Although they maintained their innocence until the end, Sacco and Vanzetti were sent to the electric chair four months later.

Fifty years after the controversial death sentence was carried out, the state of Massachusetts officially proclaimed it had not given them a fair trial.

THE BIRTH OF TALKING PICTURES

A new era of entertainment was ushered in on October 6, 1927, as Warner Brothers premiered *The Jazz Singer*, the world's first talking movie.

For almost a decade, engineers and inventors had attempted to develop a system capable of bringing the dimension of sound to the silent screen. While the potential for recorded sound was already well established, the difficulty lay in synchronizing sound with mouth movements.

Ironically, interest from Hollywood came in 1923 as Warner Brothers experienced a slump in the popularity of their films. Unlike other sceptical studio heads, Sam Warner became convinced that audiences would flock to talking pictures and hence patented a process known as Vitaphone. The system was crude. The sound, produced by 16-inch (40 cm) phonograph discs running at 33⅓ revolutions per minute, was poor even by domestic standards. The synchronization was also far from perfect.

Warners gave the public a brief glimpse of the Vitaphone experience in 1926 with the film *Don Juan*, which featured synchronized music and sound effects. However, it was *The Jazz Singer*, starring popular crooner Al Jolson, on which the first synchronized words were heard.

Although it only featured sporadic dialogue, *The Jazz Singer* created such a sensation that the silent era — and many of its greatest stars – became unfashionable overnight. Going to the movies would never be the same again.

Al Jolson, formerly a popular Vaudeville crooner, sings to his "Mammy" in the *The Jazz Singer*, the first-ever talking picture. ▼

THE RISE AND FALL OF THE "BLACK MOSES"

November 1927 saw the deportation from the United States of Marcus Garvey, one of the pioneers of black nationalism.

Born in Jamaica in 1887, the self-educated Garvey formed the

▲ **Marcus Garvey, the father of the black nationalist movement. A once-influential figure, he died in obscurity.**

Universal Negro Improvement Association (UNIA) in 1914, including in its aims the establishment of an independent black nation in Africa. Moving to the US in 1916, Garvey set up UNIA branches in Harlem and other black ghettos.

Using his own newspaper, *Negro World*, as a mouthpiece, the charismatic Garvey established a large following preaching a controversial message that blacks would never achieve equality unless they achieved economic freedom from white oppression. Although a notoriously poor businessman, Garvey nonetheless established the Negro Factories Corporation, an associated chain of retail outlets. In all cases he sought to produce goods using black labour for sale to black consumers.

Deeply unpopular with the US establishment – both black and white – Garvey and other members of UNIA were imprisoned in 1925 on mail fraud charges relating to the development of a black shipping company. After an appeal, on November 23, 1927, he received a pardon from President Coolidge. However, as a condition, Garvey was ignominiously deported to his native Jamaica, branded an "undesirable alien". Although it effectively ended his reign of influence – he died a relatively obscure figure in 1940 – Garvey became a symbolic figurehead to the black nationalist movements that emerged during the 1960s.

'28

- Islam no longer official religion of Turkey
- *Graf Zeppelin* makes first commercial transatlantic flight
- Thousands killed as earthquakes strike Bulgaria, Greece and Turkey and a volcano erupts in the Dutch East Indies
- First scheduled television broadcasts begin in USA
- First state pensions handed out in the United Kingdom
- Films released this year include *Two Tars*, with Laurel and Hardy, G W Pabst's *Pandora's Box* and Carl Theodor Dreyer's *The Passion of Joan of Arc*
- Walt Disney's Mickey Mouse makes his first appearance
- *The Threepenny Opera* by Berthold Brecht and Kurt Weill has first performance
- *The Oxford English Dictionary* is published after 70 years' work
- Books published this year include *Lady Chatterley's Lover* by D H Lawrence, *Decline and Fall* by Evelyn Waugh and *Point Counter Point* by Aldous Huxley

January
- Stalin executes or exiles all his political opponents in the USSR
- Fourteen die in London as the River Thames burst its banks
- Death of writer Thomas Hardy

February
- Jordan achieves autonomy under British mandate

March
- Dam burst kills at least 450 in California, US
- Wafd party leader Nahas Pasha becomes Prime Minister of Egypt

THE PACT TO END ALL WARS

Following the Allied victory in World War One, great figures on the world's stage turned their thoughts to how such a catastrophic conflict might be avoided in future. Most placed their faith in the League of Nations – a council that would mediate over disputes and act jointly against military aggression. The League, however, suffered a major flaw right from the beginning in that not all the principal nations of the world – most notably America – had signed up.

America's refusal to participate was the subject of bitter dispute in Congress, made worse by the fact that President Wilson had largely conceived the idea. His opponents objected to the clause which obligated military involvement in the defence of any other member under attack. Many Americans felt that too many of their troops had already given their lives in a war in which they had had no directly interest.

It was the French Foreign Minister, Aristide Briand, who suggested that if America would not join the League of Nations then at the very least their two countries could make a pact that renounced the act of war. It was US Secretary of State Frank B Kellogg who suggested that other nations might also wish to sign up to the agreement. Thus on August 27, 1928, the Kellogg-Briand Pact, also known as the Pact of Paris, was signed by representatives of 15 countries, including Great Britain and Germany. Over the coming months every other major country in the world – 60 in all – added their signatures.

In spite of its unquestionably noble aims, Briand's pact was subject to so many qualifications and loose interpretations as to be of little use other than as a general declaration that peace was preferable to war in dealing with international disputes – a view that few would disputed.

The Kellogg–Briand Pact was almost entirely ineffective; some saw it as a way for America to appease her European allies without having to make any commitment that could be called upon.

A creative politician, Aristide Briand was also notable for being among the first publicly to propose the idea of a federal Europe, although his suggestion, made at the League of Nations in 1930, was treated less than seriously at the time.

▼ **Aristide Briand (left) and Frank B Kellogg (right), declared that peace was preferable to war. Sixty other nations agreed.**

ACCIDENTAL DISCOVERY LEADS TO PENICILLIN

In September 1928, an accidental occurrence in a London medical laboratory led to one of the most important discoveries of the twentieth century – the antibiotic drug penicillin.

While working at St Mary's Medical School in London, bacteriologist Alexander Fleming noticed that during a series of experiments with the bacteria *Staphylococcus aureous* an area on the dish had accidentally become contaminated with a green mould – spores of *Penicillium notatum*. He observed that the bacteria was unable to grow on these contaminated areas which led him to believe that something within the mould – which he called penicillin – was in fact killing the bacteria. Carrying out further tests led Fleming to the amazing discovery that penicillin prevented the growth of many of the common bacteria active in human infection.

Fleming's frustrating problem was that he lacked the chemical expertise needed to isolate the active ingredient. Thus, he was aware that he had made a discovery of potentially staggering importance, but at that time was unable to develop a practical application.

It was left to others to take up his work, notably the biochemist Ernst Chain and the pathologist Howard Florey. Researchers at Oxford University, they managed to isolate and purify penicillin in 1940. Following this breakthrough they went on to carry out the first human clinical trials. The results showed that penicillin was the most potent non-toxic antibiotic yet discovered.

In 1945, the importance of Fleming's, Chain's and Florey's work was acknowledged when they were awarded the Nobel Prize for Medicine. Although some human bacteria have now developed an immunity to it, the various forms of penicillin continue to play an important role in modern medicine.

▼ **Bacteriologist Sir Alexander Fleming's discovery of penicillin turned out to be one of the most significant medical developments of the century.**

FIVE-YEAR PLAN FOR THE USSR

▲ **"To secure greatness, build socialism" – a dramatic billboard created by "constructivist" artists proclaims the progress of Stalin's first Five-Year Plan.**

On October 1, 1928, Joseph Stalin announced the beginning of the Soviet Union's first Five-Year Plan, an ambitious economic strategy aimed at widespread industrialization and the collectivization of agriculture.

During the course of the Plan, a number of significant industrial developments took place, such as the hydro-electric dam on the River Dnieper. The creation of major new industrial towns, often specializing in a single industry, saw some nine million workers move from the country to take up jobs in the new factories. The system was based around output targets set by a centralized committee. Heavy industry had to be developed to meet these quotas.

In spite of the widely shown propaganda films, however, Soviet workers were not uniformly behind the Five-Year Plan – not surprising, given the fact that the value of wages in real terms had fallen around 80 per cent since the time of Lenin's death in 1924. Stalin responded with coercion, introducing harsh penalties for dissenting voices. Workers could be imprisoned for minor workplace infringements; the death penalty became mandatory for theft from the workplace. Furthermore, the free movement of labour was prohibited, effectively meaning that without the permission of a Party official a worker was not allowed to leave his job.

The end of the first Five-Year period was hailed by Stalin as a great success and played a major role in Soviet internal propaganda – indeed, it was officially claimed that targets, including the tripling of industrial output, had been achieved within four years. Whilst the Plan contributed significantly to the creation of a modern industrial state, it was not until the dissolution of the Soviet Union almost 60 years later that the true figures were shown to have been a modest 5 per cent per annum.

▼ **The official portrait: Joseph Stalin proved himself skilfully adept at manipulating the Soviet state propaganda tools to promote his own image.**

'29

MOBSTERS MASSACRED ON ST VALENTINE'S DAY

Although it was supposed to be the day devoted to the lovers of the world, members of Al "Scarface" Capone's gang had other ideas on February 14, 1929 – St Valentine's Day.

Since prohibition had become law in 1920, a new breed of gangster had emerged in major cities throughout America. "Bootlegging", the illegal sale and production of liquor, was big business and rivalry for territorial control was intense.

The murder took place when members of the Capone gang, disguised as Chicago policemen, entered the garage of an illegal beer warehouse at 2122 North Clark Street. There they found seven members of the George "Bugs" Moran gang. Moran had run a dwindling bootlegging empire, having once been right-hand man to Dion O'Bannion, a bitter rival and victim of Capone. The Capone gang's aim was simple: put Moran out of business. They offered no negotiation or compromise, but lined their captives up against the wall and mowed them down with machine gun fire.

Gangland killings throughout this era were commonplace, but the sheer brutality of Capone's raid became headline news and has since come to symbolize the Jazz Age every bit as much as the novels of F Scott Fitzgerald. Although the police immediately knew the perpetrators of the murder, they never had enough evidence to secure a conviction.

▼ **The bloody remains of the slain gangsters. Police had insufficient evidence to convict their chief suspect, Al Capone.**

HOORAY FOR HOLLYWOOD: THE FIRST OSCARS

By the end of the 1920s Hollywood found itself at a crossroads. The birth of the talkies had made cinema more popular than ever, but a widespread public perception of moral degeneracy had left it with a tarnished image. The government took its own steps with the creation of the Hays Office, a censorship body that gave film-makers a checklist of moral acceptability. But the industry also felt a need to dignify itself. It was the legendary Louis B Mayer, head of Metro–Goldwyn Mayer, who came up with the idea of an annual award ceremony.

Named after the newly formed Academy of Motion Picture Arts and Sciences, the awards aimed at publicly rewarding excellence among the academy's five branches: actors, writers, technicians, directors and producers.

The first Academy Awards ceremony, for films made in 1927–28, took place in May 1929 in the modest (if plush) surroundings of the Hollywood Roosevelt Hotel. Among the first winners were *Wings*, a World War One flying drama and perhaps the last great film from the silent era, screenwriter Ben Hecht and producer Jack Warner. Winners were awarded "The Statuette", a 34-cm (13½ in) gold-plated figure of a man plunging a sword into a reel of film.

The awards drew their cynics, screenwriter Frances Marion observing: "The statuette is a perfect symbol of the picture business: a powerful athletic body clutching a gleaming sword with half of his head – the part that holds his brains – sliced off."

The awards have been held annually ever since, and are now

► Janet Gaynor receives her award from Douglas Fairbanks. She was widely praised for her roles in the films *7th Heaven*, *Sunrise* and *Street Angel*.

broadcast live all over the world. However, it wasn't until 1931 that a chance remark by Academy librarian Margaret Herrick – "He looks just like my Uncle Oscar" – that saw the birth of the unofficial name by which The Statuette would thereafter be known.

TENSION INCREASES IN PALESTINE

Ever a cauldron of unrest, tensions between the Arab and Jewish communities of Palestine came to a head on August 24, 1929 as the first major modern-day outbreak of violence erupted when an Arab revolt claimed the lives of 47 Jews. British troops were called upon to restore order, but further outbursts followed in Hebron. The conflict was sparked off by a dispute surrounding Jewish access to the Western Wall (better known as the "Wailing Wall"). The site remains sacred to Jews as the only remnant of the temple of Herod, and to Muslims as the site of the Dome of the Rock – the point from which the prophet Mohammed was believed to have ascended to heaven.

The situation in Palestine had become increasingly fractious throughout the 1920s following the endorsement of the 1917 Balfour Declaration, in which the British government pledged its support for the establishment of a national home for the Jewish people, by the League of Nations in 1922. When the mandate came into force Zionist rule was given to an area of Palestine on the east bank of the River Jordan. A Zionist government and political system were created and large numbers of Jews from around the world moved to the region, acquiring land and establishing new communities.

Although the terms of the mandate sought to protect the interests of non-Jews in the region, Arab leaders were not in favour of the new state. They were already strongly opposed to British rule and although it was accepted that the region was historically significant to the Jewish people, they feared a further influx of population and gradual loss of territory. Furthermore,

through its links with the World Zionist Organization Agency – the body whose pressure had brought the new state into being – the British government seemed to favour the Jews.

The Arab riots of August 1929 claimed the lives of 133 Jews. Over 100 Arabs were also killed, most of them by British troops brought in to restore law and order. In the Royal Commission Inquiry that followed, Sir Walter Shaw placed the blame firmly on Arab leaders, although he noted their territorial fears and the strong likelihood of future conflict. He couldn't possibly have imagined quite how prophetic his words would become.

▼ Argument over access to Jerusalem's sacred "Wailing Wall" sparked off a period of violent conflict between Arabs and Jews.

'29   THE WALL STREET CRASH

The 1920s' Jazz Age, so often depicted as an era of decadent living that saw the standard of living for most Americans and some Europeans rising to unprecedented levels, came to a grinding halt in October 1929. The New York Stock Exchange on Wall Street underwent a total collapse. Its repercussions were felt around the world and ushered in the depression that cast a shadow over the Western world for much of the 1930s.

From the mid-1920s, the US economy had experienced unfettered growth which reached a peak in the early part of September 1929. The first rumblings of trouble were felt earlier in the year when levels of unemployed began to rise. Wall Street, however, remained largely resiliant until a number of major fund managers began to liquidate large numbers of securities. This brought about a sudden downward trend in stock market prices. The month that followed illustrated the relative frailty of the stock market system as rumours began to breed in an atmosphere of increasing financial uncertainty. Speculators soon started to instruct their brokers to sell off their stocks, causing a further downturn in prices. This crisis of confidence quickly escalated into the sheer panic that took place on October 24, 1929 – the day that would become known as "Black Thursday".

Trading during the morning began more briskly than normal, but by midday the atmosphere

▲ **Panic on Wall Street. Thousands of investors assemble outside the New York Stock Exchange as a market collapse wipes out thousands of personal fortunes.**

had reached fever pitch. The famed ticker-tape machines could not keep up with demand. Anyone who owned shares seemed to be selling at any cost. Many of the smaller investors attempting to cut their losses had personal fortunes wiped out. It was the most disastrous morning in the history of any stock exchange anywhere in the world. Share prices stabilized and rose slightly in the afternoon when the influential bankers J P Morgan confirmed their ultimate confidence in the Wall Street system. Shortly afterwards a number of other banks and major investors began buying up large blocks of stock, certain

▶ **Easy come, easy go. Ready cash was the name of the game for this young investor who was just $100 away from bankruptcy.**

that they had reached their lowest possible level. By the time the final bell sounded at three

o'clock, a record 12,894,650 shares had been traded.

Hopes were high that "Black

$100. WILL BUY THIS CAR. MUST HAVE CASH. LOST ALL ON THE STOCK MARKET

▼In a bid to stem the rapidly rising unemployment and stimulate the economy, President Hoover announced an aid package worth $175 million.

Thursday" was a one-off consequence of an inflated market whose prices no longer reflected their real worth. Few were prepared for what was still to come. After an inauspicious start on the following Monday, the market continued to fall sharply, reaching a nadir the following day. October 29, 1929 – "Black Tuesday", as it immediately became known – saw a total of over 16 million shares traded. Prices were now so low that the New York Stock Exchange had to all intents and purposes collapsed completely. Many of America's wealthiest men were humbled overnight. Some, like James Riordan, President of the County Trust

Company, chose suicide rather than facing up to what might follow.

With its strong tradition of free trading, the US government avoided direct involvement in the money markets; over the month that followed, however, President Hoover found himself under growing pressure to take action to bolster confidence in the US economy. Congress was asked for an additional $175 million to finance a programme of municipal building in an attempt to resuscitate the construction industry which, like most others, had laid off employees by the thousand. In an attempt to prevent a further devastating crash, Hoover created a new council made up from 400 of America's top leading businessmen, bankers and captains of industry.

During the following decade increasingly desperate steps were taken to stimulate the economy, but nothing could fend off the Great Depression that followed. The consequences of the Wall Street Crash were felt around the world. The rampant speculation that had contributed to Black Thursday set the tone for the decade that followed. Share prices continued to fall for the next three years.

▲ Police were called in to deal with wild scenes of disorder outside the New York Sub-Treasury Building on Wall Street.

By December 1932, their average value was 79 per cent lower than the 1929 peak.

The specific events that sparked off the Wall Street Crash are almost impossible to pinpoint, but many theories have been put forward. Despite its importance to the American economy, the complex mechanism of the stock market – like that of the banking system – relies completely on the confidence of the investor. It also relies on a stable economic environment so that when an investor chooses to sell a company's stock it will usually be to buy others. As events proved, when a majority of investors lose confidence in the principles of the stock market, the system simply cannot sustain itself.

A factor that certainly contributed to the initial bursting of the Wall Street bubble was the

role of overseas investors. With their own economies in tatters after the war, many foreigners seized the opportunity to take a slice of the "Coolidge Boom". This huge external influx of money helped to drive Wall Street prices to an artificially high level that could never be realistically maintained – indeed, some stocks were reported to be valued at 150 times the price of the annual dividends they could yield . During the late 1920s, as Europe slowly recovered from the war years, confidence returned to their own markets and thus foreign investors began to switch from the US to companies trading on their own stock markets. By the time of Black Thursday, many of the major European investors had already sold off a majority of their holdings.

▼ Newly installed tickertape machines provide investors with up-to-the-minute details of the rise and fall of stocks and shares.

1930–39

The 1930s could be summarized as a decade of fear and paranoia. Still in the throes of the fall-out from the Stock Market collapse of October 1929, the decade began with unemployment in the West ever surpassing itself: from a figure of some 4 percent of the total work force in 1929, within three years over a fifth of the West's eligible workers could not find a living. The Great Depression, as it became known, saw widespread civil unrest throughout Europe and America as successive governments seemed either unwilling or unable to provide an answer. In America, the gloom only began lifting in 1933 with the arrival of Franklin Delano Roosevelt, who was elected as President on a financial reform ticket. Roosevelt instilled a new confidence in the banking system with his National Industrial Recovery Act (NRA). A program of massive public spending created millions of new jobs and provided aid to the most needy. By the middle of the decade, the financial gloom has slowly begun to lift. However, by this time the eyes of the world once again looked to Europe where war once again seemed to be looming.

1936 saw Spain in the midst of a bloody civil war in which a struggling Republican government was being challenged by Fascist Nationalist rebels centred around the Spanish army. As divisive a war as could be imagined, the hostility cut to the very heart of Spanish life: workers against employers; Catholics against secularists; landowners against peasants. It was also a battle of political ideologies that divided many families leaving bitter rifts and feuds that lasted for decades after the two-year conflict had ended with Nationalist dictator General Franco taking power.

However, it was in Germany that the events that would soon reshape the world were fast unfolding. After the downfall of Kaiser Wilhelm II that followed defeat in 1918, Germany had spent much of the 1920s in turmoil. Punitive demands for war reparations had destroyed the German economy and created unemployment and starvation. In 1930, Adolf Hitler, leader of the extreme right-wing National Socialists (Nazis), stepped forward to offer his own unique solutions to Germany's suffering. Laying the blame firmly on the Jews and the Communists, the charismatic Hitler quickly developed a faithful following by guaranteeing that he would restore The Fatherland to its former glory. Brought to power in 1933, the Nazis launched a reign of terror on Germany's minorities. The Jews came in for particular attack. Recognizing that they formed the backbone of Germany's business community, Hitler depicted them as a race apart, working for their own good, not in the interests of Germany. His scapegoating worked – as the decade progressed the Jews were increasingly disenfranchised and frequently herded in to ghettos.

In 1937, Hitler showed for the first time that he was happy to involve himself in the affairs of other states when he allowed a squadron of Junker and Heinkel bombers to intervene in the Spanish Civil War on the side of General Franco. This was the first time that aircraft specially designed to drop large numbers of missiles on a ground target had been deployed in combat. The raid was a devastating success, the Basque town of Guernica – a Republican stronghold – destroyed with thousands dead. These weapons of mass destruction, provided a chilling glimpse of how wars in the future might be fought.

During Hitler's first wave of repression the world was largely content to look away. This changed in 1938 when Hitler sent his armies outside of Germany's national border. Austria, Hitler's homeland, willingly joined what was now known as the "Third Reich". However, his "march into the great German future" that began as his forces stormed across the Sudeten border with Czechoslovakia was viewed as a statement of intent by many European leaders. Sure enough, on September 1, 1939 over a million German troops made a dawn invasion of Poland, an ally of Britain. Two days later, Prime Minister Neville Chamberlain told the people of Britain that war had been declared. Only 21 years after the most horrific conflict in history, Europe once again plunged into a full-scale war.

30

STALIN PURGES KULAKS

In July 1930, Joseph Stalin, leader of the Soviet Union, resumed his policy of the forcible collectivization of farms. Stalin, who had a deep distrust of the largely independent farming peasantry, had earlier attempted to persuade them to give up their land and join huge state-controlled collective farms. When this policy appeared to be failing in the face of much resistance from the independent farmers, Stalin attempted to create divisions among their ranks by identifying the more prosperous peasants, whom he called Kulaks, as enemies of the people. The term Kulak proved to be very flexible and was used, in practice, to identify anyone in the countryside who opposed Stalin's agricultural policies.

For Stalin and many others at the forefront of Soviet politics, the notion of an independent "petty-capitalist class" of farmers was unacceptable. As far as he was concerned, the independent peasant farming class was an obstacle to the construction of a true Communist state and so in December 1929 Stalin ordered their elimination.

At this time elimination did not yet mean execution, but rather the confiscation by force of Kulak land followed by imprisonment, or deportation of entire families to the frozen tundra of Siberia. Some Kulaks were allowed to remain, but only after they had joined the collective farms.

By the spring of 1930, over half of the peasant workers in the Soviet Union were working on collective farms, but the impact of this policy on productivity was disastrous, not least because of the enormously de-motivating resentment felt by those who had been coerced into carrying out Stalin's wishes. Facing predictions that the collective farms would produce only a fraction of the food previously yielded by the peasantry, Stalin was forced to back down. He announced that those peasants who wished to do so could leave the collectives. Against his expectations, the peasants left in huge numbers, forcing him to resume collectivization by means of extreme force, a policy which ultimately resulted in the deaths of over six million Russian peasants.

▼ Stalin declared war on the "Kulaks", the land-owning peasant class he believed were a threat to Communism. Soon they would be coerced into collective farms.

NINTH PLANET DISCOVERED

The search for the "missing" ninth planet came to an end on February 18, 1930, when the American astronomer Clyde Tombaugh spotted a distant object moving against the fixed background of the stars.

Astronomers had originally begun their search for the planet after irregularities in the orbits of Uranus and Neptune seemed to indicate the presence of an unseen mysterious object even further out into space.

Much of the early work on detecting the ninth planet, which was named Pluto after the Greek and Roman god of the underworld, took place at the Lowell Observatory in Flagstaff, Arizona, US. This work was carried out under the direction of Percival Lowell, founder of the observatory. Lowell had made two unsuccessful attempts to discover the planet before he died in 1916.

The successful final search began in 1929, when a purpose-built astronomical telescope, fitted with a 33-cm (13-in) objective lens, was acquired by the observatory. Clyde Tombaugh, an amateur astronomy enthusiast, was hired to carry out the painstaking survey of the night sky in search of the missing planet. It was discovered after comparing and contrasting photographs of the sky taken on consecutive nights.

Pluto, which orbits the Sun once every 248 years, is the third planet – along with Uranus and Neptune – to be discovered in our Solar System since the invention of the telescope. Aside obviously from the Earth, the remaining planets in the Solar System – Mercury, Venus, Mars and Jupiter – were known to the ancients, who observed them moving across the night sky and gave them the name planet, which means "wandering star".

▲ Clyde Tombagh, the amateur astronomer who discovered Pluto. Modern research has led some scientists to suggest that Pluto is technically not a planet but an asteroid.

CREATOR OF SHERLOCK HOLMES DIES

▼ Sir Arthur Conan Doyle, the creator of the greatest sleuth of them all, Sherlock Holmes. He remains one of Britain's most popular authors.

Sir Arthur Conan Doyle, the Scottish-born writer best known for his colourful tales of the exploits of fictional detective Sherlock Holmes, died in Crowborough, Sussex, England on July 7, 1930, at the age of 71. Born in Edinburgh, Scotland on May 22 1859, Conan Doyle graduated from the University of Edinburgh, where he studied medicine, before practising as a doctor until 1891. It was while studying at the University of Edinburgh that he chanced upon a lecturer, renowned for his deductive reasoning, who was to provide the inspiration for the character of Sherlock Holmes.

The world's most famous detective first appeared in print in 1887 in a story called *A Study In Scarlet*. Conan Doyle contributed regular short stories about the exploits of Sherlock Holmes to *Strand Magazine* from 1891 onwards. These stories also featured the fictional detective's good friend Dr Watson, the kindly if occasionally slightly dim companion who followed Holmes on his many adventures. Dr Watson's character was in stark contrast to that of Holmes' sworn enemy, the evil criminal master-mind Professor Moriarty.

Although the stories proved to be enormously popular with readers, Conan Doyle soon tired of his creation and killed him off in 1893. Such was the outcry from the public, however, that Conan Doyle was forced to bring Sherlock Holmes back from the dead by means of an unlikely plot twist.

Sherlock Holmes continues to be a popular character and versions of Sir Arthur Conan Doyle's work have been presented as radio plays, animations and films. New stories featuring Holmes, Watson and Moriarty have been written, principally for the screen, since Conan Doyle's death. The character of Holmes has also assumed cult status with the formation of the Sherlock Holmes Society in London, the Baker Street Regulars in New York (Holmes lived in Baker Street in London) and similar groups of enthusiasts in other countries around the world.

▲ "Holmes was working hard over a chemical investigation". An 1893 colour plate from Sir Arthur Conan Doyle's adventure, *The Naval Treaty*.

'30

SYDNEY HARBOUR BRIDGE NEARS COMPLETION

Sydney Harbour Bridge, considered by many to be one of the great wonders of the modern world, took a large step nearer completion in 1930 when the two halves of the bridge met in the middle. Work on this magnificent bridge began in 1924, but because Sydney Harbour has such very deep waters it was not possible to construct the bridge using the conventional temporary supports. Instead, the steel arch bridge, one of the longest of its type in the world, was constructed by cantilevering out from each bank with the aim of meeting in the middle. Despite having a span of some 500 metres (1,650 ft), the two sides were joined in the middle on August 18.

Sydney Harbour Bridge was constructed using high-strength silicon steel and is the heaviest bridge in the world to be built using this material. The bridge, a two-hinged arch, is supported at each end by pairs of enormous stone towers. Its deck, which sits 56 metres (172 ft) above the waters of the harbour, carries four railway tracks, two walkways and a road that is 17 metres

▲ One of the great feats of modern engineering, the Sydney Harbour Bridge was designed to accommodate both rail and road transport as well as walkers.

(57 ft) wide. Although the two halves of the bridge came together in the summer of 1930, work on the construction of the bridge as a whole was not completed until 1932, and the bridge still requires daily maintenance.

The bridge was just one of many designed by Sir Ralph Freeman, a civil engineer who was born in London, England, on November 27, 1880. A partner in a firm of consulting engineers called Freeman, Fox and Partners, Freeman also designed the Victoria Falls Bridge, which spans the Zambezi River on the border between Zimbabwe and Zambia and five other bridges throughout South Africa, as well as drawing up designs for the Auckland Harbour Bridge in New Zealand.

A NEW EMPEROR FOR ABYSSINIA

Ras Tafari, regent and heir apparent to the throne of Abyssinia, was crowned as emperor on November 2, 1930. On ascending the throne of his north African kingdom, he took the name Haile Selassie, which means "Might of the Trinity".

Born Tafari Makonnen on July 23, 1892, near Harer in Abyssinia, Haile Selassie was the great-grandson of Sahle Selassie. The boy's father was Ras Makonnen, chief adviser to Emperor Menilek II. Selassie was educated by French missionaries and, by virtue of his intellectual abilities, rose through the ranks to become governor of Harer province. While governor, he sought to reduce the power of the feudal nobility by creating a centralized civil service under the growing authority of the central government.

The death of Emperor Menilek II in 1913 resulted in the emperor's grandson, Lij Yasu, taking the throne. Yasu's reign proved to be short-lived, however, not least because of his strong leanings towards Islam, which made him deeply unpopular with the

NEWS IN BRIEF

August
- Catalan nationalists and Spanish republicans form an alliance calling for Catalan autonomy
- Military coup forces the resignation of the Peruvian President
- Mass protests force change of Polish government; Jozef Pilsudski becomes Prime Minister
- Unemployment in Britain rises above 2 million
- Soviet troops kill 200 strikers in Odessa
- Douglas McArthur appointed US Army Chief of Staff

September
- Nazi Party makes large gains in German elections; Hitler is denied a seat in the Reichstag because he is Austrian
- Economic depression causes Canada to pass emergency laws
- Censorship ends in Spain
- Rebels form a government in Peking under Yen Hsi-chan
- Playwright George Bernard Shaw turns down the offer of a peerage

predominantly Christian majority of the population. Realizing that his moment had come, Haile Selassie succeeded in deposing Lij Yasu in 1916. Menilek II's daughter, Zauditu, was declared Emperor of Abyssinia in 1917 and Selassie was given the title of Ras (Prince) Tafari.

Ever the progressive, Selassie succeeded in getting Abyssinia accepted into the League of Nations in 1923. In 1924, he embarked on a diplomatic mission to Europe, the first Abyssinian ruler ever to do so. He assumed the title of *negus*, meaning king, in 1928 but became Emperor with the death of Zauditu in 1930.

The invasion of Abyssinia by Italy in 1935 forced Selassie into exile. He did not assume power again until 1941 when, with British help, the Italians were driven from Abyssinia (renamed Ethiopia after 1941). Haile Selassie died of natural causes on August 26, 1975, although some claim he was strangled by the military in Ethiopia.

▼ **Ras Tafari, "The Lion of Judah", Emperor Haile Selassie of Ethiopia. His 45-year reign was only interrupted by six years of exile following the 1935 invasion by Mussolini's Italy.**

JAPANESE PRIME MINISTER ASSASSINATED

▲ **Japan's Hamaguchi Osachi, is rushed from the scene of his shooting at Tokyo's railway station. He died of his injuries more than nine months later.**

Hamaguchi Osachi, Prime Minister of Japan, was shot and fatally wounded at Tokyo Railway Station on November 14 by a member of a far-right political group. Hamaguchi Osachi, also known as Hamaguchi Yuko, first become Prime Minister of Japan while leader of Minseito, the moderate democratic party. He was re-elected in 1930 but his policies proved to be unpopular, especially with the rising radical right-wing groups in Japan.

Born in Kochi in the Tosa province of Japan on May 1, 1870, Osachi was adopted by the Hamaguchi family while still a very young child. He joined the Finance Ministry after graduating from the Tokyo Imperial University in 1895 and in 1914 he was elected to the Diet, the Japanese parliament. In 1924 he was made finance minister and then minister of home affairs by the then Prime Minister, Kato Takaaki.

Hamaguchi Osachi had the misfortune to be elected Prime Minister as the world was entering the Great Depression. At the time, the Japanese economy was suffering as a result of inflation. In an attempt to halt rising prices, Hamaguchi returned Japan to the gold standard but this, combined with the Great Depression, did enormous harm to the country's economy, triggering social unrest.

He succeeding in alienating himself from the country's powerful military leaders by attempting to impose civilian control upon them. This was a dangerous thing to do at a time when many people in Japan were beginning to harken back to the days of the great Samurai warriors and contrast those figures with the self-serving politicians they saw governing their country. Ultra-nationalist groups were not slow to exploit this feeling, presenting the Prime Minister as an enemy of Japan. Hamaguchi Osachi eventually died of his wounds on August 26, 1931.

31

EMPIRE STATE BUILDING SCRAPES THE SKY

◀ **One of the greatest landmarks of the twentieth century, New York City's Empire State Building.**

At the start of May, the Empire State Building in New York threw open its doors for the first time. The world's most famous "skyscraper", which can still be found in midtown Manhattan, on Fifth Avenue at 34th Street, was designed by the architectural firm of Shreve, Lamb and Harmon. It was officially opened on May 1 by the American president, Herbert Hoover. The building has a steel frame and its 102 floors rise together to a height of 380 metres (1,250 ft), making it the tallest skyscraper in the world, a record it held until 1954. In 1950, a 68-metre (222-ft) television antenna was fitted to the top of the building, raising the height of the combined structure to 450 metres (1,472 ft). This was reduced to 43 metres (1,454 ft) in 1985 when the antenna was replaced with one of a more modern design.

The Empire State Building became an unmissable landmark in New York, and has featured in a number of Hollywood films, from *King Kong* and the musical *On The Town* to *Sleepless in Seattle*. Although designed primarily as office space, the building has a promenade platform near the top which has proved very popular with tourists.

RECORD-BREAKING BALLOON ASCENT

The Swiss-born Belgian physicist Professor Auguste Piccard and his colleague Paul Kipfer took to the skies on May 27 aboard a balloon that had been designed by the professor. Rising to an altitude of 1,577 metres (51,762 ft), where the atmospheric pressure is just one tenth that at sea level, the two men broke all existing altitude records for flight in a balloon.

Born in Basle, Switzerland, on January 28, 1884, Piccard came from a family of academics (his father, Jules, and his brother, Jean, were professors of chemistry). Auguste Piccard became professor of applied physics at the University of Brussels in 1922, where he came up with a series of experiments for determining the nature of cosmic rays.

Unfortunately, the experiments had to be carried out at altitudes in excess of 15,240 metres (50,000 ft) in order to stand any chance of success. In order to do this, Piccard came up with a balloon of a revolutionary design which featured a pressurized cabin. This idea was unheard of at the time, but would have allowed Piccard and Kipfer to carry out their experiments in relative safety. Piccard managed to build the balloon in 1930 with the help of Belgian financiers and in 1931 made history with his record-breaking ascent.

Piccard returned to the skies again in 1932, this time reaching an altitude of 16,935 metres (55,564 ft). In later life he took to investigating the ocean depths with his son, Jacques, in a bathy-scape which was similar in design to his pressurized high-altitude cabin.

▼ **Professor Auguste Piccard prepares to make his record-breaking ascent. His achievement was driven by a desire to test his theories on the nature of cosmic rays.**

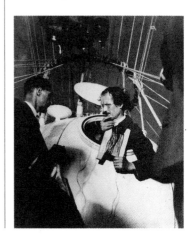

BBC BROADCASTS OVERSEAS

Television broadcasting history was made on May 8 when the BBC (British Broadcasting Corporation) broadcast overseas from London as part of a seven-year programme of experiments and investigations into the new technology. At this time the BBC had been investigating the possibility of making regular broadcasts using a system devised by the Scottish engineer and inventor John Logie Baird.

Baird had given the first successful demonstration of television in 1926, when he used his primarily mechanical approach to scan moving images, transmitting them electronically as a series of moving pictures on a small screen. The pictures were made up of only 30 lines, which were scanned around 10 times per second. Although the results were understandably very crude, they provided a practical demonstration that the technology would work. Unfortunately for Baird, the BBC ultimately opted for a superior system devised by the Marconi Company and began regular broadcasts from Alexandra Palace in London in 1936.

▲ **Alexandra Palace, the original home of the British Broadcasting Corporation. Television would play an increasingly important role in communications during the twentieth century.**

GERMAN BANKS RUN OUT OF MONEY

The German banking system had all but collapsed by July of 1931, although the cause of the collapse can be traced back as far as World War One. Under the terms of the Treaty Of Versailles, drawn up at the end of the war, Germany was obliged to make reparations to the Allies for the cost of the conflict. The Allies, in turn, intended to use this money to repay debts owing to American banks, which had provided them with financial assistance throughout much of the war. Most of the money that Germany used to make reparations came from new loans provided by the same American banks. This financial money-go-round began to fall apart after the crash of the American stock market in 1929.

Although Europe as a whole was not affected immediately, the flow of capital out of America began to slow down and by 1931 it had all but stopped. In order to pay their own debts, many Americans who had been investing abroad began to return their money to the USA, leaving many foreign economies high and dry. Britain and Austria were very badly hit by this action, but it was Germany, already vulnerable as a result of the reparations, that suffered most. In just six weeks, from the beginning of June until the middle of July, the German central bank was obliged to hand over two billion dollars-worth of gold and foreign currency. The resulting chaos led to great social unrest and was a key factor in the rise of Adolf Hitler.

▼ **Dr Curtius and Dr Bruning represent the German position at the "Seven Powers" conference. Without credit, Germany was unable to honour war reparations.**

'31

JAPAN ATTACKS CHINESE FORCES IN MANCHURIA

On the morning of September 18, 1931, Japanese forces attacked the barracks of the Chinese garrison in the city of Mukden, in the Chinese province of Manchuria. The Japanese troops, who were in the region to guard the South Manchurian railway, claimed that the railway line had been bombed. The Japanese killed between 70 and 80 Chinese troops before going on to take control of the entire city. Chinese troops were under orders from the governor of Manchuria not to return fire in the belief that the Japanese were seeking an excuse to seize control of the whole of the province. The Chinese believed that an ultra-nationalist group within the Japanese army intended to annex Manchuria before advancing into the rest of China.

The Japanese had been seeking ways of taking over Manchuria for a number of years. They had claimed the region after the Sino-Japanese War of 1894–95, but Russia, whose territories border the region, combined with France and Germany to force the Japanese to back down over this claim. This contributed to the outbreak of the Russo-Japanese War in 1904, after which Japan took control of southern Manchuria. The revolution in China during 1911 saw the Chinese assume a degree of control over the region, but in 1915 the Japanese forced China to accept a proposal, known as the 21 Demands. In return for Japanese military "protection", the Chinese granted them a 99-year lease on the region along with considerable commercial privileges.

Continued Chinese passivity after the attack on their garrison at Mukden resulted in the Japanese army taking control of the whole of Manchuria in less than five months. In 1932, the Japanese combined the three ancient provinces of Manchuria into a single satellite state, known as Manchukuo, and installed the retired former emperor of Manchuria as chief executive under their control.

◀ Japanese forces advance swiftly on the Chinese garrison at Mukden. Meeting with very little resistance from Chinese forces, Japan quickly achieved control of Manchuria.

NEWS IN BRIEF

June
- Second Five-Year Plan announced in USSR
- Commercial treaty signed between Poland and USSR
- Christian Socialist party forms new government under Karl Buresch in Austria
- Left-wing parties make major gains in Spanish general elections

July
- British May Committee report predicts large government budget deficit
- Anti-Chinese riots in Korea
- Nazi Party and German National Party form alliance in Germany
- Dispute between Norway and Denmark over territorial rights in Greenland
- German financial crisis precipitated as Danatbank goes bankrupt; all German banks close and do not open again for three weeks

August
- Yangtse River flood causes famine in China
- Resignation of British Prime Minister Ramsay Macdonald; he is expelled by the Labour Party
- Coalition government in Britain formed to balance budget deficit
- Russia and France sign a non-aggression pact
- Mahatma Gandhi arrives in Britain for discussions on India's future

DEATH OF THOMAS EDISON

Thomas Alva Edison, America's greatest inventor, died in West Orange, New Jersey, on October 18 at the age of 84. The man who was at one time referred to as the best-known American in the world went to his grave having established, either individually or jointly, a record-breaking 1,093 patents, as well as the first ever laboratory for industrial research.

Among his very many inventions, Edison is credited with having given the world the light bulb, the phonograph, the carbon-button transmitter – which is still used in many telephones and microphones to this day, the first real electrical light and power system – which was a forerunner of the national grid – the ticker-tape machine, a revolutionary type of electric railway and much of the technology that led to the development of motion pictures.

Born in Milan, Ohio, on February 11, 1847, Edison did badly at school as a result of poor hearing and even poorer

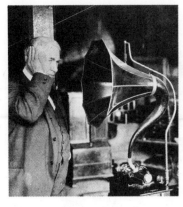

▲ An inspiration to successive generations of inventors, Edison famously viewed each failed experiment as simply another step along the path to achieving a successful result.

teaching. In 1863, having quit school four years earlier, Edison trained as a telegrapher and made a living of sorts for the next six years until the addition of a sound key to most telegraphic equipment rendered the partially deaf Edison unemployable in this field. By now, however, he was well on his way to becoming that rarest of creatures, a person who can combine the genius of invention with the more down-to-earth but just as essential skills of the entrepreneur.(Edison once famously said that genius was one per cent inspiration and 99 per cent perspiration.)

Edison married 16-year-old Mary Stilwell in 1871. She provided him with three children before her death from a brain tumour in August 1884. Two years later Edison married again, this time to Mina Miller, the 20-year-old daughter of a rich Ohio-based industrialist. In that same year, 1886, he opened a new laboratory in West Orange, New Jersey.

Although Edison continued to patent new inventions into his eighties, these were not as successful as his earlier devices. Edison will always be remembered as the man who lit up the world.

AL CAPONE BEHIND BARS

Following his arrest in June on charges of federal income tax evasion, Al "Scarface" Capone was found guilty and sentenced in October to 11 years imprisonment and ordered to pay fines and court costs of $80,000. After beginning his sentence in the Atlanta penitentiary, Capone was transferred to the newly built Alcatraz prison in August 1934 where he remained until November 1939. Suffering from advanced syphilis, Capone was released to a hospital in Baltimore, from where he eventually retired to his estate in Florida.

Capone, the fourth son of Italian immigrant parents, began his criminal career with the James Street Gang in Brooklyn, New York. He graduated to the brothel business in Chicago in 1919 before becoming involved in bootlegging as Prohibition began. By 1925, Capone was in effective control of all criminal activity in Chicago, having worked his way to the top by means of extreme violence. The most famous example of his method of dealing with the opposition came on February 14, 1929, when Capone's men, disguised as police officers, shot dead most of rival Bugs Moran's mob in a garage on Chicago's North Side – the infamous "St Valentine's Day Massacre".

The income from Capone's monopoly on gambling, prostitution and bootlegging was immense. During the 1920s, his fortune was estimated to be in the region of $100,000,000. The Chicago police force was unable or unwilling to bring him to justice, but Capone could do nothing about the Inland Revenue Service. His time in Alcatraz changed him forever and Al Capone died a broken man on January 25, 1947.

Al Capone signs the bail bond beginning his prosecution. It was the IRS that finally succeeded in getting a conviction where the Chicago police had failed for almost 20 years. ▼

'32

NEWS IN BRIEF

- USSR suffers famine
- Radio astronomy pioneered by Karl Jansky
- Vitamin C isolated
- George V makes first royal Christmas broadcast to British Commonwealth and Empire
- Sydney Harbour Bridge officially opens
- Atom split mechanically for the first time
- Subatomic particles, neutrons, discovered
- Films released during the year include Mervyn Le Roy's *I Am a Fugitive from a Chain Gang*, Rouben Mamoulian's *Love Me Tonight*, James Whale's *The Old Dark House*, Howard Hawks's *Scarface*, Ernst Lubitsch's *Trouble in Paradise*, *The Music Box* with Laurel and Hardy and *Horse Feathers* with the Marx Brothers
- Books published this year include Aldous Huxley's *Brave New World*, Evelyn Waugh's *Black Mischief*, Ernest Hemingway's *Death in the Afternoon* and Graham Greene's *Stamboul Train*

January

- Civil disobedience resumes in India; Indian National Congress outlawed; Gandhi and other leaders are arrested
- Germany refuses to continue paying war reparations
- Japanese forces in China capture Shanghai
- Communist uprising in Northern Spain is quashed
- France ends civil unrest in Morocco

POISON KILLS PHAR LAP

The world of horse racing, long considered the sport of kings, was thrown into turmoil by the apparent poisoning of the champion racehorse Phar Lap on April 5. Judged to be one of the finest racing horses in the history of the sport, Phar Lap (the name means "Lightning") had been resting at a private ranch in Menlo Park, California, while his owner, David J Davis, negotiated racing and, astonishingly, film contracts for the horse.

Phar Lap, who was normally raced and stabled in Australia, first came to the attention of horse-racing enthusiasts after winning at Rosehill, near Sydney, in 1929. From September of that year he was always placed as favourite in any race he entered. Phar Lap went on to acquire almost legendary status after winning five times in a single week during the Spring Racing Carnival of 1930. Despite earning the love and admiration of the majority of Australian punters, who rarely lost money on the horse, Phar Lap was not popular with everyone. On Derby Day,

▲ The first super star of the turf, Phar Lap, the pride of Australia, is paraded before the American public for the first time at the Agua Caliente race track barely three months before his death.

November 1, 1930, a disgruntled bookmaker, concerned to make sure that he would lose no more money as a result of the horse's astonishing winning streak, attempted to shoot Phar Lap. The horse was only saved by the brave actions of Tom Woodcock, his dedicated trainer

Woodcock accompanied the horse on the trip to the United States and was with Phar Lap on the morning of April 5, when the horse was taken ill. Despite his best efforts, Phar Lap died of stomach haemorrhaging at around midday. Subsequent investigations seemed to reveal that the horse died as a result of eating grass that had accidentally been sprayed with a lead-arsenate insecticide. The Prime Minister of Australia at the time, Joseph Lyons, described the death of Phar Lap as "a great tragedy".

LINDBERGH BABY DIES AFTER BOTCHED KIDNAP

◀ The kidnapping and murder of Charles Lindbergh Jr sent shockwaves through America. Few tears were shed when his assailant, Bruno Hauptmann, was sent to the electric chair.

On the night of March 1, 1932, the 21-month-old son of Charles and Anne Lindbergh was kidnapped from their home in Hopewell, New Jersey. The kidnapper had entered the baby's bedroom by means of a ladder and left behind a ransom note demanding $50,000. The crime made the headlines in every newspaper across America, not least because the baby's father, Charles A Lindbergh, was considered a hero by many Americans. In 1927 Lindbergh had made the first ever non-stop, solo flight from New York to Paris in a single-engined aeroplane called *Spirit of St Louis*.

Despite leaving a ransom note, the kidnapper did not, initially, contact the Lindberghs. After appeals to the kidnapper via various newspapers, it was arranged that a retired school teacher by the name of John F Condon would drop the ransom money at the Woodland Cemetery, in the Bronx, New York City, in exchange for the safe return of the Lindbergh's baby. The baby was never returned, however, having been killed either during or shortly after the kidnapping. The baby's body was eventually discovered close by the Lindbergh house on May 12.

As soon as the baby's body was discovered a well publicized hunt for the killer was launched. The serial numbers of the notes used to pay the ransom were printed in newspapers across America but it was to be over two years before one of the notes was discovered. On September

▲ The Lindbergh estate at Hopewell, New Jersey, scene of one of the most shocking crimes of the 1930s. The Lindbergh child's body was found near the house two months after his kidnapping.

15, 1934, a German-born carpenter with a history of petty crime used one of the notes to pay for gas at a filling station in the Bronx. Bruno "Richard" Hauptmann was arrested and sent for trial on January 2, 1935. Despite protesting his innocence, the evidence against him was compelling. During a search of Hauptmann's home, police found around $11,000 of the original ransom money, the telephone number of retired school teacher John F Condon, and evidence that a plank from Hauptmann's attic had been used to repair the ladder used in the kidnapping. Hauptmann was found guilty on February 13, 1935, and sentenced to death in the electric chair.

COCKCROFT AND WALTON SPLIT THE ATOM

1932 was the year that saw two Cambridge University-based physicists, Britain's John Cockcroft and Ireland's Ernest

▼ Dr John Cockcroft makes an adjustment to the pump of his "Atom Splitter". His work with Ernest Walton had a dramatic impact on life in the twentieth century.

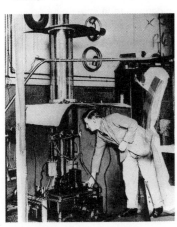

Walton, succeeded in their efforts to split atoms of lithium. By bombarding the nuclei, or cores, of the lithium atoms using a very high voltage particle accelerator, the two scientists were able to transform the atoms of lithium into atoms of helium. This was the first time that a nuclear reaction was achieved by means of artificially accelerated particles.

Cockroft's and Walton's pioneering work with their particle accelerator made their device an essential tool of any physics laboratory, putting it on a par with the microscope and the spectrometer as a means of examining the material world. The particle accelerator, a device which accelerates subatomic particles – known as elementary particles – generates up to

800,000 volts of electricity. This was used to blast a high-energy beam of protons at a group of lithium atoms. The impact of the protons altered the atomic structure of the lithium, turning it into atoms of helium. Although transmutation, as the process is called, had long been the aim of alchemists, who dreamed of turning lead into gold, this was the first time that such a feat had been achieved.

The two scientists were able to construct their particle accelerator with the support of the eminent scientist and peer Lord Rutherford, plus a much-needed £1,000 grant from Cambridge University. In recognition of their remarkable achievement, Cockcroft and Walton were jointly awarded the Nobel Prize for Physics in 1951.

'32

AMELIA EARHART FLIES INTO THE RECORD BOOKS

NEWS IN BRIEF

• Coalition government formed in Austria
• President Hindenburg forces resignation of Chancellor Brüning in Germany
• Japan and China sign armistice

June
• Constitutional monarchy formed after coup in Siam
• Nazis excluded from the German cabinet; ban on Nazi military organizations lifted
• Two men executed for their role in attempting to assassinate Mussolini in Italy

July
• Germany accepts war reparation deal at negotiations in Lausanne
• President Carmona of Portugal appoints Oliveira Salazar Prime Minister as fascist regime takes over
• Belgium reform law allows both French and Flemish to become official language
• US President Hoover orders army to end demonstration by World War One veterans in Washington
• Tenth Olympic games open in Los Angeles, USA
• Nazis become largest party in Reichstag after German elections

August
• Military-led revolt suppressed in Spain
• Adolf Hitler refuses to serve as German Vice-Chancellor under Chancellor von Papen
• Riots break out in Berlin as Nazis and Communists clash

◀ **Popularly known as "Lady Lindy", Amelia Earhart broke numerous flying records before her 1937 disappearance. Despite a rescue expedition involving 30,000 people, neither her body nor her plane were ever found.**

Between May 20 and 21, 1932 Amelia Earhart, a former social worker from Kansas, flew solo across the Atlantic Ocean, earning herself a place in the record books as the first woman ever to do so. She had made the crossing once before, back in June 1928, as a passenger. Despite having achieved fame for that flight, she felt the need to make a solo crossing in order to justify the acclaim that she had received.

Born on July 24, 1897, Amelia Earhart had worked as a nurse in Canada during World War One before moving to Boston, where she made her living as a social worker. She married the publisher George P Putnam in 1931, but retained her maiden name.

After the success of her solo transatlantic crossing she went on to make a series of well-publicized flights across the United States, doing much to raise the profile of aviation and helping to promote the interests of women pilots in what was, by virtue of military flying, a male-dominated field.

In January 1935, she took the extremely daring step of attempting to fly solo from Hawaii to California. Every pilot who had tried it before her had died during the attempt, not least because the distance to be travelled is greater than the transatlantic crossing. Earhart succeeded where all others had failed and then set her sights on a flight around the world.

She took off on her journey in 1937 in a twin-engined Lockheed Electra. Also on board with her was navigator Fred Noonan. On July 2, having already completed over two-thirds of the trip, the pair disappeared somewhere over the central Pacific region. No trace of either Amelia Earhart or Fred Noonan, or the aeroplane in which they were flying, has ever been found. Since their disappearance there has been a great deal of speculation as to their fate, with theories ranging from capture by the Japanese Navy to abduction by aliens.

The "Darling of America", Amelia Earhart concludes her record-breaking transatlantic solo flight with a successful landing at Culmore near Londonderry in Ireland. ▼

LOS ANGELES OLYMPICS

The Olympic Games got under way in August with a magnificent opening ceremony held in Los Angeles, California. Unfortunately, the extent of the growing worldwide depression could be gauged from the number of countries and athletes who declined to take part. Fewer than half of the athletes who had competed in the previous Olympic games, which had been held in The Netherlands in 1928, turned up, with many of them claiming that the cost of travelling to Los Angeles was more than they could afford.

For the first time, the Games featured an Olympic village, which had been built especially to house the male athletes. Female competitors were accommodated in a hotel in downtown Los Angeles. Track and field events were held in the newly enlarged Los Angeles Coliseum, where the crushed-peat running surface proved to be exceptionally fast. Using electronic timing and photo-finish technology, judges were in little doubt about the 10 new world records that were set at the games. America dominated the proceedings, winning 11 gold medals in track and field events.

The modern Olympic Games began in Athens, Greece, back in 1896, with events being open to all who wished to compete. There were no national teams as such and in several cases passing tourists were approached to make up the numbers in some events. Track and field competitions were held in the Panathenaic Stadium, a copy of a stadium originally been built in 330BC.

The first modern marathon was held during these Games, with runners following the 26-mile (approx 40,000 metres) route believed to have been travelled by a messenger who was sent from Marathon to Athens in 490 BC to announce the defeat of an invading army. The Olympic Games originated in Greece and some events, like the javelin, have been carried over to modern times, where they continue to be featured as a regular part of the Games.

▼ The glamorous Olympic Village was home to the world's greatest male athletes during the 1932 Olympic Games. Female competitors had to make do with local hotels.

ROOSEVELT BECOMES US PRESIDENT

As 1932 came to a close, America, along with much of the world, was in the grip of a deep depression the like of which had never been seen before. The sitting Republican president, Herbert Hoover, appeared to many voters to be doing little to help the suffering of ordinary people. In desperation, many Americans looked to the Democratic candidate, Franklin Delano Roosevelt, and his offer of a "New Deal", for a way out of the perilous situation in which they found themselves. In elections culminating on November 8, Roosevelt was elected as the new president of the United States with 22,822,000 votes to Hoover's 15,762,000, plus large majorities in both houses of Congress.

When Roosevelt finally took office on March 4, 1933, many believed that he could not have done so at a worse time. Most of the country's banks were closed, industrial output had dropped by

nearly half in just four years and more than 13 million American workers were out of a job. When Roosevelt, who had suffered a crippling bout of polio in earlier life, struggled to his feet to make his inaugural address, he famously assured the American people that "... the only thing we have to fear is fear itself". For once, it seemed as though the entire nation was behind him, and with their support he was able to preside over probably the most effective peacetime government in American history.

▼ Franklin Roosevelt (right) poses for the camera with two Georgia farm workers. He believed the key to electoral success was in reaching the ordinary working man.

'32 | THE GREAT DEPRESSION

By 1932, there was no room for doubt in anyone's mind that the western world was in the grip of the greatest economic slump in history. The Great Depression, as it became known, was triggered by the collapse of prices on the New York Stock Exchange in October 1929. Initially, the fall-out from this collapse appeared to be confined to the United States. Thousands of individual small investors lost everything as the value of stock dropped by 80 per cent between 1929 and 1932. But it was the strain placed on American banks by the declining value of stocks that sent economic shock waves through the rest of the industrialized world.

In just four years, nearly half the banks in America failed. Many Americans, having lost confidence in their country's economic system, became wary of placing their trust in any financial institution and held on to whatever money they still had. Spending and consumption as a whole dropped and with it came a reduction in output. By 1932, manufacturing production in the United States had dropped to nearly half of the 1929 level. This drop in production resulted in a greatly reduced need for workers and nearly 30 per cent of Americans lost their jobs in just four years.

Since World War One, many European countries had become indebted to the American banks, either as the result of borrowing to pay for the cost of the war or, as was the case in Germany, because of the need to pay reparations. These debts had done a great deal of damage to many European economies, especially those of Great Britain and Germany who owed the greatest debts to America. When the flow of money from America began to slow down as a result of the slump at home, these countries began to suffer also. By 1932, American investment credits to Europe had all but ceased and both Britain and Germany were in serious trouble.

German unemployment, which had begun to rise shortly after the crash of the New York Stock Exchange, had rocketed to six million by 1932. This meant that a quarter of the German workforce was without a job. In Britain the figure was not quite so high but the effects were felt just as severely. Attempting to halt the decline by protecting domestic production, most of the countries caught up in the slump began to impose new tariffs on imports, raising existing ones to unacceptably high levels and placing absolute limits on the amount of goods that could be imported even after the tariffs had been paid. The effects of this on trade as a whole was disastrous and by the end of 1932 the value of world trade had dropped to less than half that of the 1929 level.

Aside from economic miseries caused by the Great Depression, there were also other equally important consequences of the collapse of world markets. In the United States, a country founded on minimal taxation and minimal government, Franklin D Roosevelt swept to power on the promise of a "New Deal" for the American people. This created a fundamental change in the structure of the US economy, bringing with it massively increased government regulation of industry and commerce and a huge programme of public works. Despite this ambitious and courageous undertaking, the resulting effect on the US economy was not as great as most had hoped, and unemployment in the United States was still as high as 15 per cent in 1939.

In Europe the political effects of the Great Depression were rather more alarming. Europe as a whole saw a massive increase in the popularity of what had previously been extremist fringe groups, with both the Fascists and the Communists gaining

◄ The Depression signalled an unprecedented era of economic hardship as industrial output fell to half the levels of the late 1920s and over a quarter of Americans lost their livelihoods.

Fortunes may have been lost on Wall Street but the hardest hit were unskilled workers. With no prospect of employment they faced starvation. ▶

more votes than ever before. Although Britain had a brief and very minor flirtation with fascism, it was in Germany that the fascists found a natural home. Hitler rode to power on the back of resentment caused by an economy crippled by the effects of war reparations. This has led some historians to claim, with uncharacteristic certainty, that Hitler could not have risen to power without the conditions that were created by the Great Depression. The fact that Hitler was able to turn the slump around in Germany by 1936 by means of public works programmes and a massive increase in munitions production did much to cement his power base in that country.

Ultimately, it was World War

Two, sparked by Adolf Hitler's expansionist ambitions, that brought an end to the Great Depression. Britain had been unable to shake off the slump until the conflict in Europe re-opened the munitions factories, the mines and the docks, and carried many of the unemployed off to fight in France. The war in Europe also had a dramatic effect on the American economy, helping to reduce unemployment as British demand for weapons from the United States suddenly shot up. The Great Depression finally ended when America joined the war in 1941.

◀ **The economic hardship that accompanied the Depression caused widespread resentment among ordinary working people and created an environment in which extreme political parties were able to thrive.**

Overall, the Great Depression could be said to have exposed the weaknesses in the economies of the industrialized nations. After World War Two, governments were less keen to allow their economies to be regulated by market forces alone and usually sought to gain a degree of economic stability by means of taxation or legislation in the hope of avoiding a repeat of the disastrous slump which blighted the 1930s.

Like many rural Americans, these Arkansas cotton workers were forced to leave their homes in search of work. ▼

'33

NEWS IN BRIEF

- Nazi repression results in an exodus of Jews from Germany
- Flu epidemic sweeps Europe
- Films released during the year include Merian C Cooper's and Ernest Schoedsack's *King Kong*, James Whale's *The Invisible Man*, Alexander Korda's *The Private Life of Henry VIII*, Rouben Mamoulian's *Queen Christina*, and *Duck Soup*, starring the Marx Brothers
- Books published this year include *Down and Out in Paris and London* by George Orwell and *History of The Russian Revolution* by Leon Trotsky

January
- Martial law introduced in Spain
- Hitler becomes Chancellor of Germany
- Fianna Fail wins with majority of one in Irish general elections
- Edouard Daladier becomes French Prime Minister

February
- Financial crisis in USA forces temporary closure of banks
- Japanese Army advances in China; condemnation by world forces Japan's exit from the League of Nations
- Assassination attempt on US President-elect F D Roosevelt
- Reichstag in Berlin is burnt down by a Communist sympathizer

THE "BODYLINE" TOUR

The English have a long tradition of dismissing unsporting behaviour as "simply not cricket". Unfortunately, the good name of cricket itself, the very embodiment of all that is gentlemanly and honourable was dragged through the mud in January by the touring English team, who disgraced themselves with their behaviour on the field in Australia during a series of Test matches. A cable sent to the Middlesex County Cricket Club (MCC) by the Australian Cricket Board Of Control complained of

Australian batsman H M Woodful ducks to avoid another delivery by Harold "The Wrecker" Larwood. In spite of the presence of the great Don Bradman, Australia lost the Ashes. ▶

unsportsmanlike behaviour on the part of the English team, who had been applying a technique known as "bodyline" bowling – with the frighteningly quick Harold Larwood the chief exponent – to the formerly genteel game of cricket. The technique was developed essentially to intimidate the

Australian batsman by bowling short-pitched deliveries at his body with a ring of close fielders on the leg side ready to catch the ball. However, controversial bodyline proved – one English bowler refused to embrace the tactics – it helped England win the Ashes four Tests to one.

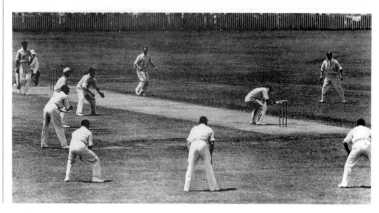

THE NEW DEAL

▲ **Franklin Delano Roosevelt (right) and secretary William H Woodlin (left), the architects of the New Deal, a policy intended to stimulate growth throughout the US economy.**

Franklin D Roosevelt had come to power at a time when it seemed that the only topic of conversation was the Depression. It was clear that something had

to be done to save the ailing American economy, but just what that should be seemed to be beyond the grasp of most people. One of the factors that made Roosevelt so appealing as a presidential candidate was his obvious confidence in his own ability to turn things around. And so it was that he rode into office on the tide of what was to become known as the New Deal.

Roosevelt promised aid to farmers, a balanced budget, ambitious building programmes designed to get America back to work and government regulation of some of the more unsavoury practices carried out under the name of capitalism. On June 16, he went before Congress and persuaded it to pass the National Industry Recovery Act. The act attempted to bring about recovery in two ways. First, the act released over three billion dollars of federal money for use in an

extensive programme of public works, with the aim of creating over a million new jobs in the process. Second, came the setting up of the National Recovery Administration, which had the task of establishing codes of practice within the business community, bringing together unions and their employers to fix working hours, set fair wages and establish production quotas.

Some have argued that the New Deal failed in the short term. The programme of public works moved too slowly to provide immediate aid to the armies of the unemployed, and the National Recovery Administration soon became bogged down in red tape and regulation. But although the New Deal did little to stimulate the economy, it did help to bring about a degree of economic stability which had previously been lacking, providing a firm basis for future growth.

MERRY-GO-ROUND IN CUBA

The eight-year reign of Cuban president Gerardo Machado came to an end after a general strike in the country sparked an army rebellion, forcing Machado to flee to Miami Beach, Florida. Machado was elected to office in 1924 on a programme of national regeneration which reflected the rising tide of nationalism in Cuba. Once in power he introduced taxation of American capital investments and promoted tourism, industry and mining. After some early successes he became increasingly dictatorial, even amending the constitution in order to extend his period in office. The Wall Street Crash of 1929 triggered an economic crisis in Cuba and Machado did well to survive a revolt in 1931.

Machado was eventually overthrown in August 1933 and Carlos Manuel de Céspedes was named as provisional president. However, an alliance of student radicals and a military junta ousted him from office during a coup on September 5. Ramón Grau San Martín, a professor of medicine at the University of Havana, was then declared provisional president of Cuba but was himself removed from office in a coup led by Fulgencio Batista y Zaldívar.

► **The turbulent island of Cuba nears anarchy as Lieutenant Villalon – the assassin of President Machado's feared chief of police – is paraded through the streets of Havana.**

ALCOHOL BACK IN VOGUE

Americans raised a glass to their new president, Franklin D Roosevelt, after he persuaded Congress to end prohibition. The abandonment of the 18th Amendment to the Constitution, which made illegal the production or sale of alcohol, brought to an end what must surely have been 13 of the darkest years in American history.

No sooner had prohibition been introduced in 1920 than normally law-abiding, patriotic citizens across the country began to apply good old American know-how to developing ingenious ways of getting their hands on alcohol. Initially, it was brought in across the borders with Canada and Mexico, or by ship from the Bahamas and Cuba. The authorities responded by increasing border controls and issuing the US Coastguard with super-fast boats with which to intercept the sea-borne smugglers. In desperation, many Americans appeared to develop a variety of ailments, all of which, coincidentally, required treatment with medicinal alcohol. Several million prescriptions were filled during the early years of prohibition, but by the late 1920s, organized gangs of bootleggers were offering under-the-counter alcohol to those who had no desire to visit their doctor.

The alcohol on offer from the bootleggers was often of highly dubious origin and quality and, in many cases, was simply corn liquor produced using illegal stills. Impurities, which might accidentally be introduced during production, were known to cause blindness, paralysis or, in extreme cases, death.

Far from ridding society of its supposed evils, prohibition had the twin effects of establishing organized crime in America and of introducing many ordinary, law-abiding citizens to the thrills of illicit behaviour.

◄ **Drinks all round – the first post-prohibition truck-load of beer leaves New York's Jacob Rupperts brewery. For the first time in 13 years Americans were legally allowed to drink alcohol.**

'33 | HITLER'S RISE TO POWER

A larm bells began to ring all over Europe in 1933 when the Nazis, led by Adolf Hitler, succeeded in taking power in Germany. At the time few could have guessed the degree to which his name and that of his party would become synonymous with all that is evil. Of all the despotic political figures who exercised dictatorial power in the twentieth century, it is unlikely that any, with the possible exception of the USSR's Joseph Stalin, attract the same degree of notoriety as Adolf Hitler.

Nazism had its roots in the Prussian ideal of a martial society, where everyone was subject to an almost military style of discipline. Combined with this belief was the arrogant Nietzschean notion that the exceptional individual was not subject to the same rules and laws as the mediocre masses. Adolf Hitler succeeded in corrupting these ideals to his own ends, convincing many Germans that they were, by virtue of their Aryan blood, a nation of exceptional individuals who had been held back from their ultimate destiny by a lack of will among their existing leaders.

This last idea appealed particularly to those many Germans who still felt bitter at what they saw as the treacherous betrayal of their country by the politicians who had negotiated the peace at the end of World War One. Germany came out badly at the end of the war and was ordered to pay over 132 billion gold marks to the Allies as reparation for the cost of the war. This had a crippling effect on the German economy. Hyper inflation in the 1920s saw the middle classes lose almost everything, driving many of these newly disaffected people into the waiting arms of the Nazi party. Hitler was also able to gather many followers by presenting himself and his party as the last line of defence

▲ Adolf Hitler, the most immediately recognizable political figure of the twentieth century. His expansionist policies lead directly to the start of World War Two.

against the Communists. Even those who had no sympathy for what Hitler was attempting to do were drawn to the Nazis as the only hope of keeping the Communists out of power.

Having established the inherent superiority of the Aryan race in the minds of many Germans, Hitler then pulled off his terrifying master-stroke by identifying what he called the enemy within. By making the Jews the scapegoats for all of Germany's troubles, he united disparate groups within the country, pulling them together under one banner, that of the Nazis, in their fight against a common enemy.

The origins of the Nazi party were humble enough, but from their first meetings in a beer cellar in Munich in 1919 the party soon expanded and began to campaign for government. By the time of the German parlia-

mentary elections in 1930, the Nazi party had grown to the point where they could claim 107 seats, which compared favourably with the Communists' 77 seats. This meant that the then Chancellor of Germany, Heinrich Brüning, was unable to form a majority government. In an attempt to avert political instability, the German President, Paul von Hindenburg, issued an emergency decree which enabled Brüning to carry on for another two years until he resigned in May 1932. More elections followed in July, and this time the Nazis won 230 seats.

In a move calculated to retain power for the old order – the Prussian élite was made up of conservatives drawn mostly from military or aristocratic backgrounds – President Paul von Hindenburg appointed Adolf Hitler Chancellor of Germany on

▼ Crude methods, such as the use of a micrometer to measure the width of the nose, were frequently applied to determine a German's racial purity.

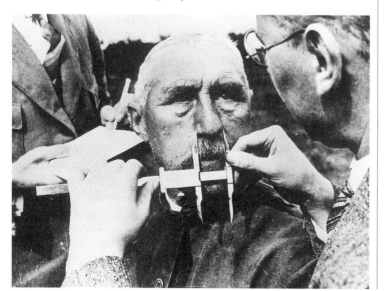

▲ Election posters urge voters to support Hitler and Hindenburg. The conservative establishment sought to control Hitler by handing him a position of high office.

January 30, 1933. Hindenburg and his supporters were labouring under the naive belief that, once in power, they could control Hitler. He was, they all argued, nothing more than a jumped-up former corporal who would soon be shown his place. Their mistake was not only foolish, it was also to prove fatal. In less than two years, Hitler had created a totalitarian state, made himself president and all but annihilated the old order.

Invoking the Fascist belief of the right of the strong to rule over the weak, Hitler began to rid Germany of those elements which he considered undesirable. Using the well-oiled propaganda machine that the Nazis had set up under the guidance of Joseph Goebbels, Hitler raised anti-semitism to a new and horrific level. One of his first actions on assuming power was to establish concentration camps. These were used initially to house the traditional enemies of the Nazi party, most notably the Communists, but the list of those who were viewed as enemies of the party was soon expanded to encompass Jews, gypsies, homosexuals and anyone who dared to speak out against the new regime.

Life was bitterly hard in the camps, but they were designed initially to crush the spirit rather than to kill the body. This changed after the outbreak of World War Two and by 1940 Hitler had established the first of the true death camps. These obscene monuments to the depths of human depravity were constructed mostly in Poland, where Hitler intended to carry out what he called the "Final Solution". His intention was to wipe the Jews, along with anyone else he deemed to be racially inferior, off the face of the planet. Auschwitz, the most notorious of these camps, had the facilities to gas and incinerate up to 12,000 people a day. Though Hitler ultimately failed in his ambitions, more than six million Jews died in his death camps.

▲ The National Socialist propaganda machine portrayed the Jewish community as the cause of their country's economic woes. Ordinary citizens were encouraged to "Buy German" and boycott Jewish shops.

▼ Throughout the decade, the Jewish population found itself increasingly disenfranchised. Official government policy would eventually result in their internment and systematic extermination.

'34

HITLER MAKES A STAND ON REPARATIONS

◀ The folly of Versailles was gradually revealed as Hitler successfully used the issue of war reparations to assert his standing among ordinary Germans.

In 1934, Adolf Hitler, by now securely in control of Germany, took the audacious step of announcing that the Fatherland would be paying no further war reparations (the payment due to the Allies for the damage done during World War One). Hitler was not slow in realizing the importance of getting Germany back on its feet after the ravages inflicted on its economy by the double body blow of the Great Depression and reparations for World War One. In an effort to overcome the effects of the Great Depression, he put in motion an ambitious programme of public works, including the start of a network of major new roads, or *autobahns*, which served the double purpose of getting many Germans back to work and establishing good roads down which he could send his tanks when the time came for the expansion of the German borders. This was allied to a much less public programme intended to rearm Germany for the conflict that would inevitably follow.

By announcing that there were to be no further payments of war reparations, Hitler was letting the world know that Germany was, or was about to become, a power to be reckoned with. Suspension of the reparations during the 1920s had resulted in the occupation of the Ruhr – Germany's industrial heartland based along the Rhine – by French and Belgian troops. Hitler was well aware that the Great Depression had left the European powers in no position to engage in armed conflict – Britain was especially keen to avoid having to rearm at a time when her economy was in such a perilous state. By declaring his intention to cease payments towards the final bill of 132 billion gold marks, he not only tested the resolve of the European powers, but also freed Germany from a crippling financial burden.

POLICE AND DOCKERS CLASH

Thursday, July 5 became known as "Bloody Thursday" after clashes between police and union members involved in the dock strike in San Francisco erupted into rioting. The strike began on May 9, with conflict coming after the Industrial Association, a group made up of employers and associated businessmen, attempted to move goods from the dock piers to warehouses in the city, a move designed to break the strike and undermine the power of the unions in the area.

The first clashes occurred on July 3, when strikers attempting to block the movement of freight found themselves facing a large police presence seemingly under the control of the employers. Rioting broke out during which police fired tear gas at the strikers. Many people were injured, including two who were shot by the police, one of them a bank teller whose forehead was grazed by a stray bullet. Several trucks were also overturned during the fighting.

Independence Day, July 4, saw little action at the docks as most people were at home celebrating with their families, but July 5 saw trouble break out on a massive scale and the conflict escalate until a general strike was declared on July 16.

Although the strike appeared, on the surface at least, to be about the pay and conditions of cargo handlers working on the San Francisco Docks, it soon took on an added significance. President Roosevelt's "New Deal" policy, in particular the National Industrial Recovery Act, had laid out the right of workers to belong to a trade union. Many employers had sought to undermine this act, or even ignore it where possible. The strike in San Francisco was to prove a testing ground for the determination of the workers to assert their rights and the resolve of the employers to continue the often unfair practices followed prior to the New Deal.

▼ **A serious casualty of the violent struggle between striking dock workers and the police, as the authorities unsuccessfully attempt to reopen the port of San Francisco.**

DILLINGER DIES

Agents from J Edgar Hoover's Federal Bureau of Investigations brought to a bloody end the career of the man who was arguably the world's most famous bank robber. On the night of July 22, 1934, FBI agents lay in wait to spring an ambush on John Dillinger as he emerged from the Biograph Theater in Chicago. This was the FBI's third attempt at capturing America's number one most wanted man and this time they got him.

Dillinger had been lured to the theatre by an old friend, Anne Sage, who was known to the Chicago police for operating a brothel. Dillinger's death brought to an end a remarkable series of bank robberies and prison escapes that had seen him make the front pages of every newspaper in America.

Dillinger, an ex-Navy man who had served on the USS *Utah* before deserting, had been a minor criminal before learning the finer points of bank robbery during a seven-year stretch in the Indiana State Penitentiary. On his release, he and his gang – whom he had recruited in prison – hit five banks in just four months before Dillinger was captured and sent to prison in Ohio. He escaped swiftly with the aid of his gang and together they proceeded to rob banks in Indiana and Wisconsin before fleeing to Tucson, Arizona, where they were picked up by local police. Dillinger was sent to serve his sentence in Indiana, at the Crown Point Jail, but famously escaped using a fake pistol carved from a piece of wood and blackened with shoe polish, forcing his way past 12 prison guards and singing a country song as he went.

Dillinger continued to carry out bank robberies and evade capture until that fateful night in Chicago when the FBI finally put an end to his career.

▲ **"Public Enemy Number One", John Dillinger (right), clearly enjoyed the period of fame during which he established himself as the most famous bank robber in history.**

'34

MOUNT EVEREST CLAIMS ANOTHER VICTIM

Hopes of a successful ascent of Mount Everest were dashed on July 19 when mountaineer Maurice Wilson died during a solo attempt to reach the peak. Wilson was not the first climber to die on Everest nor was he to be the last. To many climbers, Mount Everest was the Holy Grail of their sport and represented the pinnacle, in every sense, of achievement within their field.

The mountain peak forms part of the Great Himalayan Range in Asia, and at 8,848 metres (29,028 ft), the peak of Everest is the highest point on Earth, reaching two-thirds of the way through the Earth's atmosphere. Lack of oxygen at this altitude, combined with powerful winds and extremely low temperatures found on the upper slopes of Everest defeated many early climbers, including British mountaineering legend George Mallory.

Many believe that Mallory reached the summit in June 1924 before dying on the descent. He was last seen by colleagues close to the summit and "going strongly". His body, well preserved by ice, was found in 1999.

▲ Lost on the slopes of Everest, British climber Maurice Wilson failed to tame the world's highest peak. This feat would continue to elude adventurers until 1953.

NEWS IN BRIEF

July
- Britain begins to increase the strength of the Royal Air Force
- New government under Keisuke Okada formed in Japan
- Oil pipeline between Iraq and Lebanon opened
- Heinrich Himmler appointed head of Nazi concentration camps
- Austrian Chancellor Dollfuss assassinated by Austrian Nazis, who then fail in an attempted coup; Kurt Schuschnigg becomes new Chancellor
- US criminal, John Dillinger, shot and killed by FBI
- Death of Nobel Prize-winning scientist Marie Curie

August
- German president Paul von Hindenburg dies; Hitler takes the title "Führer" and is granted dictatorial powers
- US forces leave Haiti
- Nazi rally in the US pulls in a crowd of nearly 10,000

September
- Collapse in a Welsh pit leaves 262 miners dead
- Fascists clash with opponents in London
- Textile workers strike in USA
- Nuremburg Nazi party conference is attended by in excess of 750,000 faithful who hear Hitler claim that the Third Reich will last a thousand years
- 1,500 feared dead in hurricane in Japan
- USSR is admitted to the League of Nations

HITLER TAKES CONTROL OF GERMANY

◄ Germany's President, Field Marshal Paul von Hindenburg, and Chancellor, Adolf Hitler. Hindenburg's death allowed Hitler to assume both roles.

Chancellor, Hitler had engineered events to ensure that he had extraordinary powers. The burning of the German parliament, the Reichstag, on the night of February 27, 1933, afforded Hitler the opportunity to suspend many basic human rights and also provided the excuse for an increase in the degree of violence with which Hitler's political opponents could be persecuted (the Communists were blamed for the arson attack on the Reichstag). Hitler knew, however, that his expansionist plans would have to be put on hold unless he could take control of the German military, who swore their oath of allegiance to the President.

Having first secured for himself the post of Chancellor of Germany, Adolf Hitler assumed complete political control over the country when he was made President on August 2. Even as

In order to become President he would have to get the backing of the army.

Although there were many within the army who sympathized with Hitler's cause, they were deeply distrustful of elements within his organization. Chief among those giving them cause for concern was Ernst Röhm. Röhm was leader of the Nazi paramilitary group, the SA, who were viewed with deep suspicion by the army. The SA, which stands for *Sturm Abteilung*, or stormtroopers, were in essence a private army and had been banned under the previous regime. Although they theoretically owed their allegiance to Hitler, they were considered too much of a potential threat to the political stability of the country. While Röhm appeared to have no time for a let-up in the "revolution" that was occurring in German politics, Hitler knew that without the support of the army he would ultimately fail in his plans to expand Germany well beyond its existing borders. Despite the urgings of Hermann Goering and Heinrich Himmler, Hitler hesitated before removing Röhm until June 29, 1934. Röhm and his lieutenant, Edmund Heines, were seized and executed without trial and the SA disbanded. Satisfied now that Hitler could be trusted, the leaders of the army allowed the posts of Chancellor and President to be combined. When the current President of Germany, Paul von Hindenburg, died on August 2, Hitler became President and thereby assumed supreme command over the military, He now took on the title of Führer.

KING ALEXANDER OF YUGOSLAVIA ASSASSINATED

During the course of a diplomatic mission to France, King Alexander of Yugoslavia was assassinated, along with the French Foreign Minister, Louis Barthou, in the French city port of Marseilles on October 9. His assassin was a Croatian terrorist with links to fascist groups in Yugoslavia and Italy.

King Alexander had assumed power in Yugoslavia during a bloodless coup on January 6, 1929, which brought to an end six months of total chaos which had been triggered by the earlier assassination of Stjepan Radic, leader of the Croatian element in the country. Alexander declared Yugoslavia as a kingdom and abolished the constitution along with all political parties, trade unions and any organization that might be deemed to have a regional bias. (Then, as now, this part of Europe was being torn apart by regional conflicts.) Alexander also ordered that all locally elected bodies hand over their powers to his own royal representatives.

Alexander's aim appears to have been the creation of a Yugoslavian national consciousness, which he hoped would end the bitter rivalries between the regions that made up Yugoslavia. He attempted, where possible, to do away with regional differences in everyday matters such as taxation and to establish a set of laws with which to govern the entire country. Following the coup there was a purge of the Civil Service, such as it was, with the aim of removing corrupt and unpopular local officials. The 33 departments that had previously administered the day-to-day running of the many regions of the country were replaced with nine new ones. Of these, six had Serbian majorities, two had Croatian majorities and the final one was mostly Slovene. Yugoslavian Muslims came out of the deal badly, being unable to claim a majority in any of the new regions. Despite the best efforts of King Alexander, the various groups within the country seemed unwilling to be united as a single nation and the conflict between competing groups continues to this day.

◀ **King Alexander's personal chauffeur prevents the escape of the Croatian assassin while a cavalry officer strikes him down with his sabre.**

THE INVENTION OF RADAR

◄ Tests in London's Hyde Park provide proof of the effectiveness of radar systems as a part of Britain's defence strategy.

Perhaps the most vital invention to emerge during 1935, certainly as far as the British were concerned, was Radar (an acronym for Radio Detection And Ranging). Although the principle of Radar was understood back in the late nineteenth century, and Radar systems were developed independently by the French, Germans and the Americans, it is two British scientists working at the National Physical Laboratory, Robert Watson-Watt and A F Wilkins, who are credited with having first put the idea to practical use. Having learned that passing aircraft could cause distortion to the reception of radio signals, the two men went to work on finding ways of locating aeroplanes using radio waves.

Robert Watson-Watt's earlier work as a meteorologist, during which he spent his time trying to create devices that could be used to warn of approaching thunderstorms, led him to apply a similar approach to finding aeroplanes.

Towards the end of 1935, the two men had developed a technique of firing radio waves at possible targets and then measuring the amount of time it took for the radio waves to bounce back. The time lapse between the outgoing and incoming signal was then measured and used to calculate the distance of the aircraft from the radio emitter. By the end of the year, their system was capable of locating aircraft up to 112 km (70 miles) away.

The work of Watson-Watt and Wilkins was used to develop the world's first practical radar defence system. This proved to be a vital weapon during the Battle of Britain, giving prior warning of German attacks from the air and enabling British fighter crews to become airborne before the enemy's airplanes had even reached the British coast. Robert Watson-Watt was knighted for his work in 1942.

LAWRENCE OF ARABIA DIES

May 19, 1935 saw the death of T E Lawrence, the man who wrote *The Seven Pillars Of Wisdom* and who was more famously known in life and death as Lawrence Of Arabia. A brilliant scholar, outstanding soldier and undoubtedly one of the bravest men to serve in the Middle East during World War One, Thomas Edward Lawrence was the second of five sons produced by Sir Thomas Chapman and Sara Maden. Lawrence's father had left his wife and two daughters in Ireland in order to set up home with Sara Maden, the children's governess. The new family eventually moved to Oxford, where they assumed the family name of Lawrence.

After graduating from Oxford University with a first-class honours degree in history, Lawrence was recruited by British Intelligence and sent on a map-making expedition to northern

▼A brave and eccentric military genius, T E Lawrence was shunned by the establishment after refusing to accept honours from King George V.

Sinai, on the border with Turkey. At the start of World War One Lawrence was based in Cairo, where he continued to carry on with his intelligence duties. He soon became frustrated at the lack of progress being made against Turkey, Germany's ally in the region, and managed to persuade his superiors to let him set up a guerrilla force using Arabian tribesmen.

Lawrence's guerrillas proved to be remarkably effective, playing a key role in the Allied advance towards Jerusalem. Captured in November 1917, Lawrence was the victim of several severe homosexual assaults by Turkish troops before he was able to make his escape. The experience left him a changed man. During a reception with George V near the end of the war, Lawrence offended the monarch by refusing to accept the Order of the Bath and the DSO, thus cutting himself off from much of the British society that he had come to despise. In later life his behaviour appeared to become increasingly eccentric. Lawrence died as a result of a motorcycle accident that occurred on May 13.

CAMPBELL ZOOMS INTO THE RECORD BOOKS

The British driver Sir Malcolm Campbell caused a stir in Utah, US, when he smashed the 300 mph (483 km) land-speed barrier in *Bluebird*, his super-fast, custom-built racing car. On September 3, Campbell revved up his vehicle and set off down the Bonneville Salt Flats in near-perfect conditions for an attempt on the land-speed record. No one before Campbell had made a successful attempt on the 300 mph record under test conditions; Sir Malcolm and *Bluebird* were officially timed over the measured distance at precisely 301.337 mph (584.85 km/h).

Campbell first acquired a taste for speed while serving as a pilot in the Royal Flying Corps during World War One. From flying he went into motor racing and in 1924 he achieved a very impressive 146.16 mph (235.17 km/h) in the first version of *Bluebird*. All of Malcolm Campbell's land-speed cars and later hydroplanes were named *Bluebird*, after the play *L'Oiseau Bleu* by Belgian playwright Maurice Maeterlinck. Campbell eventually went on to establish land-speed records on a further nine separate occasions up to 1935.

Having cracked the 300 mph barrier, Campbell set his sights on the world water-speed record. In 1937, he took his hydroplane up to 129.5 mph (208.36 km/h), setting a new record. He managed to exceed this speed in 1938 and on August 19, 1939, Campbell set a world water-speed record of 141.74 mph (228 km/h), which he still held at his death in 1948. Campbell's son, Donald, followed in his father's wake, setting records for speed on both land and water. He died in an attempt on the water-speed record on Coniston Water in England in 1967.

▼*Bluebird*, driven by Malcolm Campbell, was the first land vehicle to achieve a speed of 300 mph (483 km/h). The car became one of the great icons of the "art deco" era.

NAZI LAWS PERSECUTE GERMAN JEWS

May
- Italy continues to amass troops in North Africa
- Czech Nazi party makes gains in parliamentary elections
- France and the Soviet Union agree a 5-year friendship treaty
- US athlete Jesse Owens breaks five athletics record in a day
- King George V celebrates his Silver Jubilee as British monarch

June
- Britain and Italy negotiate over Italy's expansionist aims in East Africa
- SS *Normandie* completes her maiden voyage to New York in a record 4 days, 11 hours
- Pierre Laval forms a new government in France after the resignation of Pierre Flandin
- General elections in Greece won by pro-monarchy Populist party
- Stanley Baldwin becomes Britain's Prime Minister
- Britain and Germany agree limits on the size of the German navy; France objects to them

July
- Anti-Catholic riots in Belfast
- French government assumes emergency financial powers
- Forty Italian troops die in an ambush by Abyssinian troops; the Abyssinian emperor Haile Selassie vows that he will fight to "the last man" to prevent an Italian invasion
- Ten rioting Muslims are shot dead by Indian troops

◄ **"Buy nothing from Jews!" The Nazi authorities step up their systematic persecution of Jewish businesses with a series of official one-day boycotts.**

Continuing a process of state persecution that began in 1933, Hitler's Nazis heaped ever-greater humiliation and terror on the Jewish population of Germany. Having already robbed many Jews of their livelihoods by barring them from working in the civil service, law courts and universities, as well as encouraging the vandalizing and destruction of Jewish shops and businesses, the Nazis went on to pass the Nuremberg Laws on September 15. Under the first of these laws, known as the Law of the Reich Citizen, all German Jews were deprived of their citizenship, becoming instead subjects of the state. The second of these laws, the

▶ **A humiliated Jewish lawyer is marched barefoot through the streets of Munich. His placard reads: "I am a Jew but I will never again complain about the Nazis".**

Law for the Protection of German Blood and German Honour, made illegal any sexual relations – and by extension marriage – between Jews and any citizen of Germany.

A supplementary decree was added to these laws on November 15, defining a Jew as anyone who had at least one Jewish grandparent and stating that no Jew could ever possibly be a citizen of the Third Reich.

These were the first steps on the road to the gradual segregation of the Jews from the rest of German society. Further laws followed, each seemingly more insulting or more sinister than the last. It became an offence for a Jewish household to employ any female domestic staff of German blood unless the staff member was over the age of 45. German Jewish passports had to be stamped with a red J, for *Jude*, and Jews whose surnames did not sound, in the opinion of the Nazis, "Jewish enough" were forced to adopt new, more "Jewish sounding" surnames.

The process of gradually removing every legal right of the German Jews continued until all pretence of any legal process was dropped and eventually the Nazis began transporting Jews to the extermination camps in Poland.

MUSSOLINI INVADES ABYSSINIA

Fascism extended its boundaries on October 3 when Mussolini's troops marched into the African country of Abyssinia. Italy's well-equipped and well-prepared forces, equipped with poison gas and aeroplanes, proved to be more than a match for the essentially primitive weapons of the Abyssinians. Italy's unprovoked act of aggression brought forth howls of protest from the League of Nations – which Abyssinia had joined in 1923 – but little in the way of any real action to counter the Italian forces. Britain and France, well aware of the fact that they could cut off the movement of fascist troops into Abyssinia by closing the Suez Canal to Italian shipping, sat back and considered their options carefully. Not wishing to drive Mussolini into an alliance with Hitler's Nazis, they chose instead to try for a peaceful, negotiated solution to the problem. The French were also unwilling to get involved because to do so would have placed them in violation of their existing treaties with Italy.

Mussolini, well aware of the reluctance of the League of Nations to come to the aid of the Abyssinians, added to the outrage caused by the Italian invasion. He ordered every citizen in Italy to listen to their radios while he dared the alliance to become involved in what he had earlier claimed was a dispute between the African nation and Italy dating back to 1896.

Haile Selassie, the Abyssinian leader who had been instrumental in getting his country accepted into the League of Nations, went into hiding after the invasion. He spent the next year or so organizing a guerrilla-style defence of his country but was forced to flee Abyssinia in 1936. He returned to recapture the country with the aid of the British Army in 1941.

Mussolini was able to invade Abyssinia in the knowledge that his forces would encounter very little resistance from the League of Nations. ▼

LONG MARCH TO POWER

Having lost over 90 per cent of his followers along the way, Mao Tse-tung led the Communist First Front Army into Yan'an province in northwest China on October 20 after a march lasting just over a year and covering an

The Long March was an historic event in China's transition to Communism which saw Mao Tse-tung established as the country's supreme leader. ▼

incredible 9,600 km (6,000 miles). The Communists, originally made up of 85,000 Communist troops and 15,000 administrative staff, had originally headed southwest to the Kweichow province after they were nearly crushed in battles in their former stronghold of Jiangxi with the opposing Nationalist Army, led by Chiang Kai-shek.

Chiang's army of 700,000 troops greatly overwhelmed those of the Communists and were much better equipped for open warfare. During the first three months of the march, the Communists lost over half their forces to the constant air and land attacks by the Nationalist Army. In January 1935, Mao, who had until then been on the fringes of the leadership of the Communist forces, established control over the remaining troops and led the marchers northwards, toward the relative safety of north-west China near to the border with the Soviet Union.

Once in Yenan, Mao combined his forces with the 7,000 troops of the local Red Army and by the end of 1936 further alliances with similar groups swelled the Communists ranks to around 30,000. Mao's forces moved to the nearby district of Yenan, where they established a base from which they eventually defeated the Nationalist Army of Chiang Kai-shek.

The main significance of the Long March, as it became known, was the establishment of Mao Tse-tung as the supreme leader of the Communist forces in China. With the defeat of the Nationalist forces, Mao effectively gained control of most of the country.

'36

FASCISM TAKES HOLD

NEWS IN BRIEF

• First Volkswagen factory opened by Hitler
• *Queen Mary* begins maiden voyage from Southampton
• Films released during the year include Alexander Korda's *Rembrandt*, the H G Wells--scripted *Things to Come* and Leni Riefenstahl's *Triumph of the Will*
• Sergei Prokofiev's *Peter and the Wolf* premieres
• Margaret Mitchell's novel *Gone with the Wind* published
• Eleventh Olympic Games take place in Berlin

January
• French Prime Minister Pierre Laval resigns and Albert Sarraut forms a new government
• Deaths of King George V, whose son succeeds as Edward VIII, and of British writer Rudyard Kipling.

February
• Attempted military coup in Japan forces resignation of Prime Minister Okada; Koki Hirota becomes Prime Minister
• Jawaharlal Nehru is elected President of the Indian Congress

March
• Germany re-occupies the Rhineland in defiance of the Treaty of Versailles

April
• Native South Africans gain representation in parliament
• General J Metaxas is appointed Prime Minister of Greece
• Death of Egyptian King Fuad; son Farouk succeeds

Political life in Europe after World War One was, on the whole, dominated by the rise of fascism. This political philosophy saw the state, or even race, as central to all things. The rights of the individual were negated and viewed as a small part of the whole, united under the undisputed iron will of a single leader. An example of just such a leader was Benito Mussolini, the Italian leader who first coined the word fascism in 1919. Mussolini took control of Italy in 1922 and spent the next five years establishing a fascist state, taking over industry and the legal system. By the start of the 1930s, Italy was under his sole control.

By the 1930s, the influence of fascism had spread all over the world. Ultra-nationalists in Japan sought to take control of the government and talked longingly of a return to the great days of the Samurai warrior code. The practice of harking back to an almost mythical, honourable past was and is a common feature of most fascist groups, although the validity of many of their historical claims is at best questionable. The Japanese movement was not fascist in the conventional sense of the word, but Japanese belief in their own racial superiority combined with a rigid hierarchy and a sense of destiny to produce a regime that was a natural ally to that of Nazi Germany.

Although fascism failed to find a natural home in Britain or North America, it did prove attractive to certain regimes in Latin America. Many of these regimes continued to operate along fascist lines even after World War Two had effectively rid Europe of the blight of fascism.

▲ **The founder of the British Union of Fascists, Sir Oswald Mosley, addresses a fascist rally in London.**

The reasons why fascism proved to be such a powerful force in the twentieth century is probably due, in no small part, to the effects of the Great Depression. Fascism, with its continual promise of a return to former glories and the insidious suggestion that others – usually the Jews – were to blame for present miseries, found a ready following among the disaffected. The early successes of the Nazis in Germany did much to aid the fascist movement, providing an example of a country brought back from the brink and returned to a powerful position on the international stage as a result of its rigid adherence to fascist principles.

▲ **Training a nation of warriors. Under Mussolini's guidance, a regiment of young, rifle-carrying Italian fascists provide a public display of their enthusiasm as they march through the streets of Rome.**

SOUTH AFRICA DESCENDS INTO DARKNESS

In a move designed to consolidate white rule in South Africa, the voting rights of the rapidly diminishing numbers of male black African property holders in South Africa were removed in 1936. The South Africa Act of 1909 had given the vote to white males in the region but excluded all women, black or white. White women were enfranchised in 1930 but the limited voting rights of the black and coloured South Africans – who were allowed to vote only for white candidates –

were gradually stripped away over the following years, with the voting rights of the coloured population being removed in practice in 1956.

The government of South Africa was determined to follow a policy of segregation. This was to lead ultimately to the system of apartheid – from the Afrikaans word meaning separateness. The roots of apartheid lie in the 1913 Native Land Act, which made it illegal for blacks to buy or lease land outside of

designated reserves. This policy of blatant discrimination was carried further in 1923 by the Native Urban Area Act, which sought to segregate blacks and whites in the towns and cities. The acts of 1913 and 1923, combined with the disenfranchisement of the black and coloured population of South Africa, created a firm basis for the structure of apartheid, which was established after World War Two and which was to remain in place until the 1990s.

KING EDWARD VIII PUTS LOVE BEFORE DUTY

Britain was plunged into a constitutional crisis during 1936 when it was revealed that the King, Edward VIII, wished to marry the American twice-divorced Mrs Wallis Simpson. Although the rest of the world had known about the couple's blossoming relationship for several years, censorship imposed by London-based newspaper proprietors kept the story from most of the King's British subjects. While still Prince of Wales, Edward had met Mrs Simpson in 1930, two years after she had married her second husband, Ernest. The Simpsons moved in the same social circles as the Prince and their frequent meetings led eventually to love.

The death of his father, King George V, in January 1936, made Edward both king and head of the Church of England, which was firmly opposed to divorce. Edward soon began to sound out senior figures in the Royal Family and government on the constitutional

problems that would be raised by his wish to marry a divorced woman. Neither his family, nor the government, nor the Commonwealth governments which were consulted were willing to contemplate such a marriage on the part of the king, and soon rumours of an abdication were reaching the newspapers. On December 10, the King abdicated with the words "I, Edward, do hereby declare my irrevocable

determination to renounce the throne for myself and my descendants". Parliament endorsed his abdication on December 11 and Edward's brother Albert, Duke of York, was proclaimed king, as George VI. Edward, now Duke of Windsor, married Wallis Simpson in France on June 3, 1937.

▼ **A solemn moment: Edward VIII addresses the nation in a farewell radio broadcast after his abdication.**

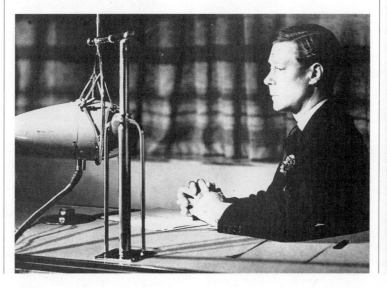

May
- Arabs and Jews clash in Palestine
- The war between Italy and Abyssinia ends with the Italian occupation of Addis Ababa

June
- French left-wing Popular Front forms government with Léon Blum as Prime Minister
- The Irish Republican Army (IRA) is outlawed by Irish Free State government

July
- General Francisco Franco leads mutinies in the Spanish Army; the Spanish Civil War begins
- German airship *Hindenburg* arrives in New York after a record-breaking Atlantic flight

August
- The black US athlete Jesse Owens wins four gold medals at the Olympic Games in Berlin
- British protectorate of Egypt ends
- Stalin executes 16 high-ranking Communists, including Grigori Zinoviev and Leon Kamenev

September
- Non-intervention pact is agreed by foreign powers over Spanish Civil War

October
- Franco is appointed head of state by Spanish nationalists
- Thousands clash with supporters of the British fascist leader Sir Oswald Mosley in London
- Thousands begin to march from Jarrow in the north of England to London to protest against unemployment

November
- The Rome-Berlin axis is declared by Mussolini
- F D Roosevelt is re-elected in US presidential elections
- London's Crystal Palace is destroyed by fire

December
- King Edward VIII abdicates

The Spanish Civil War permeated every level of Spanish life. Men, women and children from every class took up arms in a fierce war that saw the deaths of almost one million Spaniards. ▶

Several decades of in-fighting, resentment and rivalry erupted into bloody civil war in Spain on July 17, 1936, with a military revolt against the democratically elected Republican government. The coup attempt ultimately failed, but acted as a catalyst for open warfare between the many and various rival factions in Spain. Although the two sides in the war might roughly be described as Republicans and Nationalists, they were, in fact, drawn from many rival groups. The Republican side was drawn from city and agricultural workers and the educated left-wing middle classes. They faced a Nationalist enemy composed of key elements in the army, land owners and businessmen, all of whom had the backing of the Roman Catholic Church in Spain. Also thrown into this melting pot were supports of various extremist political groups such as fascists (the Falangists), Communists and militant anarchists, plus assorted Monarchists, Liberals and Socialists.

There was also a great deal of foreign involvement, due, in no small part, to the fact that neither side had the capacity to win a civil war unaided. Although around 60,000 foreigners joined the Republican International Brigade, much of the external aid during the war came from various govern-

ments. The Republicans received equipment and supplies from the Soviet Union as well as France and Mexico. But it was the essentially right-wing Nationalists who received the most help. Germany and Italy lost little time in supplying tanks, planes and even ground troops to help the side they believed would be most sympathetic to the fascist cause.

For much of the latter half of 1936, each side in the war consolidated their territories. Although the Republicans held large areas of Spain, they lost ground to the Nationalists in places such as Spanish Morocco, the Canary Islands and most of the Balearic Islands, as well as some parts of the country north of the Guadarrama Mountains. During the process of consolidation atrocities were carried out by both sides and at least 50,000 people were executed or murdered. Neither side accepted the

authority of the other to govern and so each set up a government based in different parts of the country. The Republican side was

led, from September 1936, by Francisco Largo Caballero, who was succeeded in May 1937 by Juan Negrin. The Nationalists

▲ **A French journalist intercedes to save the life of a young Spanish child caught up in the fighting. The Spanish Civil War saw human atrocities carried out by both Nationalist and Republican supporters.**

▲ A teenage girl takes careful aim as she joins the Nationalist firing line. The bitter rivalries between both sides would continue for decades after the end of war.

were led, from October 1, 1936, by General Francisco Franco.

During November 1936, the Nationalists began to advance against the Republicans and soon reached the outskirts of Madrid, but failed to take the city. The Basque region was captured in the summer of 1937, followed by Asturias. By October 1937, the Nationalists under Franco controlled the whole of the northern coast of Spain. From there they headed eastward, arriving at the Mediterranean in April 1938. With the Republicans now concentrated in Catalonia, Franco advanced his troops into that region, forcing the Republicans towards the north, where the only possible escape was by crossing the Pyrenees into France. By February 1939, over half a million Republicans, drawn equally from troops and civilians, had fled into France, to be followed shortly by the members of the beleaguered Republican government. The only territory that remained in Republican hands by March 1939 was Madrid, but in-fighting between Communist and anti-Communist factions defending the city all but handed Madrid to the Nationalists,

who marched through its streets on March 28. Any Republican groups remaining in Spain after this date either disbanded or surrendered, effectively bringing the Spanish Civil War to an end on April 1, 1939.

No one knows for certain exactly how many people lost their lives in the course of this tragic conflict, although it has been estimated to be between 500,000 and 1,000,000. It would

appear that Spain suffered unduly as a result of providing the opportunity for various factions within Europe to fight out their battles away from their own lands. Many outside Spain saw the civil war in simple terms, usually as a conflict between right and left, between fascism and Communism, or capital and labour, and lent their support according to the group they sided with. There is even a case to be

made for the claim that Spain provided a testing ground for the new weapons and techniques being developed by countries like Germany and Italy for use in the World War that every one knew was brewing.

An unfortunate feature of the civil war is the fact that the killing did not stop on April 1, 1939. Franco, determined to consolidate his control of the country, executed thousands of the captured Republicans and suspected Republican sympathizers. His new regime was further threatened by the outbreak of World War Two just five months after the fighting in Spain came to an end. Franco was determined to keep his impoverished country out of the war and lost no time in declaring Spanish neutrality but in practice remained sympathetic and supportive of the Axis powers led by Hitler's Germany.

Franco continued with this stance until 1943 when, in an act of craven self-preservation, he declared full Spanish neutrality as the tide of war began to turn away from the Nazis.

▼ A group of "Loyalist" Nationalist troops parade a troop of Republican prisoners following a hard-won victory at Somosierra in November 1936.

TENSIONS RISE BETWEEN ARABS AND JEWS

▲ **British troops stand guard along the Wailing Wall, a seemingly unending flashpoint for conflict between the Arab and Jewish communities of Palestine.**

The Arab-Jewish conflict, so much a feature of the news during the twentieth century, had its roots in a document known as the Balfour Declaration. On November 2, 1917, Arthur (later Lord) Balfour wrote, in his capacity as British Foreign Secretary, to Lord Rothschild. His letter included the following statement: "His Majesty's Government view with favour the establishment in Palestine of a national home for the Jewish people, and will use their best endeavours to facilitate the achievement of this object, it being clearly understood that nothing shall be done which may prejudice the civil and religious rights of existing non-Jewish communities in Palestine, or the rights and political status enjoyed by Jews in any other country."

Despite having made contradictory statements to French, the Russians and several Arab leaders, the British hoped that a pro-Zionist statement at this time would influence Jewish opinion in the United States in favour of the Allies. Combined with this was the belief that a Jewish community in Palestine, with strong ties to the British, would help to keep secure the Suez Canal and routes to India. Although the Balfour Declaration indicated the British desire to set up a home for the Jews within Palestine, it fell short of the hopes of the Zionists in that it did not declare that Palestine would become the principle Jewish homeland.

The council of the League Of Nations approved a British mandate over Palestine on July 24, 1922, which included provision for the Balfour Declaration. On September 22, 1922, the British announced that the Balfour Declaration would apply only to a quarter of Palestine. This meant, in theory at least, that Jewish immigration to the rest of Palestine was not covered by the British mandate.

The immediate result of this statement was to create tension between the Arab and Jewish communities. The Jews attempted to acquire as much land as possible in Palestine, and increase their numbers in the region through immigration. The Arabs sought to block both Jewish land acquisition and the influx of Jews. Inevitably, there was conflict between the two sides, which sometimes erupted into violence. The period from 1923 to 1929 was relatively quiet, however, due in some part to the decline in Jewish immigration to Palestine: more people left than arrived in 1928.

The rise of fascism in Europe from around 1930 saw a huge increase in the number of Jews seeking to enter Palestine and the Jewish population grew to the point where it accounted for some 30 per cent of the total for the region. In November 1935, the Arabs demanded an end to Jewish immigration and a freeze on any further transfers of land to the Jews. A division set out in 1937 which proposed that two-

▼ **Women troops on parade during a training exercise at the Jewish Palestinian settlement at Haganah.**

thirds of the land remain under arab control was rejected by Zionist leaders.

► **Holy territory to both Arabs and Jews alike, Palestine has remained at the heart of Middle Eastern conflict throughout the twentieth century.**

NAZI AIRSHIP EXPLODES

◄ **In one of the most spectacular air disasters of all time, within the space of less than 30 seconds the airship *Hindenburg* was reduced to smouldering wreckage.**

Cinema audiences across America were presented with the deeply shocking sight of the destruction of the great German airship the *Hindenburg* in May. The airship, the pride of the Nazi Third Reich and the largest aircraft ever to take to the skies, exploded during an attempted landing at Lakehurst Field in New Jersey on the evening of May 6. For the first time in history, a film crew was on hand to capture every moment as the airship caught fire and then exploded before crashing to the ground. Also on hand was radio presenter Herbert Morrison of the Chicago-based radio station WLS.

Morrison was in the middle of reporting the late arrival of the *Hindenburg* from its base in Germany when the unthinkable happened and the airship caught fire. Within moments, his broadcast turned from a general

description of the highly impressive airship into a macabre stream of consciousness. Unable to contain his obvious feelings of horror at what was occurring before his very eyes, Morrison's description of events began to fragment but few who heard his broadcast will ever forget the experience. Astonishingly, a number of people survived the crash, but in the 30-or-so seconds between the first flames and the crash landing, 35 people lost their lives and one more died of his injuries the next day.

The *Hindenburg* represented the embodiment of the dreams of Dr Hugo Eckener, the man who had almost single-handedly rescued the Zeppelin Company from financial collapse after World War One. By forming an unholy alliance with the Nazis, whom he openly detested, Eckener had secured the funding for the

Hindenburg, which was to have been the Zeppelin Company's flagship for the scheduled transatlantic route between Germany and North America. Having flown around the world at the helm of the *Hindenburg's* sister ship, the *Graf Zeppelin*, Eckener was convinced that the future of civil aviation lay with the great airships.

Both the *Hindenburg* and the *Graf Zeppelin* had been used as tools of propaganda during the previous year by the Nazis, who presented them as symbols of the might of the Third Reich. In reality, the fact that both airships were inflated with the highly inflammable gas hydrogen meant that they would have been extremely vulnerable to attack.

When the *Hindenburg* was originally constructed, it was designed to be filled with helium, a very much safer gas. Unfortunately, the Americans possessed the only plentiful supply of the gas and had earlier passed the Helium Control Act (1927), which effectively banned the export of helium from the United States. Although sabotage was a suspected cause of the crash, it was never proved.

'38

HOMELAND WELCOMES TRIUMPHANT HITLER

Swastikas flew over the Austrian capital of Vienna from March 14, 1938 after Adolf Hitler and his Nazi army entered the city to an enthusiastic welcome from the Austrian people. Austria holds the unwanted distinction of being the country in which Hitler was born and he returned in triumph to his homeland after persuading the new Austrian Chancellor, Artur Seyss-Inquart, of the wisdom of a union, or *Anschluss*, between the two countries.

The previous Austrian Chancellor, Kurt von Schuschnigg, had been opposed to Hitler's plans but was forced to resign. His replacement, himself a Nazi, immediately invited Hitler and his army into Austria to act as a peace-keeping force in the event of any civil disorder. Although this move was in violation of the Treaty Of Versailles, Hitler lost no time in declaring that "The German nation will never again be rent apart." As soon as the Nazis were established in Austria they set in motion a *pogrom* against the Austrian Jews, causing many of them to flee from their own countrymen in fear of their lives.

Having incorporated Austria into

▲ Hitler is given an enthusiastic welcome as he makes a triumphant return to the country of his birth.

Germany, Hitler then set his sights on the German-speaking border areas of Czechoslovakia, known as the Sudetenland. This region had been placed under Czechoslovakian control by the Treaty of Saint-Germain in 1919, a move that was resented by many Germans living there at the time. Further discrimination against Germans by Czech officials, combined with the spread of Nazi propaganda to the region during the 1930s, created an area that was ripe for the taking by Hitler.

Tensions between the Sudetenland Nazi Party and the Czechoslovakian government led to a number of concessions being made to the Nazis, yet they still continued to demand full autonomy for the region. Against

a background of rising tension in the Sudetenland, with the Czech government unable or unwilling to meet what were, in actual fact, Adolf Hitler's demands, Great Britain and France arranged to meet Germany and her Italian ally in Munich to discuss the matter on September 29.

The French were unwilling to honour their treaty with the Czechs, and the British premier, Neville Chamberlain, was determined to pursue a misguided policy of appeasement towards Hitler. No doubt fearing for the safety of their own countries, the French and British combined with Germany and Italy and demanded that the Sudetenland be ceded to Germany by October 10. Germany marched into the Sudetenland on October 5.

MUSSOLINI DECLARES FASCIST SOLIDARITY

As storm clouds gathered over Europe, and the very real possibility of war became apparent to increasing numbers of people, Benito Mussolini, the Fascist leader of Italy announced his intention to honour the Rome–Berlin Axis declared during his visit to Berlin in 1936.

Italy's invasion of Abyssinia the previous year had done much to damage Mussolini's standing within the League Of Nations and his continued desire to see Italy grow into an imperialist power ultimately drove him to form an alliance with the Nazis.

Hitler's description of Mussolini

as "the leading statesman in the world" may have done much to satisfy *Il Duce*'s rampant egomania but in reality it served only to disguise the fact, at least from the Italian leader, that the pact with Germany had turned Italy into little more than a satellite state, a process that became

NEWS IN BRIEF

- Otto Hahn becomes the first scientist to split a uranium atom, releasing atomic energy
- John Logie Baird demonstrates the first colour television
- Films released during the year include Michael Curtiz's *The Adventures of Robin Hood*, Sergei Eisenstein's *Alexander Nevsky*, Howard Hawks's *Bringing Up Baby* and Alfred Hitchcock's *The Lady Vanishes*
- Italy retains the third football World Cup after Mussolini sends the players a telegram saying "Win or die"

January
- Australia celebrates 150 years of European settlement

February
- Hitler declares himself Commander of the German armed forces
- British foreign minister Anthony Eden resigns after disagreements with Prime Minister Neville Chamberlain over appeasement of Germany

March
- Nikolai Bukharin is one of 18 senior Communists executed after show trials in the USSR
- German troops enter Austria, which is subsequently declared part of Germany
- British Prime Minister Neville Chamberlain vows to defend France and The Netherlands against Germany

April
- Franco's troops make huge advances in Catalonia
- Fascist plot foiled in Romania

complete when the Italians adopted Hitler's anti-semitic laws and began to embark upon a similar persecution of Italy's Jewish population.

▶ **Two of a kind – Adolf Hitler (left) and Benito Mussolini (right) declare a single vision of a new fascist Europe.**

WAR OF THE WORLDS SPREADS PANIC

▲ **Orson Welles convinced many Americans that New Jersey had been invaded by Martians.**

Proving the adage that you can fool all of the people some of the time, Orson Welles, the *enfant terrible* of the entertainment world, spread panic throughout much of North America with his highly original radio adaptation of the H G Wells science fiction classic *War Of The Worlds*. Under the guise of a news flash, Welles, posing as a reporter, introduced "eye-witness" accounts of what sounded like an invasion of New Jersey by technologically advanced aliens, presumed to be from the planet Mars. Quite why Martians would wish to single out New Jersey for attention was never fully explained.

In reality, this was one of a series of ground-breaking adaptations of popular novels by the Mercury Theatre, a drama group founded by Welles in 1937 with the original intention of presenting updated, modern-dress versions of the plays of William Shakespeare. Although the group was fairly popular with regular listeners, the publicity and notoriety generated by the October 31 broadcast did much to elevate the status of the group and in particular that of the group's leader, Orson Welles. Welles went on to make the classic film *Citizen Kane* in 1940, considered by many to be the greatest film ever made.

DAWNING OF THE JET AGE

In 1938, a company called Power Jets Limited demonstrated their latest invention before a far from interested group from the British Air Ministry. The company, which had been formed by Frank Whittle, a graduated of the RAF College at Cranbourne, had produced the first working prototype of the jet engine. Although the invention was confined to a workshop bench for the purposes of the demonstration, Whittle proposed that his new engine be fitted to the air force's existing fighter planes in order to give them a speed advantage over other aircraft.

Whittle had little success in convincing the men from the ministry of the advantages of his invention until German engineers, working independently of Whittle, applied their version of the technology to one of their own aircraft.

▶ **Frank Whittle (right) explains the workings of the jet engine. It was fear of invasion by Nazi Germany that would later drive the development of jet aircraft.**

On August 27, 1939, the Heinkel-built He 178, powered by a jet engine designed by Hans von Obain, took to the skies over Germany, forcing the British to take Whittle's invention seriously.

'39

NEWS IN BRIEF

- Germany launches the battleship *Bismarck*
- Films released during the year include Victor Fleming's *Gone with the Wind* and *The Wizard of Oz*, George Marshall's *Destry Rides Again*, William Dieterle's *The Hunchback of Notre Dame*, Jean Renoir's *La Regle du Jeu*, and John Ford's *Stagecoach*
- Books published this year include *The Grapes of Wrath* by John Steinbeck, *Finnegan's Wake* by James Joyce and *Goodbye to Berlin* by Christopher Isherwood

January
- Franco's troops capture Barcelona
- Hitler re-opens the Reichstag
- Death of the Irish poet William Butler Yeats

February
- France and Britain officially recognize the Spanish nationalist government under Franco
- Death of Pope Pius XI; Pius XII succeeds

March
- German troops enter Bohemia and Moravia; Hitler enters Prague, Czechoslovakia
- Poland rejects German claims to Danzig and the Polish corridor to the Baltic
- Germany annexes Memel in Lithuania
- Spanish Civil War ends as Nationalists take Madrid

▲ The aftermath of *Kristallnacht* revealed that few Jewish homes and businesses had escaped the ravages of the Nazi purge.

Jews attempting to flee Nazi oppression and violence in Central Europe faced problems entering the proposed Jewish homeland in Palestine. Although the British had earlier attempted to establish a home for the Jews in the region, objections from the majority Arab community to further Jewish immigration into Palestine led the British to declare a suspension of immigration for six months. This was done in the hope of avoiding an all-out rebellion by the Arab community, who had been protesting against the Jewish presence in Palestine since the 1920s.

▶ Jewish refugees from Germany and Austria arrive in Great Britain to begin a new life free from the terror of growing Nazi repression.

Jewish immigration to Palestine had been rising steadily throughout the 1930s, but had increased massively since the Nazis began a campaign of violent oppression against the Jews. Any doubts as to the Nazis' intentions were dispelled on the night of November 9, 1938, when an apparently "spontaneous" outbreak of violence against Jewish communities in Germany occurred. By the end of the night, several hundred synagogues had been burned down, thousands of Jews had been badly beaten and almost every known Jewish shop had been looted. The streets of many German cities where so heavily covered in broken glass that the night became known as *Kristallnacht*, or Crystal Night.

The British, although painfully aware of what was happening in Germany, were reluctant to provoke the Arab community in Palestine any further than they had already done. The outbreak of World War Two in September 1939 stiffened the British resolve to restrict Jewish immigration into Palestine for fear that it would affect the stability of the region. Despite the British attempts to restrict immigration, however, many Jews continued to enter Palestine illegally, driven by the understandable desire to escape murderous oppression at the hands of the Nazis.

FRANCO RULES SPAIN

The collapse of the Republican forces in the Spanish Civil War at the end of March effectively handed control of Spain to the leader of the rival Nationalist army, General Francisco Franco. Franco assumed command of the Nationalists on October 1, 1936, and at the same time was declared head of state. The Republicans, who still held control of several large regions of Spain, refused to recognize his government and so the civil war, which had broken out in July 1936, raged on. General Franco's Nationalist army spent the next three years fighting a particularly vicious campaign across the whole of Spain with the support and aid of the German and Italian governments. Although the Republicans received support from the Soviet Union, France and Mexico, and managed to recruit 60,000 foreigners into the International Brigade to fight against Franco, they proved to be no match for the well-trained professional soldiers of the Nationalist Army, whose numbers were further swelled by German and Italian troops. It is a measure of the determination and courage of the Republican side, however, that Franco took three years to defeat them.

After assuming power, Franco established what was to all intents and purposes a fascist dictatorship. One of his first actions was to order the mass executions of thousands of Republicans and Republican sympathizers who had opposed him during the civil war. When World War Two broke out just five months after the end of the Spanish Civil War, Franco presided over a country that was in no state to cope with further conflict. Having little choice but to declare Spain neutral, Franco in reality remained sympathetic to the Axis powers who had provided support during the civil war.

After the war Franco, the last fascist dictator in Europe, and Spain, were largely ostracized by the League of Nations and its successor, the United Nations.

▲ The Nationalist victory saw the start of an era that gave General Francisco Franco undisputed authority over Spain for the next 36 years.

WAR IN THE EAST

The origins of Japan's conflict with China in the 1930s lay in a belief, widely held in Japan, that the Japanese had an almost spiritual right to become established on an equal footing with the great imperial powers of the time. Extremist elements in the Japanese military looked with envious eyes on the great empires of others and demanded for Japan the absolute right to control the destiny of China, and ultimately rule all of Asia. Accompanying this demand was the frequently repeated claim that the denial of this "right" was an injustice that the Japanese sense of national honour could not ignore. In essence, this was little more than nationalist chauvinism in a spiritual guise, a stance that found many parallels among the fascist ideologies of Germany and Italy.

Despite the failure of a right-wing coup in Japan in February 1936, ultra-nationalist extremists still appeared to dictate much of Japan's policy towards her neighbour. Having established the puppet state of Manchukuo on the Chinese mainland in 1931, the Japanese army continued to exert an influence in Northern China. On July 7, 1937, an incident involving Japanese and Chinese troops at the Marco Polo Bridge, near Peking, proved to be the spark that led to war.

Japanese action was swift and brutal, but the Chinese Nationalists, under Chiang Kai-shek, failed to back down and soon the war began to spread. The Japanese attacked Shanghai, to the south, and by December 1937 had captured the Nationalist capital of Nanking.

The brutal behaviour of Japanese troops towards the city's residents after the capture of Nanking was one of the most disgraceful episodes of any conflict in the history of warfare – and a foretaste of their inhumanity in World War Two, but if the Japanese hoped that their barbarism would bring an end to the war they were mistaken. Japan ultimately failed in its bid to establish control over China.

▼ A Japanese landing party prepares to invade the Chinese port of Tinghai on Chusan Island.

'39 EUROPE HEADS INTO WAR ONCE MORE

On September 3, 1939, Britain and France declared war on Germany. So began World War Two, just less than 21 years after the end of World War One, the so-called war to end all wars. Against a background of aggressive diplomacy, which had seen Germany gain effective control of Austria and Czechoslovakia, Britain and France had followed a course of passive appeasement with Hitler. After the Munich agreement of September 1938, both Britain and France had hoped that Hitler would honour his promise to pursue his goals though diplomatic means. But when, in March 1939, Hitler threatened to bomb Prague into the ground unless the Czechs allow German occupation of the entire country, few observers were in any doubt as to Hitler's intentions towards the rest of Europe. A pattern of aggressive diplomacy – essentially blackmail – followed by military occupation was emerging and the other European powers began to fear that Hitler would pick them all off one by one.

Deciding on a unified show of force to try to persuade Hitler to reconsider his plans, Britain and France formed what it hoped would be a deterrent alliance with Poland and Romania on March 31. Rumours of a possible German invasion of Romania, although unfounded, proved to be the spur to the alliance. The very grave possibility of a full-scale war in Europe drew closer after August 23, when Hitler and Joseph Stalin, the leader of the Soviet Union, announced a non-aggression pact. The awful significance of the pact became clear when Germany began its invasion of Poland on September 1, with the Soviet Union attacking Poland from the east on September 17. Britain and France had little choice but to declare war on Germany on September 3,

▲ **After meeting Adolf Hitler, British Prime Minister Neville Chamberlain claimed to have secured "peace for our time".**

just two days after the invasion of Poland began.

The ferocity and speed of the German advance caught everyone by surprise. Within three days of crossing the border, Germany had cut a path right through the entire country. Just eight days after the invasion began, German troops were camped outside Warsaw. This was a powerful demonstration of what Hitler called a lightning war, or *Blitzkrieg*, and it was a tactic that he was to follow throughout the early part of the war. The start of a *Blitzkrieg* was usually marked by an attack across the border using tanks, followed by mechanized infantry and then foot soldiers supported from the air by the *Luftwaffe* (German air force).

PLAN POWOŁANIA

◀ **The people of Poland put up a spirited resistance to the Nazis, but were overwhelmed by the ferocity of the Blitzkrieg.**

◄ King George VI addresses the nation from Buckingham Palace. The King earned the respect of his people by refusing to leave London during the "Blitz".

After the Soviet Union and Germany had finished dividing Poland between themselves, the Soviet Union went on to occupy Estonia, Latvia and Lithuania before attacking Finland, which fell in March 1940. Germany continued the war at sea, with a highly effective U-boat campaign against British shipping. Many people assumed that Hitler would move east after the invasion of Poland, but the determination of the Polish defence, particularly in Warsaw, forced Hitler to change his plans. Even so, by April 1940, Germany had taken the whole of Denmark and captured vital Norwegian ports. On May 10, Hitler was finally ready to turn his attention to the west.

Using the by now tried and tested techniques of the *Blitzkrieg*, the German forces swept all before them. The Netherlands, Belgium and Luxembourg fell with awe-inspiring and shocking speed as Hitler's army of darkness headed towards their ultimate prize of France, landing stage for the invasion of Great Britain. The French defences caved in with almost indecent haste and by June 22 France was under German control. (Hitler's troops had by then managed to occupy 60 per cent of France, including the capital, Paris, while the rest of France was turned into a neutral state governed by French collaborators in the spa town of Vichy.)

In less than a year, the German army had conquered the whole of mainland Europe. Although Great Britain remained undefeated, its troops had been driven into the sea and there was little prospect of a return to Europe without significant aid from either the Soviets, who were already locked into a non-aggression pact with Germany, or from the United States. At this time the USA had little interest in getting involved in the war in Europe and had, for the most part, assumed that the German invasion of Britain was inevitable and that Britain would ultimately suffer the same fate as the rest of Europe. And so it was that Britain stood alone in its battle against the all-conquering German army.

Operation Sea Lion, as Hitler's plan for the invasion of Britain was called, was to be preceded by massive bombing raids against Britain's ports and the defeat of the Royal Air Force. It was hoped that this would reduce Britain's ability and willingness to fight back and at the same time secure the skies for the *Luftwaffe*. In preparation for war, however, Britain had wisely invested in state-of-the-art technology and the simple truth was that the Royal Air Force was equipped with some of the finest fighter aircraft in the world, flown by some extraordinarily brave and committed pilots, and had the most advanced early warning radar system in existence at this time. Combined, these facts were to prove more than a match for the German *Luftwaffe*.

◄ Rapid and repeated bombings by the *Luftwaffe* paved the way for a resistance-free land invasion by the German army.

1940-49

Within six months of the start of the 1940s, Hitler's "Blitzkrieg" military strategy had dominated much of Western Europe. Poised to invade Britain, the Nazis attempted a demoralization campaign by launching a bombing blitz on London. Here was a fundamental development of modern warfare: the fighting in World War One had largely been restricted to soldiers on the Eastern and Western Fronts; now ordinary civilians were being targeted. During the course of the war, the Nazis unleashed increasingly destructive weapons on London and other British cities, culminating in the V1 and V2 "flying bombs". Britain also used the same policy as in the horrific blanket bombing raids of Dresden and Berlin. Ultimately, Hitler's planned invasion of Britain never took place, thanks in part to the valiant war waged by the RAF in the skies above the English Channel.

The war took on a truly global scale at the end of 1941 when Japan, with eyes on territorial gains in the Pacific region launched an unprovoked attack on the United States fleet at Pearl Harbor in Hawaii. The aggression brought America into open war against the Axis powers. But from 1943, with Hitler having unsuccessfully attempted to invade the Soviet Union, the war gradually turned in favour of the Allies. In April 1945 British, American and Russian forces were able to march into the German capital of Berlin, bringing the European war to an end. Although the Soviet Union had fought on the side of the Allies, there was deep mistrust in the West for Stalin and Communism. The end of World War Two had left the Soviet Union with complete dominance of Eastern Europe. The Soviet-occupied sector of Germany gave birth to a new state – the German Democratic Republic. Gradually, the surrounding Eastern European states – Czechoslovakia, Poland, Hungary, Bulgaria, Yugoslavia and Romania – all found themselves Communist states and firmly under the influence of the Soviet Union. As Winston Churchill described it: "an iron curtain has descended across the Continent". By the end of the decade relations between East and the American-led West could be summed up in a phrase that would resonate for the next 45 years – it was a "Cold War".

The war in the Pacific dragged on for several months after the German surrender, Japan's early successes gradually being eroded by superior US forces. It was then that the USA took the most devastating step imaginable to end the war. In one of the defining moments of the twentieth century, at 8:15 on August 6, 1945, a single atom bomb was parachuted to its target in the centre of the Japanese city of Hiroshima where it detonated sending a 23,000 foot "mushroom" cloud high into the skies above the city. Over a third of the 300,000 population were killed at a stroke; many thousands more died from the effects of nuclear "fall-out". Three days later another atom bomb was dropped on the city of Nagasaki, killing a further 40,000 and creating similar devastation. These two explosions cast a long shadow over the rest of the century. It had become abundantly clear that humankind now had the power to unleash the most awesome destruction imaginable on his enemy. The powers reasoned that whoever possessed the biggest nuclear arsenal would hold the greatest influence. By the end of the decade America and the Soviet Union were engaged in an escalating arms race that gave either side the nuclear capability to destroy the entire planet.

From a moral perspective, World War Two could be said to have had a satisfactory outcome. The Nazi regime had been brutally racist in its promotion of the Aryan myth , but it was not until the discovery of the incomprehensible horror of the Nazi concentration camps that the scale of this brutality became widely known. The death camps in which the systematic extermination of Eastern European Jews had been turned into a banal exercise in industrial efficiency. There was nothing crude about this process – the camps had been designed and built by the Nazi's finest architects and engineers to operate at maximum efficiency. It is estimated that four million Jews perished in this way. Murder on such a scale remains incomprehensible. But was there anything peculiarly "German" about the rise of the Nazis and the resulting Holocaust? The unpalatable answer is that given the right set of circumstances such atrocities could probably have happened anywhere.

SOVIET INVASION OF FINLAND

Using an increasingly common rationale – that they were acting in the interests of their own security – the Soviet Union invaded Finland on November 30, 1939. After the earlier Soviet occupation of Estonia, Latvia and Lithuania – under the terms of Stalin's "Mutual Assistance Pacts" – there remained just one direct route into the USSR that was not under Moscow's control.

In October, the Soviet Union had demanded that the border with Finland be moved much further back into Finnish territory, to remove the threat of artillery bombardment on Leningrad by any occupying army. They also demanded that Finland hand over control of Petsamo, its only ice-free port, Hango at the entrance to the Gulf of Finland, and several small islands in the gulf.

While the Finns were prepared to grant most of the Soviet wishes, there was one exception – they demanded that they retain control of Hango.

When talks broke down on November 13, 1939, the Soviet Union renounced its non-aggression pact with Finland. Two days later Soviet tanks crossed the Finnish border at eight separate points while its air force mounted bombing raids on the Finnish capitol, Helsingfors.

Despite being massively outnumbered (just 200,000 troops against the entire military might of the Soviet Union), the Finns fought hard, managing to keep the Soviet forces at bay. Against all expectations, the brave Finns had brought the Soviet advance to a halt by December.

Ultimately, however, the Soviet Union was in no sense defeated. Having made a tactical withdrawal, Soviet forces regrouped and were reinforced before launching a new offensive on February 1, 1940. While the French and the British debated whether or not to assist the Finns, Soviet forces advanced successfully into Finland. On March 12, 1940, Finland was forced to surrender under terms dictated by the Soviet Union.

▲ Finnish "suicide patrols" comprising expert skiers were able to keep the might of the Soviet army at bay for almost six months.

NAZIS ENTER DENMARK AND NORWAY

The Nazi invasion of Norway was in many ways a masterpiece of planning, deception and ruthless aggression. It could be said to have started with a curious invitation-only film show at the German Legation in the Norwegian capital, Oslo, on the night of April 5.

The audience of distinguished guests, including members of the Norwegian government, were presented with a film of Germany's recent invasion of Poland. The horrific footage included scenes from the assault on Warsaw and ended with a caption that read: "For this they could thank their English and French friends".

Having left the Norwegians in no doubt as to the dangers of any kind of alliance with Germany's enemies, or to the consequences of resisting the Nazi advance, the Germans began last-minute preparations for the essentially simultaneous invasions of Norway and Denmark.

The warning signs of an impending invasion of Norway had already been made clear. On April 8, news reached the Norwegian Legation in London of sightings of German warships off the coast of Norway. News also reached Oslo of the sinking of the German troop ship, the *Rio de Janeiro,* by a Polish submarine off the south coast of Norway. Captured German troops claimed that they were heading for Bergen, on the coast of Norway, to help the

Norwegians defend themselves against the British and the French.

While the Norwegians were receiving this worrying news, events in Denmark had taken a turn for the worse. Encountering only the very slightest resistance from the Danish Royal Guard, Denmark was rapidly over-run by the Nazis on Sunday April 8. (The invasion and occupation of Denmark was so swift that news of it did not reach the Norwegians until after the invasion of their own country was under way.)

That night German warships approached Oslo from the south. At first their attack was repelled;

▲ The triumphant Nazi forces were able to reach into Scandinavia with little resistance from the small local forces.

the battle cruiser the *Blucher* and the lives of 1,000 men on board being lost.

On April 9, however, airborne troops took Oslo. Within just 48 hours, the German army had managed to put seven divisions ashore and to seize control of all the main ports in Norway. The Nazi invasion was complete.

CHURCHILL RETURNS

Winston Churchill returned on May 10 from what were later called his "wilderness years" to lead the British people in their fight against the apparently unstoppable advance of the German army. Churchill had been largely ignored when, during the 1930s, he had warned anyone who cared to listen (and many who didn't) of the danger posed by the rise of the Nazis.

After the signing of the Munich agreement, which he dismissed as a "total and unmitigated defeat", Churchill lobbied for a national coalition. Although national sentiment appeared to be on his side, the then prime minister, Neville Chamberlain, resisted this move. When Britain declared war on Germany on September 3, 1939, Chamberlain appointed Churchill to the Admiralty, where he soon proved his commitment to the task of defeating Hitler.

After Chamberlain's resignation, Churchill took over as leader of the new coalition in the twin capacity of Prime Minister and

head of the Ministry of Defence. On May 13 he stood before parliament as Prime Minister and made the first of many historic speeches, warning the British people that he had nothing to

offer them but "... blood, toil, tears and sweat". Churchill's time had arrived and he was to prove himself more than equal to the task of leading the British people during wartime.

▲ One of the grand old men of British politics, Winston Churchill's career reached its greatest peak as an inspirational war leader.

- Films released during the year include John Ford's *The Grapes of Wrath*, based on John Steinbeck's novel, Charles Chaplin's *The Great Dictator*, George Cukor's *The Philadelphia Story*, Alfred Hitchcock's *Rebecca*, Michael Curtiz's *The Sea Hawk*, Alexander Korda's *The Thief of Baghdad* and Disney's animated film, *Fantasia*
- Hattie McDaniel becomes first black actress to win an Oscar
- Bugs Bunny makes his debut
- US television company CBS makes first colour broadcast
- Be-bop develops in Minton's Playhouse, New York
- *Orchestral Variations* by Anton Webern premieres
- *Concerto de Aranjuez* by Joaquin Aranjuez premieres
- Books published this year include *The Heart Is A Lonely Hunter* by Carson McCullers, *Darkness at Noon* by Arthur Koestler, *Portrait of the Artist as a Young Dog* by Dylan Thomas, *The Power and the Glory* by Graham Greene and *For Whom the Bell Tolls* by Ernest Hemingway
- The war causes the cancellation of the twelfth Olympic games in Tokyo

'40

NAZIS LAUNCH BLITZKRIEG INVASION OF HOLLAND AND BELGIUM

▲ The Belgian government had laboured under the mistaken belief that by appeasing Hitler, a full-scale Nazi invasion could be avoided.

On the very day that Winston Churchill assumed the combined role of Prime Minister and Minister of Defence in Britain, his office was disappearing under a snowstorm of telegrams announcing the German invasion of Holland and Belgium. Just before dawn on the morning of May 10, German forces, which had been massing on the borders with the lowland countries, went into action. Artillery and air force attacks on key military positions in both Holland and Belgium were followed by the advance of German troops across a 240-km (150-mile) wide front. By May 28 it was all over and Hitler was setting his sights on France.

Neither the Belgians nor the Dutch could claim that the attack came as a complete surprise. In January, a German major had been captured after making a forced landing in Belgium. He was found to have what were undoubtedly German invasion plans for Belgium. Despite this, and despite intelligence reports which indicated that around 30 German divisions were gathering near the borders, Holland and Belgium failed to mount any serious defence. This lack of action was, in part, the result of their desire to avoid offending Hitler in the hope that he would not perceive them as a threat (and therefore leave them untouched). Unfortunately for both the Dutch and the Belgians, Hitler was not to be persuaded from mounting an invasion by their passive behaviour.

The German invasion of Holland and Belgium saw Hitler refining the tactics he had developed during the Spanish Civil War and which he had used so effectively against Poland. Known as a *Blitzkrieg* (lightning war), these tactics combined rapid armoured thrusts backed up by well-coordinated *Luftwaffe* air support and consolidated by follow-up infantry attacks.

Before the enemy knew what was happening, let alone had time to coordinate some sort of defence, German forces would destroy lines of communication and remove the country's ability to fight back by means of strikes against its key military positions. Rather than face entire armies on the battlefield, Hitler was able to paralyse a nation's defences, destroy its administration and then seize control of the country as a whole, safe in the knowledge that it was lacking organized leadership at a national level. By advancing on a wide front, it was then possible to capture land and enemy forces with the minimum loss of life or equipment being experienced by either side.

In this manner, Hitler was able to take control of most of Europe in a remarkably short space of time. In doing so, he was able to call upon the entire resources of Europe in his battles with Britain and, ultimately, the Soviet Union.

▲ A German machine gun unit defends itself against snipers hiding out in the debris from houses demolished during the Nazi invasion.

DUNKIRK EVACUATION

Towards the end of May, British forces retreating from the German advance gathered on the beaches near the French Channel port of Dunkirk. Hitler, seeing an opportunity to destroy an enemy now trapped like rats with their backs to the sea, wasted no time in unleashing the full power of his air force against the stranded men. Wave after wave of bombers dropped their deadly cargo of explosives on to the overcrowded beach and harbour at Dunkirk. Meanwhile, back in London, plans were under way to get the British Expeditionary Force (BEF) back to England.

Aware that the Belgian army was about to collapse, the British Expeditionary Force was ordered to develop a bridgehead at Dunkirk from where it could be picked up by sea. On May 26, Operation Dynamo began with the removal of the first troops from Dunkirk. On the night of May 27, the first of the famous flotilla of small boats made its way across the Channel to rescue stranded troops. The effectiveness of the evacuation was greatly increased after Admiralty officers scoured boathouses looking for suitable craft to bring the soldiers home

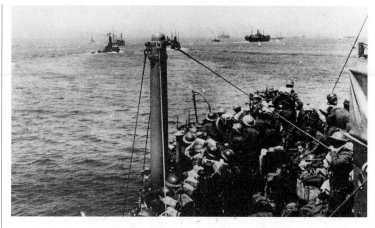

▲ In a remarkable military operation, troops from the British Expeditionary Force were evacuated from the beaches of Dunkirk.

and later put out an appeal for assistance from boat owners across England.

By May 30, what remained of the BEF was believed finally to have arrived in Dunkirk. From an original armada of around forty small vessels, the flotilla that rescued them grew to the point where over four hundred small boats of every description were being piloted by volunteers who ferried troops from the bomb- and bullet-strewn beaches to larger ships waiting out in the Channel. Between May 31 and June 1, 132,000 men were pulled out of Dunkirk in this way, but it was becoming clear that the BEF

would not be able to keep the Germans at bay for much longer.

By June 2, despite the best efforts of the Royal Air Force, it was no longer possible to pull troops out of Dunkirk during daylight hours because of the activities of the Luftwaffe. It was decided to make one last effort to remove as many men as possible on the night of June 2, and to this end more ships than ever before were dispatched to Dunkirk under cover of darkness. Unfortunately, French forces caught up in fighting at the perimeter of the beachhead were left behind as dawn broke on June 3. In a remarkable display of courage, the flotilla returned the next night and, against impossible odds, removed over 26,000 French troops from Dunkirk.

At 2.23 p.m. on June 4, the British Admiralty declared that Operation Dynamo was over. More than 338,000 troops had been rescued from the Dunkirk beaches and would one day return to fight the Germans on the mainland of Europe.

◀ In a five-day period, Operation Dynamo rescued over 300,000 Allied troops who were safely returned to mainland Britain.

October
- Princess Elizabeth makes her first broadcast to the nation

November
- Democrat candidate Franklin D Roosevelt re-elected President of the US for a third term
- Thai troops invade French territories in Laos and Cambodia
- Deaths of British statesman Neville Chamberlain, sculptor, engraver and writer Eric Gill, and press baron Lord Rothermere

December
- Death of F Scott Fitzgerald author of *Tender is the Night* and *The Great Gatsby*

'40

NAZIS TAKE PARIS

NEWS IN BRIEF
....

**World War
Two Chronology**

March
- Over 4,000 Polish army officers massacred by Soviet Army in the Katyn forest, Poland
- Soviet forces breach the Mannerheim Line in Finland
- Finland comes to terms with USSR, ending Russo-Finish War

April
- Britain breaks German "Enigma" communications code
- German invasion of Norway
- First and second Battles of Narvik in Norway between German and British warships
- British and French forces land in Norway
- German troops take Dombas in Norway
- British forces begin withdrawal from Norway

May
- German troops invade Belgium, Luxembourg and The Netherlands
- Dutch Queen Wilhelmina begins exile in Britain
- German forces cross the River Meuse near Sedan
- Rotterdam virtually destroyed by bombing
- Dutch army surrenders
- German mechanized forces begin rapid advance down the Somme Valley
- Amiens and Arras captured by German forces
- Allied line broken at Sedan; German advance splits Allied forces

With the evacuation of the British Expeditionary Force from Dunkirk, along with nearly 140,000 French troops who suddenly found themselves on British soil after fleeing the advancing German army, it was almost inevitable that France would soon fall. In many respects the war was already lost for the French, but there were a few days of relative inactivity by the Germans while their divisions re-deployed prior to the march on Paris.

Just when it seemed that the situation could get no worse, the Italians threw their hat into the ring by declaring war on the massively weakened French on June 10. It is to the eternal credit of the French army, however, that despite their desperate position they succeeded in repelling all attempts by Italian forces to cross the border into France. They were not, alas, to prove so successful in keeping the Nazis at bay.

The French had been relying on the Maginot Line to protect them from any German invasion. This was a series of fortifications running from the Swiss border near Basle, along the left bank of the Rhine and up as far as the Belgian frontier to the south of the Ardennes Forest. The Germans indulged the French belief in this increasingly unlikely scenario by keeping General Wilhelm von Leeb's army Group C facing the Maginot Line. With the fall of Belgium, however, the Germans now had a route into France that would allow them to side-step these defences entirely.

The French had considered the Ardennes Forest to be impassable to tanks, but the Germans succeeded in bringing their tanks and troops through the forest and attacking the French at the weakest point in their defences on May 12. The French belief in the impassability of the Ardennes by

▲ **A sight that many Parisians believed impossible – a regiment of Nazi troops march through the Arc de Triomphe.**

German tanks meant that they had little in the way of suitable weapons to fight off an attack by armoured divisions and they soon fell back. On May 16 alone, the Germans were able to advance 80 km (50 miles) across France.

By June the battle was all but lost. German troops marched unopposed into Paris on June 14, by which time the French government had fled to Bordeaux and was seeking a way out of its alliance with Britain.

Paul Reynaud, the French Prime Minister, was replaced by Marshal Pétain who immediately began negotiating terms with the Germans. On June 22, the French formally surrendered and France was divided into occupied territories, under German control, and unoccupied territories governed by Pétain from the new capital at Vichy, an arrangement which the majority of the French accepted without argument. Back in London, General Charles de Gaulle set to work coordinating the Free French Forces and establishing a resistance movement in the hope of one day returning to free France from German tyranny.

▲ **Hitler and other high-ranking Nazi officials survey the latest of their territorial conquests.**

THE BLITZ ON LONDON

The formal surrender of France on June 22 left Germany with just one enemy in Europe: Great Britain. After consolidating his position in France, Hitler issued an order on July 16 for the preparation of the invasion of his one

▲ Surrounded by flames, the magnificent dome of St Paul's Cathedral stands defiantly above the smoke and rubble.

remaining unconquered enemy in Europe. Aware of the considerable size and power of the British Navy and the damage that it might do to any army attempting to cross the Channel, Hitler determined to win the battle in the air first before attempting a crossing. From June to September, German and British air forces fought each other in the skies over the English Channel and areas along the south coast of Britain.

For once, the British were better equipped than the Germans, at least in the air. A superior early warning system in the form of Radar combined with the Spitfire, the best fighter plane in the world at the time, meant that despite being outnumbered more than two to one, the Royal Air Force inflicted massive damage on the Luftwaffe. By the end of August, the German air force had lost over 600 aircraft. That figure was set to rise rapidly

to around 1,700 aircraft lost to the best efforts of the RAF and Hitler was soon forced to rethink his plans.

By mid-September it was clear that Germany was losing the war in the skies over Britain. On September 17, Hitler abandoned his invasion plans but stepped up the aerial bombing campaign. The Blitz, as it became known, had begun in earnest.

The initial bombing raid had actually been against London on September 7. The Luftwaffe, under the direct orders of Hitler – who was beside himself with rage over an earlier attack on Berlin by the Royal Air Force – had launched the attack in retaliation to the RAF's actions over Germany rather than for any real tactical reasons. The bombing of London continued for 57 consecutive nights, but also spread to industrially significant regions, such as Coventry and the port of Liverpool.

▲ A milkman makes his daily deliveries through the debris, as Londoners try to carry on with life during the Blitz.

The Luftwaffe's bombing raids continued throughout the winter months. There was a brief lull during February but the bombing resumed during March and April before eventually petering out as Hitler switched his attentions to other theatres of war. Although Britain's cities would continue to be a target for the German air force, the Blitz was finally over.

▲ The aftermath – the heart of London's commercial district viewed from the gallery of St Paul's Cathedral.

- British government assumes emergency powers
- Evacuation of Allied forces from Dunkirk begins
- Boulogne captured by German troops
- Belgian army surrenders to Germany
- British troops recapture Narvik
- Fascists in Britain, including Oswald Mosley, interned

June
- German armoured troops occupy north- and southwest France
- Italy orders its ships to neutral ports
- Cease-fire in Norway
- German troops cross the River Seine in France
- Italy declares war on France and Britain
- Italian troops invade southern France
- British troops withdraw from Narvik
- German troops capture Paris
- Spanish troops occupy the International Zone of Morocco
- Soviet forces enter the Baltic States
- Soviet occupation of Lithuania, Estonia and Latvia completed
- Marshal Pétain begins armistice negotiations with Germany; anti-armistice politicians (including General de Gaulle) leave France for Britain
- Unilateral French armistice with Germany; France partitioned into German-occupied and Vichy French-controlled areas
- Armistice between Vichy France and Italy
  Japanese forces invade French Indochina
- USSR demands Bessarabia and Bukovina territories from Romania
- Romania acquiesces to USSR; Soviet forces occupy Bessarabia and Bukovina
- General de Gaulle becomes leader of the Free French
- German troops occupy the British Channel Islands

ITALY JOINS THE WAR

As the beleaguered British Expeditionary Force was attempting to evacuate its forces from Dunkirk, a new threat was looming on the horizon.

Italy had been a close ally of Germany prior to the invasion of Poland and had continued to offer moral support to the Nazis. With the apparent defeat of the rest of Europe, it seemed only a matter of time before Mussolini's Italy would join with Hitler and declare war on France and Britain.

With this in mind, British Prime Minister Winston Churchill and his French counterpart Paul Reynaud approached the American President, Franklin D Roosevelt, on May 25. Aware that Italy was likely to make territorial claims on the Mediterranean, they asked Roosevelt to contact Mussolini and make it clear that they were willing to consider any reasonable claims he might make on the region in return for peace.

Believing that he could take whatever he liked regardless of any peace deal – albeit with the assistance of the Germans – Mussolini was swift in his rejection of this approach.

At 4.45 p.m. on June 10, the Italian Minister for Foreign Affairs informed the British Ambassador that Britain should consider herself at war with Italy from midnight. A similar declaration was made to France.

With the surrender of the French on June 22, Italy was free to pursue its interests in North Africa. There were around a quarter of a million well-equipped Italian troops in the coastal provinces that stretched up to Egypt from their main base at Tripoli in Libya and they seemed poised for an attack.

With the declaration of war, the British engaged the Italians in some minor skirmishes along the border, but the real battle broke out on September 13 when the Italian army advanced into Egypt.

By September 17, the Italians had reached Sidi Barrani, where they settled for the next three months. The British took advantage of the halt in the Italian advance to send armoured reinforcements to the area.

As dawn broke on December 9, 25,000 British armoured troops attacked the Italians at Sidi Barrani. The Italian stronghold fell on December 10, and by December 15, all enemy troops had been successfully driven out of Egypt.

▲ Italian crew on the ground in the Libyan desert watching a battle between British and Axis aircraft in the skies over North Africa.

TROTSKY MURDERED

August 20 saw the death of one of the original leaders of the Russian revolution. Leon Trotsky, born Lev Davidovich Bronstein in 1879, met his end at the hand of an assassin armed with an ice pick.

Trotsky had survived an earlier assassination attempt by a group of up to 30 men armed with machine guns, but fell foul of the lone killer after bodyguards failed to notice the assassin's concealed weapon.

Trotsky had been under sentence of death ever since a show trial in Moscow, staged by his great rival for control of the Soviet Union, Joseph Stalin, had found him guilty in his absence of plotting treason against the state.

Trotsky had originally been a close ally of Vladimir Ilyich Lenin, and seemed to be the favourite to succeed him when Lenin suffered a cerebral haemorrhage in May 1922. Lenin survived but knew that his own death was imminent. He urged Trotsky to strike first at Stalin in order to gain control of the party, but Trotsky hesitated. By the time of Lenin's death in 1924, Stalin was firmly in control and Trotsky found himself increasingly isolated.

In 1926, Trotsky was dropped from the Politburo, and in 1928 he and his followers were exiled to remote regions of the Soviet Union. In 1929, he was finally thrown out of the Soviet Union and spent time in Turkey, France and Norway before ending up in Coyoacán in Mexico, where he remained until his assassination.

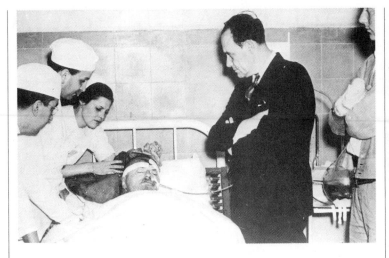

▲ Groomed by Lenin as his successor, Trotsky was outmanoeuvred and exiled by Joseph Stalin, who eventually ordered his execution.

LASCAUX GROTTO DISCOVERED

While exploring a cave in the Vézère valley near Montignac, Dordogne, in September 1939, four young Frenchmen were amazed to find what would prove to be one of the most significant displays of prehistoric art ever discovered. The cave, known as the Lascaux Grotto, consists of a main cavern with several galleries running off from it. The walls of the cave are covered with engravings, drawings and paintings of various animals, including three enormous horned aurochs, a type of European bison which is now extinct.

Also displayed on the walls are representations of ancient forms of deer, stag, oxen and horses; perhaps the most intriguing image of all is one that appears to be the form of a unicorn. Although this creature has always been considered to belong firmly to the realms of mythology, its presence in such an ancient series of paintings suggests that perhaps the myth of the unicorn was already commonplace when our Stone Age ancestors walked the Earth.

The Lascaux Grotto is thought to have been used as some sort of religious centre, where magical prehunting rituals were perhaps performed. This belief appears to be confirmed by the large number of arrows and various kinds of trap depicted in the wall paintings.

Using the carbon-14 dating technique, scientists have shown the paintings in the Lascaux Grotto to have originated between about 15,000 and 13,000 BC, a date which places them in the Perigordian period.

After the cave was opened to the public, the pictures started to fade and green fungus began to appear on some of the images. Accordingly, the grotto was closed to the general public in 1963.

▲ A detail from the main rotunda at the Lascaux Grotto, one of the earliest known examples of prehistoric painting.

- British aircraft bomb European ports
- Italian troops invade Egypt
- Japanese troops begin occupation of French Indochina
- British and Free French troops fail to take Dakar in Senegal from Vichy French forces
- Tripartite Pact between Germany, Italy and Japan agreed

October
- Passenger liner *Empress of Britain* carrying child refugees from Britain sunk by German U-boat
- Hitler and Mussolini meet at the Brenner Pass
- Germany takes control of Romania's oil production
- Free French forces take Duala in West Africa
- German lack of air dominance forces Hitler to postpone the invasion of Britain
- Burma Road supply line to China is reopened by Britain
- Greek refusal of Italian territorial demands leads to Italian invasion

November
- British forces land in Crete
- British battleship HMS *Jervis Bay* sunk in the Atlantic
- Coventry Cathedral destroyed by German bombers; later raids cause severe damage in Coventry
- British warships cripple the Italian fleet at Taranto
- Meeting between Hitler and Soviet foreign minister Molotov
- Britain launches retaliatory air raid on Hamburg
- Swiss government dissolves the Swiss Nazi Party
- Hungary and Romania endorse the Tripartite Pact

December
- Greek troops breach Italian defences in Albania and capture Porto Edda
- Greek troops overrun Italian forces in Albania
- Germany dispatches reinforcements to Italian troops in the Balkans
- British Eighth Army launches offensive against Italian forces in Libya

THE BATTLE OF BRITAIN

Shortly after Britain had declared war on Germany on September 3, 1939, the German High Command began to consider plans for a possible invasion of mainland Britain. They resolved to attack across the English Channel, coming ashore at various points along the southeast coast of England. This area of Britain had traditionally been heavily fortified as a result of several earlier historic conflicts between the British and the rest of their European neighbours – most notably the Dutch, French and Spanish – and was undoubtedly the best defended part of the coast of the British Isles.

The Germans could not have failed to have been aware of this but up until July 1940, Hitler was convinced that Britain would attempt to broker some form of peace deal with Germany.

▲ **RAF Spitfires on patrol over the English Channel during the Battle of Britain.**

◄ **RAF fighter pilots and ground crew "scramble" for their aircraft after a radar warning of incoming enemy planes.**

On July 16, however, he issued the following directive: "Since England, in spite of her militarily hopeless position shows no sign of coming to terms, I have decided to prepare a landing operation against England, and if necessary carry it out." So began the preparations for Operation Sea Lion, the German invasion of Great Britain which was supposed to bring a swift end to the war in Europe.

The German plan required that their navy create a narrow "corridor" across the Channel, protected on each side by mines and U-boats, through which men

and supplies would be ferried to the English coast.

Given Britain's superior navy, the corridor would be devastatingly vulnerable to attack unless the Luftwaffe could first clear the Royal Air Force from the skies over the English Channel. Another major consideration was the weather. From around the middle of September, the English Channel has a tendency to become fogbound. With this in mind, Hitler determined that the main part of Operation Sea Lion was to be completed by September 15.

So it was that Hermann Goering, head of the German Air Ministry, found himself with the job of destroying the RAF. Goering considered his air force to be more than equal to the task, but also believed that the British would surrender before the final invasion was mounted.

Having consolidated its position in Belgium and France during June and early July, the Luftwaffe began to make tentative strikes against British targets. This was done more out of a desire to test the opposition that to mount any serious assault.

Finally, on August 2, Goering issued the "Eagle Day" directive – an attack plan that envisaged the destruction of the British air defences prior to a landing by German forces.

In the coming battle, the British would be entirely outnumbered. Against the Luftwaffe's 1,300 bombers and 1,200 fighter aircraft, Britain could muster only 600 fighter planes. All was not lost, however, as Britain had several advantages.

Germany's bombers were incredibly vulnerable to attack from the RAF's Spitfires and Hurricanes, especially during daylight. Similarly, Germany's dive-bombers were no match for the superior speed and manoeuvrability of the RAF's fighter aircraft.

Although Germany possessed excellent fighter aircraft of their own, these were being operated at the limits of their range and were unable to stay airborne over the British coast for very long before being forced to return to base. Another advantage for Britain was that it was also ahead of the opposition in terms of Radar, which gave them a decisive advantage by robbing the attacking forces of the element of surprise.

From August 8, Germany began a period of intensive bombing of British military targets along the southeast coast and on inland to the Radar stations. Using up to 1,500 aircraft at a time, Germany

▲ Reich Marshal Hermann Goering masterminded the Luftwaffe's role in the Battle of Britain. Its defeat greatly reduced Goering's influence with Hitler.

mounted further spectacular raids on August 11, 12 and 13.

It soon became clear, however, that this was going to be no easy victory for Germany. During the period covering August 8–13, Germany lost no less than 145 aircraft. By the end of that month

the figure had risen to more than 600, while the RAF were continuing to shoot German bombers out of the sky at a faster rate than the Germans could replace them.

Realizing that this approach was not working, Hitler ordered the Luftwaffe to switch its attentions away from the coastal regions and on to Britain's cities. This was done partly in the very much mistaken belief that the British people would demand a peaceful settlement from their leaders rather than face a campaign of sustained bombing against the centres of population.

By September 15, the date that Hitler had set aside for the completion of the first phase of Operation Sea Lion, Germany was barely any nearer to dominating the skies than it had been at the start of the battle.

Although the bombing raids against Britain's cities continued

well into 1941, it was clear to all concerned that Germany was going to be in no position to launch a sea-borne assault against the British coast.

Although the RAF had lost more than 900 fighter aircraft in the course of the Battle of Britain, they had managed to shoot down around double that number of German aircraft. Germany formally abandoned the planned invasion of Britain on October 12. The Battle of Britain was over and there was no disputing the fact that the British had won.

Summing up in parliament the contribution made to the victory by the RAF, the British Prime Minister Winston Churchill made his memorable statement that "Never in the field of human conflict was so much owed by so many to so few".

▼ A German bomber drops its deadly cargo over England.

'41

- "Manhattan Project" US atomic research project, begins
- US National Gallery opens in Washington
- Mount Rushmore Memorial is completed in USA
- Films released during the year include Orson Wells's *Citizen Kane*, John Huston's *The Maltese Falcon* and Harry Watt's *Target for Tonight*
- Oliver Messiaen composes *Quartet for the End of Time*

World War Two Chronology

- Nazi Einsatzgruppen death squads begin systematic massacre of Jews in German-controlled areas of the USSR
- Transportation of German Jews to ghettos and death camps in Poland begins

January

- British troops take Bardia in Libya
- Italians forces retreat from Kenya

February

- British troops occupy Benghazi and take El Algheila in Libya
- German General Erwin Rommel arrives in Libya
- British troops in Kenya invade Italian Somaliland

March

- Bulgaria joins the Tripartite Pact alliance
- British troops launch offensive in Italian-controlled Ethiopia
- Lend-Lease Bill is approved in US

AMY JOHNSON DIES IN PLANE CRASH

On January 5, 1941 pilot Amy Johnson, "Queen of the Air" as far as the British press were concerned, drowned after crash-landing in the Thames Estuary. She had been flying a mission for the Air Ministry.

Born on July 1, 1903 in Hull in northeast England, Johnson was one of very few pioneering female aviators at a time when flying was regarded as the preserve of men.

► **Amy Johnson and the Gipsy Moth in which she made her 19-day solo flight to Australia.**

Having become interested in aviation while working as a secretary in London, Amy Johnson received her pilot's licence in 1928 and also became the first

British woman to be granted a ground engineer's licence.

In 1930 she attempted to establish a world record-breaking time for a solo flight to Darwin, Australia, from Croydon, England. Although she failed in the attempt by three days, she was still the first woman to make the solo flight, and her efforts made her enormously famous. She succeeded in setting records for a flight across Siberia to Tokyo in 1931 and in 1932 broke the record for the solo flight time to Cape Town, South Africa.

DEATH OF JAMES JOYCE

The great innovative Irish novelist James Augustine Aloysius Joyce died in Zürich, Switzerland, on January 13. Born in Dublin, Ireland, in 1882, Joyce received his education at the hands of the Jesuits, both at school and later, at University College Dublin.

He studied languages at University College but chose to devote the majority of his time to exploring his growing interest in literary matters. During this time

he managed to sell a number of reviews and short stories to various magazines. Flushed with success, Joyce resolved to make writing his occupation.

Among his best-known works are *Dubliners, A Portrait Of The Artist As A Young Man,* a largely biographical work, and *Ulysses,* which was written in a style that would later be known as "stream-of-consciousness" and which is seen as a modern parallel to Homer's *Odyssey.*

▲ **James Joyce, one of Ireland's greatest literary figures and arguably the most influential author of the twentieth century.**

ROMMEL'S AFRIKA KORPS ARRIVE IN TRIPOLI

Erwin Rommel was no ordinary tank commander. Even Winston Churchill felt compelled to comment in parliament that: "We have a very daring and skilful opponent against us, and may I say across the havoc of war, a great general". (It has been said on more than one occasion that as far as the British were concerned, the three great heroes of

the World War Two were Churchill, Montgomery and Rommel.)

Having led the Seventh Panzer division all the way to the French coast in Europe in 1940, Rommel was sent by Hitler to lead the German forces in North Africa, who were attempting to rescue the Italians.

On arriving with his advanced guard at Tripoli in Libya on

February 14, Rommel found that the Italian army was close to defeat. The growing numbers of German troops fighting under Italian command soon found themselves with a new, almost unofficial, leader who appeared to have little time for the Italian Commander-in-Chief. The feeling was mutual, as demonstrated by the rebuke that Rommel later received for advancing the Afrika Korps – the German army in North Africa – without permission from the Italians.

Rommel's apparent mastery of mechanized desert warfare soon earned him the title of "Desert Fox" as time and again he hammered the British with a combination of surprise, ingenuity and superior forces.

On March 31, he attacked the British position at Agheila. Over the next two days the British were forced to retreat, creating chaos among their ranks which led to

▲ **A Panzer division of Rommel's Afrika Korps advances rapidly through the Libyan desert.**

serious losses. In barely more than a day, he destroyed the desert flank of the British and managed eventually to push them back to

the border of Egypt. Hitler was so impressed by the efforts of his general that he soon promoted him to the rank of Field Marshal.

NAZIS ADVANCE THROUGH BALKANS INTO GREECE

The non-aggression pact between Germany and the Soviet Union, which had been agreed in August 1939, gave both countries the opportunity to divide much of northeast Europe between them. They clashed, however, over the fate of the Balkans, the easternmost peninsula of Europe.

As Nazi influence grew in Romania, the Soviets demanded the right to establish naval bases on the Bulgarian coast. The Bulgarians, horrified at the prospect of a strong Soviet presence on their territory, signed

▲ **Triumphant German troops pose on the steps of the Acropolis in Athens following the successful invasion of Greece.**

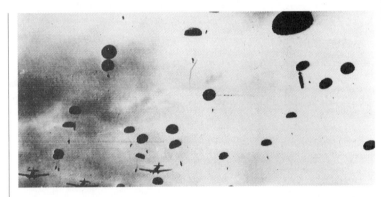

▲ **German paratroopers being dropped over Corinth in Greece as the Nazi advance continues relentlessly through the Balkans.**

a pact with Hitler in March, which should have given Germany control of the region. However, a military coup d'état in Yugoslavia, triggered by a treaty signed between Hitler and the Yugoslav regent, Prince Paul, turned that country into a potential enemy.

There was a further risk that the British would become seriously involved in the conflict between Greece and Italy. Rather than have two potentially hostile countries on his doorstep, Hitler resolved to bring them under control.

On April 6, Hitler launched a Blitzkrieg against the new government in Yugoslavia, which swept

through the country, despite fierce opposition. With the support of the Hungarians, the conflict was resolved in less than two weeks.

Meanwhile, the Italians were once again in serious trouble, this time in Greece. Mussolini, deciding to indulge in a little empire building of his own, had invaded Greece but soon found the Greeks to be more than a match for his troops. Germany stepped in, rescued the Italians and occupied Greece, reaching Athens on April 26.

With Yugoslavia and Greece now under German control, the British in North Africa were left with nowhere to retreat.

- German air raids on Britain
- General Rommel launches offensive against British forces in Libya and retakes El Algheila
- Yugoslavia joins the Tripartite Pact; anti-Tripartite Pact coup d'etat in Yugoslavia
- British forces capture Keren in Eritrea
- British naval victory over Italy in the Battle of Cape Matapan in the Mediterranean

April
- Anti-British coup led by Rashid Ali al-Ghailani in Iraq
- British forces take Italian-held Addis Abbaba in Ethiopia
- British forces take Italian-held Massawa in Eritrea
- Axis powers invade Yugoslavia and Greece; Yugoslavia surrenders to the Axis invaders, as does the Greek army
- German attack on Tobruk in Libya begins
- British troops in Greece begin evacuation

May
- Vichy France begins rounding up Jews and surrendering them to Germany
- Stalin becomes Prime Minister of the Soviet Communist Party
- Nazi party deputy leader Rudolf Hess lands in Scotland in attempt to start peace negotiations
- German airborne invasion of Crete
- British cruiser HMS *Hood* sunk by German battleship *Bismarck*
- *Bismarck* sunk by Royal Navy
- Rashid Ali overthrown by British troops in Iraq; original Iraqi government reinstated
- British troops complete evacuation of Crete

June
- Free French forces invade Syria
- Germany invades Russia (Operation Barbarossa)
- Finland declares war on USSR and invades Karelia
- German advance cuts off large Russian force near Minsk

'41

HITLER TURNS ATTENTION TO RUSSIA

Operation Sea Lion – Hitler's plan for the invasion of Great Britain – had been abandoned by the end of 1940. The operation had been a failure largely due to the courage and sheer tenacity of the Royal Air Force who fought against fearsome odds to keep Hitler's forces at bay. The arrival of bad weather in the English Channel at the start of the winter in 1940 had also made the invasion untenable. Having failed to persuade the French and Spanish to join him in a battle against British positions in the Mediterranean, Hitler now turned his attention to Russia.

On December 18, 1940, Hitler gave the order for the preparation of Operation Barbarossa – the planned invasion of Russia. This was followed by a series of campaigns in the Balkans which ensured that any advance into Russia would be on a wide front. An unlikely alliance of Romania, Hungary, Slovakia, Italy and Finland joined Germany in preparation for the invasion. Over the next few months the would-be

▲ In sharp contrast to the modern technology of the German army, Russian troops were forced to use horses to transport supplies.

invaders rallied their forces until the early hours of June 22, 1941.

Starting with an air strike, the Germans and their allies attacked Russia with the full might of 190 divisions – the greatest military force ever assembled – bringing to an end any pretence of a non-

aggression pact between Russia and Germany, and forcing Russia into the waiting arms of Great Britain and, ultimately, the United States of America.

Hitler planned to destroy the Red Army in western Russia by staging a three-pronged attack that would encircle the Russians and prevent them from dispersing into the vast territories of the Soviet Union. To this end his northern army advanced from the former Baltic states and headed towards Leningrad. His central attack force advanced from Poland with the aim of fighting

◄ The German Army had to fight its way through Russian towns and villages house by house.

their way to Smolensk and then Moscow, while the southern advance was made through the Ukraine.

In the now typical *Blitzkrieg* fashion, Hitler's combined forces of 3.6 million troops, 3,600 tanks and 2,700 aircraft blasted their way into Russia. Russia's earlier poor showing during the invasion of Finland had not gone unnoticed. Hitler had assumed that Stalin's purges of the Red Army had contributed heavily to the difficulties faced by Russia during their attack on Finland.

During the early weeks of Germany's invasion, the idea that Russia was now a spent military force appeared to be borne out. Hitler's forces met with spectacular success. Between June and

December alone, German forces captured over three million Russian troops and managed to advance hundreds of miles into Russia on some fronts. For once, however, the *Blitzkrieg* tactics that Hitler had employed so successfully elsewhere in the war began to fail.

In previous centuries, many an invading army has regretted the day it set foot on Russian territory. The sheer vastness of the Soviet Union, combined with its abundant natural resources and its severe northern winters, make it one of the greatest challenges to be faced by any invading army. Stalin had enormous reserves of manpower and, after establishing military industrial complexes beyond the Ural mountains out of the reach of the Germans, was prepared to fight a long and bitter war. Hitler knew he needed a swift victory if there was to be one at all, but by August 1941, he and his generals were in disagreement about where next to advance.

For once, Hitler's military intelligence had failed him. The astonishing advances made during the early weeks of the attack appeared now to be due,

▲ Having entered the Russian town of Vitebsk, German soldiers find nothing but burning buildings – a tactic the Russians had successfully used against Napoleon in the nineteenth century.

at least in part, to a lack of readiness on the part of the Russians. (Stalin had remained convinced that the Germans would not attempt to invade his country before 1942.) It was now becoming clear that Russia had a great deal more military strength than had previously been reported.

Rather than facing the 5,000 tanks that their intelligence had said would be waiting for them, the Germans were now staring down the barrels of 20,000

tanks. And despite their rapid advance, the Germans were taking heavy casualties: in the first six weeks of the assault, they lost 60,000 men.

The continuing advance was also proving to be more and more costly. The vast German front running the 1,600 km (1,000 miles) from the Baltic to the Black Sea stretched resources to the limit. To make matters worse, it was also apparent that Russia's less than efficient invasion of Finland

was no indication of its forces' true fighting ability.

As Hitler's army reached the great Russian cities, they found to their enormous cost that the Russian people were prepared to fight to the death rather than submit to Nazi tyranny.

An outstanding example of the Russian resolve was seen with the siege of Leningrad, which began in September 1941 and lasted until January 1944. At a cost to the inhabitants of the city of nearly 650,000 lives lost to hunger and disease, they bravely kept three-quarters of a million German troops occupied for a total of 900 days.

German troops attempting to take the Russian capital, Moscow, encountered similar examples of remarkable heroism, tenacity and skill.

Soon the fearsome Russian winter set in and Hitler realized, like Napoleon before him, that there was no easy conquest to be had in Russia.

◀ The German Army found Russia's volunteer civilian fighters to be formidable defenders of their Motherland.

'41

NEWS IN BRIEF

July
- Soviet troops retreat to the Stalin Line
- German troops break the Stalin Line and take Smolensk
- Japanese troops begin occupation of French Indochina
- German forces take Tallinn in Estonia
- Free French forces take control of Syria and Lebanon
- German forces enter the Ukraine
- Romania re-occupies Bessarabia and Bukhovina

August
- Winston Churchill and Franklin D Roosevelt sign the Atlantic Charter
- Soviet and British troops invade Iran

September
- Germans begin the siege of Leningrad
- German forces take Kiev in the Ukraine

October
- British bombing raid on Nuremberg in Germany
- Russian government moves from Moscow; German advance is 95 km (60 miles) from Moscow
- German forces take the Russian port of Odessa
- Japanese Prime Minister Prince Konoe resigns; Hideki Tojo becomes Prime Minister
- German forces take Kharkov in the Ukraine
- Germans fail in attempt to capture Moscow

SINKING OF THE BISMARCK

The German navy's most powerful warship, the *Bismarck*, a supreme symbol of the might of the Third Reich, came to the end of its short but illustrious career on May 27.

At the time of its launch in 1939, it displaced more than 52,000 tons and had a top speed of 30 knots. Armed with eight guns capable of firing 15-in (38 cm) shells, the sight of the *Bismarck* sailing over the horizon caused many a British sailor to wish he was on dry land.

Its sighting off Norway in May by a reconnaissance plane sent the Royal Navy into a frenzy. Determined to sink this symbol of German naval power, the British sent most of its North Atlantic fleet into action. After an initial contact near Iceland with two British cruisers, the mighty warship was attacked by the Royal Navy battleship *Prince Of Wales* and the battle cruiser *Hood*.

After sinking the *Hood*, the *Bismarck* headed for open seas, but was spotted again on May 26. A torpedo attack destroyed the *Bismarck*'s steering gear and again it came under heavy attack from battleships in the area.

Finally, on the morning of May 27, the once invincible battleship was sent to the bottom of the sea by three torpedoes fired from the cruiser *Dorsetshire*.

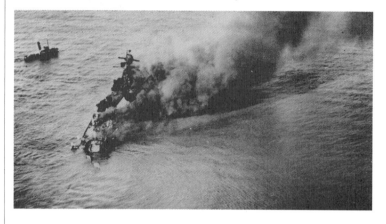

▲ **Three torpedoes from HMS *Dorsetshire* send the *Bismarck*, flagship of the German navy, to its final resting place on the bed of the Atlantic.**

ROOSEVELT FREEZES JAPANESE ASSETS IN USA

After months of threats but no action, the US government finally seized Japanese assets in America in response to Japan's continued expansion in the Far East and South Pacific region. Ever since the British and the French had become embroiled in

▲ **When General Hideki Tojo became Premier of Japan a state of outright hostility towards America quickly ensued.**

the war with Germany, the Japanese had sought to expand their empire into those areas previously under the control of these two colonial powers.

Aware of the danger that Japan posed to peace in the South Pacific region, America had attempted to halt the country's expansion plans by threatening its economy. Japan, meanwhile, attempted to convince the United States that expansion was necessary for its own survival, but at the same time grew increasingly resigned to the fact that the failure of diplomacy would lead inevitably to war.

A US embargo on the export of aviation fuel and metals to Japan came into force in July 1940 – a move which with hindsight seemed almost calculated to drive the Japanese towards an attack on the colonies.

On July 2, 1941, Japan resolved to take the Dutch East Indies. Roosevelt countered with an offer to guarantee the supply of raw materials from the colonies in return for neutrality.

Negotiations continued throughout the following months, but by this point the Japanese were firmly convinced that they could win a war against the USA in the South Pacific.

That war became inevitable after the resignation of the Japanese Prime Minister in October. His successor, General Hideki Tojo, had no interest in further negotiations with the USA and open hostilities began with a surprise attack on the US naval base at Pearl Harbor in December.

USA ESTABLISHES MILITARY BASE IN ICELAND

The USA took a step closer to joining the war in Europe when they relieved the 20,000-strong British garrison on Iceland on July 7 and established a base there.

Earlier in the war, the British had decided to occupy Iceland after Denmark fell to the Germans, exposing Iceland to attack. Faced with the prospect of Iceland becoming a staging post for long-range attacks on British shipping in the Atlantic, the British had little choice but to take over the island; its merchant fleet was already taking heavy loses while carrying essential supplies from Canada and the USA.

By April 1941, the British had established a base for merchant

▲ British and American troops erect weatherproof huts in Iceland, in preparation for the arrival of US forces there.

convey escort groups and aircraft. As German U-boats crept ever closer to US waters, President Roosevelt ordered the extension of the US security zone to include all the waters of the North Atlantic stretching as far

east as Iceland. Although the USA was, at this stage, unwilling to provide direct protection for British convoys by monitoring the zone, they were able to keep the British informed of any possible hostile vessels in the area.

ATLANTIC CHARTER

The unofficial alliance between Great Britain and the United States took a step closer to becoming a formal agreement after the leaders of both countries issued a joint declaration on August 14.

Winston Churchill had travelled in great secrecy to meet President Franklin D Roosevelt at Placentia Bay in Newfoundland. During the meeting the two men drew up the

joint declaration which became known as the Atlantic Charter.

Essentially, the agreement was a statement of common aims that declared that neither nation sought aggrandisement, territorial or otherwise, nor did they seek territorial changes without the consent of the peoples involved. They also resolved to respect or restore all sovereign rights and to promote equal access for all to

trade. They also pledged to improve labour standards, economic progress and social security. In addition, the signatories stated that they would seek to keep the seas free and to disarm potential aggressors.

Admirable as these aims were, it was the statement contained within the declaration that the two countries would seek to carry out the first five aims of the charter "after the final destruction of the Nazi tyranny" that had the greatest impact.

For a country as powerful as the USA to be seen to be making such a declaration jointly with one of Hitler's few remaining undefeated enemies amounted to little more than a thinly-veiled declaration of war which sent shock waves through the German high command.

▲ US President Roosevelt and British Prime Minister Churchill bring their countries closer together with the signing of the Atlantic Charter.

November
- German forces take Kursk in the USSR
- British aircraft carrier HMS *Ark Royal* torpedoed by German U-boat
- German re-offensive begins in an attempt to capture Moscow
- British offensive (Operation Crusader) begins in North Africa
- Soviet counter-attacks force German retreat

December
- Soviet counter-offensive to relieve Moscow begins
- British forces relieve Tobruk in Libya
- Japanese air attack on US navy in Pearl Harbor in Hawaii causes heavy American losses
- Britain and USA declare war on Japan
- Wake Island and Guam in the Pacific attacked and captured by Japan
- Japanese forces enter Malaya; British troops retreat to Singapore
- Japan begins invasion of the Philippines
- British warships *Prince of Wales* and *Repulse* sunk by Japanese aircraft
- Italy and Germany declare war on USA
- German forces near Moscow begin retreat
- Adolf Hitler takes personal control of German armed forces
- Japanese forces invade Hong Kong, which is forced to surrender
- British forces re-occupy Benghazi in Libya

ATTACK ON PEARL HARBOR

Relations between Japan and the USA, which had been strained for the better part of a decade, deteriorated to a declaration of war after the Japanese staged a surprise attack on Pearl Harbor, the US naval base on Oahu Island, Hawaii.

At just before 8 a.m. on the morning of Sunday December 7, the first wave of Japanese dive-bombers appeared over the Pacific naval base and opened fire.

No one at the base appeared to be expecting the attack. A radar operator who noticed the first wave of Japanese aircraft appearing on his monitor was told to ignore them on the grounds that the base was expecting a flight of aircraft from the USA.

The strike caught the US Navy entirely by surprise, crippling much of the US Pacific fleet in less than

▲ USS *Shaw* explodes during the unexpected raid by the Japanese air force on the US military base at Pearl Harbor. The unprovoked attack brought America into World War Two.

▲ The burning USS *West Virginia* begins its slow descent to the bed of Pearl Harbor. The attack crippled the US Pacific fleet in under an hour.

30 minutes and killing or injuring nearly 3,500 military and civilian personnel.

The attack was launched from a Japanese fleet made up of six aircraft carriers, two battleships, three cruisers and eleven destroyers. There were also 360 aircraft, which were launched from the carriers. The Japanese fleet was under the control of Vice Admiral Nagumo Chuichi and had been sent to carry out the surprise attack in the hope of crippling the entire US Pacific fleet and leaving the way open for Japan to expand throughout Southeast Asia, the Indonesian Archipelago and the South Pacific.

Against all the odds, the Japanese fleet was able to sail to a position just 445 km (275 miles) to the north of Pearl Harbor without being detected by the Americans. From here, they launched their airborne assault to devastating effect.

During the attack, the Japanese sank eight battleships, three cruisers and three destroyers and destroyed close to 200 aircraft, which never made it off the ground. Japanese losses were minimal. The best estimates place them at around 30 aircraft and fewer than 100 men.

Although the damage inflicted by the Japanese was on a massive scale, they failed to destroy the entire fleet. Of the eight American battleships that were damaged in the assault, all but two were eventually repaired. Most importantly, the Pacific fleet's two aircraft carriers were away on manoeuvres when the attack took place. The Japanese also failed to destroy the oil storage facilities at Pearl Harbor, which were essential to US operations in the region.

Reaction in the United States to the surprise attack, which had occurred before the Japanese ambassador could make a formal declaration of war against the USA, was swift and angry. President Franklin D Roosevelt described the attack as a "date which will live in infamy" – words which summed up the feeling in the country. American citizens, who had for so long claimed neutrality, were suddenly eager to enter into a war against Japan.

On Monday December 8, Congress formally declared war on Japan. The army and navy commanders at Pearl Harbor, who bore much of the blame for the way in which the base had been

caught unaware and unprepared, were relieved of duty as the USA prepared for full-scale war. Britain, until now alone in its battles against the forces of fascism, was enormously relieved when, on December 11, Japan's allies in the Axis, Germany and Italy, made a formal declaration of war against the United States. With the USA as an ally against the Germans and the Italians, the British were by now more certain than ever of the possibility of winning the war in Europe.

The earlier defeat of the French and the Dutch by the Germans had left their colonies in the Pacific region open to attack, although the Japanese had been warned off by the Americans. With the American fleet out of the way for the time being, Japan was now free to advance into Southeast Asia. In many respects the Japanese might be said to have been at war with the Chinese since at least 1937.

Just three weeks after attacking the US fleet at Pearl Harbor, the Japanese finally took Hong Kong. The leaders of the defending

▲ Miraculously, the flagship of the fleet, USS *Pennsylvania*, seen behind the wrecks of destroyers *Downes* and *Cassin*, received little damage.

forces had greatly under-estimated the fighting abilities and determination of the Japanese troops. The same mistake was also to contribute significantly to the loss of Singapore in February 1942. With the war against China beginning to loose momentum, however, the Japanese once again turned their attention on the European colonies in the Far East.

The Japanese aim was to establish a Pacific empire that would ultimately, they hoped, encompass New Zealand and Australia as well as the whole of Southeast Asia, extending at least as far west as India, which they hoped also to bring under Japanese control. To this end, the Japanese wasted no time in advancing on the Philippines and much of Southeast Asia, including Cambodia, Thailand and Burma, then under the protection of the British.

They also took the Dutch East Indies and the Malayan states

and managed to capture Wake Island and Guam from the USA.

By using a combination of surprise and extreme aggression, the Japanese were able to expand in the Pacific region up until June 1942, when, crucially, they lost the Battle of Midway, fought in the sea and air in the Pacific.

▲ Three days after the attack, President Roosevelt responded with a formal declaration of war on Japan.

Honolulu Star-Bulletin 1st EXTRA

8 PAGES—HONOLULU, TERRITORY OF HAWAII, U. S. A., SUNDAY, DECEMBER 7, 1941—8 PAGES • ★ PRICE FIVE CENTS

(Associated Press by Transpacific Telephone)

SAN FRANCISCO, Dec. 7.— President Roosevelt announced this morning that Japanese planes had attacked Manila and Pearl Harbor.

WAR!
OAHU BOMBED BY JAPANESE PLANES

SIX KNOWN DEAD, 21 INJURED, AT EMERGENCY HOSPITAL

Attack Made On Island's Defense Areas

CIVILIANS ORDERED OFF STREETS
The army has ordered that all civilians stay off the streets and highways and not use telephones.
Evidence that the Japanese attack has registered some hits was shown by three billowing pillars of smoke in the Pearl Harbor and Hickam field area.
All navy personnel and civilian defense

ANTIAIRCRAFT GUNS IN ACTION
First indication of the raid come shortly before 8 this morning when antiaircraft guns around Pearl Harbor began sending up a thunderous barrage.
At the same time a vast cloud of black smoke arose from the naval base and also from Hickam field where flames could be seen.
BOMB NEAR GOVERNOR'S MANSION

Hundreds See City Bombed
Hundreds of Honolulans who hurried to the top of Punchbowl soon after hostilities began to look, and spread out before them the whole pano-

Names of Dead and

▲ America was stunned by the Japanese act of aggression. There could only be one outcome – war between the two nations.

'42

USA INTERNS JAPANESE-AMERICANS

The surprise attack on the US naval base at Pearl Harbor at the end of 1941 came as a considerable shock to the American people. Demands for revenge against the Japanese combined with general hysteria to create a situation where many Americans became convinced that Orientals resident in the USA were probably working for the enemy.

The US government, claiming that it was being pressurized by a combination of mass hysteria, urgings from the media and requests from the military, began the forcible evacuation and relocation of anyone living on the West Coast of the United States who was known to have Japanese ancestry. This was carried out partly out of a reasonable belief that there may indeed have been Japanese spies operating on the West Coast, and also out of a desire to avoid conflict within the country.

An executive order issued on March 18 established the War Relocation Authority, the agency entrusted with the task of evacuating around 110,000 Japanese-Americans away from the coast and into ten relocation centres established in remote regions of the United States. These centres were essentially military-style barracks, located between the Sierra Nevada and the Mississippi river.

Facilities in the camps were minimal, with few constructive activities to keep the occupants busy. Among those interned in the camps were many children, who received barely any formal education during their time there.

Despite the resentment this action must have caused among the internees, over 17,000 of them were able to convince the US authorities of their loyalty to Uncle Sam and were accepted into the army, where they fought with great distinction.

The US authorities eventually compensated the surviving internees in 1988 for the suffering they had endured during their time in captivity.

◄ **Many Japanese-Americans found themselves victimized in the aftermath of the Pearl Harbor bombing.**

RAF EMBARKS ON NIGHT RAIDS OVER GERMANY

The decision by the British government to attack heavily populated German cities from the air under cover of darkness remains one of the most controversial Allied actions of World War Two. The British Chiefs of Staff decided that the most effective strikes against Germany might be those made against its people rather than its military or industrial positions. There can be little doubt that there was an element of revenge involved in the decision to attack predominantly civilian targets. Hitler had already tried to break the spirit of the British people during the Battle of Britain. The decision to bomb London on 57 consecutive nights was not made out of any desire to destroy military or industrial targets, but in the hope that the British people, driven to the brink of despair, would force their leaders to sue for peace.

A report by Winston Churchill's scientific adviser in April indicated that up to a third of the entire German population could be rendered homeless as a result of the blanket bombing of German cities. Concluding that the morale of the German people was more vulnerable than its armed forces, Sir Arthur "Bomber" Harris of RAF

Bomber Command was appointed by the Chiefs of Staff to organize a campaign of "terror" bombing.

Opening with attacks on Lübeck and the Ruhr, Harris soon began to mount his famous "Thousand-bomber raids" against German cities, destroying around one-third of the entire city of Cologne in a single night. Included among the bombs dropped were any number of incendiary devices. The resulting fires often caused as much damage as conventional bombs but when the fires got out of

control a new phenomenon appeared: the fire storm. Having exhausted the oxygen supply in the immediate vicinity, the fire storm sucked in oxygen from surrounding areas, suffocating anyone unfortunate enough to be near by when this occurred. The resulting devastation outstripped anything that the Luftwaffe inflicted on the British people.

◄ **Hitler declared that the RAF would never reach his capital, but during 1941 Berlin, Cologne and Lübeck were left in ruins.**

BATTLE OF MIDWAY

▲ **A US fighter plane limps back to its aircraft carrier having unleashed its load on the Japanese fleet in the Pacific.**

The war in the Pacific took a decisive turn during early June when the US and Japanese navies met in battle near the island of Midway.

After the surprise attack on the US Pacific fleet at Pearl Harbor in December 1941, the US Navy was left at a disadvantage as it attempted to replace and repair ships lost in the assault.

The Japanese army and air force, with the considerable assistance of the Japanese navy, were making massive gains in the Pacific region and the navy now sought to complete the destruction of the US Pacific fleet, the job it had left unfinished at Pearl Harbor.

The commander of the Japanese fleet, Admiral Yamamoto Isoroku, sent his forces out to engage the US fleet near Midway with specific instructions to sink everything in sight. This time there was to be no repeat of the Pearl Harbor fiasco.

The Americans were lying in wait for the Japanese fleet with three enormous aircraft carriers just 565 km (350 miles) north-east of Midway. In addition to these forces, the Americans also had 150 aircraft ready to take off at a moment's notice from Midway and Hawaii. Having earlier cracked the Japanese encryption codes, the USA knew just where to find the Japanese fleet. On

June 4 they attacked the Japanese from the air and quickly sank three aircraft carriers and a heavy cruiser, returning later in the day to finish off another aircraft carrier. Despite sinking the USS *Yorktown,* the Japanese were forced to retreat from the waters around Midway by June 6.

The four aircraft carriers which had been lost to the USA had contained the cream of the Japanese Navy's pilots. The loss of their four largest aircraft carriers also placed the Japanese Navy on an equal footing with the US fleet and the crushing defeat at Midway brought to an end any further expansion across the Pacific by Japanese forces.

▲ **With their ship listing heavily after being hit, the crew of the aircraft carrier USS *Yorktown* prepare to abandon it.**

'42
THE ROLE OF WOMEN THROUGHOUT THE WAR

▲ Although few women participated in the fighting, World War Two forever changed the role of women in society. After the war many were reluctant to return to their former lives.

There can be no denying the fact that the 1939–45 conflict changed the world forever. National boundaries were redrawn, dictators removed (or replaced) and old scores settled. Aircraft came into their own during the war as every side learned the importance of dominating the skies and on the technical front World War Two also gave us the fast tank, the jet engine, long-range guided missiles and, most deadly of all, the atom bomb.

But perhaps the greatest changes of all were social rather than military. World War One had underlined the stupidity of allowing large bodies of men to be led by someone whose only credentials for the job were nice manners and a title. If that war could be said to have removed much of the influence of the aristocracy, then World War Two was undoubtedly the conflict which proved that women had more to offer the world than child-minding and home-making skills.

It is generally assumed that the demands of war removed large numbers of men from their civilian work, and that it was a matter of expediency that their places were taken by the women they left behind.

At the start of World War Two, however, this was not necessarily the case. The Great Depression, which had harmed the labour market in the run up to the war, was still having an effect when war finally broke out. Indeed, the USA did not fully shrug off the

effects of the Depression until it entered the war in 1941. It is unfortunately the case that there was in place a ready-made army of cannon fodder among the mil-

▲ With Britain's men on active duty, the volunteers of the Women's Land Army were called upon to take on their roles.

lions of unemployed men in Europe and the US – men who were gratefully absorbed by the armed forces. As the conflict escalated, however, women were gradually drawn into the machinery of war in numerous and various positions.

The first and most obvious places where women made a significant contribution to the war effort were the munitions factories. It was here that they not only replaced men who had gone off to war, but also provided the additional labour required to meet the increasing production levels demanded by the war. In a sense, these were temporary jobs which would exist only for as long as the demands of war

existed. Like Christmas tree sales in December, munitions production in wartime do not reflect normal peace-time production levels of the average armaments factory. The famous Redstone Arsenal in the United States, where huge numbers of women were taken on during wartime in an effort to boost production, began to lay off its (predominantly) female staff almost as soon as hostilities ceased.

In June 1945, the management sacked 200 workers, excusing the move with the need to make "adjustments in the production schedule". More sackings soon followed and, interestingly, appeared to reflect the value that the USA placed on its different "classes" of worker. Of the first 200 workers sacked, almost all of were black and female.

By October 1945, the number of women, black or white, working at Redstone Arsenal had been reduced to zero. Similarly, Huntsville Arsenal laid off 500 women in August 1945, and a further 1,850 lost their jobs the following September.

Unions attempting to protect the rights of women working in industry at this time were faced with a dilemma. On the one hand it was intolerable to many that these women, who were doing vital work, should be treated as second-class temporary employees. At the same time, however, the unions also had the task of protecting the jobs of those men who were fighting in the war.

Women who worked directly for the military tended, on the whole, to receive a better deal. Although most countries kept women away from the front line, for reasons of sentimentality, they were still permitted to serve in large numbers in many vital non-combatant roles. More than 45,000 women, for example, served with the Canadian forces, handling every job short of sticking bayonets in the enemy. In the Soviet Union, a country which saw civilians defending their cities alongside the Red Army and fighting just as fiercely, there were no such sentimental notions about the role of women in war.

The Soviet air force had three entire regiments formed from female volunteers; these were the 586th Women's Fighter Regiment, the 587th Women's Day Bomber Regiment and the 588th Women's Night Bomber Regiment – also famously known as the "Night Witches". (The Night Witches alone were honoured with 23 "Hero Of The Soviet Union" awards.)

Women also made an impact in other areas which might not have been immediately apparent. Prior to World War Two, journalism was still very much the preserve of men. Women in journalism tended to be limited to the "women's pages", gossip columns and theatre reviews. With the coming of war, more women moved into frontline journalism and, by 1945, 127 US women had received official military accreditation to work as war correspondents.

Although many women were ultimately destined to return to roles they had adopted before the war, the principal effect of the conflict was to raise expectations. The notion that women were not suitable for certain kinds of work had been proved to be false.

This obvious equality of ability was to lead to demands for equal pay and equal treatment in the workplace. Within a generation, the daughters and granddaughters

▲ Non-combatants they may be, but these women in uniform, a general nurse and a WRAF, are in the front line on the Home Front.

of the women who had experienced the world of work for the first time during the war were marching on the streets demanding what was rightfully theirs.

▼ The need for armaments brought women back into the munitions factories. Britain's war effort would have been unsustainable without them.

'42

NEWS IN BRIEF

March
- British commando raid on Nazaire in France
- British air raid destroys Lübeck in Germany

April
- German and Italian air raids against British-held Malta
- Allies decide second front in Europe untenable in 1942
- US and Filipino troops in Bataan Peninsula surrender to Japan
- Over 10,000 US and Filipino prisoners of the Japanese die in the Bataan death march
- Germany launches Spring Offensive in USSR
- First US air raid on Tokyo by carrier-borne B-25 bombers

May
- Japanese troops take Mandalay in Burma
- British troops invade Madagascar
- Allied strategic victory in Battle of the Coral Sea
- US and Filipino troops on Corregidor surrender to Japan
- Deputy leader of the German SS Reinhard Heydrich shot by Czech resistance fighters
- German offensive in North Africa led by German General Rommel forces British retreat to Egypt
- First thousand-bomber air raid made by RAF on Cologne, Germany

June
- Allied victory in the Battle of Midway between US and Japanese aircraft carrier fleets

SECOND SIEGE OF SEBASTOPOL

The second siege of the Crimean city of Sebastopol came to an end on July 3 when the German forces surrounding it finally broke the resistance of the Russian defenders. The first siege of Sebastopol had been during the Crimean war and was a battle so bloody that the British were moved to create a new medal, the Victoria Cross, to honour the many great acts of bravery performed by the troops.

For thirty weeks leading up to June 2, the German Eleventh Army had been laying siege to the city while building up to full strength for a final assault. On the morning of June 2, the Germans opened fire on the Soviet defences with an enormous artillery bombardment from 1,300 guns, while the Luftwaffe made round-the-clock raids on the city from the air.

Sheltering behind the city's defences were some 106,000 Red Army troops, a small marine force and a group of teenagers from the Communist Union of Youth. For five solid days and nights they endured the continuous bombardment.

When the artillery finally fell silent and German troops moved in to begin mopping up operations they discovered to their surprise and shock that many of the Russians were not only still alive, but were determined to continue the defence of their city.

In a pattern that was to be seen in every Russian city that the German's attempted to take, the defenders of Sebastopol forced the Nazis to pay for every building and street in the city with their lives. When the fighting ended, the German Eleventh Army was in shreds and the city in ruins.

▲ After almost eight months of heavy fighting, the Nazis achieved a hard-won victory on the streets of Sebastopol.

RAID ON DIEPPE

At dawn on the morning of August 19, 6,000 commandos drawn mostly from British and Canadian forces began a daring raid on the heavily defended French coastal port of Dieppe. Fighting was fierce all along the beach and the cost to Allied lives of attempting the landing and trying to bring heavy guns ashore was immense. Positions of a sort were created by the sea wall, although in reality most of the men who made it to the sea wall did so simply in order to shelter from the withering fire of the German guns.

Despite the hopelessness of their situation, the commandos fought on until, at around 2 p.m., they finally caved in. French

citizens emerging from their shelters after the raid – they had been warned by the BBC to do nothing that might compromise their own safety – found a seafront in tatters, with bodies and damaged equipment lying everywhere. The Germans initially buried the almost 1,000 Allied dead in a mass grave but, in a rare display of respect for the fallen enemy, the Wehrmacht Graves Commission sent coffins to Dieppe and the dead commandos were reburied by the Germans with full military honours.

▲ The Allies lost tanks, aircraft, landing craft and other arms, as well as thousands of troops, either killed or taken prisoner, at Dieppe.

MONTY AND ROMMEL AT EL ALAMEIN

▲ **General Bernard Montgomery – "Monty" to the men of the Eighth Army – the hero of the Allied campaign in North Africa.**

The British and Axis forces met twice at El Alamein in North Africa during 1942. The first meeting saw the Axis forces, led by General Erwin Rommel, succeed in their attempts to drive the British back into Egypt – destroying most of their tank force on the way – until they eventually reached El Alamein on June 30. Once there, Rommel was put on the defensive, but still remained in position as the months passed.

In August, the British appointed a new general, Harold Alexander, to take command of its forces in the region and he in turn appointed General Bernard L Montgomery as his commander in the field. Montgomery delayed the counter-offensive against Rommel until he could be sure that the British Eighth Army was at full strength.

Allied air and submarine attacks in the Mediterranean made it difficult for Rommel to obtain supplies and equipment at El Alamein. By the time that Montgomery was ready for battle, Rommel had only 80,000 men, 210 tanks and 350 aircraft with which to fight Montgomery's 230,000 men, 1,230 tanks and 1,500 aircraft.

At 10 p.m. on October 23, the Eighth Army went into action. Just two days later, half of Rommel's tanks had been destroyed, but on the next day he succeeded in stopping the British advance with anti-tank guns. For a week the British and Axis forces played a deadly game of cat and mouse, with the British taking by far the greater number of casualties. (During the first week of fighting, the British lost four times as many tanks as the Axis forces.) By November 2, however, it was obvious that Rommel had lost the battle. He headed back towards Libya, then was eventually forced back to Tunisia.

▲ **A worthy adversary, General Erwin Rommel – "The Desert Fox" – was held in the highest regard by his enemies.**

THE COCONUT GROVE FIRE

Soldiers, sailors and airmen from the USA, on leave from the rigours of fighting World War Two, were the chief victims of a deadly inferno at Boston's famed Coconut Grove nightclub on November 28.

The club was packed well beyond its legal capacity by the addition of rival fans from that day's big football game between home-side Boston and Holy Cross.

The fire began in the newly decorated Melody Lounge at around 10 p.m. Club "MC" Mikey

▲ **Many who survived the fire at Boston's Coconut Grove were left with severe burns. Others died later from their injuries.**

Alpert had just announced the start of the floor show in the two-storey venue when flames flashed across the downstairs bar and set fire to the club's festive decorations. Within seconds the fire spread throughout the over-crowded club and, raging out of control, caused panic among the revellers.

In the ensuing blaze 433 people lost their lives, with many more dying over the following few days as a result of the terrible injuries they suffered in the disaster.

STALINGRAD AND THE EASTERN FRONT

▲ The epic battle for Stalingrad was a turning point of World War Two. Hitler's expansionist machine finally seemed to have over-stretched itself.

The war in Russia was teaching both sides some hard lessons. By December 1941, the Germans were in retreat from Moscow – a move due mainly to the fact that they had advanced beyond their own lines of supply. Stalin, mistakenly believing that the Germans were beaten by early 1942, went on the offensive. He soon found to his cost, however, that the Germans had made only a tactical withdrawal with none of

▼ Red Army troops advance toward the German line. Defeat on the Eastern front proved devastating for Hitler.

the losses that had been incurred by the Russians when they had been forced to retreat during the first few weeks of the campaign. Hundreds of thousands of Soviet troops were lost

as a result of this mistake. Stalin's error of judgement was compounded when he became convinced that the Germans would renew their assault against Moscow. Accordingly, he

concentrated his forces on the central front. Against Stalin's expectations, the German's main attack came from the south. After taking the whole of the Crimea, including Sebastopol, the Germans headed towards the River Volga and the city of Stalingrad with the intention of cutting off the whole of Russia to the south of the city and taking possession of the valuable oil-fields in the Caucasus.

By the summer of 1942, the Germans had reached the suburbs of Stalingrad and the scene was now set for one of the bloodiest and bitterest battles of the twentieth century.

Stalingrad was vital to both sides in the war. It was a major industrial centre and whoever possessed it controlled the

▲ The Nazis faced not only the might of the Red Army but stiff resistance from the civilians of Stalingrad.

transport links with the whole of southern Russia. The Germans needed to capture Stalingrad if they were ever to advance deeper into Russia, but Stalin had ordered that the city be defended to the last man. He had sent in his best general, Zhukov, to oversee the plans for the defence of the city and the Red Army was dug in and waiting grimly for the coming battle.

Hitler was equally determined to succeed in Stalingrad and ordered that there would be no retreat of German forces from the city. He sent the Sixth Army, under Friedrich Paulus, and sections of the Fourth Panzer Army, under Ewald von Kleist, to take Stalingrad.

This was to be more than a mere battle, it was to be a test of strength between the two leaders, Stalin and Hitler, and neither man was prepared to

back down or spare in the attempt to achieve supremacy.

Having reached the suburbs of Stalingrad, the German army now found itself engaged in mortal combat for every inch gained. House by house, street by street, the Red Army defended every building as if it were a fortress until they were eventually pushed back to the centre of the city by September 1942. By the following October they had been pushed back almost to the River Volga.

By now, the German's supplies were beginning to run low and soon they would have to face the Russian winter – an enemy that was just as fierce and deadly as the Red Army itself.

Stalin had been deliberately slow to reinforce his army in Stalingrad, preferring instead to build up fresh divisions for a counter-offensive in the winter

and relying on the courage, determination and skill of his forces in the city to keep the German's occupied until he was ready. November 19, 1942, was payback day.

The Russians attacked with a pincer movement to the north and south. Within four days they had surrounded the 250,000 men who remained alive from the German Sixth Army and Fourth Panzer Army, trapping them in the city of Stalingrad. German forces attempted to relieve their comrades during December, but were beaten back by both the Russians and the weather.

Hitler was aware that as long as the Russians were occupied with Stalingrad, he might still get his heavily pressed army out of the Caucasus. With this in mind, he ordered Field Marshal Paulus to hold his ground, depriving him of the chance to link up with the German forces to his rear, and also robbing him of any chance of a retreat. All that remained now was for the Germans to sit tight in Stalingrad and wait for the inevitable defeat.

No mercy was shown or expected as both sides continued the battle over winter into 1943. Finally, on January 31, and

against Hitler's express wishes, Paulus surrendered.

Two days later the last of the German troops who were still fighting laid down their weapons and surrendered themselves to the less than tender care of the Red Army. The battle for the city of Stalingrad was over, but the cost of victory (and defeat) had been immense.

Soviet forces pulled 250,000 German and Romanian corpses from the rubble of Stalingrad, although the total losses to the Axis forces are believed to have been in the region of 800,000. The Soviets fared even worse, losing over a million men in the battle to defend the city.

Probably the most significant turning point in World War Two had been reached. German forces were never to recover from the defeat inflicted on them by the Russians, who appeared to grow in strength as the Germans went into decline.

Most importantly, the weaknesses of the "Master Race" had been exposed along with the truth about the myth of Hitler's infallibility. Although the road to victory in Europe would remain long and hard, the war had finally turned decisively against the Germans.

▲ Hitler's highly trained troops, like Napoleon's over a century before, were unable to deal with the ravages of the Russian winter.

THE WAR IN BURMA

▲ The war in Burma saw British forces facing both a harsh climate and, in the Japanese, a formidable enemy.

British forces fighting in Burma found themselves facing a Japanese army of considerable ability and determination. The Japanese interest in Burma had earlier led them to train a small guerrilla force of Burmese nationals, which was placed under the command of Aung San, and to promise them independence after the country was "liberated" from the British by Japanese forces.

The Japanese advanced into Burma in 1942 and by the end of the year had taken control of the entire country. Ba Maw, Burma's original Prime Minister under the 1939 constitution, was appointed head of state by the Japanese, while Aung San was given a posi-

tion in the cabinet. In reality, however. Maw's government was little more than a front for the Japanese military.

When the British attempted to remove the Japanese from Burma they found that the enemy had dug in well. Every attempt at an advance from India into Burma was met with the strongest possible response and soon the British began to despair of ever driving the Japanese out.

Against this desperate backdrop, Brigadier General Orde Wingate began to organize and train a small long-range specialist force. Known as the "Chindits". Wingate's troops were essentially a guerrilla army, which entered

Burma from the west during February and May.

Having crossed the Chindwin River, they pressed further into enemy territory and began their guerrilla campaign with attacks on the railway between Mandalay and Myitkyina, where they succeeded in cutting Japanese lines of communication.

From there they pressed on to the Irrawaddy River, all the time receiving supplies from the air. After crossing the river, they continued to disrupt Japanese communications but soon found that the terrain offered little cover or protection. Facing the possibility of capture, the Chindits were forced to return to India and the British were obliged to rethink the assault on Burma.

▲ The "Chindit" army – Asian troops under the command of Allied officers – failed to rid Burma of the Japanese invaders.

DAMBUSTERS TRIUMPH

Flying in a group of specially adapted Avro Lancaster bombers, Royal Air Force Wing Commander Guy Gibson and his team of "Dambusters" staged a series of daring raids in Germany on the night of May 16.

The aim of the raids was to strike a damaging blow at Germany's industrial military heartland in the Ruhr Valley by blowing up and breaching its three large dams. The dams, built

in the valley, supplied water and hydroelectric power to Germany's vital armaments factories.

Previous attempts to blast the heavily defended dams had failed, either because the aircraft used for the attack had been intercepted before reaching their targets, or because the bombs they had dropped had proved relatively ineffective against the thick dam walls. Attempts on the dams using air-launched

torpedoes were foiled by the anti-torpedo nets that the Germans had placed in the water.

A British inventor, Barnes Wallace had, in the meantime, succeeded in demonstrating a new kind of bomb to an extremely sceptical group from the Ministry Of Defence.

Using the same principle that allows children to skip stones across the surface of a pond, Wallace's bomb could, if dropped at the right speed and from the correct height, bounce over the anti-torpedo nets before coming to rest against the wall of the dam. Once there, it sank below the surface of the water and exploded.

The three targets for the raid were the dams on the Eder, the Mohne and the Scorpe. While the Scorpe dam was badly damaged during the raid on the night of May 16, the dams on the Eder and the Mohne were successfully breached, causing the Ruhr Valley below to flood and killing as many as 1,300 people in its wake.

▲ The Mohne Dam shatters, draining 134 million tons of water and crippling the Ruhr Valley's 300 hydro-electric power stations.

To the Germans, the raid proved to be more of an inconvenience than a complete disaster, although the raid had successfully halted production until the dams were repaired.

ITALY SURRENDERS

September 8 was the day that Italy at last gave up its unequal alliance with Germany and officially surrendered to the Allies. Negotiations over the surrender had, however, been going on in secret for some time.

Under the surrender agreement, the Allies had offered the Italians very favourable terms, but only on the condition that they joined them in the war against Germany. Any doubts that the Italians might have had concerning surrendering to the Allies vanished after two corps of Montgomery's Eighth Army

crossed the Strait of Messina from their positions in Sicily and landed in Calabria on the Italian mainland on September 3. Prompted by the invasion of the Allies, the Italian government agreed to the terms of the surrender.

On September 9, a force made up of 170,000 US and British troops landed at Salerno, south of Naples. Although the Italians were no longer considered a threat, the Allies still had to deal with the eight German divisions in southern and central Italy.

Ever since the fall of Mussolini,

▲ Inhabitants of the town of Reggio, grateful that their war is at an end, warmly welcome an invading Allied tank crew.

who had been swept from power in July, the Germans had been preparing for the betrayal of the Italians, and when it came they were ready, if a little under strength, to step into the breach. The Sixteenth Panzer Division was waiting near Salerno for the Allies, and succeeded in keeping them out of Naples until October 5.

By the time the Italians declared war on Germany on October 13, German forces in Italy were already being reinforced and had begun to consolidate their positions throughout the country, in particular along the Gustav Line, which ran from the Garigliano to the Sangro.

▲ With a brief handshake, Italy's General Castellano (centre) gives his unconditional surrender to General Eisenhower (right).

'43

HOLOCAUST: THE PLIGHT OF JEWS AND OTHER MINORITIES UNDER THE NAZIS

▲ **Nazi troops round up Jewish women and children in Warsaw's ghetto. The majority would perish in the concentration camps of Auschwitz, Sobibor and Treblinka.**

When Adolf Hitler embarked on his planned expansion of Germany into the rest of Europe, he did so with certain aims already in mind. European countries to the north and west of Germany, such as Norway and the Netherlands, were to be incorporated into a kind of Greater Germany. Those countries where a German military administration had been imposed, such as France, were destined to become part of the European bloc under the control of Germany – in much the same way as Russia came to dominate the expanded Soviet Union after the war.

Interestingly, Hitler had quite separate plans for the Soviet Union, which was to become subject to a colonial administration that would oversee the exploitation of its resources and peoples. Hitler's plans were streaked, however, with a seam of pure evil based on racist misconceptions.

Within Germany's forces there existed a group with extraordinary powers. The SS, or *Schutzstaffel* (Protective Echelon) had been formed by Hitler in 1925 as a personal bodyguard. The organization had grown in size and power until, by the start of war in 1939, it numbered around a quarter of a million men.

Acting as a state within the state, the SS was responsible for carrying out most of Hitler's murderous racial policies – a task which they performed regardless of the existing administration within a conquered country.

Those deemed to be racially inferior according to the dictates of Nazi ideology were systematically sought out and murdered for no other reason than being deemed racially impure and therefore sub-human – very different treatment from those who were felt to be racially pure. Even so, those inhabitants of conquered countries who best resembled the Aryan ideal still suffered greatly at the hands of the Germans

Having already inflicted misery on German Jews on an unimaginable scale, Hitler moved a step closer to what he called the Final Solution – the murder of every

Jew in any country under German control – during the invasion of the Soviet Union.

As the German army advanced into western Russia and the Ukraine, SS death squads followed up at the rear, rounding up and shooting any Jew they could find. By the end of 1941, they had murdered nearly one and a half million people, but the killing did not stop there.

In January 1942, Nazis and SS leaders met for the Wannsee Conference, where the fate of Jews and other racial minorities, such as gypsies, in Western and Central Europe was decided. With

immediate effect, the order was issued to deport all Jews rounded up in these regions to camps in Eastern Poland, where they would be murdered *en masse* or cruelly worked to death as slave labour. In barely more than two years, over four million Jews died in Polish extermination camps, such as Auschwitz, Sobibor and Treblinka. The Final Solution did not, however, always proceed smoothly.

In common with other areas under their control, the Nazis had created a Jewish ghetto in Warsaw, Poland, where Jews were held prior to being sent for extermination at Treblinka. The ghetto was enclosed behind a wall 3 metres (10 ft) high and over 18 km (11 miles) long. By the summer of 1942, it was crammed full with around half a million people, thousands of whom had no housing and were dying from disease or starvation. News that they were being moved to large open-air camps in the country came as a relief. The Jews were shipped out of the ghetto at a rate of 5,000 a day, until by January 1943, their numbers had been greatly reduced.

Some of those who had been among the first to leave the Warsaw ghetto had managed to escape from Treblinka – the open-air camp in the country. They had returned to the ghetto to confirm the worst fears of those who remained.

On the morning of January 18, the SS entered the ghetto and were surprised to find themselves amid fierce fighting in the streets, which raged on for four days until the Nazis pulled out of the

ghetto. The SS returned on April 19 with 2,000 troops armed with tanks and flame-throwers against the Jewish resistance, armed only with a few captured guns and a handful of improvised bombs. Despite the one-sided nature of the battle, the Jews in the Warsaw ghetto held the SS at bay until May 16, killing hundreds of German troops in the process.

But the Jews were not the only casualties of Hitler's racially motivated policies. Although they were not persecuted to the same extent, Hitler refused to accept that the Slavic Poles and Russians were anything more than sub-humans. He lost no time in exploiting them as slaves in all but name, subjecting them to barbaric treatment and often working them to death.

Hitler's treatment of minorities in the countries that he invaded had a significant effect on Germany's progress in the war. His policy of isolating minority groups and subjecting them to horrific treatment at the hands of the SS, provided a

powerful stimulus for the creation of resistance groups.

Even those who did not suffer directly at the hands of the SS were frequently disturbed and disgusted by the activities of the Nazis and as a result were unlikely to be sympathetic to their cause.

▲ The Warsaw ghetto burns as the Jews remaining there fight back, with pathetically inadequate weapons, against the odds.

▼ Refugees of many nationalities carried their pitiful belongings along Europe's roads during the years of Hitler's tyranny.

GENETIC INGENUITY

Humankind took a step closer to understanding the mysteries of life when US bacteriologist Oswald T Avery, and colleagues Colin M MacLeod and Maclyn McCarty, reported in January that they had evidence to prove that the genetic material of living cells is composed of deoxyribonucleic acid (DNA). The existence of DNA

▲ **Eminent US bacteriologist Oswald Avery proved beyond doubt that it was DNA that carried genetic information.**

had been known since 1869, when a substance which was given the name nuclein was extracted from cell nuclei.

No one could be certain that DNA acted as the carrier of genetic information until Avery, MacLeod and McCarty were able to demonstrate its function by a series of relatively simple but ingenious experiments. Their work continued that of research that had been started by Fred Griffith in London. Prior to their groundbreaking work, there was still dispute over whether it was the various proteins or the nucleic acids in chromosomes – or a combination of both – which acted carried the genetic information.

The pioneering work of Avery, MacLeod and McCarty laid the foundations for much of the research into DNA which followed in the succeeding decades.

In 1953, Nobel Prize-winners James Watson and Francis Crick

were able to take the work of the threesome a step further by demonstrating the double-helix structure of DNA. They also showed how the stability that this structure lends to the DNA molecules allows it to be used as the template for the replication of more DNA molecules.

In 1984, British geneticist Alec Jeffreys developed a method for isolating sequences of DNA – a process which also made it possible to create an image of the isolated sequence.

Jeffreys noticed that the pattern of the sequences was unique for every living organism – with the exception of identical twins – and therefore acted as a kind of fingerprint.

DNA "fingerprinting" was later adopted by police forces the world over as a means of identifying criminals from a minimal amount of genetic material found at the scene of a crime.

US ADVANCES THROUGH SOUTHEAST ASIA

The USA renewed its campaign against the Japanese in Southeast Asia with an attack by US warships on the island of Paramishu on February 4. This was followed on February 29 by a landing on Los Negros in the Admiralty Islands.

Earlier, in 1943, the USA had begun an assault on Japanese positions throughout Micronesia, while building up forces for the truly massive campaign that would lead them to gaining

▶ **A detachment of US Marines marches towards the Japanese line on Bougainville Island in Papua, New Guinea.**

possession of Japanese islands just a few hundred kilometres from the Japanese mainland.

By the start of 1944, the USA had concentrated as many men

and aircraft in the Pacific region as it had in Europe, but it was the US naval presence in the region that ultimately tipped the balance of power.

MONDRIAN AND MUNCH: UNITED BY DEATH

▲ **By July 1944 US marines had gained control of the strategically significant Saipan Island. Victory in the Pacific was now assured.**

By the summer of 1944, the US Navy had amassed almost as many as 100 aircraft carriers in the region, allowing them to attack almost any Japanese-held position at will.

By the end of July, they had recaptured Saipan, Tinian and Guam from the Japanese, which quickly became Allied air force bases from which air strikes against the Japanese mainland could be launched.

Adopting a policy of "island hopping", the US Navy under Admiral Nimitz gradually cleared the Marshall and Mariana chains of islands, while the US Pacific army under General MacArthur began their attempt to retake the Philippines in October 1944, with the aim of blocking the sea route to Southeast Asia and cutting off Japanese communications with the Dutch East Indies.

As expected, the battle for these islands was one of the fiercest conflicts of the entire war, with the Japanese opting to fight to the death rather than surrender to the USA.

Such was the determination of the Japanese to defend at any cost that they began, for the first time, to launch the famous kamikaze suicide attacks on US warships.

At a time when war was raging across the globe, it is hard to imagine the world plunged into a deep mourning over the deaths of two profound individuals. The sentiment dominated the art world and crossed the boundaries of the conflict when two of its leading lights – Edvard Munch and Pieter (Piet) Mondrian – died within days of each other. Their deaths robbed the world of two of the most influential artists of the past hundred years.

The Norwegian painter and printmaker Edvard Munch died on January 23 at Ekely, near Oslo. A huge influence on the German Expressionist movement, Munch's work came to symbolize the anguish of modern man in his attempts to come to terms with the world of the spirit and the soul. Munch's often bleak work, best illustrated by his most famous painting, *The Scream*, reflected the grim facts of his own experience of life. The early deaths of his mother, sister,

▲ **Early influences on Edvard Munch, whose work paved the way for German Expressionism, were Gauguin and van Gogh.**

▲ **Piet Mondrian, who lived in the US for just the last four years of his life, was a major influence on the New York School.**

father and brother caused him to express the opinion that "Illness, insanity and death were the black angels that kept watch over my cradle and accompanied me all my life."

Piet Mondrian died in New York City, where he lived since 1940, on February 1. His talent had greatly influenced the Dutch abstract art movement, known as *De Stijl* ("The Style"). While his own life contained none of the obvious tragedy of Munch's, his work was to prove just as influential, particularly in the fields of architecture and graphic design. It grew out of his adoption of Cubism in Paris, where he spent much time after 1911.

Mondrian invented a new term, "neo-plasticism", which described his purely objective view of the world. His work reflected this view in its use of simple straight lines, right angles and the pronounced use of primary colours.

'44

BRITAIN INTRODUCES BAN ON TRAVEL TO IRELAND

Concerned that information about the US naval base at Derry in Northern Ireland and Allied plans for the invasion of Europe might fall into the hands of Nazi supporters in the South, Britain introduced a general ban on travel to the Republic on March 12.

To a certain extent, the Irish Republic was a thorn in the side of those attempting to coordinate the defence of the UK. Despite declaring its neutrality early in World War Two, the Republic was perceived by many in Britain as friendly to Hitler's Germany. In reality, this suspicion was born more of old enmities than of any concrete evidence of cooperation with the Nazis. While the Irish authorities did little to stop the Germans monitoring British communications from their consulate in Dublin, they did not actually encourage such activity and would probably have allowed the British to do the same thing had the situation been reversed.

The one area where Britain and Ireland may have clashed – over the use of Irish ports by British warships for the protection of its merchant fleet – was avoided by making arrangements elsewhere. Of this matter, however, Churchill later wrote, rather ominously, "… if we had not been able to do without them we should have retaken them by force rather than perish by famine".

▲ **A US marine, stationed at the Derry naval base in Northern Ireland, gets to know the locality.**

ALLIES PUSH INTO ITALY

Although the Allies had advanced into Italy in the summer of 1943 with relative ease, their progress was soon halted by the strength of the German's positions along the Gustav Line – a series of defences which hinged on the fortress at Monte Cassino.

The Germans under Kesselring were proving to be a far more formidable opposition than the Italians who had controlled the south prior to their surrender. In desperation the Allies were forced to stage a daring landing at Anzio, just 55 km (33 miles) from Rome, in order to get around the Gustav Line.

The Allies landed some 50,000 troops and 5,000 vehicles at Anzio on January 22. So unprepared were the Germans for the sea-borne assault that at first they showed little resistance. Rather than press their advantage, however, the Allies wasted a great deal of time consolidating their positions at Anzio. Meanwhile, Kesselring was able to assemble a force from his reserves and mount a counter-attack against the Allies

◀ **Following the liberation of their city, over half a million starving Romans were fed from public kitchens set up by the Allies.**

on February 3. Having left his defences at Monte Cassino untouched, Kesselring was also able to resist a new offensive against his positions there.

In May, the Allies began to strengthen their forces for the final push against the Gustav Line. On the night of May 11, the new assault began: the superior forces of the Allies soon broke through the German defences at various points along the line between Monte Cassino and the coast to the West.

With the collapse of German positions at the coast, the US forces were able to make their way north. The British went around Monte Cassino, which eventually fell to an attack by Polish troops of the British Eighth Army on May 18.

On May 23, the combined Allied force that had been holding its position at Anzio pushed forward and, despite heavy losses, soon breached the Gustav Line, which finally began to collapse.

As the various Allied forces began to link up for the assault on Rome, the Germans found themselves outflanked and outgunned. Unable to hold out against the advance, the Germans began a tactical and orderly retreat to positions 260 km (160 miles) to the north of Rome.

On June 5, amid great celebration, the Allies finally entered the city of Rome. Quick to capitalize on the propaganda value of capturing the Eternal City, President Roosevelt declared "The first Axis capital is in our hands. One up and two to go."

Despite the obvious jubilation of the Allies, the war in Italy was far from over as the German positions to the north of the city grew stronger with each day that passed.

V1S HIT LONDON

▲ Silent but deadly. With victory now slipping out of Hitler's grasp, the V2 rocket was Germany's final attempt at terrorizing London.

Londoners were presented with a terrifying new development in military technology when the Germans launched their latest weapon – the *V1* Flying bomb – on June 13. The first *V1* was launched from a catapult-ramp site at the Pas-de-Calais on the northern coast of France and sent on its way to London.

Having been the target of Hitler's Luftwaffe for so long, the

▲ Clearing up after a V2 rocket had hit became a frighteningly frequent task for England's defence workers in 1944.

hapless inhabitants of Great Britain's capital were confronted with a formidable addition to the German arsenal. The *V1* had a top speed of 580 km per hour (360 mph) and a warhead packed with 2,000 pounds of explosives. Although it was never a truly accurate weapon, it allowed the Germans to attack targets in southern England from the air without risk to their own pilots.

Londoners soon learned to recognize the approach of the deadly weapon by the characteristic sound that its primitive jet engine produced. However, no such sound was produced by the next generation of flying bombs – the *V2*.

Designed by Wernher von Braun, who later played a key role in getting the Americans to the Moon, the *V2* was the first truly modern ballistic missile. It travelled so fast that the sound that it produced was heard only after it had hit its target.

The first *V2* to hit London arrived on September 8.

THE NORMANDY LANDINGS

D-Day, June 6, saw the Allies opening their offensive against the Germans in Europe with the landing of a massive invasion force in northern France. The German High Command had been expecting the assault for some time, but for a while were undecided as to where and when the Allies would strike.

One school of thought – favoured by Rommel, among others – placed the most likely point of the landing between Calais and Dieppe, where the English Channel is at it narrowest point. Hitler, however, believed that the assault would be around the beaches of Normandy, and Rommel was eventually inclined to agree with this view. All that remained for the German High Command was to decide how best to fend off the coming invasion attempt.

Some in the German High Command believed that it would be best to mount an enormous counter-attack after the Allies had landed. Rommel opposed this plan on the grounds that the Allies' superiority in the air would

▲ The Allied push for victory in Western Europe began with Operation Overlord, a full-scale assault on the Normandy beaches.

make the build-up of the troops and equipment necessary for such a strategy extremely difficult and dangerous. Instead, he proposed that the Germans should try to stop the invasion force before it moved off the beaches.

Operation Overlord, as the Allied assault had been code-named, got under way with the landing of 156,000 men on the beaches of Normandy between the Orne estuary and the south-eastern end of the Cotentin Peninsula.

In a simultaneous assault, 83,000 British and Canadian troops came ashore on the

eastern beaches while 73,000 US troops fought their way on to the western beaches.

Although the Germans were not caught entirely by surprise when the Allies invaded, Rommel, who had done so much damage to the British in North Africa, was away from his office when the assault began, having been informed earlier that the weather in the Channel made an attack somewhat unlikely.

▲ The D-Day landings that began on June 6, 1944, broke through the Nazi line, enabling the Allies to liberate occupied France.

As expected, fighting was fierce on all fronts, but the US troops who landed at Caen suffered the worst casualties when the Panzer division which was defending the area was reinforced the following day by a second Panzer division, enabling them to hold out against the Americans until July 9.

On the whole, however, attempts by the Germans to reinforce their positions were greatly hampered by the actions of the Allied air force and by confusion and infighting in their own ranks.

German forces were plunged into further disarray by an attempt on Hitler's life by a group of senior officers, including Rommel, on July 20. By the end of the month, the Allies were able to get beyond the German positions in Normandy and begin the advance into northern France.

▲ US troops landing near the port of Caen, to face heavy bombardment from one of the two Panzer divisions in the area.

LIBERATION OF PARIS

The long-awaited liberation of Paris began on August 19, when resistance groups in the city launched an armed uprising against their Nazis oppressors.

The famed French resistance movement, which had grown to the size of a small army by 1944, came into its own after the Allies launched Operation Overlord with the beach landings at Normandy on June 6.

After breaking through German positions at Normandy, the Allies were caught briefly by a counter-attack staged by four panzer divisions. The Germans were unable to hold the Allies' advance for long, however, and soon the German position became hopeless and their defences collapsed.

The German army was now on the run, but found that its retreat was hampered at every stage by the French resistance. Blown up bridges, torn-up railway tracks and every other conceivable form of sabotage served to slow the German retreat. Having already been held up by Hitler's refusal to allow his forces to retreat and regroup in an orderly fashion, the additional harassment by the French resistance helped to prevent the Germans from establishing effective new defences against the Allied invasion.

Resistance groups in Paris, well aware of the collapse of the

▲ The Allied forces parade victoriously through the centre of Paris, returned to French rule after four years of Nazi occupation.

German defences, began the preparations to take their city back from the Nazis. With each town that the Germans had left behind on their retreat from Normandy, the resistance stepped in and removed Vichy collaborators from power, thus returning the town halls to the representatives of General Charles de Gaulle's government in exile.

But in Paris the resistance had a few scores to settle. On the same day that a US army division crossed the Seine at Mantes-Gassicourt, the French resistance went into action against their unwelcome guests.

Under orders from General Eisenhower, the invading Allied forces encircled Paris, but initially did not enter the city to take it from the Germans. That honour

was given to the free French Forces under General Jacques Leclerc. Having advanced from Normandy, Leclerc and his men marched into Paris on August 25 and accepted the German surrender. Later that day, General Charles de Gaulle arrived in the city. The following day, he led a victory parade down the Champs-Elysées before concluding proceedings with a brief speech: "I wish simply – and from the bottom of my heart – to say, Vive Paris!"

Meanwhile, having retreated back to Sigmaringen, in Germany, the Vichy government attempted to adopt the role of leaders in exile, forced to flee by the invasion of hostile Allied forces. Their supporters back in France had no such opportunity for posturing as the resistance movement began to take revenge for the atrocities committed by the Nazis and their Vichy collaborators.

No one knows for certain just how many former Vichy officials and supporters were summarily executed by the French resistance after the liberation of Paris, but the figure is believed to be in excess of 10,000. A further 800 were executed after due process of law.

▲ French civilians join US troops in the hunt for Nazi snipers as German forces are gradually forced to flee occupied territory.

- The Battle of Leyte Gulf between US and Japanese naval forces in the Pacific ends in catastrophic losses for the Japanese navy
- Japanese air force first uses Kamikaze suicide bombers
- German troops occupy Buda in Hungary
- Advancing Soviet army reaches Czechoslovakia
- US troops land in Leyte in the Philippines
- Russians and Yugoslav partisans take Belgrade
- French Provisional Government under General de Gaulle is officially recognized by USA, Britain and USSR
- General MacArthur returns to the Philippines
- Armistice between Allies and new government in Bulgaria
- Soviet army launches assault on Budapest in Hungary

November
- Incumbent Democrat candidate Franklin D Roosevelt wins US presidential election
- Liberation of Greece completed; Communist Greek partisan force ELAS refuses to demobilize and takes control of areas in Athens and Piraeus
- German battleship *Tirpitz* sunk by RAF in Norway
- Allied troops take Strasbourg
- US B-29 bombers make first raid on Tokyo

December
- Allied troops take Ravenna in Italy
- US forces invade Mindoro in the Philippines
- Battle of the Bulge begins with German offensive in the Ardennes in Belgium
- German siege of Bastogne in Belgium lifted by US forces
- US forces complete occupation of Leyte in the Philippines

'45

THE YALTA CONFERENCE

Leaders of the three main powers that were united against the Axis forces met at Yalta in the Crimea between February 4 and 11 to discuss plans for the defeat and occupation of Hitler's Germany. Present at the meeting were Prime Minister Winston Churchill repre-

▲ **Moment of glory. The "Big Three" – Churchill, Roosevelt and Stalin – decide the fate of a defeated Germany.**

senting the British, President Franklin D Roosevelt of the United States and Joseph Stalin, leader of the Soviet Union.

The leaders had already decided that a defeated Germany would be divided into "zones of occupation", which were to be administered separately by the USA, British, French and Soviets. It was also decided to confiscate or destroy Germany's military industrial might and to bring its war criminals to book before an international military tribunal.

Churchill, Roosevelt and Stalin also opted to set up a commission to look into the question of reparations. (Churchill, in particular, aware of the contribution that the Treaty Of Versailles had made to creating the conditions which led to World War Two, was wary of setting too high a figure.)

The main business of the conference was concerned with how to handle those countries in eastern Europe which had been defeated or liberated from the hands of the Nazis. This was an especially sensitive matter as the Soviet Union had claims on most of these countries.

Eventually, Stalin agreed to the setting up, in each of the countries in question, of interim administrations which would eventually be replaced by freely elected governments.

With hindsight, it is obvious that Stalin had no intention of honouring his promise to Churchill and Roosevelt. After the war had ended, Communist governments were established in Poland, Czechoslovakia, Hungary, Romania and Bulgaria and free elections were never held.

DRESDEN BLITZED

One of the greatest atrocities of World War Two occurred in February, but for once it was inflicted on the German people. Back in March 1942, the British Chiefs of Staff had come to the conclusion that Germany's greatest weakness was likely to be the morale of it people – a reasonable assumption, given that few German civilians had suffered the consequences of Hitler's hostile actions in Europe.

In the same way that Hitler had tried (and failed) to destroy the will of the British people to fight against his proposed invasion of Great Britain, the Chiefs of Staff hoped to sap the will of the Germans to continue with the war by bombing their cities to rubble.

Until 1945, the German city of Dresden had largely escaped the consequences of Allied action. The

city, considered to be one of the most beautiful in the world was often referred to as the "Florence on the Elbe". It was a treasure

▲ **Once one of Germany's most beautiful cities, in a single night's bombing Dresden was all but wiped off the map.**

house of outstanding architecture and contained some of the finest galleries in the world. Dresden, was, however, of no significant military value and was therefore almost without protection against enemy assault of any kind.

On the night of February 13, the city of Dresden was changed forever when an air force made up of 800 US and British aircraft attacked the city with a massive bombing raid.

Among the bombs dropped were a high number of incendiary devices. Soon the city was lit up by the flames of a thousand out-of-

▲ **The people of Dresden try in vain to rebuild their broken city; almost double the number died in the bombing as at Hiroshima.**

control fires, which eventually combined to form a deadly fire storm. The inferno sucked the oxygen from the atmosphere, suffocating thousands of people. Temperatures rose so high that the sewers ran with melted human fat.

By the time the raid was over more than 135,000 people – a number almost double that of victims at Hiroshima – had lost their lives in the most horrible fashion. In a single night, one of the most beautiful cities in the world had been all but wiped from the face of the Earth.

THE ALLIES CROSS THE RHINE

The British and US bombing of Dresden – on the pretext of helping the Soviet advance on the Eastern Front – was a side issue to their main task of continuing to build up their forces for the inevitable crossing of the Rhine and the final push towards Berlin.

It had been decided that the bulk of the ground forces would be with Britain's General Montgomery at the northern end of the front. In the meantime the US Third Army, under the control of General Patton, had arrived at Coblenz on the Rhine by early March. Downstream from their position, lay the US First Army under General Hodges. The First Army had already taken the bridge at Remagen, to the south of Bonn, and crossed over the Rhine.

In the meantime, the US Ninth Army, under the command of Lieutenant General William H Simpson, had reached the Rhine downriver from the First Army, near to Düsseldorf. Here, along with the Third and First Armies, they were ordered to wait until Montgomery's forces were ready to cross.

The attack finally began on the night of March 23. The Third Army seized the opportunity to cross the Rhine at Oppenheim virtually unopposed by enemy

▲ **Paratroopers from the Seventeenth US Airborne Division fill the skies over Germany's Rhineland.**

forces. At the same time, Montgomery led 25 divisions in an attack across a 48-km (30-mile) front near Wesel. The attack had been preceded by a massive bombardment of enemy positions. Wave after wave of bombers swept over the Rhine, backed up by an artillery force of more than 3,000 guns.

Such was the ferocity of the bombardment that Montgomery's divisions met with relatively little opposition and were soon able to establish positions 32 km (20 miles) beyond the Rhine.

▼ **Victory is all but assured as the Allied forces cross the Rhine and advance into the very heart of Germany.**

'45

EAST MEETS WEST IN THE INVASION OF GERMANY

With Germany rapidly approaching a state of complete collapse, the Allies, who had crossed the River Rhine in late March, pressed home their advantage and swept through Germany, reaching the banks of the River Elbe, just 95 km (60 miles) from the German capital, Berlin, on April 11.

By now, Hitler had descended into the final stages of madness as it became increasingly obvious that the end of the war was approaching fast. He began to adopt a policy of self-destruction, ordering the German people to hinder the Allied advance by destroying as much of Germany's infrastructure as possible, thereby creating a "desert" for the invading Allies. To this end he ordered the destruction of all industrial plants, power stations, gas works and food and clothing stores.

▲ Allied troops advancing from the west meet Russian troops advancing from the east on the banks of the River Elbe.

When Albert Speer, Germany's minister of war production, protested at this order he was informed by Hitler that "If the war is lost, the German nation will also perish. So there is no need to consider what the people require for continued existence." This comment followed an earlier directive which Hitler had issued the day before the Allies crossed the Rhine. It stated that the German army should wage war without consideration for the population of Germany itself.

By now, the majority of Germans had tired of the war. Their main concern was to avoid being taken over by the Soviet Red Army, who were greatly feared. It was partly because of this that the Allies met with such minimal resistance as they swept through Germany. For the time being the Soviets were being held at the Oder, but on April 16 they pressed forward, reaching Berlin on April 25. That afternoon they surrounded the city before linking up with US forces on the banks of the River Elbe later that day.

DEATHS OF THREE WARTIME LEADERS

During Hitler's descent into madness, he began to search for omens that the tide of the war might once again turn in Germany's favour. On April 12, he was reportedly overjoyed to hear the news of the death of the US president, Franklin D Roosevelt, a leader who had effectively directed the Allied forces in their battle with the Axis powers since the US joined the war at the end of 1941.

Roosevelt had proved himself to be a politician of outstanding ability from the time he was first elected President in 1933 – a position he maintained right up until the time of his death.

Under Roosevelt, the United

▲ A "kangaroo court" followed by summary execution: the bullet-ridden bodies of Benito Mussolini and his mistress Clara Petacci.

States underwent many changes as the "New Deal" policies on which he was elected were enacted, gradually bringing the USA out of the Great Depression into which it had been plunged prior to his taking office. As the 32nd President of the United States, Roosevelt was the only man to be re-elected to the post on three occasions – a measure, surely, of his remarkable abilities and immense popularity. He was succeeded as President by Harry S Truman.

April proved to be a momentous month in many ways, not least because it also saw the deaths of the two leaders of the fascist forces in Europe.

On April 28, Benito Mussolini was executed, along with his mistress, Clara Petacci, by Italian partisans who discovered *Il Duce* hiding under a pile of coats in the back of a car while they were out hunting Nazi sympathizers. Following the very briefest of trials, Mussolini was put against a wall and machine-gunned to death, before his body was hung upside down on public display in the Piazza Loretto in Milan.

Adolf Hitler also died with his mistress, Eva Braun, at his side. The couple married the night before they committed suicide in the German Chancellery on April 30. Few mourned their deaths.

GERMANY SURRENDERS

The war in Europe officially came to an end at midnight on May 8, 1945. The document declaring the surrender of German forces in northwestern Europe had been signed at Montgomery's headquarters on Lüneburg Heath on May 4. An earlier surrender document, dated April 29, had already ended the fighting in Italy on May 2.

A final surrender document which covered all the German forces was signed by Field Marshal Keitel at a ceremony at General Eisenhower's headquarters at Reims in the presence of delegations from Great Britain,

▶ **The whole of Allied Europe celebrated the end of almost six years of the bitterest conflict.**

France, the Soviet Union and the United States of America.

The killing did not stop immediately, of course. In the chaos of the final days of the war and during the first few days of peace, fanatics and victims alike continued battle. In Berlin, small gangs of SS men had roamed the streets looking for soldiers from the regular German army who had thrown down their weapons and attempted to flee from the advance of the Soviets. Any they

caught were hanged and a sign proclaiming "I betrayed the Fuhrer" left around their necks.

Leaving aside the defeated German people, most of whom were more concerned with avoiding the attentions of the Soviet Red Army than with any other consequences of defeat, the end of the war was cause for great festivity. Celebrations broke out in every Allied city that was still standing as people accepted that, in Europe at least, there was to be no more bloodshed.

▲ **One of the many thousands of street parties held throughout Britain to celebrate the Allied victory in Europe.**

'45

DISCOVERY OF THE DEATH CAMPS

NEWS IN BRIEF
....

- Allied troops take Mandalay in Burma
- Allied forces under General Montgomery cross the River Rhine and advance into the Ruhr
- Advancing Soviet army reaches Austrian border
- Soviet forces take Danzig in Poland

April
- US forces land on Okinawa in the Pacific
- Allied forces launch fresh offensive in Italy
- Provisional socialist government formed in Czechoslovakia
- Resignation of Japanese government under Prime Minister Koiso
- Japanese battleship *Yamato* sunk by US aircraft
- US forces take Hanover in Germany
- Advancing Allied forces reach the River Elbe in Germany
- Japanese kamikaze rocket gliders (baka) used at Iwo Jima
- Soviet forces take Vienna in Austria
- Soviet forces launch fresh offensive across River Oder in Germany
- US and Soviet armies in Germany link-up
- Conference to found the United Nations begins in US
- German army in Italy surrenders

As the war in Europe was coming to an end, many in the advancing Allied armies had reason to be pleased. They had survived six hard years of war, which had seen much of Europe reduced to rubble and countless millions of lives destroyed.

But as these forces marched into territories in eastern Europe, which formerly had been under German occupation, they discovered sights that would wipe the smile from the face of any civilized human being.

▲ **Saved from certain death, prisoners held at the Dachau concentration camp cheer the arrival of US troops.**

Almost immediately after coming to power in Germany in 1933, Hitler had begun to persecute the Jews. Throughout the 1930s, thousands of Jews were imprisoned in concentration camps and immense amounts of Jewish wealth was confiscated by means of punitive fines.

As World War Two approached, Jews were gradually robbed of their citizenship rights. They were barred from state schools and from entering most professions. They were not allowed to own

▶ **Journalists invited to view the full extent of the Nazi atrocities found it difficult to take in the horrors they faced.**

land or associate with gentiles, nor were they allowed entry into public buildings, such as libraries and museums.

By 1941, they were forbidden to use the telephone system or to ride on public transport. Furthermore, any Jew over the age of six was forced to wear a bright yellow badge in the shape of the Star of David.

As German forces advanced across Europe, squads of SS troops routinely murdered any Jew, gypsy or Slav they encountered, usually by means of bullets, or occasionally by herding their victims into trucks and directing the exhaust fumes from the vehicle inside.

Soon, however, the Germans became concerned about the manner in which their victims died. Their concern was not triggered by feelings of guilt, but rather by the nagging worry that the methods of extermination simply were not efficient.

On January 20, 1942, a group of fifteen leading Nazis met in the Berlin suburb of Grossen-Wannsee to discuss what was euphemistically called the "final solution of the Jewish question".

In an effort to hide Germany's activities from the eyes of the world, it was decided to deport Jews from across the German-occupied territories of Europe to extermination camps in eastern Europe, most of which were constructed in Poland.

On arrival at the camps, the Nazis' victims were to be subjected to a brief selection process, during which anyone deemed capable of hard labour or who possessed skills which might be useful to the Germans was sent to work in the camp. The rest, mostly women, children and the elderly, were marched straight to purpose-built gas chambers where they were murdered with typical German efficiency at a rate of up to 12,000 a day.

Those who survived selection must have wished they had not as they were often forced to remove the bodies from the gas chambers and, having first extracted gold teeth and fillings, shovel the dead into the waiting fires of the camp crematoriums.

So it was that as the victorious Allied troops marched across Europe they encountered the real legacy of the Nazis. During the

course of Hitler's twelve-year reign over Germany around six million Jews were murdered – more than four million of them in the concentration camps of Poland, such as Auschwitz, Belsen and Buchenwald.

Even those with the darkest imaginations could not possibly have been prepared for the sight of the survivors of the camps, who had been abandoned by the fleeing Germans. Emaciated bodies, wracked with disease and barely alive, mingled with the heaped and rotting bodies of the dead. This was the true face of fascism.

▲ They may have survived the horrors of internment but the inmates at Buchenwald would forever carry the mental scars of their experience.

THE POTSDAM AGREEMENT

The Big Three Allied powers met in Potsdam, a suburb of Berlin, on July 17 for a conference to discuss just what to do with a defeated Germany.

Their former enemy was not their only concern, however, as decisions had to be made concerning the boundaries of Poland, the occupation of Austria, the level of German reparations and the continuing war against Japan.

Although no one was admitting the fact, the most contentious item on the agenda was that of the role of the Soviet Union in eastern Europe.

Previous conferences of this nature had been largely good-humoured events, and the main players – Churchill, Roosevelt and Stalin – had buried their differences in the interest of defeating their common enemy.

Now that the enemy had been defeated, and its leader lay dead, the true nature of international politics began to surface. Now that the time had come to carve up the spoils of war, it was a case of every man – or country – for himself, and it was Churchill and Stalin who showed themselves more than willing to fight for what they felt was right.

The declaration of the conference seemed harmless enough: "It is the intention of the Allies that the German people be given the opportunity to prepare for the eventual reconstruction of their life on a democratic and peaceful basis." Eventual interpretations of this declaration, however, served to highlight the stark differences between the aims of the Western democracies and the Soviet Union.

While the Western boundaries of Poland were fixed at the Oder and Neisse rivers, and moved to include parts of the former East Prussia (a move which involved the forced repatriation of millions of Germans back into Germany), Stalin refused to allow the West to interfere in eastern Europe.

After the Potsdam conference relations between the countries that had defeated the Germans declined and they never again met as allies.

▼ Leaders of the victorious Allies meet at the Potsdam Conference. The outcome paved the way for the "Cold War" that followed.

'45 USA UNLEASHES ATOM BOMB

The world became a much more dangerous place on August 6, after the United States unleashed the full terror of the atomic bomb on the people of the small Japanese city of Hiroshima. Previously untouched by the war, the city was reduced to rubble by the blast from a single bomb – an explosion equivalent to 20,000 tonnes of TNT.

The weapon had been developed in the mistaken belief that the Germans were developing similar devices at Peenemunde, where Wernher von Braun was using slave labour to build the *V2* rocket, Hitler's most sophisticated vengeance weapon.

In reality, Hitler would have nothing to do with the relatively new field of nuclear physics – he dismissed it as Jewish science – but German scientist, Lise Meitner had been investigating the neutron bombardment of uranium, work which could have led to the creation of a fission-based weapon.

Disturbed by the implications of this and similar work, a group of prominent scientists in the United States, including Albert Einstein, wrote to President Roosevelt in 1939 urging him to instigate a research programme into the development of a weapon based on nuclear fission. (Despite popular misconceptions, this was Einstein's only involvement in the US development of the atom bomb.)

Theoretical research was carried out until 1943, when a new laboratory was opened at Los Alamos, New Mexico, under the directorship of J Robert Oppenheimer with the aim of developing a practical weapon. Two years and $2 billion later, the United States was ready to test its new weapon.

At 5.30 on the morning of July 16, 1945, Alamogordo air base was suddenly bathed in a light that was brighter than a thousand suns. The blinding flash was followed by a wave of heat that turned the desert sand to glass, and a terrifying roar as shock waves moved out from the point of detonation.

As a mushroom-shaped cloud of gas and dust rose 12,000 metres (40,000 ft) into the air, Oppenheimer, the director of what had come to be known as the Manhattan Project, muttered to himself a line from the *Bhagavad Gita:* "I am become death, the shatterer of worlds". At his side

General Grove, who was observing the test on behalf of the military, had a rather practical response: "The war's over. One or two of those things, and Japan will be finished".

Although the Japanese had been on the defensive since 1943, fighting in the Pacific region was still as fierce as ever. During 1944 the USA had succeeded in capturing Saipan, Tinian and Guam from the Japanese, while, at the same time, the British had brought a stop to the Japanese advance from Burma into India.

US forces under General MacArthur had begun to retake the Philippines in October 1944, and two months later the British started operations to take Burma back from the Japanese. By June 1945, the USA had captured Iwo Jima and Okinawa, scenes of some of the fiercest fighting in the entire war. They were now just 800 km (500 miles) from mainland Japan, whose cities were being levelled by constant air attacks.

But still the Japanese would not surrender, choosing instead to fight to the last man rather than face defeat.

By July, however, even the most fanatical elements in the Japanese military were beginning to look for ways of bringing a peaceful end to the conflict.

On July 26, Winston Churchill and the new US President, Harry S Truman, issued an ultimatum to the Japanese demanding their unconditional surrender. The ultimatum also stated that Japanese war criminals would be punished

invaded China on August 8. Fearful of Soviet incursions in the Pacific region, and with the Japanese still hesitating over the proposed unconditional surrender, Truman unleashed a second atom bomb, this time on the smaller city of Nagasaki.

The blast which devastated Nagasaki on August 9 was even more powerful than the Hiroshima explosion. On August 14, the Japanese Emperor, for once choosing to overrule his military advisors, called an end to the fighting and announced on Japanese radio that the unendurable had to be endured.

Japan surrendered unconditionally and with that final action World War Two came to an end.

and that Japan would be required to pay reparations, but went on to declare that: "We do not intend that the Japanese shall be enslaved as a race nor destroyed as a nation ...".

Unfortunately, an incorrect translation of the response from the Japanese Prime Minister, Admiral Suzuki, seemed to indicate that the Japanese would never even contemplate unconditional surrender.

By now Truman was convinced that the only way to bring an end to the war was to shock the Japanese into surrendering. Accordingly, he authorized the use of the United States' secret atomic weapon against a civilian target. The bomb that devastated Hiroshima instantly wiped an area covering 10 square km (4 square miles) off the face of the Earth. More than 66,000 men, women and children were vaporized in that first split second.

As the shock wave moved out from the point of detonation, a further 69,000 people were seriously injured and almost seventy per cent of the city was damaged or destroyed.

The killing might have stopped there if the Soviet Union had not declared war on Japan and

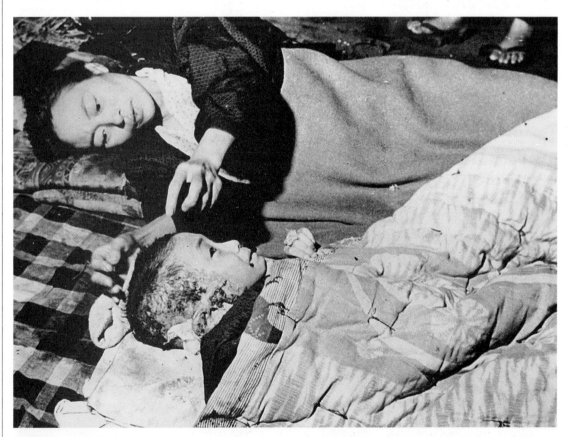

▲ Although many survived the bombings of Hiroshima and Nagasaki, the full horrors of nuclear war only emerged over the years that followed as many died from exposure to radiation.

BIRTH OF THE UNITED NATIONS

The new year began on a positive note when the first assembly of the United Nations opened on January 10 at St James's Palace in London. Delegates from 51 nations, representing around eighty per cent of the entire population of the world, met with the ultimate aim of ensuring peace on a global scale for the foreseeable future.

The United Nations, the second organization of its type to have been formed since World War One, was created to replace the League of Nations, established under the Treaty Of Versailles in 1919.

The League Of Nations had been formed to preserve the status quo established at the end of World War One, but was seriously hampered from the start by the United States' refusal to ratify the Treaty Of Versailles.

During the 1930s, conspicuous lack of action after Japanese expansion into China and Italy's invasion of Ethiopia seriously damaged the credibility of the League. During World War Two it ceased to exist in all but name.

During 1944, however, moves were made to form a new permanent body drawn from those nations that were united against the Axis powers of Germany, Italy and Japan. To this end, representatives from Great Britain, the United States, France and China – the so-called "Big Four" – met in Washington D C between August 21 and October 7, 1944.

Their aim was to draw up preliminary proposals to discuss at the United Nations Conference on International Organization, held in San Francisco in December 1944. This conference produced the Charter of The United Nations, which came into effect from October 24, 1945.

The charter set out certain aims which were to be pursued by the United Nations. In essence, these included the avoidance of war and a formal recognition of fundamental human rights.

It also set out to establish conditions under which justice and respect for the obligations arising from treaties and other sources of international law could be maintained.

Another aim was to promote social progress and better standards of life. In short, the charter had as its ultimate goal the maintenance of peace and security throughout the world.

The first assembly of the United Nations was held in London (later assemblies would be held at the permanent headquarters in New York). The assembly focused on a dispute between Iran and the Soviet Union.

Iran had complained that Soviet troops were preventing their own forces from occupying the province of Azerbaijan, thereby threatening Iran's sovereignty in the region and, most importantly, interfering with the extraction of oil from the province.

▼ **Gunners from the Royal Artillery prepare place names for the first meeting of the United Nations.**

EMPEROR HIROHITO NO LONGER DIVINE

Still reeling from the shock of defeat at the hands of the Allies and the humiliation of unconditional surrender, the Japanese sense of honour and inherent superiority was dealt a further blow in January.

Emperor Hirohito issued an imperial decree which was published in Japanese newspapers and broadcast over the radio on the first day of the new year. Under orders from the US occupiers of Japan, Hirohito was forced to declare that, contrary to well over a thousand years of traditional belief, he was not divine in origin or nature. (Since ancient times, Japanese emperors had been believed to be direct descendants of the Sun goddess Amaterasu.)

According to the new constitution of Japan, which had been drawn up by the United States at the end of the war, Japan was to be a constitutional monarchy. It had been decided that its sovereignty would rest with the people of Japan and not with its emperor, whose role was reduced to that of a figurehead.

► In a final humiliation at the hands of the Allied victors, Hirohito was forced to declare that he was not a divine being.

NATIONALIZATION IN BRITAIN

At the end of July 1945, with the war in Europe over and the war in the Far East nearing its cataclysmic end, the British people went to the polls to elect a new leader for the first time since 1935.

In a result that seemed to surprise the rest of the world, Winston Churchill, Britain's unshakeable and courageous wartime leader, was removed from office and replaced by mild-mannered Clement Attlee, leader of the Labour party. For the first time ever, Britain had a Socialist government with a clear and powerful overall majority of 136 seats.

The party had been elected on a platform of massive social reform and the nationalization of key industries and institutions. Nationalization was to be carried out with the aim of giving the government more control over the

▲ The Bank of England in the City of London. The Bank was nationalized by the UK's new Labour Government in 1946.

running of the economy in the hope of avoiding a repeat of the slump of the 1930s.

To this end, the Bank of England was nationalized with effect from March 1, 1946. Before this date the bank had been in private hands since it was incorporated by an act of parliament in 1694.

On January 1, 1947, the coal industry followed the Bank of England with the setting up of the National Coal Board. The board took control of Britain's 1,647 mines out of private hands and placed it with the then Ministry of Power.

The success of the policy of nationalization can be illustrated by the fact that, for a generation, the level of unemployment in Great Britain rarely rose above half a million people – a figure equivalent to around two per cent of the entire population.

CHURCHILL DEFINES THE "IRON CURTAIN"

June
- State elections in US-controlled zone of Germany
- Elections for French assembly held
- US Supreme court rules segregation of buses is unconstitutional
- Georges Bidault becomes President of French provisional government
- Greece takes possession of the Dodecanese Islands
- Deaths of British pioneer of television John Logie Baird and US boxer Jack Johnson

July
- Republic of the Philippines declared
- Miguel Alemán elected Mexican president
- Ninety-one people die in Jewish terrorist bomb attack on the King David Hotel in Jerusalem
- Allied powers peace conference begins in Paris

August
- German army dissolved by Allies
- Death of British writer H G Wells

September
- Conference on the future of Palestine opens in London
- Provisional government formed under Nehru in India
- King George II returns to Greece

Speaking in Fulton, Missouri, in the United States of America on March 5, former British Prime Minister Winston Churchill made his famous reference to the "Iron Curtain" between the Capitalist West and the Communist East. "From Stettin in the Baltic to Trieste in the Adriatic," he boomed, "an iron curtain has descended across the Continent."

The iron curtain to which he was referring was the ideological barrier between Stalin's Soviet Union and his neighbours in Europe and the rest of the world. Urging the United States to form an alliance with Britain to discourage any future expansion of the Soviet Union, Churchill went on to condemn Stalin's regime in words that sounded remarkably similar in tone to those he had used to describe Hitler's Germany some years earlier.

Churchill's speech was consistent with the views that he had expressed privately to President Truman at the end of World War Two. Worldwide reaction to the speech was, nonetheless, mixed. In London, a leading article in *The Times* expressed the view that: "... while Western democracy and Communism are in many respects opposed, they have much to learn from each other." In the United States, however, Senator Robertson used public interest in the speech to stress the importance of close relations between Great Britain and the United States of America in order to curb the expansion plans of the Soviet Union.

Churchill's comments were born as much from up-close observations of Joseph Stalin as they were of the Soviet Union's actions after the end of World War Two.

During the key meeting of the Allied powers at Potsdam in Berlin in July 1945, it had become apparent to Churchill that the interests of the West were no longer the same as those of Stalin and the Soviet Union. Despite assurances to the contrary, Stalin never did hand power back to those countries that came under Soviet control during the supposed interim period following the end of the conflict in Europe. This confirmed Churchill's worst fears as to Stalin's true intentions for postwar Europe.

▲ Britain's wartime hero Winston Churchill coined the phrase that would forever describe the divide between East and West.

ITALY BECOMES A REPUBLIC

Italians voted overwhelmingly to change their country from a monarchy to a republic in a referendum held on June 3. The vote immediately rendered the sitting monarch, King Umberto II, redundant; on June 14 he and any male heirs were permanently banished from Italy. Enrico de Nicola became president of the republic.

Umberto was the son of King Victor Emmanuel III, who had abdicated in his favour less than a month before. A deciding factor for many of the Italians who voted for the republic was the role that Umberto had played in the fascist dictatorship under Mussolini.

With the creation of the new republic, Italy could truly begin to rebuild itself after the ravages of World War Two. The moderate Italian Prime Minister Alcide de Gaspari oversaw the transition from monarchy to republic and

continued to act as Prime Minister of Italy until 1953.

During his time in office, de Gaspari introduced many reforms at home and also sought to bring Italy back to the international stage. To this end, he took Italy into the North Atlantic Treaty Organization in 1951 and, to gain a more influential role for his country, began to re-arm Italy that same year. He was also instrumental in the organization of the Council of Europe.

◄ Alcide de Gaspari, first Prime Minister of the new republic of Italy. With the fall of fascism, the monarchy also fell from grace.

CHINESE CIVIL WAR CONTINUES

In October fighting broke out yet again between the two sides embroiled in the long-running civil war in China.

Japan's defeat at the hands of the Allies brought an end to World War Two and with it a close to the expansionist plans of the Japanese military.

As Japanese forces withdrew from the territories they had taken in the run up to, and course of, the war there was an unseemly struggle among many factions to take control of what remained. Nowhere was this struggle more obvious or disastrous than in China, which had for so long suffered the attentions of the Japanese.

Despite the Japanese invasion, the civil war in China had continued to some degree and with the ending of worldwide hostilities had flared up again.

President Harry S Truman of the United States of America had earlier attempted to broker a truce between the two sides in the civil war – the Nationalists under Chiang Kai-shek and the Communists under Mao Tse-tung. In an effort to bring about a unified China, he had gone as far as dispatching General George C Marshall, architect of the Marshall Aid plan, to the country as his special envoy and mediator in the hope of bringing the two sides together. Unfortunately, Marshall's mission met with little success and in October hostilities broke out again.

The United States' immediate response was to impose an arms embargo on the country, but in 1947 they relented and began to supply arms to the Nationalists forces under Chiang Kai-shek. (Quite bizarrely, the US claimed that arming the Nationalists allowed them to pursue their own policy of "neutrality against the Communists".)

At this stage in the civil war, the Chinese Communists did not officially receive the military support of their counterparts in the Soviet Union. However, Stalin, depicting Mao Tse-tung as an agrarian reformer, continued to call for a coalition government in China to be formed from the rival Nationalist and Communist forces.

▼ **Members of the Communist New Fourth Army, opponents of Chiang Kai-shek's Nationalist forces in China.**

As the Allies had advanced across Europe, they found disturbing evidence to suggest that the Axis powers had indulged in murder on a massive scale.

Death is an inevitable consequence of war, but the sights and stories that the Allies encountered on their march to Berlin suggested that the fascists had slaughtered military personnel and civilians alike to an extent that had never been witnessed before in the modern world.

Even before the end of World War Two, thoughts were turning to finding the means to punish those who had stepped so far beyond the bounds of what was deemed to be acceptable behaviour – even in wartime – as to be considered criminal and therefore punishable by law.

On August 8, 1945, representatives of the United States, Great Britain, the Soviet Union and France signed what came to be known as the London Agreement. This agreement established a charter for the setting up of an international lmilitary tribunal to try those members of the Axis powers who were accused of being war criminals but whose crimes were not confined to a single country. (Those whose criminal activities were restricted to a single country were to be tried in the country in which their crimes had been committed.)

Under the terms of the agreement, individuals could be tried for crimes against peace, crimes against humanity or war crimes.

▲ Sitting in the dock, high-ranking Nazis Hermann Goering, Rudolf Hess, Joachim von Ribbentrop and Wilhelm Keitel (front, from left to right) await their fate.

Conspiracy to commit any of these crimes was also, in itself, considered a criminal offence. In addition to these charges, organizations– such as the SS – could also be declared to be criminal by their very nature, removing any question as to their legal status.

Crimes against peace involved acts of aggression in violation of treaties or agreements. Charges of crimes against humanity were to be levelled at anyone thought to be involved in mass deportations and genocide.

War crimes were simply those acts committed in violation of the laws of war. Defendants were given more or less the same rights as those of any defendants in an ordinary criminal court.

Soon after it was signed, nineteen other countries agreed to accept the provisions of the London Agreement and the first tribunal began in Berlin on October 18, 1945. It was presided over by General Nikitchenko of the Soviet Union and the defendants were twenty four former Nazis leaders, who were charged with having carried out acts which could be defined as war crimes.

In addition, various extreme elements in the Nazi organization, such as the Gestapo, were charged with being – by their very nature – criminal. On November

20, 1945, the tribunal was moved to Nuremberg (the site of the Nazis' glorious rallies less than a decade earlier) and placed under the presidency of Lord Justice Geoffrey Lawrence of Great Britain.

So began the Nuremberg Trials proper, which saw several former Nazi leaders charged and tried as war criminals by the International Military Tribunal. Between November 20, 1945, and October 1, 1946, the tribunal met 216 times before delivering its verdict.

Of the twenty-four Nazis charged with war crimes, nineteen were found to be guilty. (Robert Ley, one of the original defendants, had committed suicide while in prison; the German industrialist Gustav Krupp, whose company continues to thrive to this day, was judged to be unfit to stand trial on the grounds of senile dementia.) Three of the men – Hjalmar Schacht, Franz von Papen and Hans Fritzsche – were acquitted. Four of the defendants – Karl Dönitz, Baldur von Schirach, Albert Speer and Konstantin von Neurath – received prison sentences of between ten and twenty years. Rudolf Hess, Walther Funk and Erich Raeder received life sentences. The remaining twelve Nazis were each sentenced to death by hanging.

Martin Bormann had been found guilty and sentenced in his absence, however, and the sentence was never carried out as he was never found by the authorities. Hermann Goering also managed to escape hanging, but rather less successfully: he committed suicide on the eve of

▲ Hermann Goering, former head of Hitler's Luftwaffe, takes the oath as he enters the witness box at his own war crimes trial.

▲ Spandau Prison, Berlin. Sentenced to life imprisonment at Nuremberg, Rudolf Hess was kept here until his death in 1987.

his execution. The ten remaining defendants – Hans Frank, Wilhelm Frick, Julius Streicher, Alfred Rosenberg, Ernst Kaltenbrunner, Joachim von Ribbentrop, Fritz Sauckel, Alfred Jodl, Wilhelm Keitel, and Arthur Seyss-Inquart – were hanged on October 16, 1946.

The essential problem facing those seeking to punish the Nazis for their activities during World War Two was deciding who should be prosecuted. After the occupation of Germany by the Allies, an attempt was made to round up all those who were thought to have served the Nazis in some capacity, but it soon became apparent that there were too many people involved for this to be a practical proposition.

Millions of Germans had joined the Nazi party, although their motives for doing so were not always criminal. In the sections of Germany controlled by the British, French and USA, only 209,000 Germans out of a population of 44.5 million were prosecuted.

The figure for the Soviet sector is usually given as just over 17,000. This does not mean that the Soviets were less committed to prosecuting Nazis than their counterparts in the rest of Germany, but merely that they were less inclined to go through the legal process before executing those suspected of war crimes.

BRITAIN NATIONALIZES THE COAL INDUSTRY

One of the least exciting pieces of news to break in 1947 concerned the nationalization of Britain's coal industry.

The Labour party in power had already nationalized the Bank of England at the start of March 1946, following an election pledge to examine the possibility of nationalizing certain key institutions and industries. This motion would ensure that there was no repeat of the disastrous slump of the 1930s, and also enable the government to improve the rights and conditions of workers in those industries.

Next in line was Britain's coal industry, which at the time was one of the major employers of manual labour in the country.

From January 1, the newly formed National Coal Board came into being as a result of the passing of the earlier Coal Industry Nationalization Act of 1946. Its function was to take over the running of the mines, which had previously been in private hands, and to oversee the distribution of coal and related supplies. The board members were appointed by the minister of power and came under the chairmanship of Lord Hyndley. The National Coal Board's assets at the time included 1,647 mines, more than a million acres of land and around 100,000 miners' homes.

The nationalization of the Bank of England and the coal industry was not the end of the policy. Over time, the telephone industry, the airlines, the railways, the iron and steel industries and public utilities, including gas and electricity, would all follow suit as they, too, were taken into public ownership.

▲ **An experienced miner has some welcoming words for two young apprentices at the Lount Colliery in Leicestershire, opened in 1943.**

DISCOVERY OF THE DEAD SEA SCROLLS

One of the most exciting and significant archaeological finds of all times occurred in April: a young Bedouin boy discovered a set of earthenware jars in a desert cave at Qumran on the shores of the Dead Sea. Rolled up in the jars were several fine leather scrolls, which turned out to be manuscripts dating mostly from the first century BC and the first century AD.

Later finds, in the 1950s and 1960s, appeared to date from around the same period and allowed scholars to begin to piece together the original sections of the first part of the Bible – the Old Testament.

With a few exceptions, the scrolls are written in Hebrew or Aramaic and appear to have belonged to an ancient Jewish sect. Debate raged over just which sect had produced the scrolls. At first it was thought that they were the work of the Zealots, or perhaps an early Christian sect. There is, however, compelling evidence to suggest that many of the scrolls formed the library of a Jewish fundamentalist group called the Essenes, who are known to have been based around Qumran from about the second century BC until AD68, when an invading Roman army arrived in the region.

The scrolls relating to the Hebrew Old Testament date from around AD70 – less than forty years after the presumed death of Jesus Christ, and indicate the extent to which the Hebrew Bible had already been formalized. The scrolls have also assisted scholars in charting the history of Palestine as far back as four centuries before the birth of Christ and to trace the emergence of Christianity.

The scrolls continue to shed light on the relationship between the early Christians and the Jews. However, the information contained in the scrolls is jealously guarded by the Israeli Antiquities Authority, who have tended to restrict access to these important documents.

▲ These sections from one of the 2000-year-old Dead Sea Scrolls contain text from the Old Testament Book of Isaiah.

THE MARSHALL PLAN

While addressing a meeting at Harvard University on June 5, US Secretary of State George C Marshall put forward a plan for the rehabilitation of the many devastated European economies. His strategy, he hoped, would bring about conditions under which democracy could thrive throughout Europe.

Based on plans put forward by a committee representing sixteen of the European economies, the US Congress agreed to set up the European Recovery Program. Under this scheme, financial aid was offered to most European countries, even those occupied by the Soviets. However, the Soviets later withdrew from the program taking those countries it controlled out of the scheme in the process.

The Economic Cooperation Administration was set up under the control of Paul G Hoffman to distribute 13 billion US dollars worth of economic aid to those countries which remained involved with the plan, namely Austria, Belgium, Denmark, France, Great Britain, Greece, Iceland, Ireland, Italy, Luxembourg, The Netherlands, Norway, Portugal, Sweden,

Switzerland, Turkey, and West Germany. For the most part aid came in the form of grants to help rebuild industry and agriculture. (This also had the added bonus of helping to stabilize economies and expand trade.) The remainder of the money was paid in the form of loans.

The success of the Marshall plan is clear from the effects on the economies of the various European countries which partici-

pated. Thanks to economic aid from the US, most of the countries experienced a growth in their economies of between 15 and 25 per cent and saw the rebirth of their heavy industries in the process.

President Harry S Truman expanded the plan further to include other countries outside Europe. His scheme, known as the Point Four Program, began in 1949.

▲ The first consignment of sugar arrives at Royal Victoria Docks in London under the terms of the Marshall Plan.

NEWS IN BRIEF

May
- State elections in French-controlled zone of Germany
- Major strikes in France
- New constitution adopted in Japan
- Italian Prime Minister de Gasperi resigns; he forms a new coalition government days later
- Hungarian Prime Minister Nagy resigns; Lajos Dinnyés succeeds

June
- Government-backed economy drive brings wartime austerity rationing back in UK

July
- Conference between West European nations begins in Paris to discuss the Marshall Plan
- Dutch troops begin campaign to reassert Dutch control in Indonesia
- The National Security Act reforming US military structures signed
- The Romanian National Peasant Party dissolved

▲ As the drive for independence continued, so did violence between India's Hindus and Muslims. (Insets: top, Nehru; bottom, Jinnah.)

British colonial rule in India came to an end in August with the enforcement of the Indian Independence Act. Under the act, passed by the British parliament in July, a line of demarcation was to be drawn across India and the new dominions of India and Pakistan established by midnight on August 14–15.

The British had tried for some time to establish a single administration in India to which all power could be transferred, but the complexities of Indian politics made the task almost impossible. The essential problem was that India was a country deeply divided along political and religious lines but united in its desire to see the British leave. (Mahatma Gandhi's "Quit India" campaign neatly expressed what the majority of people in India felt about the British presence on their soil.)

The two main political/religious groups in India were the Muslims, led by Mohammed Ali Jinnah and the Hindus, led by Pandit Jawaharlal Nehru. The Sikh population of India, who had played so prominent a role in the

British Army, had naively assumed that their courage and loyalty would be rewarded in some way by the British. This proved not to be the case, of course, and their betrayal by the British left the Sikhs, led by Tara Singh, with little political influence in the country.

Civil war in India between rival Muslim and Hindu groups – which in 1946 had been particularly bloody – combined with the possibility of mutiny in the Indian army had led the British to seek a swift

transfer of power. It was clear to all observers that the situation, rather than improving, would instead grow considerably worse.

In March 1947, Lord Mountbatten had taken over as Viceroy of India with the aim of returning the country to Indian rule by June 1948. He soon realized, however, that the situation was too dangerous for him to risk the lives of British troops still stationed in the country. Rather than see more lives lost to the civil war while protracted negotiations between both sides were played out, he simply resolved to divide Punjab and Bengal and hand over control to the Muslims (who got Pakistan) and the Hindus (who got India).

Gandhi could not accept the plan and was even prepared to put up with Jinnah, the Muslim leader, as Premier of a united India rather than face partition.

Nehru, however, had tired of the fight and finally, along with Jinnah, accepted the British plan for India. During the bloodshed triggered by the mass migrations that followed the partition, more than one million people are believed to have lost their lives.

▼ Lord Mountbatten sits between Nehru and Jinnah at one of the many negotiating sessions for Indian independence.

COMMITTEE INVESTIGATES COMMUNISM IN THE USA

In a move likened later by US playwright Arthur Miller to the Salem witchhunt of the late seventeenth century, Congress agreed to the creation of a committee to investigate the extent of Communist infiltration into the United States. The House Un-American Activities Committee was set up to expose the continued rise of Communism after World War Two – a move that quickly caused outright hysteria as claim and counter-claim turned into accusation and recrimination.

On October 23, the hearings in Washington switched focus and began to investigate the extent of Communist infiltration into the entertainment industry. First on the stand was the president of the Screen Actors Guild (a man who had previously been acted off the screen by a chimpanzee), future US President Ronald Reagan. As expected, Reagan denied that the guild was under the control of Communists and was left to resume his business.

Less fortunate was a group of producers, directors and screenwriters from Tinsel Town who came to be known as the Hollywood Ten. Despite pleading the Fifth Amendment, which gives US citizens the right under the US Constitution to refuse to answer questions which may prove incriminating, the ten individuals – Alvah Bessie, Herbert Biberman, Lester Cole, Edward Dmytryk, Ring Lardner, Jr, John Howard Lawson, Albert Maltz, Samuel Ornitz, Adrian Scott and Dalton Trumbo – were charged with contempt of Congress on November 24. They were sentenced to prison terms of between six months and a year. On emerging from prison, the ten were blacklisted by the studios and most of them never worked in Hollywood again.

▼ Film stars including Humphrey Bogart and Lauren Bacall (centre) protest at the US government's anti-Communist investigations.

CHUCK YEAGER BREAKS THE SOUND BARRIER

Proving beyond a shadow of a doubt that he was "the Right Stuff", Captain Charles "Chuck" Yeager seized the Holy Grail of aviation when he piloted the Bell Aircraft Company's experimental X-1 rocket plane through the sound barrier. His mission on October 14 arguably made him the greatest ever test pilot in the US, and secured him a place in the history books.

Flying over Rogers Dry Lake in southern California, Yeager and his aircraft were dropped from a specially adapted B-29 bomber at 7,600 metres (25,000 ft). As the X-1 dropped like a stone, Yeager kicked in the rocket engines in

▲ Faster than the speed of sound, USAF Captain Chuck Yeager flies his Bell X-1 "rocket plane" into aviation history.

sequence and piloted the craft up to 12,200 metres (40,000 ft), flying faster than the speed of sound – 1,065 km per hour (662 mph) at that altitude – in the process. So secret was the project that neither the Bell Aircraft Company nor the US government announced the successful attempt until June 1948.

Yeager had served with the US Airforce based in Great Britain during World War Two, shooting down 13 enemy aircraft before being shot down himself over France (he escaped with the aid of the Resistance). Despite his immense courage and ability, he was rejected for the US space program on the grounds that he lacked a college education.

GANDHI MURDERED

On the night of January 20, while on his way to an evening prayer meeting in Delhi, Mohandas Karamchand Gandhi, known to Indians and the world as "Mahatma" or "great sage", was approached by Nathuram Godse, a young Hindu fanatic. Without warning, Godse produced a gun and shot dead the leading light of the Indian nationalism movement. The cruel irony of Gandhi's death was that he was a man who had spent most of his life advocating non-violent resistance to British rule in India.

Born in Porbandar in western India on October 2, 1869, Gandhi was raised as a Hindu, although he was also exposed to Jainism, a highly moral Indian religion which advocates non-violence. After attending the University of Bombay, Gandhi went to London to study to become a barrister. In his youth, he had imagined England to be "a land of philosophers and poets, the very centre of civilization". One might safely assume that the reality of life for a poor Indian student in late nineteenth-century England somewhat altered his views on

the English. But his treatment in London was as nothing compared to the shock awaiting him when he went to work in South Africa after his studies. His experience of South African racism made him vow to defend the dignity of every Indian and stimulated a lasting interest in politics.

On his return to India, Gandhi campaigned for the rights of the indigenous people, even exposing Queen Victoria to accusations of racism. Despite this, he supported both the British in their war against the Boers in South Africa and the British efforts

during World War One.

By 1920, Gandhi had risen through the ranks of Indian politics and turned the Indian National Congress into an effective force in the battle for independence. His programme of non-violent non-cooperation with the British authorities in India grew rapidly. By 1922, thousands of Indians were being arrested for peacefully defying British rule.

On March 10, 1922, Gandhi himself was arrested and given a six-year sentence for sedition. After two years, he was released. However, on emerging from prison, he found that his beloved Congress Party had split down the middle: cooperation between Muslims and Hindus in the fight to rid India of the British had broken down.

Gandhi continued his policy of harassing the British in his own non-violent fashion, but Indian politics were changing and a new, more aggressive and violent element had crept in.

The real tragedy of Gandhi's death was that he was the one individual who might have been able to find a peaceful solution to the problems created by Britain's arbitrary division of the country he had done so much to unite.

▲ **Gandhi's refusal to embrace violent protest won the admiration of the world, but made him enemies within his own country.**

▼ **Once the bane of British colonial rule, Gandhi's importance was later acknowledged by Lord Mountbatten, India's last Viceroy.**

NEWS IN BRIEF

- The United Nations General Assembly adopts the Universal Declaration of Human Rights
- Organization of American States (OAS) founded
- World Health Organization (WHO) founded
- Large-scale emigration from the West Indies to Britain begins
- Solid state transistor invented
- Discovery of RNA in chromosomes
- 33rpm audio records developed
- Buckminster Fuller builds first large geodesic dome in USA
- Piccard develops bathyscape for deep ocean descents
- Morris Minor car marketed in Britain
- Films released during the year include Laurence Olivier's *Hamlet*, David Lean's *Oliver Twist*, Powell and Pressburger's *The Red Shoes*, Alexander Mackendrick's *Whisky Galore*, Orson Welles's *The Lady from Shanghai* and John Huston's *Key Largo*
- Aldeburgh Music Festival in Britain founded
- *Turangalila Symphony* by Oliver Messiaen premieres
- The musical *Kiss Me Kate* opens in New York
- Books published this year include *Other Voices, Other Rooms* by Truman Capote, *The Naked and the Dead* by Norman Mailer and *Cry The Beloved Country* by Alan Paton
- Scrabble word game marketed

COMMUNISTS IN CONTROL OF CZECHOSLOVAKIA

▲ **Klement Gottwald, Czechoslovakia's first Communist president, addresses a mass rally from the balcony of Prague's Kinsky Palace.**

A loose alliance of Communist interests led by Klement Gottwald seized power in Czechoslovakia on February 25 by what was later to be termed an "elegant takeover". This was no coup in the conventional sense, but rather an attempt by the President of Czechoslovakia, Eduard Benes, to prevent a civil war and avoid the direct intervention of the Soviet Union in the running of the country.

Benes had returned to Czechoslovakia to run the newly restored state in 1945. Unlike many of the other countries which fell under the influence of the Soviet Union after World War Two, Czechoslovakia had a fairly strong democratic system, despite the fact that its postwar administration and army had been modelled closely on those of the Soviet Union.

A measure of just how open the Czech political system was at this time is clearly evident from the interim government appointed immediately after the war, under the leadership of Klement Gottwald.

The "People's Front" cabinet included members from groups. including the Communist Party, the Social Democratic Party, the Czech National Socialist Party and the Slovak Democratic Party. During the first postwar elections to be held in Czechoslovakia in May 1946, the Communists gained almost 40 per cent of the entire vote and looked set to rule Czechoslovakia under the approving eye of the Soviet Union for some time to come.

Events took a bad turn in July 1947, however, when the Kremlin, against the wishes of many in the Czech government, insisted that the US Marshall Aid plan would not be extended to include Czechoslovakia. The Soviet's lack of sensitivity over this issue reflected badly on the Communists, whose grip on power began to slip. In November 1947 they fared extremely badly in open elections held within the universities. An opinion poll carried out in January 1948 indicated that national support for the Communists had fallen to less than 25 per cent. At a time

when the Soviet Union was seeking to increase its influence in the country through the Communists, the people of Czechoslovakia appeared to be rejecting rule from Moscow.

In an attempt to maintain power, the Communists began to exercise greater control over the police force and the trade unions. Despite demands from non-Communist parties in the country to end their interference, Gottwald and his followers established "action committees". These were made up mostly from loyal trade unionists, who bypassed elected local bodies.

A further outrage occurred on February 20, when an armed 20,000-strong people's militia was set up. The force was drawn once again from the ranks of Communist supporters. The militia's march through Prague on February 22 brought events to a head. With the Soviet Union breathing down his neck and the scent of civil war in the air, President Benes handed power to the Communists, under Klement Gottwald on February 25.

BIRTH OF THE STATE OF ISRAEL

When David Ben-Gurion proudly declared Israeli independence at Tel Aviv on May 14, he brought to an end nearly two thousand years of stateless wandering by the Jewish people. There had been no official Jewish state since the founders of the First Reich – the Romans – had driven the Jews from the Holy Land, causing them eventually to disperse around the world.

Now the Jews had returned from exile, many of them survivors of the war in Europe and the relentless persecution at the hands of the Nazis. They shared no common language and their backgrounds could not have been more different.

The immigrants to Israel from Germany were mostly professional people, doctors, lawyers and lecturers who had been driven from their work and their homes by Nazis legislation. Jews fleeing from eastern Europe were often sons and daughters of the manual workers who had narrowly escaped murder at the hands of the SS. Thrown together in Israel they found a common purpose.

Dispersed throughout the world the Jews had been unable to resist the rise of the Nazis. Now, from the security of their own state, they would ensure that never again would Jewish people be so defenceless.

The Balfour Declaration of 1917 had promised the Jews a national home in Palestine. For Ben-Gurion, who was destined to become the first Prime Minister of the state of Israel, this was merely the first step towards an independent Jewish state.

In succeeding years Ben-Gurion worked to increase Jewish immigration into Palestine. On May 12, 1942, he addressed a conference of Zionists in New York where it was decided that a Jewish State would be established in Palestine at the end of the war. The resulting struggle against the British mandate in Palestine was led by Ben-Gurion, but it was the full backing of the United Nations General Assembly – and the support of the Soviet Union and the United States – that helped finally establish the state of Israel in 1948. The Jews had found the promised land.

▼ **David Ben-Gurion, the first Prime Minister of Israel, reads the Jewish Declaration of Independence.**

BERLIN AIRLIFT TRIUMPH

June 24 saw an historic declaration by the Soviet Union. In response to the decision by Great Britain, France and the United States to combine their "zones of occupation" in Germany into a single body, the Soviets announced that all previous arrangements regarding the administration of Berlin by the four Allied powers no longer applied. Furthermore the Western powers no longer had any rights over Berlin. (The Soviets had earlier withdrawn from the Allied Control Council, which had been set up to administer postwar Germany.)

When the new Deutsche Mark was introduced in the west of the city – a move viewed as a potential threat to eastern European currencies – the Soviets began a blockade of Berlin. Two days later, on June 26, the United States and Great Britain began to airlift supplies of food and other essentials into the besieged city, and in doing so sparked a crisis of international proportions.

The Soviet army of occupation in East Germany began to receive reinforcements and by the middle of July had grown in strength to forty divisions, outnumbering Western Allied forces in the country by five to one.

At the end of the month, three groups of US strategic bombers arrived in Britain where they posed an obvious threat to Soviet positions. Miraculously, and despite tensions between the two sides, the conflict did not escalate into a full-scale war.

Although Great Britain and the United States could do little to alleviate the desperate shortages of fuel and electricity, they managed to maintain food supplies to West Berlin for eleven months until the Soviet Union, under strong pressure from Western counter-measures against eastern bloc exports, lifted the blockade on May 12, 1949.

The airlifts continued, however, until the end of September, by which time well over two million tonnes of goods had been airlifted into Berlin at a total cost of over $US200 million.

▲ The "Berlin Airlift" carried out by the British and US air forces successfully foiled the Soviet attempt to isolate the city.

NORTH KOREA PROCLAIMS INDEPENDENCE

▲ President Kim Il Sung, the first leader of the Democratic People's Republic of Korea. He would remain in power until his death in 1994.

The people of North Korea proclaimed their independence on September 3, establishing the Democratic People's Republic of Korea under the leadership of President Kim Il Sung. This was the latest development in the long saga of Korea. The Japanese had been in control of the country for much of the twentieth century until they had been force to hand it over to the Allies during World War Two.

The Allies, with their seeming talent for creating trouble while attempting to act with the best of intentions, divided Korea artificially between North and South, leaving the North in the hands of the Soviet Union. The US assumed control of South Korea.

No sooner had North Korea proclaimed its independence than secret plans were drawn up for the proposed invasion of the southern half of the country with the aim of uniting Korea under a Communist government.

The invasion began on June 25, 1950 without warning. With considerable aid from China, North Korean forces advanced swiftly into South Korea and came close to taking over the entire country. In response, the West, especially the United States, sent a UN force into the country to defend the South from the Communist invasion. The resulting war lasted until July 25 1953, by which time the country was in ruins.

North Korea was effectively rebuilt by the Communist governments of the Soviet Union and China and the principal aim of its present administration remains the re-unification of Korea.

CHINESE COMMUNISTS SEIZE PEKING

Chinese Communists, under Mao Tse-tung, seized control of Peking in January in a decisive move, which brought the possibility of an end to the long-running civil war in China. This marked a major change in the tide of the war, which until the end of 1947 looked to be going the way of the Nationalist forces under Chiang Kai-shek.

Ironically, the turn around was in some part due to the actions of the pro-Nationalist US, which had begun to supply military aid to Chiang's forces in 1947. In March that year the Nationalists had advanced against the Communists and had even

▲ **Mao Tse-tung proclaims the foundation of the People's Republic of China on October 1, 1949.**

▲ **Chiang Kai-shek in typically forthright stance. US aid did not win his Nationalists the prize of mainland China.**

succeeded in overrunning the Communist stronghold at Yen-an.

Flushed with success and armed with US-bought weapons, the Nationalists expanded throughout North China and Manchuria, greatly over-extending their stretched forces in the process. As complacency set in, some Nationalist officers began to sell US weapons to the Communists, while corrupt officials diverted US aid worth up to $2 billion into their own pockets.

When the Communists counter-attacked at the end of 1947 the

Nationalists were soon driven back. After capturing Peking a little over a year later, Mao's forces headed south, heaping comprehensive defeat on the Nationalists as they went.

On August 5, the United States officially ceased supplying aid to the Nationalists, most of whom had fled to Taiwan. On October 1, 1949, the Communists at Peking declared China to be a Communist People's Republic. The new regime under Chairman Mao was immediately recognized by the Soviet Union.

BIRTH OF NATO

The Western powers formalized their alliance against the growing Communist threat on April 4 with the signing of the North Atlantic Treaty.

At the end of World War Two, the United States and the Western European powers began to dismantle their armies. But while the USA, Great Britain and France were busy putting the

machinery of war into storage, the Soviet Union was, in contrast, building up its forces in those eastern European countries over which it had control.

After the euphoria of victory had begun to fade, it became apparent that the "Iron Curtain" had truly descended across Europe, and behind it lay a former ally who was now a potential threat. The

necessarily close relationship that had been forced on the Soviet Union and the Western powers by the actions of Hitler and Nazi Germany began to fall apart as it became apparent that each side held a very different view of the way that affairs should be conducted in peace time.

Nowhere was this more apparent than in postwar Germany,

which was rapidly developing into two entirely separate states.

In March 1948, Great Britain and France signed a pact – the Brussels Treaty – with the Low Countries. The pact was a blueprint for a collective defence strategy in the face of the growing military power and influence of the Soviet Union. In reality, however, the countries that had signed the Brussels Treaty were in no position to offer any more than token resistance to any militarily enforced future expansion of the Soviet Union.

Painfully aware of the weakness of their alliance, the countries that had come together under the banner of the treaty approached the USA and Canada in the hope of expanding and strengthening the alliance. The result was the North Atlantic Treaty.

A new organization, the North Atlantic Treaty Organization, was created in order to implement the treaty and came into being on August 24 with the aim of enforcing the various declarations made in the treaty document. The main aim of the alliance was laid out in Article 5 of the treaty, which states that "... an armed attack against one or more of them (the signatories) in Europe or North America shall be considered an attack against them all; and ... if such an armed attack occurs, each of them ... will assist the Party or Parties so attacked by taking forthwith ... such action as it deems necessary, including the use of armed force, to restore and maintain the security of the North Atlantic area."

The treaty declaration was a clear and obvious statement of intent and served to define the two sides – the Capitalist West and the Communist East – in the Cold War that dominated world politics in the coming decades.

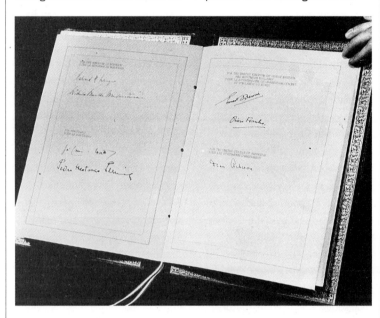

▲ The signatures of the foreign secretaries and ambassadors of the twelve initial members of Nato.

JOE LOUIS RETIRES UNDEFEATED

▲ Joe Louis, "The Brown Bomber", one of the greatest champions in the history of heavyweight boxing.

One of the giants of the boxing ring, Joe "The Brown Bomber" Louis retired undefeated on March 1, after holding the world heavyweight championship title for almost twelve straight years – a record which still stands to this day.

Born and raised in Lexington, Alabama in 1914, Louis had become the amateur Golden Gloves champion by the age of 20. As a professional he beat six previous heavyweight champions before he got his shot at the then holder of the title, James J Braddock, on June 22, 1937.

In the conclusion to a thrilling fight, Braddock was knocked unconscious in the eighth round, opening the way for Louis to assume his rightful position as king of the heavyweight boxers.

Louis went on to defend the heavyweight title no less than 25 times, finishing 21 of them with knockouts.

Unable to stay away, Joe Louis returned to the ring in 1950, but failed to achieve the same degree of success. He ended his days greeting guests as they arrived at Caesar's Palace in Las Vegas.

GERMANY DIVIDED

NEWS IN BRIEF
....

July
- Emperor Bao Dai returns to Vietnam
- Chinese Nationalist forces begin withdrawal to Formosa
- Armistice between Syria and Israel
- The "Comet" passenger jet aircraft makes first flight
- British government implements 1920 Emergency Powers Act to end dock workers strike

August
- Hungary adopts Soviet-style constitution
- New coalition government formed in Belgium
- General election held in West Germany
- Second coup in Syria
- Australian government ends coal miners' strike
- Death of Margaret Mitchell author of *Gone with the Wind*

September
- Tension rises between Yugoslavia and the Soviet Bloc
- Britain devalues sterling
- Death of composer Richard Strauss

A new Germany emerged from the ashes of defeat in 1949, or to be more precise, two new Germanies. The sectors of Germany that had been under the control of the United States, Britain and France were reorganized along federal lines. The leader of the German Christian Democratic Union in the British zone of control, Konrad Adenauer, was made President of the parliamentary council, which was given the task of producing a constitution for the proposed new German Federal Republic. Communist East Germany was left in the control of the USSR.

Adenauer had been a German politician in the early 1930s, but had been stripped of his powers when Hitler assumed the German chancellorship in 1933.

After numerous clashes with the Nazis, Adenauer was sent to a concentration camp in 1944, but survived to become Mayor of Cologne after the war.

Adenauer became chairman of the Christian Democratic Union for the whole of non-Soviet Germany in 1949. In the first elections held to decide the leadership of the new German Federal Republic, the Christian Democratic Union and their allies, the Christian Social Union, succeeded in winning 139 of the 402 available seats in the new federal parliament, the Bundestag. With a majority of just one vote, 73-year-old Konrad Adenauer was confirmed as the first chancellor of the new German Federal Republic on September 15, an office he held, against all expectations, for the next fourteen years. The first President of the new republic was Theodor Heuss, who had helped to draw up the new constitution.

Arguably the most effective politician in Adenauer's new cabinet was Ludwig Erhard. As the architect of Germany's financial recovery, Erhard steered

▲ **Konrad Adenauer, the first post-war chancellor of Germany. Almost 80 per cent of the 30 million eligible cast their votes.**

Germany down the path of welfare-state capitalism. This system left control of industry in the hands of private business interests and also left the market to decide prices and salaries. An equitable distribution of the profits generated by this system was ensured by government legislation and taxation.

In most respects this policy represented the best of two worlds: it allowed the business community to get on with the generation of profit without interference from the government, but ensured that any profits – and only the profits – that might be generated under this system were shared reasonably fairly among those who had created them.

By this approach to economic matters, the German Federal Republic underwent what would later be called an economic miracle, which saw a swift end to rationing and enormous increases in industrial output. Within twenty-five years, standards of living in the Republic were the highest in Europe.

▼ **A Communist propaganda banner hangs alongside the East–West border hailing itself as "the sector of freedom".**

START OF THE ARMS RACE

On the morning of September 23, President Harry S Truman assembled his cabinet to announce that he had some very disturbing news. "Gentlemen", he began, "we have evidence that within recent weeks an atomic explosion occurred in the USSR." The news shocked the cabinet and, when it leaked out, caused panic among the US people.

Ever since it had demonstrated the incredible destructive power of the atom bomb, the United States had sought to keep the weapon for itself. Despite being allies during World War Two, a gradual hardening of attitudes between the United States and the Soviet Union had developed into a "Cold War".

While the USSR maintained a powerful army, the US monopoly on atomic weapons meant that it was the premier military power in the world. Although it was inevitable to a certain extent that the Soviets would one day get their hands on the US atom bomb secrets – or develop one of their own independently of the USA – no one had expected them to acquire the technology quite so rapidly.

Even before the end of the war, the USSR had attempted to get access to the atomic bomb programme, resorting to using spies, where possible, in the face of a complete lack of cooperation from the USA.

The Danish scientist Niels Bohr had warned President Roosevelt that the USSR would inevitably develop their own bomb and urged the President to share atomic secrets with the Soviets so that together they could control the spread of the technology and maintain a balance of power worldwide.

Roosevelt was understandably reluctant to give up technological superiority, however, and by the time the USSR tested its first weapon, relations between the two countries had declined to the point where cooperation was extremely unlikely. (The Baruch Plan, an earlier attempt to include the Soviet Union in the atomic weapons program, had failed when the Soviets rightly dismissed the initiative as one-sided and unfair.)

As soon as both countries had atomic weapons the race was on to establish a new technological advantage; each side in the Cold War working to be the first to develop ever more deadly weapons. Having proved the effectiveness of fission-based atom bombs with the attacks on Japan, the USA began to develop a fusion-based bomb. If successful, it would be a thousand times more destructive than the original Manhattan Project weapon.

President Truman gave his approval for the highly expensive development of the hydrogen bomb in 1950. In November 1952, US scientists successfully tested the first H-bomb on a Pacific atoll. The Soviets exploded their first H-bomb less than a year later, and thus both countries became locked into a grim race to develop increasingly destructive weapons.

October
- Border clashes begin between North and South Korean troops
- German Democratic Republic (East Germany) founded
- Communist forces take Canton in China
- End of Greek Civil War
- New coalition government under Georges Bidault formed in France

November
- India adopts new constitution

December
- Execution of Bulgarian Communist Traicho Kostov in pro-Stalinist purge
- Chinese Nationalists complete withdrawal to Formosa, and declare Taipei to be the capital of China
- Achmed Sukarno elected President of Indonesia
- New coalition government under Robert Menzies formed in Australia
- Third coup in Syria

▲ An emergency meeting of the General Assembly of the United Nations convenes in Flushing, New York, following the announcement that the Soviet Union now had a nuclear capability.

1950–59

One way or another, the single most dominant issue of the 1950s was the growing ideological tension between the Communist East and the "free" West. America and the Soviet Union, now referred to as the world's two "superpowers", waged their Cold War on every possible front. A demonstration of the strength of public feeling on these issues was shown during the first few months of the decade when Joseph McCarthy, a minor US senator, began making outrageous claims about Communist infiltration in American public life. Although he could not substantiate any of his allegations he fuelled a "witch hunt" that aimed to root out Communist sympathizers. McCarthy fell from grace when he turned his attentions on the army, but the lasting outcome of his war was that in the eyes of many ordinary Americans, Communism was no longer merely an alternative political system, but the very definition of evil.

Such reasoning permeated America's foreign policy throughout the first two decades of the Cold War. That Communism, rather than the simply the Soviet Union, was the new enemy was shown by the zeal with which America waged war in Korea. When forces from the Communist North overran the Western-backed South, the USA (ostensibly under the United Nations flag) sent its troops in to fight. Quickly repelling the invaders and crossing into North Korea, victory was halted when China's newly founded Communist People's Republic announced that they were prepared to intervene. The Korean War quickly developed into a stalemate, but showed America's willingness to step in wherever Communism threatened to take hold – even in an insignificant state on the other side of the world.

During this time, propaganda was vitally important to both sides of the ideological divide. The growing public fear of nuclear war was exacerbated in 1951 when a Hydrogen bomb several hundred times more powerful than the two dropped on Japan in 1945 was tested. This gave a new impetus to the arms race. Indeed, by the end of the decade both the USA and the Soviet Union had stock-piled nuclear armaments to the point that either side had the capability to annihilate the other many times over. Those who supported this proliferation argued that the "nuclear deterrent" was necessary to prevent nuclear weapons ever being used again in conflict.

In most areas of the Cold War, the USA, by now the wealthiest nation the world had ever seen, was clearly the dominant force. However, towards the end of the 1950s this complacency was sent into shock as the Soviet Union proved that there was one area of technology in which they were several years ahead of their rivals – the "Space Race". From the launching of the *Sputnik* satellite in 1957 to the mission that made Yuri Gagarin the first man in space four years later, the Soviets were always one step ahead.

Throughout America and Europe, the 1950s also saw a shift in the social landscape. During World War Two, many of the traditional labouring jobs had been filled by women while the young working men were conscripted into the armed forces. Although this was widely assumed to have been a temporary measure, after the war there was no wholesale return to the status quo – many women had enjoyed this new found freedom and were reluctant to return to their traditional roles. The female work force would play an increasingly important role in the Western economy throughout the rest of the century.

Finally, the decade was also notable for the first emergence of a mass youth culture. By the middle of the 1950s, America's rapidly growing wealth had filtered down to its high school and college students giving them more freedom and independence than ever before. These "teenagers" sought to forge their own identities: they were not children but neither did they want to identify with their parents. This new generation gap was exacerbated by the popularity of young rock and roll singers like Elvis Presley, who shocked the adult world by presenting themselves as raw, sexual and slightly dangerous young men. Over the coming decades rock and pop music would become closely linked to an ever widening gap of ideals between youth and the establishment.

DEATH OF GEORGE ORWELL

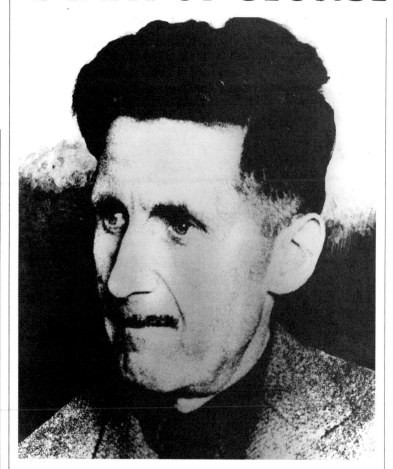

▲ **Under the pen name of George Orwell, Eric Arthur Blair became one of the most popular British authors of the century.**

Barely a year after the publication of his most famous work, *Nineteen Eighty-four,* novelist and essayist George Orwell died on January 21, 1950.

Orwell was born Eric Arthur Blair in 1903 in Bengal, where his father was employed in the Indian Civil Service. He was brought up in the environment of impoverished snobbery that characterized the British colonial "Sahibs", whose attitudes he later pilloried, describing them as "landless gentry".

Educated in England, Blair turned down a university scholarship in favour of joining the Indian Imperial Police in Burma. Here, he gained first-hand experience of the way in which the Burmese people were being abused by their colonial rulers.

Guilt-ridden for his own small contribution to these iniquities, he resigned his commission and returned to England, immersing himself in the slums and poverty of east London. As George Orwell – taking his surname from the East Anglian river – he published the semi-fictional work *Down and Out in Paris and London* (1933). The thrust of many of Orwell's early works aimed to highlight oppression and the emptiness of middle-class materialism.

Viewing himself as a socialist, Orwell set out much of his thinking in the autobiographical political essay *The Road to Wigan Pier* (1937), although the book betrayed his growing disillusionment with organized socialism. That same year found Orwell,

originally in Barcelona to report on the Spanish Civil War, fighting (and being wounded) on the side of the Republicans. *Homage to Catalonia* (1938) grew out of his experiences in Spain.

In 1945 Orwell found wealth and fame with the political fable *Animal Farm,* which takes the story of Stalin's betrayal of the Russian Revolution and transposes it to a farm where the animals overthrow their human exploiters only to experience even greater oppression at the hands of a new ruling class of animals.

It was Orwell's final book for which he will be best remembered. *1984* (1949) warns against the perils of totalitarianism, be it Communist or fascist. It describes a state in which the government distorts truth to its own ends and whose citizens, forbidden privacy, independent thinking or sexual pleasure, are under constant surveillance by "Big Brother". The book continues to find relevance wherever in the world abuse of government rule is identified.

▲ **"Big Brother Is Watching You".** *1984*, **George Orwell's most famous work, warned of the dangers of totalitarian rule.**

THE McCARTHY WITCH HUNTS

In 1950, the US reached a fever pitch of fear that Communism had infiltrated the very heart of American life. One man more than any other fuelled this paranoia, the relatively obscure Wisconsin senator Joseph McCarthy.

The McCarthy era began on February 9, 1950, when the senator addressed a Republican Women's Club in West Virginia. During his speech he claimed to have the names of 205 Communists "working and shaping policy in the State Department". His claims made national headlines, catapulting him to the forefront of public attention overnight. Although McCarthy was unable to back up any of his claims with hard evidence, he had captured the imaginations of many Americans who applauded as he proceeded to launch himself into a nationwide campaign to uncover Communist sympathizers in every walk of life.

McCarthy's crusade seemed to take on a life of its own. One of the first of a long list of victims was actress Jean Muir who was dropped from the cast of the long-running serial *The Aldrich Family* following McCarthy's claims of her affiliations. Like most, these claims were never proved. In September, 1950, against the wishes of President Truman, Congress passed the McCarran Act, making it a legal requirement for American Communist organizations to name their members on a government register. This was followed up by a ban on the issue of visas to visitors from "totalitarian states". A number of states passed their own laws making it a requirement for job applicants to sign anti-Communist affidavits.

By early 1952, McCarthy's inter-

▲ **Senator Joseph McCarthy of Wisconsin achieved overnight fame with his unsubstantiated claims of Communist infiltration.**

rogation techniques and lack of substantive evidence were attracting critics. Senator William Benton compared McCarthy to Hitler, a quip that brought about a libel action. Other Democrats began referring to the work of the Senate investigatory sub-committee, headed by McCarthy, as a "witch hunt", a phrase that took hold in some of the liberal media.

McCarthy finally came to grief when he took on the US Army, claiming evidence of Soviet sympathies among the ranks. Many who saw little harm in clearing a few

▲ **Piled high on the Senate's committee room table are the 36 volumes of the testimony given at the US Army McCarthy hearings.**

alleged "reds under the bed" felt uncomfortable at seeing the same treatment meted out to America's military. His hearings against the army began a 36-day run on national television in May 1954. It was the first time most ordinary Americans had been given an opportunity of seeing McCarthy's brutal style of interrogation in action. The regular sight of American servicemen being bullied and pilloried was unpalatable and his popularity began to decline.

Many saw McCarthy's activities as being directly responsible for heavy Republican losses in the November 1954 mid-term elections. McCarthy lost his position as chairman of the investigating committee. President Eisenhower came under pressure to support a motion censuring Senator McCarthy's activities. Although opposed to McCarthyism, "censure" was too severe a punishment for Eisenhower to mete out to a fellow-Republican. The following month the Senate voted by 67 to 22 for the milder "condemnation" of McCarthy's conduct as being "contrary to Senate traditions".

Although he vowed to continue his fight against Communism in the USA, McCarthy's influence in government was limited to those holding the most extreme right-wing views. He received little further interest until his death in 1957.

Many of his allegations were shown to have been fabricated or inaccurate – small consolation to the thousands of innocent Americans, both prominent and anonymous, who were blacklisted or found their lives upturned during one of the most extraordinary erosions of civil liberty in the history of the United States.

- Race riots in South Africa
- US President Truman gives go-ahead for production of hydrogen bomb
- Soviet Union officially recognizes Viet Minh government in Vietnam
- Death of novelist and essayist George Orwell

February
- Chervenkov (Little Stalin) becomes ruler of Bulgaria
- Mutual assistance treaty signed by USSR and Communist China
- US severs diplomatic relations with Bulgaria
- US and Britain recognize Emperor Bao Dai as ruler of South Vietnam
- Labour Party win general election in Britain

March
- Klaus Fuchs convicted in Britain of passing atomic development secrets to the USSR
- USSR announces possession of atomic bomb capability
- German Chancellor Adenauer advances ideas of economic union with France
- Death of writer Edgar Rice Burroughs

April
- Italian Somaliland becomes UN Trust Territory
- Dock workers begin strike in Britain (ends May 1)
- Britain officially recognizes the state of Israel
- Kingdom of Jordan created
- Deaths of Russian ballet dancer Vaslav Nijinsky and German composer Kurt Weill

May
- Schuman Plan for consolidation of German and French heavy industries announced
- Albania severs diplomatic relations with Yugoslavia

THE KOREAN WAR

'50

On June 25, 1950, armed forces of the Democratic People's Republic of North Korea, with the tacit support of the Soviet Union, which had equipped them, carried out a massive attack on territories across their national border in the Republic of Korea (usually known as South Korea). The attack began three years of East-West conflict, eventually involving 20 nations, that many feared would escalate into another global conflict.

Like other conflicts of the 1950s, the Korean War came about as a result of unfinished business carried over from World War Two. By 1945, Japanese forces had advanced well into the Asian mainland. At the end of the war there was a dispute among the Allies as to who would accept their surrender. It was finally agreed that Soviet forces would deal with Japanese troops in Korea north of 38° latitude ("the 38th parallel"); American troops

▲ US infantry Long Tom guns in action "somewhere in Korea". In taking on a self-styled "policing" role, the United States set a precedent that would be repeated throughout the century.

▲ A heavy US military presence was required to regain the territory taken by the invading North Koreans.

would take those in the south.

In 1947, attempting to unify what were now effectively two separate Korean states, the United Nations proposed that general elections be held. The Soviet Union refused to co-operate and after two years of fruitless negotiation a communist state was permanently established in the north and a pro-Western state was set up in the south. By mutual agreement, by the end of the decade both the United States and the Soviet Union had withdrawn most of their troops from the region.

Thus, in 1950, military forces in the south were small, and the North Korean People's Army experienced little resistance as they swarmed southward, quickly taking the capital city of Seoul. The United Nations Security Council met in emergency session, passing a resolution to halt the invasion. US General Douglas MacArthur was placed in charge of the UN effort in Korea. By the time the first UN troops arrived early in July, North Korean forces had effective control of most of South Korea, causing President

Syngman Rhee and his government to flee to the south.

Heavy UN reinforcements brought in the following month saw a dramatic turn of events. On September 15, General MacArthur launched a surprise attack, landing troops at Inchon, 160 km (100 miles) below the 38th Parallel. Supported by squadrons of B-52 bombers, the operation was a massive success, landing the marines without casualties and cutting the North Korean lines down the middle. From this position, MacArthur's forces moved inland, recapturing Seoul and restoring the government of President Rhee within 10 days. During the operation, North Korean forces were heavily depleted, with 125,000 prisoners taken.

As the allied forces advanced toward the 38th parallel, a new threat emerged. From across North Korea's border with Manchuria, Chinese Premier Chou En-lai warned that a UN crossing of the 38th parallel would be taken as a threat to the security of the Chinese People's Republic and Chinese troops would intervene. The threats were ignored and UN forces advanced into North Korea, their intention now being the re-unification of Korea. On November 24, General MacArthur announced an offensive that would take his forces right up to the Chinese border, believing that this would bring the conflict to a swift end. The following day, however, the Chinese made good their threat and 200,000 Manchurian "volunteers" entered the war. By the end of the year, MacArthur's forces had been pushed back south of the 38th parallel.

1951 began with a second Communist invasion by 500,000 troops. Heavy allied bombing meant that they were unable to gain any permanent foothold, and the battle zone eventually stabilized along the north-south border. Heavy fighting continued throughout the first six months of 1951 as the world's two great ideologies, democracy and communism, faced each other.

With Communist China now actively engaged in the conflict, MacArthur realized that the only way to achieve a swift victory was to create a blockade and bomb bases in Manchuria. This would be a heavy gamble, as the Soviet Union, though keeping a low profile during the events of 1950, had many "advisers" in the country and would be likely to come to China's aid, creating the very real danger of a global conflict. US President Harry Truman refused to sanction MacArthur's plans. Openly critical of Truman, MacArthur attempted to appeal

directly to the American people, but misjudged their mood, many Americans viewing the purpose of the Korean War with some suspicion. Outraged by MacArthur's dissent, President Truman recalled him in April and replaced him with General Matthew B Ridgway. As the President told America, "It is fundamental that military commanders must be governed by policies and directives issued to them". The controversial MacArthur returned to a "tickertape" welcome from the city of New York.

The war thereafter became something of stalemate. June 1951 saw a surprising Soviet call for a cease-fire. The first truce meetings, which took place the following month, sought to establish a demilitarized zone around the 38th parallel. These meetings were largely unsuccessful and sporadic fighting and UN bombing raids continued. There was little change until the election of President Dwight D Eisenhower in

▲ Towns and villages were razed during the bombing of South Korea, creating a major refugee crisis.

November 1952. The former Supreme Commander of Allied Forces in Europe had been openly critical of the war and had announced his intention to end it as quickly as possible if elected.

After further negotiations, an armistice was concluded on July 27, 1953, making the front line – the 38th parallel – a permanent official boundary between North and South Korea. Unification was no longer on the agenda.

The Korean War caused the

deaths of over a million South Koreans, a million Chinese and half-a-million North Koreans. Over 50,000 Allied troops were killed. The industrial base of both Koreas had been almost entirely decimated by bombing. The war also demonstrated that American foreign policy was prepared to take on a self-styled policing role wherever Communism threatened to take hold. This was a policy for which they would pay dearly in the decades to come.

▲ Civilian casualties were heavy throughout the Korean campaign, in which over a million men, women and children perished. These women are identifying the men of their village, killed by North Korean forces.

'50

NEWS IN BRIEF

....

June
- French Prime Minister Bidault resigns
- North Korean troops invade South Korea: start of the Korean War
- Egypt signs security pact with Syria, Lebanon, Yemen and Saudi Arabia
- West Germany joins the Council of Europe
- Touring West Indies side beats England at cricket for the first time in England
- England beaten by USA in football World Cup

July
- First UN troops arrive in South Korea; General Douglas MacArthur takes command
- New government under René Pleven formed in France
- Uruguay beat Brazil to win the fourth football World Cup competition
- King Leopold III returns to Belgium from exile; abdicates after anti-monarchist riots

August
- United Nations forces retreat to Southeast Korea
- Prince Baudouin sworn in as Regent in Belgium
- Soviet boycott of UN ends
- New government under Prime Minister van Zeeland formed in Belgium

September
- North Koreans launch fresh offensive against remaining UN troops in South Korea
- UN forces land at Inchon in Korea and retake Seoul

THE NEW FORM OF OPERA

April 3, 1950, saw the death in New York City of the composer Kurt Weill, the man who created a new musical form which combined opera with social satire. He is especially remembered for his collaborations with the German writer Bertolt Brecht.

Born in 1900 in Dessau, Germany, Weill's career began as a composer of abstract instrumental music, two early works, *Der Protagonist* (1926) and *Royal Palace* (1927) establishing him as one of Germany's most promising young opera composers.

He found success the following year when he teamed up with the poet and dramatist Bertolt Brecht to produce the short opera (or "songspiel" as he called it) *Die Dreigroschenoper (The Threepenny Opera)* (1928). The opera took the characters from John Gay's eighteenth-century play *The Beggar's Opera* and reinvented them in the Berlin underworld of the 1920s. One of the songs from the opera, "Morität", better known in its English form, "Mack The Knife", remains popular today. *The Rise*

▲ **Kurt Weill, one the greatest modern operatic composers, is remembered for his collaborations with Bertolt Brecht.**

and Fall of the City of Mahagonny (1929), another Weill and Brecht collaboration, satirized German life by transposing it to a mythical American city. By now, Weill's music was a unique integration of contemporary classical song forms with American ragtime jazz.

In the early 1930s, the Jewish Weill fell foul of the emergent Nazi regime and fled Germany with his wife, the actress and singer Lotte Lenya, the couple eventually settling in New York City. His many American works were created with such well-respected librettists as Ogden Nash and Maxwell Anderson, the latter contributing the words for the haunting "September Song". They lacked, however, the satirical bite of his work with Brecht.

The music of Kurt Weill has remained popular, Lotte Lenya providing many of the definitive recordings of her husband's songs until her death in 1981.

ENGLAND SHAMED

June 29, 1950, was one of the darkest day in England's sporting history as their football team, widely viewed as one of the greatest in the world, was dealt a humiliating World Cup defeat at the hands of a team from the United States, a nation with little interest in the sport.

This was the first World Cup since World War Two and the Brazilian climate was always likely to work against European sides. But after a promising 2-nil victory over Chile, England, with its great stars Matthews, Finney and Mortenson, were unable to find a way past the tight American defence. In the end they went down by one goal to nil.

They were eliminated from the

▲ **England's star striker Tom Finney is once again foiled during a brave performance from American goalkeeper Borghi.**

tournament after a 1-nil defeat by Spain.

At this time, the final stages of the World Cup were not decided by the "knockout" system used today, but by a league. This time, however, the outcome did rest on the result of the final game, Uruguay defeating Brazil to take the trophy for the second time.

RETURN OF THE STONE OF SCONE

On Christmas Day, 1950, a group of Scottish Nationalists made a defiant gesture of independence by breaking into London's Westminster Abbey and removing the Stone of Scone.

For centuries, the Stone of Scone was a part of the crowning ceremony of the Kings of Scotland. It was taken to England by the invading forces of Edward I in 1296. The stone is a small piece of sandstone marked with a simple Latin cross. According to legend, it was the pillow upon which Jacob rested his head at Bethel when he saw visions of angels. The stone found its way to Ireland around 700 BC, where it was set on the Hill of Tara, the

▲ Scotland's Stone of Scone shown in position beneath the Coronation Chair of Westminster Abbey in London.

crowning place of Irish kings. It was taken to Scotland by the Celtic Scots who invaded the region and was encased in the seat of the royal coronation chair.

When the stone was brought south it was set underneath the Coronation Chair in Westminster Abbey, thus symbolizing that whoever was crowned monarch of England was also the ruler of Scotland.

Four months after its theft, the Stone of Scone was found in Arbroath Abbey and returned to Westminster. The thieves were never discovered. In 1997, with the Scots having voted to have their own independent parliament again, the Stone of Scone was formally returned to Scotland.

THE TWO VIETNAMS

Perhaps the most notable aspect of world affairs throughout the 1950s was the way in which the newly created East-West divide permeated so many peripheral areas. At the start of the 1950s, Vietnam became a gradual focus for these hostilities.

Lying along the eastern coast of the Indochinese Peninsula, bordered by China in the north and Laos and Cambodia on the west, Vietnam had been conquered in the nineteenth century by France, becoming a French colony in 1883. In 1945, Communist leader Ho Chi Minh, supported by various nationalist groups, declared Vietnam independent of French rule. Not surprisingly, France refused to recognize the "Viet Minh" government based in Hanoi. Months of negotiation between the two parties and a truce ended in November 1946, when the French

navy bombarded Haiphong, killing thousands. The first Indo-China War had begun. In 1949 the French government set up the Associated State of Vietnam, with the "playboy" Emperor Bao Dai at its head.

This was unacceptable to both the Viet Minh and the people of Vietnam. The Communist government waged an increasingly successful guerrilla war against the French, at the same time lobbying the world for recognition. At the end of January 1950, the Soviet Union and other Eastern Bloc states officially recognized the Viet Minh government. A week later, the United States, fearing the spread of Communism in the region, threw their support behind France and the Emperor Bao Dai, providing military funding to fight the rebel forces.

Hostilities lasted until May 7, 1954, when French forces were

routed at Dien Bien Phu. A peace agreement was signed in Geneva on July 21, "temporarily" dividing Vietnam along the 17th parallel. The Communist government of Ho Chi Minh was to administer the north and Emperor Bao Dai the south, until an election in 1956 could decide who should rule Vietnam. The stage was set for the war that devastated the region in the 1970s.

▲ Ho Chi Minh, military strategist and Premier of the newly founded Communist regime of North Vietnam.

BEVAN, THE GREAT ORATOR

Internal conflict arose in Clement Attlee's Labour government in April 1951, as Aneurin "Nye" Bevan, one of the most colourful figures in postwar British politics, resigned from his post as Minister of Labour. Bevan, renowned as one of the greatest orators ever to enter parliament, was the architect of Britain's National Health Service, instituted in 1945. His resignation came in protest at Attlee's programme of rearmament at the expense of social welfare and, in particular, against the introduction of a number of national health charges.

The son of a Monmouthshire miner, Bevan left school at the age of 13 to work in one of the county's many collieries. Bevan was eventually forced to abandon the mines because of long-standing eye disease. Active in local politics, in his late twenties Bevan moved to London to attend the Central Labour College. In 1929 he was elected to the House of Commons as Labour member for the Ebbw Vale constituency in South Wales.

During the following decade Bevan made a name for himself as a razor-sharp wit with a facility

▲ One of the greatest political orators of the twentieth century, Nye Bevan was never one to shy away from verbal confrontation.

for elevating the most mundane political debate to a masterclass in the art of oration. Equally famed was his capacity to offend his opponents: throughout World War Two he was a vigorous critic of Winston Churchill – not one himself to shy away from verbal conflict – who described the Welshman as a "merchant of discourtesy".

Following Churchill's surprise defeat in the 1945 General Election, Bevan was given the position of Minister of Health in Attlee's Labour government. His two great achievements were the creation of the National Health Service and the initiation of housing programmes.

Bevan was often viewed as a thorn in the side of the Labour Party, of whom he could sometimes be as critical as he was of the opposition. He became Minister of Labour in January 1951, a position which he held for only three months. Labour was removed from power just months later as a result of a General Election. In 1955, Bevan staged his own campaign to become party leader. Defeated by Hugh Gaitskell, he accepted the post of shadow Foreign Secretary. He died in 1960.

THE "BOMB" COMES OF AGE

On May 12, 1951, a huge ball of fire erupted over the tiny Pacific atoll of Eniwetok. America had detonated the most powerful and deadly weapon the world had ever seen, the H-bomb. In 1945 America had given the world a glimpse of a possible future when atomic bombs were dropped on the Japanese cities of Hiroshima and Nagasaki. The resulting devastation was unthinkable to most. The newly developed hydrogen-based H-bomb was hundreds

▲ The H-bomb's mushroom cloud hangs over Eniwetok

of times more powerful than those used in 1945.

The US atomic project was born in 1943, when J Robert Oppenheimer set up the secret Los Alamos science laboratory in New Mexico. Among his recruits was a brilliant Hungarian-born nuclear physicist named Edward (Ede) Teller. During his time working on the A-bomb at Los Alamos, Teller began to investigate the possibility of creating an even more powerful device by causing the nuclei of a heavy hydrogen called deuterium to collide.

The use of the Hiroshima bomb had horrified many of those engaged in the project. Among them, Oppenheimer chose not to pursue nuclear weapons research any further. Indeed, in 1954 he was the subject of a board of inquiry that concluded he was a serious risk to national security. Teller, a staunch anti-communist, was vociferous in his view that the US should develop a hydrogen bomb, especially as the Soviet Union had already exploded its first atomic device in 1949. On January 31, 1950, President Truman gave him the go-ahead to develop his project.

Following the first successful H-bomb test in 1951, the United States and the Soviet Union found itself in an escalating "arms race", each nation diverting huge resources to keep pace with the other. By 1952 it was estimated that there was already sufficient nuclear weaponry in existence effectively to destroy life on earth.

Teller remained the most prominent scientist involved in the nuclear arms race, and was a major influence on Ronald Reagan's widely discredited SDI "star wars" project in 1984.

TIBET IN CHAINS

Throughout the twentieth century Tibet strove to fight against aggression from China. Following invasion by Chinese troops the previous year, on May 24, 1951, Tibet was forced to succumb to the might of communist China as the Dalai Lama, the state's religious leader, was forced to sign a 17-point pact that effectively made Tibet an "independent" Chinese state. By September, Chinese troops were occupying Lhasa, Tibet's cultural and religious centre.

Located north of the Himalayan mountains of Nepal, Tibet had first interested Chinese invaders as far back as the ninth century, but had always fiercely fought to maintain its independence. Nevertheless, by the nineteenth century there was some reliance on the Chinese Manchus for protection. At the same time, Britain also sought influence in the region as a way of gaining control over the crucial trade routes into China. This created friction between Britain and China which was only halted in 1906 with the signing of a treaty that recognized China's role in Tibetan affairs.

Following the Chinese revolution of 1912, the Tibetans themselves went on the offensive, expelling all Chinese and declaring themselves independent. The next forty years were turbulent within China and, with attention focused on internal conflicts, Tibet was able to

▲ **The Dalai Lama was forced to submit to the aggression of China, which turned Tibet into little more than a satellite state.**

▲ **Since the so-called "liberation" of 1950, the rich culture of Tibet has been persistently undermined by the rule of Communist China.**

function as an independent state. During this time it sought to isolate its unique culture and religion from the rest of the world.

The Chinese called the invasion of October 1950 the "liberation" of Tibet. Although Tibet would be theoretically free to run its own internal affairs, the holy city of Lhasa would also become a Chinese military base.

'51

NEWS IN BRIEF

March
- Purges begin in the Czechoslovak Communist Party
- European Coal and Steel Community created
- Iranian Prime Minister General Razmara assassinated
- New government under Henri Queuille formed in France
- Free Presbyterian Church founded by Ian Paisley in Northern Ireland
- US senate committee led by Senator Kefauver begins hearings on organized crime
- Jacobo Arbenz Guzman becomes President of Guatemala
- Iran nationalizes oil industry
- Julius and Ethel Rosenberg convicted of treason in USA
- UN forces advance north in Korea; MacArthur counsels prosecution of war into China
- Death of British popular composer and theatre producer Ivor Novello

KING AND COLLABORATOR?

The coronation of Baudouin I, King of the Belgians, took place on July 16, 1951. The crowning of the 20-year-old, following the abdication of his father, Leopold III, brought an end to the "royal question" which had raged in Belgium since World War Two.

On the outbreak of war, King Leopold had been appointed supreme commander of the Belgian Army. The controversy began on May 28, 1940, as he surrendered his country's forces only 18 days after the German invasion had begun. The government of Belgium, exiled in London during the Occupation, condemned the speed of his acquiescence and his decision to remain a voluntary prisoner of war. The King spent most of the rest of the war confined to his château near Brussels.

Following the Allied victory, the Belgian government returned to Brussels. For the next five years no agreement could be reached on what action, if any, should be taken against the monarch. The issue was further complicated by claims that a letter Leopold wrote to Adolf Hitler in 1942 prevented half a million Belgian women being deported to work in Germany's munitions factories.

The country was split along religious, political and regional lines. When the government decided to hold a referendum on Leopold's return from exile, 58 per cent voted in favour, most support coming from the Catholic Flemish-speaking north. Leopold's return to the traditional royal home at Laeken was widely opposed by socialists, liberals and the Walloon population of the south. In July 1950 mineworkers struck in protest, bringing Belgium to a standstill. After discussions with the government, Leopold chose to abdicate in favour of his son,

▲ The young Baudouin I, King of the Belgians. His accession to the throne brought an end to the "royal question".

Baudouin, then 19 years old.

In a tearful royal ceremony on July 16, 1951, Leopold told the people of Belgium that his abdication was the only way of reuniting and rebuilding the nation after the traumatic Nazi occupation.

THE FESTIVAL OF BRITAIN

May 4, 1951, saw the opening of the Festival of Britain, a science and technology fair that would attract over 8,000,000 visitors during the summer.

The event had been announced in December 1947, Labour minister Herbert Morrison telling the House of Commons that the government planned to mark the centenary of the Great Exhibition of 1851. Originally intended to be a "world fair", economic circumstances led to its being redesignated a national event. A grant of over £11,300,000 was provided to finance the project. Planned as a nationwide celebration, the aim of the Festival was to "demonstrate Britain's contribution to civilization, to stimulate trade and to encourage creative

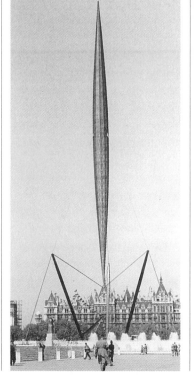

effort in British national life". Although there were regional exhibitions throughout the country, the main attraction was built on a massive bomb site on the South Bank of the Thames.

The upstream section of the site was dominated by the Dome of Discovery and the impressive Skylon, both temporary exhibits designed to show off Britain's importance in the fields of science, technology, architecture and design. Also unveiled was the Festival Hall, one of the few buildings from the event still in use, as one of London's leading concert halls.

◄ Like most of the exhibits, the Skylon was demolished by the incoming Churchill government who saw it as a shrine to socialism.

PARTNERS IN CRIME

May 25, 1951, saw the start of an intriguing mystery that would take almost 30 years to unravel in full. It would unveil international espionage operating at the very heart of Britain's establishment. The story began with the sudden disappearance of two Foreign Office officials, Guy Burgess and Donald MacLean. It would be five years before they were next seen – in Moscow, where they announced their defection and long-standing allegiance to the Soviet Union.

Burgess and MacLean had met as students at Cambridge University in the early 1930s. Communist sympathizers from "privileged" backgrounds, they were both recruited as Soviet secret agents. Following graduation, both enjoyed rapidly successful careers, Burgess working for MI-6 before joining MacLean at the British embassy in Washington. Information MacLean was able to pass on to his Soviet counterparts was especially dangerous. As secretary of

▲ With a background in MI-6, Britain's secret intelligence service, Guy Burgess was well placed as a Communist agent.

▲ Foreign Office high-flier Donald MacLean – one of the most infamous spies of the Cold War era.

the Combined Policy Committee on Atomic Development he had access to highly classified information relating to the formation of Nato. In 1950 he was further promoted and engaged in work on high-level Anglo–American diplomacy at the start of the Korean War.

It was early in May 1951 that MacLean was warned that both British and American agencies had realized that at least one spy was working at a prominent level. By the end of the month both men had vanished.

The swift disappearance indicated that there were others involved. A prominent suspect was Kim Philby, head of counter-espionage at MI-6. In 1949 he had been sent to Washington as principal liaison officer between British and American intelligence agencies, a particularly sensitive position, given the emerging Cold War. Viewed as a possible security risk, he was relieved of his position following Burgess and MacLean's defection and

resumed his former career as a journalist. In 1963, his actions coming under further scrutiny, he also defected to the Soviet Union. It transpired that he had been recruited by Burgess while at Cambridge. Unlike his former colleagues, Philby was a passionate Communist and joined the KGB in Moscow, rising to the rank of colonel. During his time as a double agent the KGB had been able to detect and eliminate a large number of British and American agents working in Eastern Europe.

After the defection of Burgess and MacLean there was considerable speculation that a so-called "fourth man" had been involved in the spy ring, arranging their passage to Moscow. Not until 1979 was it revealed that this long-sought figure was no less than Sir Anthony Blunt, an eminent art historian and Keeper of the Queen's Pictures. Blunt was stripped of his knighthood and died in 1983, having been nationally disgraced.

'51

NEWS IN BRIEF

July
- Tensions between India and Pakistan over Kashmir increase
- Iran rejects International Court judgment its over oil dispute with Britain
- New armistice negotiations begin in Korea
- Leopold III abdicates in Belgium; Baudouin swears oath as king
- King Abdullah of Jordan assassinated
- Death of Austrian composer Arnold Schoenberg: developed the "seria" or tone row method of composition and had a great influence on twentieth-century classical music

August
- Armistice talks break down in Korea
- Territorial dispute between Peru and Ecuador leads to conflict
- Britain and Iran open talks on oil dispute
- Deaths of American newspaper tycoon William Randolph Hearst and of British composer Constant Lambert

September
- Pacific Security Agreement signed by Australia, New Zealand and US
- King Talal of Jordan enthroned
- Peace treaty with Japan signed in US
- UN-brokered peace talks between Arabs and Israel begin
- Iranian troops occupy the Abadan oil fields

THE MEDIA'S FIRST TYCOON

The greatest newspaper tycoon of them all, William Randolph Hearst, passed from the scene on August 14, 1951. In 1935, at the peak of his fortune, he owned 28 newspapers, 12 magazines, radio stations and movie studios, his sphere of influence covering the whole of the United States.

Born in 1863, William Randolph Hearst was the only son of a wealthy US senator. Expelled after two years at Harvard, Hearst took over the ailing *San Francisco Examiner,* a newspaper bought by his father in 1880 as a political mouthpiece.

Within two years a combination of crusading reformism and sensational journalism had turned the *Examiner* into profit.

Looking to the East Coast, Hearst used the same recipe to transform the *New York Morning Journal*, making it one of the most influential newspapers of the day. Although he publicly supported unpopular reform issues such as anti-trust laws and the growth of labour unions, Hearst was not above fabricating the truth to achieve his aims. Indeed, anti-Spanish feeling whipped up through deliberately

inaccurate reporting largely brought about the outbreak of the Spanish-American War in 1898. During this time, Hearst also harboured the highest of political ambitions, even though these would always remain unfulfilled, leaving him to concentrate on the growth of the world's first great media empire. In spite of his failure in the world of politics, his increasingly right-wing views heavily influenced America during the first three decades of the twentieth century.

The Depression led to a downturn in Hearst's fortunes and by 1940 his business empire had dwindled, even though his own personal fortune was still one of the greatest in America. Although married in 1903, Hearst spent 30 years openly engaged in an affair with a little-known actress, Marion Davies, devoting a vast fortune in an attempt to make her a Hollywood star. He lived his final years in virtual seclusion in his lavish Californian castle, San Simeon.

Much of Hearst's life provided the template for Orson Welles's 1941 cinematic masterpiece *Citizen Kane.*

◀ **William Randolph Hearst made almost no attempt to hide his long-standing affair with the actress Marion Davies.**

AN INDEPENDENT LIBYA

On December 24, 1951, with the full support of the United Nations, the former Italian colony of Libya gained full independence. The country's first ruler was King Idris I. Formerly known as Sidi Muhammad Idris al-Mahdi As-Sanusi, King Idris was also the head of the Sanusiyah, a mystic

Sufi sect that extolled the virtues of a return to early Islamic values. By the middle of the twentieth century the Sanusiyah were the dominant indigenous political force in North Africa, galvanizing local tribes in opposition to Italian occupation from 1911 onwards.

Idris had been exiled by the Italian regime in 1922, and remained in Egypt until Britain's defeat of Italy in North Africa during World War Two. The three provinces of Libya – Cyrenaica, Fezzan, and Tripolitania – remained under British rule until 1949, when the General

Assembly of the United Nations decreed that leaders from the three provinces should decide how a new united Libya should be governed. The outcome was a constitutional monarchy, with a government formed of prominent businessmen and tribal leaders. However, King Idris assumed a position of great influence over the workings of the parliament, and also had absolute control of the army.

Once a poverty-stricken region, Libya's fortunes turned dramatically during the 1950s following the discovery of oil. During this time, opposition to the monarchy, and especially to the King's pro-Western stance and refusal to embrace the spirit of nationalism that had enveloped other parts of the Arab world, began to take hold within Libya's middle classes and military officers.

It was not until 1969, however, that a military coup led by a young army captain, Muammar al-Gaddafi, succeeded in overthrowing King Idris and turning Libya into a socialist republic.

▲ **King Idris, the first monarch of the state of Libya. He remained in power until 1969 when he was unseated by a military uprising.**

RETURN OF THE GREAT LEADER

▲ **"V for Victory". First it was the defeat of Germany in 1945; six years later Churchill celebrated an election victory.**

October 26, 1951, saw 77-year-old Winston Churchill return to the very pinnacle of British politics as he succeeded Clement Attlee as Prime Minister. Churchill had been a towering presence leading Britain's coalition war government between 1940 and 1945. In the election that followed VE Day in 1945, Churchill was surprisingly ousted from office by Attlee's Labour Party. Churchill had wanted to continue the coalition government until the defeat of Japan, but Attlee's message of social reform was more in tune with the jubilant national mood.

After his defeat, Churchill, while remaining leader of the Conservatives and an effective Leader of the Opposition, began work on what would be his greatest literary achievement, the six-volume *The Second World War*, for which he was awarded the Nobel Prize for Literature in 1953.

As Prime Minister, Churchill's main aim was to restore Britain's relationship with the United States, which he felt had lapsed in the postwar period. He gave President Truman his backing for the war in Korea. Britain was also in the throes of a trade crisis, Churchill's Chancellor of the Exchequer, R A Butler, being given the task of restoring international confidence in the pound.

Awarded the Order of the Garter in 1953, that same year Churchill suffered a stroke, which left him greatly weakened. In April 1955, at the age of 81, he resigned, handing over the leadership to his chosen successor, Foreign Secretary, Sir Anthony Eden. He remained in the House of Commons, still finding the time and energy to publish another major work, the four-volume *A History of the English-Speaking Peoples*. After his death in January 1965, he was given a state funeral.

DEATH OF THE KING

King George VI, a man who had never aspired nor expected to become monarch of the British Empire, died on February 6, 1952.

▲ **Queen Mary, mother of the late king, is flanked by her daughter-in-law and granddaughter, Elizabeth II, at George VI's funeral.**

Albert Frederick Arthur George was born on December 14, 1895, the second son of the future King George V. In 1920, after a period serving in the Royal Navy and a year's study at Trinity College, Cambridge, Prince Albert was invested with the title of Duke of York. In April 1923, he was married to Lady Elizabeth Angela Marguerite Bowes-Lyon, the youngest daughter of the 14th Earl of Strathmore and Kinghorne (now the Queen Mother). The royal couple raised two children, the princesses Elizabeth and Margaret – the former now Queen Elizabeth II.

The Duke of York was proclaimed king on December 12, 1936, following the abdication of his brother Edward VIII who gave up the Crown to marry Wallis Simpson, an American divorcee. The Duke of York took the name of George VI and was crowned in May 1937.

Before the start of World War Two, the King supported Prime Minister Neville Chamberlain's policy of appeasement toward fascist aggression from Germany and Italy. Throughout the war, he

▶ **The body of King George VI lies in state in the historic Westminster Hall. Beefeaters provide a guard of honour for the dead king.**

gave his firm support to the coalition government of Winston Churchill, even though he had called for the appointment of Lord Halifax to lead the war effort.

From 1948 onward, King George's health deteriorated following treatment for lung cancer, which eventually claimed his life. His funeral procession on February 15 was attended by thousands of mourners – a testimony to a popular king who, against the wishes of his advisors, persistently refused to leave London during the Blitz.

END OF THE AMERICAN OCCUPATION OF JAPAN

Signing a peace treaty with Japan on April 15, 1952, US President Harry Truman brought a formal end to the war in the Pacific. Japan gained full sovereignty and US occupation ended.

Between 1945 and 1952 Japan was officially under allied military occupation, ruled by the Supreme Commander for Allied Powers (SCAP), a role first held by General Douglas MacArthur. Although officially a multinational task, from the outset, the overriding influence on the occupation came from the US.

The occupation oversaw a period of immense social and institutional change. The general principles that would guide the new Japan had been outlined at the Potsdam Declaration of August 1945, the overriding aim of which was the demilitarization and democratization of the state. General MacArthur was charged with the task of developing a political system that guaranteed the rights of the individual. The bitter lessons of the overly punitive Treaty of Versailles that followed World War One had been learned, so that crucial to the achievement of the Potsdam Declaration's aims was the establishment of a sound economy that would be able to support a peaceful and democratic Japan.

During the period of SCAP rule, the old empire was disbanded, the armed forces were demobilized and millions of

Japanese civilians abroad repatriated. Additionally, nationalist organizations sympathetic to traditional Japanese values were marginalized or abolished. Perhaps the most difficult change for the Japanese people to accept came from one of the principal terms of the newly written constitution which ruled that the Emperor was no longer to be seen as a divine being but merely as a symbolic figurehead.

Fundamental changes in Japanese society were gradually brought about by widespread reforms in education and in the system of land ownership. Before the war, most of Japan's farmers lived poorly, paying high rents to wealthy landowners. As Japan's

◄ **An official peace. President Harry Truman ratifies the treaty formally signalling the end of US occupation of Japan.**

principal industry, it was clear that, unreformed, it was a major impediment to the growth of democracy. Thus, Japan's large landowners were forced to give a high proportion of their land to

the government which then sold it on to the former tenants at favourable rates. This land redistribution largely accounted for the eventual popularity of Japan's Liberal Democratic Party among the rural community.

The aim of the treaty of April 1952, signed by representatives of 49 other nations, was, in Harry Truman's own words, "To restore Japan to a position of independence, honour and equality within the world community." By the end of the month, the Allied forces were able to make a complete withdrawal from the region.

THE CHILDREN'S EDUCATOR

May 6, 1952, saw the death of Maria Montessori, the creator of the revolutionary children's education method that bears her name.

A pioneer from the very start, Montessori graduated in medicine from the University of Rome in 1894, becoming Italy's first ever woman doctor. Her initial interests were in the treatment of brain-damaged children. It was while working as director of the Orthophrenic School of Rome that she developed her "Method", which was based on the careful nurturing, with minimal constraint, of a child's creative potential and the development of initiative and self-learning.

In 1907, for the first time, Montessori applied her methods to children of normal intelligence, opening her first Casa dei Bambini (literally, "Children's House"), a school for young children in one of Rome's slum districts. Over the next 40 years Montessori schools opened all

▲ **Maria Montessori, Italy's first female doctor, who revolutionized the education of children.**

over the world, particularly in Europe, Asia and the United States of America.

In 1934, while government inspector for all Italian schools, she fled the country following the emergence of Mussolini's fas-

cists, travelling and lecturing widely throughout the world before finally settling in Holland. Today, the Montessori Method remains a popular and well-respected approach to the education of children.

- First Holiday Inn hotel built in the USA
- Gibson produce the first Les Paul electric guitars
- Leo Fender develops the Fender Stratocaster electric guitar
- British-designed Comet passenger jets begin commercial scheduled flights
- The show *This Is Your Life* debuts on US television
- *The Goon Show* begins on BBC radio
- The children's television programme *Bill and Ben, Flowerpot Men* first shown on BBC television
- Among films released this year are Fred Zinneman's *High Noon*, John Huston's *The Quiet Man*, Cecil B de Mille's *The Greatest Show on Earth*, Arthur Freed's *Singin' in the Rain*, with Gene Kelly singin' and dancing, Vincente Minnelli's *The Bad and the Beautiful* and the first 3-D film, *Bwana Devil*
- Among musical premieres are *4' 33"* by John Cage, notable as a composition consisting of silence and Sinfonia *Antarctica* by Ralph Vaughan Williams
- Books published this year include *East Of Eden* by John Steinbeck, *The Old Man and the Sea* by Ernest Hemingway, *The Natural* by Bernard Malamud, the Revised Standard Version of the Bible and *The Diary of Anne Frank*

"EVITA" DIES

▲ "Evita" Perón was loved and hated in equal measures by Argentina's underclasses – *los descamisados* – and its wealthy establishment.

January
- Anti-British riots in Egypt
- Coalition government in France collapses; new coalition under Edgar Faure formed
- King Farouk dismisses Egyptian Prime Minister
- Structure of the European Defence Community defined at conference in Paris

February
- India makes its first Test match win in cricket
- Nato approves European Defence Community initiative
- Britain declares it possesses nuclear capability
- Collapse of coalition government under Edgar Faure in France; new government formed under Antoine Pinay
- Death of King George VI of Britain; daughter succeeds as Elizabeth II

March
- Congress Party, led by Pandit Nehru, wins majority in Indian National Assembly elections
- Egyptian Prime Minister Ali Maher resigns; Nagib al Hilaly succeeds
- Military coup in Cuba; Batista returns to power
- Apartheid legislation ruled unconstitutional by South African Supreme Court
- Kwame Nkrumah of Ghana elected the first African Prime Minister of his country
- Death of Ceylonese Prime Minister Don Stephen Senanayake; Dudley Senanayake succeeds

A contradictory character who never held an official government post in a "career" that lasted barely seven years, "Evita" Perón was one of the most influential figures in postwar South American politics. Much loved by the poor and dispossessed, her death from ovarian cancer on July 26, 1952, led to widespread public mourning throughout her native Argentina.

Born in May 1919, the illegitimate daughter of a cook, Maria Eva Duarte began her adult life as a singer and actress. In her late teens she became the mistress of Colonel Juan Perón, one of a clique of military officers who in 1943 overthrew Argentina's civilian government. Backed by the military and the lower social classes, Colonel Perón effectively was Argentina's leader until he was ousted by a civilian coup in October, 1945 and imprisoned. Eva Duarte, well-known as Perón's mistress, made an appeal to the labour unions and secured his release two weeks later. On his release, Perón addressed a crowd of 300,000 from the presidential palace, declaring his intention to lead Argentina as President. He married Evita shortly afterwards. She played a major role in the election campaign which secured his position with 56 per cent of the popular vote; crucial support coming from the *descamisados* (the "shirtless ones"), Argentina's poorest citizens.

Reviled by Argentina's middle classes, Evita was an overwhelming influence on her husband. Although she was not given an official government post, she was Argentina's Minister for Health and Labour in all but name. During this time she improved the plight of the working man and diverted government funds toward schools, hospitals and orphanages. She also single-handedly fought on behalf of women's suffrage. At the same time, however, the Perónist period also saw a widespread erosion of civil liberties, many opposition figures becoming victims of "disappearances".

In 1951, although seriously ill, she declared her intention to run as Vice-President and seemed to have been accepted until the crucial military establishment made it clear that they would withdraw support for the Perónist regime if she did not stand down. She was left with no option but to comply.

Even after her death she caused controversy, Argentina's working class campaigning vigorously for her canonization. After Perón was ousted in 1955, her body was stolen by supporters of the new regime and "expelled" from Argentina – a symbolic gesture ending a period that much of Argentina's establishment had found unpalatable.

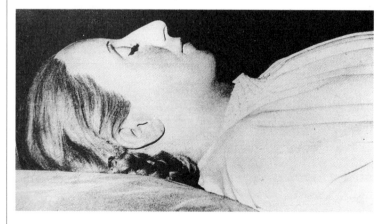

▲ The embalmed body of Eva Perón was displayed publicly until it was officially "exiled" by anti-Perónists in 1955.

ZATOPEK'S OLYMPICS

The 1952 Helsinki Olympic Games were the first to be held after the onset of the Cold War. East–West rivalry dominated the preparations, the US Olympic Committee using the hostilities as a lever to procure additional government funds for training. The Soviet Union initially refused to house their Olympians in Helsinki, preferring instead to fly them in each day from Leningrad. This plan was only abandoned when the Finns agreed to build a separate Olympic village for Eastern Bloc athletes. Throughout the games, athletes from the east and west were kept apart.

The Olympic Games themselves were dominated by one name – Zatopek. A soldier in the Czech army, 29-year-old Emil Zatopek

▲ **Emil Zatopek surges ahead of his rivals to take the gold medal for the 5,000 metres race at the Helsinki Olympics in 1952.**

established himself as perhaps the greatest long-distance runner of all time, taking both the 5,000 and 10,000 metres titles with Olympic record-breaking times. Perhaps his most notable achievement came when he also took the

gold medal in the gruelling 26-mile marathon. Winning by a clear minute and a half, Zatopek ran the fastest marathon ever at that time. Incredibly, it was the first time he had ever even attempted the distance. Zatopek's own triumph turned into a family affair as his young wife Dana took the gold medal and the Olympic record in the javelin.

The Zatopeks became a celebrated couple throughout the Eastern Bloc. Emil Zatopek rose to the rank of colonel in the Czech army, but fell from grace in 1969 when he spoke out against the Soviet occupation of his country a year earlier. His punishment was to be stripped of both his army rank and his membership of the Communist Party.

TWO YOUNG KINGS

In the space of two weeks, July and August 1952 saw a radical overhaul in the leadership of Egypt and Jordan, two of the Arab world's most prominent and volatile states.

On July 23 1952, King Farouk of Egypt – an internationally-known playboy – was ousted from power by a secret society of army officers led by the self-styled commander-in-chief of the army, Mohammed Neguib. The king had been accused of corruption and negligence, taking much of the blame for Egypt's shattering defeat by Israel in 1948. Forced to abdicate, Farouk was succeeded by his infant son, Fuad II.

In neighbouring Jordan, August 11 saw King Talal declared unfit to rule by his parliament. The 41-year-old King, who had come to power only a year earlier following the assassination of his father, the Emir Abdullah, suffered from

an untreatable mental illness. He was succeeded by his eldest son Hussein, at the time a 17-year-old student at Harrow School in England. Hussein was crowned king on May 2, 1953, his eighteenth birthday.

Hussein's early reign was overshadowed by the issue of Palestinian nationalism. In spite of his youth, the young King showed himself adept at walking a tightrope between the various conflicting parties of the Middle East while retaining close relations with the West. In April 1957, members of the pro-Palestinian National Guard attempted a *coup d'état*. Supported by loyalist Bedouins, the king was able to minimize domestic unrest. He banished purged nationalists and extremists from government, banned political parties, and created a royal dictatorship.

▲ **King Hussein of Jordan remained a central figure in the politics of the Middle East until his death in 1999.**

THE MAU MAU REVOLT

NEWS IN BRIEF
....

- King Farouk of Egypt abdicates
- Death of Eva Perón in Argentina

August
- Conference of the Pacific Council begins
- King Talal's reign over Jordan ended by parliamentary decree; Hussein succeeds
- Hungarian Prime Minister István Dobi resigns; Mátyás Rákosi succeeds

September
- New constitution adopted in Romania
- New coalition government formed in the Netherlands
- General Ibañez becomes President of Chile
- Federation of Eritrea and Ethiopia ratified by Haile Selassie
- Rocky Marciano defeats Jersey Joe Walcott to take World Heavyweight boxing title
- US Vice-Presidential candidate Richard Nixon denies charges of corruption in emotional televised speech
- Council of Europe adopts Eden Plan

October
- USSR demands departure of US ambassador
- First British atom bomb test
- USSR Communist Party holds Congress; fifth Five-Year plan adopted
- State of emergency declared in Kenya to deal with disorder caused by Mau Mau nationalists

During 1952, British rule in Kenya had been under increasing threat from the Mau Mau movement, a nationalist anti-white organization formed among the Kikuyu, the predominant tribe in Kenya. The Mau Mau advocated violent resistance to British rule and a move towards unity among the tribes of Kenya that would eventually lead to the country's winning its independence from Britain.

On October 20, 1952, after a campaign of sabotage and assassination, the government in Kenya declared a state of emergency after which a battalion of 800 British Lancashire Fusiliers were sent out to quell the uprising. What was first seen as a simple piece of military fire-fighting turned into four years of bitter guerrilla warfare which ended with the death of 11,000 rebels, 2,000 Kenyan loyalists and 100 British troops.

The conflict saw the widespread arrest of Kikuyu tribesmen, over

▲ **Over 20,000 suspected Mau Mau terrorists were routinely rounded up by the Kenyan police during the uprising.**

20,000 being placed in detention centres where numerous alleged tortures took place. In April 1953, Jomo Kenyatta, President of the Kenya African Union and known to his Kikuyu people as "Burning Spear", was tried on a charge of being a Mau Mau terrorist leader. While the British sought to present the trial as a simple criminal case, it was seen throughout the world as political repression. Although he always denied direct involvement with the Mau Mau, Kenyatta was imprisoned for seven years.

The Mau Mau became inactive after 1956. However, resistance and lobbying from the Kikuyu tribe continued and Kenya finally won independence in 1963. Jomo Kenyatta became the new nation's first Prime Minister.

HARROW RAIL TRAGEDY

October 8, 1952, saw the second worst rail accident in British history as a three-train collision just north of London took the lives of 112 people and injured over 200 others.

The story began as commuters at Harrow station boarded the 08:19 train to take them into the centre of London. Before the train had set off, a Perth–London overnight express ploughed into the back of it, demolishing four carriages and spreading debris over surrounding tracks. Less than a minute later, an outgoing express train from Euston collided with the wreckage. Within the space of a few minutes, three trains had been reduced to a pile of wreckage, the smoke from which mushroomed 15 metres (50 ft) into the air.

Emergency services from all over north London quickly arrived on the scene, but were overwhelmed by the carnage. Among the rescuers were US Air Force personnel from a nearby military base. Their expertise and prompt action was responsible for keeping the death toll down. Twelve hours after the accident, workmen were still cutting through the twisted debris, the hopes of finding survivors trapped inside diminishing by the hour.

Although an immediate investigation was launched into the tragedy, the outcome was inconclusive, with a dead train driver blamed for the accident, leading dissatisfied relatives of the victims to suspect the responsible parties were being protected by a cover-up.

▲ **The tangled wreckage of *The Night Scot* smoulders in the aftermath of a horrific three-way accident.**

LANDSLIDE FOR IKE

In accepting the presidential nomination of the Republican Party in July 1952, General Dwight David Eisenhower, the former Supreme Commander of Allied Forces in Europe, had promised that he would "wage a great crusade to total victory" over the Democratic Party. True to his word, on November 5, the Republican ticket of Eisenhower and a young lawyer named Richard M Nixon won a landslide victory over Democrat Adlai Stevenson, taking 39 states, winning the electoral college vote by 442 to 89, and collecting more than 33 million popular votes.

Since the end of World War Two, Eisenhower had been America's most respected and popular soldier. His career began at West Point, where he graduated in 1915 as one of an extraordinary class that would produce 59 generals from 164 graduates. His military career until 1942 was distinguished if low-profile, a situation that changed when he was appointed supreme Allied commander in Europe during World War Two.

He retired in 1952, a five-star general, at the end of a period as supreme commander of the Nato forces in Europe. Although some commentators had discussed a possible political career, Eisenhower chose to take up the post of President of Columbia University. This was not a successful tenure for a man who had never shone academically and mistrusted intellectuals. It did, however, allow him the time to write *The Crusade in Europe*, a best-selling work that made him a very wealthy man.

As a man of immense personal popularity, Eisenhower found himself courted by both political parties, although his conservative views made him a natural Republican. Defeating Senator Robert Taft of Ohio for the Republican nomination, Eisenhower launched a vigorous campaign that belied his age (62 years) and late entry into the political arena. Branding the Democrats and President Harry Truman as corrupt, he was a staunch critic of the Korean War, publicly declaring that if elected he would go to Korea in person in an attempt to bring the war to an end. This he achieved in 1953.

Eisenhower enjoyed two terms as President, leaving office in 1960. The Eisenhower era saw an increase in Cold War hostilities, the ending of the communist witch hunts of Joseph McCarthy and the explosion of the segregation conflict. Although he never managed to deal conclusively with such major issues, the 1950s also saw widespread prosperity for the average American. Eisenhower left office as one of the most popular presidents in history. With his military rank permanently reinstated, he enjoyed a quiet retirement on his farm in Gettysburg, Pennsylvania, where he published several volumes of memoirs. He died in 1969.

- Oil dispute causes Iran to severe diplomatic relations with Britain
- Rhône Valley dam officially opened in France
- Elections in Poland; first under new constitution

November
- Show trials of former Communist party members in Czechoslovakia
- Republican candidate Dwight Eisenhower wins US presidential election
- US explodes test H-bomb
- Death of Israeli president Chaim Weizman
- UN General Secretary Trygve Lie resigns
- New government under Marshal Papagos formed in Greece
- Communist Boleslaw Beirut appointed Polish Prime Minister
- The play *The Mousetrap* by Agatha Christie opens in London's West End

December
- Severe air pollution in London leads to many deaths
- President Eisenhower visits Korea
- Czechoslovak Communist party members convicted in show trials executed
- Nationalist riots in French Morocco
- Itzhak Ben-Zvi becomes Israeli President
- Controversial conviction in Britain of Derek Bentley for killing a policeman; Bentley did not actually fire the gun which killed the policeman but is sentenced to death
- Yugoslavia severs diplomatic relations with the Vatican
- Resignation of French Prime Minister Pinay

▲ Before his dramatic and successful entry into the political arena the former war hero General "Ike" Eisenhower had been one of the most respected men in America.

'53

NEWS IN BRIEF

- China begins its First Five-Year plan
- "Rillington Place" murderer John Christie is executed in Britain
- Discovery of double helix structure of DNA announced by Crick and Watson
- First successful open-heart surgery carried out
- *The Quatermass Experiment* debuts on British television
- Films released this year include Fred Zinnemann's *From Here to Eternity*, Henry Cornelius's *Genevieve*, George Stevens's *Shane*, Henri-Georges Clouzot's *The Wages of Fear*, Jacques Tati's *Monsieur Hulot's Holiday*, Yasujiro Ozu's *Tokyo Story* and the first CinemaScope film, *The Robe*
- Dmitri Shostakovich's *Tenth Symphony* premieres
- Samuel Beckett's play *Waiting for Godot* opens in Paris and Arthur Miller's play *The Crucible* opens in New York
- *Playboy* magazine first published
- Among books published this year are the first James Bond novel *Casino Royale* by Ian Fleming, Ray Bradbury's *Fahrenheit 541* and James Baldwin's *Go Tell It On the Mountain*. Ludwig Wittgenstein's *Philosophical Investigations*, completed in 1949, are also published this year

DEATH OF STALIN

On March 5, 1953, Joseph Stalin, the absolute ruler of the Soviet Union for almost three decades, died following a stroke, thus ending the most powerful and ruthless dictatorship of the twentieth century.

Stalin was born in Georgia in 1879, the son of a shoemaker. Much of his early life is difficult to discern, as the facts were frequently obscured by Soviet revisionist propaganda, keen to promote the personality cult of Stalinism. It is known that he came from a poor background and received little in the way of schooling: he was certainly no intellectual match for other figures of the Revolution, like Lenin and Trotsky. However, he proved to be a master of political manipulation, quicker than his rivals to see how the bureaucratic party "machine" could be used to consolidate power.

Stalin's rule saw the Soviet Union develop from a backward agricultural economy to a nuclear superpower, achieved at a terrible price. Dissenting voices found themselves "purged" – an unknown number, perhaps in the millions, died at the hands of Stalin's secret police. Industrialization and the collectivization of agriculture were carried out with a ruthless disregard for their effects on the peasant population, millions of whom starved as he ordered grain to be exported rather than used within the state.

Stalin was a successful war-time leader, especially in the postwar negotiations that gave the Soviet Union's influence free reign in Eastern Europe.

In the period leading up to his death, Stalin became insecure and paranoid. In January 1953 he announced the discovery of the "Doctors' Plot", an alleged conspiracy by nine leading physicians who had "confessed" to murdering Soviet officials using medical means. Although Stalin died before their trials could take place, it was widely believed that they were to be used as an excuse to launch a wide-ranging purge of the Communist Party. A month later *Pravda* announced that the doctors were all innocent and their confessions had been obtained using torture.

The years after Stalin's death saw the Soviet Union undergo a power struggle for leadership between Stalin's heir-apparent Georgi Malenkov and the eventual victor, Nikita Khrushchev. Then came a revision of the Stalinist era within the Soviet Union, culminating in 1956 in Khrushchev's extraordinary denunciation of Stalin's "abuse of power".

▲ Arguably the most powerful dictator in history, Joseph Stalin's later life was overshadowed by paranoid conspiracy theories.

BIRTH OF A REPUBLIC

In an effort to bring stability to its volatile political landscape, Egypt's new rulers proclaimed the country a republic on June 18, 1953. Thus the 148-year-old monarchy was abolished. It had begun in 1805 with Ottoman Viceroy Mohammed Ali and had effectively ended in 1951 with the ousting of King Farouk, representative of the tenth generation of Mohammed Ali's descendents.

The first President and Premier of the Republic of Egypt was Mohammed Naguib. The man largely responsible for the republic chose initially to remain in the shadows. Gamal Abdel Nasser had been the organizer of the revolutionary secret Free Officers group whose bloodless coup had ousted King Farouk. Nasser waited a year, to the spring of 1954, before conspiring to overthrow Naguib and name himself Prime Minister. He consolidated his position two years later when he declared Egypt a single-party socialist Arab state. He held presidential elections in which the name of Nasser was the only one on the ballot paper. Not surprisingly, he received 99.95 per cent of the vote.

Effectively a police state, Egypt underwent significant modernization under Nasser's rule, most notably in the building of the remarkable Aswan High Dam.

▶ President and Prime Minister, General Neguib leads a cavalcade through Cairo to celebrate Egypt's new status as a republic.

DEATH FOR THE ROSENBERGS

June 19, 1953, saw the execution by electric chair of the communist spies Julius and Ethel Rosenberg, making them the first American citizens to be put to death for espionage.

The Rosenbergs had been convicted in March 1951 of passing American atomic secrets to the Soviet Union. A once-active member of the Communist Party, in 1940 Julius Rosenberg joined the US Army Signal Corps as an engineer, a position that enabled him and his wife Ethel to turn

over wartime military secrets to the Soviet Union. Ethel Rosenberg's brother, Sergeant David Greenglass, who was engaged in the US government's atomic bomb project, was also indicted, having given his sister data on the US nuclear weapon program. This information was passed via a Swiss-born courier named Harry Gold, to Anatoly Yakovlev, the Soviet vice consul in New York City.

Gold first came to the notice of the authorities in May 1950 when

he was arrested in connection with the case of the British atomic spy Dr Klaus Fuchs. The Rosenbergs and Greenglass were taken into custody shortly afterwards. After agreeing to testify against the Rosenbergs, Greenglass was given a reduced sentence of 15 years. At their New York City trial in March 1951, the Rosenbergs were found guilty under the Espionage Act of 1917 which allowed the crime of espionage to be punishable by death during wartime. Even though the trial had taken place during peace time, the acts were committed while America was at war.

An appeal made in February 1953 was unsuccessful, President Eisenhower himself calling their crime "worse than murder" since it had the capacity to "jeopardize millions of innocent civilians". The Rosenbergs were given a brief stay of execution while their lawyers prepared a further unsuccessful appeal.

The Rosenbergs went to the electric chair at Sing-Sing prison. On the morning of their execution a crowd of 5,000 protesters met at New York's Union Square. Their plea was in vain.

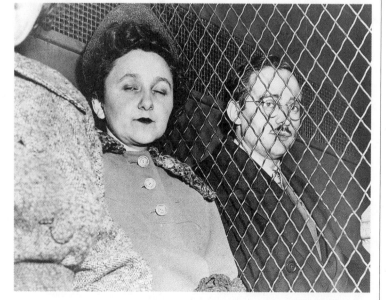

▲ In spite of protests from around the globe, nuclear spies Ethel and Julius Rosenberg prepare for the electric chair.

'53

THE CORONATION OF QUEEN ELIZABETH II

NEWS IN BRIEF

- National Party under D F Malan win majority in South African elections
- Government dismissed in Pakistan; new government under Muhammad Ali
- Social Democrats win Danish general election
- Elections held in British Guyana under new constitution

May
- Comet passenger jet crashes in India, killing all on board
- General Aldred Gruenther replaces General Ridgway as Allied Supreme Commander in Europe
- Government under René Meyer collapses in France
- Edmund Hillary and Tenzing Norgay reach the summit of Mount Everest
- Death of French jazz guitarist Django Reinhardt

June
- Coronation of Queen Elizabeth II in London
- Christian Democrats make gains in Italian elections
- Strikes in East Germany
- Anti-Communist insurrection suppressed by Soviet troops in East Germany
- General Neguib proclaims Republic of Egypt
- New government under Joseph Laniel formed in France

July
- In Ireland, Eamon de Valera wins vote of no-confidence
- Matyas Rakosi deposed as Prime Minister of Hungary, replaced by Imre Nagy

▲ The advent of television allowed the coronation of Queen Elizabeth to be enjoyed in every corner of the Empire.

June 2, 1953 saw Britain's greatest day of pageantry since the VE Day celebrations of 1945, as Elizabeth, the elder daughter of the late King George VI, was formally crowned Queen Elizabeth II.

After a long illness, King George finally succumbed to lung cancer in February 1952. The Princess, then 25 years old, had already represented him at the Trooping the Colour ceremony and at state occasions at home and abroad. In January 1952 Elizabeth and her husband Prince Philip, Duke of Edinburgh, set out on an official tour to Australia and New Zealand. En route, while on safari in Kenya, she received the news of her father's death and immediately returned to England. She was proclaimed Queen on February 8. That summer, the royal couple, with their four-year-old son Prince Charles and two-year-old daughter Princess Anne, moved from their London home, Clarence House, to Buckingham Palace, the official London home of the sovereign.

Already well-known to the British people, Elizabeth had endeared herself to them during World War Two by serving for a brief period as a second lieutenant in the Women's Army Corps, where she repaired and drove trucks. During the Blitz, she and her sister Margaret had spent most of their time at Windsor Castle, while the King and Queen remained in Buckingham Palace, which was bombed several times.

The coronation ceremony took place at its traditional location, Westminster Abbey. The coronation procession proceeded slowly through the streets of central London, packed solidly with thousands of well-wishers enjoying the spectacle. Afterwards, the Royal Family returned to Buckingham Palace where they waved to the crowds from the balcony.

As a young girl, Princess Elizabeth had not been brought up to expect that she would

▲ Flanked by her Maids of Honour, Queen Elizabeth makes her way along the nave of Westminster Abbey.

become Queen. As Duke of York, her father was second in succession to the throne. He became King following the abdication of his elder brother Edward VIII, who renounced the throne in order to marry an American divorcee.

▲ Prince Philip, Duke of Edinburgh, swears loyalty to his wife, the newly crowned Queen Elizabeth II.

EVEREST CONQUERED AT LAST

On May 29, 1953, New Zealander Edmund Hillary and the Nepalese mountaineer Tenzing Norgay became the first men to scale Mount Everest, at 8,848 metres (29,028 ft), the world's highest mountain peak. Everest had long been revered by the local people of Tibet and Nepal as "Goddess Mother of the World", and its conquest was long prized as one of man's greatest challenges.

The earliest attempts to climb Everest began in 1920. Over the following thirty years, ten missions failed as man battled against some of the harshest natural elements on Earth. The successful expedition, led by Colonel John Hunt, was sponsored by the Royal Geographical Society. Hillary, a beekeeper by profession, had already been a part of a team of New Zealanders who had made a failed attempt in

▲ **Edmund Hillary and Tenzing Norgay, the first men to conquer the peak of Mount Everest.**

1951. Tenzing, one of the mountain-dwelling Sherpa people of Nepal, was one of the most experienced mountaineers in the region, and had been employed on most of the Everest expeditions since he assisted Sir Eric Shipton's failed mission in 1935.

The operation was planned and executed with military precision, making crucial use of oxygen maintenance systems, specially insulated clothing, and portable radio equipment. Eight interim bases were set up along the way. The mission reached it's suc-

cessful climax at 11:30 on the morning of May 29. Tenzing planted the flags of Britain, Nepal, India and the United Nations at Everest's peak whilst Hillary photographed the event. They remained at the highest point on the Earth's surface for just 15 minutes before beginning their descent.

This incredible feat brought celebrity to both men, Hillary receiving a knighthood in July, 1953; Tenzing was awarded the George Cross. Hillary returned to the region in the late 1950s where he played a major role in building schools and hospitals for the Sherpa people. Although he continued his life as a great adventurer, taking part in a successful trans-Antarctic crossing, it is for the conquest of the Earth's greatest peak that Sir Edmund Hillary and Sherpa Tenzing will always be remembered.

THE RILLINGTON PLACE MURDERS

The month-long trial of John Reginald Halliday Christie, the perpetrator of a series of notorious murders at 10 Rillington Place, London took place in June 1953.

The saga began in 1949 when Timothy Evans, a barely literate van driver who lived in the top flat at 10 Rillington Place walked into a police station claiming to found the bodies of his wife and child, which he had then hidden down a drain. He later confessed to their murder but before he went to trial he accused "Reg" Christie of the murder. A tenant in the basement of same house, Christie testified at the trial. Evans was subsequently found guilty and hanged.

In March 1953, Christie disappeared. Seeing that he had also

emptied the flat, his landlord re-let it to another tenant, Beresford Brown. While attempting to put up a shelf on March 23, Brown discovered a women's body buried behind the wall. When the police arrived and began a detailed search of the house, three more bodies were found, one of them that of Christie's wife Ethel. Christie was arrested a week later.

Christie admitted the killings; three of the women had been local prostitutes and his motive had been sexual. He had invited his victims into the flat where they were subdued with gas. They were then raped and strangled.

Convicted of murder on June 25, 1953, Christie was hanged at Pentonville Prison on July 15. Although he always denied the

Evans killings, the unlikely coincidence of two unrelated murderers living in the same building led to calls for a government enquiry, even

though Evans had been hanged. Criticized by many as a whitewash, an enquiry which reported in July still found Evans to be the murderer.

▲ **Police evidence being removed from 10 Rillington Place.**

'53

BERLIN UPRISING

On June 16, 1953, the Soviet Union gave the world a demonstration – were it needed – that insurrection within the Communist territories of the Eastern bloc could not be tolerated. A workers' uprising was met by a massive show of force as Soviet tanks swept through the streets of East Berlin, overpowering the rioters. During the week that followed 20 were killed and a further 200 injured.

The events began a day earlier as the government of the German Democratic Republic (East Germany), announced that construction workers would have to increase their production quotas. This immediately led to a strike which brought 5,000 onto the streets in protest. With no response from the government, the following day the protest grew to 50,000-strong, upon which Premier Otto Grotewohl announced his decision to withdraw the new quotas. By now, however, the protests had turned into anti-Soviet riots. The Soviet embassy was besieged and the markers that divided East Berlin from the West were demolished.

With the East German authorities unable to curtail the rioting, which had now spread to miners, factory workers and railwaymen throughout the country, Soviet troops entered the scene. Their

▲ Soviet tanks roll through the streets of Berlin dispersing groups of rioting workers.

actions were swift and brutal, sealing the East–West border and cutting off the highway that linked Berlin to West Germany. East Berlin was placed under martial law and a curfew imposed.

It was another three days before law and order was restored. The Soviet authorities publicly declared the protests to be the work of Western agitators.

On July 10, the US government approved a $15 million aid package to East Berlin which began

with the creation of food camps in the west of the city. The Soviet Union demanded a halt to the practice, but the distribution continued. During that week over 10,000 crossed the border into the West. Many of them chose not to return.

The events of 1953 were just another tale in the tragic saga of a city divided against its will. A similar crisis five years later would see a further exodus to the West. This flow was dramatically halted in 1961 with the erection of the Berlin Wall. By that time it was estimated that since the end of World War Two over 2.5 million Germans had fled to the West. The Wall turned West Berlin into an island within the surrounding German Democratic Republic. Throughout the Cold War its isolation became viewed as a symbol of the freedom of the Western World.

▲ The Soviet Union proclaimed a state of martial law while the anti-Communist protests were suppressed.

WELSH BARD DIES

On November 9, 1953, Dylan Thomas, one of Britain's best-known writers of verse and prose died in New York City. He was 39 years old. The Welshman was well known for a characteristic blend of humour and pathos which can be seen – and heard – in *Under Milk Wood*, his "play for voices" for which he is, perhaps, best remembered.

Thomas began writing at a very early age, contributing numerous pieces to his school magazine, which he also edited. In his general education, however, Thomas performed poorly, disregarding any subjects in which he was not interested. He left school at the age of 16 to become a local news reporter.

His first book was published in 1934. *Eighteen Poems*, many of which had been written in his late teens, was immediately hailed by literary critics. Although Thomas was widely published and acclaimed over the next decade he made little money during most of his life. His poor business acumen and legendary drinking exploits were as much to blame as his inability to reach a wide audience with his poetry.

By the beginning of World War Two, Thomas also had a young family to support. Excused from military service because of an ongoing lung disease, he turned

▲ **Dylan Thomas struggled to make a living in the final three years of his life.**

to scriptwriting as a way of making ends meet. Throughout the 1940s he combined his literary career with working for the BBC, although even then he still struggled to survive.

In 1950, Thomas embarked on his first book tour of America, where he enjoyed a growing reputation. In 1952, *Collected Poems* was published to great acclaim on both sides of the Atlantic. For the first time in his life, Thomas saw a book by him sell in large quantities; he failed to reap the rewards, much of which were lost to the British inland revenue.

He went to New York for the third time in 1953 to oversee the first production of *Under Milk Wood*. Suffering from depression, he survived such exhausting trips by indulging in increasingly heavy bouts of drinking. During this stay in New York he took a massive alcohol overdose, fell into a coma and died.

THE BAFFLING MYSTERY OF PILTDOWN MAN

A 41-year-old scientific mystery was finally solved beyond doubt on November 21, 1953 as Piltdown Man – the supposed fossil remains of a prehistoric human – was shown to be a forgery.

The story began with the discovery in 1912 of the fossilized remains of a human-like cranium and jawbone on Piltdown Common in the south of England. The find excited scientists the world over who believed that a hitherto unknown ancestor of modern man had been found. There was never any suggestion of impropriety at this time, but certain clues emerged during the 1920s when archaeologists began to unearth remains of earlier primitive ancestors in Africa. The problem was that Piltdown Man simply didn't seem to fit into the emerging evolutionary sequence.

Many scientists became sceptical from that point onwards, but it wasn't until 1953 that scientific tests were able to provide irrefutable evidence that a deliberate and skilful hoax had been committed, using fragments of 50,000-year-old cranium, the jaw of an orangutan and a tooth from a chimpanzee.

The perpetrator of the hoax was never discovered – by the time it was uncovered, most of those involved were long dead. The finger of suspicion pointed most strongly, however, at Charles Dawson, the man who had supposedly unearthed one of his prehistoric ancestors in 1912.

▲ **The Piltdown skull, the subject of scientific controversy since its discovery in 1912.**

- Primate of the Catholic church in Poland, Cardinal Wyszynski, is placed under house arrest
- General election in Denmark under new constitution; government formed under Hans Hedoft

October
- Fears of Communist take-over of British Guyana cause Britain to send in troops, suspend constitution, declare state of emergency and arrest party members
- Prime Minister Senanayake of Ceylon retires; new government under Kotalawala formed
- Central African Federation comes into being
- General strike in Austria against Soviet occupation

November
- New government formed in Finland under the governor of the Bank of Finland
- French troops capture the village of Dien Bien Phu in Indochina
- The leader of Buganda in Uganda, Kabaka Mutesa II, deported by the governor of Uganda
- Death of US playwright Eugene O'Neill

December
- Following resolution of power struggle in Iran, diplomatic relations with Britain resume
- Israeli Prime Minister David Ben-Gurion resigns; a new coalition government is formed under Moshe Sharret
- New government under Godfrey Huggins formed in the Central African Federation
- One-party – Fatherland Front – elections held in Bulgaria
- René Coty elected President of France
- Ex-Minister of the Interior, Lavrenty Beria, executed in USSR

'54

CURE FOR POLIO

In February 1954, a vaccine for the treatment of polio (infantile paralysis) was given its first field test among children at the University of Pittsburgh. It was the culmination of seven years' research by Dr Jonas Salk.

Salk's early career saw him working with Thomas Francis on a ground-breaking vaccine for protecting against influenza viruses. In 1947, Salk began his own research on poliomyelitis (polio), a crippling disease that causes the inflammation and destruction of nerve cells on the spinal cord and, at worst, ends in muscular paralysis. A largely untreatable disease, the best course of action medical research could take was to immunize against the virus.

Salk's research isolated three separate strains of the polio virus. His first experiments, which were on monkeys, showed that by injecting a "killed" virus of each strain, antibodies were produced that would protect against the virus. Although this principle of "cancellation" was

◀ **Dr Jonas Salk, whose polio vaccine has saved millions of lives throughout the world.**

well established by the late 1940s, there was still a risk that invoking the killed polio virus could, in fact, cause the subject to contract polio. Salk's monkey experiments enabled him to gauge beyond doubt that this would not happen.

In 1952 the vaccine was tested on children who had already suffered from polio, and then on a control group who had not. The field tests of February 1954 were adjudged to be successful, and the vaccine was licensed for use by the US Food and Drug Administration in April, 1955.

The polio vaccine has undoubtedly saved the lives of millions. In 1952, 58,000 cases of polio were reported in the US; within ten years the number had dropped to below a thousand. In 1960 the virologist Albert Sabin took Salk's work a stage further, producing a polio vaccine that could be taken orally.

FIRST FOUR-MINUTE MILE

On May 6, 1954, one of sport's most famous milestone barriers was broken as Roger Bannister, a medical student at Oxford University, achieved the unthinkable by running a mile in under four minutes.

For more than twenty years experts had argued whether such a feat was physiologically possible. During the 1940s the Swedish middle-distance runner Gunder Hägg – in whose dazzling career 15 world records were shattered – had gradually shaved the mile barrier to 4 minutes 1.3 seconds in 1945. In the nine years that followed no athlete came near to bettering the record.

At the groundbreaking athletics meeting in Oxford, Bannister,

▲ **Roger Bannister crosses the finishing line as he completes his record-breaking run.**

already a British and European champion over 1500 metres, had the additional impediment of strong 24 km/h (15 mph) cross winds. His winning time was 3 minutes 59.4 seconds.

Bannister's achievement brought him overnight international celebrity. He wrote a successful account of his achievement, *The Four-Minute Mile*, then returned to his studies.

In 1963 Bannister earned a further medical degree and thereafter became a noted neurologist. He was knighted in 1979.

Surprisingly, Bannister's record was broken within six weeks when Australian athlete John Landy clocked a time of 3 minute 58 seconds. Although a "sub-four" time is still regarded as commendable, top athletes over this distance regularly manage it. In September 1993, Algerian athlete Noureddine Morceli took the record down to an incredible 3 minutes 44.39 seconds. That time has yet to be bettered.

COMPUTER AGE DAWNS

The computer made its first real inroad into the world of commerce in May 1954 as the International Business Machines Corporation (IBM) announced the sale of the first electronic computers aimed at business users. The size and expense of computers had hitherto made them the preserve of universities and science laboratories, with a highly specialized staff required to operate and programme them.

The IBM machine could process over ten million arithmetic calculations in an hour. It was mainly aimed at banks and insurance companies who, at the time, performed all of their "number-crunching" operations using departments of clerks with mechanical adding machines.

Raw information was entered into the computer's cathode-tube logic unit from magnetic tapes. After processing, the resulting data was also output on magnetic tape from which the data could then be printed out.

At this time, Thomas Watson, the president of IBM, felt that the costs involved, including the creation of a new industry of computer professionals, were prohibitively expensive. Therefore, the first machines were rented out. Although IBM charged around a quarter of a million dollars a year for the service, the potential staff savings and the commercial benefits of seeing results more quickly made it a massive success.

The rapid progress in computer development, which has accelerated over the past decade, has been such that even the lowliest modern home computer would have out-performed the first IBM business machine, which was, in effect, simply a glorified adding machine. More demanding mathematical processes would not generally be possible until the early 1960s and the development of the first widely used programming language, COBOL (Common Business-Oriented language). This allowed industry to hire its own specialist computer programmers and analysts to create tailor-made computer systems.

Computers would also undergo radical changes in size as silicon chip technology emerged. The first IBM business machines took up as much space as a small apartment.

▼ **The most basic of modern-day personal computers would be able to out-perform a state-of-the-art, 1950s mainframe system.**

'54

The sleepy town of Newport, Rhode Island was shaken up on July 18, 1954, as 7,000 music fans made a bee-line for the world's first great jazz festival.

The star of the show was singer Ella Fitzgerald, thought by many to be the greatest vocalist in the history of popular music. The modern jazz world was also well-represented by be-bop trumpet star Dizzy Gillespie, who gave an acclaimed performance. Also noteworthy were vibe-star Milt Jackson's Modern Jazz Quartet.

During the 1960s, Newport became the single most important set of dates on the jazz calendar, often acting as a stage from which new future directions in jazz were announced. Every great name in jazz from Miles Davis to Duke Ellington played at Newport at some time in their career. In the end, the Newport Jazz Festival became a victim of its own success, and in 1972 was moved to New York City.

NEWS IN BRIEF

April
- All Comet passenger jets grounded after a third fatal crash
- No conclusive result in Belgian general election; coalition government formed under Achille van Acker
- Soviet diplomat–agent Vladimir Petrov defects to Australia
- General Nasser becomes Prime Minister of Egypt
- US Air Force flies French reinforcements to Indochina
- General Zahedi re-appointed Prime Minister of Iran
- Senator McCarthy begins televised hearings on Communist subversion in US federal institutions
- First elections held in Honduras

May
- Siege of Dien Bien Phu ends; French troops surrender to Viet Minh
- US Supreme Court outlaws racial segregation in schools
- Sitting government re-elected in Australian general elections
- State of emergency declared in Buganda province of Uganda
- Death of American composer Charles Ives

June
- Coalition government under John Costello formed in Ireland
- French government falls after defeat of French troops at Dien Bien Phu; Pierre Mendès-France new French leader
- Elections held in Gold Coast; Dr Kwame Nkrumah forms new government

AMERICA IN VIETNAM

Conflict between the Soviet-backed Viet Minh rebels of North Vietnam and the Western-backed South Vietnam formally ended in July 21, 1954, with the country divided along the latitude 17 degrees north. The hostilities, however, were far from over as, tacitly encouraged by the US administration, up to half-a-million refugees fled the communist regime to settle south of the "17th Parallel".

Vietnam had been a French protectorate until the Viet Minh revolution; now, the Paris government found itself increasingly side-lined after the cease-fire, as America openly sought influence in the region. Without seeking French approval, on September

▲ **Almost a half-a-million refugees fled fierce fighting, to settle in the relative safety of the south side of the 17th parallel.**

10, 1954, President Eisenhower called for the allocation of over $10 million to help with the relocation of refugees who initially were housed in US army camps south of the border. The following month, he announced that the US government was prepared to finance intensive training for the depleted South Vietnamese army.

Meanwhile, in the north, rebel leader Ho Chi Minh returned from hiding to take up his position as premier of North Vietnam, while his generals paraded the Viet Minh armies triumphantly through the streets of Hanoi. With the final wave of French officials evacuated, the Communists celebrated their victory over the occupying forces. However, East–West tensions in the region would continue to run high.

FIRST NOBEL PRIZE FOR LINUS PAULING

One of finest scientists of the postwar era, Linus Pauling was awarded the 1954 Nobel Prize for chemistry. It was given for his work in applying quantum mechanics to molecular bonding. It was the first of two Nobel

▶ **The unorthodox Professor Linus Pauling: Nobel Prize-winning chemist, physicist and peace campaigner.**

prizes the controversial scientist would earn during his life.

An expert in both chemistry and physics, in 1958 Pauling found himself at the forefront of the anti-nuclear movement when he published the book *No More War!* He came to public notice that same year, presenting a petition to the United Nations calling for an end to nuclear testing. The petition had been signed by over 11,000 scientists from around the world. Pauling's work in this field earned him the Nobel Peace Prize in 1962, although at the same he was fiercely criticized by America's right-wing.

In his later years, Pauling's interest spread to medical matters. A number of his theories – such as the benefits of mega-doses of vitamin C – were somewhat unorthodox and viewed as eccentric by some members of the scientific community.

MASTER OF COLOUR DIES

November 3, 1954, saw the passing of Henri Matisse, one of the most important artists of the twentieth century. He died at his apartment in Nice at the age of 84. The most prominent of the Fauves, a group of painters whose strongly coloured work caused a furore when first shown in 1905, Matisse's work was characterized by a revolutionary expressive use of colour.

Born in Picardy, France in 1869, Matisse showed no real interest in art until his early twenties. Having studied law in Paris, he returned to his home town where he started working as a legal clerk. After taking some recreational drawing classes, Matisse undertook his first oil paintings while recovering from appendicitis. He quickly realized this was his true calling and abandoned law.

Returning to Paris in 1891, he took private lessons in preparation for the entrance examination to the École des Beaux-Arts. His progress was rapid and the following year he was accepted at the prestigious school on the basis of his existing work. In 1896 Matisse enjoyed his first success when his painting, *Woman Reading*, was bought by the French government.

Matisse developed the Fauvist style (its name – in English "wild beasts" – coined by the critic Louis Vauxelles), after a lengthy study of the work of van Gogh and Gauguin. Unlike the work of these post-Impressionists, however, Matisse's forceful brushstrokes created an almost violently expressive impact. Fauvism brought Matisse a degree of wealth and fame and by 1908 he had been exhibited in New York, Moscow and Berlin.

For some of his followers – artists such as Raoul Dufy and Georges Braque – Fauvism was but a stepping stone to Expressionism and Cubism. Matisse, however, retained a striking use of colour throughout his working life.

Extraordinarily prolific, Matisse worked in a number of different media, producing some 60 sculptures and experimenting with etching, drypoint, lithography and printmaking. In spite of being bedridden for much of the last ten years of his life, he continued to develop his art. In 1947 he published his own book, *Jazz*, using a technique he described as "drawing with scissors" – creating motifs cut out from sheets of paper and pasted together. His final works were large-scale pieces using this technique, and although they are stylistically very different from his best-known paintings, the dramatic use of contrasting colour remains unmistakable.

▲ **Irrespective of his chosen style, the work of Henri Matisse was characterized by an expressive use of colour.**

NATO AND THE WARSAW PACT

▲ **The Eastern Bloc responded to the formation of Nato by signing the Warsaw Pact.**

Nato – the North Atlantic Treaty Organization – had been brought into being in 1949 as a way of balancing the heavy military presence the Soviet Union built up in Eastern Europe after the end of World War Two.

Nato created a combined military force made up of troops from the US and the non-neutral states of Europe who had agreed to its formation at the Brussels conference of 1948. An awkward difficulty faced by the Western powers was how to include the Federal Republic of Germany (West Germany) in Nato's defence plans. The bitter experience of the 1930s made the West extremely wary of allowing Germany a free hand to re-equip its military strength. On the other hand, the country's size and strategic position at the centre of Europe made its involvement in some kind of defence strategy a necessity. A Soviet land attack on Western Europe, it was generally

agreed, would begin with crossing the borders of West Germany.

With broad agreement among the Allies, the matter became the centre of discussion at a nine-power conference in London in October 1954. Called to set out the terms for an end to the Allied

occupation of Germany and a ruling on Germany's re-armament allowance, the conference agreed to admit West Germany to Nato, but without nuclear weapons. On May 5, 1955, West Germany was given its sovereign independence. The Bonn parliament would be free to govern without interference from the West.

This development was a cause of major concern to the Soviet Union, now faced by a mighty consolidated armed force capable of acting on behalf of all of the Western powers. The response was swift. On May 14, 1955 in the Czech capital, Prague, the Soviet Prime Minister Marshal Bulganin and the leaders of the Eastern Bloc nations signed the Warsaw Treaty of Friendship, Co-operation and Mutual Assistance.

Known thereafter simply as the Warsaw Pact, this treaty allowed for the creation of a unified military command similar to Nato's and, significantly, the stationing of Soviet military units within all member states. Soviet Marshal

▲ **Nato meetings were impressive events in the 1950s. This meeting of political and military leaders took place in Paris in 1957.**

Ivan Konev was named as the military commander of the Eastern bloc. Among those taking part were Soviet Foreign Minister Molotov and the army chief Marshal Zhukov.

The initial signatories to the Warsaw Pact were the Soviet Union, Albania, Bulgaria, Czechoslovakia, East Germany, Hungary, Poland and Romania. Although on the surface it provided the Eastern bloc nations with military strength to match that of Nato, the Warsaw Pact went further, emphasizing the powerful stranglehold the Soviet Union had established over Eastern Europe. As a consequence, once-mighty states like Poland and Hungary were now little more than satellites at the beck and call of Moscow. Over the coming years, the positioning of Soviet military bases became a frequent focus for nationalist protests, a spate of which took place throughout Hungary and Poland during 1956, ending with occupation by the Red Army.

In the future, the Warsaw Pact would be invoked during periods of internal unrest in the Eastern bloc, most notably when the Soviet Union ordered a combined force into Czechoslovakia after the 1968 uprising. Such moves were invariably at the behest of the Moscow.

All of the original signatories, with the exception of Albania, which had refused to back the invasion of Czechoslovakia, agreed the renewal of the Warsaw Pact in 1985. However, the wave of democratic revolutions that swept through Eastern Europe in 1989, concluding with the break-up of the Soviet Union, rendered the Warsaw Pact a meaningless agreement. A final summit of Eastern European leaders formally ended the Pact on July 1, 1991.

DEATH OF A GENIUS

Albert Einstein, the world's most celebrated scientist died on April 18, 1955. Having suffered many years from a heart condition, the savant died in his sleep at his home in Princeton, New Jersey. He was 76 years old.

Born in Ulm, Germany in 1879, Einstein's early scholastic life was mediocre. Indeed, one of his school reports noted that it was unlikely that Einstein would ever

▲ **After a life of scientific achievement, in his latter years Albert Einstein worked tirelessly to promote world peace.**

"come to much". However, as a child, Einstein developed a fascination for mathematical puzzles. Eventually, after being turned away, he was accepted by the Federal Polytechnic Academy in Zürich. He graduated in 1900, albeit with a modest degree.

Quickly abandoning a career as a mathematics teacher, Einstein joined the civil service, examining new patents. It was during this time that he formulated some of his greatest scientific theories. In 1905 Einstein submitted a thesis to the University of Zürich for which he was awarded a doctorate. Among other papers

on theoretical physics that Einstein published in 1905 was one which contained the principle of his Special Theory of Relativity, the mathematics for which was expressed in the formula $E=mc^2$. In 1916 he published his General Theory of Relativity, developed from the Special Theory. Einstein was awarded the Nobel Prize for Physics in 1921.

Following the rise of the Nazis in Germany, Einstein, a Jew, was deprived of his post as director of the Kaiser Wilhelm Institute in Berlin in 1933, and went to the United States. Some of Einstein's research laid the groundwork for the birth of the atom bomb. At first, he actively promoted its development for fear that the Nazis were engaged in a similar project. Seeing the bomb used at Hiroshima altered his view.

Einstein's postwar life was largely devoted to the cause of pacifism. One of his last acts was to sign a petition of Nobel Prize winners calling on the nations of the world to renounce warfare.

'55

A NEW ERA IN TELEVISION

On 22 September 1955, 188,000 television sets were tuned in to an even that would forever change the face of broadcasting in Britain – the opening night of ITV, Britain's first independent television network.

Although the first broadcasts had been made in 1936, television in Britain only took off in earnest a decade later following an end to the blackout of the war years. Until 1954, a Royal Charter had given the British Broadcasting Corporation (BBC) a total monopoly over television in the UK. It was during the early 1950s that the subject of providing commercial competition became widely debated in parliamentary circles. In spite of considerable establishment opposition, in 1954 Parliament passed the Television Act creating the Independent Television Authority (ITA), a government body that was to be given responsibility for the regulation of a new channel financed by selling airtime to advertisers. The independent channel – called ITV – would be a national network of broadcasting organizations covering different regions of Great Britain.

On 25 August 1954, the ITA placed an advertisement in the British press, inviting "Applications from those interested in becoming programme contractors". Of the 25 organizations that applied, only four, Rediffusion, Granada, ATV and ABC, covering the majority of viewers in England, were initially deemed suitable.

The opening night of transmission saw viewers treated to live coverage of the annual Guildhall Banquet followed by Britain's first ever cash-prize quiz show. Although outwardly displaying little concern towards the ITV, the BBC upstaged their rival's opening night by killing off one of the main characters in the massively popular radio serial "The Archers".

Nonetheless, with a schedule dominated by entertainment, the ITV network became an immediate success, reshaping the face of British television. With popular shows like "Sunday Night at the London Palladium" and "Coronation Street", ITV quickly dominated the ratings.

By the end of the decade, advertising revenue had increased from an initial £2 million to approaching £100 million.

DISNEY'S THEME PARK

On July 18, 1955, the world's most famous pioneer of film animation, Walt Disney, opened a theme park in Anaheim, California dedicated to his cartoon creations. Ever modest, Disney named the 160-acre site Disneyland.

A commercial artist by training, Walt Disney had founded the Disney Studios in 1919 and started out by making simple animation advertising films. In 1927 Disney and his partner Ub Iwerks created the cartoon characters Mickey Mouse and Minnie Mouse. Making his screen debut in 1928 in *Steamboat Willie*, Mickey was a sensation and his success was the foundation on

◀ **The success of Disneyland was founded on the belief of its creator that whatever their age, everyone remains a child at heart.**

which the Disney fortune was built. During the early 1930s Disney created many more cartoon figures, such as Donald Duck and family, Pluto and Goofy.

In 1937 Disney released his cartoon masterpiece, *Snow White and the Seven Dwarfs*. It was the first feature-length animated film. A huge cinema hit, *Snow White* won a Special Oscar for "a significant screen innovation". Other children's classics followed: *Pinocchio*, *Dumbo* and the more sophisticated *Fantasia*, in which his cartoon creations were allowed to play to the music of Tchaikovsky and Stravinsky.

Behind Walt Disney's technical wizardry was an astute business brain. And while some criticized the parochialism and sentimentality of his pictures, he never deviated from his aim to produce entertainment for "children of all ages" in the knowledge that there could be no bigger market.

It was this outlook that drove his most ambitious project, the creation of Disneyland. The first plans were laid down in 1950. Using his successful films as a backdrop, Disney created a fantasy kingdom where "children" could go on a real-life adventure in a medieval castle, ride on a Mississippi paddle steamer, or wander through the Wild West. Everywhere, they could encounter Disney's most famous characters brought to life by actors.

It was a bold plan which cost $17 million to create, but Disney was confidant that he could attract up to five million visitors each year. This proved to be something of an underestimate, Disneyland quickly becoming one of the world's most popular tourist attractions – as it continues to be almost 50 years later.

ENDING THE ARMS RACE

The overriding threat to world peace during the decade that followed the end of World War Two was the escalation of armaments. America's use of nuclear bombs over Japan in 1945 had provided a glimpse of how future world conflict could end. Ten years later, the US and the USSR each possessed a nuclear arsenal capable of destroying life on Earth.

Since its formation, the General Assembly of the United Nations had put forward various plans for reducing the stockpiling of nuclear weapons. With the US and Soviet positions firmly entrenched, little progress was made.

In 1952, the UN created the Disarmaments Commission, set up in an effort to balance reduction of all armed forces, eliminate all weapons of mass destruction, and place all use of atomic energy in the hands of an international body. The Commission failed to achieve any useful results, becoming one of growing number of forums in which the ideological differences between both sides were played up to the full.

Since the end of the war, Winston Churchill had made repeated calls for a summit conference of international leaders to discuss the issues of the day. It was Stalin's death in 1953 that encouraged some Western leaders to think that a more meaningful dialogue might be possible. Thus, on July 12, 1955, the leaders of the "Big Four" nations, the United States, Great Britain, France and the USSR, convened at a summit meeting, held on neutral soil in Geneva, Switzerland.

▲ **Delegates from the United States, Soviet Union, France and Britain debate the rapid increase in the stockpiling of nuclear arms.**

One of the main issues under discussion was the reunification of Germany. The Soviet Union pressed for the creation of a neutral state and the withdrawal of US military bases; to the Western leaders free elections were the only acceptable way forward. No agreement was reached.

The most surprising development came towards the end of the summit when US President Eisenhower unveiled his "open skies" proposal. The American idea was that each of the superpowers should exchange defence installation blueprints and allow each other unhindered aerial access to make inspections. Premier Khrushchev of the USSR eventually denounced the proposal as just a scheme to allow the US to embark on espionage.

Nothing tangible resulted from the summit, although it did temporarily halt the escalating tension between the two sides. Indeed, the following month the Soviet news agency TASS announced that the current conciliatory atmosphere meant that the manpower of the Red Army could be reduced by 650,000.

May
- Premier Ngo Dinh Diem wins power struggle for control of South Vietnam; Binh Xuyen rebels forced out of Saigon in heavy fighting
- West Germany becomes a sovereign state, joins Nato
- The Western European Union, an organization for the co-ordination of European security and defence, comes into existence
- South Vietnamese government order French troops north to counter Viet Minh threat
- Warsaw Pact signed by eight Soviet Bloc countries
- USSR's Khrushchev and Bulganin make "fence-mending" visit to Yugoslavia
- Argentine government's anti-Catholic laws cause civil unrest
- Dock workers strike begins in Britain
- Conservative Party under Anthony Eden wins general election in Britain
- Railway strike begins in Britain

June
- End of British railway strike
- Pope excommunicates President Perón of Argentina, who takes dictatorial powers; government officials resign
- Italian coalition government under Mario Scelba collapses; new coalition under Antonio Segni formed
- US and UK sign deal on atomic energy
- EOKA terrorists arrested in Cyprus

'55

SCIENTISTS' DIRE WARNING

On July 9, 1955, the world's governments were given a dire warning of the potential consequences of nuclear war by some of the most eminent names working in the field of science.

Led by the celebrated British political philosopher Bertrand Russell, a group of nine leading academics, among them seven Nobel Prize winners, called for the total renunciation of warfare, warning of a possible "utter and irretrievable disaster".

At a press conference held in London, Earl Russell stressed that the protest was opposed to war in general rather than specifically nuclear conflict. It was also intended to be non-political, scientists of different persuasions coming from both sides of the Iron Curtain.

In a lengthy statement published in many of the world's

▲ Spokesperson for the scientific community, Bertrand Russell warns the world of the dangers of nuclear proliferation.

leading newspapers, Russell was unequivocal: "In view of the fact that in any future world war nuclear weapons will certainly be employed, and that such weapons threaten the continued existence of mankind, we urge the governments of the world to realize and acknowledge publicly that their purposes cannot be furthered by a world war."

The petition was given added weight by including the signature of Albert Einstein. The most famous scientist of them all, whose early work had paved the way for the nuclear age – and the atom bomb – Einstein had died three months earlier. Russell reported that it was "the last public action of his life".

Russell had hoped to elicit a response from the six world powers with a nuclear capability – US, USSR, Great Britain, Canada, France and China – his aim being the creation of a high-profile international scientific forum. With Cold War loyalties now well-established, however, the views of Russell and his eminent colleagues were politely brushed aside as the world arms race continued unabated.

NEWS IN BRIEF
....

July
- First US civil atomic energy reactor to generate electricity goes on-line
- End of dock workers' strike in Britain
- Convicted murderer Ruth Ellis hanged, the last woman to be executed in Britain
- President Perón of Argentina promises to give up dictatorial powers
- East–West summit conference opens in Geneva
- Soviet leader Khrushchev visits East Germany

August
- Revolts in southern Sudan; withdrawal of British and Egyptian troops demanded
- "Peaceful Uses of Atomic Energy" conference begins in Geneva
- USSR announce reduction in armed forces
- Police in Portuguese Goa in India kill 24 demonstrators demanding return of Goa to India; India severs diplomatic relations with Portugal
- Anti-French riots in Morocco
- Anti-French uprising in Aïn Abid in Algeria leads to massacre of Europeans in Philippeville
- Conference in London between Greece, Turkey and UK to settle the Cyprus issue begins
- Deaths of Nobel Prize-winning German author Thomas Mann and French artist Fernand Leger

WAR IN ALGERIA

The fight for independence in the French North African province of Algeria escalated as violent rebellion broke out in 25 towns across the country on August 20, 1955.

Algerian nationalism had first reared a violent head in May 1945, when 84 French Algerian settlers were massacred. The French-backed authorities responded harshly with an estimated 1,800 indiscriminate killings. The movement was subdued over the next decade, partially as a result of widespread migration. Indeed, some of the province's wealth at this time came from the 350,000 Algerians who had used their partial-French citizenship to establish themselves in the cities of France, sending money back home to support their families.

Riots first broke out in November 1954, when Muslim nationalists joined forces to form the National Liberation Front. They began low-key guerrilla activities aimed at settlers and, at the same time, started diplomatic efforts outside Algeria.

The carefully planned attacks on August 20 were led by former councillor Zirout Youssef. In 25

▲ Armed and well-organized, the Algerian rebels were prepared for a long and bitter campaign in their drive towards independence.

"LIVE FAST, DIE YOUNG"

towns, rebels under his command attacked French military and police posts and other civil bases. The aim was to cause maximum disruption to the French administration. At the same time, thousands of Muslim peasants grouped to attack the homes of Europeans. In the town of Philipville, 60 Europeans perished in a violent mob attack. As before, the response of the French authorities was unequivocal. Villages suspected of harbouring rebels were razed and, at the same time, an army of half-a-million French troops was sent to Algeria to maintain order.

Throughout 1957, fighting between the two sides was fierce. Realizing that the newly independent adjoining states of Morocco and Tunisia were aiding the rebels, the French army creating a barbed-wire border. This became the focus of fighting as a rebel army numbering 30,000 fought from Tunisia under the aegis of the Provisional Government of Algeria. When the French air force launched a retaliatory raid on Tunisia, a United Nations mission was quickly sent in to mediate.

The Paris government in turmoil, events degenerated further on May 13, 1958 as thousands of European Algerians, fearing that France would succumb to nationalist pressure, took to the streets of Algiers. With the tacit support of the French military, they were effectively free to run riot. The call of the protesters was for the immediate integration of Algeria with France. With little confidence in the Parisian government, they demanded the return of the only politician they thought capable of sorting out the mess – Charles de Gaulle. It was a call that would also be echoed throughout France.

The actor James Dean, Hollywood's first true teenage idol, died on September 30, 1955. The body of the 24-year-old star was found amongst the mangled wreckage of his Porsche Spider coupe on the Los Angeles to Salinas road. Dean had shot to fame earlier in the year in the film *East of Eden.* Although generally viewed as his film debut, Dean had actually played bit-parts in a number of Hollywood pictures before.

His status as the greatest icon of eternal youth was cemented by the two films he completed in the year of his death, both of which were issued posthumously. In *Rebel Without A Cause* (1955), Dean created nothing less than a template for future generations of misunderstood teen angst. His moody "method" style created a perfect summation of the contradictory confusion and arrogance of youth. It was also the first film to suggest that juvenile violence was not necessarily born out of poverty – Dean was "the bad boy from a good family", as the billing ran. The appeal of Dean's character transcends its period setting and continues to resonate for teenagers of the PlayStation era.

▲ James Dean in his finest role, as Jett Rink in the film *Giant*, based on the novel by Edna Ferber.

Dean's credentials for being considered a serious actor grew largely out of his performance as a Texas oil man in *Giant* (1956), his second posthumous film and one of the finest of the 1950s.

Like his older contemporary Marlon Brando, Dean was instrumental in creating an identifiable generation gap between child and adult. Unlike Brando, Dean, dying young, never lost the looks that brought him celebrity during his lifetime – and for decades after.

▼ The mangled wreckage of James Dean's beloved Porsche Spider coupe. His two greatest films were not released until after his untimely death.

THE OUSTING OF PERÓN

▲ **He who lives by the bullet – Juan Domingo Perón seized power as a result of a military coup and was overthrown in the same manner.**

The end of Juan Perón's nine-year rule in Argentina came on September 19, 1955, when a military coup swept the him from power.

An authoritarian leader, Perón had himself come to power with the help of the army in which he had been a high-ranking officer. His popularity had fallen dramatically since 1952, after the death of his popular wife "Evita".

The main thorn in the side of the Perónists was the Roman Catholic church, a highly influential body within Argentina. Not unnaturally, Perón sought to minimize the role of the church in Argentine life – a policy that angered many military officers and turned them against him. During the final year of his reign, Perón had caused outrage when he arrested 85 priests and expelled the Bishop of Buenos Aires. The Vatican's response was firm, Pope Pius XII excommunicating Perón – an unthinkable situation in a Roman Catholic state.

On June 18, 1955, a revolt was launched by officers of Argentina's navy and air force in which fighter planes bombed the government building at Plaza de Mayo. Over three hundred civilians were killed in the attack and Perón placed the country under army rule.

July and August saw massed protests by Catholics and by students calling for the resignation of the President. The protests were suppressed and numerous arrests made.

The end came swiftly when a fully fledged military coup was launched by General Eduardo Lonardi on September 16. Three days later, Perón fled to exile in Paraguay. Lonardi became temporary leader until his colleague General Pedro Aramburu took command a month later.

Although in exile until 1973, Perón continued to wield considerable influence over Argentine politics. When Perónist candidates won the presidential election in that year he returned to a hero's welcome and resumed the presidency until his death the following year.

PRINCESS MARGARET ENDS ROMANCE

After much speculation in the world's media, on October 31, 1955, Queen Elizabeth's sister, Princess Margaret, announced that her controversial two-year romance with Group Captain Peter Townsend was over, and that there would be no royal wedding.

The romance, between the handsome 40-year-old war hero and the lively, pretty 24-year-old princess, had captured the imagination of the British public. The only problem facing the couple was that Townsend had already been married and his divorce had not been sanctioned by the Church of England. This was not the first time such a dilemma had affected the royal family. Less than twenty years earlier, Princess Margaret's uncle, Edward VIII, had abdicated so that he could marry an American divorcee, Wallis Simpson. Although her position in Britain's monarchy was minor by comparison, Margaret acted in accordance with her "royal duty" and ended the courtship.

Although she was married in 1960 to a commoner – the

photographer Anthony Armstrong-Jones – there remained speculation that Princess Margaret was bitterly unhappy at having been deprived of her true love. Although the couple had two children, the attractive young princess appeared increasingly dour and removed as she carried out her public duties.

By the time "Tony and Margaret" announced their divorce in 1978 they had long since been separated. The first divorce to come so close to the English throne, Princess Margaret thereafter became something of an embarrassment to the royal family, embarking on a jet-set lifestyle, smoking heavily and creating a tabloid scandal by her affair with the "toy boy" Roddy Llewellyn. After a series of health scares in the 1980s, Margaret overhauled her way of life and thereafter chose to keep a low public profile.

▲ The glamorous face of the royal family, Princess Margaret opens a trade fair – Captain Townsend is pictured behind her.

ATTLEE BIDS FAREWELL

▲ One of the pivotal figures of Britain in the twentieth century, Clement Attlee was never so grand he would not travel on the Underground.

On December 7, 1955, Clement Attlee resigned the leadership of the Labour Party, which he had held for twenty years. During that time he had served at the very pinnacle of British politics.

A former lawyer, Attlee had become Prime Minister following the 1945 election that ousted Winston Churchill and the Conservatives in favour of the Labour party. Attlee's premiership oversaw the birth of the National Health Service and the nationalization of numerous important industries. Abroad, he actively supported the move towards independence throughout the Empire and Commonwealth.

Although returned to office in the 1951 election, Attlee's House of Commons majority was cut to only six seats, making his position extremely weak. His government crumbled as two very prominent ministers, Nye Bevan and the young Harold Wilson resigned from the cabinet over the introduction of health-service charges. Later that year, after another election, Conservatives were returned to power.

Serious ideological divides beset the Labour Party of the early 1950s. The main difficulty was the question of how socialism could fit into an affluent society. On the left of the party "Bevanites" led by the outspoken Welshman Nye Bevan stood firmly by socialist policy and favoured a move away from dependence on the US; "Revisionists" led by Hugh Gaitskell were opposed to the continued manifesto pledge towards further nationalization.

By 1955, Attlee, now 72, had become more of a figurehead than an effective leader of the Labour Party. He chose to stand down so that a new leader could be elected. Although Gaitskell won an easy victory it would be nine years before Labour came to power again, led by Harold Wilson (Gaitskell having died in 1963). As the first Earl Attlee, Attlee continued a lower-profile career in the House of Lords until his death in 1969.

November
- New coalition government under David Ben-Gurion formed in Israel
- Coup deposes Lonardi regime in Argentina; General Pedro Aramburu becomes president
- The Sultan of Morocco returns home from exile
- British water supply fluoridated in Anglesey, Wales
- Interstate Commerce Commission orders end of racial segregation of US public transport
- State of emergency declared in Cyprus
- Deaths of French composer Arthur Honegger and artist Maurice Utrillo

December
- Rosa Parks arrested for violating segregated seating laws on buses in Alabama, USA; Black Americans begin boycott of city buses in Montgomery, Alabama
- New government formed in Turkey
- Britain and Egypt agree to grant independence to Sudan
- US evacuates its consulate in Hanoi, North Vietnam
- Hugh Gaitskell becomes leader of the British Labour Party

'56

NEWS IN BRIEF

- Morocco gains independence from France
- EOKA terrorists agitate for the union of Cyprus with Greece
- USA adopts the motto "In God We Trust" by act of Congress
- "Pop" art becomes fashionable
- Films released during the year include Mike Todd's *Around the World in Eighty Days*, John Ford's *The Searchers*, Roger Vadim's *And God Created Woman*, starring Brigitte Bardot, Alain Resnais's *Nuit et Brouillard* and Satyajit Ray's *Pather Panchali*
- The show *Gunsmoke* debuts on US television
- The play *Look Back In Anger* by John Osborne opens in Britain
- Opera *Candide* by Leonard Bernstein premieres
- Opera singer Maria Callas makes debut in New York
- The musical *My Fair Lady* by Lerner and Loewe opens in New York
- First Eurovision Song Contest
- Popular tunes of the year include "Heartbreak Hotel" and "Hound Dog" by Elvis Presley and "Que Sera Sera" by Doris Day
- Beat poet Allen Ginsberg publishes the poem *Howl*
- Books published during the year include *Cider With Rosie* by Laurie Lee, *My Family and Other Animals* by Gerald Durrell and *The Fall* by Albert Camus

REVISING STALIN'S IMAGE

In a "secret" address to the Twentieth Congress of the Communist Party, held on February 24, 1956, Soviet Premier Nikita Khrushchev launched an extraordinary attack on his predecessor Joseph Stalin. Highlighting the paranoia that permeated a reign of terror in which political opponents were ruthlessly removed at will, Khrushchev declared: "Here we see no wisdom, only a demonstration of brutal force."

Such public criticism of leading Party officials was unprecedented at this time. Khrushchev went on to denounce many of Stalin's political strategies, including the battle for Kharkov during World War Two, which saw the unnecessary deaths of hundreds of thousands of Red Army troops.

Although the speech was leaked from an unknown Eastern European source, the Eisenhower administration in the US was sceptical, viewing it as a Soviet propaganda exercise aimed at creating an impression of a new regime prepared to allow greater personal freedom.

▲ **Soviet leader Nikita Khrushchev announces a new face for Soviet Communism. The image of Karl Marx towers over the background.**

CYPRUS EXPLODES

On January 10, 1956, the British government ordered a battalion of 1,600 paratroopers to the eastern Mediterranean island of Cyprus to deal with the growing number of guerrilla attacks on British military and police bases. The cause of the disturbances was the growing support for an end to British rule on the island.

British occupation of Cyprus began in 1878 with an uneasy agreement with former sovereign state Turkey. After World War One, in which Britain and Turkey were enemies, the island was proclaimed a British crown colony.

Most of the political problems experienced in Cyprus have been a result of hostilities between the Greek and Turkish populations living on the island. From the 1930s onwards a growing movement emerged among Greek Cypriots for formal unification with Greece – *enosis* – as it was called. Turkish Cypriots exercised a continuing hostility to the idea. Even before World War Two, rioting and fighting between the two sides was common in the capital, Nicosia.

In 1947 Britain's newly elected Labour government declared a move towards greater self-government for all of Britain's crown colonies. When this was made public in Cyprus, the idea was strongly rejected by the Greek Cypriots. In 1955 Georgios Grivas (Dighenis), a high-ranking Cypriot in the Greek Army, founded the National Organization of Cypriot Struggle (EOKA), believing that only by violent means would they rid the island of British rule. EOKA engaged in a campaign of bombings and assassinations of opponents of *enosis*, both Cypriot and British.

With British troops arriving on

▲ **Royal Marines stationed on the island scour the mountain villages of Cyprus in search of EOKA strongholds.**

the island, the guerrilla war escalated, reaching a peak following the arrest and deportation of Archbishop Makarios III, the head of the Greek Orthodox Church in Cyprus. Protest also spread to mainland Greece where crowds rioted outside the British embassy in Athens. In recognition of the severity of the situation, Britain recalled its ambassador from Greece.

The impact of EOKA alarmed the Turkish-Cypriot minority and they, under the leadership of Fazil Küçük, began to voice demands for a partitioning of the island. The situation, in which the governments of Greece and Turkey had hitherto played little part, began to cause growing tensions between the two states. Following the failure of the United Nations to broker any compromise

between the two sides, in 1959 Greece, Turkey and Great Britain agreed that Cyprus should become an independent republic, with neither Greece nor Turkey pressing any claims for sovereignty of the island. The first elections were held in December 1959, with Archbishop Makarios becoming the first President of Cyprus and his Turkish rival Fazil Küçük Vice-President.

INDEPENDENCE FOR MOROCCO AND TUNISIA

Britain was not the only Western state to take active steps to shed its former colonies. On March 2, 1956, France granted independence to Morocco. Less than three weeks later Tunisia was also given its independence. The French protectorates in North Africa had become difficult to administer, especially with the wave of nationalism sweeping across the territory, and creating havoc in the adjoining Algeria.

France had been the dominant influence in the region since 1830, following the invasion of Algeria. Although traditionally under the influence Spain, Morocco became a French protectorate in 1912. Strategically useful, Morocco not only possessed coastlines on the southern Mediterranean, but also on the Atlantic at Tangier. France maintained the traditional Moroccan government, the *makhzan*, although a sultan effectively held autocratic rule. In 1927, the French government approved the accession of Sultan Muhammad V, following the death of his father, Moulay Yousuf. In spite of his retiring personality, Muhammad was a key figure in the drive towards independence. When the French authorities deported him in August 1953,

▲ **Muhammad V, first ruler of independent Morocco.**

nationalist riots followed. He was allowed to return two years later and at once began negotiating Morocco's independence. In 1957 he took the title King of Morocco.

Tunisia had been under effective French rule since 1881, when an advance by Tunisian tribes into Algeria had given the French an excuse to invade. The invasion provoked a fierce civil uprising which was finally subdued by French troops in 1883. The Convention of al-Marsa the same year effectively imposed on the ruling bey of Tunisia a requirement to act only in accordance with the wishes of the French government.

A key figure in Tunisia's independence movement was a young lawyer, Habib Bourgiba, who in 1934 formed an opposition to

the main Destour (Constitution) Party. Civil unrest followed his growing popularity and in 1939 French authorities deported him to Paris. He was released during the Nazi occupation, and Tunisia enjoyed brief self-rule backed by Mussolini who saw Tunisia as a strategically useful state. When French control resumed, Bourgiba once again became a fugitive from the French authorities, only being allowed to return in 1951.

Morocco having been granted independence in March 1956, Tunisia was granted the same just three weeks later, with Bourgiba as Prime Minister. In July 1957, the traditional rule of the *beys* was abolished as Tunisia declared itself a republic, with Habib Bourgiba as its President.

'56

THE BIRTH OF ROCK 'N' ROLL

1956 can be neatly summed up in a single word: ELVIS. This was the year that a former truck driver from Tupelo, Mississippi forever lodged himself in the heart and soul of American culture. The young Presley had already made a local name for himself on Sam Phillips' Sun label, but once the tortured phrase "Ever since my baby left me" hit the national airwaves in March 1956, nothing would ever be quite the same again. Up until then, rock 'n' roll had still not found its true voice. Its greatest stars were black, in itself a commercial stumbling block in an era that saw racial tension slowly turning into a prominent national issue. Of course, there was always Bill Haley, but frankly he was already old enough to have a

▲ Elvis Presley conquered America in 1956. Over 20 years after his death, to many he remains "The King".

▲ The birth of rock and roll all but created the idea of the teenager and gave birth to the so-called "generation gap".

teenage family of his own. What young, white America wanted was a hero from its own generation. Sam Philips had known that if he could find a white kid who sounded black he would make a fortune. Although no longer on the payroll, Elvis in 1956 proved Philips right. Spectacularly right.

It was Presley's TV appearances which fuelled the public hysteria that within months turned him into America's most successful recording artist. *The Milton Berle Show* in April was seen by around 40 million viewers. Presley's hallmark suggestive gyrations caused widespread outrage among conservative America. The influential Ed Sullivan declared that he would never allow such scenes on his

show, but with Presley's popularity growing exponentially by the day the lure of ratings saw Sullivan relent. In September, "The Pelvis" – as he was now being called – performed on two of Sullivan's shows in front of a live teenage audience. Further pandemonium ensued. Although heavily criticized by Moral America, Presley pulled in the viewers like nobody before him. Sullivan invited Presley back for a third show, but this time, in an effort to appease conservatives, he ordered his cameramen to shoot Presley from the waist upwards. But the damage was already done.

The effect of such high profile publicity on record sales was predictable – they went ballistic.

"Heartbreak Hotel" was quickly followed into the national Top Ten by "I Want You, I Need You, I Love You", "Hound Dog", "Don't Be Cruel", "Love Me Tender", and "Love Me". Presley's domination of the charts was unprecedented. In all, 18 different sides hit the singles charts, cumulatively holding the top spot for over six months. During 1956, Presley products amassed an estimated $20 million.

The same month that "Heartbreak Hotel" topped the charts, saw similar success for Carl Perkins with "Blue Suede Shoes". It was truly a vintage year for rock 'n' roll. Some viewed Perkins as the greater of the two talents, but even though he wrote several classic songs he just wasn't pretty enough to create teen hysteria. Or lucky enough, either – a car crash while he was on his way to perform on *The Perry Como Show* put him out of action for months. Crucial momentum was lost, and by the time Perkins was on his feet Elvis had already swept the board.

Although harmony group The Platters managed two stints at the top of the charts, black culture had yet to make significant inroads into the nation's musical identity. However, one of the greatest names in the history of black music debuted in 1956. James Brown, a 23-year old ex-convict, cut his first disc "Please Please Please". A 6/8 R&B swinger, with his backing band the Famous Flames, Brown quickly built up a reputation as an electric performer, not to mention a fearsome band leader. Although a massive influence

▶ **The 1950s saw the rise of a new kind of teen idol. The likes of Dean and Presley were viewed by some as dangerous influences.**

of the development and identity of black music, "Please Please Please" never charted. It would be almost another ten years before he scored his first national top ten hit, and a further decade before his pioneering funk jams with the JBs.

Black music of a very different kind was also undergoing a revolution of its own. Jazz had long since become too complex for the average listener – bebop had seen to that. After a long struggle with narcotics problems, trumpeter Miles Davis cleaned up and took his modal experiments in new directions. Along with tenor man John Coltrane, over a period of 12 months the Miles Davis Quartet produced no less than six albums, among them *Workin And Steamin'* a crucial document of everything "cool."

In August, the Republicans renominated President

Eisenhower and Vice President Nixon to run for office. Three months later the team won a landslide victory over Adlai Stevenson. It was the heaviest defeat since Roosevelt saw off Alfred Landon's challenge in 1936. 1956 was also a year that saw racial tensions mounting in the Deep South. Protests against the segregated bus service in Montgomery, Alabama resulted in the arrest of 115 civil rights campaigners, including Rev. Dr Martin Luther King. At the same time riots followed a court decision to allow Autherine Lucy to become the University of Alabama's first black student.

Hollywood began to sit up and take notice of rock 'n' roll. Although most studio heads saw it as a short-lived fad, most also thought it would be around just long enough to make a quick buck. A dire genre best viewed

now through post-modern-tinted spectacles, the rock 'n' roll movie was probably at its most interesting in Frank Tashlin's *The Girl Can't Help It*. A satire on the world of public relations, it benefited from performances by some of the legends of the period, such as Fats Domino, The Platters, Gene Vincent and, most spectacularly, the great Eddie Cochran, who sizzled his way through "20 Flight Rock".

Although the Best Film Oscar went to Michael Anderson's dull odyssey *Around the World in Eighty Days*, perhaps the most notable film release of the year was George Stevens' *Giant*. At over three hours long, this Texan epic proved a fine tribute to its star, James Dean, who had died the previous year. Already, Dean and Elvis Presley were well established as America's greatest teenage icons of the 1950s.

'56 | THE HUNGARIAN UPRISING

After the hostilities of World War Two had drawn to a close, Hungary, like other east European states, found itself under near-complete domination by the Soviet Union. With Communism enforced, a new Hungarian government was headed by the Stalinist Matyas Rákosi, leader of the Workers Party. From 1948, Hungary experienced a period of widespread industrialization, following Soviet-style three- and five-year plans. All too often, however, such initiatives seemed aimed at benefiting the Soviet Union rather than Hungary. The country's rich deposits of uranium and other minerals were largely exported at the behest of Moscow. Little of this new wealth served to improve the plight of ordinary Hungarians. Furthermore, the seizure of private land by the state and the curtailing of many civil liberties made the Communist regime and Hungary's new status as "puppet" state very unpopular.

Following the death of Stalin in 1953, Rákosi was deposed and replaced by the more moderate Imre Nagy, who promised reforms, such as an end to collective labour, more consumer goods and the release of political prisoners. Although nominally a Communist, Nagy soon found his promises were unacceptable to the new regime in the USSR and in April 1955 he was dismissed from office. Rákosi was reinstated temporarily but was then removed by Khrushchev as a gesture of goodwill to Yugoslav leader, Tito, whom Rákosi had offended personally. He was replaced by his deputy, the equally unpopular Erno Gero, who pledged his support to the hard, pro-Soviet line of his predecessor.

The glimpse of reform briefly offered by Nagy provided the impetus to a period of popular protest that followed. On October

▲ The toppled statue of Stalin, a symbol of the tyranny of Soviet-style Communism to many Hungarians.

23, 1956, students in Budapest staged a procession whose aim was the presentation of a petition outlining the nation's complaints. Gero was unwilling to offer a compromise and ordered the police to fire on the crowd. What was initially a peaceful demonstration turned into open rebellion, with the Hungarian military joining and arming the protesters. Within a week the Soviet-backed bureaucracy had all but collapsed, with peasants reoccupying their land

▲ Hungarians from all walks of life took up arms in a failed attempt to free themselves from Soviet influence.

and political prisoners being released from concentration camps. Nagy was returned to power.

At the beginning of November, Nagy called for the complete withdrawal of Soviet troops from Hungarian soil. Going further, he also announced Hungary's withdrawal from the Warsaw Pact and requested that the United Nations recognize Hungary as a neutral state. This was a move too far for the Soviet Union. To the horror of the West, before dawn on November 4, over a thousand tanks of the Red Army entered Budapest from bases in Russia, Romania and Czechoslovakia. By nine o'clock, Soviet troops had entered the Parliament building, taking Nagy and other government ministers prisoner. The Hungarian army was outnumbered and quickly capitulated. A new government was announced, this time made up entirely of Communists under the leadership of János Kádár, who only weeks earlier had allied himself to the Nagy government. From that moment, Kádár was widely viewed by the people of Hungary as a traitor.

Kádár assured the Soviet Union that under his rule the "counter-revolution" would be suppressed. Sporadic fighting continued on the streets of Budapest for several more weeks, the workers applying pressure with a general strike. However, with almost no resources to hand the rebellion was quickly extinguished. Over 10,000 were killed and 30,000 injured during the restoration of Soviet rule. Although Kádár promised some reforms, the period that followed saw Hungary purged of its rebel leaders. Nagy and General Maléter, head of Hungary's armed forces, were tried and secretly executed. Much of the country's intellectual elite, who had openly supportive of the rebellion, were kidnapped by Soviet security police and transported to work camps in the Soviet Union.

Almost a quarter of a million Hungarians fled to the West, claiming refugee status.

Kádár remained a powerful figure in Hungarian politics until his death in 1989. During this time, although still deeply unpopular, Communist rule received little further challenge until the overall collapse of Communism in Eastern Europe at the end of the 1980s.

CELEBRITY WEDDINGS

▲ A match made in heaven? Sex goddess Marilyn Monroe makes a public appearance with her playwright husband Arthur Miller.

A pair of spectacular celebrity weddings occurred in 1956. On April 19, Hollywood film star Grace Kelly married Prince Rainier II of Monaco. Six weeks later, on June 26, sultry sex goddess Marilyn Monroe and New York playwright Arthur Miller were also wed.

Born into a wealthy Philadelphia family, Grace Kelly enjoyed six years as one of Hollywood's leading ladies, starring in musicals like *High Society* and the Alfred Hitchcock thrillers *Rear Window* and *To Catch A Thief* and bringing what the legendary director described as "sexual elegance" to the roles. It was while making the last film in the south of France that she met her future husband.

Following her marriage she assumed the title Princess Grace

of Monaco. Never returning to the stage or screen, the princess remained famously devoted to her husband and family until her death in a car accident in 1982.

Less devoted, Marilyn Monroe and Arthur Miller were an extremely unlikely pairing. Briefly married to baseball star Joe

DiMaggio, Monroe found success as the archetypal dumb blond, an image that would always over-shadow her underrated talents as an actress. Miller, on the other hand, with major works such as *Death of a Salesman* and *The Crucible* to his name, could arguably be rated as one of the most important figures in twentieth-century American literature. Some cynics called it a marriage of convenience – the dowdy book-worm winning the "world's sexiest woman"; the starlet who yearned to be taken seriously, gaining intellectual kudos by the association. Although their relationship was relatively brief, their marriage was not terminated until 1961. That same year, Monroe starred in *The Misfits*. Scripted for her by Miller, it was the last film she would complete before her infamous death the following year.

▲ The ceremony that transformed plain Grace Kelly into Her Serene Highness Princess Grace Patricia of Monaco.

'56

THE SUEZ CRISIS

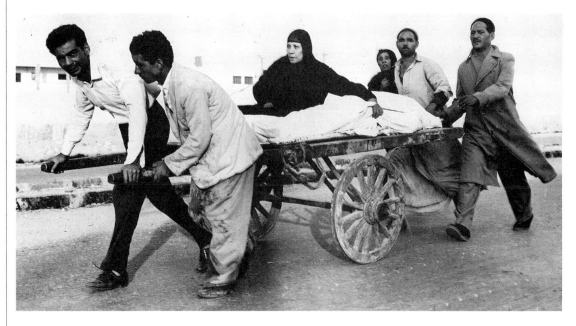

▲ Thousands of ordinary citizens of Port Said were caught up in the heavy fighting as Anglo-French troops responded to President Nasser's decision to nationalize the Suez Canal.

A major international crisis began on July 26, 1956, surrounding the use of the Suez Canal as Egypt's President Nasser announced that the waterway, then owned and operated by the Anglo-French Suez Canal Company, was to be nationalized. It was a direct reprisal for the withdrawal of offers of financial support by Britain and the United States to build a new dam at Aswan. The Western powers had become worried about Egypt's growing links to Eastern Europe and the Soviet Union. Nasser calculated that the tolls collected from ships passing through the canal – over 50 a day at its peak – would pay for the construction of the dam within five years.

Completed in 1869 after eleven years' construction, the 160-km (100-mile) Suez Canal allowed ships to pass from the Mediterranean Sea into the Indian Ocean, without having to sail around the perilous Cape of Good Hope on the southern tip of Africa. Its crucial significance to Western Europe remains as the main route for transporting petroleum from the oil fields of the Persian Gulf.

Shortly after President Nasser's announcement on July 26 that an Egyptian company had been formed to operate the canal, the area was promptly placed under martial law. Nasser's act proved problematic for Britain and France who feared that it could prevent their ships from using the canal and cutting off crucial oil supplies.

Britain's response was to freeze Egyptian assets based in the UK. Three days later, on September 1, 1956, emergency talks were held between Britain, France and the USA. With the Americans acting as a moderating force on her two allies, France and Britain secretly engaged in talks with the government of Israel, who were extremely hostile to the Nasser regime. Meanwhile, British forces were mobilized and made their way towards the Suez Canal. French troops stationed themselves on the Aegean island of Cyprus.

◀ A salvage ship moves sunken vessels that block the Suez Canal, clearing the crucial route between the West and the Indian Ocean.

Throughout August the Big Three attempted to bring Nasser to the negotiating table, warning of an imminent invasion if he refused. In London members of states for whom the canal had strategic importance met to form the Suez Canal Users Association, agreeing that tolls would be paid to them rather than the Egyptian government.

With little progress being made, on October 29, ten Israeli brigades advanced into Egypt toward the Canal, easily overpowering Nasser's forces. Vetoing a call from the US and Soviet Union for a cease-fire between Egypt and Israel, the following day, British and French bombers launched a damaging raid on military targets within Egypt, destroying over a hundred Russian-built fighter planes. This act caused outrage both in the UK and around the world. Both Britain and France were condemned at an emergency meeting of the United Nations General Assembly. With the Soviet Union threatening to intervene on behalf of Egypt, there was a genuine fear that the conflict could escalate. In Britain's parliament, meanwhile, Prime Minister Anthony Eden was severely criticized by the opposition leader

Hugh Gaitskell, who called the action "a tragic folly". This censure was followed by a massive demonstration in London's Trafalgar Square demanding Eden's resignation.

November 1956 saw Britain, France and Israel wholly out of sync with international opinion. As the UN worked towards a peaceful solution, allied forces moved further into Egypt. On November 3, Israel invaded and claimed possession of the Gaza strip. Two days later Britain and France launched an air invasion, taking Port Said and Port Fuad, thereby occupying the Canal Zone.

It was pressure from the United Nations and lack of support at home, that finally caused Britain and France to suspend their operation. On November 6, a cease-fire was agreed. Although the UN demanded the swift withdrawal of the invading armies, the victors were slow to respond. An evacuation of French and British troops finally took place on December 22 on the condition that the UN enforced free passage along the Suez Canal.

The Israeli government was less willing to cede its new territorial gains. Their troops had seen the heaviest fighting and it was

▲ Following an end to the fighting, a troop of marines hoist the White Ensign, the flag of the Royal Navy, over Port Said.

estimated that during November, 18,000 Egyptians had died and a further 12,000 had been held captive. Israel's intransigence created further instability in the region and it was six months before the Gaza Strip was evacuated and returned to Egyptian rule. This was by no means the last time that this 225 square km (140-square-mile) piece of land would be the centre of Arab–Israeli conflict.

Although Egypt suffered greatly over the crisis, its air force being decimated and Port Said levelled in fighting, President Nasser emerged as a victor and figurehead for an Arab and Egyptian nationalism prepared to take on the might of the Western world. The conflict also brought Egypt and the Soviet Union closer together, with Premier Khrushchev

later agreeing to the Aswan High Dam loan. For Britain and France, the Suez Canal adventure was disastrous. Before the campaign, they had been the dominant European powers in the Middle East; by the beginning of 1957 their influence was all but a memory. It also spelled the end of the political career of British Prime Minister, Anthony Eden. The Suez Crisis, as it became known, made his position untenable and in January 1957 he resigned. Although he cited ill health as his reason for standing down, he would most likely have been forced out of office had he not resigned. His successor was Harold MacMillan, who found himself with the task of rebuilding Britain's important relationship with the US, which had suffered badly because of the Suez offensive.

▲ Prime Minister Sir Anthony Eden tells the people of Britain that the Suez campaign is "a matter of life and death to us all".

▲ Anti-segregationist, the Reverend F L Shuttleworth (centre, right), leads a defiant protest by taking seats reserved for white passengers.

In an effort to curb the growing racial tension in America's Deep South, the first civil rights legislation to be enacted since the Reconstruction period that followed the American Civil War was passed on August 29, 1957. In spite of the creation of a Civil Rights Commission, there was clearly still widespread support for racial segregation among the white population of the South.

The race issue had most recently reached the national consciousness during December 1955 in the town of Montgomery, Alabama. A young black woman named Rosa Parks was arrested for refusing to leave a bus seat in a section intended for white passengers. In court, she refused to pay her fine and was sent to prison. Local protests erupted, led by a local black Baptist minister, Martin Luther King. Over the two months that followed, state buses were boycotted by the black population. The state's response to the boycott included the indiscriminate arrest of King and 114 others on the spurious grounds that an Alabama statute forbade organized boycotting. The draconian behaviour of Alabama's authorities shocked much of America and showed that some of the traditional divides between north and south were still very much in place.

That same month controversy raged at the University of Alabama in Tuscaloosa, as the college's first black student, Autherine Lucy, was suspended following the increasingly violent white demonstrations that greeted her daily entrance. The Alabama authorities claimed to be acting to protect her safety, but the federal court ruled in February 1956 that segregation within public education was a violation of civil liberty and that she must be reinstated. Two months later the Supreme Court ruled that segregation on buses should also be made illegal.

Although these were significant victories for King and his followers, they inflamed the passions of pro-segregationists. Many high schools in the South that were forced into desegregation found themselves the subject of violent lobbying by white extremists, the National Guard being called in to keep order in Mansfield, Texas and Clinton, Tennessee.

In June 1957, the role of Martin Luther King and his Southern Christian Leadership Conference in the civil rights struggle was acknowledged by national government. King was called to Washington to meet Vice President Richard Nixon to

▲ An empty bus heads through the campus of the all-black **A&M College** as black students continue their boycott.

discuss the proposed civil rights legislation. When the bill was discussed at a Congressional hearing, Senator Thurmond of South Carolina attempted filibustering tactics, holding the floor for more than 24 hours in an attempt to prevent its passage. Although he failed, the bill was severely weakened by the numerous amendments proposed by other Southern senators during the hearing.

Widely unpopular in the South, the new legislation met its most serious opposition in Little Rock, Arkansas. On September 2, 1957, Governor Orval Faubus achieved national notoriety by sending in the state militia to prevent black students from entering the newly desegregated Central High School. His actions brought down on him the wrath of the nation's highest authority. On September 14, President Eisenhower took direct action, demanding that Arkansas observe the Supreme Court's ruling and threatening military action. Faubus reluctantly agreed to abide by the law. Two weeks later, with 1000 US paratroopers armed with rifles and bayonets standing by, the first black students were admitted to the school. The action drew a crowd of over a thousand white protesters and during a number of violent scuffles seven were arrested.

These separate incidents were an important part of the civil rights struggle. However, while Martin Luther King and his followers may have had the law on their side, there was still a great uphill struggle against the many other covert forms of discrimination that would be far more difficult to battle. King's chosen weapon, like that of Mahatma Gandhi, was one of "peaceful resistance". While this would not always please his followers, he would remain at the very forefront of the civil rights movement until his assassination in 1968.

CANCER DEFEATS BOGIE

On January 14, 1957, one Hollywood's greatest toughguys, Humphrey Bogart, lost his fight against throat cancer.

In spite of his weather-beaten image, Bogart's upbringing was solidly prep-school, middle-class America. His father was a prominent surgeon and his mother a well-known illustrator. Born in New York City in 1899, Bogart served in the US Navy during World War One. It was here that a lip wound caused by a splinter of wood gave him the famous lisp which would become his distinctive trademark. After struggling in a succession of minor Broadway productions, in 1930 Bogart moved briefly to Hollywood where he played supporting roles in numerous gangster B-movies. Returning to Broadway, he first made an impression in *The Petrified Forest*, playing the existential killer Duke Mantee, a role he reprised successfully in the screen version in 1936.

Stardom came late to Bogart. In 1941 he established himself

▲ **Humphrey Bogart with his wife Lauren Bacall and son Stevie on a set for *The African Queen*, one of his best films.**

as one of Hollywood's biggest box-office draws playing Raymond Chandler's private eye Sam Spade in *The Maltese Falcon*. A year later came the role, that of the expatriate American club-owner, Rick, in *Casablanca*, perhaps the greatest screen romance of them all, that would guarantee him movie immortality.

Married to actress Lauren Bacall, Bogart remained a star right up until his final film, *The Harder They Fall* (1956). In a career that spanned 70 movies , there were inevitably some duds, Bogart himself claiming to have made "more lousy pictures than any actor in history". On the other hand, there was also an Oscar, for a great performance as the gin-swilling river trader, Charlie Allnutt, in a great picture, *The African Queen* (1951).

'57

The first tentative steps towards a formal economic union within Europe were made on March 25, 1957, when the leaders of six states put their signatures to the Treaty of Rome. It was the starting point on a path that would lead directly to European monetary union in the 1990s and the creation of a single European currency, the Euro.

The idea for a "European Community" was voiced as early as 1919 by, among others, the noted French politician Aristide Briand, one of the architects of the League of Nations. After World War Two, a council of European states was set up to administer the war reparation funds agreed by the Marshall Plan.

The main driving force towards the Treaty of Rome and the creation of the European Economic Community was an awareness of the appaling damage done by the history of conflict between France and Germany. In less than a century the two nations had fought three major wars (the Franco-Prussian War of 1870—71 and two world wars). The EEC was established in an attempt to promote a lasting reconciliation between the two nations. Indeed, the great hope was that by making the member states part of a single federation, all of Europe could live free from the fear of war.

The first discussions took place in 1955 in Messina, Sicily, paving the way for the Treaties of Rome that followed two years later. Signed by France, Belgium, Luxembourg, The Netherlands,

▲ **The German delegation at Rome, lead by Chancellor Konrad Adenauer (centre), put their signatures on the treaty establishing the European Economic Community.**

Italy and West Germany, the principal treaty established the European Economic Community (EEC); a second treaty saw the formation of the European Atomic Energy Community (EURATOM).

Coming into effect on January 1, 1958, the Treaty's immediate aim was the removal of trade barriers between the signatory states; this meant the elimination of the tariffs, customs duties and quotas that its members currently imposed on each other's exports. This change was to pave the way for the establishment of a unified commercial policy toward countries outside the EEC. Tariffs in imports would be standardized, thereby preventing "unfair" competition among the EEC's members.

It was intended that the member states would take contin-

uous steps towards a unified development, standardizing statutes, transportation systems, agricultural policies and general economic policies. Free movement would also be encouraged throughout the Common Market, the relaxation of national borders allowing the free mobility of labour, capital, and entrepreneurship among the members.

The first standardization of internal tariffs was implemented in January 1959. It proved to be massively successful, quadrupling trade between member states during the first half of the 1960s.

One of the most controversial areas of Common Market activity proved to be the implementation of a common agricultural policy. Although a part of the Treaty of

Rome, dissent among members meant that no system could be implemented until 1962. It was a policy that guaranteed prices for certain agricultural produce, offering protection against imports from cheaper Third-World markets. In practice, it became a subsidy on inefficient production techniques. Farmers were guaranteed payment above the market rate and thus continued to produce, irrespective of demand. This led to the farcical creation of "mountains" of produce that would never be bought. A wasteful practice, it brought the EEC a degree of notoriety.

The intention of the EEC was always to increase its membership. The terms of the Treaty of Rome laid down that any European state could request membership, but that acceptance would require a unanimous decision by the existing members after "the conditions for entry" had been unanimously agreed.

Realizing the benefits of free trade within Europe, those nations not in the first wave of EEC membership – Austria, Denmark, Norway, Portugal, Sweden, Switzerland and the United Kingdom (the "Outer Seven") – formed their own economic union, the European Free Trade Association (EFTA) which operated in tandem with the EEC.

Britain's role as a part of any European community has always been ambiguous. The postwar years saw a definite swing towards the notion of a united Europe, but, speaking in 1953, Foreign Secretary Anthony Eden had made Britain's stance clear when he stated that joining a federal Europe was "something which we know, in our bones, that we cannot do". Part of the problem was that with vestiges of the great empire of the nineteenth century still in working order, economic alliance with Europe would, inevitably, punish traders within the Commonwealth, especially in Australia and New Zealand. Furthermore, Britain felt able take this stance because of its so-called "special relationship" with the United States.

This hard line began to soften towards the end of the decade as the economic benefits of EEC membership became apparent. Eventually, in 1961, Britain

▲ The Treaty of Rome, establishing the European Economic Community, was signed in Italy's capital on March 25, 1957.

▲ As Foreign Secretary and, after 1955, as Prime Minister, Sir Anthony Eden expressed reservations about Britain's becoming too closely involved in the affairs of Europe.

applied to join, but, following a passionate and unexpected intervention by France's President de Gaulle, who feared that British agricultural subsidies would destabilize the Community, the application was not accepted. Britain eventually joined the EEC along with Denmark and Ireland in 1973. Greece followed in 1981; Portugal and Spain in 1986; and Austria, Finland and Sweden in 1995.

The European Union, as it is now known, has continued to be treated with suspicion within Great Britain. During the 1980s, the belligerent stance of Prime Minister Margaret Thatcher had the effect of isolating Britain in the eyes of Europe. As the drive for greater European integration continued apace, Britain noticeably dragged its heels. During the decade that followed, the European issue created a seemingly irreparable split in the ranks of the ruling Conservative Party and was a major factor in their devastating election defeat in 1997. It is a rift that seems likely to keep them from power for some time to come.

Meanwhile, with the single currency effective in Europe from the beginning of 1999, Britain was still showing few signs of setting up a firm, unalterable timetable for moving towards monetary union with Europe.

'57

THE SPACE RACE

On the morning of October 5, 1957, the Western World awoke with a shock to the announcement that, the day before, the Soviet Union had successfully launched and put into orbit round the Earth the first man-made satellite. The Space Age had begun and, with the Cold War in full swing, America found it unacceptable that it was the Soviet Union making the running.

Measuring 56 cm (22 in) in diameter, the 84 kg (184-lb) satellite was called *Sputnik I*. During its orbit its apogee – the farthest point from the Earth – was 940 km (584 miles). It circled the Earth every 96 minutes. *Sputnik* became the hottest news event everywhere in the world and began an obsession with the realistic possibility of space travel

that would dominate much of the coming decade. This fascination influenced many areas of modern life, from the way cars and furniture were designed to the world of the arts and entertainment.

Almost before the Americans had come to terms with the success of *Sputnik I*, on November 3, 1957 *Sputnik II* was launched. Over six times heavier than its predecessor, *Sputnik II* was launched with a passenger – a dog named Laika, which survived in space for several days, but was found dead on returning to Earth. The operation sent back important new research data on cosmic radiation.

Until 1958, America's space research had been conducted by the aeronautical agency, the NACA. Their earliest efforts had not been successful. Ten days after the Soviet success the US failed in three attempts to fire a rocket into outer space. A month after Laika had orbited the globe, the US *Vanguard* rocket chosen to launch the first tiny US satel-

▲ The first US satellite, *Explorer*, was launched by the US army's *Jupiter C* rocket on January 31, 1958.

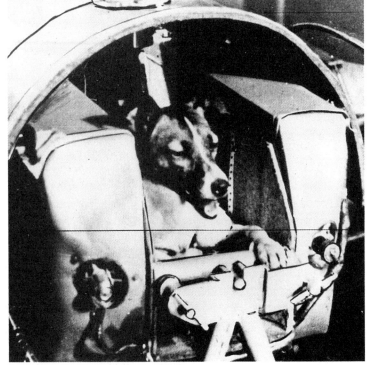

◄ Laika, the Soviet "Satellite Dog", strapped into the cockpit of *Sputnik II*. Although the dog perished during the flight, the operation yielded significant new information on cosmic radiation.

lite exploded on take-off.

Although President Eisenhower publicly declared not to care "an iota" about *Sputnik*, a sense of panic overwhelmed the administration, resulting in large sums of public money being made avail-

able for the creation of a new agency, the National Aeronautics and Space Administration (NASA). At this time, in spite of an earlier offer from Soviet premier Nikita Khrushchev to place all satellites and pilotless missiles under an international body, there was widespread belief that space could be a battleground of the future. Not only had the Soviet Union pulled off a brilliant propaganda coup, they had given a practical demonstration of an

▲ *Sputnik I*, the satellite that heralded the space age with its launch on October 4, 1957.

Earth from their 2734 km (1,700-mile) journey in good health. Piloted spaceflight was now seen as a very real possibility. At the start of the year, NASA had already selected 110 personnel for training as potential astronauts. By May these candidates had been whittled down to seven.

Little did the Americans know that in the Soviet Union a young air force major named Yuri Gagarin was already receiving similar training. Indeed, much of the Soviet space program during the late 1950s was completely unknown to the West. Information was usually garnered from the Russian news agency, Tass, which was little more than a mouthpiece of the state. Tass announcements tended, not surprisingly, to herald the triumphs of Communism over capitalism while ignoring the failures. NASA could only guess at the Soviets' next move.

At the end of the decade, it was quite clear that both sides in the Space Race were gearing up to meet the challenge of the next great milestone in space exploration – sending a man into space. This objective was viewed as more than simple nationalistic rivalry or even as proof of scientific advancement. It was nothing less than a test of the merits of two doggedly opposed ideologies. It was a race that both sides were determined to win at all costs.

important area in which they could justifiably be said to lead the world.

In February 1958, NASA finally launched its first successful satellite, *Explorer I*. Analyzing data sent back to Earth, the physicist James van Allen was able to make the first important discovery of space exploration, noting the existence of the doughnut-shaped groupings of radioactive particles that encircled the planet. These became known as Van Allen Belts. The same month, an air force pilot, Donald Farrell, underwent a week of simulated space training. Nonetheless, morale was still low as Werner von Braun, the German-born rocket scientist whose work enabled the launch of *Explorer I*, declared that US space research was two years behind that of the Soviet Union.

In the middle of 1958, NASA announced its intention to send a satellite to the Moon. As the closest planetary body to the Earth, it was always likely to be the first port of call on the progression into outer space. On October 12, 1958, *Pioneer I* took off for the moon. Although it burned up in the Earth's atmosphere, it still managed to achieve a record altitude, soaring 109,432 km (68,000 miles) above the planet.

Over the months that followed, the Soviet Union launched a series of *Lunik* satellites. The first, aimed at orbiting the Sun, easily broke the altitude record set by *Pioneer 1*. Its successor, *Lunik II*, was launched on September 17, 1959 to coincide with Premier Khrushchev's highly publicized visit to the United States. Another great Soviet propaganda coup, the spacecraft was the first man-made object to reach the Moon, crash-landing on its surface.

The first US space achievement to capture the affections of the American public took place in May 1959 when a *Jupiter* rocket launched into space a rhesus monkey named Abel and a squirrel monkey named Baker. The aim was to provide data on the impact of space travel on living creatures. Unlike the Soviet dog Laika, the monkeys returned to

▲ In 1959 a young Soviet airman, Major Yuri Gagarin, began preparations for a flight that would later bring him worldwide fame.

'58

CRASH KILLS BUSBY'S BABES

February 6, 1958 is remembered as one of the darkest days in British sporting history. It was the day that the mighty Manchester United football team was destroyed by a plane crash that took the lives of 23, among them eight of United's first-team squad.

Britain's reigning league champions, Manchester United were returning from a triumphant European Cup encounter in Yugoslavia, which had seen them defeat Red Star Belgrade to reach the semi-finals of the competition. Having reached Munich in the south of Germany, their return flight to Manchester took off in snowy conditions. With visibility poor, the plane failed to clear a house close to the end of

▲ The wreckage of the BEA Elizabethan airliner that crashed in flames shortly after taking off from Munich Airport.

▲ Eight members of Manchester United's first team – "Busby's Babes" – perished in the Munich air crash.

the runway. Seven of Britain's finest young players – Roger Byrne, David Pegg, Tommy Taylor, Eddie Coleman, Mark Jones, Billy Whelan and Geoff Bent – died instantly. Two weeks later, Duncan Edwards, still considered to be one of the greatest footballers England ever produced, also died from his injuries.

Although seriously depleted, United still reached the final of the FA Cup in May. In a highly emotional match for players and spectators at Wembley Stadium they were unable to contain Bolton Wanderers, losing two-nil.

After a life-and-death struggle, manager and guiding light Matt

Busby pulled through. He slowly rebuilt his side, finally achieving European glory in 1968, beating Portuguese side Benfica to take the European Cup. One of the goal-scorers in that match was Bobby Charlton, himself a survivor of the Munich disaster.

The passing of each anniversary is still mourned by fans at Old Trafford, Manchester United's home. Even though most were not even born at the time of the tragedy, "Busby's Babes" – as the young side were popularly known – have passed into footballing legend, both for their mastery on the field and their cruel demise.

NUCLEAR PROTEST MOVEMENT

In the United States, the arms race was presented to citizens as an issue of patriotism. It might have terrified ordinary Americans, but it was seen as a necessity. Britons, whose motherland was a more junior nuclear power, were less easily convinced. Throughout the 1950s, disparate groups,

such as the Church of England, other religious pacifists, Socialists and Communists, made their concerns heard, gradually becoming united in the cause.

The Campaign for Nuclear Disarmament was founded in the early months of 1958 with Britain's most noted arms

protester, Bertrand Russell, as its first president. The organization first hit the headlines during the Easter weekend of that year, when 5,000 protesters held Britain's first anti-nuclear rally in Trafalgar Square in the heart of London. It was to be the starting point for a 80-km (50-mile) march to the Atomic Weapons Research Establishment at Aldermaston, in Berkshire, during which the original number of marchers, 700 or so, swelled to 12,000 at the gates of Aldermaston.

The atmosphere during the three-day march was light-hearted, helped by communal singing and marching jazz bands. The novelty of the protest was viewed with curiosity, although there were a number of scuffles caused by right-wing "patriotic" groups such as the Fascist Union.

The marchers successfully reached their destination on April 4. In doing so, they had brought the nuclear arms issue to the top of the political agenda for the first time. Within two years, however, Russell had abandoned the CND in favour of the more militant

▲ Supporters of the Campaign for Nuclear Disarmament march from London's Trafalgar Square to RAF Aldermaston in Berkshire.

Committee of 100. Encouraging mass civil-disobedience, Russell, by then almost 90 years old, found himself in frequent trouble with the law, ending with a prison sentence in 1961.

The Campaign for Nuclear

Disarmament maintained a low profile until the end of the 1970s when, along with Greenpeace, it played an important role in making the British public much more aware of ecological matters than hitherto.

THE ANTI-AMERICAN LATIN STATES

It was supposed to be a communications exercise to improve relations between the US and Latin America, but when US Vice President Richard Milhaus Nixon engaged in a tour of the region in May 1958, he encountered widespread and violent protest.

America in the 1950s was desperate to stop the spread of the "Red Peril" wherever possible. However, the imbalance of wealth in many of the countries of Latin America made them fertile territory for sowing the seeds of Communism. This, in turn, led the US administration to provide financial and military support for a number of brutal right-wing dictatorships in the region, on the

▶ Anti-US fervour sweeps through Latin America, causing Vice President Richard Nixon to cut short his tour of the region.

grounds, apparently, that they were the lesser of two evils. This hardly endeared the US to ordinary Latinos who saw American interference as an indirect way of dominating the continent.

Arriving in Lima, the capital city of Peru, on May 7, Vice President Nixon was greeted by more than

a thousand protesters, calling for his immediate deportation. Six days later in Caracas, Venezuela, rioting ensued, resulting in a US military envoy being sent to protect Nixon and his wife. A public relations disaster, the tour was cancelled and the following day the Nixons were flown to American soil.

Back in Congress, Democrat senators were critical of Nixon, accusing his trip of being provocative. Although the protests were largely thought to have been organized by Communist agitators, most Latin-American politicians were critical of a US trade policy that placed tariffs on their crucial mineral exports. Nixon's ill-timed tour served only to give the Communists the opportunity to show their growing power in the Americas.

'58

The summer of 1958 saw Brussels, the capital city of Belgium, hosting the 1958 World Fair. On the outskirts of the city, the Parc des Expositions housed exhibits from all over the world, though the centre of attraction was the specially built Atomium building. Designed to look like a molecular structure, nine giant spheres were linked by tubes, each of which housed an escalator. The highest sphere housed a restaurant and offered spectacular views of Brussels and the surrounding area.

By the time the World Fair closed on October 19, more than 40 million visitors had passed through its exhibitions.

The Atomium remains one of the most extraordinary pieces of postwar architecture to be found anywhere in the world.

▲ **Reflecting the tone of the era, the Atomium remains one of the world's most unusual pieces of postwar architecture.**

NEWS IN BRIEF

March
- Tension between Syria and Saudi Arabia over accusations of Saudi-supported conspiracy to overthrow the Syrian government
- Antarctica crossed for first time by British polar exploration team
- Elvis Presley drafted into US Army for two-year stint
- Khrushchev replaces Bulganin as Soviet Prime Minister, thus holding both top jobs in the state
- Canadian Conservative party again wins general election
- Death of British suffragette activist Dame Christabel Pankhurst

April
- US President Eisenhower proposes methods for enforcing nuclear test ban
- Nationalist Party wins overwhelming victory in South African elections
- French Assembly forces resignation of government over the Tunisian affair
- Maltese Prime Minister resigns over terms for union with Britain
- United Rhodesia Party formed in Southern Rhodesia

May
- French settlers opposed to concessions to Algerian nationalists riot in Algiers, causing major political crisis
- State of emergency declared in Yemen
- President Eisenhower proposes freeze on national claims on Antarctica

DE GAULLE'S RETURN

After 12 years spent in self-imposed exile, on June 1, 1958, France's great wartime leader, Charles de Gaulle, stepped once more into the limelight as the country's Premier. The inability of his predecessors to deal with the growing crisis in Algeria had been instrumental in his return to power.

De Gaulle's return was by no

◄ **Inactive since the glory days of World War Two, Charles de Gaulle returned to the forefront of French politics on his own terms.**

means overwhelmingly popular. De Gaulle chose his acolyte Michel Debre to rewrite the constitution, and the new republic would see powers taken from the parliamentary assembly and given directly to the President himself – most notably, the power to select a Prime Minister of his choice. De Gaulle had long since made clear his opposition to political parties, a view that led some socialist politicians to fear that a mandate had been given for a presidential dictatorship.

De Gaulle won approval for his reforms. The Fifth Republic was ratified in January 1959 and de Gaulle was inaugurated as its

first President. Over the months that followed, he embarked on a tour of French colonies across the globe, declaring that drives towards independence would not necessarily be opposed.

De Gaulle was not able to solve the Algerian crisis immediately, though he quickly realized, to the consternation of European-Algerians, that a compromise solution that allied a "free" Algeria to France would be the best outcome. This attitude characterized a shrewd foreign policy towards the colonies. By 1963 most French colonies had received their independence, with military and economic aid coming from France. Thus, large areas of Africa would develop as independent French-speaking territories allied to (and influenced by) the French government in Paris.

A STAR IS BORN

The 1958 World Cup, held for the first time in Sweden, was dominated by the dazzling footballing skills of an 18-year-old Brazilian known simply as "Pele". In a career that was to last for another 20 years, Pele would become revered as the greatest-ever exponent of the world's most popular sport.

Born in 1940, Edson Arantes do Nascimento was first rejected by Brazil's major football teams until, at the age of 16, he was signed by Santos. Playing the inside left position, Pele (his adopted name), turned Santos into one of the world's greatest club sides. He burst on to the world scene in 1958, scoring a hat-trick against France in the semi-finals and two more in Brazil's five–two defeat of Sweden in the final in Stockholm.

A national hero, "*la Perola Negra*" ("the Black Pearl") led Brazil to World Cup victories in 1962 and 1970. The 1970 final – a stunning four–two win over Italy in Mexico City – saw perhaps the greatest ever international football team take permanent possession of the Jules Rimet trophy for Brazil.

The statesmanlike Pele has been the perfect ambassador for both Brazil and football, his charitable activities earning him the International Peace Award in 1977. A well-published author, actor and musician, Pele remains one of the most respected sporting legends of the twentieth century, his reputation perhaps only equalled by Muhammad Ali's.

▶ **Edson Arantes do Nacimento (right), better known as Pele, is still regarded as the greatest footballer of all time.**

RULE BY TYRANNY

On July 31, 1958, President François Duvalier of Haiti, known to his followers as "Papa Doc", faced a challenge to his authority when a small army organized by Haitian exiles advanced on the capital city of Port-au-Prince in an attempt to seize control of the island.

A former hospital physician, Duvalier was elected President in September 1957 with the avowed intention of ending the rule of the dominant mixed-race mullatos and the poverty of the black underclasses who made up the majority of Haiti's population. Duvalier was also a member of Le Groupe des Griots, a mystical circle of writers and intellectuals who embraced black nationalism and the importance of voodoo in Haitian culture.

Before Duvalier's election, the political landscape of Haiti was hugely volatile. Indeed, 1956 had seen 10 different governments fall in as many months. Defeated in the election that brought Papa Doc to power, opposition leader Louis Dejoie and former President Paul Magloire fled to the safe haven of the United States. There they organized a 100-man rebel force led by two former army officers. Landing at St Marc, the

▲ **One of the century's most ruthless dictators, "Papa Doc" Duvalier ruled over one of the world's poorest countries.**

rebels marched on Port-au-Prince where they seized control of the army barracks. After a brief period of fighting, troops loyal to Duvalier suppressed the revolt.

Duvalier took advantage of the instability, requesting that the Haitian Congress give him the right to rule by decree for a temporary period of six months. His request was granted, giving him little less than dictatorial powers which he retained until his death in 1969.

Duvalier consolidated power by reducing the size of the Haitian army and creating his own private militia – the Tontons Macoutes. This became his most important tool in a reign of tyranny that saw even the smallest glimmer of opposition brutally suppressed. Duvalier's autocratic rule was made official in 1964 when he made himself President for life – a title that few dared oppose during his rule.

'58

NEWS IN BRIEF

- King Hussein of Jordan requests British military presence in Jordan; British paratroops enter the state
- United Arab Republic signs mutual defence treaty with new regime in Iraq and severs diplomatic relations with Jordan
- Premier of Laos Prince Souvanna resigns; Phoui Sananikone succeeds
- Khrushchev meets Mao Tse-tung in China

August
- King Hussein dissolves federation of Jordan with Iraq
- Nato countries relax trade embargo with Soviet bloc countries
- Chinese Communist forces attack the Nationalist controlled island of Quernoy
- Death in office of South African Prime Minister, J G Strijdom
- Death of British composer Ralph Vaughan Williams

September
- Henrik Voerwoerd becomes Prime Minister of South Africa
- Meeting between German Chancellor Adenauer and French Premier Charles de Gaulle
- Referendum in France approves constitution giving President increased powers
- Provisional independent government of Algeria declared by Algerian rebel leader in Cairo

VOYAGE BENEATH THE ICE

On July 23, 1958, the USS *Nautilus*, the world's first nuclear-powered submarine left Pearl Harbor on what would become a historic voyage – the first undersea crossing of the North Pole.

It was no coincidence that the name *Nautilus* was chosen for such a pioneering ship. The name had already been used for one of the earliest submarine designs, built in the nineteenth century by American engineer Robert Fulton. It was also the name given to Captain Nemo's giant submarine in Jules Verne's novel *20,000 Leagues Under The Sea*.

Launched in January 1954, the *Nautilus* was powered by propulsion turbines driven by steam produced by a nuclear reactor. It was designed to be the first submarine capable of prolonged submersion and was capable of achieving a speed of 20 knots under water. The *Nautilus* also set new standards for submarine size, measuring a gigantic 97.2 metres (319 feet) and displacing well over 3,000 tons.

Skippered by Commander William R Anderson, the *Nautilus* sailed north through the Bering Strait and on August 1 left the surface at Point Barrow, Alaska, passing beneath the ice cap of the North Pole on August 3 at 11:45 a.m. It emerged two days later in the Greenland Sea. Commander Anderson and his

▶ **History in the making – USS *Nautilus* prepares to embark on its successful undersea crossing of the North Pole.**

116-man crew all received military honours in recognition of their achievement which broke every previous record for submarine travel.

The vessel was decommissioned in 1980 to begin a new life as a floating museum.

RACE RIOTS HIT THE UK

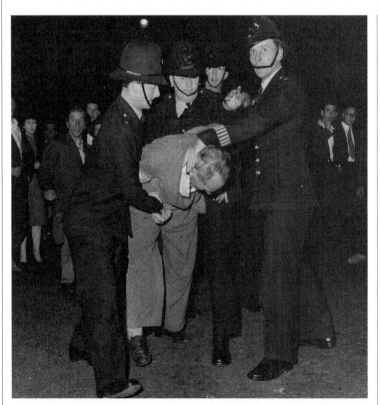

▲ **Police arrest a demonstrator during the ugly race riots that hit London's Notting Hill during the summer of 1958.**

Despite having a huge empire, peopled by many different races, Britain itself had known relatively few people of other ethnic groups and therefore had no experience of the racial tensions of countries like America. All that changed in 1958 when a series of race-inspired riots took place in London and Nottingham.

The biggest influx ever of black people into the UK, most of them hailing from Jamaica and other Caribbean islands, had occurred in the mid-1950s. It was hoped that these people, becoming integrated into British society, would relieve Britain's labour shortages. Instead, the West Indians created their own communities in many of Britain's towns and cities.

Black people found themselves the subject first of curiosity and suspicion and later of discrimination. Their situation spilled over into violence during 1958. There was serious rioting over several nights at the end of August in London's Notting Hill, an area with a high immigrant population, and violence in Nottingham. The following month, a group of white youths were convicted and jailed for "coloured bashing" in Ladbroke Grove, Notting Hill.

The violence shocked the government and the nation, several prominent people publicly airing the view that a multiracial society was impossible and that immigration should be stopped at once. Prime Minister Macmillan called for an inquiry, which was carried out by his Home Secretary, R A Butler. The tone of the ensuing report, which may seem at the very least patronizing by today's standards, says much about the attitudes of the time. Butler attributed the violence to the competitive jealousies of young white males, citing the attraction of white women to black males and the fact that black workers were seemingly happier to accept lower wages and a lower standard of living than their white counterparts. This, he continued, made unskilled labour cheaper to employ and increased rents as large groups of blacks were prepared to live in confined spaces. Furthermore, he noted the unpopularity of black families in white neighbourhoods, claiming that Teddy Boys, formerly considered a public nuisance, were being turned into "local heroes" by engaging in violent acts against young blacks.

There was no admission by the government of the existence of any fundamental discrimination against immigrants. Indeed, at this time the plight of Britain's Caribbean community gave the establishment no real cause for concern on any matter other than that of public order.

A NEW DAM FOR THE NILE

▲ **Construction work in progress on the southern entrance to Egypt's new High Dam at Aswan.**

According to President Nasser of Egypt, the construction of a new Aswan dam was the key to the future prosperity of his country. After two years of delays, his project was finally given the go-ahead on October 23, 1958.

The dam, known as the Aswan High Dam, had been a direct cause of the Suez Crisis in 1956. After promising to provide loans, the US and British governments withdrew their finance, primarily as a result of Nasser's increasingly pro-Communist line. Seeking other ways to finance the dam, Nasser unsuccessfully attempted to "nationalize" the canal, creating the 1956 crisis. In 1958, the Soviet Union stepped in with a loan of 400 million roubles and a further promise of raw materials and specialist expertise. It was a clear indication of the Soviet Union's desire to wield greater power in the oil-rich Middle East.

The ambitious scheme, which would take until 1970 to complete, involved the creation of a huge, 321 km (200-mile) reservoir in the Upper Nile, which was christened Lake Nasser. When discharging its contents downstream, the 111-metre (364-ft) Aswan High Dam was able to provide perennial irrigation for approaching a million acres of new land. For the first time, the annual flooding of the Nile was controllable.

There were further economic benefits. As a source of electricity, the dam's hydro-electric plants have provided Egypt with up to half of its total power. Furthermore, the introduction of food fish into Lake Nasser gave birth to a new fishing industry.

By the time of its formal opening in January 1971, the Aswan High Dam had cost an estimated $1,000,000,000. It remains one of the greatest engineering feats of the modern world.

'59   CUBA'S REVOLUTION

NEWS IN BRIEF

- Tensions in Indochina over North Vietnam's policies
- Antarctic Treaty limiting development in Antarctica signed
- Space race between USSR and US continues; both launch satellites and moon probes
- Crop failures in China
- Civil unrest in Central African Federation leads to the banning of several political parties
- Obscene Publications Act passed in Britain
- Trials and executions in Cuba of members of Batista regime
- Louis Leakey discovers prehistoric remains in Olduvai Gorge in Tanganyika
- Submarine plateau discovered in the Arctic
- Films released this year include François Truffaut's *The 400 Blows*, Tony Richardson's film of John Osborne's *Look Back in Anger*, Billy Wilder's *Some Like It Hot*, Alain Resnais's *Hiroshima, Mon Amour* and Otto Preminger's *Anatomy of a Murder*
- The musical *The Sound Of Music* by Rodgers and Hammerstein opens in New York
- Motown records founded by Berry Gordy
- Popular songs of the year include "Living Doll" by Cliff Richard, "Mack the Knife" by Bobby Darin and "C'mon Everybody" by Eddie Cochran

▲ **The revolutionary forces under the leadership of Fidel Castro (centre) seize control of Cuba. Che Guevara is shown on the left.**

On January 1, 1959 Cuban revolutionary leader Fidel Castro seized power in Cuba as his 800-strong guerrilla army proved too powerful for the 30,000 demoralized government troops. Castro's victory, which had the popular backing of the people, created the first communist state in the Western Hemisphere. The former dictator, General Fulgencio Batista, fled to the Dominican Republic.

Castro had graduated in law from the University of Havana in 1950. Already a well-seasoned political agitator in his student days, the young lawyer joined the Cuban People's Party, a reformist organization calling for an end to the corruption of the regime of President Carlos Prío Socarrás. Castro was chosen as a candidate for the 1952 elections. These elections never took place, being cancelled when an armed revolt saw the return of the exiled former president, Batista. Initially popular, Batista's return quickly became fearsome. In Cuba's volatile environment he set about consolidating his own position by controlling the government and violently suppressing the opposition. He also embezzled vast amounts of government funding for his own use.

Castro knew that only a popular revolution could bring down Batista. His first direct action was the organization of a rebel attack on a government military barracks in 1953. With only 160 men at his disposal he had little hope of success, but his intention was to make the attack the catalyst for a people's revolt. In the event, most of the rebels died in the attack and Castro was given a 15-year prison sentence.

Released in 1955, Castro fled the repression of Cuba to Mexico, where he organized a group of Cuban exiles into the revolutionary "26th of July Movement". In December 1956, Castro, his brother Raúl and "lieutenant" Ernesto "Che" Guevara, led an armed landing in the Oriente province on Cuba's southwest coast. Again, the rebels were defeated easily, but settled inland from where they gradually built up an army of 800 revolutionary troops. Winning a string of small victories against government troops, Castro embarked on a propaganda campaign that began to sway public support in his favour. Further victories followed throughout 1958 and finally, his army disillusioned, Batista was forced to accept defeat.

Although unquestionably leader of the revolution, Castro first installed Manuel Urrutia, a moderate liberal, as President. But Castro gradually assumed greater control. By July, already head of the government, Castro gained overall control when Urrutia resigned. Reshuffling his government at will, in December Castro placed Che Guevara – a doctor by training – at the head of the Cuban bank.

Initially, the new regime was accepted by the US, especially after it announced that it would honour existing international agreements. Indeed, in a speech given on March 22, 1959, Castro pledged that he would back the US in the Cold War. Relations quickly soured during the following year, however, as Castro's policies became increasingly radical, ending with the appropriation of all foreign businesses operating in Cuba, most of which were American. Matters worsened as Castro's wordy rhetoric took on an increasingly anti-American tone. By the beginning of 1961 America had severed both its trade and its diplomatic links with the now openly Communist island. The US thereafter became a natural home for Cuban exiles waiting in vain for Castro to be overthrown. Forty years on, he remains in control of Cuba, still seemingly with the backing of the vast majority of his people.

END OF THE EPIC

Cecil B De Mille, the man who all but created the very idea of a movie "spectacular", died at his mansion in Hollywood on January 21, 1959. He was 78 years old.

Although he started life as an actor, De Mille was there at the birth of Hollywood and quickly realized that his talents would be better used on the other side of the camera. As a producer and director he cut a fearsome character who few dared contradict.

Lavish production values characterized his epics. His first big hit was *The Ten Commandments*, a silent film first made in 1923

▲ A "cast of thousands" and spectacular sets typified De Mille's epics.

and re-made in 1956 with sound and colour. His favourite subject matter, De Mille once said, was the Bible: "Give me any couple of pages of the Bible and I'll give you a picture."

ROCK 'N' ROLL TRAGEDY

On February 3, 1959 a light aircraft crashed on to farmland outside Mason City, Iowa, killing the pilot and its three passengers. The crash left teenage rock 'n' roll fans throughout the world mourning the tragic deaths of three of the most popular singers of the late 1950s, Buddy

▲ The body of one of the three rock 'n' rollers who perished as their single-engine Bonanza plunged into a snowy field in Iowa.

Holly, Richie Valens and the Big Bopper (J.P. Richardson).

The aircraft, on which Holly had not even been due to fly, took off for the town of Fargo in North Dakota where the stars – all of whom had enjoyed million-selling hits in recent months – were due to perform. The plane fell from the sky within a few minutes of take-off.

Although Valens and the Big Bopper were popular figures, scoring hits with "La Bamba" and "Chantilly Lace", it was the death of Buddy Holly that had the greatest impact. One of a small but growing number of rock 'n' roll singers who composed his own material, Holly, at just 22 years old, had already enjoyed success with immortal classics such as "That'll be the Day" and "Peggy Sue". Ironically, his current release at the time of his death was a song called "It Doesn't Matter Anymore". Holly's potential continues to be a subject for speculation. His influence over the next generation of pop stars – such as John Lennon and Paul

▲ The influential Buddy Holly, one of the first musicians of the rock 'n' roll generation to make a name with his own material.

McCartney – was immense. In the 1970s, American singer Don MacLean documented the events of February 3, 1959 in his song "American Pie". It was, the line went, "the day the music died."

CHANDLER'S BIG SLEEP

America's premier detective novelist, Raymond Chandler, died on March 26, 1959.

Born in Chicago in 1888, Chandler spent his early life in England with his mother, and was educated at the prestigious Dulwich College in South London. Although a US citizen at the outbreak of World War One, he served in both the Canadian army and the Royal Flying Corps.

A successful petroleum executive after the war, Chandler turned to writing in his forties, having lost his job during the Depression. His first stories appeared in pulp fiction magazines; in 1939 his greatest creation, the hard-boiled Los Angeles private eye Philip Marlowe first made an appearance in the book *The Big Sleep*. The hallmarks of Chandler's great fiction were all in place by this time: complex and convoluted plot lines; Marlowe the "anti-hero", true to his own integrity even if it fell outside the law; the femme fatale who both attracted and compromised Marlowe – all of it tied together using a form of "hip" underworld dialogue that came to define the very genre.

This and many of Chandler's Marlowe series, such as *Farewell, My Lovely* and *The Lady in the Lake*, became a staple of the Hollywood film noir period, Humphrey Bogart providing the definitive characterization. From 1943 Chandler largely worked as a Hollywood screenwriter, creating thrillers like *Double Indemnity* (1944), *The Blue Dahlia* (1946), and the Hitchcock classic *Strangers on a Train* (1951).

Viewed as a "pulp" writer during his lifetime, Chandler's position in twentieth-century literature is now well established.

◄ **The greatest pulp fiction writer of them all, Raymond Chandler (centre), is now viewed as a significant literary figure.**

THE PRINCE AND THE COMMONER

If any further evidence were needed of the fundamental changes in Japanese society after World War Two, on April 10, 1959, Crown Prince Akihito, the heir to the Japanese throne, broke with a 1,500-year tradition by marrying outside of royal blood.

Born in 1933 into the world's oldest imperial family, according to Japanese tradition, Akihito became the 125th direct descendant of Jimmu, Japan's legendary first emperor. The eldest son of Hirohito, Akihito's early schooling followed the strict imperial tradition. However, the Royal Family's official loss of status that followed defeat in World War Two enabled his later education to be somewhat broader, including study of the English language and aspects of Western culture. A fine academic, he eventually graduated in marine biology.

His decision to marry a commoner, Michiko Shoda, the daughter of a wealthy businessman, caused some consternation among the people of Japan, many of whom still refused to accept the Emperor's enforced declaration that he was mortal, and not a deity as tradition had prescribed.

Akihito eventually became Emperor on January 7, 1989, following the death of his father. His reign was given the designation Heisei – achiever of peace.

► **Prince Akihito and his bride Michiko don traditional court wedding gowns for the ceremony at the Imperial Palace.**

FIGHTING FOR FISHING RIGHTS

Following World War Two, Iceland, its economy almost entirely dependent on fishing, had restricted the activities of its cod trawlers to within three nautical miles of the Icelandic coast. In 1950, nationalist politicians within the *Althing*, Iceland's government, declared that its ships would henceforth be able to fish within a 321-km (200-mile) radius, taking Icelandic fishing boats well within traditional British and German waters. The announcement infuriated the British fishing industry and began an ongoing dispute that would not be resolved until the mid-1970s.

The first dangerously aggressive clashes took place in May 1959 when a tussle between two trawlers ended with Icelandic crews firing on the British ship. Although nobody was harmed in the clash, the British government made a formal complaint to Iceland's Prime Minister. Over the coming months the Royal Navy regularly sent gunboats to protect Britain's fishing fleet. For a brief period, the Icelandic government, fearful of risking relations with its Nato partners, called on its fishermen to exercise restraint. A decade later, however, with Britain still refusing to recognize Iceland's fishing limits, the tensions exploded into what would become known as the "Cod Wars" of the 1970s.

▲ **The Royal Navy in action in the north Atlantic, protecting Britain's fishing fleet. Such operations would be repeated in the 1970s.**

EAST MEETS WEST

In an effort to halt the continuing tensions of the Cold War, the US and the Soviet Union made reciprocal state visits during 1959.

Vice President Richard Nixon began the process with a visit to Moscow in July. With President Eisenhower weakened by a heart attack, Nixon generally deputized for him in such situations. The visit started on a slightly rocky note as Nixon formally opened a US exposition in Moscow. Alongside a model of a typical American kitchen, the Vice President and Soviet Premier Khrushchev publicly engaged in a seemingly light-hearted verbal confrontation on the merits of communism versus capitalism. In spite of the geniality of their banter, clearly neither one was prepared to back down. The exchange was widely reported throughout the world and is now commonly known as the "kitchen debate".

During the tour Nixon appeared

▲ **Broad smiles all round as Vice President Nixon opens the American Exhibition in Moscow. Khrushchev smiles but keeps a step back.**

on Soviet television declaring America's desire to lift the tension of the Cold War, but concluded by saying that this was in the hands of the Soviet leadership. The tour concluded on high note with a concert given by the New York Philharmonic Orchestra, conducted by Leonard Bernstein.

Khrushchev's visit to the USA began on September 15. Although he was given a muted reception, his stay was regarded as a success. He toured widely in both urban and rural areas and captured the imagination of the American people with his ebullience. The crowning moment of his stay was a Camp David summit with President Eisenhower.

A public relations triumph for both sides, the state visits resulted in mutual co-operation agreements in the areas of education, science, culture and sport. In all, it saw relations between the two countries reach a new high point – albeit temporarily.

'59

NEWS IN BRIEF
....

July
- Heinriche Luebke elected President of West Germany
- Jamaica becomes self-governing
- US Vice President Richard Nixon visits USSR
- Fidel Castro becomes President of Cuba
- Deaths of US jazz singer Billie Holliday and German artist George Grosz

August
- Tension between China and India when Chinese troops cross into Indian territory
- United Arab Republic of Syria and Egypt resumes diplomatic relations with Jordan
- Death of sculptor Jacob Epstein

September
- Exiled Dalai Lama appeals for UN intervention in Tibet
- Mini Minor car, designed by Alec Issigonis, launched in UK
- Prime Minister of Ceylon Solomon Bandaranaike assassinated; Dahanayake succeeds

October
- Conservatives under MacMillan win British general election
- UN General Assembly calls for restoration of civil liberties in Tibet
- Pakistan reforms government structure
- Deaths of film stars Errol Flynn and Mario Lanza and of US General George Catlett Marshall, originator of the Marshall Plan

TWO NEW STATES

1959 saw the formal acceptance of the 49th and 50th states of the US. Alaska joined the Union in January and was followed in August by the Pacific islands of Hawaii. Both states were unique in that they were not linked geographically to the other 48 states of mainland America.

Alaska sits at the extreme northwest of the North American continent, bordering on the Arctic and Pacific oceans and the Bering Sea. Some 965 km (600 miles) from Washington State, Alaska, which accounts for over 20 per cent of America's surface area, and has vast areas still uncharted, is cut off from the US mainland by the Canadian province of British Columbia.

Traditionally the home to the Eskimo (Inuit), Tlingit and Aleut peoples, Alaska was first discovered by Europeans in the early 1700s, its mountains being occasionally visible from the coast of Siberia barely 80 km (50 miles) away. In 1728, the Tsar of Russia appointed the Danish explorer Vitus Bering to survey the region to discover whether it was an uncharted part of mainland Russia. Bering found the lands were divided by a 85-km (53-mile) waterway, which

▲ An Eskimo holds a symbolic 49th star in honour of Alaska's formal membership of the United States of America.

thereafter became known as the Bering Strait.

The first settlers were Russian fur traders in 1784. Thereafter, Tsar Paul I appointed the Russian-American Company to govern the territory. Depleting the region's natural wildlife during the early nineteenth century, the fur trade gradually fell into recession. In 1867, US Secretary of State William H Seward assured his place in history when he bought the territory from Russia. Its purchase ridiculed by many, Alaska was known for years as "Seward's Folly". The territory was handed over to the US military.

In 1912, the US Congress formally established the Territory of Alaska with its own legislative body. In 1946 the majority of Alaskans voted to join the Union.

Almost 3860 km (2,400 miles) from the west coast of mainland America, Hawaii, a group of volcanic islands in the central Pacific Ocean, is the remotest outpost of the United States. Originally populated by Polynesian peoples who are thought to have sailed to the islands around AD 400, Hawaii was "discovered" by British explorer Captain Cook in 1778. Over the next century the influence of European missionaries radically altered the culture of the island. Although dominated by Britain, France and America, until the end of the nineteenth century Hawaii was an independent self-governing nation. US influence finally prevailed and in 1900 Congress formally granted Hawaii status as a US territory.

Known for its exotic scenery and climate, Hawaii was described by Mark Twain as "the loveliest fleet of islands that lies anchored in any ocean". Hawaii became an international focal point on December 7, 1941 when the military base at Pearl Harbor was attacked by Japanese war planes, drawing the USA into World War Two.

WRIGHT'S LEGACY

On October 21, 1959, the Guggenheim Museum, built to house the US's finest works of contemporary art, opened in New York. The building was conceived by Frank Lloyd Wright, one of the greatest and most controversial of America's twentieth-century architects. Wright did not live to see the opening of his last great work, having died six months earlier following emergency surgery to unblock an intestinal obstruction.

▲ He may have dropped out of college, but Frank Lloyd Wright remains one of the best-known architects of the century.

Wright's remarkable career began in 1887 when, having dropped out of the University of Wisconsin, he moved to Chicago where he was employed as an architectural detailer. After a brief spell of employment under Louis Sullivan, the "inventor" of the skyscraper, in 1893, in spite of having no formal architectural training, Wright started his own practice. He quickly gained attention as one of a group of young architects that made up the "Prairie School", typically creating two-storey houses utilizing horizontal lines and gently sloping roofs. They provided a basic template for twentieth-century American residential dwelling.

During the 1920s, Wright fell foul of the Depression and a series of scandals in his personal life, and very few of his designs were built. Much of this time was spent writing and lecturing. Wright's fortunes changed with the economic upturn, and he found international acclaim with two buildings in particular: "Fallingwater" near Pittsburgh, Pennsylvania – a dramatic weekend retreat that was cantilevered across a waterfall – and the head office for the Johnson Wax Company in Wisconsin, with its famous tubu-

▲ New York's Guggenheim Museum, designed so that the paintings would become, in the words of the architect, "part of the building".

lar "mushroom" columns.

The Guggenheim Museum was commissioned in 1943. Although it appears as a giant multi-story cylinder, instead of separate floor levels there is a spiral ramp sup-

ported against the inside walls creating six different "layers" of continuous space. The centre of the spiral is opened out and illuminated by a massive glass dome.

QUIZ SHOW DEBACLE

▲ Charles van Doren (right) briefly became a national celebrity after his appearances on the quiz show *Twenty-One*.

In November 1959 the US Federal Trade Commission investigated a scandal that shocked America and brought the growing medium of television into disrepute – the allegations that big-money quiz shows had been rigged to create tension artificially and hence boost ratings. Quiz shows such as *Name That Tune* or *$64,000 Question* were among the most popular shows on television during the 1950s.

The most celebrated "ringer" was Charles Van Doren, a professor at Columbia University, whose parents were Pulitzer Prize winning poet Mark Van Doren and author Dorothy Graffe. Dan Enright, producer of the show *Twenty-One*, thought that such a distinguished competitor was certain to draw massive audiences. He was proved right as the charming, handsome, clean-cut Van Doren quickly became a national celebrity. What audiences didn't know was that he had been given the answers in advance and was merely acting out nail-biting situations during the live broadcasts. In his record-breaking run, Van Doren pocketed payments of $129,000.

Producer Enright was severely censured by the FTC and lost his job, even though he was widely believed to have acted under the instruction of the show's sponsors, Geritol, and of the management of the television network. Van Doren returned the money and, disgraced, embarked upon a low-profile teaching career.

1960–69

Popularly remembered as the decade of peace and love, the 1960s got off to a decidedly shaky start as the Cold War tensions that had dominated the postwar years prepared to reach a climax. The early optimism surrounding the news that the Soviet Union and USA had begun arms limitation talks was shattered when an American spy plane was shot down over Russia. However, it was at the end of October 1962 that the whole world held its breath as the two superpowers came as close as they ever would to a nuclear conflict. The flashpoint was the island of Cuba, less than 160 km (100 miles) off the coast of Florida. Three years earlier, a corrupt regime had been overthrown by Fidel Castro's popular Marxist revolution. America responded with a campaign of covert interference which ended with the Bay of Pigs fiasco in which a CIA-backed coup failed to overthrow Castro. Thereafter, to the horror of the USA, Cuba forged increasingly close ties with the Soviet Union. But the discovery that Soviet mid-range nuclear weapons were being shipped to the island caused an international incident that came close to outright war. What was perhaps the tensest week of the century came to an end when the Soviets agreed to remove the missiles on condition that the USA would not invade Cuba.

Much of the focus of the world was on America during the 1960s. The television was now the dominant cultural medium and much of it was exported from America. The mood at the turn of the decade was for all things new, with youth firmly topping the agenda. The election in 1960 of John F Kennedy, at 43 years old the youngest President in America's history, was symbolic of this prevailing wind. As he said at his inaugural address, "The torch has been passed to a new generation of Americans". Within three years, that spirit of optimism had soured: Kennedy had been assassinated and America was slowly become embroiled in its most embarrassing overseas campaign – Vietnam.

Essentially a continuation of the foreign policy that led America to fight in Korea, the Vietnam sideshow began when President Kennedy agreed to provide military aid to the governments of Laos and South Vietnam who were threatened by Communist invasion. But by 1965, over 150,000 US marines were engaged in battle with the Viet Cong. In spite of superior forces, the alien terrain made a swift victory impossible. By the end of the decade, with growing casualties and widespread condemnation at home, the US military was preparing to disengage. Public protest by ordinary Americans was one of the principle reasons that the USA were forced to back out of Vietnam. The same form of direct action was also responsible for raising the profile of black America's campaign for civil equality. The way in which blacks had been treated had always been something of a thorn in America's side – the legality of slavery had been one of the issues at the heart of the Civil War of the previous century. Although by the 1960s legitimate segregation had all but disappeared, widespread discrimination still existed. The figurehead of the campaign was Dr Martin Luther King, who touched the world with his famous "I have a dream" speech. Dr King espoused peaceful protest but died from an assassin's bullet.

Britain also entered the 1960s with renewed optimism. Unlike America, the previous decade had been austere for most Britons with wartime sacrifices such as rationing still in place. Now it really did seem as if the war was finally over. A new young Labour government emerged to embrace the modern world – the "white heat of progress", as Prime Minister Harold Wilson called it. "Swinging London" was now seen to be the cultural centre of the world, resonating to the music of the all-conquering Beatles.

Ultimately, however, the 1960s illustrated that the march of scientific progress was now relentless, if often born out of international conflict. When Soviet cosmonaut Yuri Gagarin became the first man in space in 1961, the US government immediately made billions of dollars available to compete with the "enemy". So it was that in July 1969, Neil Armstrong stepped down from *Apollo 11*'s lunar lander to plant the US flag on the surface of the Moon. It was the realization of Man's greatest scientific achievement.

JOURNEY INTO THE ABYSS

In January 1960, two men made the first descent to the bottom of the planet's deepest ocean trench, a feat as remarkable as the pioneering journeys into space. Aboard the bathyscape *Trieste*, Jacques Piccard and US Navy Lieutenant Donald Walsh reached the floor of the Pacific, near the island of Guam, 10,920 metres (35,800 ft) – more than 11 km (7 miles) – below the surface of the ocean.

Jacques Piccard was the son of a Swiss professor, Auguste Piccard, the inventor of the bathyscape. Originally engaged in experiments in high-altitude balloon flights, Auguste Piccard came up with the idea of exploring the ocean depths with a kind of underwater balloon.

The *Trieste*, built in Italy in 1953, comprised a steel sphere, just large enough to hold two passengers, attached to a large flotation tank filled with gasoline. Iron pellets provided ballast: with the pellets on board, the vessel would sink; once jettisoned, the flotation tank would rise to the surface.

In 1957, Piccard's bathyscape attracted the attention of the US Navy's Office of Naval Research, which had the resources to prepare the *Trieste* for a descent into the world's deepest abyss, the Marianas Trench.

On January 23, 1960, Jacques Piccard and Lieutenant Walsh squashed into the cramped observation sphere, and for five hours sank ever deeper under the Pacific, finally settling gently into the sediment at the ocean bottom. To their amazement, they watched a fish swimming past, proving that life existed even in the darkest depths. After 20 minutes on the ocean bed, they released their ballast and returned painlessly to a hero's welcome above the waves.

▼ **Second-generation pioneer, Jacques Piccard's historic descent was in a bathyscape developed with his father, Professor Auguste Piccard.**

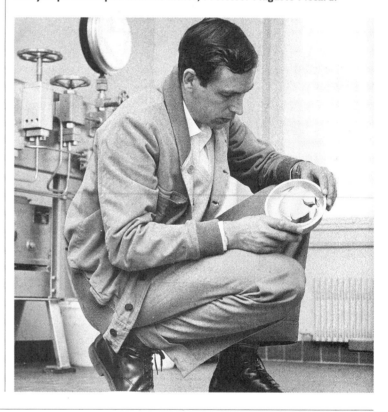

MASSACRE AT SHARPEVILLE

On February 3, 1960, British Prime Minister Harold Macmillan addressed the South African parliament with the message that "the wind of change is blowing through Africa". Both Britain and France had decided to grant their African colonies independence under black governments.

In 1960 alone, fourteen French and two British colonies became independent – including Nigeria, the most populous state in the continent. The implications of Macmillan's speech were clear: the South Africans would have to adapt to a new world in which assumptions of white racial superiority must be abandoned, or at least diplomatically disguised.

But the South African government, headed by Hendrik Verwoerd, had no intention of listening to such advice. Since 1948, South Africa had been formalizing white domination through the "apartheid" system. Every South African was assigned to a racial category, and the mixing of races was banned in every area of life. While claiming to be "separate development", the system was used to guarantee the white minority control of the best land, the best jobs and all the political power.

Only six weeks after Macmillan's speech, South

Africa's resistance to change was reaffirmed in the most brutal way possible. Two major groups, the long-established African National Congress (ANC) and the break-away Pan African Congress (PAC), led the opposition to the system of apartheid.

On March 21, they initiated a campaign of civil disobedience in protest at the infamous "pass laws" used to control blacks' access to jobs and freedom of movement. At the township of Sharpeville in the Transvaal, a large crowd of unarmed protest-ers, including a majority of women and children, approached the local police station. The police opened fire, killing 69 people and injuring 178.

The Sharpeville massacre proved to be a turning point in South Africa's internal politics as well as in its relations with the rest of the world. In its wake, the ANC and PAC were banned. The two groups reacted by espousing violence as the only way to chal-lenge the apartheid state. The following year, South Africa with-drew from the Commonwealth, declaring itself a Republic. The message was clear: there was to be no compromise between apartheid and Macmillan's "wind of change".

▼ **The Sharpeville massacre saw the beginning of 30 years of political violence that preceded an end to apartheid.**

RACE RIOTS IN THE DEEP SOUTH

In 1960, the mounting pressure to end racial segregation in the United States was provoking a violent backlash among Southern whites – a reaction that was graphically demonstrated in a race riot at Biloxi, Mississippi, on April 25, leaving ten people dead.

The most striking novelty of the year's civil rights campaign was direct action by groups of students from black campuses to defy segregation in public places. The movement took off after four black students entered the Woolworths store in Greensboro, North Carolina, on February 1 and seated themselves at the whites-only lunch counter. Despite being refused service, they returned day after day in a protest that quickly attracted the support of hundreds more black students. Media coverage helped spread the sit-in movement. It also attracted the support of Martin Luther King, the most prominent black civil rights cam-paigner, who told the students: "You now take your honoured place in the worldwide struggle for freedom".

On April 17, the Student

▲ **One of the the Biloxi protesters is questioned in the aftermath of Mississippi's worse race riot.**

Nonviolent Coordinating Committee (SNCC), which was to organize so much of the most rad-ical agitation against white racism in the 1960s, was founded at Shaw University in North Carolina.

Just over a week later, the events at Biloxi showed how dangerous the campaign of forced integration could become. The trouble started after a group of blacks installed themselves on a Biloxi beach traditionally reserved for whites only.

Hostile whites, determined to uphold their exclusive access to the beach, confronted the blacks. As tempers frayed, a gun was pulled and mayhem ensued. The disturbance resulted in the deaths of eight blacks and two whites, making it the worst race riot in the history of the state.

- The American Football League formed
- Cassius Clay wins boxing gold medal in Rome Olympics
- Films released during the year include Jean Luc Godard's *A Bout de Souffle*, Alfred Hitchcock's *Psycho*, Frederico Fellini's *La Dolce Vita* and *The Magnificent Seven*, starring Steve McQueen and Yul Brynner
- *Coronation Street* begins its run on British television
- *Beyond the Fringe*, starring Peter Cook and Dudley Moore debuts in Britain
- The play *A Man for All Seasons* by Robert Bolt is first performed
- Musical premieres include *Circles* by Luciano Berio, *Chronochromie* by Oliver Messiaen and *Threnody for the Victims of Hiroshima* by Penderecki
- Lionel Bart's musical *Oliver!* opens in London; on Broadway, Lerner and Lowe's musical *Camelot* opens
- Edith Piaf rejuvenates her career with the song "Non, Je Ne Regrette Rien", Elvis Presley releases "Are You Lonesome Tonight"

January
- Civil unrest in Algeria
- British leader Harold Macmillan begins visit to Africa
- Nationalist leader Kenneth Kaunda released from jail in Rhodesia
- US and Japan sign treaty of mutual cooperation
- End of the state of emergency in Kenya
- Death of French existentialist author and Nobel Prize winner Albert Camus in a car accident

USSR DOWNS U2 SPY PLANE

Leaders of the United States, the Soviet Union, Britain and France gathered in Paris for a Four Power summit meeting in May. There were high hopes that the summit might reduce some of the dangerous tensions of the Cold War confrontation. Instead, it turned into a blazing public row over espionage.

Since 1956, US U2 spy planes had been carrying out regular flights over the Soviet Union, taking photos of secret military installations. The aircraft flew at 25,900 metres (85,000 ft), its high altitude making it supposedly immune to interception by Soviet aircraft or missiles.

However, on May 1, 1960, a U2 plane, piloted by Gary Powers was hit by an SA2 missile and brought down near Sverdlovsk. Powers not only survived, but failed to swallow the cyanide capsule provided for him by the CIA to avoid capture and interrogation.

Believing that Powers was dead, the US repeatedly denied that the downed aircraft had been engaged in a spy mission, as the Soviets alleged. They claimed instead that the U2 had been engaged on weather research and had blown off course. After allowing the US to commit themselves publicly to these lies, on May 7, the Soviets triumphantly produced Powers at a press conference, providing full and incontrovertible evidence of the nature of his mission.

Arriving for the Paris summit, scheduled to begin on May 16, Soviet Premier Nikita Khrushchev demanded that US President Dwight D Eisenhower make a full public apology and promise never to send spy planes through Soviet airspace again. The President refused and the summit fell apart in a welter of accusations and counter-accusations.

Powers was sentenced to ten years in a Soviet prison, but

▲ **Gary Powers holds a model of the U2 aircraft which the Soviet Union claimed had been engaged in military espionage.**

served only 18 months before being returned to the West in exchange for Soviet agent Rudolf Abel in the first of many "spy swaps".

CONGO PLUNGES INTO THE "HEART OF DARKNESS"

By 1960, Britain and France, the major colonial powers in Africa, were well advanced with carefully planned programmes for handing over power to independent African governments.

Belgium, however, controller of the vast, sparsely populated, mineral-rich Congo, had done almost nothing to prepare the colony for independence. There were virtually no blacks in the civil service above the most menial levels, or in the army officer corps.

◀ **Two battalions of the Ghanaian Army fly into the Congo to join the ten-thousand-strong United Nations peacekeeping force.**

Faced with agitation from a Congolese nationalist movement led by a fiery radical, Patrice Lumumba, the Belgians precipitately announced that they were pulling out on June 30, 1960.

Lumumba became Prime Minister of an independent republic which, predictably immediately fell apart. The army revolted against its white officers and went on the rampage, giving the Belgians a pretext for sending their troops back into the Congo to "restore order". Most Europeans were evacuated on Belgian military aircraft, destroying the country's business and administration at a stroke. Meanwhile, the southern province of Katanga, which contained most of the Congo's mineral wealth, was erected into an independent state, headed by local politician Moise Tshombe, but financed by European mine owners and protected by Belgian troops and white mercenaries.

Faced with the collapse of his country, Lumumba called on the United Nations to intervene. UN Secretary-General Dag Hammarskjöld sent in a peacekeeping force, which was 10,000 strong by the end of July. The Soviet Union began to supply Lumumba's supporters, while in America CIA hatched various schemes to have him assassinated.

The UN forces did their best to protect Lumumba, but in November he fell into the hands of troops loyal to the Congo's future President, Colonel Joseph Désiré Mobutu. They handed him over to his enemies in Katanga, where he was murdered in February 1961. Confused and brutal warfare continued in the Congo for much of the 1960s.

INDEPENDENCE FOR CYPRUS

On August 16, 1960, the island of Cyprus became an independent republic after 82 years of British rule – and just six years after a British government had announced categorically that "Britain could never contemplate giving up sovereignty" over the island. The official British attitude had been changed by a resistance campaign that had made continued occupation of Cyprus too costly to contemplate.

As so often in colonial conflicts, the situation in Cyprus was far from simple. The population of the island was 78 per cent Greek. Rather than wanting independence, many of the Greek Cypriots aspired to *enosis* (union) with Greece.

The Greek government itself supported this aspiration, but it was flatly opposed by Turkey, who espoused the cause of the other 22 per cent of the island's population, the Turkish Cypriots. The fact that both Greece and Turkey were Britain's allies in Nato did not make the situation any easier to resolve.

An armed campaign to drive the British out of Cyprus and achieve *enosis* was started by the *Ethniki Organosis Kyprion Agoniston* (EOKA) in April 1955. Led by the formidable General George Grivas, EOKA launched a series of guerrilla attacks that soon soaked up a large number of British troops in counter-insurgency operations.

Meanwhile, Archbishop Makarios, the Greek Cypriots' religious leader and chief spokesman, maintained political pressure for change. Makarios was deported in 1956, but this did nothing to calm Greek Cypriot feelings.

The path to a compromise was found in 1958. The Greek Cypriots accepted that Turkey would never allow *enosis*, and settled instead for independence under a power-sharing deal that gave the presidency to Makarios. The vice-presidency was given to a representative of the Turkish community.

The British agreed to leave as long as they were allowed to retain bases at Dhekelia and Akrotiri. And so the Union flag ceased to fly in yet another corner of the British Empire.

▼ Following the end of British rule, Archbishop Makarios became first President of independent Cyprus.

- South African Prime Minister wounded by a disgruntled businessman
- State of emergency ended in Nyasaland
- President Syngman Rhee of Korea forced to resign
- Student demonstrations begin in Turkey

May
- Diplomatic incident between USSR and US caused when US U2 spy plane pilot Gary Powers shot down over USSR
- European Free Trade Association (EFTA) comes into existence
- Leonid Brezhnev becomes Soviet head of state
- US Federal Drug Administration approves oral contraception pill
- Kariba Dam opens in Rhodesia
- Major earthquake in Chile
- Military coup in Turkey deposes President Menderes; General Gürsel takes power
- Death of Russian Nobel Prize-winning author Boris Pasternak

June
- Anti-US student demonstrations in Japan
- Negotiations between General de Gaulle and provisional French government
- British Somaliland gains independence
- Congo Republic gains independence from Belgium; Patrice Lumumba becomes Prime Minister

July
- Mogadishu government gains independence, forming Somalia
- Cyprus and Britain settle terms of Cypriot independence
- Army mutiny in the newly independent Congo; Belgium sends troops to its former colony

'60

CASTRO DEFIES THE UNITED STATES

In August 1960, Cuban leader Fidel Castro proclaimed the nationalization of US-owned property worth hundreds of millions of dollars in a bold gesture of defiance towards his island country's superpower neighbour. Castro was well aware that the CIA was already plotting his overthrow and that his chances of longterm political survival were slim.

When Castro's guerrilla campaign brought him to power in Cuba in January 1959, his triumph was broadly welcomed by many US citizens. However, Castro soon showed himself to be more revolutionary than the United States had originally bargained on.

Although not initially a Communist, Castro openly promoted revolutionary movements against US-backed governments in Central America. He also used his considerable rhetorical powers to pour scorn on US imperialism in a series of widely publicized speeches.

The Eisenhower administration soon came to feel that Castro, installed only 145 km (90 miles) from Florida, was a threat to US interests. While the CIA secretly tried to organize his assassination – with the help of the mafia, who had lost out heavily when

Castro closed down Havana's notorious nightlife – the US government waged economic war on Cuba. The economy of the country depended almost entirely on exports to the United States, especially of sugar. By blocking the import of Cuban sugar, the United States hoped to bring Castro to his knees.

The nationalization of US property was one part of Castro's response to the US trade blockade. Another was to establish a special relationship with the Soviet Union, which offered to buy Cuba's sugar and, essentially, subsidize the Cuban revolution. The Cold War had come to the Caribbean.

◀ **Widespread demonstrations followed the US trade embargo; the crisis resulted in closer ties between Cuba and the USSR.**

NEWS IN BRIEF

- Breakaway republic declared under Moïse Tshombe in Katanga province of Congo; diplomatic relations with Belgium are severed
- UN forces arrive in Congo
- Japanese leader Kishi resigns; Hayato Ikeda succeeds
- Election in Ceylon won by Sri Lanka Freedom Party; Sirimavo Bandaranaike appointed Prime Minister
- New government under Amintore Fanfani formed in Italy
- End of the state of emergency in Malaya caused by Communist insurgents
- Death of creator of Britain's National Health Service, Aneurin Bevan

August
- UN demands withdrawal of Belgian troops from Congo
- Military coup in Laos
- Cyprus attains independence with Archbishop Makarios as President
- New government formed in Laos under General Souvanna Phoumi
- Seventeenth Olympic games open in Rome
- Prime Minister of Jordan assassinated; Syria implicated
- State of emergency ended in South Africa
- Death of lyricist and theatre producer Oscar Hammerstein II

KENNEDY FLOORS NIXON IN PRESIDENTIAL CONTEST

On November 8, 1960, Democratic candidate John Fitzgerald Kennedy was elected President of the United States, defeating Republican Richard Nixon. Aged 43, Kennedy was the youngest man ever elected to the White House. He was also the first Roman Catholic to hold the United States' highest office. It had been an extremely close-run contest: Kennedy's share of the popular vote was 34,227,096 against 34,108,546 for Nixon.

The election had not revealed any profound differences between the Democratic and Republican candidates on issues. Nixon, who was Vice-President under Eisenhower, defended the existing administration's record, while Kennedy attacked it. He particularly berated Eisenhower for

◀ **Kennedy's victory was widely attributed to his performance in a series of live televised debates with opponent Richard Nixon.**

allowing Cuba to become a communist thorn in the United States' side, and for allegedly permitting the Soviet Union to open up a lead over the United States in the installation of nuclear missiles – the so-called "missile gap".

But it was the contrast in image and presentation between the two candidates that made the biggest impact. Author Norman Mailer, a Kennedy supporter, described the choice as between "the stability of the mediocre" and America's "romantic dream of itself". US citizens, Mailer said, were being asked to vote "for glamour or for ugliness".

Mailer's comments were probably not far from the truth, because this was the first television election. Some 40 million US citizens now had television sets, and as many as 120 million may have watched each of the four televised debates between Kennedy and Nixon during the campaign.

The viewing public gleaned little news about the candidates' policies, but learned a great deal about their looks and self-presentation. Kennedy appeared calm, handsome and relaxed; Nixon was sweaty and pallid, with an apparently ineradicable stubble shadow and uncontrollably shifty eyes. The TV debates are generally credited with shifting enough votes to ensure a Kennedy victory.

Whatever the reason for Kennedy's narrow triumph, it meant a fundamental change of atmosphere in Washington. The new administration intended to project an image of youth, dynamism and idealism – encapsulated in Kennedy's famous inauguration speech injunction: "Ask not what your country can do for you, but what you can do for your country." The appeal to youthful idealism may have been mere rhetoric, but it was to resonate through the decade.

THE TRIAL OF "LADY C"

▲ After 32 years of censorship, the British public – "wife and servants" included – was free to read *Lady Chatterley's Lover*.

Lifting the censorship of sexually explicit material was to be one of the great themes of the 1960s, starting with a sensational trial in the autumn of 1960. D H Lawrence's novel *Lady Chatterley's Lover* – banned when it was written in 1928 because it contained four-letter words and graphic descriptions of sexual acts between a gamekeeper and the lady of the manor – was finally cleared of the charge of obscenity.

The trial was a test case deliberately embarked upon by both sides. In 1959, the law on obscenity had been changed to allow a defence on the grounds of artistic or literary merit. Soon afterwards, Penguin Books announced that it intended to publish an unexpurgated paperback edition of Lawrence's banned classic. Consequently, the Director of Public Prosecutions rose to the bait and took Penguin to court.

The tone of the often farcical case was established at the outset by the prosecuting counsel, Mervyn Griffith-Jones. Asking the jury to consider: "Is it a book that you would even wish your wife and servants to read?" Griffith-Jones felt safe in assuming that Britain was peopled by well-off patriarchs – people who regarded any description of adulterous sex as obscene, unless accompanied by a clear statement of disapproval supplied by the author.

To the prosecution counsel's evident astonishment, an array of prominent people queued up to give evidence in favour of the book's literary merit, and the jury agreed with them.

The not-guilty verdict was pronounced on November 2. A week later, Penguin's *Lady Chatterley* appeared on shelves of bookshops. A total of 200,000 copies of the first print run were sold in just one day.

'61

NEWS IN BRIEF

- Conflict in Laos continues between Pathet Lao and right-wing groups for control of the country
- Britain begins negotiations to join European Economic Community
- Peace Corps founded in the US
- World Wildlife Fund founded
- Films released during the year include Françoise Truffaut's *Jules et Jim*, John Huston's *The Misfits*, which is to be the last film of its stars Marilyn Monroe and Clark Gable, and Akira Kurosawa's *Yojimbo*
- Cellist Jacqueline du Pré makes debut in London
- Music releases include "Let's Twist Again" by Chubby Checker
- Books published this year include *The Prime of Miss Jean Brodie* by Muriel Spark, *The Agony and the Ecstasy* by Irving Stone and *Catch 22* by Joseph Heller
- France wins the Five Nations rugby championship

January

- US severs diplomatic relations with Cuba
- Referendum in France and Algeria approves de Gaulle's proposals for Algeria
- Former leader of Congo Patrice Lumumba assassinated
- Britain and United Arab Federation of Egypt and Syria resume normal diplomatic relations
- Provisional government in Rwanda proclaims republic

SUBURBS HIDE SOVIET SPIES

An ordinary suburban house in Cranleigh Drive, Ruislip, north London, was revealed as the hub of a sophisticated Soviet spy ring in January 1961. The arrest of the so-called "Portland" spies caused a media sensation, stimulating fresh questions about the state of British security in the Cold War.

The investigation that cracked the spy ring began with a tip-off from an Eastern bloc defector, Michael Goleniewski, a senior officer in Polish military intelligence. Goleniewski told the CIA of an Englishman who had been recruited by the Soviets in Warsaw in the 1950s and was now working in a naval installation. The information was passed on to MI5, who identified the man as Harry Houghton, an employee of the top-secret Underwater Weapons Establishment, Portland.

Houghton and his mistress, Ethyl Gee, were put under surveillance and soon led their watchers to their Soviet contact. On a visit to London, they were observed handing over a package to a Canadian businessman, Gordon Lonsdale, who was living in his flat overlooking Regent's Park and enjoying a high-spending, playboy lifestyle. Lonsdale's true identity was established later: he was Konon Trofimovich Molody, an officer in the KGB.

In October 1960, after a spell abroad, Lonsdale/Molody changed his place of residence, moving into a house in Ruislip with a New Zealand couple, Peter and Helen Kroger, who were

▲ The "Canadian businessman" who called himself Gordon Lonsdale was really KGB officer Konon Trofimovich Molody.

apparently harmless antiquarian booksellers. As with Lonsdale, their identities were elaborate fakes. They were later identified by the FBI as US citizens, Morris and Lona Cohen – long-established Soviet agents who had fled the United States in the 1940s.

On January 7, Special Branch arrested Lonsdale/Molody, Houghton and Gee outside the Old Vic theatre, shortly after secret documents had been handed over to the Russian in a carrier bag. At the same time, other officers raided the house in Ruislip and arrested the "Krogers". The house was packed with fascinating espionage paraphernalia, including microdot equipment, a radio transmitter hidden under the kitchen floor and materials for invisible writing.

On the face of it, the arrests were a triumph for the British intelligence services. But, along with the later arrests of SIS double-agent George Blake and Admiralty clerk John Vassall, they fuelled Cold War paranoia, and created the impression that Britain's secret military establishment was riddled with Soviet spies.

USA EYES LAOTIAN THREAT

In March 1961, the Kennedy administration initiated a drive to convince the people of the United States that it should be deeply concerned about the fate of Laos, which was involved in a complex civil war that even the US government barely understood. Laos, – a small southeast Asian country, had at one time been part of French Indochina, along with Cambodia and North and South Vietnam.

When outgoing President Dwight D Eisenhower briefed John F Kennedy on foreign affairs before handing over the reins of power, he told him: "Laos is your big problem." This was also the advice given by the CIA, which was secretly building up the forces of right-wing Laotian General Phoumi Nosavan in the hope he could win power and hold the line against the rebel forces of the Communist Pathet Lao.

On March 21, Kennedy went public about at least part of the United States' direct involvement in the Laotian civil war. During a television briefing to journalists, he announced a doubling of the number of military advisers training the Laotian government army. To explain why the fate of such a small and remote country should be significant, the President's aides turned to the "domino theory" – if any one of the

▲ President Kennedy introduces the "Laotian Problem" – until this time few Americans had even heard of the southeast Asian state.

countries of southeast Asia were to fall to Communism, it would lead to the fall of all the rest, from Thailand to the Philippines.

The press dutifully conveyed the administration message with few questions asked, although Asian experts doubted that a peculiar conflict in which the government and rebel sides were led by quarrelling royal brothers – Prince Souvanna Phouma and Prince Souphanouvong – could really be simplified to match the preconceptions of the global Cold War.

THE FIRST MAN IN SPACE

In a startling demonstration of technological prowess, on April 12, 1961, the Soviet Union won the race to send the first man into space. A massive *Vostok* rocket blasted off from Baikonur in Kazhakstan, propelling cosmonaut Yuri Alexeyivich Gagarin, aged 27, into orbit around the Earth.

Strapped into a tiny capsule 2.6 metres (8ft 5 in) in diameter, Gagarin had virtually no control of the flight. His function was to be monitored by instruments studying the effects of the launch and space travel on the human body. Achieving a maximum height of 300 km (185 miles), Gagarin had orbited the Earth once before making a parachute-cushioned ground landing near the town of Sartov.

The event was immediately recognized as an epoch-making step forward for humanity. In the United States, it caused consternation. The quality of Soviet rocket technology was seen as a threat to their military security, while the Soviet lead in space represented a major blow to US international prestige. The best that NASA had been able to do was to launch a monkey into space the previous February.

President Kennedy's response was to raise the stakes. In May he told Congress that "this nation should commit itself to achieving the goal before this decade is out of landing a man on the Moon and returning him safely to Earth." If the United States had lost one space race, they were determined to win the next.

▲ Preparing for the unknown, cosmonaut Yuri Gagarin awaits the launch of the first piloted space flight.

SLAUGHTER AT THE BAY OF PIGS

One of the first briefings John F Kennedy received after becoming President-elect in November 1960 was from CIA chief Allen Dulles and his head of covert operations, Richard Bissel. They told him of a secret plan to overthrow Fidel Castro's revolutionary regime in Cuba. An army of Cuban exiles was being trained at bases in Guatemala, ready to launch an invasion of the island. The project had a $13 million budget and the blessing of President Dwight D Eisenhower.

Kennedy seems to have had doubts about the project, but once installed in the White House gave it the go-ahead. He was concerned, however, to maintain "deniability" – he wanted to be able to distance the US government from the project if it failed. So he scaled down the planned level of US air and naval support for the invasion.

The invasion site was shifted to the Bay of Pigs – a swampy area where it was thought the Cuban exiles could establish a bridgehead without over-dependence on air cover.

The project, codenamed "JM/WAVE", had its headquarters in Miami, Florida, which became a buzzing hive of undercover activity in which CIA operatives, Cuban exiles and mafiosi conspired together to produce Castro's downfall. Whether President Kennedy was aware of the bizarre plots to assassinate or discredit Castro – ranging from murder by exploding cigar to ridicule through public intoxication with LSD – is not certain. But an invasion by around 1,300 men, with limited US support, against a Cuban army of around 200,000 obviously had no hope of success unless it coincided with the death of Castro or an armed uprising inside Cuba.

The landing force arrived off the Bay of Pigs on the morning of April 17, escorted by a small fleet of US naval vessels. Six American B26 bombers, piloted by Cuban exiles, had launched some preliminary attacks on Cuban air bases, but these completely failed to disable Castro's air force, which counter-attacked as the invaders came ashore. Isolated and under air attack, the Cuban exiles soon found themselves in desperate straits. Kennedy flatly refused to authorize air strikes by planes from the carrier *Essex* stationed off Cuba. With no popular revolt against Castro materializing, the invaders were abandoned to their fate. By April 20, almost all had been killed or taken prisoner.

The failed invasion was a profound embarrassment for the United States and its President. It raised Castro to a new pitch of domestic popularity and international prestige.

Those involved in the invasion – part of the CIA and the Cuban exiles – developed a bitter hatred for Kennedy, who they believed had betrayed their cause. Kennedy, for his part, took his revenge on the CIA when he sacked Dulles and Bissell later that year.

▼ **Cuban exile "mercenaries" who took part in the Bay of Pigs fiasco appear at their Havana show trial. They were each given 30-year sentences or offered release on a $22 million indemnity.**

MYSTIC ANALYST JUNG DIES

The Swiss analytical psychologist Carl Gustav Jung died on June 6, 1961, aged 85. In the first decade of the twentieth century, Jung was closely associated with Sigmund Freud in creating psychoanalysis. He was responsible for inventing the

technique known as "free association", in which patients reveal the secrets of their unconscious mind by responding to a word read out by an analyst with the first word that comes into their head.

In 1913, however, Jung broke with Freud, rejecting the Freudian emphasis on the overriding importance of sex in human development. As he began to explore myths, legends, folk stories and Eastern religions, his insights into the mind became increasingly mystical. He developed the idea of the "collective

▲ Carl Gustav Jung who, next to his former colleague Sigmund Freud, the most noted psychoanalyst of them all.

unconscious" from which "archetypes" surfaced in dreams and myths to guide individuals on a voyage of spiritual discovery. Jung became obsessed with mandalas – circular Oriental images representing psychic wholeness. And he explored the murky realm of coincidence, he suggested that some form of psychological causation might make related events occur simultaneously.

Strangely, by the time of his death it was Jung's wackier ideas that seemed most relevant to the age. His belief in spiritual growth and his determination to search for spiritual meaning in life appealed to a new generation that rebelled against Western materialism.

UN CHIEF DIES IN CONGO AIR CRASH

On September 17, 1961, the UN Secretary-General, Dag Hammarskjöld, was killed in an air crash near Ndola in Northern Rhodesia (now Zambia). Because Hammarskjöld had been a controversial figure, there were suspicions that the crash, which also claimed the lives of twelve other passengers, may not have been an accident.

An experienced Swedish diplomat, Hammarskjöld had become UN Secretary-General in 1953. He set out to make the United Nations an active representative of the majority of the world's states – many of them newly independent – rather than a tool of the major powers. He was anti-colonialist and deeply suspicious of the United States.

When the Congo crisis erupted in 1960, Hammarskjöld seized the chance to intervene. He

created a UN force made up of soldiers from neutral states, excluding representatives of Nato or the Communist bloc. He then used that force against what he saw as neo-colonialist and racist interference in the Congo by the Belgian army and white mercenaries, who were defending a breakaway state in the Congolese province of Katanga.

By September 1961, UN forces had fought their way into the Katangese capital, Elizabethville, forcing the Katangese leader Moise Tshombe to flee to Northern Rhodesia for safety. Hammarskjöld was on his way to meet Tshombe for peace talks when the fatal crash occurred.

Hammarskjöld was revered by many, and was posthumously awarded the 1961 Nobel Prize for peace. But the United States was relieved to see the end of his

▲ As Secretary-General, Dag Hammarskjöld raised the profile of the United Nations, especially its role in keeping world peace.

reign at the UN. His successor, U Thant, failed to sustain the role of the organization as a counterweight to the superpowers in the Cold War era.

'61

THE BERLIN WALL

In the dead of night on the warm summer weekend of August 12–13, 1961, East German soldiers, police and construction crews began erecting a barrier across the centre of the divided city of Berlin. Barbed wire and fixing posts were laid down into the cobblestone streets at the start of what was to become the most infamous monument of the Cold War: the Berlin Wall.

Since 1945, Berlin had been under the military occupation of the four victors of World War Two, the United States, Britain, France and the Soviet Union. West Berlin – the three sectors of the city controlled by the Western powers – was an isolated outpost of

▲ **Queues of refugees continue the mass exodus from the Soviet sector of Berlin to the relative freedom of the West.**

capitalism, deep inside the territory of Communist East Germany. Since the failure of a Soviet attempt to drive the Western powers out by blockade in the late 1940s, the city had settled down to a strange and anomalous existence as the only place in Europe where there was virtually free movement across the Iron Curtain – a hotbed of espionage and one of the most dangerous potential flashpoints in the nuclear standoff of the Cold War

By 1961, the open border in Berlin had become a mortal menace to the survival of East Germany. The drab, impoverished, propaganda-saturated police state ruled over by veteran Communist Walter Ulbricht could not command the loyalty of a large part of its population. West Germany was prepared to welcome them with open arms. Every month, thousands of East Germans crossed from East to West Berlin and registered at reception centres. In due course, they were flown out to West Germany, where they were given political refugee status and found accommodation and jobs. Most of those who left were young and skilled workers. By July 1961, about 30,000 people were emigrating every month. It was becoming almost impossible to find a plumber or electrician anywhere in East Germany.

Watching the people he was supposed to govern vanish to the West, Ulbricht called for Soviet backing for a decisive move to stop emigration once and for all.

Nikita Khrushchev, the ebullient, mercurial Soviet leader, saw an opportunity for scoring gains at the expense of the US. Buoyed up by the recent Soviet successes in space, he genuinely believed that socialism would soon "bury capitalism". He regarded the untried new US President Kennedy as a weak figure who might be bullied. Khrushchev regarded Berlin as the perfect place for a propaganda

◀ **Viewed from across the divide, the body of an 18-year old is carried away after an unsuccessful bid to escape to the West.**

▲ Between 1961 and 1990, Berlin's Heinrich Heine Strasse was divided by the Berlin Wall. Armed Soviet troops on the Eastern Sector were largely successful in stemming the East–West exodus.

coup. With his earthy sense of humour, he once described the city as "the testicles of the West – when I want the West to scream, I squeeze on Berlin."

In June 1961, Khrushchev and Kennedy met for the first time at a summit meeting in Vienna. In a calculated display of aggression, the Soviet leader demanded the withdrawal of the Western powers from Berlin in six months time and threatened war if they refused to go. Kennedy was shaken, believing that Khrushchev might just be mad enough to trigger a nuclear holocaust.

Returning to the United States, Kennedy called up reservists, announced a civil defence programme to build nuclear fallout shelters, and told the US people that Berlin was "the great testing place of Western courage and will." Nato military commanders worked out plans to deal with a Soviet attack on West Berlin or a renewed blockade of the city. No one in the West was expecting a wall.

At 1 a.m. on August 13, the East German news agency announced that since "deceit, bribery and blackmail" had induced "unstable elements" to leave for West Germany, "effective control was going to be established around the whole territory of West Berlin." It took two days to complete a barbed wire barricade across the line dividing East and West Berlin. Once this was complete, the East Germans began building a wall. It was 2.4 metres (8 ft) tall, made of cinderblocks and topped with barbed wire. Although the original wall was flimsy in structure compared with what it would eventually become, it was enough to deter all but the bravest from attempting to cross to the West.

The scenes of anguish and desperation in Berlin during the first weeks of the Wall made an indelible impression on all who witnessed them. Around one thousand people managed to find a way across in a last dash before the barrier was complete. In Bernauerstrasse, where the border followed the line of the backs of houses, fleeing East Berliners leapt out of high windows into jumping sheets rushed to the scene by the West Berlin fire brigade.

The Wall cut many Berliners off from their relatives and friends – people gathered at points along the Wall to hold up new-born babies to be seen by their grandparents, or to search desperately for a glimpse of a loved one.

On August 24, a man called Gunter Liften was shot while trying to reach the West. He was the first person, but certainly would not be the last, to die trying to cross the Wall.

The Western powers made no attempt to intervene to stop the Wall being built. Although publicly all Western leaders denounced it, in private there was considerable relief that a solution to the Berlin crisis had been found.

Kennedy commented that it was "a hell of a lot better than a war." With the building of the Wall, East Germany was stabilized for another quarter of a century and Berlin ceased to be a Cold War flashpoint. It was the people of Berlin who paid the price for world peace.

▼ During the lifespan of the Berlin Wall, the Brandenburg Gate – once one of the greatest symbols of German unity – was closed to the West.

'62

NEWS IN BRIEF

• Tension increases between Egypt and Saudi Arabia; several Saudi princes defect to Egypt
• Anti-immigration laws passed in Britain
• The Second Vatican Council opens
• The new Coventry Cathedral in Britain is consecrated; the original was destroyed in World War Two
• The sedative thalidomide found to cause genetic abnormalities and banned
• Films released during the year include David Lean's *Lawrence of Arabia*, the first James Bond movie *Dr No* and *The Manchurian Candidate*, starring Frank Sinatra
• The play *Who's Afraid of Virginia Woolf?* by Edward Albee opens
• The musical *A Funny Thing Happened On The Way To The Forum* by Stephen Sondheim opens in New York
• Musical premieres include the opera *King Priam* by Michael Tippet and Benjamin Britten's *War Requiem*
• The Beach Boys release "Surfin' Safari"
• Books published this year include *One Day in the Life of Ivan Denisovich* by Alexander Solzhenitsyn, *One Flew Over the Cuckoo's Nest* by Ken Kesey and *A Clockwork Orange* by Anthony Burgess
• Brazil wins the seventh football World Cup

USA ENTERS THE VIETNAM QUAGMIRE

In 1962, South Vietnam moved towards centre stage in the United States' global struggle against Communism. By the start of the year, the US-backed Saigon regime of Ngo Dinh Diem was in serious trouble. Faced with Communist-led Vietcong fighters conducting a skilful guerrilla campaign in the countryside, Diem's corrupt government was proving

▲ **A US supply ship docks in Saigon with a military cargo to protect South Vietnam from Communist forces in the North.**

both militarily incompetent and politically inept.

The US had proposed a "strategic hamlets" programme to regain control of rural South Vietnam. This was a classic counter-insurgency ploy, used successfully by the British in Malaya in the 1950s. The idea was to move peasants into secure villages protected from the guerrillas by government troops, and to provide an improved standard of living to win their "hearts and minds". In the hands of Diem's generals, however, strategic hamlets had become little more than concentration camps.

It was increasingly clear that only the direct involvement of US personnel could save Diem. Small numbers of the US elite Special Forces – the Green Berets – were sent into South Vietnam's remote mountain regions to contact the Montagnard tribespeople.

An exemplary campaign won the Montagnards' wholehearted sup-

port for the anti-Communist effort, turning their villages into centres for attack on Communist guerrilla supply routes. But this was not enough to have a decisive effect on the conflict.

In January 1962, 300 US helicopter pilots began flying combat missions with South Vietnamese forces. Other pilots sprayed Viet Cong areas with chemical defoliants. During the year, the number of US military advisers accompanying the South Vietnamese into action would rise to almost 12,000. Thirty one US citizens were killed in Vietnam in 1962.

Under constant pressure from his army commanders to commit more US forces, Kennedy gradually gave way. He would have done better to listen to French President Charles De Gaulle who advised him to stay out of Vietnam. "You will, step by step, be sucked into a bottomless military and political quagmire," said the French leader. Tragically, his prediction was accurate.

THE BATTLE FOR ALGERIA

On July 3, 1962, Algeria gained its independence from France after a bitter and complex struggle that had, by some estimates, cost a million lives. The unlikely architect of the independence agreement was President Charles de Gaulle, who had come to power in France in 1958 as the man the French generals believed could keep Algeria French.

From September 1959, when he announced his intention of giving Algerians control of their own affairs, De Gaulle became a hate figure for Algeria's European

colonists and their supporters in the French army officer corps.

They formed the OAS (Organization Armée Secrete) to wage a terrorist campaign in defence of the sacred cause of "*Algérie française*". A three-cornered fight developed between French forces loyal to De Gaulle, the OAS and the Muslim FLN (Front de Libération Nationale), which had been fighting for Algerian

◄ **The Muslim population of Algeria came together in support of the provisional government under Ahmed Ben Bella.**

independence since 1954.

In June 1960, de Gaulle began independence negotiations with the FLN. The increasingly desperate supporters of *Algérie Française* were determined to resist. In April 1961, a group of French generals in Algeria staged a revolt and seized control of major cities. But the majority of the army stayed loyal to de Gaulle and the mutiny collapsed.

The OAS, meanwhile, stepped up its campaign of bombings and assassinations, exporting terror from Algeria to France. In September 1961, an OAS hit squad ambushed de Gaulle at Pont-sur-Seine, but failed to kill him. A series of OAS bombings rocked the streets of Paris, killing and maiming many innocent people. The OAS had the secret support or sympathy of many

officers in the French police and army. When a demonstration was organized to protest at a particularly savage OAS bomb outrage in February 1962, the Parisian police attacked the protesters with such violence that nine of them were killed and more than 200 were injured.

On March 18, 1962, President de Gaulle announced the Evian agreement with the FLN, paving the way for complete independence for Algeria. The OAS chief, General Salan, was arrested the following month. The head of the new Algerian government was to be FLN leader Ahmed Ben Bella. Confronted with the triumph of their enemies, hundreds of thousands of European colonists fled from Algeria, most settling in Corsica or the south of France.

▲ **An unpopular war to most French citizens, the government issued posters declaring "For our children... Peace in Algeria".**

THE HOVERCRAFT GETS OFF THE GROUND

The development of the hovercraft showed Britain's determination to take its place at the cutting edge of technological innovation. First conceived in 1953 by English scientist Sir Christopher Cockerell, the cushioned aircraft became a reality through the support of the National Development Corporation. A prototype crossed the English Channel in July 1959.

As with so many British inventions, however, commercial exploitation of a clever idea proved difficult. On July 20, 1962, the first passenger hovercraft service was initiated across the Dee estuary, between Wallasey and Rhyl. The Vickers VA-3 carried 24 passengers on the thirty-minute journey.

In August, another service, using a larger Westland SR-N2 model, was begun across the Solent between Southsea and Ryde on the Isle of Wight.

The aim of these experimental services was to see how money could be made out of hovercraft travel. Despite the high hopes raised by this new mode of transport, its commercial potential seemed likely to be limited by its inability to function in heavy seas, and by the small number of passengers it could carry compared with conventional ferries.

▼ **The Vickers Armstrong hovercraft takes off from the beach at Rhyl marking the start of the world's first passenger hovercraft service.**

January
- Western Samoa attains full independence
- European Economic Community agrees Common Agricultural Policy (CAP)
- Prime Minister of Tanganyika Julius Nyerere retires; Rashidj Kawawa succeeds

February
- Austerity measures provoke riots in British Guiana
- General election in Malta
- John Glenn becomes first US astronaut in space

March
- Uganda attains self governance
- Military coup in Burma; Ne Win takes power
- New government under Borg Olivier formed in Malta
- France and provisional Algerian government for Algerian independence

April
- Renewed conflict in civil war in Laos
- New government formed under Alex Bustamante in Jamaica
- Prime Minister Debré of France resigns to be succeeded by Georges Pompidou
- West Indies Federation dissolved
- OAS leader General Raoul Salan is captured in Algeria
- Opposition parties boycott elections in Central African Federation

May
- Antonio Segni elected President of Italy
- Agreement reached between rival factions at peace talks on Laotian civil war
- Adolf Eichmann executed in Israel for war crimes

'62

NEWS IN BRIEF

....

- South Vietnamese army launches "Operation Sunrise" offensive against Vietcong guerrillas with massive US assistance
- Provisional government formed in Laos
- Elections in Canada

June
- New constitution adopted in Pakistan

July
- Rwanda and Burundi attain full independence from Belgium
- British Prime Minister Harold Macmillan makes radical reshuffle of cabinet
- Death of US author and Nobel Prize-winner William Faulkner

August
- Nelson Mandela arrested in South Africa
- Jamaica and Trinidad and Tobago gain independence from Britain
- Indonesia and Netherlands settle dispute over West New Guinea
- Algeria joins the Arab League
- Movie star Marilyn Monroe dies
- Deaths of US movie star Marilyn Monroe and Swiss author and Nobel Prize-winner Hermann Hesse

September
- France restores diplomatic relations with Syria, Jordan and Saudi Arabia
- Chinese troops make incursion into Indian territory
- Death of US poet and painter e e cummings

TELSTAR FLASHES PICTURES ACROSS THE ATLANTIC

The first great step in the communications revolution of the 1960s was the launch of the satellite *Telstar* from Cape Canaveral on July 10, 1962. Described as "about the size and shape of a beachball", it permitted the first live television broadcasts between Europe and the United States.

Telstar was the first satellite owned and operated by a business corporation, the US communications giant AT & T. During its sixth orbit, images transmitted from Andover, Maine, were picked up successfully by a ground station at Pleumeur-Bodou in Brittany, and less successfully at Goonhilly Downs in Cornwall, where a technical fault meant the reception was blurred and foggy.

The following day, France and Britain transmitted TV pictures to the United States – Yves Montand singing for the French, the test card for Britain.

After these initial experiments, the first live transatlantic programmes were broadcast by national networks on each side of the Atlantic on July 23.

Europe sent a twenty-minute travelogue narrated by Richard Dimbleby – shots of Lapp reindeer farmers, a hovercraft on the Solent and the Sistine Chapel – while the United States responded with a baseball game, a speech by President Kennedy and Niagara Falls.

Although the content of these early broadcasts was disappointing, the technical leap forward

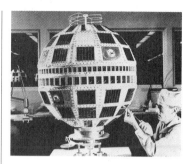

▲ The future of communication – the *Telstar* satellite was powered by solar panels which converted sunlight to electrical energy.

towards what trendy Canadian academic Marshall McLuhan was already calling "the Global Village" was impressive. It certainly captured the popular imagination: the biggest hit single of 1962 was the Tornados' would-be futuristic instrumental "Telstar".

GOODBYE NORMA JEAN

▲ Clark Gable and Marilyn Monroe in *The Misfits*, written by her then husband Arthur Miller, which was the last film either star completed.

Marilyn Monroe, one of the world's most famous and desirable women, was found dead on August 5, 1962 at her home in Los Angeles. An autopsy revealed that she had died after taking a massive overdose of barbiturates.

Monroe's life had, at first, seemed to be a rags-to-riches Hollywood fairytale. Born Norma Jean Baker, she was brought up in an orphanage and foster homes. Her breakthrough into the movies at the start of the 1950s depended entirely on her sensational physical charms, but in films such as *Gentlemen Prefer Blondes* (1953) and *Some Like It Hot* (1959), she proved she could send up her "dumb blonde" image to excellent comic effect, as well as projecting a breathy and vulnerable sexuality.

Sadly, fame did not bring Monroe security or happiness. After the break up of her third marriage to heavyweight playwright Arthur Miller in 1961, she spent time in a psychiatric clinic.

She was plagued by insomnia and lack of self-confidence. An attempt to return to the movies with a role in *Something's Got to Give* ended disastrously when she was sacked for repeatedly failing to appear on set. The studio, 20th Century Fox, opened proceedings against her for breach of contract.

One of her last public appearances was at the lavish birthday celebrations for President Kennedy held at Madison Square Gardens, New York, in May. Her memorable performance of "Happy Birthday, Mr President" is among the century's most frequently replayed film clips.

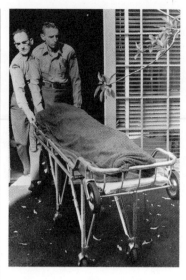

▲ **The body of the screen goddess is wheeled out of her Los Angeles home; her death is still debated by armchair conspiracy theorists.**

Whether or not she had an affair with Kennedy – a rumour so often repeated as to have taken on the status of fact – the wilder allegations that she may have been killed to stop her damaging Jack or Bobby Kennedy's reputations is left to speculation.

Monroe's death is more likely to have been a result of her insecurities and the exploitative nature of the movie business. As she bitterly commented: "This industry should behave to its stars like a mother whose child has just run out in front of a car. But instead of clasping the child to them, they start punishing the child." That child was Marilyn.

MISSISSIPPI RIOTS OVER DESEGREGATION

Eight years after the US Supreme Court ruled that racial segregation in education was unconstitutional, black people were still fighting to gain entry to whites-only schools and universities in the Deep South.

James Howard Meredith was one of the brave individuals who took on violent white prejudice by asserting his right to an integrated education, forcing a reluctant federal government to uphold the constitution.

Meredith applied to attend the University of Mississippi, known as "Ole Miss", an all-white institution. The issue was fought through the courts, until Supreme Court Justice Hugo Black ruled that the university's Board of Trustees must enroll Meredith.

In September 1962, they reluctantly announced they would comply, but Mississippi state governor Ross Barnett then stepped in to block enrolment, presenting the issue as a defence of state rights against

the federal tyranny of Washington. Each time Meredith presented himself at the university his path was blocked by Barnett and his state troopers.

President Kennedy eventually intervened, his brother, Attorney General Robert Kennedy, cynically telling an aide "The President needs a moral issue".

On September 30, Meredith arrived at the university with a bodyguard of no less than 170 federal marshals. A mob of white students responded by going on the rampage, throwing bricks and stones and setting fire to cars and buildings. Late in the evening, sporadic gunfire started, leaving two dead, including a French journalist, and more than fifty other people injured.

The following day order was restored. Under constant federal guard, Meredith went on to attend classes at "Ole Miss" and take his diploma. His courage was demonstrated – and ill-rewarded – once again four years

later. In June 1966, he returned to Mississippi on a civil rights march. After crossing the state line, he was shot in the back by a white man lying in ambush. Meredith survived to continue his part in the civil rights campaign.

▼ **Making a stand: James Howard Meredith was the first black man to take his place at the "all-white" University of Mississippi.**

'62 | CUBAN MISSILE CRISIS

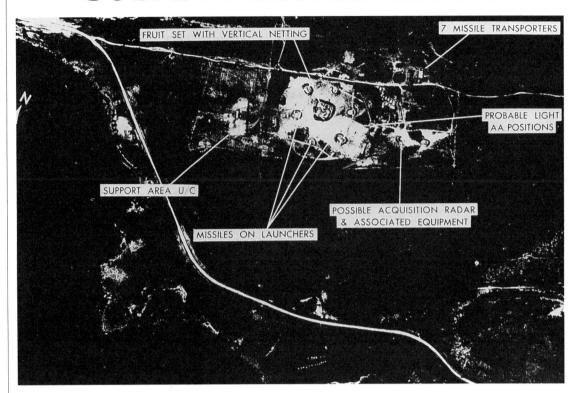

In October 1962, the world came closer to full-scale nuclear war than at any time before or since. A Soviet attempt to station nuclear missiles on Cuba led to a confrontation with the United States that easily could have triggered a global conflict.

The background to the crisis lay in the continuing efforts of the United States to destabilize, and if possible, overthrow Fidel Castro's regime in Cuba. Guessing that the Bay of Pigs invasion would not be the last US-backed onslaught he would have to face, Castro turned to the Soviet Union for arms.

Soviet fighter aircraft, tanks, artillery and air-defence missiles were soon flooding into Cuba. In the late summer of 1962, US intelligence reports began to indicate a more sinister development: bases were being built for Soviet ballistic missiles, capable of delivering a nuclear strike

◄ Soviet Premier Nikita Khrushchev meets President John F Kennedy at the Vienna "summit" that cooled the growing East–West conflict.

against the United States.

On October 14, a U2 spy plane piloted by Major Rudolf Anderson flew over the San Cristobal area, west of Havana. The high-level photographs it took were deemed to show a nuclear missile base under construction. The photos were shown to President Kennedy on the morning of October 16. They were important not just because clearly they showed someone in the process of build-

ing something, but also because they could be annotated and used as a visual aid to convince a sceptical world that the US was telling the truth.

Kennedy did not want a confrontation with the Soviets over Cuba. However, he could not avoid responding to such a potentially major shift in the nuclear balance of power, nor to such a direct challenge to US power and prestige. He called a meeting of his National Security Council, which decided that the installation of the missiles had to be stopped. If not, Cuba would be invaded to destroy them.

A fourteen-man advisory committee, "Ex Comm", was set up to help President Kennedy and his brother Bobby handle the crisis. Its military members, such as air force chief General

▲ US surveillance pictures of a Cuban surface-to-air missile site. The reaction of the US government brought the world to the brink of nuclear war.

Curtis Le May, were keen on immediate air strikes against Cuba or a full-scale invasion. They welcomed the chance for an armed confrontation with the Soviets.

This, however, was not the view of the Kennedys. They wanted the missiles out of Cuba, and were not unaware that a triumph over the Soviets would be a trump card in imminent mid-term elections. The Kennedys also wanted to avoid war if at all possible, especially a nuclear war.

On October 22, President Kennedy went public on the crisis. In a dramatic peak-time TV broadcast, he told the US people that unless the Soviets started dismantling the missile bases by 10 a.m. on the October 24, the United States would place a "quarantine line" of naval ships

around Cuba to stop and search any vessel suspected of carrying military equipment. How Soviet leader Nikita Khrushchev would respond if a Soviet ship was turned back nobody knew.

The morning that the strategy came into effect, two Soviet vessels, the *Gagarin* and the *Komiles*, approached the line of US interception ships, shadowed by a Soviet submarine. The US forces planned to draw the submarine to surface by dropping a depth charge. Fortunately, this act of war was avoided when the Soviet vessels turned back short of the quarantine line.

US Secretary of State Dean Rusk commented: "We're eyeball to eyeball and I think the other fellow just blinked." In fact, despite his readiness to make bold and provocative moves in search of an advantage in the superpower confrontation, Soviet leader Khrushchev was as keen to avoid a war as Kennedy was – perhaps more so.

He offered a deal: he would dismantle the missile bases if

▶ **Members of Fidel Castro's militia, these well-armed and trained guerrillas ensured the overthrow of Batista in 1959.**

the US promised never to invade Cuba. But then he added a second condition: the United States must remove its nuclear missiles from Turkey – which were as close to Soviet territory as the Cuban-based missiles would have been to the US.

Ironically, the United States

◀ **The Soviet ship *Kasimov* docks in Cuba with its cargo of fuselage crates for the building of Soviet IR-28 bombers.**

was planning to withdraw its Turkish missiles anyway, regarding them as obsolete. But Kennedy baulked at a "missile swap" that might have allowed Khrushchev to present the outcome of the confrontation as a Soviet success.

On October 27, he rejected the Turkish missile deal. On the same day, a U2 spy plane, piloted by the same Major Anderson whose photos had precipitated the crisis, was shot down over Cuba.

US nuclear missile crews were put on red alert and 90 B52 nuclear bombers took to the air, ready and waiting for the order to head for Russia.

Having reached the edge of the abyss, the two sides found a

timely formula to allow them to pull back. They simply ignored that the demand for withdrawal of Turkish-based missiles had ever been made.

Kennedy promised never to invade Cuba, as Khrushchev had originally requested, and the Soviets agreed not to install missiles in Cuba. On October 28, the crisis was over.

The Cuban missile crisis ushered in the beginnings of detente. During the next two years, a "hot line" was set up between the Kremlin and the White House, and a treaty was signed banning atmospheric nuclear tests.

The crisis also, paradoxically, lessened popular concern over nuclear war. The Campaign for Nuclear Disarmament (CND), so active in the early 1960s, suddenly lost its appeal. The campaign was not be revived until the 1980s.

'63

NEWS IN BRIEF

- Soviet spy Kim Philby flees from Britain to USSR
- Riots, civil unrest and killings of blacks and civil rights workers continue in the American south in campaign for desegregation of schools
- Tensions increase between Turkish and Greek communities of Cyprus
- Alcatraz, the island prison just off San Francisco, is closed
- Greater London Council (GLC) formed in Britain
- Audio cassette tape marketed
- *Syncom 2* becomes the first satellite launched into geosynchronous orbit
- Ice Age skeletons discovered in Italy
- USSR launches first woman, Valentina Tereshkova, into space
- Films released during the year include Tony Richardson's *Tom Jones*, Luchino Visconti's *The Leopard* and the epic *Cleopatra*, starring Richard Burton and Elizabeth Taylor
- The musical *Oh What A Lovely War* opens in London
- Tenor Luciano Pavarotti makes London debut
- The Beatles release "Twist and Shout" and "She Loves You"
- Books published this year include *The Centaur* by John Updike and *The Bell Jar* by Sylvia Plath

SUBMARINE MYSTERY

On April 9, 1963, the United States suffered its worst ever peacetime submarine disaster when the nuclear-powered USS *Thresher* was lost with all hands. The *Thresher* was carrying out deep-sea diving tests after a refit at the Portsmouth Naval Yard, New Hampshire. On board were seventeen civilians from the dockyard, and 112 crew.

The *Thresher* was designed to operate at depths of more than 455 metres (1,500 ft). About 320 km (200 miles) off Cape Cod, it dived. The tests were being monitored by the *Skylark*, a rescue ship, which after a short time, lost contact. The submarine was never heard from again.

The following day, the US Navy announced that the *Thresher* must have sunk to the ocean floor, at that point 2,560 metres (8,400 ft) deep. Admiral George

▲ The fated nuclear submarine *USS Thresher*, lost with all hands in a mystery that has never been solved.

W Anderson said that at such a depth "rescue would be absolutely out of the question."

Although there has never been a full explanation, it is thought that a fault must have caused the nuclear reactor to shut down, resulting in the boat sinking so deep that the weight of the ocean crushed its hull. In September 1964, the bathyscape *Trieste II* located the boat on the ocean floor, a mangled wreck that had become a coffin for 129 people.

PROFUMO SEX SCANDAL

In 1963, a scandal involving two potent taboo areas of British life – sex and the secret service –

▲ Disgraced Minister for War, John Profumo – revelations about his private life contributed to the downfall of the Tory government.

blew the lid off the political establishment and struck a mortal blow to the Conservative government. The trouble began in June 1961, when the Minister for War, John Profumo, met 19-year-old Christine Keeler by Lord Astor's swimming pool.

Keeler was living under the protection of society osteopath Steven Ward, who had introduced her to the sleek world of upper-class vice. Her looks made her immediately welcome at the sex clubs and orgies, where the more raffish members of the establishment took their pleasures. She slept with a lot of men, and Profumo was one of them.

Unfortunately for Profumo, another of Keeler's bedfellows was Eugene Ivanov, a naval attaché at the Soviet embassy.

Keeler had been pushed in Ivanov's direction by MI5, who hoped to use sexual entrapment to extract secrets from the attaché. This plot completely backfired, as Ivanov began to question Keeler about details of her pillow-talk with Profumo.

On March 22, 1963, as rumours about the affair began to surface in the press, Profumo told the House of Commons: "There was no impropriety whatsoever in my acquaintanceship with Miss Keeler."

It was a lie that could not be sustained; stories about Keeler, her friend Mandy Rice-Davies and their numerous male companions were recounted in the press in detail. On June 5, Profumo resigned from the government, forced to admit to a sexual relationship that had put Britain's secrets at risk.

The Establishment took its revenge by having Steven Ward arrested on a trumped-up charge of pimping. The trial offered more sensational newspaper copy, giving Mandy Rice-Davies the chance to produce the retort, "He would, wouldn't he?" when she referred to a man of standing who had denied her allegations of sexual impropriety. For Ward, however, it was a tragedy. Unable

▲ The Profumo Scandal created a tabloid sensation that brought 19-year-old Christine Keeler into the public eye.

to face a prison term, he committed suicide.

The Profumo affair had a massive impact largely because its public revelations of the pompous and hypocritical Establishment chimed with a widespread mood of irreverence, expressed by the new satirical media, such as the magazine *Private Eye* and its television equivalent *That Was The Week That Was*.

In October, the Prime Minister, Harold Macmillan, resigned, and Sir Alec Douglas-Home succeeded him. A year later, Labour came to power after thirteen years of Tory government – in part, at least, thanks to the charms of Christine Keeler.

KENNEDY'S GERMAN CONQUEST

The people of Berlin had been less than impressed by the reaction of the United States to the building of the Wall in August 1961. Many felt that a more positive US stance might have made the Communists back down. On June 26, 1963, President John F Kennedy visited the city in an effort to reassure its population of his country's commitment to the freedom of West Berlin – and to exploit the propaganda advantage that the Wall offered.

Despite the Communists' attempt to put a positive spin on the structure by calling it the Anti-Fascist Defence Wall, it was fairly obvious that there must be something wrong with a regime that had to use machine guns, concrete and barbed wire to contain its people.

Mobbed by cheering West Berliners, Kennedy visited the Wall at the famous US-sector crossing point Checkpoint Charlie, and at the Brandenburg Gate, where the Communists hung vast red banners to block his view.

The climax of the day was the speech Kennedy delivered from the balcony of the Schoneburg Rathaus, West Berlin's city hall. He told a crowd of 150,000: "There are many people in the world who really don't understand, or say they don't, what is the great issue between the free world and the Communist world. Let them come to Berlin. There are some who say that Communism is the wave of the future. Let them come to Berlin … All free men, wherever they may live, are citizens of Berlin, and, therefore, as a free man, I take pride in the words: *Ich bin ein Berliner*."

The people of Berlin took delight in the malicious joke that Kennedy had called himself a jam doughnut – known as a *Berliner* in German cake shops.

▼A quarter-of-a-million Germans gathered in front of City Hall to hear President Kennedy declare himself "ein Berliner".

'63

NEWS IN BRIEF

June
- British government minister John Profumo resigns
- Greek Prime Minister Constantin Karamantis resigns
- Leader of breakaway Congo republic Katanga Joseph Tshombe is forced to resign
- In Saigon a Buddhist monk commits self-immolation in protest against the war
- Death of Pope John XXIII; Pope Paul VI elected

July
- Briton Kim Philby is revealed as Soviet spy and "third man"
- Ex-ANC leader, Walter Sisulu arrested by South African paramilitary police
- Earthquake in Yugoslavia destroys the city of Skopje

August
- Nuclear test ban treaty agreed by USA, Britain and USSR
- Martial law declared in South Vietnam
- Martin Luther King leads civil rights march in Washington DC
- "Hot line" between the Kremlin and the White House installed
- Armed gang commit England's "Great Train Robbery"
- Death of French painter and developer of cubism Georges Braque

BUDDHIST SACRIFICE

On June 11, 1963, before the lenses of press photographers and TV cameramen, a Buddhist monk, Thich Quang Duc, sat down in a Saigon street, was dowsed with petrol, set light to himself and sat calmly amid the flames as he burned to death. The image, reproduced across the world, destroyed the credibility of South Vietnam's authoritarian ruler, Ngo Dinh Diem, in a single stroke.

Diem, who had run South Vietnam with the backing of the United States since 1955, was a staunch Catholic – a member of a religious minority in a largely Buddhist country. He came to depend heavily on fellow Catholics in key administrative and governmental positions.

In the 1960s, the regime's policy towards the Buddhists became ever more oppressive. In a single incident in the summer of 1963, about forty Buddhist demonstrators were killed and thousands were arrested after the government refused to allow the flying of a religious flag on

▲ **One of the most powerful images of the century, a Buddhist monk sacrifices himself in protest at the authoritarian rule of Ngo Dinh Diem.**

Buddha's birthday. Buddhist monasteries became centres of resistance to the regime, which was already fully occupied with combatting the Communist Viet Cong guerrilla movement.

Members of the regime's inner circle tried to laugh off Quang Duc's spectacular self-sacrifice. Diem's sister-in-law, Madame Nhu, derided it as a "barbecue".

However, the Kennedy administration in Washington was shaken. They already had doubts about continuing support for the unpopular Diem, now they publicly

warned him to respect Buddhists' rights or lose their backing.

By the end of August 1963, there had been six more highly publicised Buddhist suicide-burnings in South Vietnam. A new US ambassador, Henry Cabot Lodge, was sent to Saigon and soon gave approval to a group of generals plotting against Diem.

On November 1, a military coup led by General Duong Van Minh overthrew the government. Both Diem and his brother, Ngo Dinh Nhu, were murdered in cold blood.

THE GREAT TRAIN ROBBERY

Around 3 a.m. on August 8, 1963, a gang stopped the Glasgow to London Royal Mail train near Cheddington in Buckinghamshire. The raiders stole 120 mailbags holding £2.5 million in used bank notes. The daring operation was immediately dubbed "The Great Train Robbery".

Although the robbers were all essentially small-time criminals, their operation was efficiently planned and executed. Using a false red stop light, they halted the train and took over the engine, coshing driver Jack Mills.

▲ **Scene of the crime – the Great Train Robbers, in particular Ronnie Biggs, later achieved a level of folk-hero status.**

One of the gang, himself an engine driver, took the train further down the track to where a lorry was waiting.

In the meantime, other members of the gang broke into the sorting carriages and seized the mailbags. By the time the alarm was raised, they had made off into the night. However, the robbers' escape was far less efficient than their ambush; soon, most of them were under arrest.

The authorities were astonished to discover that, as journalist Bernard Levin wrote, the British public "regarded the train robbers as folk heroes, and viewed their crime with glee, their enterprise with admiration, and their fate with sympathy."

Southampton University students went as far as electing Bruce Reynolds, mastermind of the operation, an honorary life member of their union.

The courts imposed extravagant sentences of thirty years on most of those involved in the crime. Charlie Wilson, the first to be tried and charged, managed to escape from prison in 1964, but was rearrested in Canada in 1968.

Ronnie Biggs, a marginal latecomer to the scheme, escaped in 1965. Biggs fought a memorable campaign against extradition from Brazil in the 1970s.

KING'S MARCH ON WASHINGTON

On August 28, 1963, a quarter of a million people, led by Martin Luther King, marched across Washington DC to the Lincoln Memorial in a massive demonstration of support for black civil rights.

The march was in part a protest at a series of recent outrages in the southern United States, including attacks on peaceful anti-segregation demonstrators in Birmingham, Alabama, by police with clubs and dogs, the bombing of black churches and the murder of civil rights activist Medgar Evers.

It was also a gesture of support for a civil rights bill being forced through Congress by the Kennedy administration – although Kennedy originally tried to stop the March, believing it might lead to disturbances and prove counter-productive.

The March was itself an example of the integration that King so passionately preached. More than a quarter of the demonstrators were white and so were many of the speakers. The tone of the event was lofty, epitomized by the singing of the civil rights anthem "We Shall Overcome" by Mahalia Jackson.

▲ **A man with a dream, Martin Luther King addresses civil rights demonstrators gathered at the Lincoln Memorial in Washington DC.**

Media stars, Bob Dylan, Joan Baez and Marlon Brando – much associated with liberal causes – were a prominent presence.

The climax of the event was the speech in which King, basing himself on the principals of the United States Declaration of Independence, declared: "I have a dream that one day this nation will rise up and live out the true meaning of its creed – we hold these truths to be self-evident, that all men are created equal." He looked forward to "that day when all of God's children – black men and white men, Jews and Gentiles, Protestants and

Catholics – will be able to join hands and sing in the words of the old Negro spiritual: 'Free at last, free at last...' "

The speech confirmed King's status as a world political figure and earned him the Nobel Peace Prize the following year.

The integrationist liberalism of the March failed to win the admiration of all black Americans, however. Black Muslim separatist, Malcolm X, commented cryptically: "I observed that circus." Many student activists in the SNCC already believed that a more radical approach was needed to shake racism.

'63

KENNEDY'S ASSASSINATION

At 11.25 a.m. on November 22, 1963, President John F Kennedy and his wife Jacqueline flew in to Love Field, Dallas, on a whistlestop tour of Texas. Kennedy was campaigning for re-election the following year, and needed to drum up as much support as he could in a state where he was not well-liked.

There was a high expectation that there might be trouble of some kind in Dallas – a city once known as the "hate capital of Dixie". Senator William J Fulbright had told Kennedy: "Dallas is a very dangerous place. I wouldn't go there. Don't you go."

The day before the visit, right-wingers in the city handed out leaflets carrying Kennedy's portrait under the headline: "Wanted for Treason". Most Dallas schools pointedly refused to give children time off to line the presidential route.

Kennedy's motorcade headed into the centre of Dallas at noon. The custom-made Lincoln holding

▲ Following the requiem mass, the body of the assassinated President Kennedy leaves St Martin's Cathedral, Washington. His widow, Jackie Kennedy, and two children follow the coffin.

◄ A family in mourning, Jackie Kennedy is flanked by brothers-in-law Senator Edward and Attorney General Robert Kennedy.

Jack and Jackie Kennedy, plus their host, Texas Governor John B Connally and his wife Nellie, drove slowly through the smiling, waving crowds. The car was open-top – to allow the public the best view of their handsome President and his glamorous wife.

As the motorcade reached Dealey Plaza, at the far side of the city centre, Mrs Connally turned to Kennedy and commented: "You sure can't say Dallas doesn't love you, Mr President." It was 12.30 p.m.

The assassination lasted a mere five seconds. Kennedy was hit by two shots. The first wounded him in the neck and back, the second blew away the side of his head. Governor Connally was also wounded in the back and wrist. Jackie Kennedy tried to scramble out of the back of the limousine, screaming "They've killed Jack, they've killed my husband!" The horrifying scene was filmed by dress manufacturer Abe Zapruder on a home movie camera, bought especially to record the Kennedy visit.

The presidential Lincoln sped to Parkland Hospital, but Kennedy was already dead. The US people heard the news at 1.35 p.m. from rookie CBS TV presenter Walter Cronkite – the only newsman at the studio who had not gone to lunch.

In Washington there was a fear that the Soviet Union might exploit the power vacuum to launch a nuclear strike. Vice-

President Lyndon B Johnson was sworn in as President on board Air Force One, just two hours after the assassination. Jacqueline Kennedy stood beside him, still wearing the pink suit she had worn for the motorcade, now spattered with blood. Her husband's corpse was also on the plane, having been commandeered from the hospital by secret service agents. The presidential jet flew back to Washington.

Meanwhile, the Dallas police had found a bolt-action rifle and three spent cartridge cases on the sixth floor of the Texas School Book Depository, overlooking Dealey Plaza.

One of the employees in the Book Depository at the time of the assassination was Lee Harvey Oswald, who had left shortly after the killing. Later that afternoon, Oswald was arrested in the Texas Theatre movie house. It was alleged that, in the meantime, he had returned home to pick up a revolver and had used it to kill a police officer, J D Tippit, who was shot down in the street. Oswald was first charged with the murder of Tippet, and then, at around 1.30

▲ The motorcade moves slowly through the centre of Dallas. Moments later two bullets would bring a premature end to the presidency of John F Kennedy.

a.m. on November 23, with the Kennedy assassination.

The Dallas police held a press conference in the middle of the night, during which Oswald denied any knowledge of the assassination. "I'm just the patsy," he said.

Oswald was something of an oddity. He was a former US Marine who had defected to the Soviet Union, then returned to the United States with a Russian wife. He had apparently been a leftist, organizing his own "Fair Play For Cuba" Committee and handing out pro-Castro leaflets. But he also had contacts among the secret agents and mafiosi who where plotting to kill the Cuban leader. The rifle found at the Book Depository had apparently been bought by Oswald under an assumed name – a convenient snapshot was found showing him brandishing the gun.

On the morning of November 24, the police took Oswald from the city jail for transfer to the Dallas County jail. The media were notified of the move and turned up in force. As Oswald came out into the television lights, handcuffed and flanked by two detectives, a man called Jack Ruby darted forward and shot him at point blank range in the stomach. Oswald died in Parkland Hospital, almost exactly 48 hours after Kennedy.

Ruby was a nightclub owner with close mafia connections.

No satisfactory explanation of his action was ever produced. He claimed to have acted on impulse under the influence of "shock and grief" at Kennedy's death. The effect was to prevent Oswald coming to trial – as a legal case, the assassination of the President was closed.

The wave of emotion that swept the United States and much of the rest of the world in the wake of Kennedy's death was out of all proportion to his popularity when alive. Millions felt bereft and grief-stricken.

The extreme reaction was partly sympathy for the tragedy suffered by Kennedy's photogenic wife and young children. But it was also a reflection of the dangerous times – the years of the Cuban missile crisis and the Berlin Wall.

Unconsciously, people had felt that Kennedy was the hero who would shield them from a dangerous world. The hero had been slain, and many experienced the grief of the vulnerable and the unprotected.

▲ Assassin or scapegoat? The guilt of Lee Harvey Oswald has been hotly debated over the past four decades.

LBJ AT ODDS WITH THE RADICALS

▲ The 1964 World Fair at New York proved to be the unlikely setting for a civil rights protest.

- Rural insurgencies in Congo Republic but the rebels fail to take control of the country; European mercenaries aid the government to bring the rebellion under control
- Civil war again breaks out in Laos
- Palestine Liberation Organization (PLO) founded
- Race riots in New York
- Sugar industry in British Guiana crippled by strikes; civil unrest and violence ensues
- Civil Rights Act anti-discrimination laws passed in the US
- Mods versus Rockers gang conflict in Britain
- Home kidney dialysis introduced
- US launches *Mariner 4* probe to photograph Mars
- *The Sun* newspaper begins publication in Britain
- The Beatles and the Rolling Stones undertake first US tours
- Cassius Clay announces conversion to Islam and becomes Muhammad Ali
- Films released during the year include Sergio Leone's *A Fistful of Dollars*, starring Clint Eastwood, Stanley Kubrick's *Dr Strangelove*, and Pier Paolo Pasolini's *The Gospel According to St Matthew*
- The musical *Fiddler On The Roof* opens in New York
- Hit songs include "I Want to Hold Your Hand" and "Can't Buy Me Love" by the Beatles, "Fun, Fun, Fun" by the Beach Boys and "I Only Want to be With You by Dusty Springfield
- Books published this year include *Herzog* by Saul Bellow

When President Lyndon B Johnson addressed the opening of the New York World Fair on April 23, 1964 – it was the sort of occasion when general patriotic sentiments, goodwill and optimism were expected to set the tone.

Instead, Johnson was heckled by civil rights protesters, more than 300 of whom were arrested. The mounting tide of radical protest was to pursue him throughout his presidency.

On the face of it, 1964 should have been a year of triumph for the civil rights movement. Showing a far greater commitment to the cause of racial equality than his predecessor, John F Kennedy, Johnson forced a package of civil rights measures through Congress in July. One measure banned racial discrimination in employment and in all federally-funded projects. However, only days after this legislative triumph, riots broke out in Harlem, quickly spreading to other black areas of New York and New Jersey.

Poverty and oppressive policing had alienated black youth in the northern cities – to them, civil rights laws meant nothing.

The moderate pursuit of legislative change had also lost the support of young student activists. The summer of 1964 was dubbed the Freedom Summer as over 1,000 students ventured into the notoriously racist state of Mississippi in a drive to encourage black voter registration.

The reaction of local whites was violent in the extreme. In the most notorious case, three young civil rights activists, two white and one black, were murdered and their bodies sunk in a swamp.

Neither the FBI nor the federal government intervened to prevent systematic intimidation by white racists. Abbie Hoffman, one of the student radicals formed by the experience of the Freedom Summer, later wrote: "After Mississippi there was never any question what I was going to do with my life."

US student radicals were beginning to feel that the violence and racism of the Deep South were the essence of their society, rather than an aberration: a belief that was soon be strengthened by the experience of the Vietnam War.

HUNDREDS DIE IN FOOTBALL RIOT

On May 24, 1964, the National Stadium in Lima, Peru, was the site of the world's worst-ever football disaster.

Peru were playing Argentina in a vital qualifying match for the Tokyo Olympic Games. The Argentinians were leading by one goal when the home side appeared to have equalized, however the goal was disallowed by the Uruguayan referee.

For the passionate home crowd of 45,000 football-mad fans, the decision was just too much to bear. Spectators ran on to the pitch and the referee abandoned the match and was escorted off under police protection.

The fans vented their frustration by wrecking the stadium – smashing windows and ripping up seats. The police then moved in to attempt to restore order. As they advanced, launching tear gas canisters into the crowd, thousands of fans fled in panic, swarming towards the exit gates. Disastrously, most of the gates were locked. Soon people were being trampled under foot and bodies piled up six deep, crushed to death or asphyxiated.

The violent conflict continued outside the stadium for many hours. Cars and buses were set on fire and shops were looted. By the time the fury was spent, 318 people had been killed and more than 500 seriously injured.

PAPA DOC RULES HAITI

On June 14, 1964, Dr Francois Duvalier, known as "Papa Doc", introduced a new constitution making himself President-for-life of the Caribbean republic of Haiti. Duvalier had become Haiti's ruler in 1957, declaring himself in favour of a redistribution of wealth to aid "our impoverished peasant masses". However, his idea of the policy was to redistribute wealth mostly into the pockets of his family and wealthy supporters. State assets to the tune of $US500 million disappeared in this way.

In 1963, Papa Doc founded a terrorist militia, the dreaded Tontons Macoutes, who used kidnapping, torture and arbitrary execution to suppress political opposition. Surviving opponents of the regime were driven into exile. Some armed themselves and organized incursions into Haiti from the neighbouring Dominican Republic. However, Duvalier enjoyed the financial support of the United States, which regarded him as a bulwark against Communism.

Although the outrages committed by Duvalier's regime were widely denounced, the letter of the 1964 constitution was fulfilled. Papa Doc died in office in 1971, and his son, Jean Claude Duvalier, succeeded him.

◀ "President for Life" – Papa Doc Duvalier's redistribution of wealth helped line the pockets of his family and supporters.

NELSON MANDELA SENTENCED TO LIFE

On June 14, 1964, a South African court sentenced Nelson Mandela, the leader of the anti-apartheid African National Congress (ANC), to life imprisonment for sabotage and treason.

The ANC had campaigned peacefully against apartheid until 1960. But the brutal suppression of unarmed protest and the banning of the ANC forced its leaders to turn to violence. A spate of bomb attacks on government installations and other terrorist acts followed. The security forces responded with an effective crackdown on the ANC and Mandela was arrested in August 1962.

The four-hour speech made by Mandela in his own defence during the trial included a memorable statement of his faith in a multiracial society:

"I have cherished the ideal of a democratic and free society in which all persons live together in harmony and with equal opportunities. It is an ideal I hope to live for and to achieve. But if needs be, it is an ideal for which I am prepared to die."

Mandela was carried off to begin his sentence in the prison on Robben Island, from which no escape was possible. Only a remarkable twist of fate could give him back his freedom.

▲ A young Nelson Mandela in London, before his campaign against apartheid led to his imprisonment in South Africa.

'64

THE BEATLES CONQUER THE WORLD

In the history of popular culture, 1964 is the year when Britain invaded the United States. From the moment that the Beatles touched down at Kennedy Airport, New York, on February 7, the United States surrendered without a fight. The Fab Four were soon to become, in the words of John Lennon: "more popular than Jesus Christ".

As for any successful invasion, careful planning had been the key. The US record company Capitol pulled out all the stops to promote the Beatles' single, "I Want To Hold Your Hand", released in the States in December 1963.

The song was already top of the US charts by the time the Beatles arrived for a short visit built around two appearances on the immensely popular *Ed Sullivan Show* .

The TV broadcast of their airport arrival, complete with mobs

▲ The Beatles' conquest of America saw them taking the top five positions in the singles chart in April 1964 – a feat that no other artist has come close to emulating.

of screaming teenagers and a live press conference, worked up US curiosity to fever pitch.

Their first *Ed Sullivan* appearance on February 9, was watched by a record estimated audience of 73 million. By April, the Beatles held all five top places in the Hot 100 singles chart.

Although the Beatles could never have achieved success on a global scale without skilful commercial promotion, they were not a manufactured band created by marketing men. They were the product of a genuine creative upsurge among British youth in revolt against the stifling dullness of life in the Britain of the early 1960s. Clubs and art colleges had spawned a flourishing culture centred on pop music and fashion. British bands reinterpreted US music in an inventive style, using it to express their own frustrations and aspirations.

The Beatles were a product of the especially vibrant Liverpool scene, although they had acquired their professionalism and their haircuts during a spell in Hamburg. By 1962, they were the most popular group on Merseyside. Under the management of a local businessman, Brian Epstein, they eventually secured a recording contract with Parlophone.

The Beatles had their first number one single in April 1963, and by the end of that summer Beatlemania was in full swing.

Near-riots broke out at their concerts, where the screams of adolescent girls drowned the music. The country was deluged in Beatles wigs, brooches, collarless jackets and magazines.

Eager not to be square, grownups leaped on the bandwagon. By the autumn, a *Sunday Times*

▲ Mixing business with pleasure – Paul McCartney engages in beach frolics with two excited Beatles fans.

◀ They called it "Beatlemania". Wherever the "Fab Four" went they were sure to be greeted by thousands of screaming fans.

Even more surprising than the scale of the Beatles' success was the way they proved able to develop their music and style in intelligent and inventive ways. Their first film, *Hard Day's Night*, directed by Richard Lester and released in 1964, was a piece of Pop Art, full of avant-garde cinematic tricks. It was a world away from the movies by which Elvis Presley or Cliff Richard had sought to extend their careers.

For the rest of the 1960s, the Beatles remained central to the evolution of the new youth culture that connected, at different points, to avant-garde art, political protest, and experiments with mind-bending drugs.

Britain's dominance of the US pop charts in 1964 was transient and partial but it triggered a massive change in perceptions of Britain worldwide. The land of the bowler hat and Queen Victoria was reinvented as the home of the mini-skirt and the electric guitar.

music critic had called Lennon and McCartney "the greatest composers since Beethoven".

They topped the bill on the mainstream TV show *Sunday Night at the London Palladium* in October and starred at a Royal Command Performance the following month – the occasion for Lennon's famous crack: "Will people in the cheaper seats clap your hands. The rest of you rattle your jewellery."

Their album *With the Beatles*, released on the day Kennedy was shot, sold a quarter of a million copies in advance.

It is hard to appreciate the impact of the Beatles phenomenon retrospectively, because so many aspects of it have since become commonplace. For example, it is hard to recall that, until the Beatles, the "serious" press had never paid any attention to pop music as art.

The sudden appearance of articles by musicologists analysing the Beatles' use of harmony had no precedent. Nor did the irreverent style of interview that they

gave, dominated by John Lennon's caustic and surrealist-tinged wit. And nor did the fact that they wrote their own songs. Pop singers had traditionally been a carefully groomed front for the hack Tin Pan Alley tune-spinners.

The transatlantic breakthrough in 1964 transformed the whole scale of the Beatles phenomenon – and of pop music generally. Until then, the Beatles were still touring hard like any other band, appearing at local Gaumonts and Odeons throughout Britain. The members of the band were not fabulously rich, but when they visited the US for the second time, in the autumn of 1964, they played huge venues such as the Hollywood Bowl and Chicago's International Amphitheatre. Their concert in Cleveland, Ohio, was stopped by a police chief who claimed the emotional frenzy of the audience posed a health risk.

Other British pop groups – the Animals, the Dave Clark Five, and the Rolling Stones – swarmed in to the United States to expand

the bridgehead the Beatles had created. The Stones were marketed by their manager, Andrew Loog Oldham, as the anti-Beatles – loutish, inarticulate and offensive, compared to the Beatles more pleasing image. But they too had talent and a staying power beyond anything that would have been predicted at the time.

▲ The Beatles' record-breaking success in America paved the way for other British bands, such as the Rolling Stones, to follow.

'64

NEWS IN BRIEF
. . . .

May
- Aswan Dam in Egypt officially opened
- State of emergency declared in British Guiana
- 135 people die in riot at football match between Peru and Argentina
- Death of Indian Prime Minister Jawaharlal Nehru

June
- Lal Bahadur Shastri becomes Prime Minister of India
- Nelson Mandela sentenced to life imprisonment in South Africa
- Talks between Malaysia and Indonesia over Indonesian aggression collapse

July
- Nyasaland gains independence as Malawi
- Moise Tshombe becomes Prime Minister of Congo Republic

August
- US navy ship USS *Maddox* attacked by North Vietnamese forces in the Gulf of Tonkin; US aircraft make retaliatory air strike on North Vietnam
- Air strike by Turkish aircraft on northern Cyprus
- General Grivas takes command of the Greek-Cypriot National Guard
- Government-hired mercenaries arrive in the Congo Republic
- South Vietnam President Nguyen Khanh resigns
- ZANU political party banned in Rhodesia

INCIDENT IN THE GULF OF TONKIN

US Defence Secretary Robert McNamara returned from a visit to South Vietnam in the spring of 1964 convinced that a victory for the Communist-led Viet-cong guerrillas was imminent unless the United States stepped up its military involvement.

One option for the US was to launch air strikes against Communist North Vietnam, which might then call off the guerrilla war in the South. But US political leaders required a forceful pretext for commencing attacks on North Vietnam for two reasons: to convince the world that they were not engaging in unbridled aggression, and to avoid provoking China or the Soviet Union into direct

▲ **The attack on the USS *Maddox* persuaded the US government to step up involvement in Vietnam.**

military intervention in defence of Hanoi.

The US Navy was supporting secret hit-and-run raids by South Vietnamese commandos against the North Vietnamese coast in the Gulf of Tonkin. US warships regularly patrolled in sight of shore, inside North Vietnamese territorial waters.

On August 2, 1964, the US destroyer *Maddox* was sailing about 16 km (10 miles) off a stretch of coast that had been assaulted by South Vietnamese raiders only two days earlier. Three North Vietnamese torpedo boats ventured out to attack the *Maddox*, which called in air support from the carrier USS *Ticonderoga*. One of the torpedo boats was sunk and another crippled; the *Maddox* was undamaged.

The US administration sensed the opportunity it had been waiting for. President Johnson announced that any further "unprovoked military action" would lead to "grave consequences". The *Maddox*, now accompanied by another destroyer, continued its patrol along the North Vietnamese

coast. Towards midnight on the stormy night of August 4–5, the destroyers reported radar contact with five enemy vessels in attack formation. It is now almost certain that these vessels never existed. Either there had been an error in interpreting radar data, or the second attack was invented to justify an escalation of US military involvement.

Either way, Johnson had got what he wanted. He ordered immediate retaliatory air strikes. Sixty-four aircraft from the carriers *Ticonderoga* and *Constellation* set North Vietnamese ports ablaze.

More important for the future of Vietnam, on August 7, the Gulf of Tonkin Resolution was rushed through Congress. It authorized the President to take "any necessary measures" to repel an attack on US forces or to support its allies in southeast Asia – including South Vietnam. This resolution was used by successive US administrations as authorization for every act of war in Vietnam, including the large-scale deployment of US combat forces and the systematic bombing of North Vietnam, both of which began the following year.

THE WARREN REPORT

In the immediate aftermath of the assassination of President Kennedy in November 1963, his successor, President Lyndon B Johnson, set up a commission to investigate the killing. Its chairman was the highly respected Supreme Court Chief Justice Earl Warren. Other members of the commission included future Republican President Gerald Ford and former CIA director Allen Dulles.

Between February and June 1964, the Warren Commission heard testimony from 552 witnesses. It then drew up an 888-page report, which was delivered to the President on September 24. The report concluded that Kennedy had been killed by a crazed lone assassin, Lee Harvey Oswald, who had in his turn been killed by another crazed lone assassin, Jack Ruby.

This is unquestionably the outcome that Johnson had hoped for in setting up the commission. The President was especially keen that neither the Soviet Union nor Cuban leader Fidel Castro should be found to have plotted the assassination – since this would have forced the US government to take some form of drastic retaliatory action, involving a serious risk of war.

However, an opinion poll held after the publication of the Warren Report showed that only one in three US citizens believed the lone-assassin theory. Twice as many believed there had been a conspiracy to kill the President.

As paranoia about the "military-industrial complex" mounted through the 1960s, ever more elaborate conspiracy theories gained credence, centering not on

◀ **Earl Warren's 888-page report concluded that the Kennedy assassination was the work of a lone gunman.**

Communist involvement, but on a plot by, at the least, elements of the mafia and the CIA, and, at most, the highest levels of the US political establishment.

In 1978, a House Committee on Assassinations set up by Congress reversed the verdict of the Warren Report. It concluded that there had been a second gunman involved in the Kennedy assassination and hence a "probable conspiracy".

To this day no decisive evidence has ever emerged to finally resolve the most infamous murder mystery of the United States.

THEFT OF THE STAR OF INDIA

On October 30, 1964, the American Museum of Natural History in New York discovered that it had been burgled. The fabled Star of India, the world's largest cut sapphire, and twenty three other priceless stones had been stolen from the fourth floor Morgan Hall of Minerals and Gems. To its embarrassment, the museum had to admit that the burglar alarm system had not worked for some time.

The burglary was the work of two Miami beach bums, Jack "Murph the Surf" Murphy and Allen Kuhn. Their inspiration to commit the crime came after seeing the movie *Topkapi*, about a jewel theft from an Istanbul museum. The police in Florida had held the two men under surveillance for some time. They were picked up the day after the burglary and named as key suspects.

Blond and bronzed, Murphy and Kuhn quickly became media celebrities, and this was their undoing. Actress Eva Gabor saw their photographs in a newspaper and identified them as the people

who had assaulted her and stolen her jewels the previous year. Having no other option, Kuhn decided to cooperate with the authorities. He led them to

the Star of India, which was stashed in a bus-station locker. In return, Murphy and Kuhn were charged with simple burglary and only served short prison terms.

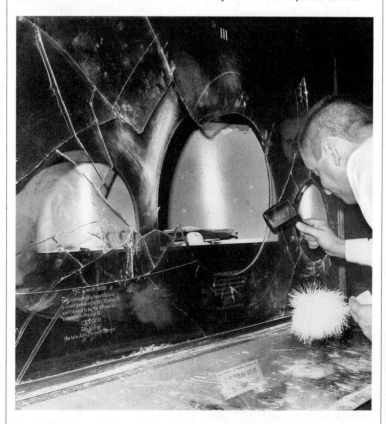

▲ **The smashed casing that once held the Star of India – while missing, the jewel was stashed in a bus-station locker.**

'65

NEWS IN BRIEF
....

- Maldives gain independence from Britain
- Crop failures in the USSR
- Monsoon rains fail in India and Pakistan, causing famine
- Oil found in the North Sea
- First space walks made by US astronaut Ed White and Soviet astronaut Alexei Leonov
- International Society for Krishna Consciousness founded
- Death penalty suspended in Britain
- Britain implements wage and price freeze in attempt to improve worsening trade deficit
- Britain accepts jurisdiction of the European Court of Human Rights
- Confederation of British Industry (CBI) founded in Britain
- LSD becomes controlled drug in US
- BASIC computer language developed
- Songs of the year include "You've Lost that Lovin' Feelin'" by the Righteous Brothers, "It's Not Unusual" by Tom Jones, "King of the Road" by Roger Miller, "Help" and "Yesterday" by the Beatles "Satisfaction" by the Rolling Stones and "I Got You Babe" by Sonny and Cher

CHURCHILL MEETS HIS MAKER

Sir Winston Churchill, Britain's pugnacious leader during World War Two, died of a stroke at his London home, 28 Hyde Park Gate, on January 24, 1965. He was 90.

The son of a raffish English aristocrat, Lord Randolph Churchill, and US heiress Jennie Jerome, Sir Winston fought in imperial wars in Sudan, India and South Africa before entering politics in 1900.

Churchill was a member of the reforming Liberal government before 1914, but later reverted to his father's Toryism. Becoming Prime Minister in 1940, in the darkest days of the war, he scorned defeatism and inspired resistance to Hitler with his lofty rhetoric. Churchill was also a prolific author, winning the Nobel Prize for literature in 1953.

The Queen had long made known her wish that Churchill should be honoured with a state funeral – the first accorded to a subject since the death of the Duke of Wellington in 1852. Sir Winston's body lay in state in Westminster Hall for three days, during which time over 300,000 people filed past to pay their last respects. The funeral was held on

▲ Over a quarter-of-a-million queued to pay their last respects to Sir Winston Churchill, Britain's great wartime leader.

January 30. Watched by a crowd of thousands that lined the streets and by millions on television, the coffin was carried on a gun carriage to St Paul's Cathedral. After the service, it was ferried by barge down the Thames to Waterloo station, and carried by train to Oxfordshire. Churchill had asked to be buried alongside his parents in Bladon churchyard, near Blenheim Palace where he had been born.

Many commentators at the time attributed the emotional response to Churchill's death to a mourning for Britain's lost empire. Most people, however, were almost certainly mourning a remarkable individual.

One of Churchill's own comments on his death, delivered on his 75th birthday, encapsulated the humour and courage that made him so well loved: "I am ready to meet my Maker," he quipped. "Whether my Maker is ready for the great ordeal of meeting me is another matter."

US TROOPS POUR INTO VIETNAM

▲ US troops carry out a successful amphibian assault on "Red Beach One" during the Tet offensive of August 1965.

By early 1965, about four-fifths of South Vietnam was under the control of Communist-led Vietcong guerrillas. They were installed only 32 km (20 miles) from Saigon, where a series of weak and unpopular military governments succeeded one another in rapid succession.

The US government felt it had no choice but to escalate its involvement in the conflict, otherwise South Vietnam would have a Communist government before the year was out.

The plan most popular in Washington was to rely on airpower, which would minimize US casualties. On February 7, after a Vietcong attack on a US military compound at Pleiku that killed nine US soldiers, US aircraft hit targets in North Vietnam. It was the prelude to a sustained bombing campaign against the North.

From March, 2 the operation known as Rolling Thunder was set in motion – a virtually unbroken sequence of raids by carrier and land-based aircraft designed to

▲ A major problem facing US troops in Vietnam was discriminating between ordinary civilians and Vietcong guerrillas.

break the North Vietnamese will to fight. The US air assault on South Vietnam was even heavier. Zones under the control of the Vietcong were battered by high-flying B52s, drenched with napalm – burning petrol – and poisoned with defoliants.

But air power was never going to be enough. On March 8, the first US combat troops – as opposed to "military advisers" – were committed to South Vietnam. US Marines stormed ashore from landing craft at Da Nang, wearing full combat gear for the benefit of the television cameras, although they were greeted on the beach by pretty Vietnamese girls in split skirts who hung garlands around their necks.

The beach party was soon over. The Marines were initially assigned to defensive duties, but during the summer US ground troops began to replace the incompetent and demoralized South Vietnamese in offensive combat. Commanded by General William C Westmoreland, the US embarked on a series of large-scale "search and destroy" operations in Communist-controlled areas. Their hope was to use the mobility provided by fleets of helicopters to bring infantry into contact with Vietcong forces, and then to deploy massive firepower from aircraft, artillery and naval vessels, to wipe out the guerrillas. It was a strategy that involved heavy "collateral damage" – the killing of Vietnamese peasants and the destruction of their villages.

Success was measured by the body count of dead guerrillas. But it was the mounting US death toll that grabbed the headlines. More than 1,350 US military personnel were killed in action during 1965. By the year's end, the number of US military personnel in South Vietnam exceeded 184,000.

FLOATING IN SPACE

On March 18, 1965, the Soviet Union proved it still had the edge over the United States in the space race, when Soviet cosmonaut Alexei Leonov became the first man to exit from a spacecraft in orbit. Leonov crawled out of the *Voshkod 2* craft 485 km (300 miles) above the Earth, turning a somersault as he emerged. He stayed outside the craft for about 10 minutes, providing a spectacular sight for television viewers in Europe who were able to watch the entire feat.

The United States could not respond in kind until June 3, when astronaut Major Edward White became the second spacewalker. White spent 14 minutes outside the *Gemini 4* spacecraft in orbit.

The US put as brave a face on it as they could, but coming second, rather than first, was not something the United States was accustomed to. They were redoubling their efforts to ensure that the first man on the Moon would be a US citizen.

► Soviet cosmonaut Alexei Leonov leaves the comparative safety of *Voshkod 2* to make the first-ever spacewalk.

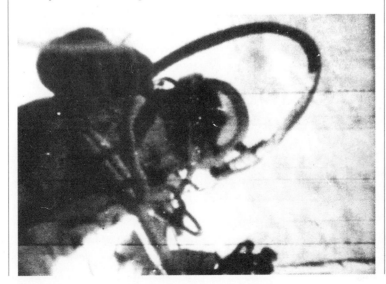

'65

The trouble caused by Fidel Castro's regime in Cuba made the United States intensely concerned to avoid any other left-wing government coming to power in the Caribbean. In the spring of 1965, this led to a large-scale US military intervention in the Dominican Republic.

Occupying two-thirds of the island of Hispaniola – Haiti is the other third – the Dominican Republic had been in a state of political upheaval since the assassination of longterm dictator Rafael Trujillo in 1961. Free elections in December 1962 had brought a mild left-winger, Juan Bosch, to power but he was soon deposed in a military coup.

The right-wing junta that replaced Bosch was itself overthrown in April 1965 in a rebellion led by Colonel Francisco Caama. The rebels invited Bosch to return from exile and lead the Dominican Republic back to democracy.

▲ The Dominican crisis showed that the US government was increasingly prepared to intervene in the politics of Central America.

This did not suit the United States. Using the excuse of protecting the lives of US nationals, US Marines went ashore on April 28 and occupied the western part of the Dominican capital, Santo Domingo. On the other side of the city, right-wing generals still controlled the San Isidro air base.

In the following days, thousands of US troops from the 82nd and 101st airborne divisions flew into San Isidro. They linked up with the Marines to form a military cordon around the part of San Domingo in which the rebel government was based.

Despite mass demonstrations against "US imperialism", there was nothing the Dominicans could do to control their own fate. However, the political solution the US then brokered proved relatively benign. US troops were progressively replaced by an Inter-American Force under Brazilian command. Free elections in 1966 produced a stable constitutional government under President Joaquin Balaguer.

MODERNIZING BRITAIN

▲ British Prime Minister Harold Wilson; his Labour government was dedicated to the "white heat" of technological progress.

In May 1965, the British government made a statement of intent that the country would eventually switch to the metric system. With a typical British sense of compromise, however, the change would only be made gradually and both metric and imperial systems would coexist for many years.

Going metric was in line with Labour's commitment, elected in 1964, to modernization and technological progress.

The Labour Prime Minister Harold Wilson had spoken of a new Britain being forged "in the white heat of the technological revolution". The government was introducing a "planned economy". This was considered a scientific step forward from the old-fashioned laissez-faire economics of the Conservatives. It would also endow the *Concorde* supersonic airliner project with a high profile.

Furthermore, adopting the metric system was also an acknowledgement that Britain's future lay in forging closer links with Europe – an intention despite the fact that the British membership of the European Common Market had been vetoed by the French President Charles de Gaulle in 1963.

DYLAN GOES ELECTRIC

US singer-songwriter Bob Dylan, born Robert Zimmerman, came to prominence in the early 1960s as the voice of self-right-eous radical protest. With his acoustic guitar, harmonica and edgily subversive lyrics, he characterized everything that folk

fans – mostly students – thought distinguished their music from "mindless" commercial pop.

But by 1965 Dylan had come to feel that the new versions of songs he had written or per-formed, currently being played by pop groups such as the Animals ("House of the Rising Sun") and the Byrds ("Mr Tambourine Man"), sounded far more exciting than the acoustic originals. After one half-rock album, *Bringing It All Back Home*, he went fully electric with the single "Like a Rolling Stone" and the album *Highway 61 Revisited.*

Deaf to the radical inventive-ness of Dylan's folk-rock fusion, traditional folk music fans felt

◀ **Bob Dylan's experiments with electric guitars shocked many of his traditional folk fans but changed the face of rock music.**

betrayed At the Newport Folk Festival in July 1965, when the singer was booed off stage after performing with an electric back-ing band. It was a phenomenon that was repeated with depress-ing regularity during the following year, including a famous occasion at London's Albert Hall in May 1966 when most of the audience walked out as soon as the elec-tric guitars went into action.

While folk fans denounced Dylan as "Judas", however, more young people turned on to his music than ever before. "Like a Rolling Stone" made it to number two in the US charts, far surpassing any of Dylan's acoustic numbers in popularity. The flow of imagery in the lyrics wedded to a driving rock backing made Dylan's recordings of this period a turning point in the history of rock music.

THE WATTS RIOTS

On August 11, 1965, in the predominantly black Watts district of Los Angeles, a local resident, Marquette Fry, was arrested by white police officers for alleged drunken driving and beaten up. A crowd gathered and began fighting with police. Watts was a poverty-stricken area plagued by racist policing – a tinder-box in which an incident like this was enough to spark a general conflagration.

Over the next two nights rioting spread through an area of about 130 square km (50 square miles). Cars and buildings were set on fire and grocery and liquor stores were looted.

Activist Jerry Furber later wrote: "People were proud. The overall mood was joyful. The looting itself was done with joy ..." The popular

slogan of the rebellion was a catchphrase coined by a local disc jockey: "Burn, baby, burn!" A later survey showed that around one in seven black residents had taken part in the riots. On the night of August 13, 2,000 National Guardsmen moved in to support

the thousands of armed police already on the streets. An 8 p.m. curfew was imposed for the next three nights, as the riots were ruthlessly suppressed. By the end, 34 people had been killed, most of them blacks shot by the National Guard or the police.

▲ **The main street of the Watts district of Los Angeles – flashpoint of violence between the black residents and white police officers.**

May
- Massive retaliatory attack by Israeli forces on village of Qalqiliya in Jordan
- Commercial tele-communica-tions satellite *Early Bird* launched
- Rhodesian Front Party under Ian Smith wins general election in Southern Rhodesia
- West Germany establishes diplomatic relations with Israel; Arab states sever diplomatic relations with West Germany in response
- Death of British aircraft designer Geoffrey de Havilland

June
- US forces in Vietnam begin offensive operations against Vietcong in South Vietnam
- Commonwealth Secretariat established in London
- Military coup in Algeria; Houari Boumedienne takes control
- Cease-fire in border conflict between Pakistan and India

July
- France begins boycott of EEC meetings
- King Constantine II dismisses Greek Prime Minister George Papandreou
- Leader of Conservative Party in Britain, Sir Alec Douglas-Home, resigns; Edward Heath elected leader in his place
- Over 125,000 US troops land in Vietnam

August
- Cigarette commercials banned from British television
- Crisis in Kashmir when India accuses Pakistan of infiltrating troops into the area
- Singapore withdraws from the Malaysian Federation

'65

* Voting Rights Act becomes law in US
* Indian troops make incursion into Pakistani territory; undeclared war follows; US and Britain suspend military aid to India and Pakistan
* Death of influential architect Charles-Edouard Jeanneret – Le Corbusier

September

* Pakistani forces in Kashmir break cease-fire agreement and advance into Kashmir
* Civil war in Dominica
* India invades Pakistan
* Stephen Stefanopoulos appointed Greek Prime Minister
* Temporary cease-fire in war between Pakistan and India
* Six army generals kidnapped, tortured and murdered in attempted military coup in Indonesia in which President Sukarno is implicated
* Death of Nobel Peace Prize-winner, philosopher, doctor and theologian Albert Schweitzer

October

* Talks on Rhodesian independence begin in London
* Fraudulent elections in Nigeria; civil unrest ensues
* Massacres of suspected Communist party members in Indonesia begin; about 400,000 killed

CREATOR OF MODERNIST ARCHITECTURE DIES

The Swiss-born French architect Charles Edouard Jeanneret, known by his pseudonym Le Corbusier, died on August 27, 1965 at the age of 77. He had lived to see the triumph of the International Style of modernist architecture that he helped create.

From the 1920s, Le Corbusier advocated a purist architecture free of decoration and adapted to the machine age.

After World War Two, he invented a system he called the "Modulor" for constructing buildings out of standard-sized units allegedly bearing a significant relationship to the proportions of the average human body. He dreamed of a Utopian *Ville Radieuse* comprising ranks of high-rise buildings surrounded by green open spaces.

The influence of Le Corbusier, as well as other modernist European architects, such as Ludwig Mies van der Rohe, was overwhelmingly preponderant in the 1950s and 1960s.

It is evident in the box-like skyscrapers of booming financial centres from Hong Kong to Frankfurt, and in the cheap high-rise housing estates that ring just about every city in the world.

It was only towards the end of

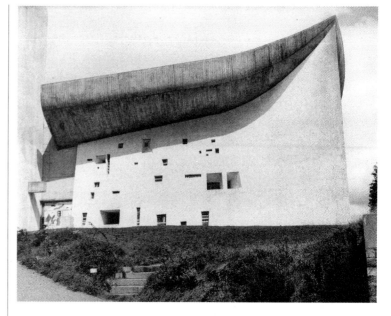

▲ The most influential architect of the century, Le Corbusier's buildings included the chapel at Ronchamp, France.

the 1960s, after Le Corbusier's death, that a reaction set in against the decoration-free high-rise style he had championed.

RHODESIA DECLARES UDI

Britain's withdrawal from its African colonies in the late 1950s and early 1960s was generally a smooth process, involving a polite handover to a friendly black African government content to maintain a special relationship with the former colonial power within the Commonwealth.

In 1963, the British-ruled Central African Federation, comprising Northern and Southern Rhodesia and Nyasaland, was dissolved into its component parts. The following year Northern Rhodesia became independent as Zambia and Nyasaland as Malawi. However, in Southern Rhodesia, a smooth transition to independence was blocked by resistance from its white settlers.

Southern Rhodesia had a white population of 220,000. Although they were far outnumbered by the approximately four million black Africans in the colony, they had put down roots and regarded the country as theirs. In a sense, the country was theirs since they owned all the best land and were used to exercising a monopoly of political power under vague British tutelage.

Many whites were profoundly apprehensive at the prospect of coming under the rule of a black government, as would happen if Britain organized independence under a democratic constitution.

In 1961, a former World War Two RAF fighter pilot, Ian Smith, born and bred in Rhodesia, created the Rhodesian Front. Its programme was to resist the imposition of black majority rule. To the astonishment of the colony's moderate political establishment, Smith's extremist organization triumphed in the elections of 1963.

During lengthy negotiations, the British insisted that a large measure of democracy must be a necessary precondition for granting independence. In April 1964, Smith became the colony's Prime

Minister, and made clear his readiness to declare independence himself if the British would not back down. In a referendum held in Southern Rhodesia the following November, the white population wholeheartedly backed Smith's stance.

The election of a Labour government in Britain, somewhat more resolutely committed to the principle of "One Man One Vote" than its Tory predecessors, made the failure of negotiations ultimately inevitable.

On November 11, 1965, Smith made a Unilateral Declaration of Independence (UDI). The British government responded by denouncing Smith and his followers as rebels, but quickly decided against attempting military action to regain control of the colony. Instead, economic sanctions were imposed, which British Prime Minister Harold Wilson fondly prophesied would bring down the Smith regime in weeks.

However, since Rhodesia's neighbours, white-ruled South Africa and the Portuguese colonies of Mozambique and Angola, supported UDI, sanctions were ineffectual. They were, in any case, covertly evaded by major multinational corporations, including oil companies. As the collapse of the Rhodesian regime failed to materialize, the British government made desperate efforts to lure Smith into renouncing UDI.

In December 1966, Wilson met Smith for talks on board a British warship, the *Tiger;* another meeting followed in 1968. Although Britain was now prepared to accept the token presence of a few black Africans in the Rhodesian government as a sufficient concession to the principle of majority rule, Rhodesia refused to budge.

Smith used draconian emergency powers to suppress any political opposition among the

▲ **Rhodesian leader Ian Smith refused to compromise in his negotiations with British Prime Minister Harold Wilson.**

black majority. In the years that followed, the white population of Rhodesia, as it was now called, enjoyed prosperity and security.

It was not until 1975 when Portuguese rule collapsed in Mozambique and Angola that military pressure from black guerrillas would begin to undermine the UDI regime.

MEETING IN SPACE

On December 15, 1965, US astronauts achieved the first rendezvous in space.

The two space capsules involved were *Gemini 6*, manned by Walter P Shirra and Thomas P Stafford, and *Gemini 7*, with Frank Borman and James A Lovell aboard.

Gemini 6 was launched from Cape Canaveral to meet up with *Gemini 7*, which had already been in orbit for eleven days.

Shirra, piloting *Gemini 6*, gradually manoeuvred the craft until, on its fourth orbit, it arrived alongside *Gemini 7*, about 315 km (195 miles) above the Pacific. The two space vehicles then orbited the Earth twice in tandem, about 3 metres (10 ft) apart.

The space rendezvous was vital to the US programme to land a man on the Moon. It was planned to involve a lunar module separating off from a command ship to touch down on the Moon surface, and then rejoining the command ship for the return to Earth.

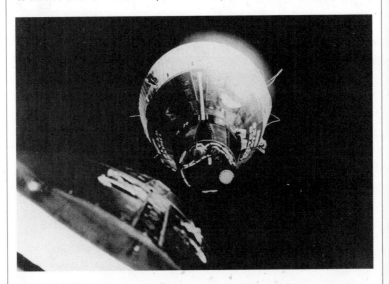

▲ **An early US triumph in space as the *Gemini 6* and *Gemini 7* capsules prepare to make their historic docking.**

'66

THE VIETNAM WAR TAKES ITS TOLL

NEWS IN BRIEF

- Tensions rise between Syria and Israel over border clashes
- Red Guard ideological police formed in China
- US forces in Vietnam begin using chemical defoliants
- US passes extensive legislation for the regeneration of US inner cities
- Black Panthers, militant black rights group, founded in US
- South Africa extends apartheid laws to South-west Africa
- Laker Airways formed
- British steel industry nationalized
- US and USSR both land probes on the Moon
- Fuel injection system devised for cars developed in Britain
- Masters and Johnson publish the report *Human Sexual Response*
- Measles vaccination developed
- Films released during the year include Lewis Gilbert's *Alfie*, starring Michael Caine, James Hill's *Born Free* and Fred Zinneman's *A Man For All Seasons*
- Gene Rodenberry creates the US television show *Star Trek*
- *Thunderbirds* debuts on British television
- *Anthony and Cleopatra* by Samuel Barber is the first production at the new Metropolitan Opera House, New York
- Songs released this year include "The Sounds of Silence" by Simon and Garfunkel, "Strangers in the Night" by Frank Sinatra and "Good Vibrations" by the Beach Boys

By the end of 1966, there were around 385,000 US troops engaged in the Vietnam War. US combat forces had largely replaced the South Vietnamese in the struggle against the Vietcong guerrillas, who were now increasingly supported by North Vietnamese infantry units infiltrated into the South. An epic conflict was unfolding between the technologically most advanced nation in the world and a lightly equipped peasant army clad in black pyjamas and sandals.

The US commander in Vietnam, General William C Westmoreland, felt that strategic limitations imposed by politicians made it hard for him to achieve a decisive victory. He was not allowed to use nuclear weapons, or to invade Communist North Vietnam. He was also prohibited from sending ground forces into neighbouring Laos to block the Ho Chi Minh Trail – the network of supply routes funnelling arms and men from the North into South Vietnam. Both North Vietnam and

▲ Helicopters were among the few vehicles capable of penetrating the alien terrain of Vietnam.

Laos were subjected to conventional air attack on a massive scale, and special forces carried out secret raids into Laos to attack the Trail. However, the resupply and reinforcement of the Vietcong could not be stopped.

Massive "search and destroy" operations, such as the onslaught on the Vietcong-controlled Iron Triangle north of Saigon in early 1966, involving more than 20,000 US troops, inflicted a certain number of casualties on the Vietcong and temporarily overran their bases. But since the guerrillas would never commit themselves to a full-scale battle, the effect of such operations was temporary. The Vietcong soon filtered back into the areas from which the US forces had swept them.

The classic aim of counter-insurgency warfare was to win the "hearts and minds" of the local people, denying the guerrillas the popular support on which they ultimately depended. But the US Marines favoured the slogan: "Get them by the balls and their hearts and minds will follow".

In General Westmoreland's words, the way to win back Communist-dominated areas was "to remove the people and destroy the villages". This

▲ The growing casualties among US troops unfamiliar with guerrilla warfare gradually began to turn public opinion in America.

created Free Fire Zones in which anything that moved could be blasted away. It also created a vast refugee problem – there were more than 1.5 million South Vietnamese peasants in over-crowded refugee camps by 1967.

The sufferings of the rural Vietnamese were at least partially conveyed to the US people by television. One broadcast, showing US troops setting fire to village huts with their cigarette lighters as distressed peasants looked on, had a particularly disturbing impact.

But opposition to the war in the United States was still restricted to a small minority of radicals. The gung-ho single "Ballad of the Green Berets" by Sergeant Barry Sadler, released in March 1966, sold over a million copies. Martin Luther King's outspoken opposition to the war lost him support among black Americans, many of whom were proud to see blacks fighting for their country in the desegregated army, especially in elite formations such as the airborne divisions.

US troops were not alone in fighting in Vietnam. In the course of 1966, South Korea, the Philippines and Thailand lent their support, and Australia and New Zealand made a small, somewhat reluctant, military contribution. But the United States' European allies, including Britain, stayed out of the war, offering polite diplomatic support – except for France, which denounced US policy and withdrew from the military side of Nato.

More than 5,000 US military personnel died in Vietnam in the course of 1966, without their commanders being able to offer any imminent prospect of victory. As the number of body bags coming home mounted, US citizens were bound to start asking whether the war was worthwhile.

ENGLAND WINS THE WORLD CUP

▲ Was it or wasn't it? Geoff Hurst's shot easily beats the German keeper, but some believe that the ball did not fully cross the line.

In July 1966, the football World Cup finals were held in England for the first, and so far only, time. The event had an inauspicious prelude in March, when the Jules Rimet trophy – the World Cup itself – was stolen from an exhibition in Westminster Hall. It was fortunately found in a London garden by an inquisitive dog called Pickles.

The tournament itself was marred by some outrageous foul play and violence. Pelé, the world's most famous footballer, was kicked out of the competition, and after England's victory over Argentina in a fierce quarter-final match, manager Alf Ramsey acrimoniously described the Argentinians as "animals".

Portugal, with its star striker Eusebio, was one of the best

▲ One of the great "gentlemen" of British football, the late Bobby Moore celebrates the greatest day in English football.

teams in the finals. So, more surprisingly, were North Korea, who beat Italy and went 3–0 up against Portugal, only to lose 5–3. But England appeared increasingly strong as the tournament progressed. By the time they beat Portugal 2–1 in the semi-finals, players, such as Bobby Charlton, Geoff Hurst, Alan Ball, Martin Peters and captain Bobby Moore, were looking the equal of any in the world.

The final took place at Wembley on July 30. England's opponents were West Germany, a team hinged around the formidable Franz Beckenbauer. Germany scored first, but goals from Geoff Hurst and Martin Peters seemed to have given England victory when, with seconds to go to the final whistle, Germany equalized.

Early in extra time, a shot from Hurst hit the underside of the crossbar and appeared to bounce out of the goal. The Russian linesman, however, ruled that the ball had crossed the line and England were ahead. At the end of extra time, with spectators running on to the pitch and BBC commentator Kenneth Wolstenholme intoning "They think it's all over ...", Hurst completed his hat-trick to leave England 4–2 winners.

MAO LEADS THE CULTURAL REVOLUTION

In Communist China, 1966 was the year of the Great Proletarian Cultural Revolution – one of the most astonishing mass movements in history. In September 1965, Chairman Mao Tse-tung had called for an attack on "reactionary bourgeois ideology" in Chinese art, music and literature. With the backing of Mao's wife, Jiang Qing, officially favoured intellectuals were soon describing the Chinese "cultural garden" as overgrown with "anti-socialist poisonous weeds".

In 1966, weeding out "bourgeois elements" in the cultural sphere grew into an attempt to revolutionize all areas of Chinese life. Mao had long denounced his fellow Communists in the Soviet Union for abandoning the revolutionary spirit and becoming complacent bureaucratic "revisionists". He now saw an opportunity to push China's Communist revolution into a new phase. His shock troops were to be the young.

Thousands of schoolchildren and students were issued with arm bands declaring them "Red Guards". In May 1966, Mao reviewed mass parades of Red Guards in Peking, chanting

▲ **Members of the Young Red Guard gather to recite the thoughts of their leader, Mao Tse-tung, in unison.**

Maoist slogans and waving copies of the "Little Red Book" – the *Thoughts of Chairman Mao*.

Mao was ritually praised as the "great teacher, great leader, great supreme commander, great helmsman". When he swam in the Yangtze River in July, to prove his enduring good health, the Chinese media pronounced the feat a triumph for the revolution. But the Red Guards were told

that all authority apart from Mao's was to be scorned.

In August, the Central Committee of the Communist Party endorsed the Cultural Revolution. Schools and universities closed, their pupils and students forming Red Guard bands to sweep the country clear of "old customs, old habits, old culture and old thinking".

Every aspect of "bourgeois" culture was attacked. Temples and works of art were destroyed. All "luxuries" from jazz records and chess sets to playing cards and silk clothes were confiscated and burned in giant bonfires. Libraries were shut or ransacked.

Authority figures – such as teachers, Communist officials, administrators and anyone with a good education – were publicly

◄ **Chinese students loyal to Mao Tse-tung demonstrate against "Revisionism", their term for Soviet-style Communism.**

humiliated. The Red Guards paraded their victims through the streets with dunces' caps on their heads and placards around their necks. They were forced to confess in public to imaginary crimes, admitting the most absurd counter-revolutionary acts.

Children were encouraged to denounce their parents. Attacks spread to anyone wearing glasses, anyone old. Amid the licensed violence, thousands were beaten to death. Millions were imprisoned or sent to the countryside for "re-education" through hard labour.

Although it was manipulated by Mao and his associates, the Cultural Revolution unleashed real anger and aspirations among young people, who were growing up in a repressed society.

It also allowed workers to make demands for better pay and conditions. As China degenerated into anarchy, there was a real risk that the revolution might escape Mao's leadership and develop its own programme. In February 1967, the army was drawn in and told to restore some kind of order.

Estimates of the death toll caused as a direct result of the upheaval vary wildly, but at least 400,000 people are thought to have died. Many years would pass before China fully recovered from the damage caused to its economic and intellectual life.

▲ The windows and doors of a large department store are covered in "dazeabo", newspaper prints of the proclamations of Mao.

ARCHITECT OF APARTHEID ASSASSINATED

▲ The pro-Nazi Dr Hendrik Verwoerd (right) was viewed by his assassin as being too moderate in his treatment of non-whites.

On September 6, 1966, South African Prime Minister Hendrik Verwoerd was assassinated while sitting in parliament. He was stabbed to death by Demetrio Tsafendas, a parliamentary messenger.

Ironically, Tsafendas accused Verwoerd of being too kind to blacks and Coloureds and of failing to do enough for poor whites like himself.

An Afrikaaner nationalist, Verwoerd had adopted a pro-Nazi stance during World War Two. As minister for native affairs from 1950, he was one of the chief architects of the apartheid policy of racial separation and white domination. He became Prime Minister in 1958, reinforcing the suppression of opposition to the apartheid system and taking South Africa out of the British Commonwealth. Verwoerd had survived an earlier assassination attempt in 1960.

Verwoerd was succeeded as Prime Minister by Balthazar Vorster, previously minister of justice and another nationalist hardliner. Vorster upheld the apartheid system and no relaxation of it was in prospect.

- Civil rights demonstration in Missouri, US
- US bombs Haiphong and Hanoi in Vietnam
- Death of French avant-garde artist Jean Arp

July
- Race riots in US
- Congo Republic cities Stanleyville renamed Kisingani and Leopoldville becomes Kinshasa
- End of seaman strike in Britain
- France withdraws from Nato
- Israel makes reprisal air attack on Syria
- Common Agricultural Policy agreed in the EEC
- Assassination of Nigerian ruler Major-General Johnson Aguiyi-Ironsi; Colonel Yukubu Gowon takes power
- British Colonial Office closed
- Death of US jazz pianist Bud Powell

August
- Conflict between Malaysia and Indonesia ends
- Fighting between Israeli and Syrian troops
- Major earthquake kills thousands in Turkey
- Death of US comedian Lenny Bruce from drug overdose

September
- Massacres of the Igbo tribe by Hausas in Nigeria
- Prime Minister Verwoerd of South Africa killed by disgruntled white; B J Vorster succeeds
- Rhodesian High Court rules Ian Smith's government illegal
- Race riots in San Francisco, US
- Bechuanaland gains independence from Britain, becoming Botswana

DISASTER IN ABERFAN

▲ **Rescue workers search in vain for survivors buried beneath the slag heap that engulfed part of the village school.**

One of Britain's worst peace-time disasters occurred at the Welsh mining village of Aberfan on October 21, 1966. It was 9.15 a.m. and the children at the village's Pant Glas Junior and Infants School were just settling down to lessons after morning assembly – at which they had sung "All Things Bright and Beautiful" – when they heard a sound like thunder and felt the ground begin to shake.

Like many Welsh pit villages, Aberfan was dominated by a tip of waste from the nearby colliery.

Heavy rain had destabilized the tip, and that morning it slid on to the village in a fatal avalanche. The school lay full in its path and within seconds it was buried under a tide of black slurry.

Local people, including miners from the local Merthyr Vale colliery, rushed to the scene. Reverend Kenneth Hayes, whose son was among the victims, later recalled the terrible scene: "I went up the road and turned the bend. I could see nothing but a mountain of black waste."

Joined by the emergency services, people frantically began trying to dig children out. But there were only five survivors. In all, 116 children and 28 adults lost their lives.

The impact was especially extreme in such a self-contained, tight-knit community. The few surviving children led isolated lives – one pointed out that there were no longer enough local kids even to play a game of football.

Local people felt particular bitterness against the National Coal Board, which adamantly avoided taking responsibility for the tragedy – the tip had been sited on top of a natural spring.

The disaster was a tragic reminder of the reality of life in Britain's declining industrial areas in the 1960s, far from the superficial glitter of "Swinging London". In Aberfan, the accumulated waste of Britain's industrial past had buried the generation of the future.

▲ **A nation mourns in the aftermath of a disaster that all but wiped out a generation of the village of Aberfan.**

FLORENCE FLOOD DISASTER

On November 4, 1966, the worst floods ever recorded devastated the city of Florence. Many art treasures were at risk as the River Arno burst its banks and water rose to 1.8 m (6 ft) above street level through two-thirds of the Italian Renaissance city.

The famous east doors of the Baptistry, cast in bronze by Lorenzo Ghiberti in 1452 and described by Michelangelo as the "Gate of Paradise", were torn from their hinges and swept away.

The 600-year-old Ponte Vecchio, the bridge in the centre of Florence, survived the battering of the storm, but more vulnerable treasures, including ancient books housed in the National Library were ruined.

About 180 people died in the flooding. The world's intense concern for Florence's works of art and lack of concern for its people led to earnest debates about the relative value of cultural artifacts and human lives.

▲ **The raging River Arno bursts its stone-paved banks, flooding the famous Renaissance palaces and museums of Florence.**

BLACK PROGRESS – FOR SOME

One outstanding result in the November 1966 US mid-term elections was the victory for African American Edward W Brooke, who was elected to represent Massachusetts in the Senate. A Republican, Brooke easily defeated the Democratic candidate, former Massachusetts Governor Endicott Peabody.

Brooke became the first black senator since the nineteenth century (a substantial number of blacks gained political office in the period immediately after the Civil War). He was elected by an overwhelmingly white electorate, since Massachusetts has one of the lowest percentages of black voters anywhere in the United States. Brooke's triumph was a sign of the opportunities opening up for blacks at the highest levels of power.

In the same year, Robert C Weaver became the first black man to hold a US Cabinet appointment, and in 1967 civil rights lawyer Thurgood Marshall was successfully nominated as a justice in the Supreme Court.

But the relevance of the success of this elite – and of middle-class blacks in general – to lives of the majority of African Americans was doubtful. Many found that young radicals such as Stokely Carmichael and H Rapp Brown, deploying the aggressive rhetoric of Black Power, expressed their frustration and anger more adequately.

▲ The Republican Edward W Brooke who became the USA's first African-American senator.

CARTOON KING DISNEY IS DEAD

Walt Disney, the king of US family entertainment, died on December 15, 1966 after surgery for lung cancer. He was aged 65.

Disney's rise to fortune began in 1928 when, in association with Ubbe Iwerks, he created the immensely popular cartoon character Mickey Mouse. Mickey was followed by a whole menagerie of successful Disney cartoon animals in the 1930s, including Donald Duck, Goofy and Pluto.

With all their associated merchandizing, these comic shorts generated enough money for Disney to make a full-length animated feature movie. *Snow White and the Seven Dwarfs*, released in 1938, was a box office hit that transformed the status of animated films.

▲ The king of children's animation, Walt Disney created a business empire that continues to flourish over 30 years after his death.

Discontent with Disney's way of running his cartoon factory led to a mass resignation of animators in 1941.

Most critics feel that the quality of Disney movies never recovered, at least during his lifetime. But the Disney Company continued to prosper.

The Disneyland amusement park at Anaheim, California, opened in 1955, quickly became one of the world's greatest tourist attractions.

Disney died at a time when the prestige of his company was being resurrected by the success of *Mary Poppins* in 1964, and the imminent release of *The Jungle Book* – an animated feature recapturing much of the storytelling power of the classic Disney period.

December
- Kurt Kiesinger becomes West German Chancellor
- U Thant re-elected Secretary-General of UN
- Harold Wilson and Ian Smith meet to resolve Rhodesia dispute; Rhodesia subsequently rejects British plan for Rhodesian independence, which calls for black majority rule. Ian Smith declares a republic.
- New constitution approved in referendum in Spain
- Customs union achieved by members of European Free Trade Association
- Yugoslav Communist dissident Milovan Djilas released from jail
- Death of US film-maker and businessman Walt Disney, creator of Mickey Mouse

'67

NEWS IN BRIEF

- Hundreds of thousands die in Red Guard militia purges of "traditionalists" in China; Chinese government fails to control the Red Guards, causing much civil unrest and industrial disruption
- Power struggle in Aden between The Front for the Liberation of Occupied Yemen (FLOSY) backed by Egypt and the Marxist-oriented National Liberation Front (NLF)
- US General Westmoreland initiates "search and destroy" operations in Vietnam; US military announce "… the war is being won …"
- The world's largest hydroelectric project, the Krasnoryarsk Dam, is completed in Siberia
- Foot-and-mouth disease epidemic in farm animals in Britain
- The "summer of love" becomes the zenith of the hippie social revolution in the West
- Colorado becomes first US state to legalize abortion
- British bank rates rise and Britain obtains loans and International Monetary Fund in economic crisis
- Britain renews campaign to join the EEC
- First black judge appointed to US Supreme Court

US ASTRONAUTS ENGULFED BY FIREBALL

On January 27, 1967, three US astronauts were killed when their spacecraft caught fire at Cape Canaveral (at that time known as Cape Kennedy). The men were Virgil I Grissom, Roger B Chaffee, and Edward H White. They were the first casualties in the US space programme.

At the time of the accident, the astronauts were practising for a launch scheduled to take place on February 21. They were in the cabin of the spacecraft on top of the *Saturn 1* rocket that would be used to blast them into space. An electrical fault is thought to have caused a spark that ignited the pure oxygen atmosphere inside the cabin.

Instantly engulfed by flames, the astronauts could not exit from the cabin because a gantry was blocking the escape system. Rescuers attempting to release them were driven back by dense smoke and flames.

The men were taking part in the *Apollo* programme for a manned Moon landing, and the disaster was a major setback for NASA's hopes of getting a man on the Moon by the end of the decade.

However, 1967 brought compensatory spectacular progress in the *Surveyor* programme of unpiloted Moon flights. Three US space vehicles were successfully landed on the surface of the Moon, sending back television pictures of the terrain that awaited the first Moonwalker.

▲ The *Apollo* space programme began tragically when astronauts Virgil Grissom, Edward White and Roger Chaffee died in a flash fire.

THE WRECK OF THE TORREY CANYON

▲ The broken wreck of the *Torrey Canyon* is battered against the rocks of the Seven Stones Reef off the coast of Land's End.

At Easter 1967, Cornwall was the site of the world's first major oil-tanker disaster.

On March 19, the tanker *Torrey Canyon*, carrying about 120,000 tons of crude oil, was attempting the difficult passage between Land's End and the Scilly Isles en route to the refinery at Milford Haven in south Wales.

Disaster struck when the tanker hit the Seven Stones reef and stuck fast, with a hole ripped in its hull. Oil began to flood out, carried by currents and the prevailing winds towards the Cornish coast, where it would pollute tourist beaches and destroy marine life.

The first response was to send Royal Naval vessels with thousands of gallons of detergent to spray on the oil slick. But within five days of the original accident, the crude oil had spread out to cover approximately 1,800 square km (700 square miles) of ocean and had begun to drift ashore. Worse was to follow, for the wave-battered vessel then began to break up, releasing even more of its liquid cargo.

The British government decided on the radical step of dropping incendiary bombs and napalm on the stricken tanker. The aim was to set fire to the oil remaining in the tanker's hold and burn it off.

To the humiliation of the air force commanders, in front of large crowds of Easter holiday-makers lining the Cornish cliffs – including Prime Minister Harold Wilson, who always holidayed in the Scillies – the bombers at first failed to hit their stationary target. The bombing was ultimately declared a success, but over 160 km (100 miles) of the Cornish coast had been polluted, requiring a massive clean-up operation.

The *Torrey Canyon* disaster gave fresh impetus to concerns about the environment that were mounting through the 1960s, and would lead to the creation of Friends of the Earth in 1970 and Greenpeace the following year.

ALI PUNISHED FOR VIETNAM PROTEST

On April 30, 1967, one of the greatest boxers in the history of the sport, Muhammad Ali, was stripped of his world heavyweight title by the US boxing associations because of his refusal to be conscripted to serve in the Vietnam War.

Under his original name of Cassius Clay, Ali had come to prominence as an amateur when he won a gold medal in the 1960 Rome Olympics.

Turning professional, he took the world heavyweight title in February 1964, defeating the formidable Sonny Liston. By that time, he had already become a disturbing figure for the boxing establishment. His frantic interview style and endless bragging – "I am the greatest" , his early catchphrase – earned him the nickname "the Louisville Lip".

But it was obvious that Ali was a boxer with an unprecedented blend of good looks, style and brains. His performances inside the ring were light-footed and arrogant. Outside it, he knew just how to keep his opponents off balance with his sharp wit and unpredictable aggression.

In the same year that he won the heavyweight title, he joined the Black Muslims and changed his name to Muhammad Ali, rejecting Cassius Clay as a "slave name". However, the US boxing authorities, who were willing to accept a boxer such as Liston,

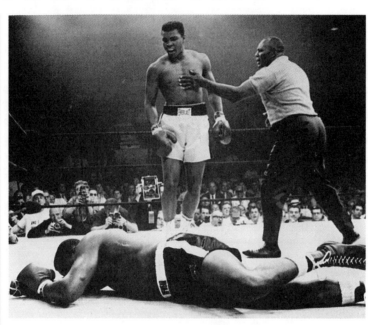

▲ **Muhammad Ali told the world "I am the greatest" – many of us still agree with him.**

with his prison record and known criminal connections, were horrified by the smart, outspoken black champion who had joined what was widely regarded as a subversive anti-US political organization. For years, officials refused to accept Ali's new name and stubbornly referred to the boxer as Clay.

In February 1966, the Louisville draft board, organizing conscription into the army for the Vietnam War, classed Ali as 1-A fit for induction. His lawyers fought a long battle to reverse this decision, but failed.

By April 1967, Ali had a choice – either to accept the draft, or to refuse and face prosecution. The

Black Muslims were wholly opposed to participation of any sort in the "white man's war". Ali's personal attitude was summed up in his famous phrase: "No Vietcong ever called me nigger". He refused to be inducted.

In June 1967, Ali was sentenced to five years in prison and a $10,000 for draft evasion. Once again, his lawyers tackled the case, taking their appeal to the Supreme Court, which eventually quashed the conviction in 1970.

Ali returned to the ring, still the greatest boxer in the world, and won back the heavyweight title twice to prove it.

'67 VICTORY IN SIX DAYS

After the Suez Crisis of 1956, peace prevailed between Israel and its Arab neighbours for more than a decade. But for both sides the situation was unsatisfactory. The Arabs refused to accept the permanent existence of a Jewish state in Palestine, while Israel longed to expand to more secure frontiers. Most dissatisfied of all were the Palestinian Arab refugees living around Israel's borders, who longed to return to what they considered their homeland.

In 1964, the Arab countries set up the Palestine Liberation Organization (PLO) to represent Palestinian Arabs. Egypt armed a PLO "liberation army" dedicated to the destruction of Israel. Syria backed another Palestinian guerrilla force, El Fatah, led by Yassir Arafat. By 1967, Palestinian guerrilla attacks had become a serious nuisance to the Israelis, who retaliated with punitive military strikes into Jordan and Syria.

Israeli and Egyptian forces were separated by the Sinai

▲ Following an awesome display of military strength, Egyptian prisoners of war are lined up by their Israeli captors in the Sinai Desert.

desert, where UN peacekeepers were stationed.

On May 16. 1967, Egyptian President Abdul Gamal Nasser sent his troops into the Sinai and ordered the UN peacekeeping force to leave. Six days later he announced he was closing the

Straits of Tiran to Israeli shipping. Nasser's actions were greeted with widespread popular enthusiasm throughout the Arab world. Jordan, Syria and Iraq hastily joined Egypt in a military alliance.

Israel also prepared for war. The aggressive General Moshe Dayan was brought into the government as defence minister. The Israeli armed forces were mobilized. Despite much heated rhetoric, it was unclear whether the Arab states would launch an all out attack on Israel. The Israelis did not wait to find out.

At dawn on June 5, the Israeli Air Force launched a series of pre-emptive strikes against the Egyptian Air Force, destroying more than 200 aircraft, mostly on the ground. Without air cover, the Egyptian ground forces in Gaza and Sinai were doomed. After four days of heavy fighting, Israeli tanks reached the east bank of the Suez Canal, having destroyed the bulk of the Egyptian army.

It was a similar story on Israel's eastern front. The

▲ During the six days of the conflict General Moshe Dayan's Israeli army all but wiped out the Egyptian military machine.

Jordanian and Syrian air forces were both eliminated on the first day of the war. The Jordanian army put up fierce resistance, but had been driven out of East Jerusalem and the West Bank by June 7, when a cease-fire was agreed. With Egypt and Jordan effectively defeated, on June 9 Israel turned its attention to Syria, seizing the strategically vital Golan Heights in a combined tank and infantry assault.

By the evening of June 10, the war was over. In six days, Israel, with a population of 2.5 million and armed forces totalling 275,000, had defeated Arab states with a combined population of over 40 million and armed forces numbering 395,000. The war had cost 689 Israeli lives; the Arab death toll was estimated at around 13,500.

Yet it proved impossible for the Israelis to turn this astonishing military triumph into a longterm political victory. President Nasser survived as ruler of Egypt and was soon receiving massive military aid from the Soviet Union, which also poured arms into Syria and Iraq.

Israel was forced to turn to the United States for a balancing supply of the latest military hardware. Within two years of the end of the Six-Day War, the Middle East was engaged in a furious arms race, with serious potential for super-power confrontation.

Even more important in the longterm was Israel's failure to legitimize its occupation of the West Bank, East Jerusalem and Gaza, with their large Palestinian Arab population. In 1969, Fatah leader Yasser Arafat became the head of the PLO. Israel was soon the target of a spectacular campaign of international terrorism, combined with intense political pressure to accept demands for a Palestinian homeland.

BIAFRA BREAKS AWAY

The Biafran tragedy had its roots in the ethnic diversity of Nigeria, a vast country with a population of around 50 million in the 1960s. The main ethnic groups were Muslim Hausa and Fulani in the north, Catholic Ibos in the east, and Anglican and Muslim Yorubas in the west. However, around half the population belonged to other smaller ethnic groups. The Muslim northern tribes and the Ibos had a deep-rooted antipathy.

The civilian regime established in Nigeria at independence in 1960 did not last long. In January 1966, Major-General Johnson Ironsi, an Ibo, took power after a military coup. A fear of Ibo domination sparked a violent response in the north, where thousands of innocent Ibos were massacred.

At the end of July, there was a second coup. This time, northern army officers seized power. As a result, General Ironsi was tortured and murdered.

After the second coup, General Yakubu Gowon, an officer from a minority Christian tribe, came to power. He tried to end the massacres in the north and to reassure the Ibos, but his efforts were in vain. Hundreds of thousands of Ibo civilians and soldiers fled to the Ibo heartland in the east in search of safety.

The military governor of Nigeria's Eastern Region was Colonel Chukwuemeka Ojukwu. He was an Ibo who came from a wealthy background and had been educated at Oxford.

Ojukwu refused to accept Gowon's plan to create a new 12-state federal structure in Nigeria. After several lengthy but futile negotiations, Ojukwu declared the Eastern Region independent as Biafra on May 30, 1967.

Ojukwu probably hoped for the support of multinational oil companies, since Nigeria's major oilfields were in Biafra. But Federal government forces soon conquered the oil-producing areas, as well as the Biafran capital, Enugu.

At the end of 1967, General Gowon announced that he expected a rapid victory. Instead, the world was to witness a tragedy in slow motion that made Biafra synonymous with mass starvation.

▲ **Heavily armed soldiers patrol Biafra during its bloody and tragic conflict with Nigeria.**

- Referendum on independence in French Somaliland; self-rule declined
- UN Secretary-General U Thant proposes peace plan for Vietnam war; US accepts but North Vietnam rejects

April
- Nationalists foment unrest and violence in Aden
- Border incidents between Syrian and Israeli troops
- New constitution adopted in South Vietnam
- Renewed fighting between Greek and Turkish communities in Cyprus
- Military coup in Athens led by Colonel Georgios Papadolous; civil government deposed

May
- Rioting in Hong Kong
- Britain, Ireland and Denmark apply to join the EEC
- De Gaulle makes statement against British entry to the EEC
- UN withdraws peacekeeping force from Sinai
- Egypt closes the Gulf of Aqaba to Israeli shipping; Israel and Arab nations begin mobilizing
- Igbo-dominated Eastern Region of Nigeria declares independence as Biafra, under Colonel Odumegwu Ojukwu; Nigerian government under General Yakubu Gowon refuses to recognize Biafra's secession
- Death of British poet John Masefield

June
- Six-Day War between Arab nations and Israel
- Egypt closes the Suez Canal and Arab states suspend oil supplies to Britain and USA
- USSR severs diplomatic relations with Israel
- China explodes hydrogen bomb
- British soldiers killed by Arabs in Aden
- Summit meeting between US President Johnson and Soviet Premier Kosygin

'67

By the mid-1960s, the Haight Ashbury district of San Francisco, California, had spawned a subculture of young drop-outs, dubbed "hippies". In 1967, media interest came close to transforming the hippie lifestyle and its vague ideology – the rejection of individualism and private property, belief in "peace and love", taking of hallucinogenic drugs, faith in the wisdom of the East – into a massive youth movement.

The tone of the year was set by the Be-In in Golden Gate Park, San Francisco, in January. This mass celebration of the cult of amorphous love was advertised as the "Gathering of the Tribes",

▲ **Thousands of young hippies flock to Speaker's Corner on London's Hyde Park to attend the "Legalize Pot" rally.**

▲ **The American cast of *Hair*, a rock musical that presented an unthreatening, watered-down version of hippie culture.**

although one jaundiced observer, Emmet Grogan, described it as "actually more a gathering of the suburbs". Thousands of middle-class US kids sat on the grass listening to Jefferson Airplane and smoking dope, chanting mantras and holding balloons bearing anti-war slogans.

Wide media coverage ensured that the event would be imitated, as was the first major open-air pop festival, held at Monterey in June. Britain soon had its own Love-In, in Hyde Park, and a pop festival, at Woburn in August.

That summer London tinkled with the sound of cow bells and the chant of Hare Krishna first made itself heard in Oxford Street. Cults flourished, from Transcendental Meditation to druidic earth-worship.

The underground magazines *IT* and *OZ* were sold on the streets, with their novel "psychedelic" imagery. Thousands of young people set off on the overland trail to India, establishing out-posts of hippiedom in Nepal, Goa and Afghanistan. The more business-minded made fortunes bringing back Indian fabrics or Afghan coats – the entrepreneurial spirit also flourished in the Summer of Love.

However, the vast majority of British people under 30 had not a whiff of marijuana, let alone a taste of an Acid tab. Most participated in the Summer of Love through media images, particularly of pop stars.

George Melley cynically described the whole pop world as "dressing like mad prophets, and talking about love and vibrations and flying saucers." With their long hair, droopy moustaches, granny glasses and experimentation with drugs, the Beatles were the world's most powerful advertisement for alternative style and culture. For the launch of their single "All You Need is Love" in June, they organized an international TV link-up in the hope of spreading the benign but woolly philosophy of their guru, the Mahirishi Mahesh Yogi.

In the United States, the issue of Vietnam gave the slogan "Make Love Not War" a real potency. Many young people in the US saw a crossover between radical politics and hippie lifestyles. They brought a fantastical new element to the anti-war movement in 1967.

Before the year's largest anti-war demonstration, the march on the Pentagon in October, Jerry Rubin and Abbie Hoffman, founders of the Yippie movement, told the media they intended to use magical powers to levitate the Pentagon building 90 metres (300 ft) into the air.

Owseley, known as the supplier of the world's best acid, announced he had invented Lace, a hippie alternative to the police's anti-riot weapon, Mace. Whereas Mace caused temporary blindness, Lace made you "want to take your clothes off, kiss people and make love".

It is not clear who was most annoyed by such fantasies – the authorities or the straight serious-minded leaders of the anti-war protest movement. But during the march on the Pentagon, a symbolic confrontation of lifestyles – the hippie ethos against corporate America – was certainly achieved. Photographed by the world's press, young girls put flowers in the barrels of soldiers' guns. When the media had turned their backs on the scene, the same young girls were clubbed by the US forces of order. The Pentagon did not rise off the ground, and the Vietnam War went on regardless.

The mass marketing of the Summer of Love inevitably diluted its message near to vanishing point. The record that represented the West Coast hippie scene to most of the world was not the Grateful Dead's first album, which flopped, but Scott Mackenzie's dreamy "If You're Going to San Francisco (Wear Some Flowers in Your Hair)".

The musical *Hair*, which opened off Broadway in October, was to show again how marketable an unthreatening version of the hippie vision could be.

▲ One of the slogans of the era may have been "Never trust anyone over thirty", but the hippie revolution appealed to some old-timers.

The mood of the Summer of Love had its aesthetic successes, such as Procul Harum's Bach-based "Whiter Shade of Pale", the work of Jim Morrison and the Doors, and the first emergence of psychedelic band Pink Floyd. But it was the Beatles, as usual, who seemed to express its quintessence in the experimental single "Strawberry Fields" (accompanied by arguably the first pop video) and the first concept album, *Sergeant Pepper's Lonely Hearts Club Band*, with its celebrated cover designed by Pop artist Peter Blake and his wife.

But the Summer of Love was also when the Beatles fairy story began to crack up. In August, while the Beatles were meditating with the Mahirishi in Wales, their manager, Brian Epstein, killed himself. At the end of the year, their Christmas TV film *Magical Mystery Tour* flopped.

Meanwhile, Haight Ashbury had turned into a crime-ridden tourist attraction. Young people wanting to drop out were now heading out of the city to rural communes where various forms of the simple life could be practised. One of these communes was inhabited by Acid-inspired prophet Charles Manson and his Family, whose murders in 1969 would throw a dark retrospective shadow over the subculture of peace and love.

▲ John Lennon, Paul McCartney and George Harrison with the Maharishi Mahesh Yogi, on whose left-hand side stands Mia Farrow.

'67

NEWS IN BRIEF

July
- Race riots in US cause extensive damage to inner cities of many major US cities
- Conflict between white mercenaries and army troops in Congo
- Civil war in Nigeria begins between Biafran troops and Nigerian government forces
- Communist round-up by government in Hong Kong; State of emergency declared in Hong Kong
- Homosexuality decriminalized in Britain
- Death of influential US jazz saxophonist John Coltrane

August
- Martin Luther King advocates campaign of civil disobedience by black Americans
- British embassy in Peking set on fire by Red Guards
- British troops begin withdrawal from Aden
- Belgium suspends aid to Congo Republic
- British playwright Joe Orton killed by his lover K L Halliwell, who commits suicide

THE POUND IN YOUR POCKET

On November 18, 1967, sterling was officially devalued by 14.3 per cent, falling from an exchange rate of $US2.80 to $US2.40. It was an overwhelming blow to the political prestige of Prime Minister Harold Wilson's Labour government, which had struggled to maintain sterling's value ever since taking office in October 1964.

In an effort to reassure the British public, Wilson told them in a television broadcast: "It does not mean, of course, that the pound here in Britain, in your pocket or purse or in your bank, has been devalued."

The Labour government had inherited a massive balance of payments crisis from its Conservative predecessors, Britain's exports being wholly inadequate to finance its imports. It was this endlessly debated "trade gap" that put downward pressure on sterling, officially held at the same level against the dollar since the aftermath of World War Two.

▲ Before Harold Wilson made his address to the British people, few had even heard of the term "devaluation".

In 1966, faced with around five per cent inflation and unemployment rising to almost half a million – regarded as crisis levels at the time – the government tried to impose a freeze on wages, prices and profits. The policy was intended, among other things, to lower imports by reducing spending power and boost exports by cutting costs. It had only a limited effect. Trade union leaders endorsed the policy, but shop stewards opposed every attempt to block wage rises and there was a rash of unofficial strikes.

Devaluation had always been an alternative policy advocated by some Labour politicians as the quickest and most painless way of making British goods more competitive abroad. But there was no disguising the fact that it had been resorted to under duress after pressure in the international markets had become irresistible.

BRITAIN WITHDRAWS FROM ADEN

By the mid-1960s, Britain had given independence to all but a few far-flung remnants of its empire. With a Labour government from 1964 keen to cut defence spending wherever possible, there was soon talk of withdrawing from all commitments "east of Suez". One of these was the port city of Aden and its hinterland, the South Arabian Federation.

In February 1966, the government announced that it intended to leave Aden in 1968.

The British garrison had been dealing with sporadic terrorist attacks in Aden since December 1963. The announcement of Britain's imminent departure inspired the two would-be liberation organizations, the Front for the Liberation of Occupied South Yemen (FLOSY) and the National Liberation Front (NLF), to new levels of activity. More than 500 terrorist attacks took place in 1966, increasing to almost 300 a month in 1967. As casualties rose, Britain decided to cut and run, advancing the date of withdrawal to November 1967.

Even then, it was difficult to manage the withdrawal with any degree of dignity or pride. By the summer, some areas of Aden, notably the city's Crater district, had become out of bounds for British forces. A mutiny by local police in June showed how far the disintegration of colonial control had gone. Honour was restored by the Argyll and Sutherland

Highlanders, under the idiosyncratic command of Lieutenant-Colonel Colin Mitchell – a man that the popular press nicknamed "Mad Mitch".

In early July, in a demonstration of extraordinary bravado, the Argylls retook Crater without suffering a single casualty.

By the autumn, FLOSY and the FLN were far more occupied with fighting one another over the future control of an independent South Yemen than they were with attacking the British. On November 29, the last of the British troops quit the colony in good order.

In the words of journalist Bernard Levin, "amid a skirl of pipes and a flurry of sand, Britain's troops left the Middle East, where so many of her sons had laid their bones, for ever."

▶ **Troops of the Argyll and Sutherland Highlanders were sent in to restore order in Aden in 1967.**

FIRST HEART TRANSPLANT

On December 3, 1967, at Groote Schuur hospital in Cape Town, South Africa, Dr Christiaan Barnard carried out what is generally accepted as the world's first successful heart transplant. The patient, Louis Washkansky, died less than three weeks later.

Washkansky, a 53-year-old grocer, had suffered a series of heart attacks and had only days to live when the Barnard and his a five-man surgical team offered him the chance of a transplant.

The heart came from a 25-year-old woman who had died in a car crash. The transplant operation was deemed a success because the implanted heart functioned successfully, if only for a short period of time.

Wahskanshky's condition soon began to deteriorate, apparently because the drugs he was given to prevent his body rejecting the new heart made him vulnerable to infection. He developed lung complications that finally killed him 18 days after the operation.

Dr Barnard went on to achieve what might more properly be considered the first successful heart transplant on January 2, 1968. The patient on that occasion, Philip Blaiberg, lived for a year and a half after the operation.

The development of heart transplants was one of a series of advances in the treatment of heart complaints in the 1960s. At the start of the decade, British doctors produced the first pacemaker. In 1966, Dr Michael E de Bakey, implanted an artificial heart pump in a patient who died five days later.

In 1967 the technique for heart by-pass operation was developed by Rene Favaloro in Cleveland, Ohio. In April 1969 the first total artificial plastic-and-metal heart was implanted in a patient at St Luke's Episcopal Hospital in Houston, Texas, in a failed effort to keep him alive until a human heart could be found for a transplant.

▲ **South Africa's pioneering surgeon, Professor Christian Barnard. Heart surgery is now a relatively standard medical practice.**

VIOLENT END FOR A MAN OF PEACE

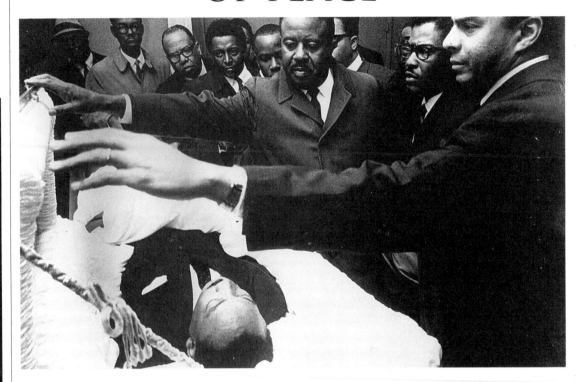

▲ **Prominent civil rights leaders stand alongside the body of the murdered Martin Luther King. An apostle of peaceful protest, his views had been increasingly at odds with a new generation of militant black nationalism.**

On April 4, 1968, Civil Rights campaigner Martin Luther King Jr stepped out on to the balcony outside his room at the Lorraine Motel, Memphis, Tennessee, for a breath of fresh air before dinner. As he leaned over the balcony rail to talk to one of his associates, Reverend Jesse Jackson, standing below, King was hit by a shot fired from a high-powered rifle. He was rushed to St Joseph's Hospital, but died without regaining consciousness.

Born in 1929, King was a Baptist minister in Montgomery, Alabama, when he first came to prominence as a campaigner against racial segregation. As leader of the Southern Christian Leadership Conference from 1957, his fearless campaign of non-violent civil disobedience drew the attention of the world to the brutality of white racism in the United States. More than any other single individual, he was responsible for securing progress on civil rights in the first half of the 1960s.

By 1968, however, King was looking for a new role. Younger, more aggressive black spokesmen were grabbing public attention, articulating the mood of violence and despair that had exploded in riots in the ghettos of US cities every summer since 1964.

King wanted to put his non-violent campaign back at the centre of the political stage. He recognized that many people felt civil rights made no difference to their lives, since their real problems were low incomes, poor housing, and lack of basic facilities.

King's answer was to launch the "Poor People's Campaign". This was to be a movement on behalf of all the economically disadvantaged – not only African Americans, but also poor whites, Hispanics and Native Americans. King planned a Poor People's March on Washington for April 1968. The marchers would establish a camp in the capital called Resurrection City, and would stay there until their demands for a federal programme to end poverty were met.

King came to Memphis as part of his efforts to get his new campaign off the ground. The city's garbage workers – mostly black – had been on strike for two months. By being seen to support their demands for better pay and conditions, he would be able to demonstrate his new concern for the practical problems of the poor.

On April 3, on the eve of the assassination, speaking at the Memphis Masonic Temple, King seemed to hint that he might not live long: "Like anybody, I would like to live a long life. Longevity has its place. But I'm not concerned about that now. I just want to do God's will. And he's allowed me to go to the mountain. And I've looked over. And I've seen the promised land. I may not get there with you."

The death of the apostle of non-violence triggered the most destructive wave of civil disturbances in US history. As news of the assassination spread, blacks took to the streets across the country, looting shops and setting fire to cars and buildings. More than 100 cities were affected, including Baltimore, New York, Boston, Chicago, Detroit, and Washington DC.

Troops were deployed to protect the White House as rioters took over the capital's city centre

and burned parts of it to the ground. It took 21,000 federal troops and 34,000 National Guardsmen to restore order. In their wake, the riots left 46 people dead and more than 3,000 injured.

Meanwhile, the police attributed the assassination to a lone gunman, James Earl Ray, who had been staying at a boarding house in sight of the Lorraine Motel. Ray was eventually arrested at Heathrow airport, London, in June. He was returned to the United States, pleaded guilty to the killing and was sentenced to life imprisonment. Ray later protested his innocence. Just before his death in 1998, he told a television interviewer: "I was not the trigger man. I didn't know anything about the killing."

King's widow, Coretta Scott King, continues to campaign for an investigation to reveal her husband's real killer.

▲ It was a day that she had feared and that he had prophesied – Mrs Martin Luther King mourns the tragic death of her husband.

"RIVERS OF BLOOD"

In 1968, race and immigration were key issues on the British political agenda. The Labour government had introduced a Race Relations Act to outlaw racial discrimination in employment and housing. On the other hand, in February 1968, Home Secretary James Callaghan rushed a new Immigration Act through parliament removing the right for

Commonwealth citizens with British passports to enter Britain. The act was a panic response to an influx of Kenyan Asians, who were being driven out of East Africa by the racist policies of the Kenyan government.

All British political parties, apart from the small newly-formed National Front, were officially committed to racial harmony. But on

April 20, 1968, Enoch Powell, a member of the Conservative shadow cabinet, made an extremist attack on the concept of a peaceful multiracial Britain.

Speaking in Birmingham, he expressed a vision of future racial conflict, using the sort of classical reference that came more naturally to him than to his audience: "As I look ahead I am filled with foreboding. Like the Roman I seem to see 'the river Tiber foaming with much blood'"

Simplified by headline writers as "rivers of blood", the speech caused a political sensation. Powell was sacked from the shadow cabinet by Tory leader Edward Heath. However demonstrations by groups of workers, including dockers and Smithfields' meat porters, supported his views. Furthermore, an opinion poll showed that as many as 75 per cent of the population broadly agreed with his views.

▲ Enoch Powell makes his notorious "Rivers of Blood" speech that would cast him into Britain's political wilderness.

'68

In 1968, student riots, sit-ins, demonstrations and protest movements occurred across the world – in France, West Germany and Italy, Northern Ireland, Poland and Czechoslovakia, the United States, Mexico, and Japan. Together they were an explosive expression of the anti-authoritarianism and idealism of Sixties youth.

Because of the massive expansion of universities in the 1960s, students were a far less privileged group than they had been in the past. Only a small minority of students were heavily politicized, bent on world revolution – Trotskyist, Maoist, or "New Left". However, much larger numbers were at least vaguely critical of Western society, regarding it as oppressive, racist, and militaristic. The ideas of thinkers, such as Herbert Marcuse and Wilhelm Reich, with their critique of the repression of desire in a consumer society, influenced far more people than ever read their books. Furthermore, protests against the Vietnam War mobilized large numbers of otherwise apathetic students.

The most sensational events occurred in France. On the night of May 10–11, 1968, French riot police battled with student demonstrators in the Latin Quarter of Paris, storming hastily improvised barricades thrown up in the narrow streets.

The brutality displayed by the police won the students massive popular support. On May 13, a million people demonstrated in favour of the students in Paris, and the following day the Sorbonne was occupied.

Over the subsequent days, a spontaneous wave of revolt swept France. Not only was almost every university and secondary school occupied by students or pupils, but workers took over their workplaces. Workers occupied factories, bank clerks took over banks, librarians occupied libraries. By May 22, 10 million workers were on strike. Food and fuel supplies broke down.

▲ **Students and police clash in the streets of Paris during the May demonstrations of 1968.**

The government of Charles de Gaulle seemed powerless, but neither students nor workers had any serious plans for taking control of France. Inspiring slogans such as "All power to the imagination" and "Be realistic: demand the impossible" captured the Utopian mood of the moment. But in the real world, they led nowhere. De Gaulle did a deal with the Communist trade unions to buy the workers off with hefty pay rises, then called a snap general election, which his party easily won. By mid-June, the students had drifted off for their summer holidays.

Nowhere else in the world did student revolt have as wide an impact. In West Germany, the attempted assassination of student leader Rudi Dutschke by a right-wing extremist on April 12, sparked off widespread rioting, in which two people died. Frankfurt University was occupied and temporarily renamed "Karl Marx University". But the German students lacked popular support.

In Mexico, students rioted during the Olympic Games, held there in October.

In the United States, the student occupation of Columbia University, New York, in April was repressed by the police with extreme brutality. But most of the energies of US students were focused on the anti-Vietnam War movement.

Britain managed only a pale reflection of these dramatic events. Both Essex University and Hornsey College of Art were briefly occupied by students in 1968, but this was hardly a revolutionary threat to society.

Most young Sixties Britons, like their Victorian ancestors, regarded acts of revolt as events that rightly happened abroad.

SECOND TRAGEDY HITS KENNEDY FAMILY

In March 1968, President Lyndon B Johnson announced he would not be seeking nomination as Democratic candidate in the November presidential elections. As soon as Johnson withdrew, New York Senator Robert Kennedy, younger brother of the late JFK, put himself forward as a candidate. His intention, he declared, was to bring a speedy end to the Vietnam War.

Kennedy's candidature annoyed supporters of Senator Eugene McCarthy, who, up until

▲ Four years after the death of President Kennedy, tragedy once again hits one of America's most prominent families.

that time, had made the running as an anti-war candidate against Johnson. However, Kennedy won the support of many Democrats who wanted a leader with an idealistic commitment to peace and to the cause of underprivileged minorities.

On June 5, Kennedy won the vital California Democratic primary, easily defeating McCarthy. Late in the evening, he made a triumphant speech to campaign workers in the ballroom of the Ambassadors Hotel in Los Angeles. He then left for a press conference, taking a short cut through a kitchen. There a Palestinian immigrant, Sirhan Sirhan, shot him five times with a handgun. Kennedy died in hospital in the early hours of June 6.

The assassination of Robert Kennedy, following so soon after the killing of Martin Luther King, and only four years after the death of his brother Jack, understandably fuelled suspicions of a conspiracy.

▲ Bobby Kennedy's popularity was based on an anti-Vietnam ticket. But he was not popular with all Democrats.

Sirhan Sirhan's motive seems clear, however. He had been outraged by Kennedy's outspoken backing for Israel in the Middle East conflict, and shot him on the first anniversary of the Six-Day War.

AROUND THE WORLD IN 354 DAYS

On July 4, 1968, a 59-year-old greengrocer from Portsmouth, Alec Rose, completed a 45,860-km (28,500-mile) solo voyage around the world in his small yacht *Lively Lady*. A crowd of around 250,000 people gave him a tumultuous welcome back to his home town, from which he had set out 354 days earlier.

Rose's feat followed the success of another British lone yachtsman, 65-year-old Francis Chichester, in 1967. Chichester

▲ Sir Alec Rose receives a heroes welcome in Portsmouth Harbour after the successful completion of his epic voyage.

had also completed a solo round-the-world voyage, on board his yacht *Gipsy Moth IV*, setting out from and returning to the port of Plymouth via Sydney.

Chichester was knighted after his return in a public ceremony at Greenwich; Alec Rose also received a knighthood.

The two men were a focus of great patriotic enthusiasm, reflecting a feeling at the time that Britain still had much to offer to the world in terms of endeavour and invention.

'68

TURNING POINT IN VIETNAM

At the start of 1968 there were almost half a million US military personnel in Vietnam. Some 16,000 US troops had already died in the fight to hold the line against Communism. Yet US military and political leaders could see no prospect of a successful end to the war, which was damaging the country's finances and its international prestige.

Before resigning in the autumn of 1967, Defence Secretary Robert McNamara admitted to President Lyndon B Johnson: "The picture of the world's greatest superpower ... trying to pound a tiny backward nation into submission on an issue whose merits are hotly disputed, is not a pretty one." Such doubts about the war were shared by increasing numbers of US citizens.

The North Vietnamese Communist leadership, always acutely aware of the psychological and political aspects of warfare, felt the moment was

▲ **The average age of US troops in Vietnam was 19 – even Republicans wanted "to bring our boys home".**

ripe for a decisive blow that might crack the American will to fight.

On January 21, 1968, North Vietnamese troops infiltrated the South and laid siege to the US firebase at Khe Sanh, awakening US fears of a military catastrophe of the kind inflicted on the French at Dien Bien Phu in 1954. But for the Communists, the siege of Khe Sanh was primarily a diversionary move. The main blow was to fall on South Vietnam's towns and cities.

The major offensive was set for the night of January 31, during the Tet holiday, when the South

Vietnamese would be most off their guard.

Viet Cong guerrillas and North Vietnamese troops launched simultaneous attacks on over 100 urban areas throughout South Vietnam. Militarily, the Tet Offensive was a disaster for the Communists. They could not hold any of the towns or cities they occupied. The last to be recaptured was Hue, retaken by US Marines three weeks after Tet. Communist losses in the urban fighting were heavy – perhaps as many as 30,000 dead.

But the Tet Offensive was a political triumph. The shock to US opinion was profound. In Saigon, guerrillas briefly occupied part of the US embassy. American journalists asked why, after three years of large-scale military involvement, their troops were fighting in their own embassy compound. The towns and cities were recaptured at the cost of massive damage inflicted on local people and their property. A US officer famously said of a town in the Mekong delta: "We had to destroy it to save it."

Journalists questioned whether it made sense to claim to be defending South Vietnam when US forces spent most of their time bombing and napalming its people.

The US media have been accused of "snatching defeat from the jaws of victory" in Vietnam through their excessively pessimistic descriptions of the situation there in 1968. But the "credibility gap" between journalists and the military had become unbridgeable because endless upbeat briefings from army press officers had simply not been matched by the real events.

▲ **As the Viet Cong continued to advance the war spread to the towns and cities of South Vietnam.**

The Johnson administration had also lost faith in its military commanders. As the battle for Khe Sanh still raged – the siege was finally lifted at the beginning of April – General William C Westmoreland asked for another 200,000 troops and permission to launch offensives across the border into Cambodia and Laos.

Johnson asked his new defense secretary, Clark Clifford, to look into the chances of success if this escalation of the war was authorized. Clifford reported that the generals had no convincing plan for winning the war: "All that can be said is that additional troops would allow us to kill more of the enemy …" Westmoreland would never get his extra troops.

On March 31, Johnson announced that bombing raids on North Vietnam were to be scaled down in an attempt to induce the Communists to take part in peace talks. In effect, he was publicly accepting that the United States could not win the war.

In June, Westmoreland was replaced as US commander in Vietnam by General Creighton Abrams. The new commander's aim was to achieve "Vietnamization". The South Vietnamese army was to be turned into an efficient fighting force capable of defending its own country without the involvement of US troops. This was a longterm policy, however.

Throughout 1968 the US continued to bear the brunt of fighting. In terms of casualties, it was their worst year of the entire conflict – 14,592 US servicemen were killed in action, and more than 80,000 wounded.

Such losses were totally unacceptable to almost the entire US public. They wanted the sacrifice of US troops to stop. Even the

▲ By 1968 the US government made the tacit admission that they could not win in Vietnam.

Republican candidate in the 1968 presidential elections, lifelong anti-Communist hardliner Richard M Nixon, committed himself to "bringing the boys back home". But in all other ways, America was bitterly divided over the war.

Opinions ranged from student radicals who identified with the Viet Cong in their struggle against "American imperialism" to gung-ho Cold War warriors who were in favour of "nuking" North Vietnam.

The most dramatic confrontation between anti-war protesters and the authorities came in August at the Democratic party convention in Chicago. When about 10,000 anti-war protesters turned up outside the convention to support anti-war candidate Senator Eugene McCarthy, Chicago Mayor Richard Daley unleashed his police force.

In what was described as a "police riot" on the eve of August 25, the forces of order clubbed demonstrators and passers-by in a display of indiscriminate brutality. Johnson's vice-president, Hubert Humphrey, was chosen as Democratic candidate and duly lost to Nixon in November.

By the time the elections were held, US bombing of North Vietnam had been halted completely. In January 1969, peace talks between the US, South Vietnam, North Vietnam, and the South Vietnamese Communists opened in Paris. Peace, however, was still many years away.

▲ Cowboys in a strange land – the world's most powerful military force was unable to operate effectively against the guerrilla tactics of the Viet Cong.

'68

NEWS IN BRIEF
....

July
- Treaty of Non-Proliferation of Nuclear Weapons signed by 61 countries
- Biafra refuses food aid from Britain because Britain is selling arms to Nigeria
- Couve de Murville becomes French Prime Minister
- Warsaw Pact countries declare Czechoslovak political reforms unacceptable; Czech leader Alexander Dubcek refuses to compromise

August
- Israeli airforce bombs suspected Palestinian terrorist bases in Jordan
- Basque separatist terrorists kill police chief in Spain
- Nigeria refuses to allow Red Cross access to Biafra
- Soviet forces invade Czechoslovakia; Dubcek and other Czech leaders arrested and taken to Moscow; Dubcek is later released
- France explodes hydrogen bomb
- Anti-Vietnam war demonstrations at the Democratic Party convention in US in which Hubert Humphrey selected as Democrat presidential candidate
- Thousands die in earthquakes in Iran

PRAGUE SPRING TURNS TO WINTER

In March 1968, Alexander Dubcek, first secretary of the Czech Communist Party, announced a programme of wholesale reforms designed to create "socialism with a human face". Czechoslovakia had been a hardline Communist state since 1948. Dubcek abolished censorship, freed political prisoners and legalized non-Communist political groups. His reforms ushered in the "Prague Spring" – a time of intense political debate, popular enthusiasm and cultural inventiveness, in which students played a leading part.

Dubcek appealed to the Soviet Union to accept that these changes were not a threat to the Communist system or to the unity of the Soviet-led Warsaw Pact, to which Czechoslovakia belonged. However, the conservative bureaucrats of the Kremlin were not impressed. In the first week of August, Dubcek held a tense meeting with Soviet leader Leonid Brezhnev in Bratislava. A deal seemed to be struck, setting some limits to Czech liberaliza-

▲ **Finding the reforms of the Prague Spring unacceptable, the Soviet Union crushed the Dubcek regime.**

tion, but accepting most of the reforms. Brezhnev and Dubcek embraced, wreathed in smiles, in front of the world's press.

Less than three weeks later, on the night of August 20–21, Soviet and other Warsaw Pact forces invaded Czechoslovakia. The Czech army obeyed orders not to resist, but angry crowds swarmed on to the streets of Prague to demonstrate their hostility to the

Soviet invaders. While they jeered the Soviet tanks, however, Dubcek was surreptitiously whisked off to Moscow, where he was forced to agree to cancel all reforms and accept a Soviet army of occupation.

From that time on until the collapse of Soviet Communism in the late 1980s, Czechoslovakia remained one of the most repressive states in the Soviet bloc.

GETTING HIGH

By 1968, drugs were one of the biggest political and social issues in the Western world. When the decade began, the recreational drugs scene was dominated by fall-out from the pharmaceutical industry, which was flooding Western society with barbiturates and amphetamines. These were the drugs of choice for Mods on Brighton beach, or Andy Warhol's entourage in his New York Factory.

But by the mid-1960s fashion was shifting to marijuana and a variety of hallucinogens, including mescalin and LSD (lysergic acid diethylamide or – more succinctly – Acid). There was nothing new about any of these substances – even LSD had been synthesized before World War Two. But in the 1960s these drugs began to be promoted by a small number of intellectuals as the key to a spiritual and social revolution.

Two contrasting gurus of hallucinogenic experience were Harvard psychology lecturer Timothy Leary and novelist Ken Kesey. Leary published an article in 1963 saying that mass-produced hallucinogens would open the eyes of Western society to the spiritual essence of life and the meaninglessness of materialism. When Harvard sacked him, Leary became a public campaigner for the Acid experience, founding the "League for Spiritual Discovery" and holding an "Acid Mass" in New York.

Ken Kesey, author of the subversive novel *One Flew Over the Cuckoo's Nest,* took a less reverential view. He drove a Day-Glo painted "magic bus" across the United States in 1964 to advertise the psychedelic experience. He also arranged "Trips Festivals" in California with the aid of the Grateful Dead and their sound-engineer-cum-alternative-chemist Owsley. Kesey's "Pranksters" seem to have been the first to associate the Acid experience with light shows, very loud music and crazy dancing.

Through the second half of the 1960s, the use of marijuana and hallucinogens spread from a small minority of hippies, alternative artists and "turned-on" students to wider circles of youth, especially in North America.

The drugs remained at least vaguely associated with "peace and love", although they were also the cheapest and most effective way of getting high available at the time.

Until the mid-1960s, laws against marijuana were not strictly administered and LSD was not illegal. But as use of the drugs increased and became identified with a revolt against authority and the work ethic, official paranoia set in.

In Britain, personalities as unlikely as future Tory minister Norman St John Stevas and broadcaster David Dimbleby publicly supported the decriminalization of marijuana in 1967. In the same year, the sentencing of Rolling Stones Mick Jagger and Keith Richards for possession was condemned even by *The Times*. But the harshness of drugs legislation and the enthusiasm with which police pursued drugs offenders grew relentlessly.

Leary was eventually given a 10-year prison sentence on a marijuana-related charge in 1970, after years of police harassment.

▲ **Calls for the decriminalization of marijuana have persisted since the 1960s. It's use now constitutes a relatively minor offence.**

"TRICKY DICKY" ELECTED

In November 1968, Republican Richard Milhous Nixon was elected President of the United States, scoring a narrow victory over the Democratic candidate, Vice-President Hubert Humphrey.

It was a remarkable political comeback for Nixon. As Vice-President from 1952, he lost to John F Kennedy in the 1960 presidential race. Two years later, he was also beaten when he stood for governor of California, and seemed to write off any further political career, telling journalists bitterly: "You won't have Nixon to kick around any more".

Nixon's victory owed much to dissensions and difficulties in the Democratic ranks. The decision of President Johnson not to stand for a second term had opened up a struggle for the Democratic nomination, marked by furious

▲ **A split in the Democrat ranks brought Richard Nixon to the White House. His period in office would be a memorable one.**

in-fighting, especially over the Vietnam War.

The assassination of Robert Kennedy in June took away the party's most convincing anti-war leader. The defeat of the other anti-war candidate, Senator Eugene McCarthy, at the riot-torn Democratic convention in Chicago in August, alienated many party activists.

Nixon's election marked a distinct swing to the right in US politics. Student protests, drug-taking and riots in black ghettos had convinced many Middle Americans that it was time for a call to order.

The United States was already deeply divided; under the Nixon presidency, the confrontation between the advocates of change and the guardians of order was to be pushed to new extremes.

BIAFRA STARVES

The Biafran tragedy began with an Ibo rebellion in Nigeria's Eastern Region in May 1967. Colonel Chukwuemeka Ojukwu, the local military governor, declared the oil-rich region the independent state of Biafra. Ojukwu's forces were soon driven back by Nigerian Federal government troops, and by May 1968 independent Biafra had shrunk to a landlocked rump entirely surrounded by Federal forces.

If the Federal side had been able to carry on to a swift victory, much suffering would have been avoided. But they were incapable of delivering a decisive blow. While Federal bombers carried out rather ineffectual raids on Biafran territory and troops engaged mostly in desultory skirmishes, the Biafrans organized a brilliant propaganda offensive.

Colonel Ojukwu engaged a public relations firm, Markpress of Geneva, to present his cause to the world. At first Markpress played the religious card, representing the Biafrans as good Catholics besieged by Muslim hoards. This went down well in the United States, but the effect was spoiled once the Federal government managed to make it clear to world opinion that many on its side, including the Nigerian leader General Yakubu Gowon himself, were also Christians.

Markpress then turned to a humanitarian appeal against "genocide by starvation". Isolated and crowded with refugees, Biafra was undoubtedly threatened by famine. Pictures of starving children circulated by the public relations firm provoked indignation around the world.

In August 1968, foreign aid agencies began to airlift emergency food supplies into Biafra. At the same time, the French government decided to back Biafra, and French arms began to flow into the country, airlifted from francophone Gabon and the Ivory Coast.

Biafran military resistance was also stiffened by the arrival of European mercenaries, mostly

▲ **The hapless victims of war, tens of thousands of Biafrans starved to death as their leaders fought on regardless.**

under the nominal command of Colonel Rolf Steiner.

Nigeria's main backers were the unlikely pairing of Britain and the Soviet Union. The British government refused to be deflected by mounting protests against the starvation in Biafra. Britain still counted on a swift Federal victory to solve the crisis. But in September 1968, with Biafra reduced to an area about 100 km (60 miles) long and 50 km (30 miles) wide, Steiner's mercenaries counter-attacked to such an extent that the Federal troops were driven back in disarray.

Unable to conquer Biafra, Nigeria settled for bombing and blockade. As the conflict dragged on through 1969, both tactics led to worldwide criticism. Most indignation was stirred up by the blocking of emergency food.

General Gowon argued that food relief was being used to mask airlifts of arms. When an attempt to reach an agreement between the federal government and Biafra on a method for ensuring food supplies failed, each side accused the other of bad faith. Throughout the year, thousands of Biafrans died every week. It was a nightmare scenario of civil war, mass starvation and political cynicism on all sides, that was to be witnessed again in Sudan, Ethiopia and Somalia in the following decades.

CONCORDE GETS OFF THE GROUND

On March 2, 1969, the Anglo-French supersonic airliner *Concorde* made its maiden flight in Toulouse, France.

The British prototype, *Concorde 002*, followed with its maiden flight a month later. The idea for the air-

liner had first been floated in 1960. In November 1962, Britain and France had agreed to split the development costs, initially calculated at almost £200 million. By 1969, the estimated cost had risen to four times that figure.

The British and French governments claimed that they hoped to sell 400 *Concordes* at £10 million a piece when the aircraft came into service in 1974. But even while the maiden flights took place, severe doubts were being

voiced about the aircraft's commercial viability.

Concorde was said to be too noisy to satisfy US environmental regulations and felt to carry too small a payload to be commercially effective.

Meanwhile, in February 1969, Boeing flew the first 747 jumbo jet. Once again, Britain had displayed its technological brilliance, but it was the United States that had had the commercial acumen to back the right project.

▲ **Two great symbols of British achievement: *Concorde* is seen flying above Nelson's Column in the centre of London.**

DEATH OF A ROLLING STONE

On the night of July 2–3, 1969, former Rolling Stone Brian Jones took a midnight dip in his swimming pool at his home Cotchford Farm in Hartfield, Sussex. In the early hours of the morning his body was found floating in the pool. A doctor pronounced him dead at 3 a.m. A coroner's court subsequently attributed his death to alcohol and drugs.

Jones had quit the Rolling Stones the previous June, saying: "I no longer see eye-to-eye with the others over the discs we are cutting." The Stones had hurriedly found a replacement, Mick Taylor, in time for a free open-air concert in Hyde Park scheduled for Saturday July 5. Reluctant to abandon the concert in the wake of Jones's death, Stones lead singer Mick Jagger decided to turn it into a tribute to his memory.

An estimated 250,000 fans turned up for the event. Jagger opened with a reading from Shelley's *Adonis*, accompanied by

the release of a cloud of white butterflies. The 75-minute act that followed has become a rock music classic, largely because it was filmed for a Granada television documentary.

The occasion was anything but a display of pure peace and love. Hell's Angels provided heavy security and groups of skinheads roamed the periphery of the crowd looking for stray hippies to prey on. This atmosphere of edginess suited the Stones' image well enough, however, with a repertoire of numbers that included "Sympathy for the Devil" and "Street Fighting Man".

▲ **The original leader of the Stones, Brian Jones had been overshadowed by the emerging talents of Mick Jagger and guitarist Keith Richards.**

MAN ON THE MOON

The moment when US astronaut Neil Armstrong stepped on to the surface of the Moon was an event in human history to which no correct date can be assigned. For people in the eastern United States, it happened on the evening of July 20, 1969, for Britons it happened in the early hours of the July 21, but what date was it on the Moon?

The *Apollo 11* mission had blasted off from launch complex 39A at Cape Kennedy (the name by which Cape Canaveral was known from 1963 to 1973) at 9.37 a.m. local time on July 16. Aboard were mission commander Armstrong, lunar module pilot Edwin "Buzz" Aldrin, and command module pilot Michael Collins. The flight to Moon orbit took three days and was completely uneventful.

For the Moon-landing, Armstrong and Aldrin moved into the lunar module, dubbed *Eagle*, which undocked from the command module for the computer-controlled descent to the Sea of Tranquillity. About 90 metres (300 ft) above the Moon surface, the astronauts realized they were heading towards a boulder-strewn crater and took over from the computer to guide the module to a flatter area. Armstrong described the final seconds as nerve-racking, because stirred up lunar dust obscured his view of the ground. He later said: "It's quite important not to stub your toe during the final phases of touchdown."

The first word spoken on the surface of the Moon was "Houston", as Armstrong

▲ *Saturn V* **awaits blast off to the Moon on the launchpad 39A at Cape Kennedy on July 16, 1969.**

announced the successful landing to the control centre in Texas: "Houston. Tranquillity base here. The Eagle has landed."

It took six hours of rest and preparation before Armstrong was ready to climb out of the module. The US was aware of the importance of this moment being seen on television, so they had arranged for a camera to film Armstrong climbing down to the Moon surface. He was supposed to say: "That's one small step for a man, one giant leap for mankind." However, in the excitement of the moment he fluffed his line, leaving out the

"a" in front of "man" and thus rendering the sentence meaningless – although no one seemed to notice.

Later joined by Aldrin, Armstrong spent two and a half hours walking in Moon dust. Looking like two overgrown babies in romper suits playing in a sandpit, the astronauts collected rock samples and set up experiments, such as installing a seismograph to measure moonquakes and a laser reflector to allow an exact measurement of the distance from the earth to the Moon. Armstrong took photos of

▲ *Apollo 11* **mission commander, Neil Armstrong leaves a his mark on the soft lunar surface.**

Aldrin, as would any tourist who had just arrived somewhere new and interesting. The fun was briefly interrupted by a phone call from President Nixon in the White House. To mark the spot where the landing took place, the astronauts left a plaque expressing the noble sentiment, "We came in peace for all mankind". But so that mankind did not forget exactly who had come in peace, they also planted the Stars and Stripes.

After 22 hours on the Moon surface, the lunar module took off to rendezvous with the command module, which was still in lunar orbit. An uneventful return journey led to a splashdown in the Pacific off Hawaii. The mission had lasted exactly 8 days, 3 hours and 18 minutes, while the splashdown was just 10 seconds behind schedule.

Fears had been expressed before the moonflight that the astronauts might inadvertently bring back Moon viruses or bacteria that could decimate the population of the Earth, which would have no natural resistance to such alien infections. As a precaution the astronauts were transferred directly to a Mobile Quarantine Facility – a large sealed container – in which they were transported to Houston. They were not released until August 10, when exhaustive tests had failed to identify the presence of any alien organisms.

▲ **President Nixon congratulates the three crew members of the *Apollo 11* mission, who were quarantined on their return to Earth.**

There followed the traditional tickertape parade in New York and a whistlestop tour of 25 countries in 35 days.

Before the *Apollo 11* launch, President Nixon had said that the mission would have "profound meaning for generations to come". But precisely what meaning was not clear.

In September 1969 the rocks brought back by the *Apollo 11* astronauts went on show at the Smithsonian Institution in Washington D.C. Public interest was intense and thousands queued up to get a close-up view of a chunk of the Moon.

It is fair to say that many found the sight disappointing. No one denied that the Moon landing had been a technological triumph, but it was somewhat disconcerting that all it had produced was a collection of rocks and some dust.

The moonwalk, watched by an estimated 600 million people, was undoubtedly the greatest television event that had ever occurred worldwide. The mere fact that direct pictures could be relayed from the Moon was startling evidence of the pace of technological progress, only seven years after the first live transmission across the Atlantic.

When the second manned moonlanding was made the following November, the television camera broke down and the unfortunate astronauts, Charles Conrad and Alan Bean, became invisible men, forgotten by both the public and by history.

In truth, by the time it took place the first manned moonshot was already a little anachronistic. With its mix of hopeful idealism, aggressive nationalism, macho endeavour, and technological optimism, it really belonged to the Kennedy years, rather than to the doubt-ridden late Sixties. It is not surprising that the *Apollo* programme was abandoned only three years later.

Even though in a sense it was pointless and wasteful, the landing of a man on the Moon was also the wondrous fulfillment of a long-nourished science-fiction fantasy that captured the imagination of the world.

◀ **"That's one small step for [a] man, one giant leap for mankind": Buzz Aldrin follows Armstrong onto the surface of the Moon.**

'69

NEWS IN BRIEF
. . . .

March
- Border clashes between USSR and China
- British gangsters the Kray brothers sentenced to life imprisonment
- British troops re-establish legal government in British dependant Caribbean island of Anguilla
- Military coup in Pakistan; General Yahya Khan takes power
- Anti-Soviet demonstrations in Prague

April
- Peace in the Middle East summit opens in New York
- Arab terrorists attack Israel; Israel makes reprisal air raids on Jordan
- Alexander Dubcek demoted from position of First secretary of the Czechoslovak Communist Party to President of the Federal Assembly
- Post offices bombed by Republican terrorists in Ireland
- Nigerian troops capture capital of breakaway state of Biafra
- French President Charles de Gaulle resigns; Alain Poher succeeds
- Death of Bolivian President Rene Barrientos in helicopter accident

THE MANSON MURDERS

Towards the end of the 1960s, thousands of dropout US hippies were deserting city districts such as San Francisco's Haight Ashbury to search for the natural life in the open country. They established rural communes, where nudity, sexual experimentation, dope-smoking, and tripping on Acid were the norm.

One such commune, apparently much like the others, was set up by Charles Manson and his "Family" in the desert outside Los Angles.

Manson was a disturbed individual who had spent most of his life in various forms of correctional institution. He had drifted into the Haight Ashbury scene in 1967

▲ The hapless victim of a random murder Sharon Tate happened to be in the wrong place at the wrong time.

and gathered around him a following of young middle-class dropouts, mostly female. Uprooted from their social background and spaced out on drugs, they found Manson irresistibly charismatic. Succumbing to an almost hypnotic fascination, they followed him out into the desert to pursue a savage alternative life of Acid trips and orgies.

Basing himself on a drug-inspired interpretation of the Beatles track "Helter Skelter" and on a reading of Revelations – every madman's favourite book of the Bible – Manson convinced himself that a race war was imminent. He believed that blacks and whites would ultimately destroy one another, drowning the society of the United States in a tide of blood. Manson set out to trigger this apocalypse, which he saw as wholly desirable, by ordering his Family to carry out a massacre of privileged Whites.

On August 9, 1969, he led four of his young followers into Beverley Hills and sent them on their mission. In two nights of mayhem they killed eight people. First they hacked to death movie actress Sharon Tate, wife of the director Roman Polanski and eight months pregnant. They also killed three of her house guests and a

▲ The charismatic Charles Manson claimed that the Beatles' *White Album* had influenced his killing spree.

passer-by. Before leaving, they scrawled abuse of the "pigs" on the walls in blood.

The following night, the group butchered Leno and Rosemary Bianca, wealthy supermarket owners who lived nearby.

In December, Manson and three members of the Family, Susan Atkins, Leslie Van Houten and Patricia Krewnwinkel, were arrested and charged with the murders. Their trial caused a sensation. Defiant and unrepentant, all the defendants were found guilty in March 1971.

The killings were seized upon by conservatives as a chance to discredit the hippie ethos of tribalism, rock, drugs, mysticism, and vague revolutionary aspirations.

WOODSTOCK

In mid-August 1969, some 400,000 people, mostly young and white, gathered at Bethel in upstate New York for the Woodstock Music and Art Fair.

They crowd listened to Jimi Hendrix, Janis Joplin, Joan Baez, the Who, Joe Cocker, Jefferson Airplane, and many other notable performers of the time. Despite heavy rain and poor facilities,

most of the audience seemed to have a good weekend.

This innocuous occasion was immediately trumpeted by *Time* magazine as "one of the most significant political and social events of the age". This was certainly not because it represented a summation of the music of the time – the list of those missing from Woodstock included the

Beatles, the Rolling Stones, Bob Dylan, Simon and Garfunkel, the Doors, Stevie Wonder and Led Zeppelin. The extraordinary and significant fact about Woodstock was the absence of trouble.

Filmed with the intention of creating an instant legend, Woodstock occurred at a time of intense anxiety for the young in the United States. There had been violent confrontations between police and students on college campuses, and at rock festivals earlier in the year – at Denver, Palm Springs and Los Angeles. The following December there were to be several deaths at the Rolling Stones concert at the Altamont Speedway in California.

At Woodstock, peace and goodwill prevailed. The police held off from drug busts, despite the circulation of large amounts of marijuana and other substances. It was profoundly reassuring to Middle America that a large selection of their children should come together without causing or coming to any harm.

▲ The era of peace and love reached its peak with the Woodstock Festival, but the hippie dream would soon turn sour.

TROOPS GO INTO ULSTER

On August 14–15, 1969, British troops were deployed on the streets of the Northern Ireland cities of Londonderry and Belfast to restore order after a savage outbreak of sectarian violence. They were expected to stay for a few months.

The violence had come as the result of a brave civil rights campaign by Catholics, especially students, demanding equal rights in the Protestant-ruled province, where Catholics suffered widespread discrimination in areas such as housing and employ-

ment. When civil rights marchers were brutally attacked by Protestant thugs, the overwhelmingly Protestant Royal Ulster Constabulary provided little protection. As pressure for reform mounted, so did the determination of Protestants to prevent it.

On August 12, the annual Protestant Apprentice Boys' parade sparked rioting in Londonderry. In the Catholic Bogside district, barricades were thrown up and youths fought the RUC with stones and petrol bombs. The Bogsiders declared

the area "Free Derry" and resisted repeated onslaughts in which Protestant rioters fought side by side with police.

On August 14, the first British troops were deployed in Londonderry in an attempt to stop the fighting. However, that night, the violence spread to Belfast. Protestant extremists from Belfast's Shankill district rampaged through the Catholic Falls Road, burning houses and attacking the inhabitants. The police joined in, driving armoured cars through the Falls and opening fire with machine guns. Eight people were killed.

The following day, British troops arrived in force. Their mission was to restore order and protect the Catholic population. They were generally welcomed in Catholic areas – British soldiers were photographed drinking cups of tea provided by friendly Catholic housewives. The British government promised reforms and the crisis seemed over. In reality, a war was about to begin.

▲ Armed police and troops were to become a common sight on the streets of Northern Ireland after 1969.

DAWN OF BLACK POWER

The Black Panther movement was a part of the upsurge of Black Power assertiveness among African Americans in the second half of the 1960s. A large number of young blacks were disillusioned with the ideals of Martin Luther King's civil rights movement, based on non-violence and the pursuit of racial integration. They wanted to assert a separate black identity and fight back if attacked.

The Black Panthers came to national prominence in May 1967, with the headline-grabbing activities of the Oakland branch of the movement, founded by two part-time students, Bobby Searle and Huey P Newton. Exercising their legal right to bear arms, Oakland Panthers strode into the Californian state capitol brandishing loaded automatic weapons. The image of these macho, hip blacks in leather jackets, berets and shades, heavily armed and openly defying white power, carried enormous appeal for black youth. Imitators set up Black Panther groups across the country. The Panthers won support in the criminalized ghettos as the civil rights movement never had.

Newton and Searle were soon joined by journalist Eldridge Cleaver, author of *Soul on Ice,* who became their "Minister of Information". Later, West Indian-born Black Power student leader Stokely Carmichael was also briefly a prominent member of what became the Black Panther Party.

For the white authorities, the Black Panthers were their worst nightmare come true. The FBI began a systematic campaign of harassment and violence. A favourite tactic was to provoke an armed confrontation. The Panthers could then either be gunned down or arrested for shooting back.

In April 1968, Cleaver was arrested after a police raid in which the movement's treasurer, Bobby Hutton was shot dead. In October, Newton was charged with murder after a shoot-out with police. In the course of 1969, about 350 other Panthers were arrested nationwide, including Bobby Seale.

The Panthers were also torn by internal dissensions. Seale led them into an alliance with white Marxist student radicals who shared their interest in revolutionary violence – people such as Mark Rudd who would soon form the terrorist group Weatherman. But for Carmichael and many others, this was a betrayal of the black separatist ideal.

By the end of 1969, both Cleaver and Carmichael had fled to exile in Africa, where they bickered about these finer points of the revolution. The other leaders were in jail and the Black Panther movement was essentially defunct. Martin Luther King had been right when he pointed out the practical flaw in the appeal for blacks to resort to violence – the white men had more guns and were prepared to use them.

▲ Viewed as a major threat by the white authorities, the Black Panthers soon attracted the wrath of the FBI.

ANTI-WAR PROTESTS SPREAD

◄ Yoko Ono and John Lennon – created the most famous peace anthems of the period.

Protest against the Vietnam War entered the US mainstream in 1969. There had been opposition to the war ever since it began, and some very high profile personalities had put their freedom in jeopardy for the cause – those arrested at one time or another included baby expert Dr Benjamin Spock, novelist Norman Mailer, folk singer Joan Baez and world boxing champion Muhammad Ali.

But the majority of US citizens were not impressed by protests that seemed to them unpatriotic, such as witnessing students carrying Viet Cong flags. Nor did they approve of the disorder associated with protest, even though much of this was created during police assaults on demonstrators by police.

The National Moratorium days called in October and November 1969 by moderate peace groups were therefore a great triumph. Hundreds of thousands of people demonstrated for peace in a dignified and non-violent manner that earned the respect of those who had been alienated by the extremism of student radicals. Protest was becoming respectable.

MASSACRE AT MY LAI

In November 1969, a military enquiry confirmed that US troops had carried out a massacre of Vietnamese civilians in the hamlet of My Lai. The facts would never have come to light without the efforts of GI-turned-journalist Ronald Ridenhour. Having seen a photograph that had been taken of some of the bodies, Ridenhour set about investigating persistent rumours of an atrocity.

The massacre occurred on March 16, 1968. C Company of First Battalion, 20th Infantry was ordered to attack and destroy My Lai, which was situated in an area where US troops had suffered heavy casualties. The company commander, Captain Ernest L Medina, was reportedly told that there were 250 Viet Cong guerrillas in the hamlet and that the civilian population would have left for market before his men arrived.

At sunrise, helicopters landed the company near the hamlet. Lieutenant William Calley led a 30-man platoon into the collection of thatched-roof huts, throwing grenades through the windows. As people ran out, they were mown down with automatic fire. It was immediately obvious that the only people present were women, children and the elderly. There was no counter-fire. But the platoon was possessed by what one eyewitness called "a contagion of slaughter". Old men were stabbed with bayonets; young girls were raped and then blown up with grenades and groups of civilians were led to a ditch and gunned down in batches.

It is estimated that 200 civilians were massacred at My Lai, though the total may be as high as 700. Although senior officers must have been aware of what had happened, they made no effort to investigate it or discipline those responsible. Even after overwhelming evidence of the massacre became public knowledge, the army was extremely reluctant to take action.

In the end, only five people were court-martialled, and only one of those, Lieutenant Calley, was found guilty. Sentenced to life imprisonment, he served only three and a half years before he was released on parole.

▲ Lieutenant William Calley at the court martial that convicted him.

1970-79

E ver searching for an angle on which stories can be hung, the media has often vainly attempted to group newsworthy events in convenient ten-year blocks, as if the world suddenly made an identifiable characteristic shift at the turn of each decade. That attitude was never more starkly illustrated than the transition between the 1960s and the 1970s. The spirit of freedom and social revolution that had seemingly characterized the final years of the 1960s had reached its zenith in the summer of 1969 with the Woodstock Festival. But the dawning of the new decade seemed to bring about a widespread realization that through all the posturing of the "peace and love" era, the world hadn't really changed all that much. The anti-Vietnam protest movement, largely comprising students, continued unabated. Although not supported by most of America to whom their actions were "unpatriotic", the nation was genuinely shocked when in May 1970 National Guardsmen opened fire on a demonstration at Kent State University killing four students and wounding many more. Americans had become used to seeing footage of this sort treatment routinely meted out to protesters in the Eastern bloc, but this was Ohio.

Meanwhile, although America had continued gradually to withdraw its forces from Vietnam, the war still lingered on with heavy casualties on both sides. It was not until the Viet Cong took the Southern capital of Saigon in 1975 that US troops were forced to make a final dramatic departure. A similar ideological civil war was also raging in nearby Cambodia. Again, in spite of support from the US, the existing government fell to Communist forces that brought Pol Pot to power. During a four-year reign, Pol Pot's Khmer Rouge committed the most appalling atrocities on which millions of Cambodians were brutally slaughtered.

The early 1970s were also noteworthy for events at the White House. In 1972, Richard Nixon had been elected president for a second term with a landslide victory – further proof perhaps of America's innate conservatism during this supposedly liberal period. Victory quickly turned to scandal as reporters from the *Washington Post* uncovered a conspiracy to spy on the Democrat national headquarters during the run-up to the elections. The plot was traced to Nixon himself and within two year, accused of a cover-up and facing impeachment, Nixon became the first president in American history to resign from office.

The 1970s can also brought a menacing new word to the world's vocabulary – "terrorism". The majority of these violent acts could be traced to the increasingly confusing hostilities in the Middle East. Since the formal creation of the state of Israel in 1948, the perennial conflict between Christian and Arab peoples had stepped up. Egypt and Jordan had frequently waged war with Israel, and the roaming forces of the Palestinian Liberation Army – a powerful lobby for the creation of a permanent Palestinian state – created further instability. Forcibly evicted from Jordan, the PLO settled in Beirut, already the scene of periodic inter-faction fighting. Thereafter, the city became a bloody battle ground for the next decade.

Britain, too, had its own share of conflict throughout the 1970s as sectarian violence proliferated in Northern Ireland between catholic nationalists who sought reunification with the South and pro-British Protestant unionists. The decision by the Conservative government to send in troops in 1971 created bitterness amongst the catholic minority, driving many to side with the Irish Republican Army. The following year, many Protestants were also alienated as direct rule saw the suspension of the provincial government over which they dominated. Thereafter, Northern Ireland became a flashpoint for brutal acts of terror committed not only by the IRA and their loyalist counterparts but also the British army. Sorting through the seemingly insolvable problems of Northern Ireland would be among the highest priorities of every British government that followed.

Through the decade, the Cold War had quietly persisted. Some progress had been in limiting the arms race – by now a notable financial drain on both sides – but contact was otherwise limited. However, the intentions of the Soviet Union came into question once again in the dying days of the decade when the Red Army invaded Afghanistan, ostensibly to assist the beleaguered President Karmal against attack from the rebel mujaheddin forces. In spite of the protests of the outside world, the Soviet Union would remain in place for eight crippling years in what would become their very own "Vietnam".

THE "CHICAGO SEVEN" CONSPIRACY TRIAL

In August 1968, serious clashes occurred between anti-war demonstrators and police during the Democratic Convention in Chicago. Despite an official report that blamed the violence on the police, seven leading white radicals were arrested and charged with inciting a riot. The trial, in February 1970, turned into an often farcical confrontation between US counter-culture and reactionary authority.

The accused included pacifist David Dellinger, Yippie student anarchists Abbie Hoffman and Jerry Rubin and prominent student radical Tom Hayden. Tried and convicted separately was Black Panther chairman Bobby Seale. All were determined to subvert the trial and turn it into a propaganda

▲ **Abbie Hoffman (left) and Jerry Rubin (centre), two of the ringleaders of the so-called "Chicago Seven".**

circus, draping the defence table with the Viet Cong flag and repeatedly denouncing a "fascist" United States and its police "pigs".

The judge, Julius J Hoffman, cantankerous, eccentric and biased, plastered the accused and their lawyers with citations for contempt of court and at one point had Bobby Seale gagged and shackled to stop his interruptions.

Although the case against the Chicago Seven was extremely weak, five of them, like Bobby Seale, were convicted on riot-related charges.

THE BEATLES SPLIT

▲ **Paul and Linda McCartney. After leaving the Beatles he became one of the top-selling solo artists of the 1970s.**

When, in April 1970, Paul McCartney released his first solo album and announced he was leaving the Beatles, it was the culmination of a slow-motion break-up that had begun two and a half years earlier.

The group had never recovered from the death of their manager, Brian Epstein, in August 1967. Since then they had drifted apart, although the four still came together for recording sessions until well into 1969, producing some of their best music on the *White Album*, *Abbey Road* and *Let It Be* albums.

Many looked to the personal relationships of Paul McCartney and John Lennon for the split. McCartney had met New York photographer Linda Eastman, while Lennon had become involved with New York-based Japanese performance artist Yoko Ono.

Meanwhile, Apple Records, the idealistic company the Beatles had set up to escape from the established music labels, had evolved from generosity into chaos. The four knew they needed a new business controller, but could not agree on who it should be. John, George and Ringo opted for New York accountant Allen Klein, while Paul wanted to rely on Eastman and Eastman, the New York law firm run by Linda's father. This business split led to acrimony and, ultimately, litigation.

It was an unhappy end for a band that would forever symbolize the youthful, optimistic face of the 1960s. Nostalgia would continue to fuel rumours of a band reunion until John Lennon's violent death in 1980 definitively closed the door on the Beatles' era.

APOLLO 13: THE GREAT ESCAPE

Launched on April 11, 1970, *Apollo 13* was the third manned lunar landing mission. The crew were James Lovell, Fred Haise and Jack Swigert, a late replacement for Ken Mattingly who had contracted German measles.

The first two days of the flight were uneventful. Then, on April 13, at 9.08 p.m. US eastern standard time, the crew heard a loud bang. As warning lights flashed on, Swigert told ground control: "Houston, we've had a problem here."

One of the service module's two oxygen tanks had exploded. This had severely damaged the other tank, from which oxygen was rapidly escaping. Once the oxygen was gone, the command module would be dead – without electricity, light, or water.

▲ The mission that almost turned to tragedy – the crew of *Apollo 13* safely emerge following successful splashdown in the Pacific.

About 322,000 km (200,000 miles) from Earth, the crew's only chance of survival was to transfer from the command module to the lunar module, which had its own supplies of power, water and oxygen for use during the moon landing. These supplies were only intended to last for 45 hours, however. The return to Earth would take 90 hours. By using every available source of oxygen – including the portable supplies meant for moonwalking – and cutting power use to a minimum, survival was possible.

Apollo 13 orbited the Moon and then manoeuvred into position for the journey back to Earth. The trip was extremely uncomfortable: water consumption had to be reduced to one-fifth of normal intake and sleep was almost impossible, as the temperature in the module dropped close to freezing.

After four days of high anxiety, the module splashed down safely on April 17 in the Pacific Ocean near Samoa . The mission was classed as a "successful failure" because of the experience gained in rescuing a crew from space.

FROM CAMBODIA TO KENT STATE

On April 30, 1970, US ground forces crossed the border from South Vietnam into Cambodia. Vietnamese Communist guerrillas had long been operating from bases inside neutral Cambodia, and US President Richard Nixon had secretly authorized massive bombing raids against Cambodian targets in 1969. But, as far as the US public knew, this was the first time that US forces had violated Cambodian territory.

The widening of the war sparked a wave of anti-war protests across the United States. The authorities were in an aggressive mood, inspired by the likes of California Governor Ronald Reagan, who backed the use of force to subdue campus protest: "If it takes a bloodbath," Reagan said, "then let's get it over with."

Kent State University, Ohio, was one of the more apathetic campuses. However, on May 4, 1970, students there organized a mass demonstration against the Cambodian incursion. The Ohio National Guard was called out, with instructions to open fire if there was any trouble.

With virtually no provocation, national guardsmen fired into a crowd of unarmed students, killing four people, two of them young women. Ten days later, another two student protesters were shot dead at Jackson State, a black campus in Mississippi.

These events shocked young Americans, marking another step in the radicalization of student opinion. They guaranteed that anti-war protests would become even larger and more frequent.

▲ An anti-war protester at Kent State University falls to the ground as the Ohio National Guard fire into an unarmed crowd.

THE END OF BIAFRA

In 1967 Biafra had declared itself independent of Nigeria, leading to conflict between the

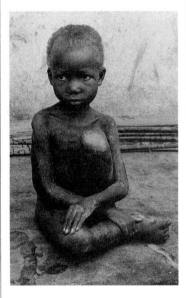

▲ **Never ending circle – the plight of the victims of the war in Biafra would later be echoed in similar tragedies in Ethiopia and Somalia.**

two territories. By the start of 1970, after three years of civil war, the Biafran forces controlled only a small area surrounded by federal troops and morale at last cracked. Biafran soldiers discarded their arms and uniforms and mingled with refugees.

On January 10, at a final meeting of the Biafran cabinet, the leader of the breakaway state, General Chukwuemeka Ojukwu, agreed to hand over to his chief of staff, General Effiong. Ojukwu then fled to the Ivory Coast. General Effiong broadcast Biafra's surrender on January 12.

Biafra was to spend 1970 coming to terms with defeat and counting the cost of a war that had turned into a humanitarian tragedy.

A large part of the motivation behind the Biafran breakaway had been the Ibo population's fear of

massacre at the hands of military leaders from northern Nigeria who dominated the Nigerian federal government. There was a widespread expectation that mass killings would follow the surrender. However, Nigeria's leader, General Yakubu Gowon, took the official line that the Ibo people had been led astray by "the tyranny and deceit of Ojukwu and his gang". Although not realistic, this attitude formed the basis for a policy of reconciliation. On the whole, the people of Biafra were treated in an exemplary fashion by Gowon's forces once the fighting stopped.

Inevitably, deep scars remained from a war in which around a million people lost their lives, mostly through starvation or from diseases associated with the extremes of malnutrition.

NASSER'S DREAM REALIZED

In July 1970, the Aswan High Dam was completed on the Nile in southern Egypt. Approximately 4 km (2.5 miles) wide and 115 metres (375 ft) high, the dam was intended to increase the amount of cultivable land in Egypt by a third and double the country's electricity supply.

Building the dam was an obsession of Egypt's leader Gamal Abdal Nasser. When the West refused to finance the dam in 1956, Nasser took over the Suez Canal as an alternative source of funding – an action that precipitated the Anglo-French invasion. From 1960, the Soviet Union provided both the cash and the technical expertise to get the dam built, in return for Egypt's becoming an ally of the Soviets.

The dam created the world's largest artificial lake, Lake

Nasser, stretching almost 500 km (310 miles) south across Nubia into Sudan. Thousands of Nubians had to be relocated from villages submerged by the lakewaters. The temple complex of Abu Simbel also had to be moved to higher ground in a rescue operation organized by Unesco.

Nasser died in September 1970, before the effects of the dam could be seen in full. They have proved to be, at the very best, mixed. The ecology of the Nile has been severely disrupted, undermining the natural fertility of the soil on which peasant agriculture depends.

▲ **The dream of President Nasser, the Aswan High Dam – the world's greatest artificial lake.**

HIJACK AT DAWSON'S FIELD

In September 1970, Palestinian terrorism became headline news around the world, when a coordinated series of skyjackings ended in the spectacular destruction of three airliners at the desert airstrip of Dawson's Field in Jordan. At a stroke, the terrorists shifted the fate of the long-ignored Palestinian people near to the top of the world's political agenda.

The skyjackings were the work of the Popular Front for the Liberation of Palestine (PFLP), led by the extremist George Habash. The PFLP had begun a campaign of international terrorism, targeting airliners, in 1968. Airport security was universally lax, with few checks to stop arms or explosives being carried on to flights. Emboldened by a series of successes, by 1970 the PFLP was ready for a major propaganda coup.

On September 6, 1970, PFLP commandos simultaneously hijacked three airliners bound for New York from European cities – a Swissair DC-8, a TWA Boeing 707, and a Pan Am jumbo jet. Two hijackers also tried to take over an El Al jet flying from Amsterdam, but this attempt was foiled. One hijacker was killed and the other, Leila Khaled, was captured and handed over to the British authorities at Heathrow, where the airliner landed.

The Pan Am jumbo was flown to Cairo and blown up on the ground after the crew and passengers had been moved off. The other two airliners were flown to Dawson's Field. Holding over 300 passengers hostage, the terrorists began negotiations for the release of Palestinian prisoners. On September 9, they were

joined by another airliner, a BOAC VC-10, hijacked en route from London to Bahrain, with another 115 passengers and crew on board.

King Hussein of Jordan was profoundly hostile to the Palestinian terrorists and ringed the airstrip with tanks. But it was impossible to attack without precipitating a bloodbath. By September 12, the release of most of the hostages had been negotiated, but 54 passengers and crew remained in terrorist hands. They were taken from the aircraft and driven away on a bus. Then the three airliners were blown up in a spectacular desert firestorm, broadcast on television around the world. At the end of the month, the PFLP released all

their hostages, and in return Switzerland, Britain, West Germany and Israel all freed Palestinian prisoners – including, in Britain, Leila Khaled.

By then, King Hussein had taken his revenge, attacking and overrunning Palestinian guerrilla bases in Jordan. The Palestinian fighters, mostly owing allegiance to Yasser Arafat, were forced to move to Lebanon. More than 3,000 were killed in the fighting in Jordan and their ability to launch raids on Israel was curtailed. Yet, in the longer term, Dawson's Field unquestionably contributed to a growing international recognition of the importance of the Palestinian question. As a form of propaganda, terror worked.

▲ **Hijacker Leila Khaled helped place the "Palestinian Question" at the forefront of world politics.**

- Police station attacked by Irish republicans in Londonderry, Northern Ireland
- West German ambassador to Guatemala kidnapped by left-wing guerrillas

April
- Vietcong launch fresh offensive in South Vietnam
- More British troops are sent to Northern Ireland
- Thirty schoolchildren killed in Israeli air raid on Egypt
- US *Apollo 13* mission to the moon aborted due to explosion on board
- Clifford Dupont becomes president of Rhodesia
- Gambia becomes a republic
- China places satellite in orbit
- US and South Vietnamese troops invade Cambodia and attack Communist bases

May
- US air raids on North Vietnam
- Demonstrations in USA against US invasion of Cambodia
- Police kill two Black students at Jackson State College in the USA
- Severe flooding in Romania
- Palestinian terrorists kill 12 in attack on school bus in Israel
- Portuguese troops attack nationalist guerrilla bases in Angola
- Incumbent government defeated in general election in Ceylon; Bandaranaike appointed Prime Minister of Ceylon
- Severe earthquake kills more than 70,000 in Peru

June
- Tonga attains independence from Britain
- Fighting between PLO and Jordanian army in Jordan, followed by cease-fire
- Conservative Party wins British general election; Edward Heath becomes Prime Minister

'70

NEWS IN BRIEF

· ·

- Alexander Dubcek expelled from the Czechoslovak Communist Party
- US troops withdraw from Cambodia
- Fresh negotiations begin on entry of Ireland, Norway, Denmark and Britain into European Community

July

- British charter jet crashes in Spain, killing 112
- Egypt accepts Rogers Plan for peace in the Middle East
- Protesters throw tear gas canisters into the British House of Commons, forcing end of Parliamentary session
- Death of Portuguese dictator Antonio Salazar

August

- Israel accepts US-proposed Rogers Plan for peace in the Middle East
- First 90-day truce between Israel, Egypt and Jordan
- Israeli, Egyptian and Jordanian representatives meet UN mediator

September

- Salvadore Allende wins Chilean presidential election
- King Hussein declares martial law in Jordan after PFLP terrorists hijack three jets and blow them up in Jordan
- Death of Egyptian President Gamal Abdel Nasser; Anwar Sadat succeeds
- Deaths of US author John Dos Passos, German author Erich Maria Remarque and French Nobel Prize-winning author François Mauriac

JIMI HENDRIX FOUND DEAD

On September 18, 1970, superstar guitarist Jimi Hendrix was found dead at the flat of his girlfriend, Monika Danneman. He was 27 years old. A coroner's inquest found he had died of "suffocation from inhalation of vomit" after mixing alcohol and drugs.

Born in a poor black neighbourhood of Seattle in 1942, Hendrix enlisted as a US paratrooper in 1961 but was soon invalided out of the service. He was already a respected guitarist when he moved to London in 1966 and formed a three-piece band, the Jimi Hendrix Experience. The following year he had his first hit with the single "Hey Joe", and his appearance at the Monterey rock festival caused a sensation.

Hendrix had an extraordinary ability as a guitarist and achieved an unprecedented range of sound and expression. His talent would have been sufficient to guarantee him stardom, but he was also encouraged to attract attention by

▲ Jimi Hendrix, the man who all but defined the art of rock guitar, at one of his last performances – the 1970 Isle of Wight Festival.

deliberately cultivating a "wild man" image – a reputation thought suitable to a black performer in the almost exclusively white world of progressive rock. His stage act included much sexual posturing and the occasional destruction of a guitar, which was obligingly worked up by the press as scandalous.

By 1969, the strains of pop stardom had begun to weigh upon Hendrix. As well as the usual problems associated with unlimited access to drugs and women, he came under pressure to identify with the black radicalism that was rampant in the United States in the late 1960s. He formed an all-black group, the Band of Gypsies, but this soon foundered. His last notable performance was at the Isle of Wight rock festival in August 1970. His death, followed a fortnight later by that of singer Janis Joplin, seemed to mark the definitive cracking up of the Sixties rock scene.

DE GAULLE DIES BUT HIS REPUBLIC LIVES ON

Charles de Gaulle, the founder of the French Fifth Republic, was buried on November 12, 1970 in a simple grave in the church of his home village, Colombey-les-Deux-Eglises. It was a humble end for a man not noted for his modesty.

De Gaulle's standing on the world stage – and his estimate of his own importance – was better reflected in the glittering requiem mass held at Notre Dame cathedral in Paris on the same day, attended by some eighty heads of

state, from the Shah of Iran and the Emperor of Ethiopia to the presidents of the United States and the Soviet Union.

Born in 1890, De Gaulle's formative experience was World War One. It confirmed his high-minded patriotism and taught him that tanks and aircraft in combination held the key to modern warfare. The belief that the failure of the French generals to adopt De Gaulle's revolutionary military ideas led to the fall of France in 1940 was probably a myth, but

underpinned his self-appointed role as leader of the Free French in exile during World War Two. Although he was quick to claim credit for the liberation of Paris in August 1944, he still failed to secure the role he craved as leader of postwar France.

His chance came in 1958, when the faction-torn Fourth Republic collapsed under the strain of the Algerian conflict. De Gaulle stepped forward to seize the reins of power. He drew up a new constitution focusing power in the hands of a strong presidency and was duly elected president himself.

At first De Gaulle was widely regarded as a militaristic right-wing strong man, but he proved a more complex political figure than anyone had anticipated. He rapidly gave independence to France's African colonies, including Algeria, and established a close relationship with West Germany as the lynchpin of the new Europe.

Seeing the United States as the chief threat to France's independence, he took France out of the military side of the Nato alliance and developed an independent French nuclear armoury. He rejected Britain's application to join the European Community in 1963, chiefly because of the close relations the British maintained with the US.

Re-elected for a second seven-year term in 1965, he survived the student uprising and general strike of May 1968, but resigned the presidency the following year after a defeat in a referendum on the relatively unimportant issue of regional government reform.

De Gaulle always had a despairing sense that France was essentially ungovernable – hence his famous comment: "Nobody can simply bring together a country that has 265 kinds of cheese." But his Republic survived him, with minor modifications, as France's most effective system of government in the twentieth century.

▲ The death of Charles De Gaulle was received with the same sense of national loss as the passing of Winston Churchill in Britain.

POLISH RIOTS ROCK COMMUNISTS

Poland was the most consistently restless of the Soviet Union's satellite states in Eastern Europe. A blend of nationalism and Catholicism formed the basis for acts of defiance whenever the Communist government ran into difficulties.

The head of the Polish government in 1970 was Wladyslaw Gomulka, who had come to power in 1956 as a liberal Communist, promising to free the country from the oppression of the Stalinist years. Over time, however, he had come to be seen as just another ageing party boss.

In December 1970, riots broke out in the port of Gdansk (formerly Danzig) in protest at the rising prices of food. The rioting soon took on a more political character, with attacks on Communist Party buildings. The disturbances were eventually suppressed by armed militia, with considerable loss of life.

To appease popular opinion in the wake of the riots, Gomulka "resigned" on December 20 and was replaced by Edward Gierek, presented – as Gomulka had been in 1956 – as a liberal reformer within the Communist system. Again, it was an image not destined to last long.

▲ Wladyslaw Gomulka – the veteran leader of Poland's "liberal" Communist regime.

DEATH OF A FASHION ICON

NEWS IN BRIEF

- US probe *Mariner 9* orbits Mars and send back pictures
- Soviet probe *Mars 2* orbits Mars; probe *Mars 3* lands on Mars
- Environmental pressure group Greenpeace founded
- Intel develops the micro processor
- Endoscope developed
- Films released during the year include William Friedkin's *The French Connection*, Peter Bogdanovich's *The Last Picture Show*, Stanley Kubrick's *A Clockwork Orange*, Luchino Visconti's *Death in Venice*, Robert Altman's *McCabe and Mrs Miller*, Monte Hellman's *Two Lane Blacktop*, Bernardo Bertolucci's *The Conformist* and Don Siegel's *Dirty Harry*
- *Columbo* starring Peter Falk debuts on US television
- *The Prisoner of Second Avenue* by Neil Simon opens in New York
- The musicals *Godspell* by Stephen Schwartz and *Jesus Christ Superstar* by Andrew Lloyd Webber and Tim Rice open in New York
- Books published this year include *The Tenants* by Bernard Malamud, *Rabbit Redux* by John Updike, *Maurice* by E M Forster, *The Day of the Jackal* by Frederick Forsyth and *August, 1914* by Alexander Solzhenitsyn
- Popular songs of the year include "My Sweet Lord" by George Harrison, "What's Going On" by Marvin Gaye and "Maggie May" by Rod Stewart
- Albums of the year include *Tapestry* by Carol King

▲ At the pinnacle of the fashion world for half a century, Coco Chanel gave the world her "No 5" perfume and "the little black dress".

On January 10, 1971, Gabrielle "Coco" Chanel, one of the most influential fashion designers of the twentieth century, died in her suite at the Paris Ritz. The luxurious circumstances of her death were in striking contrast to her humble origins. Born in 1883, Chanel was orphaned at an early age and worked for a pittance for a milliner. By 1914, she was able to open her own dress shop in Deauville. Her breakthrough came in the 1920s when she opened her own couture house in Paris that soon became the source of a fashion revolution.

Responding to the needs of the liberated women of the postwar period, Chanel designed practical but stylish clothes. Credited with freeing women from corsets, her chemise dresses and collarless jackets had widespread appeal. Chanel was associated with a wide range of durable fashion features, from the "little black dress" to the wearing of costume jewellery, bobbed hair, and the vogue for suntans. Her perfume Chanel No 5 was first marketed in 1921 – five was her lucky number.

Coco Chanel retired in 1938 to concentrate all her energies on a dazzling social life among the wealthy Parisian elite, which continued largely untroubled through the German occupation. In the 1950s, she returned to fashion design, successfully creating new ranges that were the essence of Parisian chic. After her death, her fashion house continued to operate, coming under the control of Karl Lagerfeld in 1983.

THE POUND GOES DECIMAL

In February 1971, the time-honoured British institutions of the shilling, the florin, the sixpence and the half-crown were finally consigned to the dustbin of history as the new decimalized currency took over. No longer would foreigners be asked to puzzle over a system with 12 pence to the shilling and 20 shillings to the pound – or demand to know why pounds, shillings and pence should be written "L" "s" "d" for short.

A decision to keep the pound at its old value meant that the new penny, set at one hundreth of a pound, would be worth almost two and a half old pence.

The reception accorded to the new pennies was not improved by the failure to find a satisfactory way of referring to them. Without being able to say "ten pence", since this referred to the old currency, people resorted to the ugly reference "ten pee" – a pronunciation which has persisted ever since.

▶ Converting between decimal coinage and "the old money" was a confusing business for many Britons.

THE BLOODY BIRTH OF BANGLADESH

Pakistan, the Muslim state created through the partition of British India at independence in 1947, was an inherently unstable structure created by linking two ethnically and linguistically diverse areas that were more than 1,600 km (1,000 miles) apart.

West Pakistan was the dominant partner, largely because Punjabis predominated in the Pakistani armed forces. East Pakistan was more populous than the West, but its Bengali population was systematically discriminated against and excluded from political power.

From 1958 to 1969, Pakistan was under the military rule of Field Marshal Ayub Khan. During this period, Sheikh Mujibur Rahman emerged as the leading political figure in East Pakistan, heading the Awami League. Sheikh Mujib's demands for a large measure of autonomy for East Pakistan led to his imprisonment by the military regime in 1968. The following year, however, Ayub Khan was overthrown. His successor, General Yahya Khan, released Sheikh Mujib and organized free democratic elections.

Yahya Khan had seriously underestimated the strength of Bengali resentment against rule from West Pakistan. The resentment was increased by the government's inadequate response to the catastrophic typhoon and tidal wave that struck East Pakistan in November 1970, killing more than 150,000 people.

The elections, held the following month, were a triumph for the Awami League. Not only did it gain an overwhelming majority of the vote in East Pakistan, but it also won a clear majority of seats in Pakistan's national assembly, giving it the democratic right to form the government of the whole country. It was an outcome entirely unacceptable to the military rulers of Pakistan.

At the start of March 1971, Yahya Khan announced that the opening of the national parliament was being postponed indefinitely. Sheikh Mujib responded by calling a general strike in East Pakistan, which went into a state of virtual insurrection. On March 25, Yahya Khan announced a campaign to "restore law and order", and widespread arrests of members of the Awami League began. The following day, Sheikh Mujib declared East Pakistan independent as Bangladesh – that is, Free Bengal.

There followed one of the worst genocidal massacres in the blood-soaked history of the twentieth century. The Pakistan army easily overcame Bangladeshi military resistance and had total control of the country by the end of April.

Abetted by Islamic fundamentalist militias, the army then embarked on a campaign of terror and extermination, aimed at groups believed to be most in favour of independence. These included all Awami League members, all educated Bengalis, such as doctors, teachers and students and all Hindu Bengalis – about 10 per cent of the population.

Using mass murder, mass rape and the burning of villages, the Pakistani army and its allies laid the country waste. At least one million people were killed; according to some estimates, a more likely figure is two to three million. Around 10 million refugees fled across the border to makeshift camps in India, where many died of hardship and disease.

By the summer of 1971, the Bengalis' only hope was for a military intervention by India – which is what, finally, was to occur.

▲ **Almost a tenth of the population of East Pakistan is thought to have perished in the brutal struggle for independence.**

JAZZ LEGEND DIES

▲ Louis Armstrong, one of the pioneers of jazz improvization. His nickname, "Satchmo", was an abbreviation of "Satchel Mouth".

Louis "Satchmo" Armstrong, considered by many to be the greatest figure in the history of jazz, died on July 6, 1971. Armstrong's life story was something of a rags-to-riches fairytale.

Born in New Orleans in 1900, Armstrong was brought up in extreme poverty. He learned to play cornet in his teens while incarcerated in the city's "home for coloured waifs".

By 1923, when Armstrong made his first recordings with King Oliver's Creole Jazz Band in Chicago, he was already the leading jazz trumpeter of his day, surpassing all others in bravura technique and sensitivity. Between 1925 and 1928, he performed and recorded with small ensembles, the *Hot Five* and *Hot Seven*, in sessions now seen as some of the finest jazz ever played.

By the 1930s, Armstrong was an internationally famous entertainer, fronting big bands in diluted versions of jazz for mass consumption. While never hitting the peaks of his earlier performances, he continued to produce music of high quality through to the 1960s, mostly with his *Louis Armstrong All Stars*.

At the time of his death, he was known as the singer of the heart-warming hit singles "Hello Dolly" and "What a Wonderful World".

MYSTERIOUS END FOR MORRISON

Following the deaths of guitarist Jimi Hendrix and singer Janis Joplin, the world of rock lost another legend on July 3, 1971, when Jim Morrison, lead singer of the Doors, was found dead in his bath in his Paris apartment. He was 27 years old.

Morrison was a would-be visionary poet who drifted into rock in the Acid-inspired West Coast scene of the mid-1960s.

In typical style, The Doors took their name from a poem by English mystical poet William Blake, popularized by veteran hallucinogen-experimenter Aldous Huxley: "If the doors of perception were cleansed/All things would appear infinite."

The Doors had a massive hit with the erotic "Light My Fire", but many of their songs had more metaphysical themes – "Break On Through (to the Other Side)", for example.

Morrison's stage performances attracted the unfriendly attentions of the authorities, both for their eroticism and their appeals to revolution. In 1969, he was arrested in Miami, and the wave of success began to falter.

At the time of his death, Morrison had gone to Paris to

▶ The Doors featuring singer Jim Morrison (centre), one of the most important rock bands of the late 1960s.

concentrate on his poetry. He was buried in the city's Père Lachaise cemetery. Despite rumours that his death was drug-related, its cause has remained a mystery.

INTERNMENT IN NORTHERN IRELAND

At dawn on August 9, 1971, units of the British Army were sent into Catholic areas of Northern Ireland with orders to arrest 450 individuals suspected of supporting armed subversion. They were to be interned – held without charge or trial in special camps.

The British government had introduced internment reluctantly in the face of a deteriorating security situation. In the event, it only served to make matters worse.

When British soldiers had first arrived on the streets of Northern Ireland two years earlier, they had been largely welcomed by Catholics in the Protestant-ruled province. The first shots fired at British soldiers in October 1969 were from Protestant gunmen, outraged by drastic measures to reform the Protestant-dominated police. In the course of time, however, the British troops found themselves inevitably drawn into close cooperation with Northern Ireland's Protestant authorities, and thus into conflict with the Catholic population.

The alienation of the Catholics was exploited by the Provisional IRA, a recent breakaway from the long-established – and by this time relatively moderate – Irish Republican Army. The Provisionals were committed to achieving a united Ireland through armed struggle against the British "occupiers" and their Protestant allies. During the course of 1970, the Provisionals' ranks were swelled by a flood of recruits. With funding flowing in from sympathizers in the United States, the Provos began to arm themselves for an assault on British power.

On February 6, 1971, a British soldier, Gunner Robert Curtis, was shot by a Provisional sniper in Belfast: he was the first British fatality in the conflict. The Ulster government then declared that Northern Ireland was "at war with the Provisional IRA". Many Catholic districts became in practice "no-go areas" for the British

cal disaster. The Catholic areas rose in open revolt and fighting against the British army spilled over into communal violence. Over the next two days, 23 people were killed and hundreds of buildings were burned out.

Many of the internees were

▲ A soldier searches a Belfast civilian. Internment was one of the British government's more controversial policies in Northern Ireland.

Army, as any army patrol would face, at best, rioters throwing bricks and petrol bombs, and – at worst – sniper fire.

From the security of these safe havens, the Provisionals launched a bombing campaign against commercial targets throughout the Province. By July, the number of bombings was approaching 100 a month.

Unable to contain the rapidly worsening situation, the British government acceded to demands from the head of the Northern Ireland government, Brian Faulkner, for the introduction of internment.

The implementation of this measure on August 9 was a politi-

subjected to interrogations that a commission of enquiry later admitted was "ill-treatment". Fourteen prisoners were subjected to in-depth interrogation involving sensory deprivation. This was later condemned by the European Court of Human Rights as "inhuman and degrading".

In effect, the British authorities had tainted themselves with arbitrary arrest and near-torture. And the net result was only to crank up the violence to a new pitch.

In the seven months before internment, thirty people died in the Northern Ireland troubles. In the five months that followed, 143 lost their lives as the bombings and shootings spiralled.

CHINA JOINS THE UNITED NATIONS

In November 1971, representatives of the Chinese People's Republic took their place in the United Nations, ending an anomaly that had excluded one fifth of the world's population from representation in the "world parliament" for over twenty years.

When the Chinese Communists, led by Mao Tse-tung, triumphed in China's civil war and proclaimed their People's Republic in Peking in October 1949, their defeated enemies, the Chinese Nationalists under Chiang Kai-shek, took refuge on the island of Formosa, known as Taiwan.

The Nationalists refused to acknowledge the Communist victory and continued to claim to be the legitimate government of mainland China. They were backed in this stance by the United States.

Nationalist China had been one of the founder members of the United Nations and held one of the five seats in the Security Council, alongside the Soviet

▲ **Their presence at the United Nations for the first time signalled world recognition for the Chinese People's Republic.**

Union, the United States, Britain and France. Despite the evident fact that the vast majority of Chinese were under the rule of the Communist government in Peking, Chiang Kai-shek's island regime continued to hold this elevated status.

In the 1970s, however, under the guidance of President Nixon's foreign policy adviser Henry Kissinger, the United States embarked on a policy of detente with Communist China, as well as with the Soviet Union. This inevitably involved recognizing the Communists as China's legitimate government. The United States hoped to admit Communist China into the United Nations while allowing Nationalist China to keep its seat, but this ploy was defeated by a vote of the UN General Assembly, which expelled Nationalist Taiwan in October 1971.

JAPAN RESTLESS IN PROSPERITY

By the early 1970s, Japan had established itself as the world's second largest industrial power. In the manufacture of many consumer goods, including cars, radios and televisions, it was catching up with, or had already overtaken, the USA.

This remarkable recovery from the devastation of World War Two

◄ **Wartime enemy Emperor Hirohito receives a royal reception on his first visit to Britain.**

had not been accompanied by a full normalization of relations between Japan and the rest of the world. There remained widespread bitterness, both in East Asia and Europe, about Japanese war crimes. At the same time, many Japanese resented their country's current status as a demilitarized subsidiary ally of the United States.

The survival of wartime Emperor Hirohito on the Japanese throne was a special focus of resentment for many foreigners. In October 1971, the Emperor made a state visit to Britain and was received by the Queen at Buckingham Palace, but the crowds that turned out to see him were mostly silent and hostile.

The following month, the other side of the coin was on view when thousands of Japanese were arrested during violent mass demonstrations against the continuing presence of a US military base on the island of Okinawa, even after its official return to Japanese sovereignty.

Some anti-US feeling was displayed by student radicalism imbued with anti-imperialist rhetoric. But far more deeply rooted in Japan was a harking back to military glory and the imperial past.

In November 1970, Japanese novelist Yukio Mishima had committed *sepuku* – ritual suicide – in a gesture that was designed to reawaken his country to its heroic traditions. His shocking action seriously shook the prestige of Japan's postwar ruling elite.

In the face of such attitudes, it was impossible for Japan's rulers to make a public apology for war crimes or to admit war guilt – the only gestures that might have appeased hostile opinion in Europe and East Asia.

THE BIRTH OF BANGLADESHI INDEPENDENCE

▲ **India responded decisively to Pakistan's aggression – victory resulted in independence for Bangladesh.**

After East Pakistan's declaration of its independence as Bangladesh in March 1971, the Pakistani army instituted a reign of terror against the Bengalis, intended to crush the independence movement once and for all. The Bangladeshi leader, Sheikh Mujibur Rahman, was carried off to imprisonment in West Pakistan.

The crucial factor in any resolving of the conflict was India's attitude to it. Deep hostility existed between India and Pakistan, the two countries having fought a war as recently as 1965. It was clearly in India's interest to see Bangladesh become independent, since this would fundamentally weaken Pakistan, more than halving its population and resources. Indian Prime Minister Indira Gandhi allowed the Bangladeshis to set up a government-in-exile in India and gave her backing to Bangladeshi guerrillas, the Mukti Bahini. But she hesitated to commit herself to open war.

From the summer through to the autumn of 1971, Pakistan and India manoeuvered for international diplomatic support and made their military preparations. Pakistan's leader, General Yahya Khan, rightly believed he could not hold Bangladesh against an Indian onslaught. He decided to seize the initiative by attacking India from West Pakistan, hoping that a quick victory in the West would force India to accept Pakistani terms in the East.

On December 3, 1971, the Pakistani air force launched preemptive strikes against Indian airfields in the West. The Indian response was swift and decisive. Aided by the Mukti Bahini, the Indian army surged into Bangladesh, advancing swiftly against demoralized Pakistani troops surrounded by a hostile population. Within a fortnight, they had established complete control of the country, including the capital, Dacca. Meanwhile, the Pakistani offensive in the West petered out.

In January 1972 Sheikh Mujibur Rahman returned from imprisonment to become the first leader of independent Bangladesh. In Pakistan, Yahya Khan handed over to the civilian rule of Zulfiqar Bhutto. There were to be no happy endings, however. Before the end of the decade both men were dead, Sheikh Mujibur murdered with his family in a military coup in 1975, and Bhutto executed in 1978 after a military takeover in Pakistan.

'72

FROM BLOODY SUNDAY TO BLOODY FRIDAY

▲ British troops stationed in Belfast stand guard over Loyalist housing bombed by the IRA.

The worst single year in the history of the Northern Ireland conflict had to be 1972. In the course of twelve months, a total of 467 people, including 103 British soldiers, lost their lives in the violence that convulsed the Province.

The year opened with the tragedy known as Bloody Sunday. The predominantly Catholic Civil Rights Association had decided to mount a campaign of marches to protest against internment – a bold attempt to wrest back the initiative from the men of violence.

On January 30, a highly publicized march set off from the Creggan estate in Derry. When it was turned back from its planned route by an army barricade, a small number of rioters began throwing stones. British paratroopers pursued the rioters and opened fire near the Rossville Flats. Thirteen Catholic civilians were shot dead and another twelve wounded. The Widgery Tribunal, set up to investigate the event, admitted that "none of the deceased or wounded is proved to have been shot while handling a firearm or bomb".

Since it happened in full view of the media, the massacre caused a sensation around the world. In Dublin, the British embassy was burnt down. The Official IRA's response was a botched car-bombing at the Parachute Regiment's Aldershot barracks, which killed five cleaning women, a gardener and a Roman Catholic chaplain.

In Northern Ireland, the Provisional IRA raised its terrorist campaign to a new pitch. Through the spring of 1972, bombings were a daily occurrence – in a single two-day period in mid-April, forty explosive devices were planted across the Province. Although aimed at "economic targets", the bombs inevitably caused civilian deaths and horrific maimings. The security forces also suffered mounting casualties, chiefly from sniper fire. Not to be left out, Protestant paramilitaries stepped up their activities, targeting Catholics in a series of sectarian killings.

Desperate to regain control, on March 24, British Prime Minister Edward Heath suspended the Stormont government, taking over direct rule of the Province. The newly appointed Northern Ireland Secretary, William Whitelaw, and his military advisers were unable, in these early weeks, to reduce the level of violence. Solidly in control of Catholic districts of Belfast and Derry that were out of bounds for the security forces, the Provisionals felt confident they could persuade the British to give up and go home.

▲ Thousands attend the funeral of the 13 victims of Bloody Sunday on Creggan Hill in Belfast's Bogside.

In June, the Provisionals put out feelers for peace talks with the British government. Publicly, the government said they would not talk to terrorists, but privately they agreed to look for a deal.

On June 26, the Provisionals declared a truce and in the first week of July a delegation including Gerry Adams – released from internment so he could take part – and Martin McGuiness met Whitelaw for secret talks in London. The meeting did not go badly, but on July 9 the cease-fire predictably broke down with a clash between Catholics and British troops on the streets of Belfast.

Over the following eight days, fifteen British soldiers were killed in the Province. The bombing campaign was resumed with unparalleled ferocity, culminating on the afternoon of July 21 – the day later referred to as Bloody Friday – when nineteen bombs exploded in Belfast city centre in an hour. Nine people were killed and 130 injured. Graphic television pictures depicting the maimed victims and the remains of bodies being scooped into plastic bags shocked viewers.

The horror of Bloody Friday lost the Provisionals much support among Northern Ireland Catholics and gave back the initiative to the British government. On July 31, the army swept into the "no-go" areas in force, using armoured bulldozers to demolish barricades. They met little resistance.

Troops were permanently installed in strongpoints inside the Catholic districts. The loss of their safe havens was a serious blow to the Provisionals, and the level of bombings and shootings was almost halved in the following months, they would never again get close to driving the British out by force.

FINAL US FLING IN VIETNAM

▲ **South Vietnamese marines escort a blindfolded Viet Cong prisoner of war to be interrogated.**

From 1969 onward, the United States desperately wanted to extricate itself from the Vietnam War, but was also determined not to accept a Communist victory. While peace talks in Paris stalled, President Richard Nixon went ahead with the gradual withdrawal of US troops from South Vietnam. At the same time, he widened the war, authorizing incursions into Cambodia in 1970 and Laos in 1971. By the spring of 1972, Nixon could claim considerable success. The South Vietnamese army had taken over ground combat duties from the US, and the major part of South Vietnam was under the control of government forces.

On March 30, 1972, however, the war entered a new phase. Abandoning guerrilla warfare, the North Vietnamese launched a conventional invasion of the South, with tanks and heavy artillery. On May 1, they captured the northern city of Quang Tri and there were fears that South Vietnam might disintegrate. However, the United States deployed its air power to massive effect, both against targets inside North Vietnam and against the forces invading the South.

New "smart" weapons made the bombing far more effective than ever before.

With the Communist forces driven back to mere toeholds around the borders of South Vietnam, the North Vietnamese proposed peace in October on the basis of a cease-fire in place.

Under domestic pressure to end the war, Nixon could hardly refuse, but still preferred to go out with a bang. From December 18 to 30, strikes by B52 bombers devastated the two major cities of Haiphong and Hanoi. Finally, on January 23, 1973, a peace agreement was signed in Paris – the US war in Vietnam was over.

▲ **Running scared – South Vietnamese children flee for their lives following an accidental napalm attack by the US airforce.**

- The musical *Grease* opens in New York
- Books published this year include *Invisible Cities* by Italo Calvino, *Watership Down* by Richard Adams, and *The Joy of Sex* by Alex Comfort
- Popular songs of the year include "Let's Stay Together" by Al Green and "Long Haired Lover from Liverpool" by Jimmy Osmond

January
- Over one million unemployed in Britain
- US president Nixon authorizes space shuttle program
- British coal miners strike
- President Mujibur Rahman resigns to become Prime Minister of Bangladesh
- Pakistan leaves the Commonwealth
- Three hundred and fifty Soviet Jews arrive in Israel
- Death of King Frederik IX of Denmark; daughter succeeds as Margrethe II
- Deaths of US poet John Berryman and French singer and actor Maurice Chevalier

February
- Britain recognizes Bangladesh
- New Zealand Prime Minister John Holyoake retires; John Marshall succeeds
- Third largest diamond in the world, the Star of Sierra Leone, discovered
- US President Nixon begins visit to China

'72

The Six became the Ten when Britain, Ireland, Denmark and Norway signed the Treaty of Brussels, on January 22, 1972, committing them to join the European Economic Community (EEC) on January 1, 1973. In the event, there were only nine, Norway having held a referendum in 1972 which rejected entry into Europe.

Many people British people believed that they should also have had a chance to vote on the issue – all opinion polls showed a solid majority of the population opposed to EEC membership. There was already a controversial agreement among European leaders to progress towards a more complete European Union.

Britain's entry into Europe was a personal triumph for Edward Heath, British Prime Minister since 1970. A fervent pro-European, he had been the chief negotiator when Britain first attempted to join the EEC, only to see British membership vetoed by France's President Charles de Gaulle in 1963. De Gaulle vetoed another British application to join, initiated by Harold Wilson's Labour government, in 1967. It was only the French leader's fall from power in 1969 that opened the door to a fresh British approach.

Britain had negotiated special deals to maintain some of its privileged trading links with the Commonwealth. Nevertheless, both the Conservatives and Labour were split over the EEC. Generally, the Conservatives were more in favour of Europe than the Socialists. The left wing of the Labour Party was opposed and, after Labour's election victory in 1974, forced Harold Wilson to call a referendum on membership. Held in 1975, this produced a large majority of around two to one in favour of Europe, partly in acknowledgement of a *fait accompli*, but also thanks to a lavishly funded campaign mounted by the pro-European lobby.

▲ Although decided by referendum, Britain's entry into the Common Market was bitterly opposed by many.

NIXON IN CHINA

On February 21, 1972, Richard Nixon stepped on to the tarmac of Peking airport, becoming the first US president to set foot in the People's Republic of China. The scale of the diplomatic revolution encompassed in this simple act could be measured by comparison with the recent past.

Until 1971, the United States had not officially recognized the existence of Communist China and the only diplomatic contacts between the two countries had been conducted through their respective ambassadors to Poland. All trade and travel between the United States and China had been banned.

Both sides had begun to see this situation as irksome. China's relations with the Soviet Union had deteriorated to the point at which open fighting broke out on the border in 1969. This split left China isolated, and crucially short of the technological expertise that the Soviets had once provided.

Despite their hostility to Western imperialism, the Chinese leaders saw the need to find friends in the West and import Western technology. For their part, Nixon's policy advisers, especially Henry Kissinger, wanted to pursue a global strategy of detente with the Communist powers.

Nixon's lifelong record as a fanatical anti-Communist protected him against accusations of "going soft on the Reds".

On the first day of his China trip, Nixon met Chairman Mao Tse-tung in the Forbidden City. Television images and press photographs of the two men chatting and joking together impressed the world with the transformation that was taking place. Nixon and his entourage then embarked on a week of sightseeing, while intensive diplomatic negotiations went on behind the scenes.

Their result was apparently unspectacular – an agreement to disagree on most topics, including, crucially, the status of Taiwan, still recognized by the United States as the legitimate government of China. But a giant step had been taken towards a new relationship between China and the West, soon reflected in massive deals for the import of advanced technological goods.

The US drive for detente continued with a summit meeting between Nixon and the Soviet leader, Leonid Brezhnev, in

▲ A historic visit to the Great Wall of China was part of Nixon's trip to the Communist state.

Moscow the following May – also a first visit for a US president.

Although more important to world peace, the Moscow meeting was less spectacular because it formed part of a long series of

negotiations, designed to reduce nuclear armouries and prevent nuclear wars. The first Strategic Arms Limitation Treaty was signed between the two superpowers later in the year.

A NEW SPACE AGE

The launch on March 2, 1972 of the *Pioneer 10* space probe, bound for the planet Jupiter, showed the direction that space exploration was taking in the 1970s.

The heroic age of the 1960s "space race" was over. There was a new era of superpower co-operation in space, culminating in

the link-up of a US and a Soviet spacecraft in July 1975. With national prestige no longer at stake, budgets for space programmes were slashed. The US staged its last crewed Moon landing in December 1972.

Both the United States and the Soviets turned their attention to investigating the solar system

with less prestigious but more cost-effective unmanned missions such as *Pioneer 10*.

In terms of scientific progress, these missions far surpassed the achievements of the *Apollo* programme. A Soviet craft landed on Venus in 1975, and a US craft on Mars the following year, sending back data that transformed our understanding of these planets.

In 1977, Nasa launched the space probes *Voyager 1* and *Voyager 2* on an even more ambitious journey to the end of the solar system and beyond.

Attempts were made to fix the popular imagination on these projects – *Voyager 2* carried a video disc intended to communicate with aliens in some distant galaxy (one of the items on it was Chuck Berry performing "Johnny B Goode").

However, it was only with the space shuttle programme of the 1980s that space rediscovered its mass appeal.

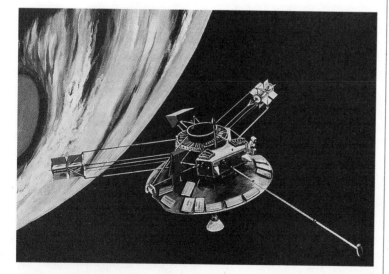

▲ An artist's impression of the *Pioneer* space craft passing close by the surface of the planet Jupiter.

May

- Oil discovered near Villahermosa in Mexico
- Quang Tri falls to North Vietnamese forces
- US blockades North Vietnamese ports
- Governor of Alabama and candidate for Democratic presidential nomination in US, George Wallace paralysed in assassination attempt
- President Nixon arrives in Moscow and meets Soviet leader Leonid Brezhnev
- Ceylon changes name to Sri Lanka
- USA and USSR sign treaty restricting anti-ballistic missile sites
- Deaths of the Duke of Windsor, former King Edward VIII, British poet Cecil Day Lewis, founder and head of the US FBI J Edgar Hoover and of British actress Dame Margaret Rutherford

June

- Red Army Faction leaders Andreas Baader and Ulrike Meinhof captured in West Germany
- Iraq nationalizes London-based Iraq Petroleum's oil fields in Kirkuk
- Police arrest five intruders at break-in into Democratic Party headquarters in Washington
- The Susquehanna River breaks its banks and floods the Wyoming Valley in the US
- The US Supreme Court rules the death penalty to be a "cruel and unusual" punishment and therefore unconstitutional

'72

ANGELA DAVIS STANDS TRIAL

▲ **Black political activist Angela Davis remained a thorn in the side of the White American authorities throughout the 1970s.**

In May 1972, a young black Communist, Angela Davis, stood trial in San Jose, California, on charges of murder, kidnapping and criminal conspiracy. Davis had become a Communist as a student in the 1960s, under the influence of left-wing intellectual Herbert Marcuse. She first came to public attention in 1969, when she was sacked from her teaching job at UCLA (University of California at Los Angeles) because of her political allegiance.

Davis became involved in campaigns on behalf of black prisoners, and in particular took up the case of George Jackson. Arrested for his part in a minor robbery in 1960 at the age of 18, Jackson was still detained in Soledad prison in 1970. In that year, he and two other prisoners were charged with the murder of a prison guard. The defence of the three "Soledad Brothers" became a radical cause.

On August 7, 1970, Jonathan Jackson, George's brother, led an attempt to kidnap a judge from a courthouse in San Rafael, intending to demand the Soledad Brothers' release. In a bloody shoot-out with police, Jonathan, two of his accomplices and the judge were killed. Two weeks later George Jackson was shot dead in San Quentin prison, allegedly while trying to escape.

Angela Davis was arrested after the courthouse shoot-out because guns used there were registered in her name. There were widespread protests at the gravity of the charges brought against her on the flimsiest of evidence. Radicals who believed the US was a racist country in which the dispensing of justice was a mere charade expected a guilty verdict to be a formality. But the all-white jury at her trial was clearly equally unimpressed by the evidence against her. On June 4, the jury found Davis not guilty and set her free to continue her career as a radical critic of US society.

MASSACRE AT LOD AIRPORT

In the early 1970s, Palestinian terrorists fighting to destroy the state of Israel formed close contacts with terrorist groups in other countries around the world. One of the most brutal acts of the international terrorist network these contacts created was the massacre at Lod airport, Tel Aviv, on May 30, 1972.

At about 10 p.m., 116 passengers who had just arrived on an Air France jet filed through passport control into the baggage area. Unnoticed among them were three Japanese terrorists belonging to an organization called the Red Army, which had links with the Popular Front for the Liberation of Palestine (PFLP). Their luggage, which came through on the conveyor belt, contained sub-machine guns, ammunition and grenades. They calmly unzipped the bags, pulled out the weapons, and opened fire.

As security guards struggled to respond, the terrorists emptied magazine after magazine of ammunition, sweeping the airport building with prolonged bursts of fire. They threw grenades in the direction of knots of civilians who had huddled together in an attempt to find shelter from the onslaught.

▶ **The chilling aftermath of one of the worst acts of international terrorism at Lod airport in Tel Aviv, Israel.**

The attack lasted four minutes. Two terrorists died in the baggage hall, one blown up by his own grenade. A third ran out on to the runway, discarding his weapon, and was caught by an El Al mechanic. Twenty-six other people were killed and hundreds were seriously wounded.

THE POULSON AFFAIR

▲ A distinguished politician, Reginald Maudling fell from grace following the revelations of his links with John Poulson.

In July 1972, Reginald Maudling, the Home Secretary in the Conservative government and a potential prime minister, was obliged to resign after he was shown to be linked to Leeds property developer John Poulson, the subject of a police inquiry into corruption.

The Poulson case blew the lid off the cosy world of favours and bribery that had grown up during the years of rapid urban redevelopment in the 1960s.

A self-made millionaire, Poulson had created Europe's largest international architect's practice. He was also at the centre of a web of corruption. Individuals such as Scottish Office civil servant George Pottinger and Newcastle Labour councillors T Dan Smith and Andy Cunningham received favours from Poulson, ranging from meals at the Dorchester and suits from Saville Row tailors to Mediterranean cruises.

The scandal came to light when Poulson went bankrupt in 1972. At trials held in Leeds in 1973 and 1974, he was sentenced to prison terms of five and seven years, to run concurrently.

AMIN EXPELS ASIANS

In August 1972, Ugandan ruler General Idi Amin Dada announced that he was expelling all of his country's Asian population, reckoned to number about 80,000 people. Since the majority of them had British passports, they would expect to find refuge in Britain, alongside the thousands of Asians forced out of neighbouring Kenya in the late 1960s.

A largely uneducated Muslim, Amin had risen through the ranks of the colonial King's African Rifles to become Commander-in-Chief of the Ugandan army after independence. In January 1971, he overthrew the civilian head of government Milton Obote and declared himself president. His rule quickly proved corrupt and brutal, rooted in a narrow tribalism. He formed close links with Libyan leader Colonel Muammar Gaddafi and with Palestinian terrorists.

The expulsion of Asians, which took place in conditions of the utmost brutality, was widely approved of by other African governments. Introduced into East Africa by the British in the nineteenth century, the Asians were resented by Black Africans because they constituted a business class with a generally higher standard of living. Amin's motivation was simply the desire for plunder, but the Asians' departure inevitably contributed to a steep decline in the Ugandan economy.

▲ The Asian community was crucial to Uganda's economy, which quickly faltered following their expulsion.

- South Vietnamese forces recapture Quang Tri
- The *Washington Post* reports existence of a secret fund controlled by Nixon's campaign finance chairman
- Ugandan dictator Idi Amin orders 8,000 Ugandan Asians to leave within 48 hours
- Death in UK of Lord Fisher of Lambeth, former Archbishop of Canterbury

October
- USA and USSR sign SALT I missile control agreement
- The *Washington Post* reports connection between Watergate break-in and campaign of political sabotage and espionage conducted on behalf of US President Nixon
- EC summit agrees monetary union by 1980
- Liberal Party under Pierre Trudeau wins general election in Canada
- Deaths of British anthropologist Dr Louis Leakey and Russian-born US aviation pioneer Igor Sikorsky

TERROR AT THE OLYMPICS

▲ **Britain's most notable Olympic triumph in Munich was 33-year-old Mary Peters, who took the gold medal in the women's Pentathlon.**

The 20th Olympic Games were held in Munich in August and September 1972. They should have been memorable for sporting achievements: the 22-year-old US swimmer Mark Spitz won a record seven gold medals – four for individual events and three for team relays; gymnastics for the first time established itself as one of the most popular Olympic events, largely through the breathtaking performances and personal charm of the tiny 16-year-old Soviet gymnast Olga Korbut, winner of three golds and a silver and British hearts were warmed by the victory of Mary Peters in the pentathlon.

But all sporting considerations were overshadowed by the eruption of Middle Eastern terrorism into the games.

Early on the morning of September 5, eight Palestinians belonging to the Black September terrorist group climbed over a perimeter fence into the Olympic village and headed for the building where the Israeli Olympic team was staying. The Palestinians were armed with Kalashnikov automatic weapons and grenades. As they burst into the Israeli quarters, there was a violent struggle in which weightlifter Joseph Romano and wrestling coach Moshe Weinberg were killed. Some

Israelis escaped through the windows or the rear door, but nine athletes and officials were taken hostage. The terrorists demanded the release of 200 Palestinian prisoners from Israeli jails and free passage out of Germany.

The building was soon surrounded by about 300 armed Bavarian police. The Israeli government made it clear to West German Chancellor Willi Brandt that they did not intend to comply with any of the demands of the terrorists.

The police were told to devise a plan to rescue the hostages. It was decided to pretend to accept the demand for an aircraft to fly the terrorists and their hostages out of the country. However, the police would attack the plane at the airport.

This turned out to be a misguided plan. After dark, the terrorists and their trussed hostages were flown to the military airport of Furstenfeldbruck, where a Lufthansa airliner was waiting for them. So were five police marksmen hidden on the control tower roof. Four of the terrorists had dismounted from the helicopters when the marksmen opened fire, killing three of them. However, the five other terrorists remained in control of the hostages who were still tied up inside the helicopters.

A raging firefight developed, in which one policeman was shot dead. Just after midnight, in a final act of defiance, a terrorist threw a grenade into one of the helicopters, which exploded into flames. Two more terrorists were killed as they tried to make their escape, while the other three were captured. All the hostages were dead.

This fiasco for the security forces led directly to the development of specialist anti-terrorist squads.

▲ **The terror of Munich – a masked Palestinian gunman stands guard outside the Israeli team headquarters.**

EARTHQUAKE IN NICARAGUA

On Christmas Day 1972, an earthquake struck Managua, the capital of the Central American state of Nicaragua. A series of tremors over a two-hour period damaged or destroyed about three-quarters of the buildings in the city. Around 10,000 people died in the devastation.

The earthquake was a major natural disaster; it was also a turning point in Nicaragua's troubled political history. At that time, the country was ruled by the US-backed dictator Anastasio Somoza Debayle and his feared National Guard. The Somoza family had run Nicaragua since 1935, amassing an enormous fortune in the process. A guerrilla movement, the Sandinistas, had been set up in the 1960s to fight against the Somoza dictatorship, but it had enjoyed little success and only limited popular support.

The earthquake, or rather its aftermath, seriously undermined

▲ The earthquake that devastated Nicaragua seriously weakened the grip of the ruling Somoza dictatorship.

the Somoza regime. As most of Managua's 350,000 population fled from the ruins, fearing further tremors, the National Guard moved in to loot and pillage. A force of US troops was eventually sent to restore order in the city, which was an important centre for US business interests – over 3,000 US citizens were in Managua at the time of the earthquake, including millionaire recluse Howard Hughes.

Outrage at the National Guard's behaviour was compounded by the scandal of the regime's exploitation of international aid, which flooded in to finance relief work and reconstruction. Much of the money was rumoured to have gone into the pockets of Somoza and his associates, either directly or indirectly – for example, the rebuilding of the city was contracted to companies owned by the dictator.

Opposition to the regime was reinforced in every sector of Nicaraguan society. As a consequence, the Sandinistas, once a small fringe group, grew into the spearhead of a broad popular revolt against the Somoza dictatorship.

THE CHESS COLD WAR

It is always said that the United States will never take a sport seriously until they win at it. This is certainly true of chess. World championship contests in that Soviet-dominated game had received little coverage in the Western media until 1972, when US competitor Bobby Fischer defeated the reigning champion, Russian grandmaster Boris Spassky, in Reykjavik, Iceland.

Fischer was an eccentric individual who hardly ranked as a typical all-American boy. However, the press was happy to present the championship as a reflection of the Cold War superpower confrontation and its well-established cultural stereotypes – Fischer as the inventive, imaginative exemplar of a free society, Spassky as the disciplined, dour, but potentially sneaky "Russki". In this form, the championship captured the imagination of millions who had no chance of understanding the subtlety of the manoeuvres on the board.

Fischer's victory made him a national hero, but the aftermath was bathetic. After failing to agree terms for a defence of his title against Anatoly Karpov in 1975, Fischer was stripped of the world championship. He never played competitive chess again.

▶ America's Bobby Fischer (left) during his epic struggle with existing champion, the Russian Boris Spassky.

'73

WOUNDED KNEE

In the wake of the civil rights campaign on behalf of African Americans in the 1960s, other ethnic groups began to assert their claim for rights. Among these were Native Americans, still universally known at that time as Indians – "a name," said one protester, "given to us by some dumb honky who got lost and

thought he'd landed in India". Their case was brought to wide public attention in 1970 by Dee Brown's bestseller *Bury My Heart at Wounded Knee*, a harrowing account of the injustices perpetrated by whites in their conquest of North America.

The most radical of the groups campaigning for "Red Power" in the early 1970s was the American Indian Movement (AIM). On February 27, 1973, about 300 AIM militants took over buildings in the Sioux reservation at Wounded Knee, South Dakota, the site of a notorious massacre

◀ **Two armed members of the American Indian Movement stand guard at the Sioux reservation at Wounded Knee.**

of Sioux by US cavalry in 1890 – especially famous because of its use in the title of Dee Brown's book. As FBI agents put the militants under siege, the media flocked to the site to provide largely sympathetic coverage. Celebrities such as Marlon Brando and Jane Fonda declared their support for the militants.

The siege lasted two months, during which time two Native Americans were killed and a federal marshal was severely injured in sporadic exchanges of gunfire. The occupation ended on May 8. The AIM militants had only limited support among Native Americans, who mostly rejected their extreme radicalism, but their action was an unquestionable propaganda triumph.

PICASSO PASSES ON

On April 8, 1973, Pablo Picasso, the most influential artist of the twentieth century, died at his home in Provence aged 91. Picasso was astonishingly versatile, both in the range of media he explored, from painting and engraving to sculpture and ceramics, and in the wide variety of styles in which he worked. His inexhaustible energy and fertile imagination made him one of the most prolific artists of all time.

Picasso was born in Malaga, Spain, in 1881. After moving to Paris, in 1906 he embarked on the ground-breaking experiment known as Cubism, subverting almost every principle of Western art. After World War One, he worked in a dizzying range of

▶ **The founding father of the Cubist movement, Pablo Picasso was arguably the most influential artist of the century.**

styles, from neo-classicism to surrealism. His most famous work, *Guernica*, exhibited in 1937, was both a gesture of support for the Republican side in the Spanish Civil War and a protest against war in general.

Picasso remained in the avant-garde all his life. The works of his old age, many involving a disturbingly overt depiction of sexual acts, continued to puzzle and challenge both the critics and the public.

COUP IN CHILE

On September 11, 1973, the Chilean armed forces, led by army commander-in-chief General Augusto Pinochet Ugarte, overthrew the democratically elected government of Salvador Allende Gossens in a violent coup. Allende tried to organize resistance from the presidential palace, which was bombed and strafed by air force jets. His body was found in the ruins of the building.

Allende was a Marxist socialist, but not a Communist as his opponents often alleged and Western journalists carelessly repeated. He was elected president in 1970 in a tight-fought contest and governed through a left-wing Popular Unity coalition of socialists, communists, and radicals. The coalition government embarked on an ambitious programme of socialist reforms, including the breaking up of large estates in the countryside, and the nationalization of banks, copper mines and other major industrial concerns, some of which were wholly or partly American-owned.

Most South American countries at this time were under the rule of right-wing military dictatorships, backed by the Americans as a bulwark against Marxist revolution. Chile was exceptional in the region for its long tradition of democracy, but the US military establishment and business interests were nervous that this might open the door to a Communist takeover. In 1970, the CIA had backed an effort by the communications giant ITT to prevent Allende's election by mounting a "dirty tricks" campaign. After his election, covert American intervention to destabilize the regime continued.

This was not the only reason for the serious difficulties Allende soon encountered. Left-wing groups, who regarded the government as too moderate, seized land illegally and occupied factories. The failure to stop these revolutionary initiatives increased the fears of the middle and upper classes, already alienated by reforms that threatened their comfortable lifestyles. As the economy faltered, inflation raged out of control, reaching an annual involved in left-wing politics, trade union leaders, academics, journalists, social workers, and many loosely involved in liberal or humanitarian causes. A notorious case was that of folk singer Victor Jara, well known for his left-wing views. He was arrested on the day of the coup and taken to Santiago's boxing stadium. For four days he was tortured, his hands and wrists broken. Finally he was machine-gunned

▲ **"President Allende's Last Day"** – the Chilean leader is shown shortly before his death at the hands of General Pinochet's coup.

rate of 150 per cent. Chilean military leaders came to believe that they alone could save the country from a descent into chaos. They were encouraged in this view by the CIA, which was actively involved in the run-up to the coup.

The coup was followed by a reign of terror. At least 5,000 people were killed, tens of thousands were tortured and around 250,000 were interned as political prisoners in concentration camps. Victims included anyone to death and his body was thrown into the street.

Heading the new military regime, General Pinochet dissolved Congress, outlawed opposition parties, and imposed strict controls on the media. This did not prevent some conservatives in the United States and Britain hailing him as a saviour of liberty. They pointed to his introduction of free market reforms, ending price controls and reversing nationalization. Military rule was to last in Chile for 17 years.

YOM KIPPUR WAR

▲ **The Egyptian government viewed the Yom Kippur war as a moral victory despite its eventual military defeat.**

The Israeli victory over its Arab neighbours in the 1967 Six-Day War failed to create the basis for a stable peace in the Middle East. Egypt and Syria were determined to recover territory they had lost in the Sinai and the Golan Heights respectively. The Middle East conflict had also become subsumed under the Cold War, with the United States supplying state-of-the-art military technology to Israel, and the Soviets backing Egypt and Syria.

Egypt's radical leader Gamal Abdel Nasser died in 1970 and his place was taken by Anwar Sadat. Making a realistic assessment of Egypt's situation, Sadat believed the only way to drive the Israelis from the Sinai was to induce the Americans to force the Israelis to make concessions. In 1972 he expelled Soviet military advisers from Egypt, but the United States showed no signs of rewarding this move. Sadat decided the only way to unblock the situation was to launch a limited offensive that would compel the Americans to intervene.

On October 6, 1973, on the Jewish holiday of Yom Kippur, Egyptian troops launched an assault across the Suez Canal and breached the Israeli Bar-Lev Line. Egyptian tanks and infantry flowed across pontoon bridges into Sinai. The Israelis, who had so easily defeated their Arab neighbours in 1956 and 1967, had grown complacent about their military superiority. But the Egyptians were now equipped with Soviet anti-aircraft and anti-tank missiles. When the Israelis counter-attacked, they suffered heavy losses on land and in the air. Large-scale battle was also joined on the Golan front, with Syrian and Israeli tanks locked in combat.

The Israelis quickly recovered from their initial shock, and once more proved their tactical superiority. On 15 October, Israeli forces crossed the Suez Canal to the west bank and cut off the Egyptian armies in Sinai from their supply bases. Egypt faced total military catastrophe. The superpowers agreed that it was time to call a halt. On October 22, the United Nations passed a resolution framed by the United States and the Soviet Union calling for an immediate cease-fire. When the Israelis continued to advance the following day, the Soviet Union threatened to send in its own troops to defend Egypt. The United States responded by putting its nuclear forces on red alert, but also pressured Israel into calling a halt.

The Israelis were profoundly shocked by their losses in the war – 1,854 dead and a similar number wounded. Egypt celebrated what its people felt to be a moral victory, despite the eventual military defeat. As Sadat had intended, the United States was subsequently drawn into an effort to broker an even-handed peace in the Middle East that bore fruit by the end of the decade.

BRITAIN'S THREE-DAY WEEK

In mid-December 1973, British Prime Minister Edward Heath announced that, from the start of the New Year, factories and businesses would only be allowed to use electricity for three days a week. Most of them, of course, would have to shut down for lack of light and power. In another energy-saving measure, television programmes were to stop at 10.30 every evening.

The declaration of a three-day week was the climax of a pro-longed confrontation between the government and workers in nationalized industries. Since 1970, the Heath government had been battered by nationwide strikes – in 1972, a record 24 million working days had been lost through strike action. One of the most powerful unions was the National Union of Mineworkers (NUM). In February 1972, the miners had won a large pay rise after a strike that caused power cuts and short-time working in industry.

When the NUM called an over-time ban in late 1973, the government decided the moment was ripe for a showdown. The declaration of a three-day week was a pre-emptive blow, intended to mobilize popular opinion against the miners while coal stocks were still adequate. The ploy proved a failure. In February 1974, the miners came out on strike, with the active support of the rail and power unions. Heath called an immediate general election on the the issue: "Who runs the country?" He lost by a narrow margin, and Labour leader Harold Wilson was able to form a government committed to full cooperation with the unions.

◄ **Working by lamplight became a common experience for the people of Britain during the "Winter of Discontent".**

OIL SHEIKHS SHAKE THE WORLD

The Yom Kippur War precipitated a crisis in energy supplies that had a seismic effect on the world economy. Western Europe, Japan and, to a much lesser extent, the United States, had become heavily dependent on oil supplies from Arab countries in the Middle East. Led by Saudi Arabia, these countries united to use the "oil weapon" against the West. At the height of the war, they announced sharp reductions in oil exports and a complete embargo on supplies to the United States and the Netherlands, the two Western countries most closely identified with Israel.

These measures caused panic and temporary petrol shortages in some countries, but were shortlived. By March 1974, oil supplies were generally back to normal. But the price of crude oil had quadrupled during the crisis. Through the Organization of

▲ **Sheikh Yamani of Saudi Arabia, one of the perpetrators of the "oil weapon" that crippled the West during 1970s.**

Petroleum Exporting Countries (OPEC), the oil producers worked to hold prices at their new level by regulating output.

As a consequence of this huge price hike, the rulers of some of the Arab states, such as Kuwait, Bahrain and Saudi Arabia, suddenly became fabulously rich. Inflation surged in all oil-importing countries, and unemployment followed as economies fell headlong into recession. The search for alternative energy sources quickened, with France, for example, embarking on a massive nuclear power programme. And new oil fields in difficult areas, such as those just being explored in the North Sea, were suddenly potentially profitable.

At 2.30 a.m. on June 17, 1972, five men carrying cameras and bugging devices were arrested after breaking into the offices of the Democratic National Committee at the Watergate complex in Washington DC. Campaigning for the US presidential elections the following November was in full swing, with the incumbent Richard Nixon looking set to win another four years in the White House. Nixon's Democratic opponents struggled to make an issue of the Watergate break-in, but despite clear links between the burglars and Nixon's Committee to Reelect the President (CREEP) – one of the burglars, James W McCord, was CREEP's director of security – the case failed to catch fire. Denying he had any connection with this "third-rate burglary", Nixon duly won by a landslide. His triumph was to prove shortlived.

▲ **A poster showing those apprehended in the aftermath of the Watergate scandal. One figure escaped prosecution – President Nixon.**

The trial of the Watergate burglars had already opened by the time of the election. Indicted along with the five men arrested in the building were former CIA operative Howard Hunt and former FBI agent Gordon Liddy. Hunt and Liddy had planned and organized the break-in. It later emerged that they were members of a secret White House team known as the "plumbers" – because they would stop government leaks. The plumbers had been assembled in 1971 after defense expert Daniel Ellsberg leaked a secret report on the Vietnam War, the Pentagon Papers, to the press. Hunt and

◀ **Richard Nixon, known after Watergate as "Tricky Dicky", chose live television to announce his resignation.**

Liddy organized a burglary at the office of Ellsberg's psychiatrist in an effort to find material that would discredit him. They moved on to surveillance and "dirty tricks" activities against the Democrats, acting under the orders of CREEP, which was headed by former attorney-general John Mitchell.

The burglary trial, conducted by Judge John Sirica, ended in January 1973 with prison sentences for all the accused. Sirica was not satisfied that the truth had come out in court, however, and ensured that investigation of the case continued. It was also being pursued by two young journalists from the *Washington Post*, Bob Woodward and Carl Bernstein, guided by an anonymous informant dubbed "Deep Throat" after the famous porn movie of the time.

By April 1973, the wall of secrecy protecting the president had been breached. White House legal counsel John Dean agreed to talk, detailing the involvement of presidential aides and the President himself in a cover-up. At the end of the month, Nixon's top White House staffers, Bob Haldeman and John Ehrlichman resigned: Ehrlichman had directed the activities of the "plumbers", while Haldeman was heavily implicated in the post-Watergate cover-up. A fortnight later, a Senate Watergate committee began televised hearings. Still insisting he was innocent, Nixon had former solicitor general Archibald Cox appointed as a special prosecutor to investigate the affair.

For the next 15 months, as the tale of the Watergate conspiracy unravelled, the cornered President battled for his political life. Dean testified that Nixon,

Haldeman and Ehrlichman had all conspired in a cover-up after the break-in, but on its own his evidence was not enough. In July 1973, a former White House aide sensationally revealed that conversations in the presidential Oval Office had been secretly taped. The tapes clearly constituted a vital source of evidence, and Nixon was ordered to hand them over. Nixon's response, on October 20, was the "Saturday Night Massacre". He sacked Cox and abolished the post of special prosecutor. He also fired his attorney-general, Elliot Richardson, and deputy attorney general William Ruckelshaus for refusing to sack the special prosecutor when told to do so.

Reported in the press as a kind of coup d'etat, the drama of October 20 only brought the presidency into further disrepute. A new prosecutor was appointed and the wrangle over the tapes went on, with the White House grudgingly releasing more and more material. The discovery of the inexplicable "accidental" erasure of a tape covering a key conversation between Nixon and Haldeman raised further suspicions of White House skullduggery. Meanwhile, Nixon's Vice-President, Spiro Agnew, had been forced to resign

▲ Investigative journalists Robert Woodward (left) and Carl Bernstein (right) of the *Washington Post* uncovered the events of Watergate.

because of unrelated tax evasion charges, and Ehrlichman was being prosecuted for his part in the Ellsberg burglary.

Desperate to restore his popularity, Nixon gave an extensive televised press conference in November. He told the public: "People have got to know whether or not their president is a crook. Well, I'm not a crook. I've earned everything I've got." But few Americans were by then prepared to believe him. As the content of conversations in the Oval Office was revealed through the tapes, people were also disturbed by the general cynicism and vulgarity they revealed – transcripts were peppered with the phrase "expletive deleted", which Nixon later claimed concealed the word "damn", but was generally believed to hide more salty ejaculations.

The protracted end-game dragged on. In March 1974, a federal grand jury indicted Nixon as a co-conspirator in the Watergate cover-up, but still he clung on as the lamest of lame-duck presidents. In the last week of July, the Supreme Court ruled that 64 tapes the president had been holding back, claiming "executive privilege", must be handed over, and the House Judiciary Committee recommended the impeachment of the president on grounds of obstruction of justice.

On August 8, 1974, Nixon announced his resignation. Vice President Gerald Ford was sworn in the following day, declaring hopefully: "Our long national nightmare is over." But the Watergate affair had seriously undermined the p ower and prestige of the presidency, which would not begin to recover until the 1980s.

In all, 19 officials from the Nixon White House staff and reelection campaign spent time in prison, including Mitchell, Erlichman, Haldeman, and Dean. But Nixon himself was given a "full, free, and absolute pardon" by President Ford.

▲ Richard Nixon embraces his daughter, Julie Eisenhower, following his decision to resign from office.

'74

SOLZHENITSYN IN EXILE

On February 13, 1974, the novelist Alexander Solzhenitsyn was deported from the Soviet Union to West Germany. The expulsion order followed the publication of the first volume of his massive study of the Stalinist prison-camp system, *The Gulag Archipelago*, in the West.

Solzhenitsyn was himself a survivor of the camps, where he had been imprisoned from 1945 to 1953. During the Soviet cultural thaw under Nikita Khrushchev, his novel of camp life *One Day in the Life of Ivan Denisovich* was published to general acclaim both in the Soviet Union and abroad. However, his outspoken criticisms of the Soviet system soon brought him once more into conflict with the authorities. His later novels, such as *The First Circle* (1968), were banned in the Soviet Union and he was expelled from the Soviet Writers' Union. In 1970, Solzhenitsyn was awarded the Nobel Prize for Literature, pro-

▲ Exiled to a life in the West, Nobel Prize-winning author Alexander Solzhenitsyn became the most celebrated of Soviet dissidents.

voking more venomous attacks in the Soviet press. It was made clear to him that if he went to Sweden to collect the prize he would never be allowed to return.

By the time of his exile, Solzhenitsyn was the most famous Soviet dissident and a hero to many in the West. He was greeted with reverence as a sage, and mobbed by journalists like a pop star. The wide support for his courageous stance against Soviet

censorship and injustice could not, however, obscure the fact that many of his views – such as his expression of support for General Pinochet in Chile and his belief in religion as the key to the rebirth of Russian greatness – could seem provocatively right-wing or eccentric in a Western context. Ill at ease with publicity, he soon retreated to well-defended seclusion in the United States.

DC-10 AIR DISASTER

On March 3, 1974, a Turkish Airlines DC-10 bound from Paris to London crashed only minutes after taking off from Orly airport. All 346 people on board

were killed, making it the worst air disaster up to that time.

The aircraft broke up at an altitude of about 3,000 metres (10,000 ft) and plunged into the

Forest of Ermonville outside the town of Senlis. Parts of the wreckage were (11 km (7 miles) away and mutilated bodies were scattered over a wide area. Initial concerns that a terrorist bomb might have caused the crash proved false. The victims included a large number of English rugby supporters returning from a match in Paris.

The crash focused mounting concerns about air safety as both the number and size of airliners increased yearly – jumbo jets had come into service at the start of the decade. Only three years later, 583 people were killed in an air disaster at Tenerife.

▲ One of the engines of the Turkish Airlines DC-10 that crashed shortly after leaving Orly airport.

THE PATTY HEARST KIDNAPPING

The Patty Hearst saga began on February 4, 1974. The 19-year-old daughter of the chairman of the Hearst media empire, she was living with her boyfriend Steven Weed in Berkeley, California. At 9 p.m., two men and a woman, heavily armed, forced their way into her apartment. They beat Weed to the ground and dragged Patty to a waiting car, forcing her into the boot and driving off after firing a few shots at neighbours who might have been tempted to intervene.

The kidnappers were a small group of would-be revolutionaries, the Symbionese Liberation Army (SLA), led by ex-convict Donald DeFreeze, known as Cinque Mtume. Many such groups had sprouted in the United States since the late 1960s, as the era of student radicalism and black power agitation soured into violence. Two SLA members had already been arrested for the murder of an Oakland school superintendent, and Patty was kidnapped as a hostage to obtain their release. However, the kidnapping of the Hearst heiress caused such a media sensation that the SLA soon began to think much more could be made of it.

For 57 days, Patty was kept bound and blindfolded in a closet, only allowed out to use the bathroom. Taunted, threatened and fearing for her life, she agreed to record a message saying she was being well treated and calling on her father to meet the SLA's demand for the distribution of $70 dollars-worth of food to every poor person in California. Gradually she began to succumb to their version of the world – that her father was a "corporate pig" who cared more about money than he did about his own daughter.

On April 3, Patty released a sensational taped statement: "I have been given the choice of being released in a safe area or joining the forces of the Symbionese Liberation Army and fighting for my freedom and the freedom of all oppressed people. I have chosen to stay and fight …" Twelve days later, she was videoed by a security camera as, armed with an automatic weapon, she covered her SLA colleagues while they robbed a San Francisco bank.

Adopting the name Tania "after a colleague of Che in Bolivia", Patty became an established member of an SLA three-person guerrilla squad. She was absent on an armed mission when the FBI found the SLA's "safe house" in the Watts district of Los Angeles. On May 18, the police launched a wholesale armed assault on the building, setting it on fire and incinerating or asphyxiating all those inside, including Donald DeFreeze. It was an operation conducted with an extraordinary brutality and a disregard for life that could have been expressly designed to confirm the SLA's vision of America as a "fascist" state.

With two other SLA members, Patty Hearst went on the run, disappearing into the radical "underground". After participating in a number of other urban guerrilla operations, she was eventually arrested in September 1975. After a highly controversial trial, she was sentenced to seven years for armed robbery.

▲ **From WASP to terrorist, in a surprise turnaround Patty Hearst went from hostage to joining the Symbionese Liberation Army.**

- Popular songs of the year include "The Way We Were" by Barbra Streisand, "Waterloo" by Abba; among the albums released is *Tubular Bells* by Mike Oldfield

January
- USA adopts 55mph national speed limit
- Israel and Egypt sign disengagement treaty
- Deaths of US film producer Sam Goldwyn, British author James Pope-Hennessy and Greek Cypriot leader General George Grivas

February
- The *Mariner 10* space probe reaches Venus
- Grenada attains independence from Britain
- British coal miners begin strike
- Pakistan recognizes Bangladesh
- New constitution adopted in Sweden
- USA and Egypt resume diplomatic relations
- Labour win British general election, but with no overall majority

'74

FLIXBOROUGH CHEMICAL DISASTER

At 4.53 on the afternoon of June 10, 1974, a massive explosion occurred at a chemical plant at Flixborough, outside Scunthorpe on Humberside. The explosion killed 28 workers and devastated an entire village. People 6.5 km (4 miles) distant from the scene were buffeted by the blast. About 100 houses were wrecked and the factory itself was reduced to a twisted, blackened shell.

The Nypro plant was engaged in cyclohexane oxidation, a stage in the production of nylon. After a pipe feeding one of the reactors on the site developed a leak, a temporary pipe had been constructed to replace it. A leak from this pipe led to about 40

tons of gaseous cyclohexane escaping in a minute, until the vapour cloud ignited with devastating effect.

The main lesson drawn from the subsequent enquiry into the Flixborough disaster was that housing should be sited away from chemical plants and other dangerous industrial locations.

◀ **One of over 100 houses wrecked after a vapour cloud exploded above the Nypro chemical plant in Flixborough.**

RUSSIAN DANCER BARYSHNIKOV DEFECTS

On the evening of June 29, 1974, the Soviet Union's foremost male ballet star, Mikhail Baryshnikov, defected to the West. He was in Toronto, Canada, touring with the Bolshoi Ballet.

The memory of the 1961 defection of Rudolf Nureyev, the greatest Soviet dancer of the previous generation, meant that the Soviet authorities were on the look-out for a defection attempt. KGB men routinely assigned to watch any Soviet group travelling abroad were watching Baryshnikov with special care. But in a carefully planned manoeuvre, he gave them the slip. As the Soviet group were walking towards a bus that was going to drive them to their hotel, he broke away and ran to a waiting car with the KGB in futile pursuit.

After his defection, Baryshnikov performed first with the American Ballet Theater and then with the New York City Ballet, under George Balanchine. He also starred in several Hollywood movies, including *The Turning Point* (1977) and *White Nights* (1985).

◀ **Mikhail Baryshnikov shown alongside partner Natalia Makarova in a scene from his celebrated *Don Quixote*.**

JUAN PERÓN DIES

On July 1, 1974, Argentina's leader Juan Domingo Perón died after a long and tortuous career that had made him one of the most significant figures in twentieth-century South American history.

Born in 1895, Perón rose to prominence as one of the army officers who carried out a military coup in 1943. He organized a personal militia modelled on Mussolini's Blackshirts, and built up mass support through a mixture of force and propaganda. His popularity was enhanced by his marriage to actress Eva Perón, known as Evita, in 1945. The following year he was elected president, and set about creating an authoritarian dictatorship.

By 1955, with Evita dead and the economy on the skids, the army and Argentina's privileged classes took their revenge on the populist dictator. He was deposed in a military coup and exiled to Spain. However, the Perónist movement remained the most popular political force in Argentina. In 1973, they won free elections and Perón returned in triumph to resume the presidency.

His death ended the chance of a Perónist revival. He was succeeded by his second wife and vice president, the former dancer Maria Estela Martinez de Perón, known as Isabelita. But she was deposed in a military coup in March 1976, and sentenced to five years in prison for alleged corruption. Argentina returned to military rule, entering the era of "disappearances" of political opponents and, ultimately, the misguided Falklands War.

▲ **After almost twenty years in exile, Perón made a triumphant return to his homeland in 1973, shortly before his death.**

BRANDT SPY SCANDAL

In May 1974, the West German Chancellor Willy Brandt was forced to resign after it was revealed that one of his closest aides was an East German spy.

▲ **West German Chancellor Willy Brandt was forced to resign when it was revealed that one of his aides was an East German spy.**

This security scandal was especially ironic in that Brandt had been pursuing a highly successful policy of rapprochement with the Soviet bloc, particularly with East Germany.

A Social Democrat, Brandt first won international renown as mayor of West Berlin from 1957 to 1966 – the period of the building of the Berlin Wall and the famous visit to the city by US President John F Kennedy. His resilient leadership of the West Berliners' resistance to Communist pressure won him many admirers. Elected West German chancellor in 1969, he embarked on a series of ambitious foreign policy initiatives known as *Ostpolitik*. These essentially involved accepting the result of World War Two, including the division of Germany and the loss of German territory in the east to Poland.

In March 1970, Brandt met the head of the East German council of ministers, Willi Stoph, at Erfurt in an epoch-making gesture that opened the way for official recognition of East Germany. The process of detente was bitterly opposed by right-wing nationalists in West Germany, dedicated to German reunification and the destruction of Communism, but

brought many practical benefits, particularly for Berliners, as lines of communication across the Wall were restored. It also contributed to a general reduction in international tension, earning Brandt the Nobel Peace Prize in 1971.

Brandt's nemesis was Gunter Guillaume. The East German espionage service, under spymaster Markus Wolf, sent Guillaume into West Germany in the 1950s as an ostensible political refugee. He joined the Social Democrats and patiently worked his way up through the ranks. He won Brandt's confidence and, despite doubts expressed by West German counter-intelligence, was given a place on the chancellor's staff. He had access to many top-secret documents, including important Nato papers.

The unmasking of Guillaume was received with evident glee by Brandt's political opponents, who linked the misjudgement to his "soft" line on Communism. The chancellor's prompt and honourable resignation saved his political reputation, however, and he continued to play a senior role on important committees. Brandt's successor, Helmut Schmidt, continued his *Ostpolitik* and kept the Social Democrats in power until 1982.

74

TURKEY INVADES CYPRUS

▲ **Turkey launched its military invasion of Cyprus following fears of its increasingly close ties with Greece.**

After Cyprus became independent of Britain in 1959, fighting soon broke out between the Greek majority and Turkish minority populations, leading in 1964 to the intervention of a UN peacekeeping force and to effective partition on communal lines, with Turkish enclaves scattered across the island. Many Greek Cypriots remained dedicated to *enosis,* the union of Cyprus with mainland Greece. They built up an 18,000-strong National Guard, commanded by officers of the Greek army, and opposed to the relative moderation of the Cypriot President, Archbishop Makarios.

On July 15, 1974, the National Guard overthrew Makarios, storming the presidential palace, and established former terrorist, Nikos Sampson, in his place. The coup had the full support of the government of the "Greek colonels", the military regime that had ruled Greece since 1967. Makarios fled to the safety of a British base area and was flown out to London.

The coup was a clear breach of the terms of the independence agreement that both Turkey and Britain were committed to uphold. On July 20, the Turks launched an invasion of the island by sea and air, ostensibly to protect the Turkish minority, but more importantly to prevent Cyprus becoming a part of Greece. Within two days, despite some stiff resistance, the Turkish invasion force was in control of a substantial part of the island. Sampson fell from power after only a week in office, and the military government in Athens was also overthrown, discredited by its failure to anticipate or resist the Cyprus invasion.

Over the following month, the Turkish forces cautiously extended their area of control until they held the whole northern part of the island from Famagusta to Lefka. Greek Cypriots were driven southward, while Turks living in the south of the island fled north to the protection of the Turkish army. By mid-August, Cyprus was divided into a Greek Cypriot south and a Turkish Cypriot north, separated by the so-called Atilla Line.

THE FALL OF HAILE SELASSIE

On September 12, 1974, an officer of the Ethiopian army drove to the imperial palace in Addis Ababa where the octagenarian Emperor Haile Selassie had for some time been living in almost total impotence and isolation. The officer read out an act of deposition, and the Lion of Judah was taken off to prison, where he would die the following year. It was an undignified end for a dynasty that claimed to trace its origins back to King Solomon and the Queen of Sheba.

Disenchantment with imperial rule in Ethiopia had gathered pace since the early 1960s. Rebellions in Eritrea and the Ogaden had forced the Emperor to expand and modernize his army with the help of the United States. The essentially feudal structure of the

▶ **The "Lion of Judah", Emperor Haile Selassie was deposed in a bloodless coup by an officer of the Ethiopian army.**

Ethiopian government and society had inevitably come to seem archaic to army officers exposed to increasing contacts with the outside world. The inadequate response to a terrible famine that began in 1972, and in which an estimated 200,000 Ethiopians lost their lives, threw a spotlight on the corruption and incompetence of the ruling elite.

By the start of 1974, there were widespread mutinies in the army, anti-government demonstrations by students, strikes, and peasant revolts. In June, a revolutionary committee of junior army officers, known as the Derg, was formed, and it was this body that eventually overthrew the emperor and seized power. Tragically, it proved far more oppressive than Haile Selassie had ever been. Under the leadership of Mengistu Haile Mariam, the Derg was to lead Ethiopia into a nightmare of red terror, warfare, and starvation.

IRA BLITZ ON BRITAIN

From 1973 onward, the Provisional IRA extended its campaign of bombing and shooting from Northern Ireland to mainland Britain. They set up "active service units", tight-knit groups of experienced personnel, to operate on the mainland. Attacks were primarily aimed at prestige targets or at off-duty soldiers.

Through 1974, the number and destructiveness of the bombings mounted alarmingly. On February 4, a bomb blew apart a coach carrying servicemen and their families along the M62 motorway, killing nine soldiers and three civilians. Westminster Hall, part of the Houses of Parliament, was bombed in June and the Tower of London in July. In October, a bomb was left in a pub in Guildford frequented by soldiers; five people were killed, including four military personnel. The bombing of another soldiers' pub, this time in Woolwich, in early November left two dead. These were only the most notable in a spate of explosions during this period.

The bloody climax came in the Midlands in mid-November. On November 14, an IRA bomber, James McDade, was blown to bits by his own device which he intended to plant at Coventry telephone exchange. As IRA sympathizers gathered for McDade's funeral, the authorities

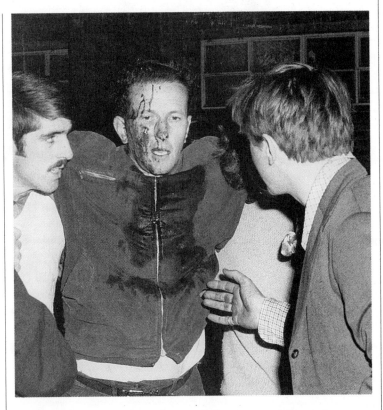

▲ One of the victims of the bombing of the Horse and Groom in Guildford, a pub known to be commonly used by soldiers.

announced that demonstrations in his memory were banned. Apparently in retaliation for this, on the evening of November 21, bombs were left in two crowded pubs in Birmingham city centre, the Mulberry Bush and the Tavern in the Town. A belated and inaccurate telephone warning left no chance for the pubs to be evacuated. In the ensuing explosions, twenty-one people were killed and over 180 injured, many seriously, in the carnage that resulted.

The Birmingham bombings triggered the passage of the Prevention of Terrorism Act, giving the police extensive new powers. Unfortunately, the police response to the bombing campaign had already been to arrest anyone they thought they could pin the bombings on and make sure the charges stuck by fair means or foul. The result was a series of major miscarriages of justice, while the terrorist campaign continued unabated into 1975.

75

AMERICA FAILS IN VIETNAM

In 1973, US Secretary of State Henry Kissinger and North Vietnamese Politburo member Le Duc Tho were jointly awarded the Nobel peace prize for negotiating an end to the Vietnam War. But everybody knew the war was not really over. US forces had been withdrawn – the last military personnel left on March 29, 1973 – but fragmentary fighting between the forces of South Vietnam and the Communist north continued where the two sides had been left facing one another by the "cease-fire-in-place".

South Vietnam's President Nguyen Van Thieu, in power since 1967, had established a viable government, but his country remained utterly dependent on the United States. The Americans had moulded South Vietnam in their own image, leaving behind a nascent consumer society whose swollen cities required large imports of petrol and consumer goods to function. South Vietnam's armed forces were also structured around high-tech equipment that required expensive fuel, munitions and servicing. Only US subsidies could keep South Vietnam functioning.

Two major events knocked the supports from under South Vietnam. One was the quadrupling of world oil prices in the wake of the Yom Kippur War, which massively increased the bill for the country's petroleum imports. The other was the collapse of the power of the US presidency as Richard Nixon foundered in the morass of the

▲ Government troops and villagers read about the cease-fire agreement signed in Paris on June 14 that will brought an end to the Vietnam conflict.

Watergate scandal. Congress reasserted its control over US foreign policy. By the War Powers Resolution of November 1973, it took away the president's power to make war without prior congressional approval, effectively nullifying the promise Nixon had given to send in US forces again if the Communists threatened to take over the South. The following year, Congress also slashed the military aid budget to South Vietnam, cutting off the country's financial lifeline.

The position of American client regimes in neighbouring Cambodia and Laos was equally perilous. In Cambodia, the United States had been responsible for destroying an essentially stable society, through the large-scale bombing of rural areas by fleets of B-52s from 1969 to 1973, and through conniving in the overthrow of the neutral Cambodian ruler Prince Norodom Sihanouk in 1970. The effect of the bombing and political disruption was to turn the tiny Communist Khmer Rouge movement into a large-scale guerrilla organization, supported by Sihanouk who was still recognized by many Cambodians as their legitimate ruler. By 1974, Sihanouk's

American-backed replacement, General Lon Nol, was in control of just one-third of Cambodia.

In Laos, American intervention had been dominated by a desire to block the Ho Chi Minh Trail, the complex system of supply routes from North Vietnam to the South that ran inside the Laotian border. But years of massive aerial bombardment and military incursions had failed to interrupt the supply route or prevent the Laotian communists, the Pathet Lao, growing in strength.

Throughout 1974, the North Vietnamese covertly built up their forces in South Vietnam's border

▲ **Hundreds of thousands gathered in New York's Central Park to celebrate an end to the war in Vietnam.**

regions. In December, they embarked on an exploratory offensive, to check out South Vietnamese resistance and the American response. It was an outstanding success. By January 7, 1975, they had captured the province of Phuoc Long, without provoking any reaction from the United States. With confidence boosted, North Vietnam's military supremo General Vo Nguyen Giap ordered a major spring offensive.

On March 10, 1975, the North Vietnamese struck at the strategic centre of Ban Me Thuot in the Central Highlands. Within four days, the South Vietnamese had decided to abandon the entire Highland region to concentrate their forces on the defence of Saigon. This intended strategic withdrawal degenerated into a rout. Hundreds of thousands of soldiers and civilian refugees choked the roads in a panic flight from the advancing Communist forces. By the start of April, half of South Vietnam was in Communist hands and the South Vietnamese army was

melting away.

The US Congress had no intention of authorizing any further military aid to South Vietnam. On April 23, as North Vietnamese forces closed in on Saigon, President Gerald Ford announced that the United States would not regain its sense of pride by "refighting a war that is finished as far as America is concerned". But the US administration refused to authorize a wholesale evacuation of Americans and compromised South Vietnamese, pinning their last hope on inducing the North Vietnamese to stop short of total victory and accept the establishment of a coalition government in Saigon.

President Thieu resigned and was replaced by the neutralist General Duong Van Minh on April 28. By then, North Vietnamese tanks and artillery were in the suburbs of Saigon. There was to be no compromise. The last-minute panic that ensued stripped the Americans of any shred of dignity. Helicopters ferried between the roofs of buildings in Saigon and US aircraft carriers, taking Americans citizens and small numbers of Vietnamese to safety. Many thousands of South Vietnamese who had loyally supported the

Americans were abandoned to their fate – even records of the people who had aided US intelligence were not destroyed.

On April 30 a North Vietnamese tank crashed through the gates of the presidential palace in Saigon, and a single soldier ran forward to raise the flag of the Provisional Revolutionary Government. Then the sequence was repeated for TV cameras, which had missed the symbolic moment the first time round. After 30 years, the struggle to create a unified Communist-led Vietnam was over.

Meanwhile, the teenage soldiers of the Khmer Rouge in Cambodia had marched into Phnom Penh and begun clearing the city of its population, driving hundreds of thousands out to the Killing Fields. The following June, the Pathet Lao occupied the Laotian capital, Vientiane. For the first time in its history, the United States had suffered comprehensive defeat.

▲ **A US helicopter lands on a rooftop in Saigon to help with the evacuation of foreigners from South Vietnam. They are transported to navy ships waiting off the coast.**

'75

THE BAADER-MEINHOF GANG

At the end of the 1960s, a handful of the young would-be revolutionaries who had participated in the student protests of the period turned to terrorism, seeing themselves as urban guerrillas taking on international capitalism and imperialism. In West Germany, a dropped-out art student, Andreas Baader, and his girlfriend Gudrun Ensslin firebombed two Frankfurt department stores in April 1968. They were soon joined by a fashionable left-wing journalist, Ulrike Meinhof, who was so impressed by their direct action that she left her husband and her glamorous lifestyle to join the revolutionary underground, becoming Baader's lover.

Baader was soon arrested, but was laxly allowed out of prison under guard for study periods. In May 1970 Meinhof led an armed raid on a library where he was studying and carried him off in a silver-grey Alfa Romeo – they always showed a taste for smart, expensive cars.

The Baader-Meinhof gang, or Red Army Faction (RAF) as they called themselves, soon became part of an international terrorist network through contact with Palestinian terrorist groups who provided arms and training. Back in Germany, they began full-scale urban guerrilla operations in 1972, killing four people in bomb attacks on US army bases and blowing up the Hamburg offices of the Axel Springer press empire. Baader and Meinhof were soon arrested, however, along with many of their colleagues. A high-security prison and courthouse were built especially to contain them, at Stammheim, Stuttgart.

The remains of the Red Army Faction now devoted its efforts to getting them out of prison. A complex series of bloody dramas ensued. In February 1975, a leading West German politician, Peter Lorentz, was kidnapped. In return for his safety, of the gang were released and allowed to join their Palestinian friends in the Middle East. When the West German embassy in Stockholm was taken over by an RAF commando the following April, however, the government took a tougher line. No prisoners were released, so the terrorists blew up the embassy building, killing four people.

The RAF was now fully involved in international terrorism. Its members took part in the kidnap of OPEC oil ministers in Vienna in December 1975, a propaganda coup masterminded by the Venezuelan terrorist known as "Carlos". But while the tempo of terrorist attacks mounted, a slow-motion tragedy was enacted at Stammheim. One RAF leader, Holger Meins, died after a hunger

▲ Andreas Baader, founder of the Red Army Faction, built up links with terrorist groups throughout the world.

▲ Ulrike Meinhof, a former journalist who was attracted to the glamour of Andreas Baader's urban guerrilla image.

strike in 1974. In May 1976, Ulrike Meinhof was found hanged in her cell. According to the authorities she had committed suicide, but her lawyers insisted she had been murdered. More deaths were to follow.

In October 1977, RAF terrorists simultaneously took hostage a leading industrialist, Hanns-Martin Schleyer, and, with the aid of Palestinians, hijacked a Lufthansa airliner to Mogadishu, Somalia. But a specialist German anti-terrorist squad, helped by the British SAS, stormed the airliner, killing three of the terrorists and freeing the hostages. In revenge, Schleyer was murdered.

Inside Stammheim, according to the official version of events, in despair at the failure of the Mogadishu operation, Baader and another RAF leader, Jan-Carl Raspe, shot themselves, and Gudrun Ensslin hanged herself. No evidence has been found to support the widely voiced conjecture that they were murdered by the authorities.

PORTUGAL'S "CARNATION REVOLUTION"

U ntil the 1970s, the politics of the Iberian peninsula had remained ossified in the form of right-wing authoritarian regimes set up in the 1930s. In Portugal, the ageing dictator Antonio Salazar had a stroke in 1968, but his regime continued under Marcello Caetano. There was mounting discontent, however, both at Portugal's economic backwardness and at the cost of the country's colonial wars in Africa, where it was fighting guerrilla forces in Portuguese Guinea, Angola and Mozambique.

On April 25, 1974, the Caetano regime was overthrown in a military coup organized by left-wing junior army officers of the clandestine Movimento das Forcas Armadas (MFA). The virtually bloodless coup was greeted with scenes of popular jubilation in Lisbon and the red carnation was adopted as the symbol of a peaceful revolution.

The country's new leader was a conservative senior army officer, the monocled General Antonio de Spinola, who had agreed to front the coup. Many of the officers of

▲ **Mario Suares, the moderate socialist who was able to take advantage of Portugal's bloodless revolution.**

the MFA, were Marxist revolutionaries, however, and the hitherto banned Communist Party quickly emerged as a powerful force in the industrial areas of Portugal. Unable to block the swing to the left, General Spinola resigned in September 1974.

The country was deeply split. While in the south, factories were occupied by their workers and peasants took over large estates at gunpoint, in the Catholic-domi-

nated, traditionalist north there were violent attacks on Communist Party offices. In March 1975, Spinola tried to launch a counter-coup, but it failed. Elections in April gave a majority to Mario Soares's moderate Socialist Party, but power remained with a Supreme Revolutionary Council of Marxist officers, inspired by the flamboyant Captain Otelo de Carvalho.

For a time it seemed Portugal might become a Marxist state, probably modelled on Castro's Cuba. In the following months, several of Portugal's colonies became independent, including Mozambique and Angola. Then in November 1975, moderate members of the MLA, led by Colonel Ramalho Eanes, ordered the arrest of Carvalho and about 100 other left-wing officers, claiming they were planning a coup. The operation met with little resistance. Eanes became chief of staff and was elected president in 1976. With Soares as Prime Minister, Portugal was firmly on the path to liberal democracy.

▲ **Communists and Maoists join together in the centre of Lisbon to celebrate the downfall of the Caetano dictatorship.**

'75

BRITAIN SUFFERS ECONOMIC CRISIS

In July 1975, inflation in Britain was running at an annual rate of 26 per cent. The apparently uncontrollable inflationary spiral was a result of the huge rise in oil prices during 1973–74, large wage rises dictated by powerful trade unions, and uncontrolled government spending. Public expenditure had increased from around 40 per cent of the country's Gross National Product (GNP) in the early 1960s to almost 60 per cent by 1975. Unemployment was still low by later standards, but rising fast – from virtual full employment at 2.6 per cent of the workforce in 1970 to 4.1 per cent in 1975. It would increase still further to 6.2 per cent by 1977.

Trying to master this difficult situation was the Labour government of Harold Wilson. In 1974 the government had tried to win union cooperation for voluntary wage restraint through a "social contract", offering improved social services and price controls in return for low pay rises. By July 1975 this was clearly not working. Chancellor of the Exchequer Denis Healey introduced compulsory wage controls, limiting wage rises to a maximum of £6 a week and freezing all incomes of £8,500 a year and above. Price controls were tightened and limits imposed on government spending.

Despite these measures, Britain was forced the following year to go to the International Monetary Fund (IMF) for a loan of over £2 billion. As a condition of the loan, the government was forced to impose severe cuts in spending on health, education, and all other social services. Ironically, the potential salvation of the British economy, North Sea oil, began to come ashore in 1975, but it would not be available in substantial quantities until the end of the decade.

▲ "What Crisis?" – Chancellor of the Exchequer Denis Healey (left) claims that Britain's economic problems are under control.

CIVIL WAR IN ANGOLA

The revolution in Portugal in April 1974 had immediate consequences for the country's African colonies, including mineral-rich Angola. The new left-wing Portuguese regime was favourably disposed toward the guerrilla movements that had fought for independence since the 1960s and wanted to hand over power to them as quickly as possible.

In Angola there were three rival guerrilla organizations, the Marxist MPLA led by Agostinho Neto, the FNLA under Holden Roberto, and Jonas Savimbi's UNITA. The Portuguese agreed to hand over power to a coalition government including all three movements, but this deal quickly fell apart. After sharp fighting, the Marxist MPLA succeeded in expelling the two other groups from the capital, Luanda. They turned to South Africa, the United States and Zaire for support, while the MPLA invited Cuban "instructors" to aid its forces.

Independence was set for November 11, 1975. By then, Angola was in the grip of a full-scale civil war with heavy foreign involvement. A South African force invaded the country in October from South West Africa (now Namibia) in support of UNITA. The FLN, backed by Zaire and stiffened by a contingent of British mercenaries, advanced on Luanda from the north. On November 7, Cuban combat troops began to pour into Luanda and were deployed to defend the MPLA's power base.

Armed by the Soviet Union, the Cubans swiftly routed the FNLA offensive and forced the South

NEWS IN BRIEF

June
- Suez Canal reopens
- Algiers Agreement between Iraq and Iran on the Shatt al-Arab waterway signed, ending the Kurdish war in Iraq
- Mozambique becomes independent from Portugal
- Indira Gandhi, Indian Prime Minister, declares state of emergency in India, imposes press censorship and imprisons political opponents

July
- Portuguese colonies of Cape Verde Islands, São Tomé and Principe all attain independence
- Comoros unilaterally declares independence from France
- US spacecraft *Apollo 18* docks with Soviet *Soyuz 19* spacecraft
- Coup in Nigeria deposes General Gowon; Brigadier Murtala Mohammed takes power
- In referendum, UK votes to remain in EEC

August
- British inflation at its highest
- The "Birmingham Six" are convicted of IRA bomb attacks on Birmingham in Britain
- President Mujibur Rahman of Bangladesh assassinated; Khandakar Mushtaq Ahmed succeeds
- Deaths of ex-Emperor Haile Selassie of Ethiopia, Irish statesman Eamon de Valera and Soviet composer Dmitri Shostakovich

Africans to withdraw southward. By early 1976, with 13,000 Cuban troops at its disposal, the MPLA was established as the effective government of Angola. Its triumph was shortlived. With the backing of the Ovimbundu people of southern Angola and with support from the United States and South Africa, UNITA was to prove capable of sustaining a guerrilla campaign into the 1990s that would ruin Angola's economy and take a heavy toll on its population.

▲ Backed by the United States and South Africa, the UNITA rebels led by Jonas Savimbi waged war on the Marxist MPLA government.

FRANCO ERA ENDS

On November 20, 1975, after a lingering final illness, General Francisco Franco Bahamonde, dictator of Spain since 1939, died. For many years, Franco had been preoccupied with the survival of his regime after his death. As long ago as 1949, he had declared Spain officially a monarchy, though without a monarch. During the 1950s, he secretly chose the young Juan Carlos, grandson of Spain's last ruling king, Alfonso XIII, as his official heir, and began schooling him in the attributes he would require to continue Francoism without Franco. Juan Carlos's position as successor was made official in 1969, and he duly ascended the throne once the dictator was dead.

Few anticipated in 1975 that the restoration of the monarchy would lead Spain towards liberal democracy. Franco had forced Juan Carlos to swear in public to uphold the principles of the Francoist state. He had also left him hedged in by the Francoist military and political establishment. Yet the desire for change in the country was strong. Pessimists foresaw an outburst of popular protest leading to violence that would provide the excuse for a brutal crackdown by Francoist officers.

But Juan Carlos turned out to hold very different ideas from those Franco had tried to instil in him. He was convinced that an orderly progress to democracy was both possible and necessary for Spain. He did not accept Franco's view that Socialists, or even Communists, were necessarily "enemies of Spain".

In July 1976, the King appointed the 43-year-old Adolfo Suarez as Prime Minister. A politician who had worked for Franco all his life, Suarez did not frighten Spain's military leaders. But he made the move to democracy with decisive speed. In November 1976, he forced a proposal for universal suffrage through the Francoist parliament; it was approved by over 90 per cent of the Spanish people in a referendum the following month. Both the Socialist and Communist parties, banned since the civil war, were legalized. Against all the odds, Spain had embarked on a largely peaceful transition to liberal democracy within a constitutional monarchy.

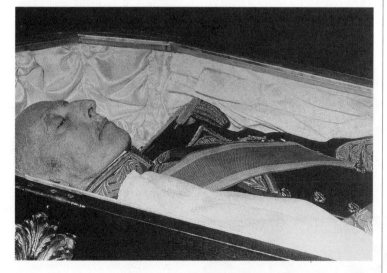

▲ For 35 years General Franco held absolute power in Spain. His death paved the way for the birth of a new democracy.

'76

CONFLICT IN THE SAHARA

The area of North Africa known until 1976 as the Spanish Sahara was a thinly populated desert zone bordered on one side by the Atlantic Ocean and, inland, by Morocco, Mauritania and Algeria. This apparently unprepossessing territory, a Spanish colony since the nineteenth century, happened to contain the world's largest deposits of phosphate, along with considerable quantities of iron ore.

In the 1970s, Spain came under pressure to leave the Sahara, both from the territory's neighbouring states and from a local independence movement, the pithily named Popular Front for the Liberation of Saguiet el Hamra and Rio de Oro – Polisario. The Spanish initially agreed to hand over to Polisario, which was generally acknowledged to have the support of the population of the territory. But Morocco's ruler King Hassan coveted the region's mineral

▲ The "Green March" saw 350,000 Moroccans marching under the flag of Islam into the Spanish territory of Polisario.

wealth. In November 1975, he organized an extraordinary propaganda coup, the "Green March", in which some 350,000 unarmed Moroccans marched under the green flag of Islam across the border into the Spanish colony.

Seeking the easiest way out, the Spanish government then changed tack and did a deal with Morocco and Mauritania. When the Spanish pulled out on

February 26, 1976, the Moroccans and Mauritanians moved in to partition the territory between them. Backed by Algeria, Polisario set up a government-in-exile and embarked on a guerrilla war to liberate their country from this new occupation. Another apparently permanent war zone was added to those already dotted across the map of independent Africa.

HAROLD WILSON RESIGNS

On March 16, 1976, Britain's Labour Prime Minister Harold Wilson announced that he was resigning from office. The

news came as a total surprise to insiders as well as to the general public. Despite awesome political problems, ranging from raging

inflation and mounting unemployment to union militancy and IRA terrorism, there was no obvious reason why Wilson should have quit. He had won two general elections in 1974 and could have been expected to govern Britain for at least another three years.

Rumours were soon spreading that Wilson had been forced to quit by a threat to reveal some scandal or secret about his past. It was later revealed that there

◀ Harold Wilson's resignation shocked Britain. Many believed that he was the victim of a secret service coup.

had indeed been a plot to oust him, hatched by disgruntled MI5 officers. According to former MI5 officer Peter Wright's sensational book *Spycatcher,* published in 1986, the idea was to leak to the press secret files containing allegations against Wilson and some of his colleagues. According to the wildest theories circulating in secret service circles, endorsed by the paranoid American counter-intelligence chief James Angleton, Wilson was a full-blown Soviet agent. Angleton believed that Wilson's predecessor as Labour leader, Hugh Gaitskell, had been murdered by the KGB in 1963 so they could get their man to the top.

Unfortunately for the conspiracy theorists, there was not only no shred of truth in the allegations against Wilson, but also no connection between the MI5 plot and his resignation. In fact, the MI5 men did not carry through their plan – it was quashed by more senior officers.

It is now known that Wilson in fact resigned because of the onset of Alzheimer's disease, which had begun to impair his faculties. Preferring to remain discreet about this, he spent a short spell performing useful duties in the House of Lords before retreating into private life. He was replaced as Prime Minister by James Callaghan, who led the government until the defeat of Labour in the 1979 elections.

HOWARD HUGHES DIES

On April 5, 1976, Howard Hughes, one of the world's richest and strangest men, died of a stroke while on a flight from Mexico to Texas. He was 70 years old.

Born in 1905, Hughes was 18 when he inherited his father's fortune, made through the invention and manufacture of an oil-drilling bit. He used the money as a springboard for the creation of a vast corporate empire, as well as for the indulgence of his own obsessive interests.

As a producer, he was a leading player in Hollywood during the early years of sound movies. His notable productions of the early 1930s included the classics *Hell's Angels, The Front Page* and *Scarface.* In 1943, he produced and directed *The Outlaw,* starring his own discovery, Jane Russell, whose bra for the film Hughes designed himself.

But from 1932 until the late 1940s, his passion was aviation. He established the Hughes Aircraft Company and designed the H-1 racer for himself to fly. As a pilot, Hughes broke virtually every speed record in the 1930s, including a round-the-world flight in 91 hours and 17 minutes in 1938 that won him a congressional medal.

His innovative approach to aircraft design got him into trouble during World War Two, when he received millions of dollars of government finance to develop a mammoth wooden flying boat. Known as the *Spruce Goose,* it was the world's largest airplane, but also one of the world's biggest

▲ **The creator of a wealthy business empire, Howard Hughes frequently indulged himself in his greatest interests – aviation and cinema.**

white elephants. Hughes flew the eight-engined monstrosity for a short distance in November 1947, just to prove it could fly, but this did little to deflect criticism of the waste of public funds.

Around this time, Hughes began to suffer psychological problems, partly as the result of a serious air crash. Nominally in control of huge corporations in the aerospace, electronics and airline sectors, he became increasingly reclusive, apparently obsessed with the risk of infection through dirt or human contact. He ran his business empire from sealed hotel suites, moving between locations in his private jet. It was a sad decline for a man who had been one of America's more interesting billionaires.

COD WAR CRISIS

In June 1976, Britain and Iceland agreed to end the third of the "Cod Wars" that had brought these two essentially friendly nations absurdly close to armed conflict. The Cod Wars grew out of a worldwide phenomenon: the depletion of fish stocks in the face of over-fishing. Between 1950 and 1970, world fish catches rose from 20 million tonnes to almost 70 million. For countries such as Iceland, heavily dependent on offshore fishing, the threat to livelihoods was acute.

Iceland's response to the fisheries crisis was to unilaterally extend its fishing limits – the distance from the Icelandic coast inside which only Icelandic fishing vessels were allowed to operate. The limits were extended from 7 km (4½ miles) to 20 km (12 miles) in 1958, then to 50 km (30 miles) in 1972, and eventually to 320 km (200 miles) in 1975. Each time, Britain rejected the new limits, which cut ever deeper into the traditional fishing grounds of British trawlers.

The pattern of conflict in the three Cod Wars – 1958–61, 1972–73, and 1975–76 – was the same. British trawlers disregarding the new fishing limits were harassed by Icelandic gunboats, which cut their nets and sometimes sent boarding parties aboard. Britain responded by sending in Royal Navy vessels to protect its trawlers. The "warfare" largely consisted of attempts by British frigates or fishery protection vessels to manoeuvre between the gunboats and the trawlers they were harassing. This not infrequently lead to collisions. In the third Cod War, 15 out of the 20 British frigates deployed off Iceland were damaged in nine months.

The 1975–76 conflict was the most serious of the three, leading Iceland and Britain to break off diplomatic relations. At one point, an Icelandic gunboat, the *Thor*, actually fired a live round at British vessels. The agreement reached in June to end the dispute was largely favourable to Iceland. There was no escape for British fishermen from the trap of declining fish stocks and mounting international competition.

▲ **A fleet of British trawlers make their feelings clear as they prepare to enter Iceland's newly extended fishing zone.**

THORPE CASE SCANDAL

In May 1976, Jeremy Thorpe, the leader of the British Liberal party since 1967, resigned in the face of what he described as "a sustained press witchhunt and campaign of denigration". The "witchhunt" concerned his relations with Norman Scott, usually described as an "unemployed male model". Scott had alleged that Thorpe seduced him as a young man, leading him into homosexuality. This allegation Thorpe hotly denied.

The issue might have been expected to fade from public attention after Thorpe's resignation and his replacement as Liberal leader by the clean-cut David Steele. But there was much more to the story than had immediately appeared. Police began investigating an apparently unlikely allegation by Scott that Thorpe had plotted to have him murdered. Amazingly, enough evidence began to emerge to suggest that Scott's allegations should be taken seriously. In December 1978, a Devon magistrates court committed Thorpe and three associates for trial at the Old Bailey in London on the charge of conspiracy to murder.

The "trial of the century", as it was billed at the time, opened in May 1979. The jury heard crown prosecutors assert that an airline pilot, Andrew Newton, had been paid £5,000 by Thorpe and three associates, George Deakin, David Holmes and John le Mesurier, to kill Scott. The motive was the threat posed by Scott, an aggrieved ex-lover, to Thorpe's political career. It was alleged that

Newton had bodged the murder, succeeding only in shooting Scott's dog, a Great Dane called Rinka (hence the scandal is sometimes referred to as "Rinkagate").

The trial judge, Mr Justice Cantley, is generally agreed to have been heavily disposed in Thorpe's favour. In his summing-up, he emphasized the defendant's standing as "a Privy Counsellor, a former leader of the Liberal Party, and a national figure with a very distinguished public record". On June 22, after three days' deliberation, the jury found all the defendants not guilty. Thorpe claimed to be completely vindicated by the verdict, but he had been shown, at the very least, to have been involved with some shady characters in an unpleasant business, and his reputation and political career – he lost his seat at the next election – were left in tatters.

▶ **The court may have found him innocent, but Jeremy Thorpe's distinguished political career was demolished.**

WORLD'S RICHEST MAN DIES

The American oil tycoon Jean Paul Getty died on June 6, 1976, at his home, Sutton Place, outside London. He was 83. His fortune was estimated at around $4 billion, making him probably the richest man in the world.

In a sense, Getty could claim to be a self-made man. He inherited around $15 million from his father, also a successful oil man, in 1930, but by then he had already become a millionaire in his own right, showing a gambler's instinct for acquiring concessions and companies at the best price and the right moment. He was known for his parsimony, famously installing a pay phone for guests in his English mansion. Married and divorced five times, he left three sons and several grandchildren.

Getty had built up a priceless collection of works of art, much of it displayed in the J Paul Getty Museum in Malibu, California, which Getty himself never visited. His death made the museum the most richly endowed art institution in the world, and its aggressive purchasing policy, backed by almost limitless funds, played a major role in the huge inflation of art auction prices from the 1970s onward.

◀ **A self-made tycoon. J Paul Getty started out with $15 million and ended up the richest man in the world.**

April
- New constitution adopted in Portugal
- James Callaghan elected leader of the British Labour party, becomes British Prime Minister
- Thai government defeated in general election
- Pol Pot becomes Cambodian Premier
- US President Ford extends US fishing rights 320 km (200 miles) off-shore
- Spain withdraws troops from the Sahara
- Western Sahara partitioned between Mauritania and Morocco
- Pakistan and India resume full diplomatic relations
- New coalition government formed in Thailand
- Indian supreme court rules that the government can imprison political opponents without trial
- Italian coalition government collapses
- Deaths of German-born French artist Max Ernst, Nobel prize-winning Danish biochemist Henrik Dam, US industrialist and film maker Howard Hughes, British film director Sir Carol Reed and South African-born actor Sid James

May
- Elias Sarkis elected president by Lebanese parliament
- Suicide in prison of Red Army Faction leader Ulrike Meinhof
- Deaths of influential Finnish architect Alvar Aalto and German existentialist philosopher Martin Heidegger

'76

THE YEAR THE EARTH SHOOK

1976 was a year of major earthquakes. Tremors in Guatemala in February, in northern Italy in May and in Turkey in November each left thousands dead. But all other natural disasters paled beside the catastrophe that struck the city of Tangshan, in China's Hebei province, on July 28. In the most destructive earthquake of the century, 242,000 people are officially estimated to have died, with another 164,000 seriously injured. Initial reports, still believed by some authorities, put the death toll much higher, at a monstrous 650,000, with 779,000 injured.

An important mining and industrial centre, Tangshan was at the epicentre of the earthquake. It was virtually obliterated. The shock waves were so powerful that there was heavy damage even in Beijing, about 160 km (100 miles) away. Faced with this colossal human tragedy, the Communist government, true to its principles of absolute self-reliance, refused all offers of aid from foreign governments and the United Nations. Instead, medical and rescue teams were drafted into Tangshen from all over China. The People's Liberation Army played a leading role both in the immediate relief effort and in reconstruction, which began almost immediately. By September, the government was trumpeting its achievement in reopening coal mines, rebuilding bridges, and restarting production in steel works.

The earthquake occurred only six weeks before the death of China's ruler, Mao Tse-tung In Chinese tradition, a political upheaval is expected to be heralded by a natural cataclysm. Although such an attitude was derided by Communists as outdated superstition, many Chinese people must have been struck by the coincidence between these two earth-shattering events.

▲ Tangshan, with its vast honeycomb of coal mines beneath the city, was obliterated by the most destructive earthquake of the century.

RAID ON ENTEBBE

On June 27, 1976, an Air France A-300 airbus on a flight from Tel Aviv to Paris was hijacked by four terrorists, two of them, Wilfried Böse and Gabriele Kröcher-Tiedemann, members of the German Baader-Meinhof gang and two belonging to the Popular Front for the Liberation of Palestine (PFLP). Holding the 12 crew and 256 passengers at gunpoint, they forced the pilot to fly the plane to Libya, where it refuelled, and then on to Entebbe International Airport in Uganda.

The destination had been chosen well in advance. Uganda's ruler, Idi Amin Dada, was a declared enemy of Israel and friend to the Palestinian cause. When the airliner landed at Entebbe, it was greeted by leading Palestinians and Ugandan army units. The crew and passengers were led off to be held hostage in a disused airport terminal building.

The hijackers demanded the release of 53 terrorists, most of them imprisoned in Israel, but some in jails in West Germany, Kenya, Switzerland, and France. As a "goodwill" gesture, they set free all the passengers and crew who were not Jewish. This left them with 105 Jewish hostages held at the airport. The terrorists felt totally secure. They were 4,800 km (3,000 miles) from Israel, in the heart of Africa, and could depend on the support of the Ugandan army and air force to repel any Israeli raid.

This was, however, an underestimation of the Israelis' implacable determination to resist terrorist demands. Despite the great risks involved, Israel decided to mount a rescue operation. On July 3, a

▲ Scenes of hysteria greet the hostages in Tel Aviv following their safe return from their kidnapping in Entebbe.

force of four Hercules transport aircraft packed with troops took off from the southern tip of Israel bound for Entebbe. Two Boeing 707s flew in support to provide a communications centre and medical facilities.

The Israeli plan was for the first Hercules to land under cover of darkness close behind a sched-uled British cargo flight, gambling on the Ugandan air traffic controllers failing to notice them. Astonishingly, the gamble worked. Without any alarm being raised on the ground, the Hercules landed safely and disgorged troops and vehicles on to the tarmac.

The assault on the airport building where the hostages were being held was brief and brutal. There were 13 terrorists and almost 100 Ugandan troops in the building, but most were asleep and all were caught completely unprepared. The Israelis had orders to kill all the terrorists, which they did, shooting some of them at close range while unarmed and still half asleep. More than 30 Ugandan soldiers were also killed, while the rest fled. Three of the hostages also died in the hail of Israeli gunfire. Only one Israeli soldier lost his life.

The other Hercules aircraft landed and the hostages were taken aboard to be flown to free-dom. Before one o'clock on the morning of July 4, the Israelis were heading for home. They were greeted at Ben Gurion airport with scenes of popular rejoicing. There was a tragic epilogue to the opera-tion as one passenger, 75-year-old Briton Dora Bloch, was in hospital when the raid took place. She was never seen again, presumably murdered by the vengeful Amin.

HAPPY BIRTHDAY USA

July 4, 1976 was the 200th anniversary of the American Declaration of Independence, the founding act of the United States. It occurred at a time of untypical self-doubt for Americans, in the wake of the Watergate scandal, setbacks for the economy, and the fall of Southeast Asia to Communism. Vice President Nelson Rockefeller marked the occasion with a downbeat remark about the "insuperable problems" the country faced. But most of his fellow citizens recognized an opportunity to celebrate feeling good about themselves and

▶ Citizens of the USA were jubilant as they celebrated their bicentennial – this huge birthday cake was typical of the revelry.

partied from coast to coast.

In New York, hundreds of thou-sands watched a fleet of tall ships progress up the Hudson River. In Washington, laser beams wrote "Happy Birthday, USA" in the sky at the climax of the largest of a myriad of firework displays. In Boston, they celebrated 1776 by making a pancake measuring 190 cm (76 in) across, and in Wisconsin enthusiasts spun a world record 1,776 frisbees into the sky.

- Former Japanese Prime Minister Kakuei Tanaka charged with accepting bribes from US aero-space company Lockheed
- Britain severs diplomatic relations with Uganda, following disappearance of Entebbe hostage Dora Bloch
- New coalition government under Giulio Andreotti formed in Italy
- Twenty-first Olympic games open in Montreal, Canada; boycotted by African nations

August
- Rioting in South African townships
- Trinidad and Tobago attain independence from Britain
- Ex-Prime Minister of Japan Tanaka indicted on corruption charges
- Earthquakes and tidal wave kills 7,000 in Indonesia
- Resignation of French Prime Minister Jacques Chirac
- Violence breaks out during the Notting Hill Carnival in Britain
- Mexico devalues the peso, causing high price rises for goods
- Deaths of German film director Fritz Lang and British actor Alastair Sim

September
- US spacecraft *Viking 2* makes soft landing on Mars
- Death Chinese leader Mao Tse-tung
- British Trident and Yugoslav DC9 collide in mid-air in Yugoslavia, killing 176
- Forty-four years of socialist rule ends when a centre-right coalition under Thorbjorn Falldin wins Swedish general election
- Elias Sarkis installed as President of Lebanon
- Emergency wage increase won by Mexican unions to mitigate inflationary price rises
- Ian Smith accepts plans for majority rule in Rhodesia

'76

THE MONTREAL OLYMPICS

▲ **Perfect ten – Nadia Comaneci, a 14-year-old gymnast from Romania, was without doubt the star of the Montreal Olympics.**

The 1976 Olympic Games in Montreal marked another stage in the politicization of sport that was threatening to tear the competition apart. South Africa had already been banned from Olympic competition because of its racist policies, but 22 black African countries nonetheless boycotted the Montreal games in an anti-South Africa protest. They withdrew because New Zealand was allowed to take part, although a New Zealand rugby team had toured South Africa. This mass boycott set a trend that was imitated by the United States at the next Olympics and by the Soviet Union and its allies at the one after that.

The star of the Montreal games was the 14-year-old Romanian gymnast Nadia Comaneci, who won three gold medals and scored the first perfect 10 in the history of Olympic gymnastics. The other most notable feature of the games was the outstanding success of East German women athletes and swimmers – which are now known to have been at least partly based on the use of banned drugs.

MAO'S DEATH AND THE GANG OF FOUR

At ten minutes after midnight on September 9, 1976, Mao Tse-tung, the leader of Communist China since its foundation in 1949, died after a long illness. More than 300,000 people filed past his body lying in state in Peking's Great Hall of the People. On the orders of the Communist Central Committee, every Chinese citizen observed the funeral ceremony on September 18, either watching on television or listening to a radio broadcast.

This impressive display of unity and discipline was not matched by harmony in the higher ranks of the ruling elite. The most prominent figure during the period of mourning was Hua Kuo-feng, recently appointed vice chairman of the Communist Party and thus, in principle, Mao's designated successor. However, also prominent at the ceremonies were Mao's widow, Jiang Qing, and three of her close associates, Wang Hongwen, Zhang Chunqiao, and Yao Wenyuan. These four were known as radicals within the Communist leadership, enjoying Mao's special protection and approval. They had made the running during the extremist period of the Cultural Revolution and advocated the purest form of egalitarian politics, with no concessions to free enterprise or foreign influence.

Four weeks after Mao's death, Western political commentators were still confidently discoursing upon the lengthy power struggle that would ensue when, to general astonishment, Hua announced the arrest of the four radical leaders

▲ **The West had expected a bitter struggle for power following the death of Mao Tse-tung, the father of Chinese Communism.**

and their detention at a secret location. Henceforth known as the "Gang of Four", they were pilloried for committing every kind of political crime and misdemeanour, from failing to make the trains run on time to perverting the young from the true course of Marxism.

The comprehensive and uncontested defeat of radical Maoism shifted China's political issues to fresh ground. A major absentee from the funeral ceremonies had been Deng Xiaoping, one of the old guard of Communist Party leaders, but a consistently pragmatic influence. During the Cultural Revolution period, he had been sent to work in a tractor factory as part of his "re-education". In 1976, he was once more out of favour following the death of his closest colleague, Chou En-lai, whose influence had protected him. But in 1977 Deng made a comeback to the party leadership. He would soon prove capable of ousting Hua and directing China on a startling new path to capitalist enterprise.

CARTER IS PRESIDENT

In November 1976, Democratic candidate Jimmy Carter, a 52-year-old peanut farmer from Plains, Georgia, was elected the next president of the United States, scoring a narrow victory over the incumbent President Gerald Ford.

Carter's victory owed much to the strength of his support in his native Deep South – he was the first Southerner elected to the White House for over a century – but it was also due to the impression of religion-based morality and honesty he conveyed, properties in high demand in the aftermath of the Watergate scandal. It could be said that American voters chose the candidate who was least like Richard Nixon.

Carter promised a programme reflecting many of the concerns of the liberal opposition in the United States over the previous decade – full civil rights, better health care, energy conservation, a foreign policy based on respect for human rights, reductions in nuclear arms, and bridging the gap between the people and their government. But the fates were to prove unkind to Carter, confronting him with economic decline at home and further blows to American power and prestige abroad.

▲ **President Jimmy Carter (left) and Vice President Walter Mondale (right) celebrate a Democrat victory.**

DEATH OF BENJAMIN BRITTEN

The celebrated English composer Benjamin Britten died on December 4, 1976 at the age of 65. Britten first came to prominence in the 1930s, when he was often associated with the poet W H Auden – they notably provided the music and verse for the famous 1936 documentary film *Night Mail*. Britten was a pacifist and, like Auden, left for the United States at the start of World War Two.

Returning to England, Britten established his claim to be regarded as a major composer with the 1945 opera *Peter Grimes*. With this and a string of other music dramas, including *Billy Budd* and *The Turn of the Screw*, he almost single-handedly created a British operatic tradition. In 1962, his choral setting of the requiem mass and poems by Wilfred Owen, *The War Requiem,* was premiered in Coventry Cathedral, recently rebuilt after its devastation by German bombs in 1940. The work was a popular and critical success, capturing the anti-war mood of the time. In his later years, Britten was increasingly preoccupied with the annual Aldeburgh Festival of which he was the presiding genius.

Britten's work reflected not only his pacifism, but also his homosexuality, though often in a veiled or allusive form. His lifelong companion was the singer Peter Pears. Only six months before his death, Britten had been made a life peer.

◀ **One of Britain's greatest composers, Benjamin Britten (right) photographed with his partner, opera singer Peter Pears.**

November
- Democratic candidate Jimmy Carter wins US presidential election
- Ban on political parties lifted in Egypt
- Deaths of Surrealist painter and photographer Man Ray, US sculptor Alexander Calder, originator of the mobile, French writer and politician André Malraux and British architect Sir Basil Spence, designer of the new Coventry Cathedral

December
- Ruling Liberal Democrats returned to power with reduced majority in Japanese elections
- Liberian oil tanker runs aground near Nantucket, USA causing major oil spill
- Coalition government under Yitzhak Rabin collapses in Israel
- Takeo Fukuda becomes Japanese Prime Minister

'77

- Attempted coup within the MPLA in Angola crushed; the MPLA conducts a purge and becomes officially a Marxist-Leninist organization
- Tamil separatist movement gathers pace in Sri Lanka
- Cholera epidemic in Arab states
- USA and USSR extend national waters to 320 km (200 miles)
- Indian birth control programme halted by scandal over botched operations and forced sterilizations
- State funding of elective abortions halted in the US
- Record low temperatures in the USA lead to major rivers freezing over in January and February
- A baby mammoth frozen in ice is discovered in the USSR
- Britain takes loan from the International Monetary Fund
- CFCs banned in the USA
- Fibre optic cable communication systems pioneered
- After years of governmental resistance, South Africa finally begins television transmissions
- New River Gorge Bridge completed in West Virginia, USA, becoming the world's longest steel arch bridge
- Sectarian bombings and killings continue in Northern Ireland and on British mainland
- Pompidou Centre opened in Paris
- Seven new nuclear power generators go on-line in the US
- One new nuclear power generator goes on-line in Japan

GARY GILMORE EXECUTED

On January 17, 1977, just after 8 a.m. local time, convicted murderer Gary Gilmore was executed by firing squad in a disused cannery in Utah State Prison. He was the first person executed anywhere in the United States for 10 years, during which time the Supreme Court had imposed an effective freeze on the death penalty.

Gilmore had been arrested in July 1976 in Provo, Utah, suspected of brutally killing two college students on consecutive nights. At the time he was already on parole from a 12-year sentence for armed robbery. Tried and found guilty the following October, Gilmore refused to appeal against the death sentence passed on him, and requested a firing squad as the mode of his execution.

The execution, originally set for November, was delayed by the American Civil Liberties Union (ACLU), which insisted on appealing the case despite Gilmore's desire to die. The ACLU knew that the case had the potential to open the floodgates to a general resumption of capital punishment. Appeals in different courts continued up to the morning of January 17, when the Supreme Court refused a last request for a stay of execution.

In the end, Gilmore got his way. He had twice tried to commit suicide while in prison. His cryptic last comment as he was led away to face the firing squad was "Let's do it".

▲ **Refusing to appeal against his death sentence, murderer Gary Gilmore was executed by firing squad as he had requested.**

CATASTROPHE IN THE CANARIES

The introduction of jumbo jets at the start of the 1970s, capable of carrying payloads of more than 300 passengers, led to gloomy predictions of massive air catastrophes. No-one, however, had quite foreseen the catastrophe that occurred in March 1977 – a collision between two jumbo jets on the ground.

The disaster happened on March 27 at Los Rodeos airport on Tenerife, one of the Canary Islands. Weather conditions were bad, with poor visibility, and the airport was under strain because nearby Las Palmas airport had been temporarily closed. Among the aircraft that had been diverted to Tenerife from Las Palmas were two Boeing 747s, one a Pan Am charter flight from Los Angeles, the other belonging to the Dutch airline KLM. The KLM jet was accelerating for take off when it ran into the Pan Am aircraft taxiing on the same runway.

Both aircraft were engulfed in flames. All 241 passengers and crew on the KLM flight were killed. Of the 380 passengers and crew on board the Pan Am aircraft, 342 died, some of severe burns a considerable time after the event. The total death toll of 583 has remained an unenviable world aviation record. The crash was eventually blamed on confused instructions from the airport control tower and the failure of air traffic control radar systems to show aircraft on the ground.

▲ **The burnt-out skeleton and tailplane of the Pan-Am jumbo jet litter the runway of Tenerife's Santa Cruz airport.**

DISASTER HIGHLIGHTS NORTH SEA OIL RISKS

In April 1977, the exploitation of the oil deposits beneath the North Sea produced its first ecological disaster. A blow-out occurred at a drilling platform, the Bravo rig, in Norway's Ekofisk Field when a valve was being changed. Oil gushed hundreds of metres into the air, as the workers on the platform were hastily evacuated. Over an eight-day period, more than 34 million litres (7.5 million gallons) of crude oil poured into the ocean, creating an oil slick 72.5 km (45 miles) long and 48 km (30 miles) wide. The gusher was eventually sealed by emergency teams using hydraulically operated rams.

There was no question of the oil spill causing any slowdown in the rush to develop North Sea oil production, however, spurred on by the world energy shortage since 1973. The first oil had come ashore in Britain in June 1975, and by 1977 776,000 barrels a day were being produced – a small quantity compared with the over 9 million barrels a day produced by the USA and Saudi Arabia, but far from insignificant.

▲ The massive expansion of oil production in the North Sea was not without its problems.

LEBANON FALLS APART

Until the 1970s, Lebanon had been an unusual Middle East success story. A state of apparently unmanageable ethnic and religious diversity, including such exotic medieval survivals as Maronite Christians and Druze Muslims, it had managed to hold together since independence at the end of World War Two and had become one of the region's most prosperous business centres. Pressures built up, however, and they eventually blew Lebanese society apart.

One element was the growing radicalism of many Lebanese Muslims, discontented with a traditional power-sharing arrangement that favoured the Christian minority. Another was the growing Palestinian presence. There had been large Palestinian refugee camps in Lebanon since the foundation of Israel in 1948, but from 1971 onwards the country became the main base for the substantial forces of Yasser Arafat's Palestine Liberation Organization.

In 1975, Lebanon exploded into civil war. Radical Shiite and Druze Muslims, the latter led by the charismatic Kamal Jumblatt, took on the Maronites, who in their turn carried out attacks on Palestinian camps and, where possible, massacred their inhabitants. This inevitably drew the PLO forces into the conflict on the Muslim side. The capital, Beirut, was split into warring sectors, with gunmen occupying what had been until recently thriving international hotels and luxury apartment blocks.

By 1977, the chaos in Lebanon had invited the intervention of a predominantly Syrian peacekeeping force, which had tried to enforce a series of cease-fires, each broken almost as soon as it was made. In March, a new twist was given to the conflict when the Druze leader Jumblatt was assassinated in his stronghold in the Chouf mountains. The Druze responded with massacres of Christian villagers, chosen not as the most likely culprits but as the most available victims. Lebanon had become a shambles, and was set to remain one of the world's most persistent troublespots into the 1990s.

▲ Teenage Christian girls, all members of the right-wing Phalangist Party, man the barricades as Lebanon's civil war descends into chaos.

TURMOIL IN PAKISTAN

In July 1977, a military coup in Pakistan overthrew the government of Zulfikar Ali Bhutto, ending a brief spell of civilian rule that had begun at the time of the secession of Bangladesh six years earlier.

Born in 1928, Bhutto was a man of aristocratic background who had been educated at Oxford University – where his daughter Benazir was also a student in the 1970s. In 1967, he founded the Pakistan People's Party, which won a massive majority in West Pakistan in elections held under General Yayha Khan's martial law regime in 1970. When the defeat of the Pakistan army by India allowed East Pakistan to become independent as Bangladesh the following year, General Khan handed over power to Bhutto.

The establishment of a democratically elected civilian government was widely welcomed. Bhutto embarked on an ambitious programme of constitutional and social reforms. His plans for the modernization of Pakistan brought him into conflict with Islamic fundamentalists in the country, who were buoyed up by the rising tide of traditionalist fervour sweeping the Islamic world, from Algeria and Egypt to Iran and Afghanistan.

Elections in the spring of 1977 confirmed Bhutto in power with a large majority. But the result was contested by Islamic fundamentalist parties, who engineered a campaign of protest that led to widespread disturbances.

On July 5, the army stepped in. General Zia ul-Haq, the chief of staff of the Pakistan army, seized power and put Bhutto under arrest. He was eventually charged with plotting the assassination of a political opponent and condemned to death. Despite a worldwide campaign against the sentence, Bhutto was hanged on April 4, 1979.

▲ **General Zia ul-Haq, the former chief of staff of the Pakistan army who lead the coup that brought an end to the Bhutto regime.**

ELIZABETH'S SILVER JUBILEE

1977 was the twenty-fifth anniversary of the accession to the throne of Queen Elizabeth II. After some hesitation, the authorities, backed by the Conservative press, decided to make this the occasion for major festivities. The Silver Jubilee turned out to be a party enjoyed by almost everyone.

The celebrations began on June 6 with the lighting of a chain of bonfires around the British coast from Land's End to the Shetlands, in imitation of the beacons lit to warn of the Spanish Armada's arrival in 1588 under Queen Elizabeth I. There was a Thanksgiving Service in St Paul's Cathedral and a banquet in the Guildhall. But the more impressive were the popular festivities at local level. Across Britain, neighbours organized street parties, with much food, drink, and goodwill being consumed amid the waving of Union Jacks. It may not have been the unifying celebration of monarchy and traditional patriotism that some commentators wishfully described – after all, the Sex Pistols were near the top of the hit parade with their aggressive "God Save the Queen". But it was an impressive display of the continued existence of an underlying local community spirit in Britain, something most people had long thought dead and gone.

▲ **The Silver Jubilee of Queen Elizabeth showed that Britain still had a taste for patriotic fervour with street parties taking place in every town.**

ANARCHY IN THE UK

By the mid-1970s, the phase of hippie popular culture that had flowered in the second half of the 1960s – with its ethos of "peace and love", its search for spiritual fulfilment through drugs and Eastern mysticism, its hi-tech concept albums, and its millionaire rock superstars – had wilted. British youth and the British music and fashion scene were ready for something new and different: they found it in punk.

The true origins of punk lay in New York, where underground bands inspired by the example of Iggy Pop were creating a raw, hard-driven musical sound and exploring subversive sartorial modes, including ripped clothing and prominently displayed safety pins. An entrepreneurial English couple, agit-pop mastermind Malcolm McLaren and dress designer Vivienne Westwood, picked up on the New York scene and brought it to Britain, giving it their own twist. Through their clothes shop Sex in London's King's Road, Mclaren met the young lads who were to become the Sex Pistols.

Punk took off in Britain in 1976 through bands such as the Sex Pistols, the Damned, and the Clash. Their fast, primitive music was greeted as a return to the crude rebellious roots of rock 'n' roll, a breath of fresh air after the "arty" rock of the hippie era. Political commentators hooked on the protest lyrics shouted over the background of ear-damaging guitars presented punk as the expression of an alienated young generation confronted with a future on the dole. To punk's street following, gigs were a raucous, riotous explosion of misbehaviour.

In December 1976, the Sex Pistols scandalized conservative opinion by engaging in a foul-mouthed dispute with presenter

▲ "Don't know what I want, but I know how to get it …" – the Sex Pistols were viewed as the figureheads of the Punk movement.

Bill Grundy on early evening television. McLaren saw such confrontations as an opportunity to achieve commercial success while simultaneously subverting the system. They certainly succeeded in winning massive publicity, ensuring that punk would be the style of 1977

Across the country, groups of young people, most with neither the ability nor the inclination to play music, climbed up on stage and called themselves bands – one of the best, the Adverts, performed a song appropriately called "One Chord Wonders". Performers adopted names such as Poly Styrene, Siouxsie, and Dee Generate. The most extreme youth fashions ever seen flourished on the streets, from Mohican hair cuts, Doc Martens, black rubbish sacks, and skin-piercing safety pins, to art-school-ironic chainstore kitsch.

Punks were in principle opposed to the established music business

and independent labels sprang up to accommodate them. But bands such as X-Ray Spex and the Stranglers were soon appearing on Top of the Pops, comfortably absorbed as the latest pop novelty in the endless and meaningless turnover of styles. The Sex Pistols were, as McLaren intended, less easily recuperated. Their single "God Save the Queen", provocatively released for the Silver Jubilee, was banned from radio and television, ensuring it would be a chart-topping hit.

By January 1978, when the Sex Pistols split up, punk was past its peak, although the next wave of performers – Elvis Costello, Blondie, Talking Heads – were heavily influenced by its example. The more extreme punk styles continued to survive as the uniform of a dwindling minority, eventually becoming a tourist attraction featured on postcards alongside Beefeaters, red telephone boxes and the British bobby.

- British aerospace and ship-building industries nationalized
- Incumbent Congress Party defeated in elections in India
- Lib-Lab pact between Liberal and Labour parties in Britain
- Morarji Desai replaces Indira Gandhi as Indian Prime Minister
- Human rights activist Anatoly Scharansky arrested by Soviet police
- Assassination of Lebanese Muslim leader Kamal Jumblatt

April
- Red Army Faction terrorists murder the West German attorney general responsible for the Baader-Meinhof prosecution
- Investment bank Kohlberg Kraus Roberts pioneers leveraged buy out
- Spanish Communist Party legalized
- Newspaper publisher Jacubo Timmerman arrested and subsequently tortured in crackdown on government critics in Argentina
- Zia ur-Rahman becomes President of Bangladesh
- US president Carter imposes national energy programme, urging energy conservation

May
- Swing to the right in British local elections
- Hanafi Muslim guerrillas seize three buildings in Washington DC, USA
- South Moluccan terrorists hijack a train at Assen in the Netherlands, taking 51 hostages
- Six policeman in Britain jailed on corruption charges

PEACE PRIZE FOR THE PEACE PEOPLE

In October 1977, two Catholic women from Andersonstown, Belfast, were awarded the Nobel Peace Prize for their initiative in starting a grass-roots peace movement in the province. Betty Williams and Mairead Corrigan

◀ **Betty Williams (left) and Mairead Corrigan (right) were awarded a Nobel Prize for their grass-roots peace movement.**

were, in fact, being belatedly awarded the prize for 1976, the award having been delayed through a technicality.

Williams and Corrigan started their peace initiative in August 1976 after three Catholic children in West Belfast, relatives of Corrigan, were killed by a Provisional IRA getaway car that was being pursued by an army patrol. They organized marches and rallies in which Protestant and Catholic women appeared side by side to protest against

both Republican and Loyalist terrorism, braving attacks and abuse from sectarian mobs. Many former neighbours, long separated by the Troubles, reestablished contact across the sectarian divide.

The women's Ulster Peace Movement, later renamed the Peace People, attracted worldwide attention, and Williams and Corrigan became celebrities. But although the movement succeeded in temporarily reducing the level of violence in Northern Ireland, its long-term effects were limited by its lack of a political programme beyond the simple ideals of non-violence, peace and justice

"SON OF SAM" TERRORIZES NEW YORK

During the spring and summer of 1977, New York was terrorized by a bizarre series of murders carried out by a killer who dubbed himself the "Son of Sam". In cryptic, incoherent notes left at murder scenes and in letters to the press and police, the killer explained that he was under orders from his "papa" to get blood, and that he would not stop killing until he was dead himself.

In August, a loner called David Berkowitz was arrested for the "Son of Sam" killings. He was alleged to have murdered six young women and one man and injured seven others. A .44 revolver used in the killings was found in a paper bag on the front seat of his car. All he said when charged was "You got me." Despite doubts about his sanity,

Berkowitz was judged fit to stand trial in 1978 and pleaded guilty. He was sentenced to life imprisonment for each of the murders.

Berkowitz's story was a sad tale of descent into madness. Rejected by his natural parents,

◀ **David Berkowitz – the "Son of Sam" – had shown an inclination towards psychotic violence since his childhood.**

he had been adopted at birth by a Jewish couple in the Bronx, Nathan and Pearl Berkowitz. Even as a teenager he showed signs of disturbed behaviour, including torturing and killing small animals. In 1971, he joined the army, hoping to serve in Vietnam and "die for a cause". In the event, he never saw combat, but did learn to handle guns effectively. Honourably discharged from the service in 1974, he moved back to New York, becoming increasingly paranoid and disturbed. He committed a series of arsons, and began to hear a voice telling him to kill. His first attacks on women were carried out at Christmas 1975.

In 1976 Berkowitz moved to upstate Yonkers and became involved in an intense fantasy life involving some of his neighbours and acquaintances, whom he imagined to be officers of a Satanic legion. The source of the voice ordering him to kill, Berkowitz declared, was a 6,000-year-old demon communicating through a dog that belonged to one of these neighbours, Sam Carr. The whiff of Satanism in Berkowitz's story was enough to spark off another of the conspiracy theories so loved by Americans. It was soon being alleged that the "Son of Sam" killings were the work of more than one person – that Berkowitz's talk of an organization devoted to Satan worship was not a fantasy, but a reality. Far-fetched theories circulated linking the "Son of Sam" killings to hippie murderer Charles Manson.

In the 1990s Berkowitz declared that he had become a born-again Christian – that "Son of Sam" had become "Son of Hope" – and publicly backed the Satan-cult theories so popular with American Christian fundamentalists. Sceptical observers pointed out, however, that it was not uncommon for long-term prisoners to suddenly declare themselves "born again" when angling for a chance of parole.

THE KING IS DEAD

Early on the morning of August 16, 1977, Elvis Presley, one of the founders of rock 'n' roll, was found dead on a bathroom floor at Graceland, his home in Memphis, Tennessee. He was 42 years old.

The son of a Mississippi farm-worker, Presley became the first successful white singer to perform black rhythm and blues, although he also drew on the white country music tradition. By 1956 he was the most popular singing star in the United States, adored by teenagers and provoking hostile commentaries from moral conservatives, offended by the overt sexuality of his pelvis-gyrating stage performances.

The turning point of his career was a two-year spell of national service in the army from 1958 to 1960. He never regained his ascendancy in the world of rock, steered by his manager "Colonel" Tom Parker into a decreasingly successful career as a film star and balladeer. By the 1970s, he had degenerated into an overweight Las Vegas nightclub performer given to popping too many pills.

None of this, however, had diminished Presley in the eyes of his millions of devoted fans. About 75,000 people attended his funeral and Graceland was set to become a place of pilgrimage. By the time of his death, he was reckoned to have sold at least 155 million singles, 25 million albums, and 15 million EPs. Songs such as "Hound Dog", "Love Me Tender", "Blue Suede Shoes", and "All Shook Up" remain pop culture classics.

▲ The irreplaceable "King" – over 20 years after his death, Elvis Presley still enjoys massive popularity.

- Elections in Sri Lanka; new government under Junius Jayawardene formed
- Somalia invades Ethiopia
- Oil begins pumping through the Alaskan pipeline
- German banker murdered by his grand-daughter, a Red Army Faction member
- Death of emigré Russian author Vladimir Nabokov

August
- Eleventh Chinese Communist Party Congress held
- US Department of Energy founded
- US space probe *Voyager 2* launched to explore the outer planetary system
- Rhodesian Front under Ian Smith win Rhodesian elections
- Death of Russian-born sculptor Naum Gabo

'77

September

- US President Jimmy Carter and Panamanian President Torrijos sign treaties for phasing out US control of the Panama Zone; later in month Panama regains control of Panama Canal Zone
- Red Army Factions terrorists kidnap the head of the German Industries Federation, Hans Meyer Schleyer after killing his driver and three bodyguards
- US space probe *Voyager I* launched to explore the outer planetary system
- Laker Airways begins Skytrain service from Britain
- Panama regains control of the Panama Canal Zone following treaty with the USA
- Nuclear Non-Proliferation Treaty signed by 15 nations, including USA and USSR
- Black activist Steve Biko is found dead in a police cell in South Africa
- Deaths of US poet Robert Lowell, British-born American conductor Leopold Stokowski and opera diva Maria Callas

October

- Intermittent power failures caused by union industrial action in Britain
- USSR adopts revised constitution
- Military coup in Thailand
- The world's last known case of smallpox reported in Somalia
- German terrorist Andreas Baader found shot dead in his prison cell in West Germany

THE DEATH OF STEVE BIKO

In September 1977, 30-year-old black activist Steve Biko died after suffering fatal head injuries while in the custody of South African police. An official inquest found that he died after hitting his head against a wall while violently attacking his captors; no one was prosecuted for his death. Evidence presented to the Truth and Reconciliation Commission since the end of apartheid in South Africa, however, has confirmed suspicions that Biko died of brutal ill-treatment and that a cover-up disguised the torture to which he had been subjected and the failure to provide prompt medical care when he was gravely injured. He had been kept naked in handcuffs and leg irons, and severely beaten.

Steve Biko had emerged as a leader of black resistance to apartheid in South Africa while a student in the late 1960s.

▲ **The authorities claimed Steve Biko had died while on hunger strike, but his body showed that he had been severely beaten.**

Influenced by the Black Power movement in the United States, Biko rejected the philosophy of racial integration dear to the imprisoned African National Congress (ANC) leader Nelson Mandela. Instead, he advocated the principle of "black consciousness", arguing that blacks would hold the key to political freedom only once they stopped feeling inferior to whites.

With the ANC leaders either in prison or in exile, Biko was the most prominent anti-apartheid activist inside South Africa in the first half of the 1970s. He was especially revered by young blacks, and his ideas made an important contribution to igniting the 1976 riots in the Soweto township outside Johannesburg which shattered the complacency of the apartheid regime.

BOAT PEOPLE FLEE VIETNAM

The aftermath of the comprehensive Communist victory in Southeast Asia in 1975 was bitterly disillusioning for liberals in the West, who had hoped the region's new rulers would prove undogmatic and seek the widest possible popular support. Instead, in Cambodia the massacres perpetrated by the Khmer Rouge exceeded even the worst prophecies of anti-Communist hawks, and in Vietnam, although no large-scale atrocities occurred, the transformation of the South into a socialist society was conducted with a total disregard for freedom or human rights.

Some 200,000 people who had served the South Vietnamese regime during the Vietnam War were sent to "re-education camps", where they were subjected to a harsh regime of physical labour and mental indoctrination. Around a million city dwellers were forcibly relocated to the war-ravaged countryside, a measure that made economic and social sense, but which caused great suffering and distress. The Communist regime made life very

▲ **Fleeing the oppression of the Khmer Rouge, almost a million South Vietnamese are thought to have left their homeland during the 1970s.**

difficult for religious groups such as Buddhists and Catholics and the ethnic Chinese were hard hit by a crackdown on private business, the source of most of the Chinese community's livelihood. Even apart from the specific abuses of Communist rule, life was inevitably hard in a war-shattered country cut off from most foreign aid for reconstruction because of continuing disputes with the United States.

By 1977, thousands of people were fleeing Vietnam every month, most taking to small, unseaworthy wooden boats that they hoped would carry them across the Gulf of Thailand or the South China Sea. Escape was a desperate venture – it is estimated that almost a quarter of those who set off died on their journey. Many of the boat people succumbed to disease. Some boats wandered lost in the vastness of the ocean until their food and water ran out. Many died at the hands of pirates who preyed upon the small boats, robbing the passengers of all they possessed, raping the women, and sometimes murdering for good measure.

The scale of the exodus through the late 1970s was vast – swelled by a mass flight of ethnic Chinese in 1979 when relations between Vietnam and China deteriorated to the point of open warfare. In all, about 800,000 boat people reached Hong Kong, Malaysia, Thailand, Indonesia, and the Philippines. More than half a million of them were able to move on to asylum in the West. Tens of thousands of others remained in refugee camps for many years, eventually facing more or less forced repatriation.

DEATH OF A COMIC GENIUS

On Christmas Day 1977, Charlie Chaplin, regarded by many as the greatest comic genius in the history of cinema, died at his home at Vevey in Switzerland, aged 88.

Born in London in 1889, Chaplin went into movies in 1913 after learning his trade in the music halls of England. He soon invented the character of the Tramp, with bowler hat, baggy trousers and cane, becoming one of Hollywood's biggest stars. The advent of sound movies at the end of the 1920s inevitably checked his career, since his act was essentially pantomime and not adaptable to verbal repartee. His few films of the 1930s and 1940s, such as *Modern Times* and *The Great Dictator*, are widely admired, but he never recovered the popularity he had enjoyed in the silent-movie era.

Chaplin was often a controversial figure. He married four times, always to a bride in her teens. His political views earned him the hostility of right-wing Americans, and in 1952, under pressure

▲ **Silent star Charlie Chaplin in his best-loved character – the loveable tramp with a bowler hat and cane.**

▲ **The exhumed coffin of Charlie Chaplin was found buried in a maize field close to his home on Lake Geneva.**

from McCarthyite witchhunters for alleged Communist affiliations, he vowed never to set foot in the United States again. He did return in 1972, however, to receive his second special Academy Award. He was knighted in 1975.

In a bizarre footnote to Chaplin's death, in March 1978 his coffin was stolen from Vevey cemetery, presumably in an effort to extort money from his family in exchange for the return of the body. The coffin and body were found in the nearby town of Noville two months later.

'78

NEWS IN BRIEF

* Economic refugees known as the "Boat People" flee from Vietnam
* OPEC raises oil prices
* G7 nations hold first meeting
* US air industry deregulated
* The British newspaper *The Times* suspends publication following failure of negotiations with print unions over the adoption of new technology
* First recombinant DNA product (human insulin) made
* A previously unknown moon orbiting Pluto is discovered and named Charon
* Soviet astronauts break record for length of time in space
* Soviet space probes *Venera 11* and *12* land on Venus
* Excavations begin on the tomb of ancient king Philip of Macedon in Greece
* Films released during the year include Michael Cimino's *The Deer Hunter*, Terrence Malick's *Days of Heaven*, Ermanno Olmi's *The Tree of Wooden Clogs*, *Grease*, starring John Travolta and *Superman*, with Christopher Reeve as the comic strip hero
* The soap opera *Dallas* debuts on US television
* The play *Betrayal* by Harold Pinter opens in London
* The musicals *The Best Little Whorehouse In Texas* opens in New York and *Evita*, by Andrew Lloyd Webber and Tim Rice opens in London

SUPERTANKER STEERS INTO DISASTER

On the morning of March 17, 1978, the *Amoco Cadiz*, a supertanker carrying 223,000 tons of crude oil, was sailing off the coast of Brittany when its steering failed. In heavy seas, it began to drift towards the rocky shore. A West German tug responded to a rescue call, but a towline thrown aboard broke. The tanker drifted on to the rocks off Portsall and was holed, releasing a flood of crude oil into the Channel.

Cliffs and beaches along a 360-km (225-mile) stretch of the Brittany coast were covered in oil. An estimated 30,000 seabirds died as the pollution spread, along with 230,000 tons of crabs, lobsters, and other fish. Oyster beds vital to the local economy were destroyed.

It was Europe's largest oil tanker disaster. Local Breton communities fought a long battle for compensation for the disaster. Finally, in 1988, a federal judge in Chicago found Standard Oil of Indiana guilty of negligence and awarded $85.2 million in damages.

▶ The supertanker *Amoco Cadiz* breaks in two spilling its cargo of crude oil into the English Channel off the coast of Brittany.

TERRORISTS MURDER MORO

Political terrorism was a prominent feature of Italian life in the 1970s. Between 1969 and 1980, there were more than 10,000 recorded terrorist incidents in the country, and 214 people died as a result of terrorist acts. Some of the most notorious outrages, such as a bombing at Bologna railway station in 1980 that killed 84 people, were carried out by right-wing neo-Fascist groups. But the most prominent terrorist band was the *Brigate Rosse* – the Red Brigades – a Marxist movement which, like the Baader-Meinhof gang in West Germany, had grown out of the failed student revolts of the late 1960s.

In 1978, the Red Brigades kidnapped the most prominent figure in Italian political life, Aldo Moro, the president of the ruling Christian Democrat party and a five-times Prime Minister of Italy. On March 16, Moro was driven from his Rome apartment for his habitual morning prayers at the church of Santa Chiara. There was an armed bodyguard in the front seat of his car and two more in another car following behind. In Via Fani, Moro's car was forced to stop by two

▲ The body of former Italian Prime Minister is discovered slumped in the back of a Renault car in the centre of Rome.

vehicles obstructing the road. Immediately, terrorists appeared from all sides, spraying the bodyguards and Moro's driver with bursts of automatic fire. Moro was carried off in a trunk in the back of a van and imprisoned in a concealed room in a shop in the centre of the city.

The Red Brigades issued a communiqué saying that Moro was being interrogated and that he would be subjected to a "people's trial". The Italian government declared that there would be no negotiations with the terrorists. Moro was allowed to write a series of letters to his family and Christian Democrat colleagues, in which he protested with mounting bitterness at their refusal to discuss a deal. On April 15, the Red Brigades announced that the "people's trial" had taken place and that Moro had been sentenced to die.

Moro's letters became even more desperate. He accused the Christian Democrats of "easy indifference and cynicism" during his "40 days of awful suffering", and appealed to them to save him from "the solitary fate of the political prisoner condemned to death". His pleas were not heeded. After long hesitation and a fierce internal debate, the Red Brigades decided to carry out their sentence. Moro's body was found on May 9. He had been shot dead and left in the back of a car in central Rome.

The results of the murder were almost entirely unfavourable to the Red Brigades. A tough new anti-terrorist crackdown almost halved the level of terrorist activity within a year. Those left-wing activists who had sympathized with the Red Brigades were mostly nauseated by the crime and withdrew their support. The group quickly went into a decline from which it never recovered.

UMBRELLA ASSASSINATION

On September 15, 1978, a Bulgarian defector, Georgi Markov, died in a London hospital three days after being admitted with a high fever. An examination of his body revealed that there was a circular area on the back of his right thigh that showed signs of inflammation. At the centre of the inflamed area was a puncture mark about two millimetres in diameter. Under the skin doctors found a tiny metal sphere pierced with four minute holes. It was made of an alloy of platinum and iridium, a material mostly used in the aerospace industry. A coroner's inquest concluded that this metal pellet had been used to introduce poison into Markov's blood stream, and that this was what had killed him.

Markov was an employee of Radio Free Europe and a well-known opponent of the Bulgarian Communist regime of Todor Zhikov. The day before his admission to hospital, he had felt a sudden sharp pain in his thigh as he stood in a bus queue at the Aldwych in central London. Turning around to see what had caused the pain, he saw a man running off. This was, it

▲ **Georgi Markov, the victim of a bizarre murder.**

is now known, an agent of the Bulgarian secret service. He had stabbed Markov with the ferrule of his umbrella, which contained the poison-filled sphere.

Markov was not the only person attacked in this way. After his death, another Bulgarian exile, Vladimir Kostov, came forward to report a similar incident in Paris the previous August. He had felt a sharp pain in his thigh one day when leaving the metro, and this had been followed by a high fever – from which, however, he recovered. A medical examination revealed that Kostov had an identical perforated metal sphere under his skin. Doctors established that the poison used was ricin, a toxic derivative of castor oil.

'78

LAST DAYS OF WHITE RULE IN RHODESIA

▲ **Robert Mugabe (left) and Joshua Nkomo (right), the two leading members of Zimbabwe's Patriotic Front.**

In March 1978, the white government of Rhodesia gave up its attempt to maintain the former British colony as an exclusively white-ruled state. The white Rhodesian leader, Ian Smith, invited moderate black leaders Bishop Abel Muzorewa, Ndabaningi Sithole, and Chief Jeremiah Chirau to join a multiracial Executive Council that would organize democratic elections. But this "internal settlement" kept stringent guarantees for the preservation of white interests and privileges, and the leaders of the guerrilla movements fighting to bring down the Smith regime would have nothing to do with it.

At the start of the 1970s, Smith and his supporters had been full of confidence. They had declared their independence from Britain and weathered economic sanctions with ease, thanks to the support of South Africa and the Portuguese colonists in neighbouring Mozambique. An attempt by African nationalists to mount a guerrilla campaign had

failed miserably and the main nationalist leaders, Joshua Nkomo and Robert Mugabe, were in detention.

In 1971, the British government had agreed to a proposal for a settlement that would have maintained white rule, with the proviso that black majority rule would follow at some unspecified date in the future. The British sent a commission to Rhodesia to check whether this settlement would be acceptable to the majority of the population – believing that the blacks were fundamentally subservient and ignorant people who had no special desire to govern themselves. To the astonishment of the British, however, the African population made it abundantly clear that they found the proposed sell-out utterly unacceptable, and the agreement collapsed.

From that point, the situation began to slip out of Smith's control. In 1974, a revolution in Portugal was the prelude to independence for Mozambique under a left-wing government prepared to provide bases for a guerrilla war against Rhodesia. South Africa decided that Rhodesia was becoming indefensible, and

▲ **After 15 years of self-styled independence, at midnight on April 14, 1980, Rhodesia officially became Zimbabwe.**

NEWS IN BRIEF

April
- Retirement age raised to 70 in the US
- Israel begins staged withdrawal from Lebanon; UN controlled buffer zone created
- Tornado kills 600 in India
- Coup in Afghanistan; president Daud deposed and murdered and Mur Muhammad Taraki takes power
- Death of British literary critic F R Leavis

May
- Mercenaries stage coup in the Comoros; exiled former president Abdallah returned to power
- Rhodesian special forces kill over 90 opposition supporters
- Italy legalizes abortion
- US launches *Pioneer 1* space probe
- PLO agree to stay outside UN-controlled buffer zone in Lebanon
- First legal casino in America outside Nevada is opened in Atlantic City, New Jersey
- Death of Australian statesman Sir Robert Menzies

June
- Naomi James completes solo round-the-world yachting trip in record time
- Head of the Iranian secret police arrested by the Shah
- Israel completes withdrawal from South Lebanon; Christian militias take control of some areas

began to put pressure on Smith to reach some form of settlement with the nationalists. Nkomo and Mugabe were released from detention, and a series of inconclusive negotiations and conferences was undertaken against a background of intermittent guerrilla war.

In 1977, Nkomo and Mugabe joined together in the Patriotic Front to promote an escalation of the guerrilla campaign by their respective forces, the Zimbabwe People's Revolutionary Army (ZIPRA) and the Zimbabwe African National Liberation Army (ZANLA). Nkomo's ZIPRA had support among the Matebele people, while the strength of Mugabe's ZANLA was based on the Shona of eastern Rhodesia. Although the white regime's counter-insurgency forces inflicted heavy casualties on the guerrillas and carried out raids against bases in neighbouring countries, the scale of the guerrilla warfare quickly became too much for them to contain in the long term.

The March 1978 agreement failed to improve the security situation, nor did the election of Abel Muzorewa as the country's first black prime minister in June 1979. It was plain that no peace could be achieved without involving the Patriotic Front. In September, the British government (Conservative again since the election of Margaret Thatcher in May) promoted all-party talks at Lancaster House which hammered out a new agreement for a cease-fire, fresh elections, and much reduced safeguards for the white minority. For a transitional period between December 1979 and April 1980, the country briefly became a British-ruled colony again, before being formally granted independence as Zimbabwe, under the rule of election-winner Robert Mugabe.

THE CAMP DAVID PEACE ACCORDS

▲ In the role of peacemaker, President Jimmy Carter stands between Israeli Prime Minister Begin (left) and President Sadat of Egypt (right).

In the aftermath of the 1973 Yom Kippur War, the United States embarked on the active pursuit of a settlement that would satisfy the Arabs as well as Israel. Since Israel was heavily dependent on the US for military supplies, the Americans had the leverage to induce the Israelis to make concessions. On the other hand, the existence of a powerful Jewish lobby in Washington, backed by millions of voters, limited the extent to which US administrations could be seen to browbeat Israel. Egypt's ruler, President Anwar Sadat, was desperate for a peace settlement, but unwilling to alienate other Arab states by appearing to sacrifice the sacred cause of the Palestinians.

Between 1973 and 1976, US Secretary of State Henry Kissinger made the running with a series of meetings dubbed "shuttle diplomacy". His initiatives foundered on Israel's refusal to do more than withdraw from part of the occupied Sinai. The chances for peace seemed even dimmer when rightwing Likud leader and former terrorist Menachem Begin became Israeli prime minister in May 1977. The new US administration of President Jimmy Carter became deeply frustrated by Begin's refusal from the outset to countenance any concessions on the

Palestinian question.

Sadat decided that a bold piece of gesture politics might break the deadlock. In December 1977 he visited Israel, an unprecedented step for an Arab leader, and even addressed the Knesset. But the gesture failed to wring any response from the Israeli hardliners. When President Carter summoned Begin and Sadat to a meeting at Camp David on September 5, 1978, an agreement looked as far off as ever. By this time, however, Sadat was becoming desperate for some return on his investment in the peace process, and Carter was frantic to achieve a marketable foreign policy success. Begin was bullied into accepting a minimal level of concessions: a complete withdrawal from the Sinai and vague promises of future action on the Palestinian question. In return, he would get peace with Egypt – effectively ending the chronic insecurity that had plagued Israel since its foundation.

Hailed in the West as a triumph of diplomacy and rewarded with the Nobel Peace Prize for Sadat and Begin, the Camp David agreement was immediately rejected by the Palestinians and almost all the Arab states. It left Sadat isolated and vulnerable to Egyptian Islamic extremists.

'78

NEWS IN BRIEF

September
- Muhammad Ali regains world heavyweight boxing title from Leon Spinks
- Earthquake kills 25,000 in Iran
- Resignation of South African Prime Minister B J Vorster; P W Botha elected as new leader
- New constitution adopted in Nigeria
- Tuvalu attains independence from Britain
- Death of German aircraft designer Willy Messerchmitt

October
- Conflict intensifies in Beirut
- Collapse of Swedish coalition government; new government formed under Ola Ullsten
- Border skirmishes between Tanzanian and Ugandan forces
- *The Little Red Book*, a collection of Mao Tse-tung's writings, is denounced in China

THE POLISH POPE

After the death of the much-loved liberal Pope Paul VI on August 6, 1978, Cardinal Albino Luciani was elected to replace him, taking the name John Paul I. An Italian of lowly origins, the new Pope was expected broadly to continue the policies of his predecessor. But on the morning of September 30, he was found dead, apparently of a heart attack, after only 33 days in office.

Thrown back into conclave in October, the cardinals came up with an almost totally unexpected replacement, the Polish Archbishop of Cracow, Cardinal Karol Wojtyla. Taking the name of John Paul II out of respect for his predecessor, Wojtyla was the first non-Italian to be elected pope since Adrian VI in 1522. His election was a triumph for cardinals from Third World countries who had been pressing for an end to

▲ **Pope John Paul II, formerly Cardinal Wojtyla of Cracow, was the first Pontiff to take a high profile in world affairs.**

the Italian monopoly of the papal throne. It was also, however, a victory for conservatives within the Church. John Paul II was not only a fervent anti-Communist, but also an opponent of liberal policies on birth control and social reform.

At 58, the new pope was the youngest pontiff of the twentieth

century. He soon made it apparent that he intended to exceed his predecessors both in his tireless travels to show himself to the faithful around the globe and in his determination to make the papacy a powerful influence in world affairs.

This influence was shown almost immediately in Eastern Europe. The election of the Polish Pope was greeted with wild enthusiasm in his Communist-ruled native land. The tide of popular feeling was too strong for the authorities to hold out against, and in June 1979 John Paul II was allowed to make an official visit to Poland, the first papal visit to a Communist state. The excitement generated by the Pope's visit had a direct influence on the rise of the Solidarity movement in Poland, which opened up the first cracks in the monolith of the Soviet bloc.

VICIOUS BY NAME ...

On October 13, 1978, Nancy Spungen, girlfriend of the former Sex Pistols' bass player Sid Vicious, was found dead in the room the couple were sharing at New York's Chelsea Hotel. She

◄ **Former Sex Pistol Sid Vicious was found dead the morning after a party. He had taken a massive heroin overdose.**

had died of stab wounds. Vicious was arrested, charged with second-degree murder, and taken to Riker's Island prison.

Born John Beverley in 1957, Vicious had been signed up for the Sex Pistols in March 1977. He was chosen by the band's manager Malcolm McLaren because his musical incompetence was matched by his talent for violent abuse. Vicious and Spungen shared a heroin habit, and their condition deteriorated after the break-up of the Pistols in early 1978. Vicious continued to perform intermittently, and had a hit

with his shambolic performance of "My Way". The purpose of his American trip was to assemble a new act with Johnny Thunders, formerly drummer with punk band the New York Dolls.

No one knows what actually happened in the Chelsea Hotel – probably Vicious himself did not know, given the quantities of heroin, barbiturates and alcohol he had consumed. But the event evidently left Vicious with no desire to go on living. He attempted suicide while inside Riker's Island prison. After his release on bail at the start of February 1979, his new girlfriend Michelle Robinson and his mother Ann Beverley threw a party, during which he collapsed. The following morning, he was found dead of a drug overdose.

CULT COMMITS MASS SUICIDE

In November 1978, 914 people, including 276 children, died in a mass suicide at a commune in the Guyana jungle. They were members of a cult known as the People's Temple. The commune was called Jonestown after the cult's founder and leader Jim Jones.

Jones had founded the People's Temple in Indianapolis, where it initially functioned as a refuge for the homeless, sick and unemployed. When reports began to emerge of strange and possibly illegal activities within the cult, he led his followers first to California and then to Guyana to avoid investigation and harassment.

The beliefs of the People's Temple were certainly weird enough to merit the interest of investigators suspicious of the power of pseudo-religious cults. Jones taught his followers that the world was soon to end in a nuclear war. The members of the Temple would all die together and be translated to a new life on another planet. In preparation for this moment, they practised mass suicide, pretending to take poison and falling to the ground.

The real mass suicide was triggered by the arrival at Jonestown of an investigative visiting party consisting of Californian Congressman, Leo Ryan, and a group of journalists. The Congressman had heard that members of the Temple were being held against their will and subjected to sexual and other abuses. The visit seemed to go off all right, until some members of the Temple decided that they wanted to leave with the visitors. As the party of visitors waited at the local airstrip to return to the

▲ **Bodies of hundreds of members of the People's Temple are strewn around the deadly vat of cyanide-laced Kool Aid.**

United States, Temple security guards opened fire, killing Ryan and four other people.

Jones then gathered his followers together and ordered them to commit suicide by drinking Kool-Aid laced with cyanide. Most did so willingly, though a small number of reluctant members were murdered by Jones's henchmen, and a few escaped into the jungle. Jones himself died from a bullet wound to the head.

THE KILLING FIELDS

▲ **Pol Pot, leader of the Khmer Rouge guerrilla force, has been branded one of the most evil dictators of the twentieth century.**

On Christmas Day 1978, Vietnamese forces invaded Cambodia, known at the time as Kampuchea. Within a fortnight they had captured the capital, Phnom Penh, overthrown the Khmer Rouge government, and installed a regime favourable to themselves – the United Front – under a former Khmer Rouge political officer, Heng Samrin. To justify their invasion, the Vietnamese invited journalists to visit the scenes of Khmer Rouge atrocities. Photographs of the pyramids of skulls harvested from the "Killing Fields" ensured Cambodia a leading position in the twentieth century's catalogue of horrors and earned one Khmer Rouge leader, Pol Pot, a place alongside Hitler and Stalin as a notorious author of genocide.

The atrocities began as soon as the Khmer Rouge guerrillas took power in Cambodia in April 1975. The Khmer Rouge leadership were Marxist intellectuals devoted to the idea of a total social revolution that would make an absolute break with the past. Individuals were to be "reconstructed" – their old lives stripped away through terror and the values of the new society inculcated in their place. To carry out this "reconstruction", the leadership had at its disposal an army of illiterate peasants, mostly teenagers, hardened by the brutalities of guerrilla war and hostile to city dwellers and the educated classes.

There were about 3 million people living in Phnom Penh when the Khmer Rouge took over. The city was cleared at gunpoint, the entire population driven out into the countryside to set up "new villages" out of nothing. A million more people were set to the same task from other Cambodian cities and from rural areas regarded as politically unreliable. The clearing of the cities was accompanied by many atrocities and massacres, with teachers, civil servants and students particular targets. Hundreds of thousands more died under the harsh regime of the new villages, racked by famine and disease, and liable to public execution for even minor infringements of insanely restrictive rules: acts punishable by death ranged from holding a long conversation with one's spouse to picking wild berries to eat.

This "ruralization" by no means constituted the only horror of the Khmer Rouge regime. Genocidal massacres were perpetrated against minority ethnic groups, especially the Muslim Cham, but also Vietnamese and Thais, the persecution of ethnic Vietnamese providing one of the reasons for the 1978 invasion of Cambodia by the Vietnamese army. There was also a political reign of terror targeted at individuals, initially prominent figures from the old regime, but later Khmer Rouge members suspected of being critical of the leadership or of having strayed from the party line.

Pol Pot, Cambodian prime minister from 1976, emerged as the strong man of the regime. When the Vietnamese invasion swept the Khmer Rouge from Phnom Penh, it was he who led the continued resistance, as the movement reverted to the guerrilla existence from which it had come. Despite the indisputable evidence of the atrocities committed by Pol Pot's regime, which was responsible for the deaths of between a million and 2.5 million people, the Khmer Rouge guerrillas enjoyed practical support and diplomatic recognition from China, Thailand, and Western governments opposed to the growing power of the Soviet-backed Vietnam.

▲ **The aftermath of the Khmer Rouge genocide program shows human skulls heaped up inside the Tuoi Sleng extermination camp.**

IRAN'S ISLAMIC REVOLUTION

The Shah of Iran, Mohammed Reza Pahlavi, fled Teheran on January 16, 1979, pushed into exile by the rising force of Islamic fundamentalism sweeping through Iran. By February 1, a 78-year-old religious leader, the Ayatollah Khomeini, who had masterminded the Shah's downfall, was back in Iran from the exile into which the Shah had forced him, to the acclaim of most of the Iranian population.

The Shah had been a modernizer and Westernizer, in the secular tradition pioneered by Turkey's Kemal Atatürk in the 1920s. He resented the lingering power of the Shi'ite mullahs, centred on the city of Qom. One of his many reforms of the 1960s was to distribute land from large estates to small peasant landholders. Most of these large estates were the property of religious foundations. After Islamic demonstrations in Qom were put down in 1963, Ayatollah Khomeini went into exile to plot the Shah's downfall.

Until the 1970s, the Shah's regime looked secure. He was supplied with modern military hardware by the United States and other Western states, who saw him as a bastion against Communism. His secret police, Savak, cracked down on any sign of dissent. Revenues from oil production financed both grandiose state projects and a Western-style consumer lifestyle for the urban middle class.

But the insidious propaganda of Khomeini and the mullahs, denouncing the Shah as the agent of the Devil, found a wide hearing among the mass of poorer Iranians. Tape recordings of Khomeini calling on the "dis-

▲ The Shah of Iran, Mohammed Reze Pahlavi, who tried to Westernize Iran but was deposed by Islamic fundamentalists.

possessed" to rise up against their "oppressors" circulated in secret. At the same time, the US administration of President Jimmy Carter, installed in 1976, made continued support for the Shah dependent upon improving human rights and reining in Savak.

In 1978, a spiral of popular protest mounted, each new demonstration stimulated by the brutality of the suppression of the one before. By the end of the year, demonstrations, involving a million people each, were occurring daily in the capital. The use of helicopter gunships and tanks against the demonstrators only created more martyrs for the cause. In any case, troops could soon not be relied upon to put down the protests. With only lukewarm backing from the United States, by 1979 the Shah had no choice but to go.

The new fanatical Shi'ite government regarded the United States as Satan and was prepared to breach any international law in the cause of its revolution. The price was paid by the Iranian people, not only forced to wear Islamic clothing and submit to puritanical morality, but arrested and executed in their thousands in a religious reign of terror, and led into a futile war of attrition with neighbouring Iraq.

▲ The image of Ayatollah Khomeini became well-known throughout the world as the face of radical Islam.

- The plays *Bent* by Martin Sherman and *Amadeus* by Peter Shaffer open in London
- The musical *Sweeney Todd* by Stephen Sondheim opens in New York
- The group The Police release the album *Regatta de Blanc*
- Popular songs of the year include "Le Freak" by Chic, "I Will Survive" by Gloria Gaynor and "My Sharona" by the Knack
- Books published this year include *The Executioner's Song* by Norman Mailer, *The Book of Laughter and Forgetting* by Milan Kundera, *A Bend in the River* by V S Naipaul and *Sophie's Choice* by William Styron
- Fifteen die after severe weather conditions strike the Fastnet yacht race in Britain
- First £1 million transfer deal completed in British football

January
- Truck drivers' strike in Britain
- Islamic fanatics incite violence in Iran
- China and USA begin normal diplomatic relations
- Shakpur Bakhtiar appointed Prime Minister of Iran
- Earthquake kills 1000 in Mexico
- Tanzania invades Uganda
- Pope John Paul II visits Latin America
- Coalition government collapses in Italy
- Deaths of US jazz composer and virtuoso double bassist Charles Mingus, German Nobel prize-winning physicist Max Born and US industrialist and politician Nelson Rockefeller

'79

NEWS IN BRIEF
....

February
- Chinese troops begin cross-border raids into Vietnam
- USA suspends aid to Somoza regime in Nicaragua due to human rights abuses
- The US ambassador to Afghanistan is abducted by Muslim extremists in Kabul; local police attempt rescue and the ambassador is killed in the following battle
- The US embassy in Tehran is seized briefly by Muslim demonstrators
- Elections in Bangladesh won by the Nationalist Party
- Loyalist killers the "Shankhill butchers" convicted and imprisoned in Northern Ireland
- St Lucia gains independence from Britain
- War breaks out between North and South Yemen
- Rhodesian war planes attack guerrilla bases in Zambia
- Deaths of French film director Jean Renoir and of Nobel prize winner for physics and inventor of holography Dennis Gabor

THREE MILE ISLAND

▲ **The nuclear power plant at Three Mile Island – the scene of America's first major nuclear accident.**

Three Mile Island is a nuclear power plant 16 km (10 miles) south of Harrisburg, the state capital of Pennsylvania. On March 28, 1979, it became the site of America's first serious nuclear accident, an event that dealt a fatal blow to the US nuclear power industry.

The accident was the result of a combination of technical failure and human error. A valve stuck in the open position, allowed water to evaporate from the cooling system of the plant's Unit 2 reactor. Misunderstanding what was happening, operators stopped the flow of emergency cooling water to the core, and temperatures increased dangerously inside the reactor. When it was eventually discovered that water had evaporated from the core, new water was added. Unfortunately, it was cold and shattered the extremely hot uranium fuel rods.

Little of the radioactivity from the damaged fuel escaped into the environment. The remote threat of a core meltdown was soon discounted as safety measures swung into action. But there was intense public concern, verging on hysteria, and Pennsylvania Governor Dick Thornburgh advised the evacuation of children and pregnant women from around the plant.

The power company soon settled a sum of compensation for local residents. Most attempts to sue the company for health damage blamed on the accident failed in the courts. Despite the outcry, Three Mile Island's Reactor 1 was still in operation 20 years later. But the accident was followed by intense pressure from protesters and lobbyists demanding an end to the building of new nuclear power plants in the United States.

AMIN'S RULE OF TYRANNY ENDS

◀ **Often viewed as a figure of fun in the West, General Idi Amin headed one of Africa's most brutal dictatorships.**

General Idi Amin Dada came to power in Uganda in 1971, after overthrowing President Milton Obote in a military coup. He ruled the country as dictator for the next eight years, imposing a regime that became infamous for its brutality and corruption. His crimes ranged from tribal massacres to the mass expulsion of Asians and the murder of prominent individuals, including the Archbishop of Uganda, who was killed in 1977.

Amin was a Muslim and his rule increasingly depended on Islamic support provided by, among others, Sudanese, Libyans, and Palestinians. But Islamicization was not popular in Uganda, a largely Christian country, and caused unrest in the armed forces. The collapse of the Ugandan economy, a consequence of the arbitrary confiscation of Asian and foreign businesses and the rapacious predations of Amin and his entourage, destroyed any popular support the dictator might have enjoyed.

In the autumn of 1978, Amin

decided on war as the solution to his mounting political problems. Julius Nyerere, the ruler of neighbouring Tanzania, had been a consistent critic of Amin and supported the exiled Obote. In October, Amin's troops invaded Tanzania and occupied a border area of the country. It was a move that totally backfired. Tanzania seized on the attack as a pretext for a counter-invasion.

In March 1979, 10,000 Tanzanian troops, with a small force of Ugandan exiles, advanced into Uganda. Despite aid from Colonel Gaddafi of Libya, who flew in a substantial body of troops to defend Amin, Kampala fell to the invaders on April 10. Amin fled to exile in Saudi Arabia.

THATCHER ENTERS NO 10

On June 4, 1979, Conservative leader Margaret Thatcher became Britain's first woman Prime Minister. She had guided the Tories to a substantial general election victory, with 44 per cent of the votes cast and 339 seats in the House of Commons, compared with Labour's 37 per cent vote share and 269 seats.

Labour had been in power since 1974, but for the last two years it had not enjoyed an overall majority in the House of Commons, depending on the backing of minority parties to continue to govern. The "Lib-Lab Pact", the agreement of the Liberal Party to broadly support the government, fell apart in the autumn of 1978. At this point, Prime Minister James Callaghan could have called a general election, that he could reasonably have expected to win.

The government had been trying to hold down wage rises in the face of growing opposition, especially from public sector workers. Between January and March 1979, dustmen, health service workers, grave-diggers, and many others went on strike for varying periods of time. Callaghan made the mistake of appearing complacent in the middle of what the *Sun* newspaper dubbed "the winter of discontent".

It was not strikes that brought down the government, however, but devolution. By 1979, the government was dependent on the support of Scottish Nationalists in

▲ **Margaret and Denis Thatcher prepare to move into number 10 Downing Street, their home for the next decade.**

the House of Commons. In referendums held in March, voters in Scotland and Wales failed to back a proposal that would have given them a measure of home rule. The government dropped its devolution legislation, and the Scottish Nationalists withdrew their support. On March 28, the government lost a vote of confidence in the Commons and was forced to call an election.

The Conservatives had taken the novel step of employing an advertising agency, Saatchi and Saatchi, to mastermind their propaganda during the election. A hoarding advertisement showing a dole queue, with the slogan "Britain isn't working", was

especially effective – although unemployment was low by the standards Britain would soon get used to.

The election was a watershed in British politics. After a 15-year period dominated by Labour – Labour governments had been in power for all but four years during that time – the Conservatives were to rule for the next 18 years. What is more, they were to overturn many of the principles accepted by both parties since World War Two, including the commitment to a welfare state and the acceptance of a "mixed economy", with a powerful state sector coexisting with private enterprise

March
- US space probe *Voyager I* reaches Jupiter
- Referendums in Scotland and Wales reject devolution from Britain
- Iran resumes selling oil, albeit at a much higher price
- New Jewel Movement stage coup in Grenada; Maurice Bishop takes power
- European Monetary System operational
- New civilian government takes power in Brazil
- End of war between North and South Yemen
- British ambassador to the Netherlands killed by the IRA
- Peace treaty between Egypt and Israel
- British Conservative politician Airey Neave killed by IRA car bomb

April
- Anthrax outbreak in USSR caused by accidental release of spores from biological weapons research institute; exact casualty figure unknown due to Soviet press censorship
- Iran declared Islamic Republic
- Former leader of Pakistan Zulfikar Ali Bhutto executed
- First multiracial elections in Rhodesia
- End of the Tokyo Round of GATT negotiations
- Yusufu Lule becomes President of Uganda
- Over 100 children killed during demonstrations in the Central African Empire

79

DEATH OF THE DUKE

NEWS IN BRIEF
....

May
- Left-wing guerrillas seize embassies in El Salvador
- Ruling Liberal Party loses Canadian general election ; Joe Clark becomes Prime Minister
- Deaths of US film actress Mary Pickford and West Indies-born author Jean Rhys

June
- Rhodesia changes name to Zimbabwe-Rhodesia
- Huge oil-well blow out in the Gulf of Mexico causes the world's worst environmental pollution incident; conventional techniques fail to cap the well and oil continues to gush out for months
- Resignation of South African President Vorster in political scandal
- Military coup in Ghana; Lieutenant Jerry Rawlings takes power
- Summit meeting of US President Jimmy Carter and Soviet Premier Leonid Brezhnev in Vienna; SALT II nuclear weapon treaty signed
- Atlanta's metropolitan rapid transit system opens

▲ The epitome of the American hero, throughout his career John Wayne remained one of Hollywood's fiercest patriots.

On June 11, 1979, Hollywood actor John Wayne died after a long fight against cancer. He was 72. Born Marion Morrison, and nicknamed "Duke" from his youth, Wayne first achieved fame under his professional name in 1939, playing the Ringo Kid in John Ford's classic Western *Stagecoach*. From then on he embodied the traditional virtues of American manhood – especially the determined use of violence in a good cause – in a string of successful war movies and Westerns, including *Red River* (1948), *She Wore a Yellow Ribbon* (1949), and *The Alamo* (1960).

Wayne's off-screen personality fitted well with his screen persona. He was a hawkish super-patriot who took a leading role in the drive to uncover Communist fellow-travellers in Hollywood at the height of the Cold War. In the 1960s, he campaigned in support of America's war in Vietnam, making *The Green Berets* in 1968 as his tribute to the US fighting men.

Wayne won widespread admiration in 1976 when, himself struggling with terminal cancer, he starred in the film *The Shootist* as a former killer dying of the same disease. He was married three times and had seven children.

EUROPEAN ELECTIONS

The first direct elections to a European Parliament were held on June 7, 1979. This should have been an epoch-making event in the progress away from a Europe of nation states, but the reaction of most voters across the continent was boredom and indifference. This was especially true of Britain, suffering voting fatigue only a month after a general election. Less than one in three registered voters turned up at the polls. Most of those who did bother to vote backed the Tories, who won 60 of the 81 Euro-seats allotted to the United Kingdom. Labour took 17 seats, with one for the Scottish Nationalists and three going to Ulster Unionists. In Europe as a whole, however, victory went to social democrat parties.

Voters' lack of enthusiasm for Europe was shared by the new Prime Minister, Margaret Thatcher. By the end of the year, she had embarked on an aggressive campaign to cut Britain's contribution to the EEC budget. Thatcher made it clear that she would fight every attempt to chip away at British sovereignty.

▲ Simone Veil, the French Minister of Health, casts her vote in the first round of European parliamentary elections.

BIRTH OF THE SANDINISTAS

By the mid-1970s, the dictatorial rule of the Somoza family in Nicaragua, in place since 1933, was widely discredited. Almost all sections of Nicaraguan society hated and feared Somoza's National Guard and were outraged by the flagrant corruption that had allowed President Anastasio Somoza Debayle to amass a fortune estimated at $900 million. After Jimmy Carter became US President in 1977, committed to a foreign policy based on human rights, Somoza also lost the wholehearted support of the Americans, on which he had always depended.

Resistance to Somoza was spearheaded by the Sandinistas, a Marxist-led guerrilla movement originally founded in 1962. The Sandinistas' original plan, inspired by the example of Cuba's Fidel Castro, had been to start a guerrilla campaign in the country-side. This proved impossible to sustain, however, because of the ruthless counter-insurgency tactics of the National Guard, who were prepared to use carpet bombing, helicopter gunships, and chemical defoliants on a large scale, with a total disregard for loss of life among the peasants.

Around 1977, the Sandinistas decided to abandon their narrow Marxist base and form a broad alliance with any groups prepared to oppose Somoza. The situation rapidly evolved from guerrilla war to mass insurrection. From January 1978 onwards, the capital, Managua, and other cities were rendered ungovernable by a series of riots and general strikes in protest at the oppressive actions

of the National Guard.

In February 1979, the Sandinistas launched a full-scale offensive. Without support from the Nicaraguan people or the United States, President Somoza was doomed. In July he fled to exile in Miami. Amid scenes of general enthusiasm, the Sandinistas took power, setting up a Junta of National Reconstruction, headed by the Marxist Daniel Ortega. Much of Somoza's National Guard fled to neighbouring Honduras and Costa Rica, soon to form the nucleus of the Contras, the guerrilla army that, in the 1980s, would be used by a new US administration less concerned for human rights to attack the Sandinistas and terrorize the Nicaraguan population.

▲ **Supporters of the Sandinistas gather in the capital city of Managua to celebrate the fall of President Somoza.**

MOUNTBATTEN KILLED BY IRA BOMB

On August 27, 1979, the Queen's cousin, Earl Mountbatten of Burma, was killed by the Provisional IRA. Lord Mountbatten was holidaying with his family in County Sligo, in the Irish Republic. A bomb was placed on board his boat, *Shadow V*, moored in Mullaghmore harbour. Shortly after he set out on a fishing trip with members of his family, the bomb was exploded by a terrorist with a radio remote-control.

Killed alongside Lord Mountbatten were his 15-year-old grandson, Nicholas Knatchbull, and a 15-year-old Irish boy, Paul Maxwell. His daughter, Lady Brabourne, her son Timothy, her husband Lord Brabourne, and

her mother-in-law, the Dowager Lady Brabourne, were all seriously injured in the blast. The Dowager Lady Brabourne later died of her injuries.

► **The funeral of Earl Mountbatten of Burma, one of Britain's great war heroes and the IRA's highest profile victim.**

On the same day, 18 British soldiers were killed at Warrenpoint in Northern Ireland, the biggest death toll suffered by the British army in a single incident in the Province. The massacre occurred on a stretch of road separated from the Irish Republic by Carlingford Lough. Two bombs were exploded by remote control from across the Lough. Firing into the Republic in an attempt to hit the terrorists responsible, the soldiers only succeeded in shooting dead an English tourist.

Most of the soldiers killed at Warrenpoint were members of the Parachute Regiment, the formation responsible for the killing of 13 Catholics on Bloody Sunday in 1972. After the events of August 27, a slogan painted on a wall in a Catholic area of Belfast read: "13 gone not forgotten, we got 18 and Mountbatten".

'79

On November 21, 1979, Prime Minister Margaret Thatcher confirmed, in answer to a parliamentary question, that Sir Anthony Blunt, a leading art historian and Surveyor of the Queen's Pictures, had been a Soviet spy. His guilt had been strongly hinted at in a recent book, *The Climate of Treason*, by biographer Andrew Boyle. Blunt was promptly stripped of his knighthood, although this was all the punishment that would befall him.

Blunt had been one of a group of upper-class students who were converted to Communism while at Trinity College, Cambridge, in the 1930s, and recruited by Soviet intelligence. Two of the Cambridge spies, Donald MacLean and Guy Burgess, fled to Russia in 1951. A third, Kim Philby, was exposed in 1963. The following year, a tip-off led to the interrogation of Blunt, who had worked for MI5 during World War Two. The wily aesthete did a deal with his interrogators, agreeing to tell them everything he knew – including his own part in the escape of Burgess and MacLean – in return for immunity from

prosecution and total secrecy, allowing him to continue his distinguished career with an unblemished public reputation.

Blunt's eventual exposure was traceable to elements within MI5 who were unhappy that he had escaped punishment. The same MI5 officers, who included Peter Wright, the author of *Spycatcher*, were convinced that a fifth Soviet spy had worked in British intelligence, and that the Fifth Man was Sir Roger Hollis, the director-general of MI5 from 1956 to 1965. This startling allegation was, however, dismissed by Thatcher in 1981 as almost certainly untrue.

◀ **Following a life at the very heart of the British establishment, Anthony Blunt was finally exposed as a former Soviet spy.**

NEWS IN BRIEF

October
- General election in Japan
- President Romero of El Salvador deposed after several weeks of violence
- President Zia of Pakistan cancels imminent elections
- Shah of Iran is allowed to enter the USA for treatment of cancer, against the advice of the US ambassador in Tehran
- Vaclav Havel and other dissidents convicted of subversion by Czechoslovak government
- South Korean president Park Ghung-hee assassinated by the Korean secret service
- St Vincent and the Grenadines gains independence from Britain
- Death of British aeronautical designer and inventor of the "bouncing bomb" Sir Barnes Wallis

November
- New Conservative government in Britain announces wide-ranging spending cuts
- Oil tanker catches on fire after collision in Galveston, Texas; oil spill causes severe pollution
- US embassy in Iran seized, with over 60 hostages, by Muslim extremists demanding the repatriation of the Shah
- The Islamic Revolutionary Council under Ayatollah Khomeini takes power in Iran
- US places embargo on Iranian oil
- Iranian assets in America frozen by the USA

MOTHER TERESA WINS PEACE PRIZE

Mother Teresa, the head of the Roman Catholic Order of the Missionaries of Charity, was awarded the 1979 Nobel Peace Prize for her tireless work on behalf of the world's poorest people.

Born in 1910 of Albanian parents, Mother Teresa's original name was Agnes Gonxha Bojaxhiu. She was brought up in Skopje, Macedonia. In 1928 she went to a convent in Calcutta, India, run by the Sisters of Loretto. She taught at the convent school until the 1940s when, moved by the plight of Calcutta's destitute street people, she set out on her own to fulfil a mission to aid them. She established the Missionaries of Charity in 1950, devoted above all to the care of the sick and dying. Recognized by Rome in 1956, the missionary order spread its activities to other countries, but Mother Teresa remained based in Calcutta. She was awarded the first Pope John XXIII peace prize in 1971. Her reputation for selfless devotion to the needy made her an obvious candidate for the Nobel, although she found herself in some strange company – other winners of the peace prize in the 1970s included former Israeli terrorist Menachem Begin and Henry Kissinger, US foreign policy supremo during the latter stages of the Vietnam War.

▲ **The "living saint", Mother Teresa of Calcutta devoted her entire life to caring for some of the world's poorest people.**

THE SOVIETS GO INTO AFGHANISTAN

The Soviet Union's war in Afghanistan, which was to contribute in no small measure to the eventual collapse of Soviet Communism, began in December 1979. Its origins lay in complex power struggles inside Afghanistan and hopeless misrule by the Afghan government.

Afghanistan had effectively become a Soviet client state in the 1950s, under the rule of General Mohammed Daoud Khan, although at first with very little direct involvement of the Soviet Union in its internal affairs. Daoud's grasp on power was increasingly contested, however, by Marxist radicals eager to modernize the largely tribal country on Soviet lines. Two Marxist factions, known as Khalq and Parcham, united to overthrow Daoud in a bloody coup in April 1978.

In a predictable post-coup power struggle between the two factions, Khalq lost and its leader, Babrak Karmal, took refuge in Eastern Europe. A Parcham government, headed by President Noor Mohammed Taraki and Prime Minister Hafizullah Amin, embarked on a programme of sweeping reforms which they attempted to impose on the traditionalist Islamic tribes. Measures such as the raising of the status of women and the provision of education for girls were anathema to tribal leaders, as was the breaking up of large landholdings. Soon the mountainous country was in revolt, with local chieftains taking up arms, proclaiming themselves the Mujaheddin – the warriors of god. In March 1979 there was a popular uprising in the city of Herat and anti-government demonstrations in Kabul.

The Soviet Union favoured the more moderate Khalq faction and regarded the actions of the Parcham government with dismay. There were by now large numbers of Soviet advisers in the country, many of whom came under attack as the revolt spread. In September 1979, Prime Minister

▲ **Fighting against the odds, a troop of Mujaheddin rebels pose triumphantly on the wreckage of a downed Soviet Sikorsky helicopter.**

Babrak Karmal was flown in to take over as head of government. Soviet troops managed to establish control of the main Afghan towns and cities, securing major airfields and other important communication centres.

Whether the Soviet action was

Amin had President Taraki killed and seized absolute power. Convinced that under Amin the situation could only worsen, the Soviets faced the choice between withdrawing their advisers from Afghanistan or intervening to take control themselves.

Just before Christmas 1979, the Soviets began sending troops into Kabul, ostensibly to aid Amin in his fight against the rebels.

On December 27, Soviet troops assaulted the presidential palace, overcoming fierce resistance from units of the Afghan army. Amin was killed and Khalq leader

strictly an "invasion", as was always said in the West, is doubtful – the Russians were not "invited" into Afghanistan, but neither were American troops into South Vietnam. It was certainly not evidence of "Soviet expansionism". But it ruined the process of detente between the USSR and the West, and opened a running sore in the Soviet flank. War against Afghani Mujaheddin was to prove as brutal and disillusioning for the Soviets as the struggle against the Viet Cong had been for the Americans.

1980-89

For Great Britain and America, the decade was dominated by two political leaders whose periods in office so characterized their times that the 1980s are often now described as the Thatcher and Reagan eras. Britain's first female Prime Minister, Margaret Thatcher had taken office in 1979. The "Iron Lady" stamped her authority over successive Cabinets and oversaw a decade in which Britain shifted dramatically to the right. A firm believer in "the market", Thatcher's monetarist policies enabled the wealthy to thrive. The dominance of the political right ensued throughout most of the West, but perhaps most dramatically in the United States following the election of Ronald Reagan. Well known to movie audiences, former-actor Reagan had been political active since the late 1950s. His massively successful terms in office were characterized by outspoken views on Communism – he dubbed the Soviet Union the "Evil Empire" – and a policy of non-interference in the economy that was extreme even by America's standards. After a decade of weak leadership that followed the Vietnam war and the Watergate debacle, America viewed Reagan's strength and determination as a restoration of international pride. Even when a scandal emerged around the illegal provision of covert financial aid to anti-Communist guerrillas in Nicaragua, public support for Reagan hardly diminished. When he stepped down in 1988 his successor as party leader, George Bush, won an easy victory over the Democrats.

In spite of numerous noble international attempts at securing peace in the region, the Middle East was still highly volatile. However, during the 1980s a new unsettling force emerged – Islamic fundamentalism. This revolution had started in 1979 with the expulsion from Iran of the pro-American Shah. He was replaced by a government dominated by Shi'ite Musims, in particular the Ayatollah Khomeini. In 1980, with American influence in Iran now non-existent, neighbouring Iraq, led by the unpredictable Saddam Hussein, took the opportunity to launch an invasion of Iran's oil fields. Khomeini responded with a *Jihad* – a holy war – which raged for eight years destroying the economies of both states.

The 1980s also saw the emergence of a new kind of threat, one that seemed to endanger the very future of humankind – AIDS. An incurable disease that attacked the body's immune system, it was discovered that AIDS was transmitted by sexual contact or transmission of blood. At first, mainly intravenous drug users and male homosexuals seemed affected – two groups of people that elicited little public or official support. It was only when it became clear that the "Gay Plague" could also affect heterosexuals that concern grew. Although a cure is still yet to be developed, some successes in preventing the full onset of AIDS for those infected by the HIV virus (from which AIDS develops) has been achieved. While the spread of HIV has been curbed in the West, it is in the underdeveloped nations of the world where the spread still goes unabated.

It was the dying months of the decade that saw the most dramatic turn of international events since World War Two. One by one, popular uprisings in the states of Eastern Europe saw the mass rejection of Soviet-style Communism. This trend could be traced to the start of the decade when Polish shipyard worker Lech Walesa's Solidarity movement engaged in a fight for civil rights. Although the Communist government responded with violent repression, support for Solidarity was such that by the end of the decade it had become a legitimate ruling political party with Walesa as President of Poland.

The weakening of the Communist grip could in part be laid at the hands of the Soviet Premier Mikhail Gorbachev. A "Kennedyesque" figure, "Gorby" introduced a new openness to Soviet dealings with the outside world and was less strident in his attitude towards Eastern Europe. The "Velvet Revolution" that ousted Communism from Czechoslovakia would in earlier decades have been met by the gunfire of Red Army tanks. As other Eastern European states followed suit, finally and dramatically, the Berlin Wall – for 28 years a symbol of Cold War tensions – came tumbling down. Within a year, the German Democratic Republic no longer existed. Germany was once again unified.

It was only a matter of time until the revolution that Lenin had launched at the dawn of century finally ran out of steam. After a lingering on powerless for over a year, in 1991 the mighty Soviet Union was dismantled. The Cold War was now over.

MOUNT ST HELENS ERUPTS

May 18, 1980 saw one of the most spectacularly violent volcanic eruptions of recent times as Mount St Helens, at the peak of the Cascade Range in the southwest of Washington State, erupted. It was the first such occurrence in North America since Mount Lassen erupted in 1917.

Dormant since 1856, Mount St Helens first showed signs of renewed activity on March 27, 1980 as a steady stream of ash, steam and small rocks burst from its crater. The state authorities ordered the immediate evacuation of villages that might be in danger from mud slides or lava flow. Although geologists had warned of potential volcanic activity two years earlier the eventual violence of the eruption took them by surprise.

Mount St Helens continued to murmur over the six weeks that followed, a second minor eruption taking place on April 22. During this time the gradual increase in pressure from the magma within the volcano created a bulge on the north slope of the 2950.5-metre (9680-ft) peak. On the morning of May 18, the volcanic peak exploded

▲ The sleeping giant, Mount St Helens sends its plume of steam and ash 180 metres (600 ft) into the skies above Washington State.

with a force measuring 5.1 on the Richter scale. It was the greatest volcanic eruption ever measured in North America. The lateral air blast carried molten ash and stones 19 km (12 miles) from the volcano's summit. The blast was felt more than 160 km (100 miles) away and created a cloud of ash that masked the sun for nearly a week.

The power of the blast destroyed ten million trees. Sixty people were killed, mostly as a result of mudslides and flooding of the Toutle River valley. Minor eruptions continued until October. By the time all volcanic activity had ceased, the summit of Mount St Helens had been reduced to 2438 metres (8000 feet).

DISASTER IN THE NORTH SEA

▲ The beleaguered rig Alex Kjaelland having been towed into Stavenger for refloating. The four upturned legs pierce the surface of the fjord.

On March 28, 1980, the Alexander Keilland, an oil platform owned by Phillips Petroleum capsized in strong winds. It was the worst tragedy to hit the North Sea oil industry since production first became possible in 1975.

Based in Norwegian waters, the platform, used as a floating hotel, was turned on its back when hurricane-force gales hit the region. Many of the 200 men on board were cast into the North Sea; others were trapped inside. In spite of being a relatively busy shipping region – 20 vessels were within a radius of 80 km (50 miles) of the rig – the appalling weather conditions made rescue attempts very difficult, while the freezing waters of the northern-most area of the North Sea made survival for more than a few hours unlikely. Eventually, only 100 men were saved.

An inquiry recorded that the collapse was a freak occurrence in unusually violent weather conditions, and was reluctant to make recommendations that would inhibit oil production. Since 1975, oil has been a crucial factor in Britain's economy and Britain is now the world's sixth largest oil-producing nation.

DEATH OF THE MAESTRO OF MYSTERY

April 29, 1980 saw the death of Alfred Hitchcock, Hollywood's king of suspense. He was 80 years old.

Born in London in 1899, Hitchcock joined the fledging British film industry after study-ing engineering at the University of London. His first work was designing title cards. Quickly pro-gressing, by 1925 he had directed his first feature film. The following year he made *The Lodger*, about a man suspected of being Jack the Ripper. Leaving the audience on the edge of their seats until the very last frame, it was the first of over eighty sus-pense-filled films Hitchcock would make during a distinguished fifty-year career.

Hitchcock was one of the first great directors to understand the mechanics of film-making and how audiences could be manipu-lated. His hallmarks were surprise – "Always make the audience suffer as much as pos-sible" – or a slow build up of tension – "There is no terror in a bang, only in the anticipation of it".

In 1939 after establishing a world reputation with such classic British thrillers as *The Thirty Nine Steps* (1935) and *The Lady Vanishes* (1938), Hitchcock moved to Hollywood where his debut film, Daphne Du Maurier's *Rebecca*, won him an Oscar. During the next twenty years he

▲ The king of suspense, Alfred Hitchcock was responsible for many of the greatest Hollywood thrillers.

made some of the greatest films of the period, including *Spellbound* (1945), *Strangers on a Train* (1951), *Rear Window* (1954) and *Vertigo* (1958).

An endearing characteristic of each of Hitchcock's films from 1940 onwards was a single fleet-ing cameo appearance, invariably away from the centre of action. His celebrity was such that audi-ences delighted in spotting the man who was, after all, the *true* star of his films. It was a view with which Hitchcock would also have agreed, having been famously quoted as saying "actors are like cattle"; when his star of the moment, Carole Lombard, took offence his retort was "What I said was, actors should be *treated* like cattle."

'80

NEWS IN BRIEF

- Human rights activist Archbishop Oscar Arnulfo Romero assassinated whilst holding mass in El Salvador
- Basque regional parliament opens in Spain
- Deaths of French author and critic Roland Barthes and US athlete Jesse Owens

April
- End of steel workers strike in Britain
- Race riot in Bristol in Britain
- USA institutes trade embargo and severs diplomatic relations with Iran
- Israeli raid against Palestinian bases in Lebanon
- Coup in Liberia; President William Tolbert and 27 other government officials executed
- Rhodesia attains full independence as Zimbabwe with Canaan Banana as President
- Philippine passenger ferry collides with oil tanker; over 300 killed
- US attempt to rescue hostages in Tehran fails
- Samuel K Doe suspends Liberian constitution and takes dictatorial powers
- Queen Juliana of the Netherlands abdicates at age 71 in favour of daughter Beatrix
- Death of French existentialist author Jean-Paul Sartre

STORMING THE EMBASSY

On April 30, 1980 the world of international terrorism hit London dramatically as five masked gunmen forced their way into the Iranian embassy, taking captive 19 hostages. Among the Iranian officials held at gun point were three Britons. A police cordon was immediately placed around the embassy.

The gunmen were identified as Iranian Arabs and issued a series of demands which included the release of political prisoners held by the Ayatollah Khomenei.

Following negotiations, the kidnappers released five of the hostages. Over the days that followed they grew increasingly impatient as no formal response came from Iran. They informed the British authorities that if their demands were not met they would begin killing the hostages.

True to their word, on May 5 two hostages were shot. The response was a spectacular attack by the British Special Air Service (SAS), who abseiled into the embassy. Three of the five gunmen were killed instantly. All of the remaining hostages were safely released.

▶ **The siege of the Iranian embassy brought the SAS, with their motto "who dares wins", to the attention of the British public.**

MOSCOW OLYMPICS

On July 19, 1980, Soviet Premier Leonid Brezhnev formally opened the 22nd Olympic Games in Moscow, the first to be held behind the Iron Curtain. They would turn out to be the most politically sensitive since the Berlin Olympics of 1936.

Controversy had started in March when President Jimmy Carter announced that in protest against the Soviet invasion of Afghanistan US athletes would not be taking part in the Olympics. The world's dominant sporting nation, the US's absence immediately lowered the level of competition. Sixty other nations followed Carter's boycott, including West Germany and Japan. A number of other nations who refused to pull out made compromise protests by not attending the opening ceremony or choosing to receive medals to the tune of the official Olympic anthem. In all, 81 teams and 5,000 athletes took part – the lowest number since Melbourne in 1956.

As far as sporting excellence was concerned, the Moscow Olympics were a grave disappointment. Athletes complained about the restrictive security, and the crowds were sometimes openly hostile. There was even a suggestion that officials were biased

▲ **British athlete Sebastian Coe celebrates a famous gold medal victory. He would later pursue a less auspicious career in politics.**

against Western athletes. However, in the end, few eyebrows were raised at the total domination of the Eastern bloc, with the Soviet Union taking 195 medals in all, 80 of them gold. There was good news for Britain, however, as middle-distance athletes Steve Ovett and Sebastian Coe continued their world-beating rivalry, Ovett pipping Coe for gold in the 800 metres, and Coe taking his revenge in the metric mile.

Four years later, the political hostilities continued as Soviet Union and other Communist nations retaliated by boycotting the Los Angeles Olympics. The official view was that their athletes might be endangered by such an overtly anti-Communist country – the wider view was a fear of a new wave of defections to the West.

THE BIRTH OF SOLIDARITY

September 22, 1980 saw the formation in Poland of Solidarity, the first independent trade union to exist in the Eastern bloc. The struggle and successes of Solidarity during the 1980s played an influential role the move towards Perestroika that eventually brought an end to the Communist domination of Eastern Europe. It also launched a charismatic shipyard electrician named Lech Walesa on to the world's political stage.

July 1980 had seen a wave of unrest spread throughout Poland. Centred around the northern port of Gdansk, workers protested at a sudden government-controlled rise in food prices. On August 14, some 17,000 workers at the Lenin Shipyards staged a strike and barricaded themselves inside the plant. During the sit-in, Lech Walesa, a former shipyard worker whose previous anti-government protests had lost him his job, climbed over the shipyard fence to join the workers. A strike committee was created with Walesa elected leader. The aim was not only to co-ordinate strike action in Gdansk, but throughout the whole of Poland.

The committee issued a list of political demands that include the right to strike and to form free labour unions. Walesa called a national strike. The government first responded by arresting 28 leading members of the strike committee. Then, fearing

▲ **The Polish Solidarity movement successfully captured the imagination and support of many in the West.**

that a nationwide revolt could result, on August 31, following a meeting between Walesa and Deputy Minister Mieczyslaw Jagielski, the government conceded to the strikers' main demands.

Ten million workers throughout Poland proceeded to form and join independent regional unions. On September 22, 1980, delegates from 36 unions met in Gdansk and formally united under the name Solidarity. Walesa was elected chairman.

The birth and success of Solidarity was unprecedented in an Eastern European Communist state, and gave the people of Poland a thirst for more liberal reforms. The strikes had seen the toppling of the hard-line party leader Edward Gierek, who had been replaced by the outwardly sympathetic Stanislaw Kania.

However, developments in Poland caused a growing concern in the Soviet Union that the country must develop "along the socialist path". At the end of 1980, fearing Soviet intervention, Nato launched its own warning to leave Poland to its own destiny. Such action would effectively have halted the East–West arms limitation talks, and perhaps resulted in economic sanctions. But Solidarity's next great struggle would not be from outside of Poland's border. Early in 1981, Kania was replaced by the Soviet-trained General Wojciech Jaruzelski. Strongly opposed to the very existence of Solidarity, Jaruzelski within months held the offices of Premier, First Secretary of the Party, and Commander-in-Chief of the armed forces. On December 13, 1981, he announced martial law in Poland.

May
- Race riots in Miami, USA following acquittal (by all-white jury) of white policemen of murder in custody of black suspect
- EC imposes trade sanctions on Iran
- President Fernando Belaunde elected President in Peru
- EC agrees to a rebate on British contributions to the EC
- Death of President Josef Tito of Yugoslavia causes power vacuum in Balkans

June
- Violence in South African townships leads to over 30 deaths when protesters clash with police
- Death of Japanese Prime Minister Masayoshi Ohira; Zenko Suzuki replaces him in July
- Severe ethnic violence in India causes more than 1,000 deaths
- Deaths of UK holiday camp pioneer Sir Billy Butlin, US writer Henry Miller

July
- New Hebrides gains independence as Vanuatu from Britain and France
- Deaths of the Shah of Iran (of cancer in Eygpt), British actor and film star Peter Sellers, scientist and author C P Snow and African statesman Sir Seretse Khama, first President of Botswana

80

IRAN-IRAQ WAR

September 22, 1980 saw the start of a major Middle Eastern conflict that would continue intermittently throughout the 1980s, as Iraqi armed forces launched an invasion of Western Iran. Their goal was to seize total control of the oil-producing region of Khuzistan, then jointly run by the two states. The war also launched Iraq's leader Saddam Hussein on to the world's political stage – one he has rarely exited since.

The agreement to administer Khuzistan jointly was made when a treaty was signed between the two nations in March 1975. However, the Islamic revolutionary rule of Ayatollah Khomeini that followed the exile of the Shah of Iran in 1979 had created new tensions in the region, and these were exacerbated by the call from Iran's government for a Shi'ite revolution in Iraq.

Saddam Hussein was a skilful political opportunist and his sudden invasion took the world by surprise. With Iran's new regime still poorly organized, Iraqi forces were easily able to capture the city of Khorramshahr but, although they were surrounding the Iranian oil centre of Abadan by the middle of October, they were then forced back by Iran's Revolutionary Guards.

Fighting continued until May 1982 when the invading Iraqi troops were forced out of Iran. Financially crippling to both sides – oil production in both states was severely curbed during the conflict – Saddam sought peace with Iran. By this time, however, in the eyes of Khomeini the situation had become a jihad – a holy war – and Iran vowed to continue until Saddam Hussein was toppled from power.

The Iran-Iraq war was unusual among other major world conflicts in that although both nations were bitter enemies, they were also openly hostile to both the values of the capitalist West and Communist East.

◀ **Invading Iraqi troops stand guard over an abandoned police fort 16 km (10 miles) within the borders of Iran.**

THE REAGAN YEARS

They said it could only happen in America, and on November 4, 1980 it *did*: Ronald Reagan, star of numerous 1940s Hollywood B-pictures, was elected 40th president of the United States. At 69 years of age, Reagan was the oldest man to have been elected to the White House.

Born in Tampico, Illinois in 1911, Reagan graduated from Eureka College and took a job as a sports announcer. Following the lure of Hollywood, Reagan took acting lessons and went on to play in over 50 movies between 1937 and 1964. His career peak came in the early 1940s, when he often played sympathetic all-American patriots. He is especially remembered for a moving performance in the acclaimed small-town melodrama, *Kings Row* (1942), though most of his films were undistinguished low-budget supporting features.

Reagan first became involved in politics in the late 1950s as his acting career went into decline. In 1959 he became President of the Screen Actors Guild, publicly vowing to combat supposed Communist sympathizers within the industry.

By now a staunch right-wing Republican (as a young man he had been a Democrat), Reagan successfully ran for governor of California in 1966 and was returned again four years later.

Reagan lost the Republican presidential nomination to Gerald Ford in 1976, but was nominated in 1980. With his espousal of traditional American values and a promise to "put America back to work again", he won a landslide victory over President Jimmy Carter.

Reagan and his second wife Nancy were a genial "First Couple" and very popular with the public. Supremely at ease in front of the media cameras, Reagan was able to project a relaxed sense of confidence which Americans found reassuring, even when his foreign policy took an increasingly provocative anti-Communist stance.

Like Margaret Thatcher in Great Britain – with whom R eagan enjoyed a closer "special relationship" than any previous leaders of the two countries – his domination of his country's politics for most of the 1980s was such that the decade is still widely described as "The Reagan Era".

▲ The film star President, Ronald Reagan, seen with his wife Nancy, remains one of the most popular American leaders of the century.

BEATLE MURDERED

On December 8, 1980, music fans the world over were stunned to hear the news that John Lennon, former member of the Beatles, the most famous pop group of all time, was dead. The 40-year-old musician had been returning from a recording session to his Manhattan apartment when he was shot twice from close range as he left his limousine.

The assassin was a 25-year-old fan named Mark Chapman. He had purportedly stalked his idol for days, even at one point asking for an autograph. Chapman did not resist arrest, nor give any reason for committing the murder. His plea of insanity was rejected and in August 1981 he was sentenced to life imprisonment.

Emerging from Liverpool at the start of the 1960s, by 1964 the Beatles had become the world's biggest-selling pop group. Public appearances were invariably met with hysteria, popularly called "Beatlemania". Their later albums, such as *Revolver* (1966), *Sgt Pepper's Lonely Hearts Club Band* (1967) and *Abbey Road* (1969), were milestones in an era that saw pop music's emerging credibility as an art form.

By the time the Beatles had split in 1970, Lennon was already a well-established political protester, the peace "bed-ins" with his wife, the Japanese artist Yoko Ono, having made headline news the world over. His music had also taken a more political direction, Lennon penning such popular anthems as "Give Peace a Chance" and "Imagine".

Dormant during the second half of the 1970s, alcohol, drugs and a well-publicized split with his wife kept him away from the music world. Re-united with Ono in 1980, Lennon's first album in half a decade, *Double Fantasy*, was released shortly before his death.

▲ A once vociferous peace protester, former Beatle John Lennon was stalked and shot by one of his own fans.

October
- British Labour Party adopts unilateral nuclear disarmament policy
- Bomb explodes in synagogue in Paris, killing four
- Chancellor Helmut Schmidt re-elected in German elections
- Earthquakes kill over 20,000 in Algeria
- James Callaghan resigns as leader of the British Labour Party
- IRA prisoners in the Maze prison in Northern Ireland begin hunger strike

November
- US space probe *Voyager I* reaches Saturn
- Michael Foot elected leader of the British Labour Party
- Gang Of Four put on trial for treason in China
- Earthquake in southern Italy kills thousands
- Deaths of US movie actor Steve McQueen and US actress Mae West

December
- Fresh Soviet offensive in Afghanistan
- Portuguese Prime Minister Francisco Carneiro killed in air crash; Francisco Pinto Balsemao replaces him
- Milton Obote elected President in Uganda
- Iran demands ransom for US hostages in Iran
- Anti-Soviet demonstrations in Iran protesting at the Soviet invasion of Afghanistan
- Deaths of US social commentator Marshall McLuhan, creator of the Kentucky Southern Fried Chicken chain Harland Sanders, British politician Sir Oswald Mosley and playwright Ben Travers

'81

IRANIAN HOSTAGE CRISIS

The Iran hostage crisis, which had lasted for 444 days, finally came to an end on January 19, 1981 as US and Iranian government officials meeting in Algiers reached an accord, agreeing the release of frozen Iranian assets. The following day, which was the day of Ronald Reagan's inauguration as the 40th President of the United States, the hostages were flown home.

The crisis had begun on November 4, 1979 as a mob of 500 students, supporters of Iran's new Islamic revolutionary government, stormed the US embassy in Tehran. 52 hostages were held captive. The siege coincided with the anniversary of the shooting of fellow students by the troops of the now-deposed Shah. The Iranians were now outraged that the Shah had been allowed medical treatment in the US. Their initial demands were the extradition of the Shah in exchange for the hostages. President Carter refused and ordered the freezing of billions of dollars-worth of Iranian assets in America.

In April 1980, with negotiations between the two sides frozen, President Carter authorized a foolhardy military raid on Tehran. It was widely opposed by the American people since the head of the Iranian government, the Ayatollah Khomeini, had already announced that the hostages would be killed if military action was used. Eight helicopters carrying commandos were dispatched. Before they were able to reach their destinations, they were called back after three had been grounded by technical failures. Attempting to refuel, one helicopter collided with a transport plane, killing eight servicemen. It was a public relations disaster for President Carter.

With little progress throughout the year, in November the Iranian

▲ At a public reception for the 52 hostages, President Reagan warned that future terrorist acts would be met with force.

government agreed terms for the release – a payment of $24 billion. After negotiations the offer was rejected, but this had at least opened the doors to a negotiated settlement, even if publicly the US held a firm line on trading with terrorists. The final agreement came on January 19, 1981. On return to the US, the 52 hostages were given an emotional "yellow ribbon" state reception.

NEW POLITICAL PARTY FOR BRITAIN

On January 25, 1981, four prominent members of Britain's Labour Party resigned, announcing the formation of the Social Democratic Party. The first significant new political party in Britain for almost 80 years, it

▲ Britain's own "Gang of Four" (from left to right) Bill Rodgers, Shirley Williams, Roy Jenkins and Dr David Owen.

became an important contributing factor to Labour's impotence during the Thatcher years.

In what they called the "Limehouse Declaration", former cabinet ministers Roy Jenkins, Bill Rodgers, Shirley Williams and Dr David Owen, made plain their view that the Labour Party under the leadership of Michael Foot was moving too far towards the political left. Their avowed aim was to prevent the lurching extremes of changes of government between the two main parties in favour of a more centrist line that they felt was more in keeping with the desires of the public.

The formal founding took place two months later on March 26 with Jenkins as party leader. Although it was hoped that the SDP would draw moderate dissidents from both parties, of the 14 MPs in the House of Commons who pledged allegiance, only one was a Tory. Some SDP policies, such as electoral reform and European integration, overlapped with those of the Liberals and the two parties quickly formed what would become an uneasy alliance.

In 1983, the Alliance, as it was formally known, polled almost a quarter of the popular votes; the "first past the post" system of British politics meant that the votes translated into very few parliamentary seats. Following the election, Jenkins stood down in favour of David Owen. Owen's leadership, and the tacit suggestion that he was the leader of the Alliance, created a rift with the Liberal leadership. At the 1987 election, Owen and the

Liberals' David Steel presented themselves as joint-leaders, though their clear rivalry and the comic caricaturing of "The Two Davids" by the media led to a disastrous campaign.

Following the election, Steel called for a full merger of the two

parties. Rejected by Owen and the few SDP members in the Commons, in 1988 the call was accepted by the party's National Committee and ordinary membership. Owen resigned, leaving David Steel to head a new Liberal Democratic Party.

REAGAN SHOT IN ASSASSINATION ATTEMPT

On March 30, 1981, newly inaugurated Ronald Reagan came close to being the first US President to be assassinated since the death of John F. Kennedy in 1963.

After addressing a union convention at Washington's Hilton Hotel, Reagan left the hotel foyer and made for his waiting limousine. As he was about to get in six shots rang out from close range and the President, critically wounded, was bundled into the car which sped off to the George Washington University Hospital where he underwent emergency surgery.

The would-be assassin was 25-year-old John Hinckley who had waited for the President among a group of TV and news reporters. The shooting was captured on film in dramatic detail. Hinckley, a "drifter" from Colorado, was quickly pinned down and arrested

by police. Reagan's press secretary, James Brady, and two plain-clothed security guards who had tried to "take" the bullets were also seriously wounded.

Ever media-conscious, Reagan's only immediate comments were humourous quips, as he apologized to his wife: "Honey, I forgot to duck." In spite of his 70 years, Reagan's recovery was remarkable and by April 11 he was able to returned to the White House.

◀ **President Reagan greets crowds outside the Washington Hilton seconds before John Hinckley's attempt on his life.**

DISTURBED SUMMER

The summer of 1981 was a season of stark contrasts as the hysteria surrounding the forthcoming marriage of Prince Charles to Lady Diana Spencer was interrupted by periodic youth rioting in some of the country's poorest areas.

With unemployment having spiralled over the two million mark, the hardest hit group were school leavers from minority cultures. The signs of trouble to come first emerged on April 11, 1981 when hundreds of predominantly black youths rampaged through the London suburb of Brixton. With the police powerless to react, the riot-

ers looted and burned out dozens of shops and offices. In early July, the focus of attention shifted to the Toxteth area of Liverpool, where a standoff resulted in over 100 police injuries.

The rioting was seen as racially motivated by a Conservative government that always fell shy of making a connection between unemployment and crime. However, it served to highlight the alienation of a growing social

▶ **Black youths take to the streets of Brixton. London's Metropolitan police were widely perceived as the "enemy".**

grouping. By a peculiar quirk of fate, the zeitgeist of the summer of 1981 was captured succinctly in one of the season's biggest hits, "Ghost Town" by The Specials, an inter-racial pop group, which summed up the mood of the moment: "Government's left the youth on the shelf ... people are getting angry."

81

ENDGAME FOR THE YORKSHIRE RIPPER

On May 22, 1981, one of Britain's most notorious serial killers, Peter Sutcliffe, was found guilty of the murder of 13 women between 1975 and 1980. He was sentenced to life imprisonment, with a rider that he must serve at least 30 years.

Sutcliffe, a long-distance lorry driver, chose his victims by cruising the red-light districts of Bradford and Leeds. The violent nature of the murders – the victims, mostly prostitutes, were killed by hammer blows and then mutilated with a knife – quickly led police to deduce that they were the work of the same man. Long before Sutcliffe's discovery and arrest, the murderer had being christened "The Yorkshire Ripper" by the British media.

Sutcliffe was not an especially cunning criminal. The fact that he eluded the police for so long was more down to luck; during the massive police investigation of the murders he was even once

▲ **A retouched police photograph showing the likeness of Peter Sutcliffe at the wheel of his truck.**

questioned before being released. In the end, his capture was a simple matter of routine policing: he was stopped as a suspected kerb-crawler. Giving a false name, he failed a police check against his car registration and was arrested. He quickly confessed to the killings.

His trial began on May 5, 1981. Although his guilt was not a matter for dispute, his sanity was. Sutcliffe pleaded diminished responsibility, claiming that God had spoken to him, ordering him on a mission to rid the world of prostitutes. The jurors were unmoved by his claims.

February
- Gro Brundtland becomes Prime Minister of Norway, first woman in the post
- Fighting breaks out between ZANU and ZAPU rivals in Zimbabwe
- British government imposes large budget cuts on universities
- Strike threat causes British Coal to halt mine closure plant
- Coup attempt in Spain fails; General Milano del Bosch and 19 other officers arrested
- Death of US rock singer Bill Haley

March
- First London marathon race held
- Deaths of British intelligence head Sir Maurice Oldfield, motorcycle champion Mike Hailwood and US publisher De Witt Wallace, founder of *Readers Digest*

April
- Food rationing begins in Poland
- Fighting between Arab peacekeeping force and Lebanese militias
- US launches first space shuttle, *Columbia*
- Death of undefeated American world heavyweight boxer Joe Louis

ASSASSINATION ATTEMPT ON POPE

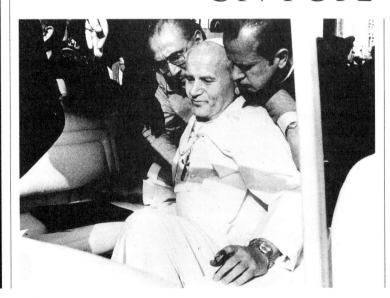

May 13, 1981 saw an attempt on the life of Pope John Paul II as he paraded in an open-top car through St Peter's Square. He was shot twice in the abdomen and was rushed to Rome's Gemelli Hospital where a section of his abdomen was removed. His recovery was speedy and complete.

The gunman was a 23-year-old

◄ **Pope John Paul II falls into the arms of his aides seconds after two bullets were fired into to his abdomen from close range.**

escaped Turkish criminal named Mehmet Ali Agca. A political activist, Agca was on the run from Turkey's authorities having murdered the editor of the newspaper *Millyet* in 1979. When he was arrested, Vatican police found a baffling note claiming that his assassination of the Pope would be protest against imperialism by the superpowers.

In July, Agca received a life sentence. Turkish authorities suggested that he was part of a right-wing conspiracy that sought to punish the pope for his support of the Solidarity union in his native home, Poland. Six others were tried but were acquitted following a lack of real evidence.

Born Karol Wojtyla, when John Paul II became pope in 1978, he was the first non-Italian to be chosen in 456 years.

IRISH HUNGER STRIKES

▲ **The making of a martyr. Young IRA supporters embark on a roof-top publicity campaign in support of the convicted terrorist Bobby Sands during his ill-fated hunger strike.**

1981 saw a renewal of violent protest breaking out in Northern Ireland. The impetus for this nationalist protest was a series of hunger strikes by inmates at the high-security Maze Prison.

At the start of March 1981, Bobby Sands, a Sinn Fein party candidate for the coming election, who was serving a sentence for his role in a bombing campaign, announced that he was on hunger strike, in protest at his treatment by the British authorities. His demand, like that of other convicted members of the Irish Republican Army (IRA), was that he should be treated as a political prisoner rather than a criminal. Two weeks later, Sands was joined on his protest by Francis Hughes, another convicted bomber.

The escalating hunger strikes within the Maze proved to be the focal point of a series of violent clashes between demonstrators and the British army patrolling the streets of the province. The violence worsened on May 5, when, after 66 days of refusing food and drink, Bobby Sands died, just weeks after winning a parliamentary seat. Hughes followed a week later. Both were given IRA "military" burials.

The deaths sparked a new campaign of nationalist terror. On May 19 an IRA bomb killed five soldiers on patrol in Northern Ireland. Two months later the campaign moved to Britain's mainland when a bomb exploded at a bandstand on London's Regents Park, killing eight soldiers and injuring 51 civilians. Meanwhile, in the Maze the hunger strikes continued, with a total of ten IRA inmates eventually starving themselves to death.

May
- USA expels Libyan diplomats
- François Mitterrand elected French President
- Italian cabinet resigns over Masonic links revelations
- Failed coup in Pakistan; President Ziaur Rahman assassinated
- Deaths of Rastafarian reggae singer Bob Marley and Polish primate Cardinal Stefan Wyszynski

June
- Clashes between the PLO and Israel in Lebanon begin
- Israeli air strike destroys nuclear reactor in Iraq
- Incumbent government defeated in elections in Ireland; new coalition government formed with Garret Fitzgerald as Prime Minister
- President Ferdinand Marcos re-elected in one-sided elections in Philippines
- Socialist victory in French general elections
- Iranian President Bani Sadr flees Iran; Mohammed Ali Rajai succeeds
- Iranian chief justice and four other government officials killed in bomb attack in Tehran

July
- Fighting between Israeli forces and PLO in southern Lebanon
- Cease-fire between the PLO and Israel
- Panamanian leader Omar Torrijos Herrera killed in air crash; Colonel Manuel Noriega succeeds
- Death of "International Style" architect Marcel Lajos Breuer

'81

ROYAL EVENT OF THE DECADE

August

- MTV begins broadcasting on US cable television
- Solidarity union protest in Warsaw
- President Reagan dismisses striking air traffic controllers
- Tax and budget cuts passed in the USA
- Two Libyan fighter jets shot down by US navy aircraft
- US space probe *Voyager 2* reaches Saturn
- Iranian Prime Minister, President and an army officer killed in bomb explosion in Tehran
- Deaths of British actress and singer Jessie Matthews and Austrian conductor Karl Bohm

September

- Crackdown on Muslim extremists and dissidents in Egypt
- Crackdown on dissidents and Solidarity union in Poland
- Huge Warsaw Pact military manoeuvres in the Baltic
- French ambassador in Beirut assassinated
- Aide to Ayatollah Khomeini, Ayatollah Madani, killed in grenade attack in Tehran
- British Honduras gains independence as Belize
- First woman judge is appointed to the US Supreme Court
- France abolishes death penalty
- Deaths of Italian Nobel Prize-winning author and poet Eugenio Montale and German architect Albert Speer

▲ The Royal Kiss. Prince Charles and his bride Princess Diana celebrate their marriage in the traditional manner.

July 29, 1981 was formally declared a public holiday throughout Great Britain in celebration of the marriage that day of the Prince of Wales to Lady Diana Spencer. The event was televised and watched by an audience numbering hundreds of millions throughout the world.

As heir to the throne, Prince Charles' romances, from his student days at Cambridge, had always roused considerable interest. However, throughout 1980, rumours began to circulate of a growing relationship between the prince and 20-year-old Lady Diana Spencer. Demure, of aristocratic lineage and, above all, highly photogenic, Diana was rarely out of the public eye from the announcement of her engagement by Buckingham Palace on February 24, 1981 to her tragic death in August 1997.

Princess Diana was born in 1961 at Park House on the Queen's Sandringham estate. As a child she often played with the princes Andrew and Edward. She hardly excelled at school (she would later describe herself as "thick as a plank") and after a period spent at finishing school in Switzerland she returned to England to work as a kindergarten teacher.

The marriage took place in St Paul's Cathedral. Diana was resplendent in a pale ivory dress designed for her by the relatively unknown Elizabeth and David Emmanuel. Her train flowed a full 7.5 metres (25 feet) behind her as she took the four-minute walk up the aisle to the altar. Prince Charles wore the full dress uniform of a Royal Naval officer.

The marriage ceremony lasted an hour after which they drove in a gilded horse-drawn carriage back to Buckingham Palace. Tens of thousands basked in the summer sunshine, lining the streets to welcome the newly-weds.

At first, the Royal marriage – which had been billed as a fairy-tale event – seemed as if it might have been a match made in heaven. Eleven months later, Diana gave birth to Prince William, second in line of succession to the British throne. Two years later a second son, Prince Henry (known as Harry), was born.

As the decade progressed rumours of a rift in the marriage were widely rumoured as the couple seemed to spend more and more time apart. Although there was a clear age gap, more significantly there seemed to be an insurmountable culture gap: the exuberant Diana with her love of parties, fashion and pop; and Charles the serious-minded, angst-ridden critic of modern architecture with a penchant for long walks in the wilderness of the Scottish Highlands.

The problems became more acute for Princess Diana as she began to find the constant attentions of the world's press and paparazzi intrusive. Little wonder – by that time she was probably the most famous (and certainly the most photographed) woman in the world. It was clear that something, at some stage, was going to give.

▲ The wedding captured the imagination of the British public, many of whom looked to Charles and Diana's future as King and Queen.

DEATH OF THE PEACE MAKER

President Anwar Sadat, the ruler of Egypt and the man who helped to create a historic peace between Egypt and Israel, was assassinated by a member of his own armed forces on October 6, 1981.

Sadat and a number of international guests were seated in a grandstand viewing a military parade held in remembrance of the Arab-Israeli war of 1973. A group of marching troops suddenly broke away from the procession and ran towards the stand, firing machine guns and lobbing hand grenades into the crowd. Ten people, including Sadat, were killed and another 40 were wounded.

Sadat had been an original member of Gamal Abdel Nasser's Free Officers organization and played a prominent role in the coup that de-throned the Egyptian monarchy in 1952. Throughout the Nasser era he had held a number of high offices and when Nasser died following a heart attack in 1970, Sadat, as Vice President, was seen as his natural successor.

As a military leader, Sadat enjoyed considerable popularity at

▲ President Sadat was widely viewed as a voice of moderation in the unpredictable political climate of the Middle East.

home following the Arab-Israeli war, in which Egypt managed to reclaim territory held by Israel. However, it was his efforts as a peacemaker that both created his reputation as an international statesman and incurred the wrath of the Islamic fundamentalists within Egypt.

His peace programme began in November 1977 when he made a historic visit to Israel, taking his

proposals for a "lasting peace" to the Knesset (the Israeli Parliament). Sadat and the Israeli Prime Minister Menachem Begin worked tirelessly to secure agreement, in spite of internal hostilities on both sides. Their efforts were publicly acknowledged when in 1978 they were jointly awarded the Nobel Peace Prize. The negotiations were concluded on March 26, 1979 when the age-old enemies signed a historic peace treaty.

Thereafter Sadat's popularity fell dramatically in the Arab world. His standing within Egypt reached rock-bottom as the public dissent that followed was suppressed, often in a brutal manner. He also began taking a firm line on religious extremists, having made 1,500 arrests after the Coptic order and the radical Moslem Brotherhood were both outlawed.

The trial of Sadat's assassins and suspected conspirators was turned into a public spectacle, the 24 men accused being held in an iron cage. Reaching a verdict on March 6, 1982, the trial judges sentenced five assassins to death, a sentence which was carried out six weeks later.

The day after Sadat's assassination, his Vice President, former air force chief Hosni Mubarak, was named as successor. He initially declared his intention of maintaining the peace agreement with Israel. However, the Israeli invasion of Lebanon in 1982 heralded a cooling of relations between the two states. Thereafter, Mubarak sought to cultivate improved relations with other Arab states. He also took a more moderate line than Sadat in containing labour and religious protest at home.

▲ President Sadat lies fatally wounded, the victim of a group of renegade Egyptian soldiers.

'82

NEWS IN BRIEF

- Tylenol capsules laced with cyanide by unknown party in the USA; seven die and Tylenol withdrawn from sale
- US unemployment at a record high
- Spain ends blockade of Gibraltar
- Crops fail for fourth consecutive year in the USSR
- Ban on whaling declared by Whaling Commission
- The US space shuttle makes first successful mission
- Compact Disc (CD) audio system launched
- Artificial heart transplanted into human recipient
- Films released during the year include Andrzej Wajda's *Danton*, Ridley Scott's *Blade Runner*, Steven Spielberg's *E.T*, Werner Herzog's *Fitzcarraldo*, Sydney Pollack's *Tootsie*, Ingmar Bergman's *Fanny and Alexander* and Richard Attenborough's *Gandhi*
- *Cheers* debuts on US television
- *The Boys From The Blackstuff* by Alan Bleasdale debuts on British television
- The play *Noises Off* by Michael Frayn opens in London

UNEMPLOYMENT: THE SCOURGE OF BRITAIN

January 1982 saw unemployment in Great Britain shoot over the three million mark, the first time such a figure had been known since the depression of the 1930s. Britain, like other European countries, was still suffering the aftermath of a recession during the 1970s and the figures for those out of work had been edging towards three million during the first two years of the decade.

The monthly announcements of employment figures have traditionally been made by the Secretary of State for Employment. Norman Tebbit explained that January had seen a sharp rise of 130,000 from the previous month. This he attributed to the particularly severe weather of December 1991. Tebbit's comments drew criticism from the opposition – at this time, the Labour Party was still committed to the principle of full employment – who blamed the government's fierce anti-inflationary policies for strangling British industry.

During the course of the 1980s, unemployment figures gradually diminished and by the end of the decade there were fewer than two million registered Britons out of work.

◀ With dole queues growing, Norman Tebbit suggested that the unemployed should "get on their bikes" in search of work.

SOCIALISM IN FRANCE

1982 saw the continuation of France's socialist phenomenon. While the aftermath of the 1970s recession had led the rest of Europe towards a broadly conservative consensus, the newly elected President François Mitterrand continued to bring his radical socialist election pledges to fruition.

When the presidential term of the incumbent, Giscard d'Estaing, came to an end in May 1981, it seemed likely that he would be elected to serve a second term. Nonetheless, bucking the opinion polls, Giscard was narrowly defeated by the socialist Mitterrand. Dissolving France's legislative body, the National Assembly, Mitterrand called an election. The Socialists won a clear majority of seats.

Mitterrand named Pierre Mauroy, a militant socialist, as Prime Minister and set about enacting a series of wide-ranging reforms. Most controversial was the nationalization of France's banking sector and other key industries. He also created a programme of social-based reforms, including the setting of a minimum wage, increased levels of social security, increased tax rates for the very wealthy and the regulation of private education.

Within a year, Mitterrand's socialist experiment had failed almost completely. Investment levels fell as the wealthy moved their capital abroad, and exports declined, creating further unemployment. Furthermore, in June 1984, Mitterrand's perceived attack on private education met fierce public hostility from almost a million people who demonstrated in Paris.

With the popularity of his government dwindling rapidly, Mitterrand replaced Mauroy with the moderate Laurent Fabius. Mitterrand's compromise satisfied nobody and served merely to stoke a general mood of discontent that pervaded France until the 1986 National Assembly elections. This environment of dissatisfaction brought a surprise success to Jean-Marie Le Pen's National Front, who fought a vigorous xenophobic campaign based around the expulsion of immigrant workers.

The Socialist Party lost control of the National Assembly and although Mitterrand's presidency still had two years to run he named the Gaullist Jacques Chirac as his new Prime Minister. For the rest of his term, Mitterrand concentrated his efforts on foreign policy, leaving domestic matters to Chirac. Personally popular, Mitterrand succeeded in winning a second term as President in 1988, but this time his attempts to create a socialist National Assembly failed.

► **Against the flow of European politics, Françoise Mitterrand sought to bring a socialist revolution to France.**

THE BRAINWASHING CULT

More commonly used for sports or entertainment, New York City's Madison Square Garden was the romantic setting, on July 1, 1982, for one of the most unusual marriage rituals ever seen. It was here that 2,075 couples, all members of the Unification Church – or the "Moonies", as they have become popularly known – were wed in a mass ceremony.

Since its formation in Korea in 1954, the Unification Church has courted controversy, not least through the activities of its founder, Sun Myung Moon. The "bible" of the Unification Church is "The Divine Principle", a work

that outlines how at the age of 16, Moon saw a vision of Jesus Christ, in which he was chosen to fight the forces of darkness, one of its manifestations being the spread of Communism. The church employs a strict code of conduct among its members, including abstinence from alcohol, tobacco and all other drugs, as well as pre-marital sex. It exerts an unusual degree of personal control, even as far as choosing marital partners.

Sun Myung Moon founded the church after his teachings brought about his expulsion from the Presbyterian Church. During the 1960s, from his base in

South Korea, he used the Unification Church, which already numbered over two million followers, to create a billion-dollar business empire. He moved his base to the United States in 1971 where over the next ten years he recruited around 50,000 new members, mostly young, disaffected people from middle-class families.

The methods used by the "Moonies" to recruit new members created considerable controversy, parents claiming that their children had been "brainwashed" or indoctrinated against their wills. Although a number of investigations were made into these allegations, there seemed to be no evidence of any illegal activity. The same was not true, however, of the way in which Moon had financed his empire. In May 1982 an eight-week court hearing in New York City found Moon guilty of tax evasion. He eventually served a prison sentence in 1984. Although the Unification Church still exists, its world membership is now thought to be less than 250,000.

▲ **Sun Myung Moon, leader of the Unification Church, presides over the simultaneous marriage of over 2000 couples.**

- Books published this year include *Chronicle Of A Death Foretold* by Gabriel Garcia Marquez, *The Safety Net* by Heinrich Böll and *The Color Purple* by Alice Walker
- Popular songs of the year include "A Town Called Malice" by the Jam, "Golden Brown" by the Stranglers, "Ebony and Ivory" by Paul McCartney and Stevie Wonder and "Our House" by Madness
- Italy wins football World Cup

January
- Vatican and Britain resume diplomatic relations
- Food prices increased drastically by Polish government; riots follow and civil unrest leads to curfew in Gdansk

February
- Collapse of Laker Airways
- Joshua Nkomo dismissed from Zimbabwean government
- Official receiver called in to the De Lorean car plant in Northern Ireland
- Fighting in Kampala, Uganda between rebels and government forces
- Irish general election, caused by defeat of Garret Fitzgerald's coalition government, brings Charles Haughey to power
- Deaths of British artist Ben Nicholson and US jazz pianist Thelonius Monk

March
- US trade embargo imposed on Libya
- Guatemalan dictator Romeo Lucas Garcia deposed
- Military coup in Bangladesh
- Deaths of British statesman R A Butler (Lord Butler of Saffron Walden) and German composer Carl Orff

April
- UN passes resolution demanding withdrawal of Argentine troops from the Falklands
- Israeli diplomat assassinated by terrorist in Paris

'82 THE FALKLANDS WAR

On April 2, 1982 the people of Britain woke up to the unexpected news that one of her colonies, the Falkland Islands, had been invaded by Argentina. It heralded the beginning of a two-month state of war between the two countries. Strategically unimportant to Britain, the Falklands' invasion was at first treated by the media as something of a joke. Within a month, however, the situation had erupted in a war that ended with the deaths of 700 Argentinian soldiers and nearly 300 British marines.

Before the invasion, many Britons had never heard of the Falkland Islands and very few knew that this was the most violent manifestation of a series of confrontations that dated back over one and a half centuries.

Situated 480 km (300 miles) off the southeast coast of Argentina, the Falklands were first sighted by an Englishman, Captain John Strong, who landed there in 1690. The two main islands were named East Falkland and West Falkland in honour of naval leader Viscount Falkland. During the eighteenth century, they became a subject of minor discord between Britain and Spain, who occupied the West and East islands

▲ "The Empire Strikes Back". British troops prepare to embark on the long journey to liberate the Falkland Islands.

respectively. In 1820, when Argentina gained independence from Spain, it made its own claim for sovereignty over what the South Americans referred to as Las Islas Malvinas (named after a group of early explorers who had arrived from the French port of St Malo). Nonetheless, by 1841, Britain had taken a firm hold over the Falklands. A British governor was appointed and Argentinians were deported. By the end of the nineteenth century a small community of around 2,000 Britons lived on the Falklands.

During this time, and beyond, Argentina continued to demand territorial rights. In 1964, the fate of the Falklands was placed in the hands of the United Nations.

Argentina's claim was based on ancient treaties forged during Spain and Portugal's conquest of the New World. The heart of the argument was essentially a geographical proximity that few could deny. Britain countered, however, using the UN benchmark of self-determination – Britain had administered the islands for over a century and the population of the Falklands was British and, above all, wished to remain so. The UN took neither side and merely invited both parties to hold peaceful discussions to solve the matter. This was the official situation at the time of the invasion.

The timing of the Argentinian invasion was somewhat baffling,

▲ Royal Marines from Britain's "task force" await instructions to advance on the settlement at Goose Green.

but was generally attributed to an ill-conceived bout of sabre-rattling by the country's new military leader Lieutenant General Leopoldo Galtieri. Argentina had already lost its sovereignty battle for the Beagle Channel islands with Chile. Galtieri felt that this reflected badly on both his leadership and the morale of his country, already stricken with a crumbling economy. With the widespread support of most Argentinians, on April 2, 1982 Galtieri's troops landed on East Falkland and quickly overran the 84 Royal Marines that were stationed at Port Stanley, the island's one and only town.

The invasion caught Britain unprepared. With intelligence reports having failed to warn the government of the impending attack, British Foreign Secretary Lord Carrington came under heavy criticism. He was left with no option but to resign. Prime Minister Margaret Thatcher immediately announced a 320-km (200-mile) war zone around the

islands. Amid a jingoistic fervour whipped up by the British tabloid media, a task force of Royal Marines departed for the Falklands. Their 13,000-km (8,000-mile) journey would take them three weeks.

The first signs of fighting began on May 1, as the task force was attacked by Argentinian aircraft. The following day saw the first significant casualty of the war as Argentinian ship, the *General Belgrano* was sunk by a British submarine as it allegedly sailed towards the war zone. Over 350 Argentinian sailors drowned. The tone of the rhetoric used by the British government was captured succinctly by *The Sun* newspaper with its triumphal headline, "Gotcha!" However, opposition members of parliament criticized the sinking of the *Belgrano* as it had been 58 km (36 miles) outside the exclusion zone. After the war, evidence mounted to indicate that the cruiser had, in fact, been sailing away from the war zone when the missiles were fired.

▲ The highly trained British forces won an easy victory over General Galtieri's taking 13,500 prisoners of war.

There was never really any doubt that in a war situation Argentina would provide little match for the superior British forces, and after bitter fighting that saw the loss of five ships, on May 21 Royal Marines landed at Port San Carlos, on East Falkland. Thereafter British infantry advanced southward capturing settlements at Darwin and Goose Green. On May 31, the

Argentine garrison at Port Stanley was surrounded. On June 14 General Galtieri announced his country's surrender as 13,500 Argentinian troops were made prisoners of war.

The defeat was viewed in Argentina as a national humiliation. Three days after the end of the conflict, General Galtieri resigned as both President and commander in chief of the army. The military junta that had ruled Argentina since 1976 had suffered a serious loss of credibility and the following year democracy was returned to Argentina with the election of Raúl Alfonsín.

In Britain, the Falklands War proved to be a turning point for Prime Minister Margaret Thatcher. Before the war her ratings had fallen to their lowest point. But Thatcher basked in the Churchillian role of war leader and in the General Election of June 1983 was returned to government with a landslide majority. Her reputation as the "Iron Lady" was now established beyond all doubt.

◀ An Argentinian shell explodes on the deck of HMS *Antelope*. During the conflict the Royal Navy lost five vessels.

ISRAEL IN LEBANON

▲ **A grieving Lebanese woman is led away from the scene of an Israeli bomb attack in which she had been made homeless.**

On June 6, 1982 the volatile peace of war-torn Lebanon was once again demolished as Israel sent a massive invasion force of over 60,000 troops and tanks across its borders into Lebanon's southern regions. The aim was ostensibly to prevent the continuation of raids by the Palestinian Liberation Army (PLO) into northern Israel.

Lebanon had always been a nation indelibly divided along sectarian lines. During the 1970s open warfare between Christian and Muslim militia groups had ravaged the country. The PLO's involvement in Lebanon dated back to 1970 when, having been driven out of Jordan, it settled its headquarters in the south of Lebanon. From then on, the PLO had launched periodic sorties across the border into northern Israel. At the request of Israel, the predominantly Christian Lebanese government began to curtail PLO activities within Lebanon. This led to the PLO's joining forces with Lebanese Muslims during the growing conflagration. Thus was created one of the most complex of war zones, with both warring sides made up of many independent factions, often with their own mutually exclusive agendas.

During 1975, as the Muslim/PLO coalition gained the upper hand in the conflict, neighbouring Syria, fearing that Israel, its bitter enemy, might intervene, sent in an army of 20,000 troops. In 1978, with Syria effectively occupying Lebanon, the United Nations sent a peacekeeping force that attempted in vain to enforce a cease-fire between the warring factions.

In 1981, the focus of conflict shifted to Israel and the PLO. On July 17, Israeli forces launched a bombing raid on the PLO headquarters in West Beirut. Periodic skirmishes continued until June 6, 1982 when the Israeli army crossed the Lebanese border. By June 9, the Israelis were within sight of Beirut and engaged in bitter fighting with both the PLO and Syria.

From a military angle, the Israeli invasion was a great success. Syrian forces were defeated and the PLO were forced out of South Lebanon to regroup in West Beirut. However, the campaign was condemned by the US Secretary of State, Alexander Haig, who "ordered" Israeli leader Menachem Begin to pull back. Haig warned that if Israeli aggression continued then the Soviet Union may be prepared to intervene on the side of Syria. Within Israel, Begin had been branded a warmonger by opposition leader Shimon Peres and others in the Knesset, the Israeli parliament. On July 3, 100,000 students marched through the streets of Tel Aviv demanding peace in the Middle East.

▲ **Palestinian Liberation Army leader Yasser Arafat (right) directs the defence of Beirut as the Israeli advance continues.**

Relations between Israel and the Western world were further strained at the end of July when Israeli jets bombed the densely populated areas of West Beirut, killing 120 and injuring over 200. Most of the victims were ordinary Lebanese citizens. Further attacks continued throughout August. Israel finally agreed to end their siege of Beirut on August 21 when the PLO agreed to pull out of the city. Most of the PLO's leaders were offered exile in Yemen. Meanwhile, many ordinary Palestinians were left in refugee camps to await their fate.

On August 23, the Christian Phalangist leader, Bashir Gemayel, was elected President of Lebanon. However, three weeks later, before his inauguration, he was assassinated in a bomb explosion. In revenge for the killing, Phalangists – seemingly with the tacit support of the Israeli army – brutally massacred hundreds of Palestinians at the refugee centres at Sabra and Shatila. The bloody images of murdered Palestinians, including elderly men, women and children, brought the Israeli government condemnation from all over the world. A peace protest in Tel Aviv brought close to 200,000 on to the streets.

With the withdrawal of the Israeli army in June 1985, it was business as usual in Lebanon as the Christian and Muslim factions continued their ongoing encounter. Meanwhile, twenty-five years of civil war and foreign occupation had brought the Lebanese economy to its knees. It has been estimated that up to a quarter of million Lebanese have been killed in the fighting. Furthermore, a quarter of the country's population – including most of the educated professionals – has fled abroad. The conflict goes on.

TWILIGHT TRAGEDY

▲ **Tragedy on the film set – the wreck of the helicopter that took the life of actor Vic Morrow and two Vietnamese children.**

On July 23, 1982, a tragically bizarre accident occurred during the making of the film *Twilight Zone: The Movie.* in Indian Dunes, California. A helicopter being used in the filming went out of control and decapitated actor Vic Morrow and two children. The film was based on the famous sci-fi/paranormal television series of the 1960s which invited the audience to enter a world in which strange happenings were the norm – "a place," the announcer intoned each week, "we call the twilight zone".

The film was made up of four independent stories. It was during a sequence in which Vic Morrow found himself mysteriously trans-ported to a violent war scene in Vietnam that a helicopter containing one of the film crews was accidentally hit by flying debris from a special effects explosion on the ground. Its tail rotor hit, the helicopter spun out of control, catching Morrow and the two Vietnamese children in its rotor blades. Morrow, a child star from the film *The Blackboard Jungle*, although perhaps best remembered for the 1960s World War Two TV action series *Combat*, was killed instantly.

In 1992, the film's director John Landis and four other production officials were cleared in court of having any responsibility for the three deaths.

'82

NEWS IN BRIEF

September

- Lebanese President-elect Bashir Gemayel killed by bomb; Amin Hemayel succeeds
- Israeli forces take West Beirut
- Coalition government collapses in Germany
- Massacres of Palestinians by Christian Phalangist militia in Lebanon
- Elections in Sweden won by Social Democrat party
- UN peacekeeping forces land in Lebanon
- Deaths of Princess Grace of Monaco (Grace Kelly) after car accident, and of British RAF hero Group Captain Sir Douglas Bader

October

- New government under Helmut Kohl formed in West Germany
- US imposes trade sanctions on Poland
- President Reagan declares war on drugs
- De Lorean motor plant in Northern Ireland closed; John De Lorean arrested in USA
- Socialist government under Felipe Gonzalez elected in Spain
- Death of Canadian pianist Glenn Gould

UP FROM THE DEEP

In a seminal event in the history of nautical archaeology, October 11, 1982 saw the climax of an incredible 17-year operation to raise a sixteenth-century British warship from its watery grave off the coast of the south of England.

Built in 1510, the 500-ton *Mary Rose* was known to have been one of Henry VIII's favourite vessels. It was thought to have been named after his favourite sister, Mary, and the emblem of the Tudor family, the rose.

The *Mary Rose* sank during an engagement with the French navy during the Battle of Spithead. The French, while not formally at war with Britain, had launched an invasion of the Solent waters around the Isle of Wight. It was not, in fact, at the hands of French cannons that the *Mary Rose* perished with most of her crew of 500, but because of human error. It would seem that while attempting to turn, she took on water in the lowest row of gun ports that had accidentally been left open after firing.

The wreck was first discovered by accident in 1836 when a local fisherman snagged his gear. A diving expedition led to the discovery of a number of bronze cannons. However, the modern story was largely the obsession of a man named Alexander McKee. He began searching for the wreck in 1966, discovering it four years later.

The operation cost an estimated £4 million to complete. The hull was successfully raised by drilling holes through the main structural timbers into which huge metal backing plates were then bolted, allowing the strain of lifting to be spread evenly. Along with the *Mary Rose*, over 17,000 artifacts were discovered – a treasure trove that provided a unique glimpse of Tudor England. The ship now stands on display in Portsmouth Harbour.

▲ **After almost 500 years on the sea bed, the hull of Henry VIII's warship *Mary Rose* rises from its watery grave.**

SOLIDARITY IN CRISIS

1982 saw Poland in turmoil. Under military rule, on October 26, 1982, the independent union movement, Solidarity, was outlawed. It looked as if the hard-won gains of the 1980 general strike had been overturned at a stroke.

Although extremely popular in Poland, and widely supported in the West, Solidarity was seen by the Soviet Union as a danger to the security of Eastern Europe. On February 9, 1981, General Wojciech Jaruzelski had come to power charged with the task of bringing order to Poland. In September 1981, the Central Committee of the Soviet Communist Party issued a dire warning to the Polish government that "anti-Sovietism had reached dangerous limits" in Poland. The government in turn charged Solidarity with endangering Poland's continued freedom with their demands for further reform.

Although threats from the West made direct Soviet action unlikely, Soviet influence over Poland's leadership was considerable. As the strikes continued to cripple Poland's economy, and calls came for a national vote on the future of the government, on December 13, 1981, General Jaruzelski announced martial law. Within days, strike actions were brutally crushed by troops and union leaders, including Lech Walesa, the President of Solidarity, were arrested.

The suppression continued into the new year, and only the intervention of the influential Roman Catholic church resulted in an easing of martial restrictions. During August, with most of Solidarity's leaders still in captivity, a number of illustrations of the depth of anti-government strength were given as protest rallies were held in Gdansk, Warsaw and Krakow.

General Jaruzelski's final move against the union came on October 8, 1982, when Solidarity was formally dissolved by the Polish Parliament. In its place were put a number of smaller unions with vastly diminished powers to strike. A month later, Walesa was released from prison.

Although illegal, Solidarity continued as an underground movement and Walesa was offered a job at the Lenin Shipyards in Gdansk where he had once worked as an electrician. He continued to play a prominent role in the conflict until the fall of Communism in 1989. Martial law was formally lifted in July 1983, although by this time, many of its most repressive features had been written into Poland's civil law.

▲ As government suppression of Solidarity increased, the second anniversary of the birth of movement was met by widespread rioting.

SOVIET LEADER DIES

When the leadership of any superpower changes hands, the implications for the rest of the world are inevitably considered. So it was that on November 10, 1982, the West speculated about future East-West relations as the Soviet news agency Tass announced the death of President Leonid Brezhnev, who had led the Soviet Union for the previous 18 years.

Brezhnev had emerged in the struggle for power that accompanied the removal of Nikita Khrushchev in 1964. Officially, the leadership was collective, Brezhnev sharing power with Prime Minister Aleksey Kosygin and President Nikolay Podgorny. By following a harder Communist line than his predecessor, by 1970 Brezhnev had effective control of the Soviet Union. His

foreign policy, that the Soviet Union had the right to intervene when another Communist country came under threat (whether that threat was internal or external), was known in the west as the "Brezhnev Doctrine". At home he was criticized for the over-production of arms at the expense of all other areas of the economy.

The man whom Brezhnev saw as his natural successor was Konstantin Chernenko, but two days after his death, the Central Committee of the Soviet Communist Party announced that the new General Secretary would be Yuri Andropov, the former head of the KGB. Over the year that followed he showed himself to be a gentle reformer, pledging himself to stamp out the corruption and cronyism that had thrived throughout the Brezhnev years.

► After 18 years of Cold War rule, the death of Leonid Brezhnev signalled the first signs of reform within the Soviet Union.

'83

STARS WARS FANTASY

In one of the most unexpected developments of the Reagan era, on March 23, 1983, the President of the United States appeared on national television to announce a proposed new system that would protect America from nuclear attacks coming from the Soviet Union.

The project was called the Strategic Defense Initiative (SDI), although it would be popularly dubbed "Star Wars". The SDI was planned to defend the nation by intercepting missiles in flight using particle and projectile beams directed from satellites in orbit around the Earth. Much of the necessary technology, Reagan admitted, would take until the end of the century to develop.

Although – or, perhaps because – huge research funds were set aside by Congress, the SDI did not win the whole-hearted backing of Americans. In spite of the presence of the "father of the H-bomb", Ede Teller, on the project, many prominent scientists argued that it was fanciful science fiction and simply not technically feasible. Meanwhile, many politicians and diplomats felt that there was a danger that SDI might impede future arms-control and limitation agreements, and even set off a new arms race.

In any event, little real progress was made in the development of the SDI and when the Soviet Union was dismantled in 1991 the project was soon deemed to be no longer necessary.

▲ President Reagan announces his "Star Wars" defence strategy on American national television.

THE RIGHT TO DIE

A vocal supporter of voluntary euthanasia, Arthur Koestler took his own life on March 3, 1983. Suffering from leukemia and Parkinson's disease, the 77-year-old novelist swallowed an overdose of sleeping pills at his London home. His wife Cynthia, twenty years younger than him and thought to be in good health, committed suicide at the same time.

Born in Hungary, Koestler was an active Communist in his youth. After attending the University of Vienna he worked as a journalist, corresponding on the Spanish Civil War. Imprisoned by the fascists, he became disillusioned with totalitarianism in any form. His first successful novel, *Darkness at Noon*, published in 1940, reflected his growing cynicism with political totalitarianism, and much of his work from this period was concerned with political morality.

A British citizen from 1948, Koestler's later works, such as *The Act of Creation* (1964), an investigation into the creative process, and *The Ghost in the Machine* (1967) examined the workings of the human mind.

▲ Writer Arthur Koestler became the most famous proponent and exponent of the principle of voluntary euthanasia.

THE GREATEST FAKE

In April 1983, historians prepared themselves for what might have been one of the most exciting discoveries of the twentieth century as the German general-interest magazine *Stern* announced the acquisition of a 60-volume collection of Adolf Hitler's diaries. The story was an immediate sensation, as it had long been hoped that such a journal – said to start before the Nazis came to power in 1933 and end days before Hitler's suicide in 1945 – might exist.

The reaction of experts was more sceptical, especially as Hitler was known to have hated dealing with paperwork, preferring to dictate everything to his secretaries. What helped convince *Stern's* management that they had the real thing was a declaration by the emi-

▲ The "Hitler Diary" (left) shown alongside a published book from which some of the faked texts were allegedly copied.

nent British historian Hugh Trevor-Roper (Baron Dacre), an expert on the Third Reich, that they were authentic.

It was only when the diaries were passed to an American expert in studying hand-writing, that the plot began to unravel. Studying the entries along with other known examples of Hitler's script, Charles Hamilton was unequivocal: the diaries were "patent and obvious forgeries".

With the management of *Stern* still harbouring doubts, the scandal climaxed on May 11 when a minor *Stern* reporter admitted that he had bought the diaries from a calligrapher in Stuttgart named Konrad Kujau. Although no convictions were ever made on the basis of the fiasco, Kujau having fled the country, embarrassment was widespread. Henri Nannen, *Stern's* publisher, was forced to resign from the magazine. It seemed that the innermost thoughts of the architect of National Socialism would forever remain hidden.

THATCHER'S LANDSLIDE

On June 9, 1983, British Prime Minister Margaret Thatcher won a second term in office, this time with a vastly increased majority in the House of Commons. The Conservative landslide was remarkable in that only a year earlier opinion polls had shown her government to be deeply unpopular with the electorate.

This turnaround was largely attributable to two factors. There was no doubting that Thatcher still basked in the jingoism surrounding the Falklands War of 1982. Evoking the memory of Winston Churchill's wartime leadership, she managed to stoke a nationalistic fervour that was out of all proportion to what was a relatively minor international incident. The war significantly enhanced Margaret Thatcher's reputation as the "Iron Lady".

The Labour Party also played a

spectacular part in its own defeat. Under the leadership of Michael Foot, Labour fell foul of in-fighting between its political wings. When four prominent ex-cabinet ministers defected to found the Social Democratic Party, the so-called left wing was able take a more prominent role. The media, largely sympathetic to Thatcher and the Tories, was able to portray the

"Loony Left" in opposition as a serious socialist threat to Britain.

With such a majority in the House of Commons, the right-wing "Thatcher Revolution" was allowed to continue unopposed. It would take the Labour Party almost a decade to form an effective opposition, and another 4 years after that before they would at last come to power.

▲ Margaret Thatcher (centre left) celebrates a famous election victory. The architect of her success was party chairman Cecil Parkinson (right).

83

THE UNITED STATES AND CENTRAL AMERICA

In February 1979, a revolution by the Sandinista National Liberation Front (FSLN) overthrew President Anastasio Somoza Debayle, ending 46 years of dictatorship and misrule in Nicaragua by the Somoza family. A military government – the National Reconstruction – was formed with the Marxist Daniel Ortega as its leader. Nicaragua by this time was in a state of ruin. The fighting had taken the lives of 30,000 people and left half a million without homes.

▲ Pope John Paul II takes mass during his 1983 visit to Nicaragua. The hoardings in the background celebrate the victory of the Sandinista Liberation Front (FSLN).

◀ Condemnation of America's covert war against the Sandinista government was widely echoed around the world.

The Sandinista government immediately set about a programme of radical social reform. Property formerly owned by the exiled Somoza family and their supporters was expropriated. The economy – what was left of it – was nationalized. A constitution was drawn up assuring all citizens fundamental individual rights and civil liberties.

In 1981, Nicaraguan foreign policy first provided a glimpse of future troubles. Nicaragua's closer relations with Cuba and the Marxist regime of Fidel Castro was unacceptable to the US, whose fiercely right-wing President, Ronald Reagan, feared the spread of Communism throughout poverty-stricken Central America. Up to this point, the US government had provided crucial economic aid to

Nicaragua. This was now withdrawn. Worse was to come. Reagan authorized a budget of $20 million for the Central Intelligence Agency (CIA) to recruit and train a counter-revolutionary force to impede the Sandinistas. This new force – referred to as the "Contras" – was easily established since many of Somoza's formidable National Guard who had fled across their national borders to Honduras and Costa Rica were waiting for such an opportunity to return. By 1984 there were at least 15,000 Contras engaged in a fierce guerrilla war.

Reagan's involvement in Nicaragua was not entirely popular in America. But as "the focus of evil in the modern world," as Reagan put it, Communism in all forms was to be combatted, especially so close to the USA. Nonetheless, an amendment put forward by Senator Edward Boland of Massachussetts in April 1983 made covert aid to

▲ The presidency of Violetta Barrios de Chamorro's National Opposition Union was firmly backed by the USA.

the Contras illegal. In June 1983, formal diplomatic relations between the USA and Nicaragua were ended after a number of CIA-backed assassination plots were uncovered. Nicaragua expelled three diplomats who were suspected of being CIA agents; the US countered by ordering the closure of the Nicaraguan embassy in Washington.

In spite of Congress's ruling of illegality, three years later it was revealed that financial aid to the Nicaraguan rebel forces had continued long after it was banned. The "Iran-Contra" scandal that saw the sale of US arms to Iran and the funds channelled back to the contras was a major embarrassment to the final stages of Reagan's presidency.

The war against the Contras was brutal and wasteful of Nicaragua's already pitiful economic reserves. In an effort to stop the fighting, the government agreed in November 1984 to hold democratic elections. The result was a clear victory for the Sandinistas, and with the support of 63 per cent of the electorate, Daniel Ortega continued as

President. Despite the presence and authorization of a team of international observers, the Reagan administration refused to accept that the elections had been fair. Limited in its ability to influence either the war or Nicaragua's internal politics, the USA turned to economic measures as a way of destabilizing the Nicaraguan government. In 1985, President Reagan announced a trade embargo; furthermore, the USA used its influence with the World Bank to block development loans previously earmarked for Nicaragua. This had the effect of decimating the Nicaraguan economy during the second half of the 1980s. Dramatic inflation rates mirrored those of Germany in the 1930s – in 1988 alone, prices rose by an average of 30,000 per cent.

In the 1990, with Nicaragua beset by poverty and unemployment, an election was called. This time, the US-backed National

▶ President Reagan took a very firm line on Marxist activity in Nicaragua when it was so close to America's back door.

Opposition Union won by a small margin. Violetta Barrios de Chamorro was named as the President. Unsurprisingly, the new government espoused conservative policies. With US aid, private enterprise was reintroduced and a degree of stability was brought to Nicaragua's political divide. Austerity measures were adopted in order to bring inflation under control. The rebel Contra forces were demobilized and the national army, most of whom were still loyal to the Sandinistas, was cut back by 80 per cent. Intermittent violence continued throughout the 1990s, however, often among former Contras (*Recontras*) and demobilized

Sandinistas (*Recompas*).

Ultimately, the story of Nicaragua is one of many contradictions. In an economically insignificant state, a criminal totalitarian dictatorship was overthrown by a popular revolution. Civil rights were introduced on an unprecedented scale. And yet simple ideological differences led the Reagan administration to brand the Sandinistas as "government out of the barrel of a gun". Systematic sabotage by the US government, via the CIA, slowly crippled the Nicaraguan economy until the government could no longer function. Many across the globe felt that in this case the US had taken the role of self-styled policeman of the world altogether too far.

'83

SOLIDARITY ON THE WORLD STAGE

▲ Solidarity leader Lech Walesa, the popular recipient of the 1983 Nobel Peace Prize.

On December 10, 1983, the Western World gave formal recognition to the advances made in Poland by the independent trade union Solidarity when its leader, Lech Walesa, was awarded the Nobel Peace Prize.

At the ceremony that took place in Oslo, Walesa's wife Danuta accepted the £129,000 prize on behalf of her husband who had been denied permission by the Polish authorities to attend the event. She received a standing ovation as she read out the acceptance speech he had written. His words told of the pride felt by the millions of members of Solidarity that the free world acknowledged their struggle.

The award failed to meet with the approval of the Soviet Union, who had already warned the Polish government of the threat to Eastern-bloc unity posed by Solidarity. Indeed, the BBC reported that on the night of the award ceremony, the Soviet jamming of their overseas services was stepped up noticeably.

THE US IN LEBANON

▲ The gutted ruins of the US marine headquarters in Beirut following a car bomb attack.

For the second time in the space of six months, the US peacekeeping force in Lebanon found itself the victim of a ruthless terrorist attack. On October 23, 1983, a Mercedes truck containing over 2000 pounds of explosive drove past security gates and crashed itself into the US marine headquarters in Beirut. Within seconds the four-story building was reduced to a pile of burning rubble. Amidst the debris were the bodies of 216 US marines.

The subject of bitter fighting that had started in 1975, Lebanon, and in particular the city of Beirut, was beset by a complex war among seemingly irreconcilable Christian and Muslim factions. Eventually, Israel came of the aid of the Christian militia, waging war on the Palestinian Liberation Organization (PLO). In an attempt to keep the factions apart, peacekeeping forces from the US, France and Italy arrived in Lebanon in 1981. Their presence was not always welcome.

At the same time as the explosion on the US military base, an attack on French peacekeeping troops in Beirut killed another 58. A group calling itself the Free Islamic Revolution Movement based in Iran claimed responsibility for the two attacks.

Only six months earlier the US embassy in Beirut had been damaged by a similar lone suicide bomber, who had killed 60 in his raid. Such attacks served to focus attention on President Reagan's foreign policy that had made the US the self-styled peacekeepers of the world.

▲ The bodies of US marines are dug out of the debris. The bomb was alleged to have been the work of Iranian terrorists.

NEWS IN BRIEF

July
- New laws limiting trade union powers passed in Britain
- Unrest by Tamil separatists causes curfew to be imposed in Sri Lanka
- Martial law lifted in Poland
- Deaths of Spanish film maker Luis Buñuel, British actor David Niven and US engineer and architect Buckminster Fuller

August
- Libyan air-strike on Faya-Largeau in Chad; French paratroopers sent to Chad, but Libyan forces take Faya-Largeau
- Military coup in Guatemala
- Martial law ended in Pakistan
- Philippine opposition leader Benigno Aquino assassinated on return to Manila from exile
- Oil tanker runs aground off Cape Town, South Africa causing severe pollution
- Resignation of Israeli Prime Minister Menachem Begin

September
- Korean 747 airliner shot down by Soviet aircraft over Soviet airspace; 269 die
- Israel begins withdrawal from Lebanon; fighting between rival Lebanese factions breaks out
- Anti-government protests in Chile on tenth anniversary of coup

GRENADA INVADED

On October 25, 1983, the US again showed itself capable of heavy handedness when it came to foreign policy as a force of over 2,000 marines stormed the former British colony of Grenada to suppress a Marxist military coup.

The West Indian island had gained its independence from Britain in 1974 with Eric Gairy as the state's first premier. Political factions fought violently during the remainder of the decade, however, and in 1979, while Gairy was abroad, a bloodless coup brought the socialist People's Revolutionary Government (PRG) to power. The new Prime Minister was the moderate Maurice Bishop. On October 19, 1983 a military coup deposed and assassinated Bishop in favour of his radical deputy Bernard Court, making Grenada an unequivocally Marxist state. This was the cue for the US invasion.

With Grenada's military outclassed in every area by the US marines, the pre-dawn invasion was over almost as soon as it had begun. The island's governor general, Sir Paul Scoon, took over government until democratic election could be held in December 1984.

The action taken by the US was given a hostile reception around the world. The United Nations Security Council passed a resolution deploring the act as a

▲ **Ever vigilant to the threat of Communism on its own doorstep, the US was easily able to suppress Grenada's Marxist regime.**

"flagrant violation of international law." President Reagan was unrepentant. He had successfully signalled the message that any other West Indian or Central American states embracing Marxism did so at their own peril.

UPROAR OVER NUCLEAR BOMB FILM

On December 10, 1983, 15 million British television viewers tuned in to watch a controversial film about the aftermath of a nuclear bomb, three weeks after it had debuted in the United States. *The Day After* showed what might have followed after a Soviet nuclear attack on a small town in Kansas.

The film was strongly opposed by the British government who were firmly behind the idea of a nuclear deterrent. Defence Minister Michael Heseltine claimed that the film gave a one-sided account of the nuclear issue and would play into the hands of the protest movements which proved such a headache to Conservative governments throughout the 1980s. Heseltine insisted that Yorkshire Television, who had bought the American-made film, gave an opportunity for the pro-nuclear defence to put its case. The network agreed to a panel discussion but Heseltine pulled out when he discovered that Monsignor Bruce Kent, who was a prominent member of the Campaign for Nuclear

◄ **What if the Soviets attacked Kansas? Nuclear devastation as shown in the controversial film *The Day After*.**

Disarmament (CND), would also be joining the debate.

Some criticized the film's credibility. The British Medical Association said the scenes of a busy but orderly hospital dealing with the critical burns and injuries of thousands of survivors were unrealistic. As they said, medical staff were just as likely to have been victims as civilians and that hospitals would quickly be overwhelmed to the point of chaos.

The very fact that *The Day After* topped the viewing ratings on both sides of the Atlantic was an indication of the very real fear felt by many millions of ordinary people about the possibility of nuclear conflagration.

'84

TUNISIAN FOOD RIOTS

During January 1984 over 100 Tunisians were killed in unrest that followed the government's decision to raise the price of bread by 125 per cent. By the time the official announcement was made on January 1, riots had already spread throughout the country.

The price rises were made in an effort to combat a massive budget deficit. The economy of Tunisia, an oil-producing state, had suffered from the drop in prices of crude oil and the situation was worsened by a poor harvest and a reduction in the number of tourists to the country. By late 1983 the government was forced to reduce imports and cut its substantial cereal product subsidies, which had kept the cost of bread at the same level since the early sixties.

The Tunisian authorities claimed

▲ **The dramatic increase in the cost of bread sent ordinary Tunisians rioting in the streets.**

the economic situation was only a contributory factor in the riots, blaming Islamic fundamentalists for organizing the demonstrations. Some independent reports con-

firmed that groups opposed to President Bourguiba's pro-Western policies played a part in encouraging the rioters.

Violence soon escalated to an uncontrollable level and the government declared a state of emergency on January 3. A curfew was imposed on the country's capital as armoured trucks and tanks were drafted in to clear the streets. Two days later, negotiations to agree compensatory wage increases began and an emergency law was passed freezing rent levels for the remainder of the year.

By January 6, the government had backed down completely, reversing the price rises, and order was finally restored. Schools and universities, closed during the riots, reopened on January 11 and the curfew was lifted at the end of the month.

RESIGNATION OF CANADIAN PRIME MINISTER

▲ **Pierre Trudeau, the Canadian Liberal Prime Minister, was one of the leading lights of his country's independence movement.**

Pierre Trudeau, the Prime Minister of Canada announced his decision to step down from power on February 29, 1984. His time in office included overseeing the freeing of Canada from its final ties with Britain, the defeat of the Quebec independence movement in a 1980 referendum and the promotion of international peace initiatives.

From 1968, Trudeau enjoyed a lengthy period as leader of Canada's Liberal Party and Prime Minister. The Liberals were only defeated in 1979, when Trudeau first resigned. He was persuaded to come back and the party won again in 1980.

The son of a millionaire, Trudeau's background was in the legal profession. His first decade

in leadership was characterized by domestic economic problems and the question of Quebec separatism, to which he was firmly opposed. In the early eighties he reformed the constitution, instigating a charter of human rights and broader federal economic powers, and negotiated the transference of the sovereignty of the 1867 Canadian constitution from Britain to Canada.

But by late 1983 his future was in doubt. One Liberal ex-minister said, "I believe it's time for Mr Trudeau to go. He has completed his agenda and I do not know what he sticking around for." In February 1984, Trudeau concurred, saying it was "the appropriate time for someone else to assume this challenge."

THE BELGRANO LEAK

Controversy over the sinking of the Argentinian cruiser *General Belgrano* dogged the Conservative government long after the end of the Falklands War. On August 18, 1984 a senior civil servant at the Ministry of Defence, Clive Ponting, was charged with breaking the Official Secrets Act by passing documents related to the affair to Labour MP Mr Tam Dalyell.

"I did this because I believed that Ministers were not prepared to answer legitimate questions from an MP about a matter of considerable public concern simply in order to protect their own political positions," Ponting claimed.

Tam Dalyell, who had been actively pursuing the case since the war, said the documents showed that the *Belgrano* had reversed its course for home 11 hours before it was torpedoed by a British submarine. He argued that the sinking ended chances of a peaceful resolution to the conflict. Prime Minister Thatcher later replied that "the precise position and course of the *Belgrano* at the time were irrelevant" and added that diplomatic action to reach a solution was "pursued vigorously".

Tam Dalyell praised Ponting's conduct, saying, "the civil servant who jeopardizes his own career for the public good is possibly the noblest Roman of them all".

Clive Ponting was tried and acquitted in February 1985.

▶ **Clive Ponting (right) broke the Official Secrets Act by leaking documents that implicated a government cover-up.**

THE BRIGHTON BOMBING

▲ **The IRA bombing of the Grand Hotel could easily have resulted in the deaths of many members of the ruling British government.**

The morning of October 12 should have been a routine day during another Conservative Party Conference. But breakfast news programmes were carrying a very different story that day, as Britain woke up in unified horror to reports of the carnage created by an IRA bomb which destroyed the main conference hotel.

The bomb, consisting of 20 pounds of commercial explosive, went off at 2.54am in a sixth-floor bathroom of Brighton's Grand Hotel. Some guests plunged several floors as an entire section of the front of the hotel collapsed. Prime Minister Thatcher, working in the lounge of her suite on the text of her conference speech, escaped injury, but a total of five people died.

No government ministers were killed, although the dead included popular MP Sir Anthony Berry and Roberta Wakeham, wife of the government Chief Whip. John Wakeham was himself pulled from the wreckage, as was Norman Tebbit, Secretary for Trade and Industry, among a total of 30 people who were admitted to hospital. Norman Tebbit would not be able to return to the House of Commons until January the following year and his wife Margaret was paralysed from the neck down.

Margaret Thatcher won widespread praise when she arrived punctually at the conference that morning. It was, she said, an attempt "to cripple Her Majesty's democratically elected government."

In claiming responsibility for the attack, the IRA said, "today we were unlucky, but remember - we have only to be lucky once: you will have to be lucky always."

84

NUCLEAR POWER AND ECOLOGY

The 1980s saw the strong emergence of a number of anti-nuclear protest movements throughout Europe, aimed at ending both the proliferation of nuclear arms and the environmental perils of nuclear energy.

The 1980s saw Britain with a powerful right-wing government. A massive majority in the House of Commons enabled it to enact a number of controversial policies with little parliamentary opposition. The official stance on both nuclear weapons and nuclear energy was clear. The government intended to arm Britain with both Cruise and Trident missiles.

▲ Demonstrators wearing skull masks and carrying a model Cruise missile protest outside Britain's nuclear missile base at Greenham Common.

◀ Support for the Campaign for Nuclear Disarmament (CND) reached peak levels in the early 1980s.

Furthermore, nuclear energy was viewed largely as a safe and cheap fuel of the future.

The announcement of Britain's new nuclear arsenal triggered a number of well-attended rallies in London and other cities, organized by the Campaign for Nuclear Disarmament (CND). Thereafter, for the next two years, the focus of attention moved to Greenham, the military installation where the Cruise missiles would be based. It was on Greenham Common, alongside the base, that an all-female protest movement began. The Women's Peace Camp was set up to provide a permanent protest vigil. Intermittent attempts by the authorities to eject them were answered with considerable resistance.

The problem for the British anti-nuclear movement in the early 1980s was ultimately one of image. The media coverage of the women of Greenham Common usually painted them as misguided members of the "Loony Left" or simply "feminists". In short, they lacked the "Middle England" respectability essential to bring about greater support.

In other parts of Europe, the anti-nuclear movements enjoyed more tangible success. In Germany, the "Greens" organized a political party out of 250 ecological and environmentalist groups. So successful were they in spreading their message that at the 1983 Bundestag elections they were able to poll over 5 per cent of the vote, giving their views genuine representation in parliament.

Following this success, "Green" parties were formed all over Europe. Although in Britain, neither the Green nor the Ecology parties ever came close to having an elected member of parliament, their high-profile campaigning made them an effective lobby. Their success can ultimately be judged by the fact that by the end of the decade all the main political parties in Britain, even if they had not shifted their stance on the nuclear question, had been forced to acknowledge that the environment was now a major political issue.

A noteworthy shift in public opinion during the 1980s was the drive toward ecological awareness. Although not overtly political - at least not in the parliamentary sense – the organization that spearheaded

▶ **The activities of the "Greenham Common Women" paved the way for other forms of environmental "direct action".**

the movement was Greenpeace, a multinational group, sponsored by voluntary contributions. Greenpeace engaged in non-violent protest wherever government agencies or large corporations acted to the detriment of the environment or the endangering of any forms of life. Greenpeace were effective at shaming their targets with the creation of maximum adverse publicity. They also crossed over with the general anti-nuclear movement in that many of their highest-profile campaigns involved attempts to stop nuclear testing.

An important aspect of the heightening of ecological awareness was the educating of ordinary consumers to think about the use of the Earth's natural resources. An early target that showed how powerful a tool a mobilized public could be was in the use of spray cans. When scientists revealed that the cans that most people used for household cleaning released gases that damaged the Earth's ozone layer initial calls for action by environmentalists were largely ignored by industry. It was only when con-

sumers had been educated that they started actively looking for alternatives. As sales of spray cans fell, the manufacturers realized it was in their own interests to supply ozone-friendly alternatives. Spray cans in their original form are now rarely seen.

So successful were the environmental pressure groups that by the start of the 1990s, ecology played a major part in the advertising of household goods – even though in many cases the claimed benefits of the packaging were marginal.

At the end of the day it is difficult to assess how much progress has resulted from public pressure. In the case of nuclear arms, as far as government agencies were concerned, the trimming of the world's nuclear arsenal in the mid-1980s was driven more by their crippling costs than environmental considerations. Then, too, at the end of the decade the crumbling of Communism meant there was no ideological Cold War left to fight.

Similarly, whilst public appetite for all things green continues to grow, the efforts of millions of

ordinary people is to some extent rendered insignificant by the levels of industrial pollution unleashed around the world, or by the potentially catastrophic practice of felling the rain forests. Calls by scientists and environmental bodies to cut back pollution are regularly acknowledged by governments who are then unwilling to impose stringent regulations on their own heavy industry.

Britain in the 1990s saw a number of violent clashes at the sites of government road-building schemes as direct action by environmental protesters – self-styled "eco-warriors" – attempted to halt the building of highways destroying natural countryside. Man's increased dependence on the car looks set to become the ecological battleground of the next century. In spite of improvements in car engine manufacturing, gases emitted from car exhausts are still one of the most significant polluters. Although nearly all drivers are aware of this fact, it seems to be one environmental sacrifice that the public is not yet prepared to make.

'84

NEWS IN BRIEF

June
- Troops end siege of the Amritsar temple in India with large loss of life
- British rebate to EC agreed at EC summit meeting
- British unions hold day of action in support of striking coal miners
- Deaths of French philosopher Michel Foucault and US film maker Joseph Losey

July
- Kidnapping of exiled former Nigerian politician Umaru Dikko foiled in Britain
- Britain expels two Nigerian diplomats over Dikko affair
- British High Court rules ban on unions at GCHQ illegal
- Twenty shot dead when unemployed security guard goes on a killing spree in a McDonald's in California
- End of dock workers' strike in Britain
- Death of British actor James Mason

August
- Upper Volta becomes Burkina Fasso
- Violence between Tamils and Sinhalese in Sri Lanka
- Olympic Games, boycotted by the USSR, open in Los Angeles
- Court of Appeal overturns High Court decision on illegality of unions at GCHQ in Britain
- Deaths of British actor Richard Burton, British playwright and author J B Priestley and US author Truman Capote

REFORM IN CHINA

▲ **Deng Xiaoping surprised the world with a move towards a new form of "open" Chinese Communism.**

October 1984 saw an unexpected announcement by Chinese premier Deng Xiaoping of wide-ranging economic reforms that would allow for the limited birth of capitalism in the Communist republic.

Deng had been a significant figure in the Chinese Communist Party since the 1950s; however, his belief that national economic growth depended on creating an incentive for individual gain rather than workers striving towards a common state goal lost him favour with Mao Tse-tung. During the Cultural Revolution of the late 1960s, Deng was stripped of his governmental responsibilities. The decade that followed saw him swing in and out of fashion: "rehabilitated" in 1973 by premier Chou En-lai; ostracized when the Maoist Gang of Four seized power in 1976; returned to public office following the trial and imprisonment of the Gang of Four.

Deng's consolidation of power during the 1980s allowed him to make the reforms he believed were necessary for China's long-term growth. The most surprising of his October 1984 announcements were the plans to allow China's state-owned enterprises greater autonomy. This would mean an end to state-controlled pricing – the dictates of the market place would now create competition among businesses. Alien notions of "supply and demand" were suddenly being aired. Furthermore, Chinese business would be encouraged to take a greater interest in international trade.

Mao might well have been turning in his grave at the very thought of these notions, but among China's student population, there was a thirst for even greater Westernization. Their growing demands, however, would soon lead to an outright confrontation with the Chinese government. And as the massacre of Tiananmen Square in 1989 would show, the right of the individual to voice his or her demands was by no means yet on China's agenda of reform.

REVENGE KILLING

On October 31, 1984, the bitter violence that always seems to have underpinned the political struggle between India's rival factions reached a new extreme as Prime Minister Indira Gandhi was shot dead by two Sikh bodyguards while walking in her garden. The killing was said to be in revenge for the armed attack she had ordered four months earlier on the Golden Temple of Amritsar, the holiest of Sikh shrines.

Indira Gandhi was a part of India's political heritage. The daughter of Jawaharial Nehru, India's first prime minister following independence, she acquired the name Gandhi through marriage – neither she nor her husband were related to Mahatma Gandhi. She first became Prime Minister in 1966, representing the New Congress Party, and served two further terms until defeated in 1978. After serving two brief prison sentences on charges of corruption, she again took the premier's office in 1980, this time as leader of the breakaway Congress (I) Party – the "I" stood for "Indira".

At this time a number of India's states were actively seeking greater independence from central government. The Sikhs of the Punjab were especially violent in their demands for autonomy, so much so that on June 2, 1984 the Indian army was sent in to quash the unrest. Four days later, with the violence still growing, Gandhi ordered her troops to storm the Golden Temple. The attack left over 450 Sikh fatalities. It was a fool-hardy political judgement that effectively ended any possibility of a peaceful, political settlement between the two sides. And she paid for the decision with her life.

The same day as Indira Gandhi was assassinated, her son Rajiv was sworn-in as Prime Minister. Although the eldest of her two sons, the mild-mannered Rajiv Gandhi had avoided politics in favour of a career as an airline pilot. It was his younger brother Sanjay who had been groomed by

▶ **The body of Indira Gandhi is slowly carried to the funeral site on the River Ganges.**

the family to continue India's great political dynasty. When Sanjay died in an air crash in 1980, however, Rajiv was reluctantly forced to reassess his future.

As the violence continued after his mother's death, Rajiv Gandhi failed to subdue the various separatist movements. In November

1989, under suspicion for a number of financial improprieties, he resigned as Prime Minister.

Continuing to lead the Congress (I) Party, Rajiv Gandhi was assassinated in May 1991 by a Tamil separatist. With his children too young to rule, his death brought an end to the Nehru dynasty.

BHOPAL CHEMICAL DISASTER

India was beset by a second national catastrophe in the wake of the assassination of Indira Gandhi as on December 3, 1984, a pesticide plant in the central Indian city of Bhopal became the scene of the worst industrial accident in history. During the early hours of the morning, 45 tons of the poisonous gas methyl iso-cyanate escaped from an underground storage tank and drifted over an area populated by almost quarter of a million people. There were 2,500 fatalities, many

of whom were still sleeping when they died.

The accident created chaos in the streets of Bhopal as at least a further 50,000 victims were temporarily debilitated by the gas, blinded, vomiting or unable to breathe. Unprepared for a disaster of such a scale, the local hospitals were unable to deal with the large number of patients urgently needing treatment.

The accident at the plant, which was owned by the American Union Carbide corporation, was caused

directly by a damaged valve in one of three giant underground storage tanks. However, the investigation that followed established that poor safety procedures and under-staffing at the plant were responsible for an accident that need never have happened.

Arriving the following month in Bhopal to inspect the damage, Warren Anderson, the Chairman of Union Carbide, was briefly arrested by the Indian authorities. Shortly afterwards, on the authorization of newly elected Prime Minister Rajiv Gandhi, lawyers began a $15 billion law suit against Union Carbide. The legal proceedings were finally concluded in 1989 as the company was forced to pay out a sum of $470 million to the victims and the families of those who perished.

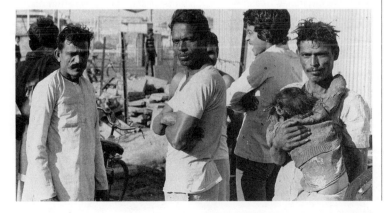

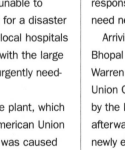

◀ **The Union Carbide factory at Bhopal in India was the scene of one of the world's worst ever industrial accidents.**

'85 THE COAL MINERS' STRIKE

On March 3, 1985 the executive committee of the National Union of Mineworkers (NUM) voted by 98 to 91 to bring to an end the year-long strike that had paralyzed Britain's coal industry. What had begun as an ordinary labour dispute had escalated into a symbolic confrontation between the union movement and the government. There was little doubt as to which side had won: in a blaze of media attention, prime minister Margaret Thatcher hailed the announcement as a "famous victory". The defeat effectively neutered the power of the trade union movement. The heady days of the 1970s when the Trades Union Congress was powerful enough to topple a government were now in the past.

The origins of the dispute were in an announcement by the National Coal Board (NCB), the employers of Britain's nationalized coal industry, at the beginning of 1984 that a number of so-called "uneconomical" mines would be closed with a loss of 20,000 jobs. With a new round of pay talks between the NUM and the NCB about to start, the pit closures became a part of the negotiations. While the NCB, under the tough leadership of American Ian MacGregor, offered an overall 5.2 per cent pay increase, he was resolute that the pit closures were not a matter for discussion.

With talks quickly reaching a deadlock, NUM leader Arthur Scargill called for all-out industrial

▲ The use of Britain's police force was brought into question during the miners' strike. Many saw them as more concerned with enforcing government policy than the law of the land.

action in March 1984. At once, 153 of Britain's 174 mines went on strike. However, it was the refusal of a number of mines to join the dispute that caused the violent escalation that soon brought the mineworkers into open conflict with the government. The so-called "scabs" of Nottinghamshire and Kent – the strike breakers who crossed the NUM picket lines – were organized by less militant union officials. Although they supported the aims of Scargill and the NUM, they refused to strike unless there was a national ballot of mineworkers. The NUM refused their demands.

The months that followed saw

an eruption of violence as secondary pickets – "flying pickets", as they became known – travelled from Wales and Yorkshire where support for the strike was strongest, to the pits of Nottinghamshire to lobby the strike breakers. Their attempts to blockade the mines became increasingly heated and soon the police were ordered in to escort workers through the picket lines. May 29 saw a riot break out at the Orgreave coking plant where pickets and police fought openly. Forty-one policemen and 29 miners were injured in a day of fierce fighting. The police blamed the presence of Arthur Scargill for inflaming the mood of the

pickets; the NUM claimed, with some justification, that their basic right to picket was being openly violated. This latter issue was exacerbated over the coming months as police cordons were placed on main roads around Nottinghamshire and miners from outside the county were turned away. It was the first time a British government had resorted to such draconian measures to intervene in a labour dispute in the twentieth century.

On June 7, 1984 the striking miners, still with considerable public sympathy, held a mass demonstration outside of the Houses of Parliament. Once again, the protests turned into a battle between the strikers and police. One hundred and twenty miners were arrested. With the South Wales branch of the NUM refusing to pay the fines handed out by the courts, on August 1 the government ordered the seizure of the union's assets. Without the ability to provide their members with strike pay, the dispute, it was thought, would soon collapse. When the case reached the High Court at the beginning of October, the NUM was fined £200,000. Arthur Scargill was handed a personal fine of £1000

for contempt of court. The court further ruled that, because there had not been a national ballot of all union members, the miners' strike was, in fact, illegal.

Although the violent clashes continued, with the onset of the winter months, more and more strikers found themselves financially unable to sustain their protest. By November, almost a third of the pits were working again; by the beginning of February 1985, over half of Britain's miners had returned to work. Although Arthur Scargill and

the NUM fought to the bitter end, it became clear that it was a battle that the miners would never be able to win.

At the end of the day, the NUM achieved little during the year-long dispute. Indeed, the once-powerful union was split as moderate Nottinghamshire miners broke away from the NUM to form their own union. Arthur Scargill, painted by the media as the villain of the piece, quite quickly slipped from the public gaze. The depth of feeling caused by the strike was such that many of the

small mining communities were torn apart by their allegiances. It was the single most devastating event in the recent history of Britain's labour movement.

The only real victors were the Conservative government. With a significant governmental shift to the political right during the 1980s, the Thatcher cabinet had relished the chance to take on the trade union movement. It was only because of the split in the ranks of the miners themselves that such a one-sided victory was made possible.

▼ Defeated and demoralized, in March 1985 the striking miners finally returned to work.

'85

GORBACHEV TAKES THE REINS

▲ A new face on the world stage, Soviet leader Mikhail Gorbachev presented himself as a man with whom, in the words of Margaret Thatcher, the West could "do business".

NEWS IN BRIEF

- World oil prices collapse in price war
- Savings and Loans financial institutions begin failing in the US
- Indian guru Bhagwan Shree Rajnesh arrested in Oregon by US authorities
- South Africa abolishes laws forbidding inter-racial marriage
- Scanning Tunnelling Microscope developed
- Films released during the year include Akira Kurosawa's *Ran*, Peter Weir's *Witness*, Terry Gilliam's *Brazil*, Sydney Pollack's *Out of Africa* and Claude Lanzman's documentary *Shoah*
- The play *Biloxi Blues* by Neil Simon opens in New York
- The musical, *Les Miserables*, based on Victor Hugo's novel, opened in London
- Samplers begin to transform pop music production
- Popular songs of the year include "Material Girl" by Madonna, "Everybody Wants to Rule the World" by Tears for Fears and "Don't You Forget About Me" by Simple Minds
- Books published this year include *The Accidental Tourist* by Anne Tyler, *Lake Woebegone Days* by Garrison Keillor and *The Good Apprentice* by Iris Murdoch

Following the death of Leonid Brezhnev in November 1982 it had been widely supposed that the mantle of Soviet leadership would be passed to Konstantin Chernenko, the man Brezhnev believed should follow him. In the event, the new leader of the USSR turned out to be Yuri Andropov, head of the KGB. His rule proved to be brief. A mild reformer, Andropov became ill shortly after coming to power and was rarely seen in public. Following his death in February 1984, he was succeeded by former rival Chernenko. It quickly became clear, however, that Chernenko was seen as only an interim leader. Like Andropov, he was in poor health and died in March 1985 after a little over a year in office. His successor was Mikhail Gorbachev, at 54, the youngest member of the

Politburo, the Soviet "parliament". Although little was known of Gorbachev in the West, he had been a rising star of Soviet politics for most of the decade.

A law graduate of Moscow University, Gorbachev had always seen his career advancing from within the Communist Party. He first made an impression as a leading member of Komsomol – a youth organization intended to groom future Party members. In 1971 he was made a member of the Central Committee of the Communist Party, and nine years later was elected to the ruling Politburo.

As Soviet Premier, Gorbachev's initial concerns were in economic matters. He sought an increase in productivity via technological modernization. His rise to power also created a renewed optimism in the West. After the stagnation

of detente with the US that followed the Soviet invasion of Afghanistan at the end of 1979, Gorbachev called for worldwide arms reduction. The first round of arms talks were held with President Reagan in November 1985. Although little tangible progress was made, the two premiers talked extensively for six hours.

Gorbachev's emergence as a world statesman was swift. He presented the world with an unexpected face of the Soviet Union, one which was youthful and progressive. Within his first year in office he had forged significant personal relationships with many of the leaders of the Western world. Few, however, could quite predict the effect his reforms would have on the future shape of the Soviet Union and Eastern Europe

TWIN SOCCER TRAGEDIES

May 1985 saw Britain's soccer season end on a tragic and bitter note as two unrelated incidents left almost 100 dead, close to a thousand injured and the reputation of British football in tatters.

May 11 was supposed to be a day of celebration in the Yorkshire city of Bradford. It was the last game of the season and the home side, Bradford City, had already accumulated enough points to win the third division championship. A capacity crowd turned out to greet their local heroes.

The day turned to disaster shortly before half time as a small fire broke out in one of the grandstands, creating panic among the fans who surged forward down the stand and over on to the football field. Within five minutes, the 76-year old wooden stand was an inferno. In all, 56 fans were either burned to death or killed in the crush. Hundreds of others were seriously injured.

The disaster focused attention on the general state of some of Britain's football stadiums, especially among the lower division where grounds like Bradford City's had seen little change or improvement since the end of the war.

It was an altogether more sinister disaster that struck less than four weeks later as reigning English champions Liverpool took on Juventus of Italy in the final of the European Cup. The game was held at the Heysel Stadium on the outskirts of Brussels in Belgium.

The organization surrounding the match on May 29 was notably poor. Policing was inadequate, the stadium was not equipped with closed circuit television equipment and, worst of all, segregation of the rival supporters was badly organized. A large number of Liverpool fans were said to have been drunk on arrival and while waiting the start of the game baiting between the two sets of fans grew increasingly hostile. When a group of Liverpool fans launched a charge at the Juventus area of one of the stands, the Italians tried to move out of the way. However, forced against a concrete wall they were faced with no way out. The wall quickly collapsed under the pressure, killing 39 and injuring over 400. The fighting spilled over to the football field as the small police presence struggled to keep back the advancing Liverpool fans. The victims were almost all Juventus supporters.

English football had hit a new nadir. Even though football-related violence was actually no worse in the UK than it was in many other European countries, the phenomenon had become widely known as an "English Disease". It was a reputation exacerbated by the Heysel Stadium disaster.

Although the British government demanded a short, sharp solution to the problem, for all its tough rhetoric, the only real outcome was the banning of the sale of alcohol at football matches. A compulsory identity card system was investigated but rejected as unworkable.

The implications were greater for the football teams themselves. The British Football Association, wanting to be seen to be taking a stand, immediately banned English clubs from the following season's European campaigns. In June, UEFA, European football's governing body, extended this to an indefinite ban. It was the best part of a decade before an English presence was again seen in European football at club level.

▼ **Panic ensues as helpless Juventus fans are crushed in the scramble to escape after the collapse of a wall at the Heysel Stadium during the European Cup Final.**

'85

NEWS IN BRIEF

May
- Sikh extremists explode bombs in India, killing over 80
- USA imposes economic sanctions on Nicaragua
- Police in Philadelphia, USA, firebomb house to end siege; 11 die in ensuing conflagration and 200 made homeless
- Tamils attack provincial city in Sri Lanka; over 100 die in fighting
- Cyclone in Bangladesh kills over 10,000
- Death of French artist Jean Dubuffet, developer of art brut

June
- Fifty-two die in car bomb explosion in Beirut
- Air India jet blows up over sea near Ireland; all 325 passengers and crew on board killed
- Death of British statesman Lord George-Brown (George Brown)

July
- State of emergency declared in South Africa
- Eduard Shevardnadze replaces Andrei Gromyko as USSR foreign secretary; Gromyko becomes President
- Military coup in Uganda; Milton Obote exiled and General Tito Okello takes power
- Alan Garcia Perez becomes new President of Peru

LIVE AID

At midday on July 13, 1985 veteran English rock band Status Quo took the stage at London's Wembley Stadium. The opening chords of their famous anthem "Rockin' All Over The World" rang out, signalling the start of Live Aid, the most ambitious live music festival ever attempted.

The project had been initiated by Bob Geldof, the singer with top Irish band The Boomtown Rats. Geldof had been moved by the reports of the 1984 famine in Ethiopia and was unimpressed with the efforts of Western governments to relieve the crisis. His first move was the organization of the all-star Band Aid single "Feed The World". Released at Christmas 1984, with all profits going to the famine, "Feed The World" was already on the way to becoming the biggest-selling single of all time.

The Live Aid concerts took celebrity fund-raising to a new height. Organized in Britain and the US, two massive concerts were planned to take place at the

▲ **Organizer Bob Geldof leads a chorus of the Live Aid anthem "Feed the World" in the finale to the biggest live event since Woodstock.**

same time, with two-way video links joining Wembley Stadium in the UK to Philadelphia in the USA. Both broadcasts were transmitted live throughout the world, every network providing a credit card hotline where donations could be made.

The shows themselves were memorable, featuring stars from every generation of pop music, from Paul McCartney, Mick Jagger and Bob Dylan up to U2 and Madonna. Notable performances came from Queen, with flamboyant singer Freddie Mercury proving himself to be perhaps the greatest of rock's stadium showmen. The spectacle reached a stunning climax with all of the shows' stars taking the stage for a unique rendition of "Feed The World".

A astounding popular achievement, Live Aid raised more than £50 million for famine relief.

RAINBOW WARRIOR SUNK

In the movement to make the world more ecologically aware, Greenpeace, an international environmental protection organization funded by voluntary donations from all over the world, has been the leader in the field. Greenpeace was founded in 1971 primarily to oppose US nuclear testing in Alaska. As unofficial representatives of a growing number of people who saw ecological matters being persistently ignored by governments and multinational corporations, Greenpeace widened its targets to protect

endangered species and take "direct non-violent action" against those committing crimes of pollution. Its aims were often achieved by publicizing covert activities and thus shaming the culprits. As many of its targets acted in an official government-approved capacity, Greenpeace soon made important enemies.

The organization hit the world's headlines on July 10, 1985 when *Rainbow Warrior*, its well-known ship which was often at the centre of Greenpeace protests, was sunk by two explosions while

berthed in Auckland Harbour, New Zealand. The vessel had been preparing to sail to Mururoa Atoll in the South Pacific to protest against French nuclear testing in the area. A Greenpeace member on board the *Rainbow Warrior* was killed in the explosion.

This was the first terrorist act ever committed on New Zealand soil and police launched a massive investigation. Their investigations led to the arrest of two French nationals, Dominique Prieur and Alain Mafart, for the attack. Suspicion grew that the two were agents acting on behalf of the French government. President Mitterrand launched an inquiry which, after 17 days, concluded there was no French connection. Leaked French government documents would soon prove otherwise.

With condemnation abroad and at home growing, the truth finally emerged, proving a national embarrassment for France. Documents showed that Defence Minister Charles Hernu and Admiral Pierre Lacost, of the DGSE, France's secret service, not only knew about the action, but had authorized it. They had, according to Mitterrand, hidden the information from the government inquiry. The two officials lost their jobs and many

also felt that Mitterrand should have offered his own resignation.

Five French officials who leaked the truth to the press were convicted of breaching official secrets legislation. Meanwhile, in New Zealand the two agents

who had planted the bombs – now revealed to be Captain Prieur and Major Mafart of the DGSE – were both given sentences of seven and ten years to be served concurrently in New Zealand.

▲ The sinking of the Greenpeace ship *Rainbow Warrior* became a major embarrassment for the French government.

MEXICAN EARTHQUAKE

On September 19, 1985 at 7:18 AM, a massive earthquake measuring 7.8 on the Richter scale struck beneath the Pacific coast of Mexico. Although the epicentre of the earthquake was some 370 km (230 miles) southwest of Mexico City, it was here that the highest intensity was felt. Skyscrapers and other buildings were levelled, resulting in an estimated 9,500 deaths.

The main reason the disaster centred so prominently on one of

the world's most highly-populated urban areas was largely due to Mexico City's unique geography. The city was originally a series of small inland islands. During the time of the Aztecs, the surrounding lake was gradually drained and filled in to create one giant plain. Thus with a softer soil foundation, the ground movement beneath Mexico City caused by the earthquake and its aftershock was shown to be five times greater than that of the surrounding areas.

The disaster was compounded by the existence of skyscrapers and other high-rise buildings. The only comparable metropolitan disaster of this scale was the 1971 Los Angeles earthquake. Here, the potential damage was reduced by the creation of buildings specifically constructed to deal with natural tremors. In Los Angeles, however, the frequency of the seismic waves were less than one second; in Mexico City they were several seconds long, approaching the natural frequency of a skyscraper. This resulted in a greater sideway motion which ultimately caused the collapse of 20 multistory buildings; at least 50 others were so badly damaged that they had to be demolished.

Ten years on, evidence of the earthquake could still be seen in parts of Mexico City.

◀ **The Infant General Hospital was among the many buildings demolished during the Mexico City earthquake.**

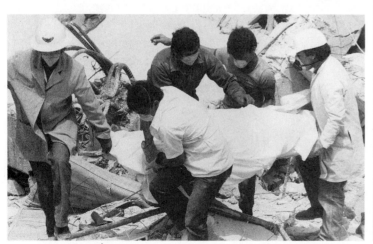

August
- Black miners in South Africa strike, demanding end of state of emergency
- Japanese airliner crashes into a mountain, killing 520 passengers and crew
- Iraqi air strike on Iranian oil installations on Kharg island in the Persian Gulf
- Coup in Nigeria; Ibrahim Babanguida takes power
- Death of President of Guyana Forbes Burnham; Desmond Hoyte succeeds

September
- Khmer Rouge Army commander Pol Pot resigns; Sol Senn succeeds
- US imposes economic sanctions on South Africa
- EEC imposes economic sanctions on South Africa
- Britain expels Soviet diplomats for alleged espionage
- Death of British fashion designer Laura Ashley

October
- Israel attacks PLO headquarters in Tunis, killing over 60
- Riots in Tottenham, London; one police officer killed
- Deaths of US film maker and actor Orson Welles and US actor Yul Brynner

November
- President of Tanzania Julius Nyerere resigns; Ali Hassan Myingi succeeds
- Volcano erupts in Colombia, killing more than 25,000 people
- Anglo-Irish agreement signed between Ireland and Britain
- Egyptian airliner hijacked to Malta; stormed by Egyptian commandos, 60 die in ensuing gun battle
- Deaths of influential French historian Fernand Braudel and Cambodian leader Lon Nol

THE NEW PLAGUE

▲ **Rock Hudson was the first major celebrity to die as a result of AIDS. His death brought the disease to the public eye.**

October 2, 1985 saw the first high-profile death to result from Acquired Immunodeficiency Syndrome (AIDS), as Hollywood superstar Rock Hudson succumbed after a long illness. The disease is transmitted either sexually or via the blood; thus many of the early victims were homosexual men or intravenous drug users who shared their needles. Although Hudson was famed for playing macho romantic leads, often alongside Doris Day, his homosexuality had been an open secret in Hollywood for decades. In July 1985, his physical appearance noticeably wasted, he made the announcement that he had the disease. Hudson's death three months later brought AIDS to the forefront of the public consciousness for the first time.

The first case of AIDS was dis-covered in California in 1981. Two years later it was found that the disease was caused by the Human Immunodeficiency Virus (HIV). The virus attacks and destroys the human immune system, the body's natural defence against disease. Without such resistance, the body is unable to fend off infections which eventually result in death. An individual who has acquired HIV is said to be "HIV positive". Currently, no vaccine or cure has been developed, although improvements in drug treatments continue to lengthen the time of delay between the onset of HIV and the full development of AIDS.

The AIDS "epidemic", as it is often described, caught the governments of the West unprepared and often in an uncomfortable position. Since the disease usually occurred as a result of the victim's lifestyle, some homophobic politicians were tempted to take the moral high ground. However, by the end of the 1980s, the fastest growing group to become HIV positive were heterosexuals. Whilst scientists searched for a cure, it became clear that prevention was the only way to stop the spread of the disease. Governments in Britain and America launched "safe sex" campaigns urging couples,

▲ **The Gay Rights movement fought hard to make the public aware of the plight of AIDS sufferers.**

irrespective of their gender preferences, to use contraceptives. Again, this angered some moral campaigners who argued that the best protection against AIDS was an end to sexual promiscuity.

While such preventative measures have been highly effective in combating the spread of HIV in the West where, by 1996, heterosexual intercourse accounted for 70 per cent of all new cases of HIV, statistics show that such methods have been ineffective among the underdeveloped nations of the world. By 1998 it was estimated that there were

▲ In Britain, the Terence Higgins Trust became an important centre for information and advice relating to HIV and AIDS.

well over 20 million HIV carriers in the world, two-thirds of whom lived in southern Africa; a further fifth lived in Southeast Asia. By the end of the century there had been an estimated seven million AIDS-related deaths.

Although the attempts by science to find a cure have so far failed, a number of anti-HIV drug treatments, such as azidothymidine (AZT), have been developed. These can be used on their own or in combinations. A major problem, however, is that some of the newer treatments that may prove to be most effective are prohibitively expensive.

A YEAR OF TERRORISM

1985 saw a stark increase in the trend for small self-interest groups to achieve political persuasion by violent means. Much of the kidnapping, hijacking and bombing that occurred throughout the year was based around the complex situation in the Middle East, but other outrages were carried out by nationalist terrorists in Ireland, Sikh extremists in India and Basque Separatists in Spain. Sadly, in most cases,the victims of the violence were ordinary members of the public.

At the beginning of March an explosion at a Shi'ite mosque in Beirut killed 15 and injured 70; less than a week later a car bomb in the same area destroyed the headquarters of the Islamic Shi'ite Revolutionary Party of God – known as Hezbollah. The culprits were thought to have been Israeli agents. A revenge attack took place on June 14, when a TWA jet with 104 Americans on board was hijacked. Taking off from Athens, the plane was seized by two Hezbollah gunmen, who killed one of the passengers. Beirut airport at first refused the plane permission to land, until

▲ Hijack at sea – the *Achille Lauro* sets sail from Alexandria with its cargo of PLO terrorists and US hostages.

the pilot reported that the gunmen had started beating the passengers. The Hezbollah men demanded that Israel release 700 Palestinian prisoners. Israel refused and on June 30 the remaining hostages were freed. The two gunmen were arrested.

There was a hijack at sea in October when Palestinian Liberation Organization terrorists seized an Italian cruise liner, the *Achille Lauro*, sailing from Alexandria in Egypt with 60 Americans on board. Once again, the hijackers, who killed an elderly passenger, demanded the release of PLO prisoners in Israel. With little likelihood of suc-

cess, the hijackers gave in when the Egyptian government offered them safe passage out of the country. However, their supposed flight to freedom was intercepted by US naval fighters who forced a landing in Sicily.

Palestinian terrorists saw out the year in a spectacular fashion, but this time there was no demand – just action. On December 30, two simultaneous attacks were carried out at airports in Rome and Vienna. In each case, the target was the check-in desk of the Israeli El Al airline. The sieges created chaos as groups of gunmen lobbed grenades and fired indiscriminately into crowds of holiday makers. There were 14 fatalities and well over a hundred serious injuries. Four terrorists were killed in the fighting with armed police. The savage attacks were ostensibly in retaliation for Israeli attacks on the PLO headquarters, the terrorists coming from a hardline breakaway group headed by the Palestinian Abu Nidal.

In spite of any amount of tough talking by the governments of the world, and the tightened security that inevitably followed, the trend towards such direct action still shows no sign of ending.

▲ One of the two Hezbollah gunmen emerge from the cabin door of the TWA jet. 104 US hostages were on board.

'86

SPACE SHUTTLE DISASTER

January 28, 1986 will be remembered as the blackest day in the history of man's exploration of space. Barely seventy seconds after take off, the *Challenger* space shuttle exploded spectacularly in the skies over Cape Canaveral. All seven astronauts on board were killed instantly. Reaching an altitude of 16 km (10 miles) above the surface of the Earth, when *Challenger*'s main engines were boosted to full power, the shuttle unexpectedly erupted in a huge ball of fire. The tragedy was seen by thousands watching from the Florida coastline and millions who had tuned in to watch the live television broadcast.

The space shuttle was the first manned spacecraft designed for re-use and had been one of NASA's greatest successes in the recent history of the space programme. Originally announced in 1969, the shuttle was planned to have the means by which astronauts could reach a permanently manned space station. Eventually, budgetary cutbacks meant that only the shuttle was made operational. Bearing a closer visual resemblance to an aircraft than a traditional space capsule, the shuttle made its first flight in April 1981.

After the initial glare of publicity, few of the first 24 shuttle flights were deemed newsworthy – most were engaged in relatively obscure scientific research which held little appeal for the public. There was, however, renewed media interest in the doomed twenty-fifth space shuttle launch because the seven-man crew included Christa McAuliffe, a young school teacher who was to have been the first ordinary civilian in space. NASA were inundated with applicants, some, like country singer John Denver, even offering huge sums of money for the honour.

The investigation and clear-up operation took almost six months to complete. A flotilla of boats scoured the Florida coastline for debris and clues as to the cause of the explosion. It would not be until the middle of March that the crew compartment would be found with the remains of the seven astronauts.

1986 was to have been a significant year for NASA with ten other shuttle launches planned. All were immediately cancelled pending the outcome of the inquiry. In June 1986, a 256-page report concluded what some experts had been speculating from the start – that the explosion was caused by a weak joint in the shuttle's solid rocket boosters. There was considerable controversy when it was revealed that a year earlier a NASA engineer had voiced his concerns over the possibility of just such an accident.

▲ A spectator watches in horror as the *Challenger* space shuttle explodes in the skies above Cape Canaveral.

WALDHEIM'S DARK PAST

Preparing for the Austrian Presidential elections, leading candidate Kurt Waldheim, twice secretary-general of the United Nations, received a severe setback when claims were made about his wartime activities. In March 1986 the World Jewish Congress uncovered records that they believed showed Waldheim to have participated in the deportation of Yugoslav and Greek Jews to Nazi death camps. They were allegations that Waldheim denied.

Born in 1918, Kurt Waldheim had served as a volunteer in the Austrian army before beginning his university studies in 1937. Conscripted into the German army at the start of the war, he served on the Russian front until he was wounded in 1941. It was the three years that followed that remained in question. Throughout his successful diplomatic career, Waldheim claimed to have spent the war years between 1942 and 1945 as a law student in Vienna. The documents uncovered by the World Jewish Congress, suggested that he had, in fact, been a staff officer stationed in the Balkans.

With an alternative past now in the open, Waldheim admitted that there were elements that he had chosen to rewrite. He confirmed that he had been a Nazi officer during this time, but strenuously denied that he had ever "participated in any sort of cruelties". He claimed to have acted merely as an interpreter. Furthermore, he

▶ **Dr Kurt Waldheim admitted he had been a Nazi officer during the war but denied that he had been involved in the genocide.**

saw no reason to withdraw from the presidential election.

Held on June 8, 1986, the election gave Waldheim a large majority of the votes. His main opponent, the socialist Dr Kurt Steyer, controversially alleged that the revelations about Waldheim's past had aroused anti-Semitic feeling within Austria and thus contributed to his victory.

Although the victor, Waldheim, perhaps because of his dark past, conducted a low-profile presidency that saw little participation in international affairs.

BABY DOC TAKES HIS LAST BOW

On February 7, 1986, following three months of violent protest all over the West Indian state of Haiti, President Jean-Claude Duvalier, known as "Baby Doc", was forced to flee the country. His flight brought to an end almost thirty years of dictatorial rule by two generations of the Duvalier family.

In 1964, having served for seven years as elected President of Haiti, François "Papa Doc" Duvalier designated himself "President for life". In spite of the periodic unrest that had always permeated the Haitian political climate, Duvalier consolidated his position with the creation of the Tontons Macoutes, his own private militia. Before his death in 1971, Duvalier nominated his son, 19-year-old Jean-Claude, as his successor.

"Baby Doc" Duvalier's regime unsuccessfully sought a degree of international respectability. Under the rule of his father, Haiti had earned a justifiably poor reputation for civil rights. This had led to a withdrawal of economic aid from the USA and a fall in tourism. All in all,

◀ **Jean-Claude "Baby Doc" Duvalier, son of one of the most infamous and brutal dictators of the twentieth century.**

Duvalier presided over the poorest country in the Western Hemisphere.

In December 1985 popular protest grew as Haitians increasingly complained about unemployment, the appalling standard of living and a lack of political freedom. The wave of demonstrations at first met with violent resistance from the Tontons Macoutes, but it was clear that the situation was in danger of plunging into civil war. On February 7, 1986, Duvalier fled Haiti on a US air force jet, to take up exile in France.

Over the coming days the violence grew, much of it centred around the mausoleum of Papa Doc in Haiti's capital, Port-au-Prince. Demonstrators homed in on the once-dreaded, blue-shirted Tontons Macoutes , now a police force without a leader.

It is debatable whether Haiti was vastly better off without Duvalier. The first "democratic" elections in January 1988 were widely believed to have been fixed, and the elected President, Leslie Manigat, was deposed within six months. Two further military coups took place before elections brought Jean-Bertrand Aristide, a Roman Catholic priest, to power in 1991. The political turmoil continued during the 1990s as Aristide was deposed and exiled by the military. This led the United States to impose a trade embargo, resulting in tens of thousands attempting to flee Haiti in small boats bound for the United States.

Haiti remains one of the most politically volatile states in the world.

'86

CHERNOBYL – THE NUCLEAR NIGHTMARE

The city of Chernobyl in the northwest of the former Soviet republic of Ukraine was largely unknown to the Western world. It was, at best, a name on a map. Sixteen kilometres (10 miles) outside the city stood a small industrial town called Pryp'yat, built largely to serve the workers at the nearby Chernobyl nuclear power plant. It was a name that would soon find itself forever embedded in the minds of anyone who had ever harboured fears about the perils of nuclear power. On April 26, 1986 a series of explosions in one of the power plant's four reactors created a giant fireball that smashed through the concrete roof of the reactor, releasing radioactive material into the atmosphere. The worst accident in the history of nuclear power, it was also an acci-

▲ **A British scientist shows one of the paper filters on which the first signs of radiation from Chernobyl were detected.**

dent that the Soviet authorities first attempted to cover up.

The first of the four reactors at the Chernobyl plant started producing electricity in 1977. The

three other reactors were gradually added over the next eight years. The station had a total generating capacity of 4,000 megawatts, contributing a significant proportion of Ukraine's energy needs.

The accident can be attributed almost entirely to human error. On April 25, 1986 technicians at the Number 4 reactor attempted an ill-conceived experiment. The reactor's power-regulation supply and emergency safety systems were shut off while the control rods were removed from the reactor's core. In the early hours of April 26 the chain reaction in the core went out of control, resulting in a series of massive explosions. As a result, the surrounding area was exposed to radioactivity. A partial meltdown of the reactors core also occurred.

The following day, Pryp'yat's 15,000 inhabitants were evacuated. At this stage, the radioactivity

◀ **During the days that followed the Chernobyl accident, helicopters permanently circled the plant taking radiation measurements.**

was carried by strong winds throughout the Soviet Union in the northeast and deep into Europe in the west. The outside world first became aware that something had gone wrong on April 28 when geographical centres in Sweden, Finland and Denmark began monitoring unusually high levels of radioactivity. That there had been some kind of nuclear occurrence was now evident but it would be a further two days before the Soviet news agency Tass reported the accident at Chernobyl to the rest of the world.

It was almost another week before radioactivity leaking from the reactor core was contained. Later in the year reactor number 4 was sealed in a massive envelope of concrete and steel.

Like many of the effects of radiation, the physical aftermath of the Chernobyl accident can never truly be quantified. Although 32 people died as a direct conse-

quence of the explosions, many others who worked on containing the disaster were contaminated by fatal levels of radiation and died later. Some experts in the West speculated that more than 20,000 people, mostly in Ukraine, would eventually die as a result of diseases caused by Chernobyl. There was also a further environmental cost as millions of acres of forestry in northwestern Ukraine were contaminated by the deadly radioactive isotopes. It is thought that the contaminated agricultural areas around Pryp'yat and Chernobyl will be unsafe for thousands of years to come.

Above all, at a time when the world's nuclear industry seemed to be taking the upper hand in the propaganda wars for the expansion of nuclear energy production, Chernobyl provided a timely example of the potential devastation of what was, thankfully, a relatively small nuclear mishap.

▲ **A grieving widow stands alongside the graves of those who died during the Chernobyl disaster.**

REAGAN'S WAR ON TERRORISM

▲ **President Reagan – seen here with Mikhail Gorbachev – declared that there would be no deals with terrorists.**

On April 15, 1986, the US controversially stepped up its avowed war on suspected terrorists when a series of bombing raids was launched on military targets within Libya. President Reagan claimed to have irrefutable evidence that Libya was now a major centre for terrorism and had been instrumental in the recent bombing of a Berlin disco that had clearly been aimed at US servicemen.

The US government acted with the full support of Britain's Prime Minister Margaret Thatcher, who authorized the use of British military bases in the operation. In two separate attacks, F-111 bombers based in Great Britain struck targets in Tripoli, and A-6 and A-7 fighters launched from aircraft carriers in the Mediterranean targeted military installations around Benghazi.

Initial reports suggested that Libya's leader Colonel Gaddafi had been killed in the bombing.

However, he emerged unscathed the following day to denounce President Reagan. The foreign media were invited to photograph hospitals and residential neighbourhoods that had also been devastated by the raids. In the weeks that followed, thousands of US and British nationals were expelled from Libya.

Outside the US, support for the operations was less enthusiastic. Britain's opposition leader, Neil Kinnock, was outraged, declaring that the Prime Minister now had "blood on her hands". The vast majority of the British public were also opposed to the action. France had even refused permission for US aircraft to fly over her airspace, an act, it was alleged, that doubled the length of the mission. It would not be the last time that the governments of Britain and the US were isolated by world opinion over military action in the Middle East.

86

CHALLENGING APARTHEID

▲ **The path that lead to end to the Apartheid system would prove to be a long and violent one.**

As sanctions from the West looked more likely by the day, during May 1986 the South African government faced growing opposition not only from the anti-apartheid movement, but also from extremist white nationalist groups within the country.

On May 22 the Afrikaner Resistance Movement, led by Eugene Terre' Blanche, disrupted a meeting in the Transvaal at which Foreign Minister Pik Botha was due to give a speech. Wearing swastika-style armbands and brown uniforms, the group stormed the hall and police used tear-gas to break up the fighting between rival supporters. While Terre' Blanche denied that his movement was racist, he also rejected the concept of power-sharing and was reported to be in favour of disenfranchising Jews in South Africa. Elsewhere in South Africa, some peaceful protest continued despite the unrest, with a strike on May 1 involving around a million black workers

Perhaps seeking to appease the Afrikaner nationalists, or in some kind of acknowledgement of the inevitability of sanctions, the South African government seemed to abandon much of its limited apartheid reforms during 1986, passing a series of harsh anti-African National Congress measures throughout the year. On May 19, South African forces carried out raids against alleged ANC targets in Botswana, Zambia and Zimbabwe

Less than a month later, a report to the Commonwealth from independent observers concluded that there was no real move from the South African authorities toward ending apartheid or creating political freedom. Despite the reservations of Britain, Germany and America's President Reagan, who felt that sanctions would only damage the people of South Africa and not affect the political system, limited economic and trade measures came into effect during the rest of the year.

It was estimated that less than 10 per cent of trade to the European Community was blocked. The figure was not high enough seriously to damage South Africa's economy, but was a clear indication of the regime's growing isolation from the international community.

▲ **Eugene Terre' Blanche, leader of the Nazi-styled Afrikaner Resistance Movement, staunch opponents of reform.**

CAMEROON DEATH CLOUD

On August 21, 1986, when a cloud of poisonous gas killed upwards of 1,700 people in the area over just one night, it was clear to the people of Wum in Cameroon that an evil lake spirit was to blame. Scientists believed the cause was less supernatural, but found it just as difficult to pin down. Most suspected that the disaster was due to the volcanic base of Lake Nios releasing a silent, deadly and odourless mix of hydrogen sulfide and carbon dioxide through the water. The result, however, was the same: an undetectable cloud of death that was blown silently into the surrounding villages.

'When I woke up in the morning,' said one survivor, "my five children were dead. My baby was dead in my hands." Local officials knew of the scale of the disaster, yet the relief effort didn't get under way until President Biya visited the area two days later.

The authorities were poorly equipped for the size of the task. Rescuers had few gas masks and were worried that gases might have lingered. Eventually, rain and wind dispersed the fumes, but also dissolved the basic tracks into the region.

The government called for international assistance, including a mission from Israel, which had just that week resumed diplomatic relations with Cameroon. Despite the huge influx of supplies and workers, the rescue attempts were not well organized and progress was slow.

In all, 3,000 people were evacuated from the immediate area and several hundred ill survivors were taken to hospital

▲ The mysterious "death cloud" claimed the lives of almost 2,000 people and many thousands of animals.

in Wum. At the same time, hundreds of Cameroon soldiers were involved in trying to prevent further contamination by burying the victims in hastily dug mass graves. Even after this grim work was complete, thousands of animal carcasses still littered the

valley, a grim reminder of the scale of the tragedy.

Scientists continued to debate the cause of the cloud and whether the conditions for it could arise again. Uncertainty remained, yet most villagers elected to stay on in order to keep their farms.

INSIDER DEALING ON WALL STREET

Few represented the greedy ethos of the money-obsessed 1980s better than Wall Street dealer Ivan Boesky. When it was announced that he had confessed to insider dealing on November 14 the revelation sent share prices plummeting.

Boesky worked in the high risk market of hostile takeovers. He was an expert arbitrageur, someone who would trade in a firm which he guessed might be about to be taken over, hoping to make a profit if the company was indeed targeted and its price rose. The problem was that Boesky was paying an investment banker named Dennis Levine for advance word of companies that were about to become involved in takeovers, a strictly illegal practice.

When federal investigators caught up with him, he agreed to

cooperate in exchange for having just one count of felony brought against him and paying a fine of $100 million. It was quite a comedown for the man who had now gone from being a bright young thing with 300 phone lines in his office (and even three in his car), to allowing himself to be recorded on the phone by the authorities in an effort to bring others to justice.

Just a year before he had been quite open about his lust for money, saying in a speech to a business school graduation ceremony that "Greed is all right, by the way. I want you to know that. You can be greedy and still feel good about yourself."

Some commentators felt that Ivan Boesky's cautionary tale would lead to a new dawn of morality and a backlash against greed. Others felt the results of fur-

ther investigations could be catastrophic for the US economy if a wide enough conspiracy was uncovered. Nobody knew who would be named next. What was certain was that the day after Boesky was brought down, everyone working on Wall Street felt a whole lot less self-confident.

▲ Ivan Boesky accrued a massive personal fortune on Wall Street through the illegal practice of "insider dealing".

'87

GORBACHEV ANNOUNCES POLICY OF POLITICAL RECONSTRUCTION

Early this century, years of stagnation in Russia had been swept away by revolution. Facing the same problem seventy years later, General-Secretary Mikhail Gorbachev responded by announcing far more gradual reforms than the Bolsheviks had undertaken and a move towards greater openness.

Addressing the central committee of the Communist Party on January 27, Gorbachev laid the blame for economic decline on previous administrations, particularly that led by Brezhnev. Socialism, he believed, remained rooted to the theories of the 1930s and 1940s, the Stalinist era. His vision of modernizing the Party and the Soviet Union was based on two central planks:

perestroika (restructuring) and *glasnost* (openness).

In practice, *perestroika* would involve gradually relaxing controls over the behemoth that was the Soviet economy. Over time, the power of the bureaucrats would be reduced and eventually corruption would be eliminated. The ultimate goal was to introduce democracy to the Soviet Communist Party.

"A house can be put in order only by someone who feels that he owns the house," Gorbachev told the meeting.

Glasnost was the process of opening up the activities of state and public organizations to greater public scrutiny But any change was bound to be resisted by those who benefited from

▲ With the ascent of Mikhail Gorbachev, the words *glasnost* and *perestroika* entered the world's popular vocabulary.

maintaining the status quo. There had already been speculation that opposition was mounting when the meeting at which Gorbachev intended announcing his new measures was delayed by a month. It was clear that the road to modernization was not going to be easy to travel.

AQUINO QUASHES COUP IN PHILIPPINES

President Cory Aquino of the Philippines faced an attempted army coup in January when 500 troops attempted to seize seven key installations in Manila. Some of the soldiers were loyal to the deposed President Marcos, others were unhappy at the way the government had dealt with Communists in the country.

At the end of the first day of the coup, January 27, it became apparent that the troops, led by Colonel Oscar Canlas, had only succeeded in seizing a broadcast-

ing facility. The building was put under siege as negotiations began to end the situation peacefully.

It was also reported that Marcos had been in contact with support-

▶ Supporters of the exiled President Marcos receive severe beatings from troops loyal to Cory Aquino.

ers from his home in exile in Honolulu, Hawaii. The day before the coup his wife Imelda apparently purchased $2,000 worth of military equipment and Marcos was said to have chartered an airliner back to Manila. The American authorities then denied permission for the former Philippines leader to leave Hawaii.

The siege continued until January 29 and although at one point it seemed as if the broadcasting company building might be stormed by dissident troops, last-minute negotiations averted further conflict. Colonel Canlas and his men left the building voluntarily. As a result of the coup, 400 army personnel were court martialled

ANDY WARHOL DIES AT 59

In the future, claimed Andy Warhol, everyone will be famous for 15 minutes. By the time of his death on February 22, 1987, Warhol had gone over his own limit many times.

One of the leading exponents of Pop Art, he was born, the son of Czechoslovak immigrants in Pittsburgh, on August 6 , 1928. By 1963, relocated to New York, Warhol had refined a style based on simple adverts and comics, and achieved notoriety through his pictures of tins of Campbell's soup (*One Hundred Cans*, 1962). The repetition of the images reflected the emptiness of American culture. Warhol had cultivated an enigmatic image of the artist as distant from his work.

By the mid-sixties, he was more concerned with experimental films, and pioneered multi-media with The Exploding Plastic Inevitable — involving the group Velvet Underground playing in front of projected films and light. Following an attempt on his life by one of his entourage at his studio, The Factory, in 1968, he began to concentrate on commissioned portraits. It wasn't until the 1980s that he returned to painting with the new generation he had inspired, who included Jean-Michel Basquiat and Francesco Clemente.

His death followed a routine gall-bladder operation and 2000 people attended a memorial service – even then, it was said some expected this most enigmatic of artists to stage a comeback.

▲ **One of the founding fathers of Pop Art, Andy Warhol, one of the greatest icons of 20th century popular culture.**

200 DIE
AS FERRY CAPSIZES
NEAR ZEEBRUGGE

The capsizing of the *Herald of Free Enterprise* was a disaster made all the more shocking by the speed at which it happened The roll-on-roll-off car ferry left the port of Zeebrugge at 7.00pm on March 6, 1987. Less than a kilometre out of the harbour, the ship turned over and nearly 200 passengers and crew died.

Owned by Townsend Thoresen, the ferry had bow doors which had not been properly closed. Water quickly poured into the ship which, destabilized, turned over on its side. Although the disaster had happened so quickly that there had not been time to send an SOS, rescuers were soon on the scene.

Teams of divers went into the freezing water to try and free people trapped in the submerged section of the ship. The rescuers had to work fast as victims were most at risk from exposure. Survivors were hauled up through broken port-holes as rescuers worked against the elements.

An enquiry was held to establish the cause of the disaster, which concluded that three members of the crew were to blame. Their union in turn said responsibility lay with the management. The result was a new law designed to ensure far harsher penalties for crew and ship owners at fault in future.

◄ **The wreck of the Townsend Thoreson ferry *Herald of Free Enterprise*, capsized off the coast of Zeebrugge, Belgium.**

January
- Iran launches new offensive in war against Iraq
- Eight high-ranking Mafia members jailed in New York
- South Korean student activist Park Chong Chol tortured and killed by South Korean police
- President of Ecuador and entourage kidnapped by arm rebels demanding release of jailed air force commander
- South Korean police chief and interior minister forced to resign over Park Chong Chol killing
- Terry Waite disappears, feared kidnapped, in Beirut
- New coalition government under Franz Vranitzky formed in Austria
- Violent demonstrations at print union picket line in East London
- Helmut Kohl re-elected Chancellor in West Germany
- Failed coup in the Philippines

February
- Colombian drug cartel leader Carlos Rivas arrested and then extradited to the USA
- Soviet government releases over 100 political prisoners
- Fianna Fail under Charles Haughey wins election in Ireland
- USA lifts economic sanctions on Poland imposed during Communist crackdown on Solidarity
- Syrian troops enter Beirut
- White House Chief of Staff Donald Regan replaced by Howard Baker following criticism in the Tower Report on the Iran-Contra affair
- Death of US kitsch piano king Liberace

87

DEMOCRATS IN DISARRAY

With little more than a year before a new round of US presidential elections, in May 1987 the Democratic camp took a severe blow as one of its leading contenders, Senator Gary Hart, pulled out of the race. This followed dramatic revelations in a newspaper that Senator Hart had been engaged in an illicit affair

▲ The alleged affair between Donna Rice (above) and Senator Gary Hart was denied by both parties, but ended his campaign.

with a 27-year-old model.

Hart, claiming innocence, confidently invited the media to investigate his character as fully as they saw fit. What emerged was that the Colorado senator had taken the model, Donna Rice, on a secret holiday on board a friend's yacht. Much was further made of the unfortunate naming of the vessel – "Monkey Business".

Hart rejoined the race for nomination in December, but was condemned by fellow Democrats as arrogant and his challenge ultimately amounted to little.

With Hart out of the race, the Reverend Jesse Jackson decided to stake his claim in what could have made him America's first black president. A civil rights campaigner with Martin Luther King in his youth, Jackson was widely respected and popular among the party faithful.

In September another candidate fell by the wayside. Senator Joseph Bidden, the head of the Senate Judiciary Committee was a Washington insider rather than a public figure. His campaign

ground to a halt when it was discovered that a widely publicized speech, in which he painted himself a self-made man from a poor background contained phrases identical to some in a speech given months earlier by Britain's Leader of the Opposition, Neil Kinnock. Shortly afterwards it was disclosed that he had admitted to a charge of plagiarism while a student at law school.

In the primary elections to decide on presidential candidates, the eventual victor was Michael Dukakis, a senator for Massachusetts. A self-confessed liberal, he chose as his running mate Lloyd Bentsen, a right-wing Democrat. Although defeated, Jesse Jackson continued to be a influential presence in the Democratic Party.

The eventual presidential campaign was not especially noteworthy. With the popular outgoing President Reagan forced by the constitution to step down after two terms in office, his Vice President, George Bush went on to win an easy victory

IRAQ ATTACKS US FRIGATE

With tensions high in the Persian Gulf, a result of the ongoing war between Iran and Iraq, the UN had approved the presence of US warships in the region as protection for the crucial oil routes from the Middle East to the rest of the world. However, on May 22, 1987 the

► The beleaguered American frigate USS *Stark*, following the missile attack by Iraqi airforce jet fighters.

NEWS IN BRIEF

March
- Resignation of Italian Prime Minister Bettino Craxi
- Tamil separatists blow up train bridge in India; 22 die in ensuing train wreck
- Ouadi Doum recaptured by Chad troops from Libyan forces in ongoing conflict
- Afghan military plane shot down by Pakistan inside Pakistani air space
- Death of American film comedian and singer Danny Kaye

April
- Syrian troops end Shi'ite militia siege of Palestinian refugee camps in Lebanon
- Elections in Fiji won by coalition dominated by ethnic Indians
- Portugal agrees to return Macau to Chinese control in 1999
- Tamil separatists kill 127 in attack on convoy in Sri Lanka
- Bomb explodes in Colombo, Sri Lanka, killing over 100
- IRA remote control bomb kills senior Ulster judge Sir Maurice Gibson and wife
- USA bars Austrian President Kurt Waldheim because of alleged Nazi past
- Hari Holkeri becomes Prime Minister of Finland
- Death of Italian writer Primo Levi

conflict took an unexpected turn as Iraq launched a bizarre attack on a US frigate.

The USS *Stark* had not even activated its radar system, so when one of the crew reported Iraqi jets flying towards the vessel no action was deemed necessary – after all, there was no official hostility between Iraq and the US at this stage. Exocet missiles launched from the Iraqi fighters tore into the *Stark*'s upper deck. In the resulting fire 37 US sailors lost their lives. In the investigation that followed, Captain Glen Brindel came under heavy criticism for not maintaining a state of operational alert.

The official view was that the attack was simply an error, the Iraqis having mistaken the USS *Stark* for an enemy warship. Some, however, chose to view it as a warning from Iraq's leader Saddam Hussein not to interfere in Gulf affairs. Although the US was not prompted to take any retaliatory action, it was the first outward signal that the relationship between Iraq and the United States could easily deteriorate.

THE GUITAR MAN

June 3, 1987 saw the passing of the virtuoso musician Andres Segovia, the man who brought respectability to the guitar and gained acceptance for the instrument in the elite world of classical music. A self-taught maestro, Segovia was always proud to declare himself his "own master and pupil".

Born in Spain in 1893, Segovia studied music and composition in Granada. Against the wishes of his teachers and parents, he gradually abandoned all other instruments in favour of the guitar. Under his own extraordinary tuition, Segovia refined and redefined the accepted playing techniques developed over the previous century.

By the age of 16 Segovia had already made his first professional recital. In 1919 he first enjoyed international acclaim as he toured South America. In 1924 he made his Parisian debut, performing before an audience that included Manuel de Falla and Albert Roussel, both of whom would later compose seminal works for the guitar. Segovia's debuts in Moscow (1926) and New York (1928) were greeted with similar enthusiasm. Thereafter, he toured widely throughout world, astounding audiences with his unprecedented virtuosity on an

▲ **Andres Segovia, the greatest virtuoso the guitar has ever seen. His work made the instrument respectable to the classical music fraternity.**

instrument that was still largely unfamiliar to the masses, and looked upon as just a crude folk instrument by the classical establishment.

Not only was Segovia the greatest maestro the instrument has yet seen, he was responsible for making the guitar a truly international instrument. Not least of all, Segovia also greatly increased the guitar's classical repertoire, since many of the finest twentieth-century compositions were written specifically for him.

Segovia's impact can still be seen in the generations of fine players who followed in his footsteps. Master-classes he held during the 1950s produced important players of the calibre of John Williams.

Segovia continued giving recitals until he was well into his eighties. His own recordings are still held up as the benchmarks against which all newcomers are measured.

May
- Elections in South Africa won by National Party
- IRA terrorists killed in attack on police station in Northern Ireland
- Egyptian government severs diplomatic relations with Iran over Egyptian Muslim extremist links with Iran
- Coup against Indian-dominated government in Fiji
- West German teenager, Mathias Rust, lands light plane in Red Square in Moscow
- Head of the Soviet Air Defence force is dismissed
- Death of American actress Rita Hayworth

June
- Lebanese Prime Minister Rashid Karami assassinated by bomb in his helicopter
- Meech Lake Accord agreed by Canadian provincial governments, granting Quebec special status
- Amnesty granted to army officers involved in human rights abuses in Argentina
- Anti-government protests in South Korea
- Conservative Party under Margaret Thatcher re-elected in Britain
- State of emergency declared in Panama to counter growing anti-government unrest
- Lynden Pindling re-elected Prime Minister of the Bahamas amid allegations of involvement in drug trade
- Karolly Grosz becomes Hungarian Prime Minister
- Deaths of US dancer and actor Fred Astaire and comedian Jackie Gleason

'87

THE GREAT GALE

In the early hours of October 16, 1987 the southeast of Great Britain was hit by hurricane-force winds, causing widespread devastation and millions of pounds worth of damage. Amid collapsing trees and flying debris, 17 people were known to have died and hundreds were injured. It was the worst storm to hit Britain since records began.

With railway lines blocked by fallen trees, many trains services were out of action for almost a week, causing widespread disruption for London commuters.

The winds, which were measured at over 177 km/ph (110 mph), came as something of shock to the British public, even though 36 hours beforehand weather centres in Holland had accurately predicted what would happen. It was a major embarrassment for Britain's Meteorological Office, whose well-known weather man Michael Fish confidently reported on national television that "there is no chance of a hurricane." The official expla-

▲ The wreckage of a car crushed by a tree during the hurricane-force winds that hit the southeast of England.

nation was that "the storm built up over an area of sea with little shipping" and hence was not monitored carefully.

Although insurance companies were hit heavily, a price tag could not be put on some of the damage. In the Chelsea Physic Garden, rare trees, some dating as far back as 1673, were snapped like twigs. It was estimated that the Royal Botanical Gardens at Kew would take at least 30 years to recover from the damage. As an official put it: "It looks as if a giant has just stepped across the garden."

Apart from tree surgeons, glaziers and roofing contractors, who flourished in the aftermath, the only other group that might have taken advantage of the pandemonium were ornithologists who could have spotted several species of rare birds blown hundreds of kilometres inland.

BLACK MONDAY

▲ Panic reigns during the "Black Monday" collapse of the stock markets of London and New York.

October 19, 1987 saw the worst ever day on the London stock exchange as £50 billion was wiped off the value of shares in a single day's trading. That fateful day, commonly known as "Black Monday", represented a 10 per cent fall in the market.

The drop was even more dramatic in the US where the Dow Jones industrial average fell by over 500 points, leaving shares worth an average of 22.6 per cent less than they had been at the start of the day. Even at its worst, the October 1929 collapse that ushered in the Great Depression only managed a 13 per cent fall over a single day.

The trauma felt by the world's stock markets brought a sudden ending to a five-year bull market, one which had seen a 350 per cent rise in share prices. Although it didn't trigger a second depression as some analysts had feared – by the end of October, half of the losses had been recouped – October 19, 1987 is widely viewed as the end of the eighties boom. A recession slowly followed which lasted into the early years of the next decade.

Black Monday was not a result of one single factor. Like its precursor fifty years earlier, stocks and shares had become overvalued. The crises in London and other markets were a direct consequence of panic on Wall Street.

Of concern of most investors was America's continuing trade deficit and inability to balance its budget. Some also blamed the advent of computerized trading systems which they argued had turned the stock market into one great unpredictable gamble.

As with all sudden market downturns, it was the smaller companies that were hit the hardest. The well-established stocks were quickly able to regain ground as investors bought at bargain low prices in the reasonably sure knowledge that they would be a reliable long-term bet.

POPPY DAY BOMBING

November 8, 1987 will be remembered as the day that the IRA carried out one of its most callous bombings in Northern Ireland. At a Remembrance Day parade in the small town of Enniskillen a bomb was detonated, killing eleven and injuring 60. Among the victims were a number of women and children.

The bombing followed reports that the IRA had restructured its organization into a number of small semi-autonomous service groups. The change was thought to have followed a number of successful intelligence operations, making crucial information leaks less likely.

The horror of the carnage reported in the media brought widespread condemnation from all sides of the community. Sensing the outrage, some, like Bishop Brian Hannon sought a positive outcome: "I hope the Enniskillen massacre will be a catalyst for peace within Northern Ireland." The IRA, however, remained resolute that there was no peace. As their tersely worded statement read: "The British army did not leave Ireland after Bloody Sunday."

It was a poignant event in the history of the "Irish issue", signalling a stepping up of violent protest by the IRA. However, it

also saw a resurgence of a vocal cross-community opposition to terrorist activities by either side. Also poignantly, the funeral of the victims was held on November 15, two years to the day that the governments of London and Dublin signed an agreement giving the south a consultative role in the running of Ulster. It had been hoped that such a concession to the nationalists in the north would be taken as an act of good faith. Such optimism was in vain.

This was merely the latest in a succession of unsuccessful attempts to solve a problem whose resolution would never seem able to satisfy both the loyalist and nationalist communities.

▲ The Enniskillen bombing shocked communities on both sides of the Irish issue, but the violence continued.

'87

IRAN-CONTRA AFFAIR

▲ **A true patriot? Lieutenant-Colonel Oliver North prepares to testify in the "Irangate" affair.**

NEWS IN BRIEF

November

- French security services intercept arms shipment on ship bound for Ireland
- ANC leader Govan Mbeki released from jail in South Africa
- Coup in Tunisia; Habib Bourguiba deposed; Zine al-Abidine Ben Ali takes power
- Arab nations summit opens in Jordan
- Death of Niger President Seyne Kountche; Colonel Ali Seibou succeeds
- Bomb in the International Airport in Beirut kills 5
- Fire at Kings Cross underground station in London kills 30
- Li Peng appointed Chinese Prime Minister
- State of emergency declared in Bangladesh
- Elections in Haiti halted by political violence; 34 die
- North Korean terrorists explode bomb on South Korean plane; 115 die as plane crashes over Burma
- Deaths of American writer James Baldwin and British broadcaster and writer Eamonn Andrews

November 18, 1987, brought an end to the worst crisis to hit Ronald Reagan's presidency as the seven-month "Iran-Contra" Congressional hearing in the US came to an end. The scandal concerned the secret supply of weapons by the US government to Iran for use in their war against Iraq and the subsequent channelling of payments to the Nicaraguan "Contra" rebels.

The scandal came to light in November 1986 when it emerged that during the previous year the National Security Council (NSC)

had organized the sale of anti-tank and anti-aircraft missiles to Iran in an attempt to secure the release of American hostages being held in Lebanon by Shi'ite terrorists thought to be under Iranian control. Rear Admiral John Poindexter, head of the NSC, and his assistant Lieutenant-Colonel Oliver North had handled the $48 million payment. Such bargaining was in direct contravention of President Reagan's public policy regarding hostages: "there will be no deals with terrorists".

To mask the financial transac-

tions, the proceeds of the arms sales were diverted to the Nicaraguan "Contra" rebels who were being supported by the US in their attempts to overthrow the Marxist Sandinista government. This violated a law passed in Congress in 1984 banning the giving of military aid to Nicaragua. The ban reflected public concern at the deepening US involvement in Central America.

When the scandal became public, Congress immediately launched a series of investigations. Meanwhile, the President's advisers attempted to limit the damage. Both Poindexter and North were removed from their posts at the NSC and on December 30 President Reagan spoke to the American people, acknowledging that "mistakes had been made", although it was notable that he refused to condemn the operation as an error. He remained adamant that he had not known about nor authorized the operation.

Further revelations emerged early in 1987. It became clear that William Casey, head of America's

▼ **A common point of view – many ordinary Americans looked upon North as a patriotic hero.**

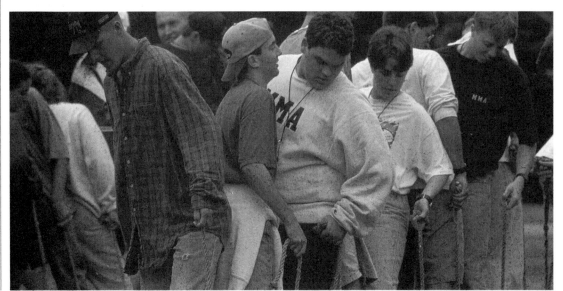

Central Intelligence Agency (CIA) had been involved in the planning. Too ill to testify, Casey died in May 1987 during the hearings. Poindexter and North, who had taken the fifth amendment – the right to remain silent – were eventually indicted. While on the stand during July 1987, North made it clear that he had always acted on the instructions of his superiors, and he had assumed that the chain of command went right up to the President himself. Following the testimony of his secretary, Fawn Hall, it also became evident that considerable efforts had been made to destroy incriminating evidence. Again, North claimed he was simply following orders, most of which conveniently seemed to end with the late William Casey. In spite of his admissions, North deeply impressed many of the millions of ordinary Americans who tuned in daily to watch the televised trial. It was clear that his belief in the operation – to save the lives of American hostages and fight the threat of Communism in Central America – was fuelled by a deep patriotism. He emerged from the hearings as something of a heroic figure.

No prosecutions were made as a result of the hearings. The Congressional report, however, was unequivocal in its condemnation of the President. Even if, as Reagan always claimed, he had neither known about nor authorized the double operation, the affair showed disturbing evidence of "disarray at the highest level of government".

Although Reagan's personal popularity dropped as a result of the Iran-Contra scandal, he weathered the storm. The scandal left a huge cloud of doubt surrounding American foreign policy, however, the inevitable question of how many other covert operations had taken place undetected being left unanswered.

MAKING THE WORLD A SAFER PLACE

▲ **The signing of the Intermediate-Range Nuclear Forces Treaty (INF) signalled a new era in East-West relations.**

December 10, 1987 saw the first fruits of a new relationship between East and West that followed the rise to power of Mikhail Gorbachev. The US and the Soviet Union signed the Intermediate-Range Nuclear Forces Treaty (INF), agreeing the terms for which both sides could reduce their nuclear arsenal.

The three-day talks in Washington defined intermediate- and short-range nuclear weapons as having a firing range of 480 km (300 miles) to 5,500 km (3,400 miles). The treaty also included land-based missiles that could be equipped to carry a nuclear warhead. Over the next three years, 2,619 missiles would be dismantled, two-thirds of them deployed in the Soviet Union. The agreement also set out the conditions under which each side would be able to inspect opposing bases to verify that missiles and their launchers had been destroyed.

During the INF talks a number of other areas of East-West conflict were also discussed, but with less successful outcomes. A major bone of contention on the Soviet side remained Reagan's futuristic Strategic Defense Initiative (SDI), at that time being viewed as a serious option. Matters of foreign policy were also the subject of discord, Reagan highlighting the continued Soviet presence in Afghanistan; Gorbachev, unwarranted US interference in the Middle East and Central America. As ever, the fundamental ideological differences remained intact.

Although the INF treaty dealt with only around 10 per cent of the total nuclear arsenal, no agreements were reached on the more critical issue of long-range weaponry. The talks reflected well on the two leaders and signalled the closest relationship between East and West since the beginning of the Cold War. To even the most cynical of observers this was patently a positive step.

December
- USA and USSR sign INF (Intermediate Nuclear Forces) treaty for reducing nuclear weapons
- Mafia trial in Sicily ends with over 300 defendants jailed
- Rae Tae Woo elected President of South Korea
- Gustav Husak resigns post as First Secretary to the Czechoslovak Communist Party
- Ferry collides with oil tanker in the Philippines and sinks; more than 1500 passengers killed
- Rival Zimbabwean politicians Joshua Nkomo and Robert Mugabe reach agreement; their ZAPU and ZANU parties are to be merged
- US dollar reaches record low

'88

DEATH ON THE ROCK

On March 7, 1988, three IRA terrorists were gunned down at point-blank range by plain-clothed members of the Special Air Service (SAS). The incident took place in Gibraltar, the tiny British possession on the southern Mediterranean coast of Spain. The three victims, two of whom had already served long prison sentences for terrorist activities, were Sean Savage, Daniel McCann and "commander" Mairead Farrell.

British intelligence had known that an IRA service unit was at work in Gibraltar. Information they had discovered led them to believe that they were planning to bomb a local changing the guard ceremony. Indeed, the day after the shooting, a white Renault car rented by the terrorists was dis-covered with 140 pounds of plastic explosive concealed in it. Had the plot succeeded the lives of up to 50 soldiers who would have been involved in the parade could have been endangered.

There was some controversy as to whether there been any genuine attempt to capture the suspects. The official report claimed that when challenged, the two men and one woman made as if to escape, so that, given their high-risk status and the fact that they may have been armed, a shoot-to-kill policy was the only option. A local witness, however, reported that the terrorists were given no warning before the shooting, making the incident little more than an authorized execution. A number of later media reports tended to confirm this latter view, even though there was very little real public sympathy for the fates of the three victims.

A week later, the "Death on the Rock" saga, as it became known, took a further twist. In the eyes of the IRA their three "soldiers" had died on active service and thus, on March 16, were given a military-style funeral. The Belfast cemetery service was an emotionally charged affair, attended by a crowd of 5,000. The British army had chosen not to police the event. As the three bodies were being lowered into the ground a lone gunman emerged, lobbing grenades and shooting indiscriminately into the crowd. Three were killed and 50 injured. Eventually the man was brought down and given a severe beating

▲ **Mourners for the three IRA terrorists killed by British troops in Gibraltar take cover behind a gravestone as an unknown gunman fires into the crowd.**

before the police intervened.

The incident was unusual in that both nationalists and loyalists were traditionally scrupulous in their observation of sectarian funerals. It later transpired that the Protestant gunman had been working alone. He had evidently tried on a number of occasions to join the loyalist Ulster Defence Association (UDA) but had been turned down. He was believed to have been on drugs at the time of the attack.

Three days later a further related incident took place that would send shock waves throughout the whole of Great Britain. Two British soldiers in their car found themselves inadvertently caught up in the midst of an IRA parade. The mood of the crowd was suspicious and ill-tempered – hardly surprising following the funeral shooting. It was here, and in the full glare of television cameras that the two hapless corporals, Derek Wood and Robert Howes, were pulled out of their car and lynched. They were beaten unconscious, stripped and taken away to nearby wasteland where they were shot dead.

It was not known why the two soldiers were even there. Although the IRA claimed that they were on a reconnaissance mission, the British army maintained that they were not on active duty.

The heightened paramilitary activity on both sides of the "troubles" since the Enniskillen bombing of November 1987 looked poised to continue indefinitely. The peace agreements unsuccessfully brokered in 1985 by Margaret Thatcher and the Irish prime minister Garrett Fitzgerald were now dead and buried, and the IRA was preparing to step up its "war" outside Northern Ireland and on mainland Great Britain.

TV SINNERS

▲ In an attempt to save face, Reverend Jimmy Swaggert makes a tearful plea for God's forgiveness on live television.

For the second time in a year the head of an American TV evangelical ministry was shown publicly to have fallen well short of the standards he might have demanded of his congregation.

On February 21, 1988, one of America's most prominent "televangelists", Jimmy Swaggert, went on the air to admit that he had committed a "sin of the flesh". Swaggert was forced to make the admission after photographs of the 52-year-old preacher visiting a young prostitute became public. Swaggert was the founder of the Assembly of God programme which at its peak brought in funds of £140 million and was seen on cable television channels the world over.

Only a year earlier Swaggert had publicly denounced fellow televangelist Jim Bakker as "a cancer on the body of Christ" when it was revealed that he had also succumbed to the charms of another woman. Bakker and his wife Tammy were well known on the Praise The Lord television network whose members each year subsidized their ministry to the tune of $100 million. Bakker claimed to have been "wickedly manipulated" into sleeping with the woman. He had then succumbed to blackmail to protect his reputation.

It was later revealed that the PTL ministry and its associated Heritage USA Christian theme park were already under investigation for misappropriation of funds. Eventually, in October 1989, Bakker was called to appear in court where he was convicted on 24 counts of fraud. His punishment was a fine of $500,000 and 45 years in prison.

88

THE END OF THE AFGHAN OCCUPATION

The West had been horrified in December 1979 when the Soviet Union, attempting to prop up an ailing Communist regime, launched what the outside world saw as an unwarranted invasion of Afghanistan. It signalled an end to detente between the Soviets and the West, and a significant downturn in relations between the two.

The protests of the West were brushed aside and Soviet troops proceeded to engage in a debilitating war against rebel forces, ostensibly in defence of the pro-Soviet Najibullah government. Based in rural mountain strongholds, the mujaheddin (literally meaning "strugglers") proved more than a match for the highly trained Soviet troops. It quickly became evident that it was a war the Soviet Union could not win.

Over 100,000 Soviet troops were brought into Afghanistan, occupying the major cities and towns of the country. This tactic drove the rebel forces into Afghanistan's harsh rural terrain. Attempts to suppress the mujaheddin inevitably failed as the rebel forces, divided into small mobile units and employing guerrilla tactics, proved elusive. It was the acquisition of US-funded rocket

▲ **Crowds line the streets of Kabul, the capital city of Afghanistan, to watch the final departure of a convoy of Soviet tanks.**

missile launchers that enabled the mujaheddin to sustain their defence. The stalemate that ensued saw Soviet planes rarely able to target their enemy effectively, but the rebels periodically able to inflict costly losses on the Soviets. The rebel ranks comprised many small rival factions. Indeed, their only unequivocal bonds were Islam and a hatred of the Soviet occupation. As such, they were only ever likely to succeed through attrition.

Opposition to the Afghan War, often called the "Soviet Vietnam", grew within Soviet Union. The

costs, both in financial and military terms, were high. Finally, in April 1988, President Gorbachev signed a United Nations initiative in Geneva under which Soviet troops would leave Afghanistan. The evacuations took place between May 1988 and February 1989.

The mujaheddin refused to acknowledge the Geneva agreement and continued to wage war against the Afghan government. Eventually, in 1992, they stormed the capital of Kabul and President Najibullah was ousted. Afghanistan was duly proclaimed an Islamic republic.

NEWS IN BRIEF

May
- Coup in Pakistan; Mohammed Zia ul-Haq takes power and dissolves national assembly
- Islamic Jihad free three French hostages in Beirut
- François Mitterrand re-elected President of France
- János Kádár deposed in Hungary; Károly Grosz takes power
- Soviet Communist Central Committee votes to limit the term of office of officials
- Ronald Reagan begins visit to Moscow

June
- Three day anti-apartheid strike by black workers in South Africa
- Military coup in Haiti; President Leslie Manigat deposed, General Henri Namphy takes power
- Police kill approximately 3000 demonstrating students in Rangoon, Burma
- Death of British writer and broadcaster Russell Harty

July
- Soviet Communist conference endorses Gorbachev's reforms
- Explosion and fire on North Sea Piper Alpha oil rig kills over 160
- Iranian passenger jet shot down by mistake by US warship in the Gulf; all 286 on board killed
- Carlos Salinas de Gortari elected President of Mexico

THE AYATOLLAH ENDS THE WAR

In August 1988, after several years of military deadlock, the Iran-Iraq war was brought to an end as the Iranian economy had been brought close to collapse by the war effort. The conflict had begun in September 1980 when Iraqi armed forces invaded western Iran. By early 1982 the

invaders had been repelled and fighting continued intermittently along the border between the two. Although Iraq, under the leadership of Saddam Hussein had sued for peace since that time, Iran's Islamic republic, led by the Ayatollah Khomeini, had vowed to fight "to the last drop his blood".

The six years that followed saw the war follow a rather pointless direction that achieved little other than the crippling of both economies and the death of over a million soldiers and civilians. Persistent advances were made by Iranian ground troops which were easily repelled by Iraq's superior weaponry. During this time, Iraq had the benefit of financial support from oil-rich Saudi Arabia. Furthermore, although the Western powers felt little fellowship towards either nation, Iraq was seen at this time as the lessor of the two evils and received tacit support. Ironically, arms that were legally sold to Iraq during this time by the US and Great Britain would in only a few years be turned back on their makers as Saddam Hussein took on the Western world with his invasion of Kuwait. Iran was only able to number Libya and Syria as its allies.

From the mid-1980s, the United Nations had attempted a conciliatory position, its principle objects being to see the war at an end and the full resumption of oil supplies, which were regularly interrupted as the warring states made periodic attacks on each other's oilfields. A UN peace plan put together at the start of 1988 was finally accepted by the Ayatollah and a cease-fire followed in July. In 1990 Iraq and Iran restored full diplomatic relations.

► The end of the crippling conflict between Iran and Iraq saw the exchange of thousands of prisoners on both sides

• Dictator of Burma General Ne Win resigns as President; General Sein Lwin succeeds, but Ne Win retains control; thousands of protesters killed by police in subsequent crackdown
• Jordan cedes the West Bank to the PLO

August
• Cease-fire in conflict between South Africa, Angola and Cuba in Namibia and Angola
• Pakistani ruler Zia ul-Haq killed in aircraft explosion; Benazir Bhutto succeeds
• Burmese premier General Sein Lwin replaced by U Maung Maung
• Deaths of British ballet choreographer Sir Frederick Ashton and Italian car designer and manufacturer Enzo Ferrari

September
• Worst floods in 70 years cause devastation in Bangladesh, killing thousands and leaving millions homeless
• End of strike in Poland
• Coup in Haiti deposes General Henri Namphy
• Tennis player Steffi Graf wins "Grand Slam", only the fifth person to do so

October
• Mikhail Gorbachev becomes President of reformed Soviet government
• End of war between Chad and Libya
• Death of British car designer Sir Alec Issigonis, creator of the Morris Minor and the Mini cars

POLITICS AND DRUGS

The 1988 Olympic Games were held in the South Korean capital of Seoul. Although less controversial than other Olympic Games in recent years, both politics and drugs made their mark on the proceedings.

The Olympics came at a time when the political situation in Korea was considerably volatile. In June, two months before the Games were due to start massed demonstrations took place throughout South Korea as students demanded reunification with the North. Over 60,000 policemen were called out to quell the rioting.

North Korean authorities complained to the Olympic committee, claiming that they should be given co-host status. When this was refused they boycotted the event, with Cuba and Ethiopia joining their protest.

The most infamous moment of the Seoul Olympics came in the 100 metres event when Canadian Ben Johnson put in an extraordinary performance that made the other finalists seem as they were jogging by comparison, clocking a time of 9.7 seconds. Johnson was stripped of his gold medal a few days later when the results of a dope test showed that he had used illegal performance-enhancing steroids in his Olympic preparations. Nine other Olympic competitors, mostly weightlifters, were disqualified for drug abuse.

The Seoul Olympics made an overnight star out of an American track athlete Florence Griffith Joyner. "Flo-Jo", as she became affectionately known, was one of the most glamorous women to have ever graced an Olympic track. She made her mark with three gold medal victories.

The biggest upset of the Games was the elimination of the US basketball team, who fell in an early round to Yugoslavia. The eventual winners were the Soviet Union, who also ended up at the head of the table with a record-breaking 132 medals.

◄ The star of Seoul, the late Florence Griffith Joyner was perhaps the greatest female track athlete of all time.

'88

A DICTATOR FALLS

NEWS IN BRIEF
....

November
- Republican candidate George Bush wins US presidential election
- People's Party under Benazir Bhutto wins election in Pakistan; she becomes Prime Minister, a position once held by her father
- Conservative Party under Brian Mulrooney wins Canadian general election
- Deaths of British socialist and life peeress Jennie Lee and Greek shipping heiress Christina Onassis

December
- Soviet premier Mikhail Gorbachev addresses the UN and announces unilateral Soviet troops and arms reductions
- Thirty-four die in train crash in Clapham, London
- Anti-deforestation campaigner Francisco Mendes assassinated in Brazil

On September 11, 1973, Chilean armed forces launched an attack on Santiago's presidential palace, killing President Allende. The coup d'état brought General Augusto Pinochet to power. During fifteen years in power which saw an unprecedented suppression of all dissent, Pinochet fought against many attempts to allow Chile to return to being a democracy. Then, on October 5, 1988, he was forced to put his leadership to a plebiscite. The people of Chile spoke – and 55 per cent of the voters called for his removal.

The rise of Pinochet was supported by the US, who had taken an active part in the overthrowing of the Marxist Allende's government. He was also initially popular among political moderates, although this was because many saw the military rule as a transitional period that would allow a return to the stability that preceded Allende.

However, within six months, Pinochet has assumed a dictatorial position and immediately launched into a brutal repression of Chile's liberal opposition. By 1976 over 100,000 had been arrested, a very significant number of whom simply "disappeared", never to return to their families. Chile quickly gained an international reputation for its civil rights abuses.

With the reintroduction of a free-market economy, Chile experienced a mild economic boom during the late 1970s. In March 1981 a new constitution was introduced. Under its terms, Pinochet would serve as President for a further eight years; eight years after that a candidate chosen by the military junta would be submitted to a referendum.

During the next eight years of Pinochet's rule opposition from centre-left political groups such as the Democratic Alliance and the Roman Catholic church grew. As Chile's economy began to experience problems his popularity began to fall. As expected, the military junta chose Pinochet as their sole candidate for the 1988 plebiscite. With over half of the voters opposed to Pinochet, according to the terms of the constitution he was forced to stand down. The result was greeted with jubilant street parties – for many it represented nothing less than the liberation of Chile.

In the event, matters were slow-moving. The first elections for 16 years were finally held in December 1989. The victor was the Christian Democrat Patricio Aylwin. According to the terms of the constitution, this would by no means be the end of General Pinochet, however. Under the 1981 constitution he was entitled to remain head of the armed forces for a further eight years.

In fact, it would be 1998 before Pinochet finally stepped down. Remaining as a powerful right-wing senator in the government, with powers to personally appoint a fifth of the senate, regardless of whether or not they had been elected, he was able to block liberal reforms, especially moves to take action against those responsible for the human rights violations that followed his rise to power.

Although a number of generals and other high-ranking officers were brought before a tribunal to reveal their "individual truths", an amnesty meant that they could not be prosecuted, even if evidence was found suggesting they were guilty.

◀ **General Augusto Pinochet, the "Strong Man" of Chile, remained a powerful figure long after his removal from office.**

LOCKERBIE BOMBING

▲ **The wreckage of Pan-Am Flight 103 lies strewn across the small Scottish border town of Lockerbie. The suspected Libyan terrorists still await trial.**

The small Scottish border town of Lockerbie found itself unwittingly at the centre of a major terrorist incident on December 21, 1988 as a Boeing 747 jumbo jet travelling from London to New York exploded, falling from the sky. All 259 crew and passengers on board Pan-Am Flight 103 died and another 11 people were killed by the debris that landed on houses and roads below.

Investigators analyzing the wreckage were quickly able to deduce conclusively that the accident was deliberate sabotage, caused by a bomb explosion.

The immediate suspects were terrorists from Iran. In July, an Iranian passenger jet had been downed by a US warship, a crewman on board the USS *Vincennes* having mistaken it for a hostile F-14 fighter. Most of the 290 victims were Iranian, and although President Khomenie described it as "one of the biggest crimes of any war" he maintained that Iran would not seek revenge.

Finding the true culprits eventually turned into an epic struggle as it slowly emerged that the terrorists were Libyan. In the early 1990s the US government publicly named two Libyan nationals, both known terrorists, whom they suspected of being responsible for the crime. Libyan leader Colonel Gaddafi refused to extradite them claiming that the strength of public feeling would make it impossible for them to receive a fair trial.

Years of slow diplomacy followed, and the likelihood of a trial taking place was boosted in 1998 when the Libyan government agreed that the suspects could be tried in Holland, under Scottish law, and with a Scottish judge presiding. In April 1999, the two Libyans arrived in Holland and the judicial proceedings, expected to last many months, began.

ARMENIAN EARTHQUAKE

On December 7, 1988, the northwestern part of the Soviet Republic of Armenia, near the border with Turkey, was devastated by an earthquake measuring 6.9 on the Richter scale. The town of Spitak, with a population of 50,000, was left without a building standing. Over three-quarters of Armenia's second city, Leninakan (since renamed Gyumri), was also destroyed. Over 100,000 people were believed to have perished and half a million left homeless.

The improvement in US-Soviet relations that followed President Gorbachev's *glasnost* policy was clearly illustrated as the Soviet Union accepted a generous aid offer from the US – the first such occurrence since World War Two. Planes were flown into Armenia containing urgently needed medical supplies.

▶ **A man searches through the unmarked coffins for the body of his brother, lost in the earthquake that devastated Armenia.**

'89

FATAL CHARM

▲ Handsome, witty, charming, confident and well-educated – Ted Bundy seemed to be the very antithesis of the stereotypical sex attacker.

Almost ten years after he had been sentenced to die in the electric chair, on January 24, 1989 serial murderer Ted Bundy was executed.

Bundy was an enigma among violent criminals. Psychological profiling has tended towards the view of sex attackers as pathetic inadequates with little in the way of self-esteem. And yet Bundy was handsome, well-educated, witty and charming. He had studied law, worked as a counsellor at a Crisis Clinic and even been a political volunteer. And yet in the space of four years Theodore "Ted" Bundy brutally murdered an unknown number of women. The police estimated it could have been as many as 40; some suggested it may have been twice that number.

It was in 1974 that Washington State police first began to suspect that a serial murderer was at large as more and more young women were reported missing. During 1975 the disappearances gradually shifted to Colorado and Utah. Bundy was first identified after he approached a young woman alongside a lake near Seattle. Refusing to go with him, she later heard Bundy introduce himself as "Ted" to another girl, whose mutilated body was later found nearby. Able to construct a photofit picture, a police appeal drew a list of 3,000 suspects, including Bundy. Little progress was made, however; more women disappeared and more bodies were discovered.

Bundy was finally caught by police in Salt Lake City when he was stopped in his car for driving through a series of red lights late at night. A number of incriminating items were found. A search of his flat revealed more clues. Finally, hairs found in his car were shown to match those of one of the victims. Ted Bundy appeared in a Salt Lake City court during November 1976. Claiming he was innocent, Bundy maintained that he was being framed by the police. The murders were not proven, but the judge sentenced him to 15 years for "aggravated kidnapping".

In December 1977 Bundy escaped from prison. Making his way to Florida, he embarked on a second reign of horrifying terror as he broke into a college campus and brutally murdered two female students.

Once again it was Bundy's erratic driving that led to his arrest and conviction. Standing trial in Florida, this time he was found guilty of murder and on July 23, 1979 was given the death sentence. For the next ten years he became adept at delaying the inevitable by occasionally offering information as to where the bodies of his victims might be found. When his time ran out in 1989 few mourned the passing of America's most notorious serial killer.

BLASPHEMY OR FREE SPEECH?

An extraordinary series of events began to unfold on February 14, 1989 as the author Salman Rushdie found himself the object of a death threat from Islamic fundamentalists. Rushdie's "crime" was the publication of his third novel, *The Satanic Verses*, in which a fictional character was interpreted by some as satirizing the prophet Mohommed. Under Islamic law this represents blasphemy punishable by death. It was the Ayatollah Khomeini, the revolutionary Islamic leader of Iran, who announced the fatwa – the call for Rushdie's execution.

Published in summer 1988, *The Satanic Verses* was quickly condemned by British Muslim leaders.

▶ **A crowd of angry British Muslims demonstrate against the author Salman Rushdie and his book, *The Satanic Verses*.**

By the new year the protests had spread throughout the Islamic world, with violent demonstrations taking place in Pakistan that left six dead and almost 100 injured.

Few doubted that Khomeini's threat was a serious matter. A reward of £3 million was even offered to the executioner. Rushdie had no choice but to go into hiding. Despite government protests, the Ayatollah refused to lift the death sentence. Most Western governments condemned the action as an attempt to suppress free speech.

Although an award-winning novelist, the Anglo-Indian Rushdie was barely known to the ordinary public until this time. Ironically, *The Satanic Verses* became an international bestseller, reaching a far wider public than the minority audience to whom Rushdie's books usually appealed.

Rushdie, however, was unable to take much joy from his high profile. It was not until the late 1990s that he was able to emerge from hiding.

ECOLOGICAL NIGHTMARE

One of the worst man-made ecological disasters in history took place on March 24, 1989 when the supertanker *Exxon Valdez* ran off course in the waters of Prince William Sound on the Alaskan coast. Running aground on the Bligh Reef, the tanker's hull

was pierced and its cargo of 50 million litres (10.9 million gallons) of crude oil emptied into the sea. The catastrophe inflicted incalculable damage on Alaska's ecosystem and all but wiped out much of the region's economically crucial fishing industry.

The Exxon Corporation, owners of the tanker, were heavily criticized both for the slow response of their clean-up operation and their apparent reluctance to take full blame. Alaska was left with a 800 km (500-mile) oil slick drifting slowly towards the mainland,

◀ **An oil-drenched guillemot, one of the victims of the *Exxon Valdez* disaster that polluted 800 km (500 miles) of the Alaskan coastline.**

eventually polluting thousands of kilometres of the coastline. Beaches had a 30-cm (1-ft) coating of crude oil, killing off all forms of wildlife and polluting the food chain for other reliant species.

Five months after the disaster the State of Alaska launched a massive lawsuit against the Exxon Corporation. In 1990, as a direct consequence of the *Exxon Valdez* catastrophe, the US Government passed the Oil Pollution Act which imposed unlimited liability on shipowners found guilty of polluting. After a lengthy legal wrangle, Exxon agreed a settlement of $1 billion. However, the environmental damage was too great even to begin to attach a price to it.

'89

HILLSBOROUGH DISASTER

▲ **Victims of the Hillsborough Stadium Disaster, in which 95 fans were crushed to death. Although many questioned the conduct of the police no responsibility was ever attributed.**

The tragedies of May 1985 that had seen 56 deaths in a blaze at Bradford and 39 the same month at Belgium's Heysel Stadium sent a message to the world that all was not well with the state of English football. The quick-fix solutions offered by the football authorities to deter direct intervention by the British government largely involved treating football fans like potentially dangerous animals. Policing was increased and at football grounds all over the country wire fences were erected to prevent violence spilling over on to the field. On April 15, 1989 the short-sightedness of this policy was laid bare in a catastrophe that resulted in 96 fans being crushed to death.

The game was an FA Cup semi-final between Liverpool and Nottingham Forest. As was traditional, the match was held in a neutral venue – in this case, the Hillsborough Stadium in Sheffield,

South Yorkshire. The problems began a few minutes before the start of the match as police took the decision to relieve the intense crowd pressure that had built up outside the stadium by opening the gates and letting Liverpool fans in without checking their tickets. This quickly created a problem of overcrowding as Liverpool supporters surged forward to find a good view. Six minutes into the game, panic set in, forcing people forward and crushing them against the concrete and steel fencing.

The aftermath turned into a major controversy as blame was sought. Most put the blame on poor policing. *The Sun* newspaper had its own ideas, running under the headline "The Truth", a story documenting the allegedly appalling behaviour of Liverpool fans. Creating outrage, to this day *The Sun* remains widely boycotted throughout Liverpool.

An official investigation into the Hillsborough disaster conducted by Lord Justice Taylor controversially concluded that the deaths were accidental. In spite of the apparently defensive and evasive reactions of senior officers during the inquiry, South Yorkshire police were cleared of responsibility. Lord Justice Taylor also commented critically on the poor state of sporting arenas in Great Britain, in particular those – like most used in football – in which most spectators were forced to stand. By enforcing all-seater stadiums the sequence of events that resulted in the Hillsborough tragedy could not recur. While this move was not wholly popular with regular football supporters, for whom standing on the terraces was a part of the sport's great tradition, it was overwhelmingly responsible for the gentrification of football that took place during the next decade.

NO DEMOCRACY FOR CHINA

Two months of student unrest amid calls for Western-style democracy in China came to a violent climax on June 3, 1989 as tanks and troops of the People's Liberation Army invaded Peking's Tiananmen Square, indiscriminately firing into a crowd of protesters. The ruthless suppression that followed saw 2,600 students dead and a further 10,000 injured.

The protests emerged following the death of former general secretary of the Chinese Communist Party, Hu Yaobang, on April 15. Hu had been forced to resign two years earlier for "mistakes on major issues of cultural policy", as he set about dismantling the cult of personality that still surrounded Mao Tse-tung. His unwillingness to stamp out a previous wave of student unrest proved to be his downfall. Over 100,000 students in Peking marked his funeral.

The protests grew more severe during May, with over 200,000 students staging a day-long demonstration throughout Peking. With hundreds of students arrested, many continued their protests in jail by refusing to take food or drink. On May 17, a massed rally

▲ The drive for democracy within China came from the student body, many of whom were former supporters of Hu Yaobang.

of almost a million marched in support of the hunger strikers.

The 100-acre concrete site of Tiananmen Square, the home of the annual meetings of the National People's Congress, thereafter became the focus of growing provocation between the authorities and the students. On May 30, art students unveiled their own symbolic gesture as they erected a 9-metre (30-ft) plaster statue alongside the hal-

lowed Monument of Revolutionary Heroes overlooking the square. Entitled the Statue for Democracy and Freedom, it outraged the Peking government.

On June 3, with no sign of the protests abating, the People's Liberation Army – previously having refused to intervene – brought chaos as they launched their fierce attack on Tiananmen Square. Over the coming days the brutal suppression of the protesters sent shockwaves around the world. This conflict created perhaps the single most dramatic image of the decade as a lone, unknown student stood before a row of tanks refusing to let them pass.

By the end of the month the pro-democracy movement had been driven underground, branded "traitors to the people" by Prime Minister Li Peng. Those identified as leaders of "counter-revolution" were executed and well over a thousand others were arrested for their part in the demonstrations.

The events of June 1989 had the effect of isolating China from its growing integration with the industrialized world as conservative Maoist influences came to the fore. In 1992, however, general secretary Deng Xiaoping sought a resumption of economic reform with the encouragement of private enterprise and a growth of the free market. This necessitated forging new trading relations with the West. Although China is now a major trading partner of many Western countries, known civil rights violations continue to impede close links with the West.

◄ One of the most stirring images of the century – a lone student halts a procession of tanks in Peking's Tiananmen Square.

'89

THE WALL COMES TUMBLING DOWN

There could be no more symbolic vision of the sudden downfall of Communism, than the collapse of the ultimate divide between East and West, the Berlin Wall. On November 9, 1989, the East German authorities – hard-line Communists having been driven from power the previous month – succumbed to the wave of democratization that was sweeping through Eastern Europe, and that would soon see the literal disintegration of the Soviet Union. They opened up the Berlin Wall and the country's borders with the German Federal Republic (West Germany), and citizens from either side were free to move between the East and West. Less than a year earlier, East German leader Erich Honecker had predicted that the Berlin Wall would stand

▲ The cracks begin to show – a West Berliner pokes his head through one of the many holes that seem to have sprung up overnight in the Berlin Wall.

for a hundred years.

The "Berliner Mauer" was erected during the night of August 12, 1961. Initially built from barbed wire and cinder blocks, the Wall was a result of a law passed by the Volkskammer, the East German parliament, to prevent the steady flow of skilled and professional workers who were fleeing from East Berlin to the more prosperous West. Over the months that followed, the barbed wire was replaced by a 4.5-metre (15-ft) concrete wall. Watchtowers manned by machine gun units were placed at strategic intervals along it. Unmanned areas were protected by electrified fences and minefields. In spite of this high security, over 5000 East Germans made their way safely to the other side in the Wall's 28-year history. Around 200 were shot dead while attempting a crossing.

The background to the sudden change of events in Eastern Europe could be traced to the glasnost reforms of Soviet Premier Mikhail Gorbachev. With an improvement in the relationship between the two

Superpowers, the Soviet Union weakened its hold over its eastern European satellite states. In an odd turnabout, the hard-line East German government was highly critical of the Gorbachev regime. Indeed, for a time during 1988, some traditional Soviet publications were banned for being subversive.

The Berlin Wall first became ineffective in May 1989 when the newly liberalized Hungarian government tore down the barbed-wire fencing that lined its border with Austria. During the months that followed, East Germans seeking asylum in the West were able to travel freely through Hungary and into Austria. Hungary's actions angered Premier Honecker, who accused the West German government in Bonn of financing the operation.

Thereafter, events progressed with an unassailable momentum. In an attempt to stem a swiftly

▲ A young family from West Berlin make their first visit to the Brandenburg Gate, closed to Westerners for almost 30 years.

deteriorating situation, on October 18, the Politburo of the Socialist Unity Party (SED), East Germany's only political party, replaced Honecker with the equally hard-line Egon Krentz, formerly the head of security. With the flow of refugees to the West now being viewed as a national embarrassment, on November 9, the East German government announced new travel regulations making it officially possible to cross from East to West without having to pass through Hungary and Austria. It was largely the ambiguity of this declaration that led East Berliners to believe that the Wall had now been effectively opened. At the stroke of midnight, thousands gathered at the Wall's official crossing points demanding to be let through. Overwhelmed, the border guards had no choice but to stand by and watch.

During the night that followed the Berlin Wall became the setting for one of the greatest impromptu celebrations in Germany's history. Thousands of jubilant Berliners climbed on top of the wall, tearing away the barbed wire to begin a night of unprecedented revelry. It was an historic moment that would lead directly to the unification of the two Germanies. Although it would be many months before the Berlin Wall was physically dismantled, from November 9, 1989 it was as if it had never existed.

The end of the Berlin Wall also signalled the end of the German Democratic Republic. Surprisingly, perhaps, at first only a small proportion of the thousands who made the historic crossings from East to West chose to remain

▶ **A distant, tragic memory of a time when families and friends risked their lives to communicate across the Berlin Wall.**

▲ **Crowds gather as an East German bulldozer demolishes the Berlin Wall along the Potsdamer Platz, once again the centre of a united city.**

there. The numbers grew, however, as protests for greater democratization became widespread throughout East Germany. By the end of November, with no place for a "Stalinist" like Krentz, Hans Modrow came to power. A moderate Communist in the

mould of Gorbachev, Modrow recognized that the GDR was facing a struggle for survival and quickly announced the first multi-party elections. The elections that took place in March 1990 saw the Communists soundly beaten. The victors were the Christian

Democrats – an eastern counterpart to Helmut Kohl's ruling party in West Germany. Under the leadership of Lothar de Maizière, a broad coalition was formed with other democratic parties with one goal in mind: unification with West Germany.

With both governments committed to this end, the only obstacle was the Soviet Union, which cited security fears as a major objection to a unified Germany working within the Nato alliance. These were lifted following Chancellor Kohl's guarantee of a German financial aid package to help the ailing Soviet economy.

On October 3, 1990, the West German Bundestag and the East German Volkskammer ratified a treaty of unification bringing 45 years of division to an end. Before the decade had ended, the parliament of the united Germany had returned to Berlin.

THE VELVET REVOLUTION

The Prague Spring of 1968, during which a combined Eastern bloc military force invaded Czechoslovakia, brought an end to the reforms of Alexander Dubcek. In April 1969, he was replaced by Gustav Husák, a Slovak hard-line Communist. Although the bloody purges that characterized other failed uprisings in Eastern European states were avoided, many professionals, intellectuals and artists were cast out of the Communist Party, forcing them to accept menial jobs in order to survive. During the 1970s, dissent among these groups saw the birth of an underground resistance movement, Charter 77. In January 1977 they presented a signed petition airing their grievances against the Husák regime. Once again, the Communist authorities responded by filling up the prison cells.

Signatories to the Charter 77 petition played an important role in the events that led up to 1989's Velvet Revolution, the movement that ended Communist control of Czechoslovakia. On November 17, 1989 the Czech authorities, influenced by the Gorbachev reforms in the Soviet Union, permitted a public demonstration to commemorate the 50th anniversary of a student march in Prague that had been suppressed by the occupying German authorities. It was soon evident that the gathering was a thinly veiled pro-democracy protest, and once again the streets of Prague were the scene of brutal police beatings. This set off a nationwide series of pro-democracy demonstrations and strikes, mostly organized by the opposition group Civic Forum.

The Communist rulers were forced to acknowledge that they could not combat popular dissent on such a grand scale and a coalition was formed between the Communists and Civic Forum. On December 9, 1989, the long-standing President Husák was forced to resign. His place was taken by the spokesman of Civic Forum, Václav Havel, also one of Eastern Europe's most noted post-war literary figures. Havel became Czechoslovakia's first non-Communist president in over 40 years.

The role of the new regime was complicated by Czechoslovakia's status as a federal republic: after the Prague Spring national governments had been set up for both the indigenous Czech and Slovak peoples. The first free elections were held in June 1990 and saw Civic Forum win decisive majorities in both parliaments. Thereafter, tensions between the Czech and Slovak factions weakened the federation, eventually resulting in the inevitable creation of two independent states – the Czech Republic and Slovakia.

▼ **Noted Czech playwright Václav Havel, an unlikely presidential figure.**

CEAUSESCU DEPOSED

The winds of change that swept through Eastern Europe during 1989 manifested themselves in very different ways. In Hungary and Czechoslovakia the transitions from Communism were relatively smooth and bloodless. In Bulgaria, the Communists even won the country's first free elections. It was in Romania that the downfall of the ruling regime followed the bloodiest and most dramatic course of events, reaching a climax on Christmas Day 1989 with the execution of President Nicolae Ceausescu and his wife. Photographs of the hated couple's bullet-ridden bodies were proudly displayed in Romanian newspapers and on television screens.

From the abdication of King Michael and the proclamation of the Romanian People's Republic at the end of 1947, Romania had conspicuously modelled itself on political and economic templates provided by the Soviet Union, in particular, on Stalin's principles of centralized planning and development of heavy industry.

By the 1960s, led by Gheorghe Gheorghiu-Dej, Romania had began to evolve its own brand of Communism. This led to gradual estrangement from the Soviet Union, quickening after Khrushchev's denunciation of Stalin. After Gheorghiu-Dej's death in 1965, Nicolae Ceausescu, a neo-Stalinist, took over, proceeding to promote a cult of personality of which Stalin himself would have been proud. He consolidated power by filling key positions with cronies (among them his wife, Elena) and within a decade, had turned Romania into a powerful police state geared to operate on his merest whim. Whilst poverty among his people

▲ **Dramatic pictures broadcast on Romanian television of the executed dictator Nicolae Ceausescu.**

was the highest in eastern Europe, Ceausescu was able to live like a king. Incredibly, this powerful, 24-year reign was overturned within the space of a single bloody week.

The Romanian revolution began on December 17, 1989 in the Transylvanian city of Timisoara, home to many of Romania's two million ethnic Hungarians. During the previous decade, Ceausescu had attempted to weaken ethnic uprisings, enforcing the use of the Romanian language in all schools and banning the publication of books in Hungarian. When 10,000 anti-government demonstrators marched through the streets of Timisoara, Ceausescu's response was swift: tanks and security forces were immediately sent in, firing indiscriminately into the crowds. Thousands of men, women and children were mercilessly gunned down

The brutal suppression in Timisoara shocked Romania. Ceausescu publicly blamed Hungarian provocateurs, but when he addressed the people from his palace in Bucharest his speech was interrupted by persis-

tent heckling from the growing crowd of protesters. On December 22, with demonstrations spreading throughout the country, troops from the Romanian army mutinied. A fierce battle was waged between the army and the Securitat, Ceausescu's personal security force. As many as 50,000 are thought to have perished in the week-long revolution.

With no possibility of restoring their rule, the Ceausescus attempted to flee Bucharest, but were captured and tried by a military tribunal. They were found guilty of mass murder and corruption and summarily executed by firing squad.

Although Europe's last dictator had been removed from power, Communism was so entrenched in Romanian life that the sudden introduction of a Western free-market economy was by no means a natural consequence. Throughout the 1990s, economic progress was slow and although democratic elections were introduced, many of the former Communists continued to hold positions of power.

1990–99

W ith so much significance being attributed to the turn of the century, the final decade of the second millennium was always likely to be something of anti-climax. As it happened, much of the 1990s was concerned with mopping up the fall-out from the dramatic events in Eastern Europe. Although "free", the harsh realities of world economics now faced the states whose fates had previously been inextricably linked to the Soviet Union. For many of these nations, the idea of free international trade was an unknown entity which threw some into economic chaos. Nowhere was the dramatic switch to capitalism more starkly illustrated than in the former Soviet Union itself. When the Mighty Empire was finally felled in 1991, President Gorbachev – he man who had done so much to end the Cold War– was effectively redundant. As the decade progressed an elite class of Russian capitalist emerged, wealthy beyond their wildest dreams. But most ordinary Russians discovered that whilst they might now have the freedom buy a Big Mac or make anti-government protests without fear of being shot, their standard of living had fallen dramatically. As the ruble underwent a complete collapse, workers could not be paid and inflation spiralled out of control.

It was, however, the dramatic dissolution of Yugoslavia that cast its greatest shadow over the 1990s. At the start of the century, the ethnically mixed states of the Balkans had vied for power. Relatively stable during the Cold War, Yugoslavia enjoyed greater independence than many other Communist states largely due to Stalin's policy of leaving the volatile region well alone. In 1991, with Communism all but collapsed around them, Bosnia, Slovenia, Macedonia and Croatia announced their secession from the federation. Serbia, the most powerful state, and controller of the Yugoslav army, sought to keep the region together. Under the leadership of President Slobodan Milosevic, Serbia's aim was clear– total dominance over the former Yugoslav states creating a "Greater Serbia". Fighting was centred over Bosnia, with its sizable Serb population. It quickly became clear that Bosnia's Muslims were being forcibly evicted from their homes This policy of "ethnic cleansing" shocked the world and eventually brought Nato into its first ever armed conflict. It was not until 1995 that a peace agreement was brokered.

In the Middle East, the West found a new pariah in President Saddam Hussein of Iraq. His invasion of Kuwait in 1990 was defeated by the combined forces of the United Nations. Throughout the decade he would recurrently perform military acts that would incur the wrath of the United Nations. But in spite of the heavy bombing of the region, Saddam Hussein remained very much in power.

Britain saw the end of an era when Margaret Thatcher was ousted following internal wranglings of the Conservative Party. Thereafter, successive Conservative governments were torn apart by internal disputes over the issue of Britain's involvement in the European Community. Complacent after 18 years in office, the General Election of 1997 came close to annihilating the Tories as Tony Blair's "New Labour" manifesto brought him into power with a majority that even his most fervent supporters found hard to believe.

As the decade drew to a close, Balkan brutality once again became a focal point as a civil war broke out in the Serbian territory of Kosovo. Milosevic sent in the Yugoslav army to suppress the Kosovo Liberation Army, but simultaneously cleared the region of the ethnic Albanians. In March 1999, Nato intervened, carrying out nightly bombing raids on Serb targets. It took almost three months of bombing before Serbia agreed to a negotiated settlement. In the meantime, over a million Kosovans were forced to flee to neighbouring states. When Nato troops occupied Kosovo following Serbia's withdrawal, the world once again looked on in horror as evidence of the most appalling brutality surfaced: mass graves filled with the charred remains of men, women and children. Nato was charged with the difficult task of keeping the peace between the returning refugees and the Serb minority.

NELSON MANDELA WALKS TO FREEDOM

At around 4 p.m. on February 11, 1990, Nelson Mandela, his wife Winnie at his side, walked out of the gates of Victor Verster prison, near Cape Town in South Africa, a free man after 27 years' imprisonment. He was met by a crowd of 2,000 supporters (the maximum number allowed by the authorities) together with numerous news cameramen and reporters. The crowd roared as the 71-year-old black nationalist leader raised his right fist. Two hours later he emerged on the balcony of City Hall in Cape Town before a crowd of 50,000 people, who had been waiting to greet him since the morning. "Nelson Mandela – the nation welcomes you home" read one enormous banner. Once again, he raised his fist to the jubilant crowd, and began to speak: "Friends, comrades and fellow South Africans, I greet you all in the name of peace, democracy and freedom for all!" The final phase in South Africa's apartheid era had begun.

Just nine days earlier, on February 2, President F W de Klerk had opened parliament with a speech that signalled his intention to dismantle the apartheid system. "The time for negotiation has arrived," he said, as he announced the lifting of the bans on the ANC and more than 30 other illegal organizations; promised freedom for political prisoners, including Nelson Mandela; suspended capital punishment; and removed press restrictions imposed by the State of Emergency. For the first time in nearly 30 years the words and pictures of Nelson Mandela and other black activists could appear in South African newspapers.

President de Klerk's speech came four years after increased rioting in the black townships had led the government to impose a State of Emergency and the international community to step up trade sanctions on South Africa, in an attempt to encourage political reform. For the past two years there had been regular meetings between Mandela and a secret government committee, feeling their way toward this new beginning for South Africa.

◀ **Nelson Mandela salutes the crowds of well-wishers who greet his long-awaited release from the Victor Verster prison.**

NEWS IN BRIEF

• President Gorbachev granted emergency powers to deal with the collapsing USSR economy

• Tribal violence erupts between Xhosas and Zulus in South Africa

• Clashes between Serbs and Albanians in Kosovo, Yugoslavia

• General Aoun surrenders in Lebanon, ending rebellion

• Namibia gains independence from South Africa under President Sam Nujoma

• EC members, with the exception of Britain, vote for second stage of economic and monetary union at summit meeting in Rome

• Anti-government unrest in Kenya after suspicious death of opposition politician

• Trial for fraud and other crimes of businessmen involved in the Guinness takeover of Distillers in Britain

• USA and Britain enter recession

• Hubble space telescope put in orbit; a fault in its lens is then discovered

• Films released during the year include Jean-Paul Rappeneau's *Cyrano de Bergerac*, starring Gerard Depardieu, Kevin Costner's *Dances With Wolves*, Martin Scorsese's *GoodFellas*, David Lynch's *Wild At Heart* and Stephen Frears' *The Grifters*

POLL TAX LEADS TO VIOLENCE

The most unpopular measure of Margaret Thatcher's eleven-year period as UK Prime Minister was the "community charge", universally known as the "poll tax", devised to replace local rates. Its introduction in England and Wales in April 1990, a year after it had come into force in Scotland, caused widespread disturbances in many parts and culminated in serious rioting in central London.

Under the old rating system, local government revenue had been raised from householders on the basis of the size of their property. In a rough-and-ready way, the rates tended to take more money from the well-off and less from the poor. The poll tax, in principle, imposed a standard charge for every adult in a given local government area, irrespective of his or her income – although there were reductions for those on benefit. It was backed up by draconian laws to prevent non-payment. The level of the poll tax was officially set by local councils, but in fact it was manipulated by the government under complex rules that – or so it seemed to some – ensured that flagship Conservative councils such as Wandsworth were able to set astonishingly low levels.

Disturbances started in early March, as crowds of protesters gathered at town halls across the country, where the level of the local poll tax was being fixed. In some places, including Bristol and the London districts of Brixton and Hackney, there were serious clashes with police. On Saturday March 31, an estimated 300,000 people gathered in Trafalgar

► **Panic on the streets of London – an unprecedented period of civil disturbance peaks with the Trafalgar Square riot.**

Square to protest against the poll tax and hear calls from speakers for a campaign of civil disobedience to make the new tax uncollectable. The rally was ending when police pushed forward in force to clear the crowd. Missiles were thrown and a chaotic melee

ensued. Small groups of demonstrators started fires and ran amok through shopping streets, smashing windows and terrifying passers-by. Scattered fighting continued through the evening. More than 300 people were arrested.

THE SUPERGUN AFFAIR

Early in 1990, MI6 and other European intelligence agencies received reports that key machine parts for a long-range artillery piece were about to be exported from Britain to Iraq. This "supergun" was an experimental weapon capable of firing a 36-inch diameter shell, fitted with a conventional, biological or even nuclear warhead, to distances in excess of 320 km (200 miles). Complicating matters further, on April 2, the gun's maverick

◄ **The piping at the heart of the "supergun" scandal. The exporters claimed it was an oil pipe when it was clearly a gun barrel.**

Canadian designer, Dr Gerald Bull, was mysteriously killed in Brussels. The finger of suspicion pointed at Mossad, the Israeli secret service, whose government feared that Iraq was planning to use the gun against Israel.

During the Iran-Iraq War, an arms embargo had been imposed on the warring nations. Despite some later relaxation of the embargo terms, the intelligence agencies decided to prevent the supergun's export. On April 11, British customs officials seized at the port of Teesside crates which were described as containing "petroleum piping" which was, in fact, parts of the supergun barrel. A week later a British driver was arrested in Athens

when his truck was found to be loaded with supergun parts. Finally, in May, Italian authorities impounded more parts for the gun in the port at Naples.

While these arrests were being made, there was confusion over who had given authorization for British companies to work on the order. The company that had made the barrel parts, Sheffield Forgemasters, claimed that they were not breaking any arms embargo. A spokesman for the company said that, "after the initial approach was made by someone on behalf of the Iraqis, the company was given the green light by the Department of Trade and Industry".

The precise role of the British authorities in this whole, murky business was to develop into the "Arms for Iraq" scandal that bedevilled the Conservative government during the 1990s.

YELTSIN ELECTED RUSSIAN PRESIDENT

NEWS IN BRIEF

March
- Soviet government permits citizens to own private businesses
- Lithuanian parliament votes to secede from the USSR; Vitautas Landsbergis elected President of Lithuania; 3 weeks later Soviet troops enter Lithuania, seizing army deserters
- Iranian-born British journalist, Farzad Bazoft, hanged for spying in Iraq
- Israeli coalition government collapses
- Labour Party returned for 4th term in elections in Australia

April
- Prisoners at Strangeways Prison in Manchester riot and take it over in protest at conditions
- Robert Mugabe wins presidential elections in Zimbabwe
- Greek election won by New Democracy Party under Constantine Mitsotakis
- Election in Hungary won by centre-right coalition
- USSR halts oil supply to Lithuania
- Death of Swedish-born actress Greta Garbo

May
- Latvia unilaterally declares independence from USSR
- Greek President Constantine Karamanlis re-elected
- Estonia unilaterally declares independence from USSR
- North and South Yemen unite to form the Republic of Yemen

▲ **Boris Yeltsin addresses a crowd of mineworkers following his election as President of the Russian Republic. A controversial figure, Yelstin would remain in office throughout the 1990s.**

On May 30, 1990, Boris Yeltsin was elected President of the Russian Soviet Federated Socialist Republic (RSFSR), by far the largest of the 15 Republics that made up the Soviet Union. Stretching from the Baltic to the Pacific, the RSFSR covered more than three-quarters of the Soviet Union's land area, contained more than half its population, and included the two most important Soviet cities, Moscow and Leningrad. Its leader clearly would have a powerful base from which to challenge the wavering authority of the USSR's President Mikhail Gorbachev. Yeltsin defeated a candidate favoured by Gorbachev, Aleksandr Vlasov.

Born in Sverdlovsk in 1931, Yeltsin had risen through the ranks of the Communist Party, becoming first secretary of his native region in 1976. It was Mikhail Gorbachev who appointed Yeltsin to the powerful position of party chief in Moscow in 1985. His thoroughgoing assault on corruption in the capital and his blunt, no-nonsense manner rapidly won him a reputation as a rising star of the *glasnost* era. In 1987, however, his outspoken criticism of the slow pace of economic and political reform angered the Soviet party leadership and he was relegated to a minor post in the bureaucracy. Election as a deputy to the new Soviet Congress in 1989 gave him a chance to bounce back into the limelight.

Yeltsin was ideally placed to exploit the rapid deterioration in Gorbachev's authority. The Soviet President's gamble on achieving a reform of the Soviet political and economic system that would make a Communist Soviet Union work was visibly failing. The half-hearted economic reforms had only succeeded in plunging the economy into a downward spiral, imposing hardship on much of the population and provoking widespread discontent. The continued pursuit of political reform gave this discontent numerous chances to express itself – most memorably when Gorbachev was booed by protesters at the annual May Day parade in Moscow in 1990.

Gorbachev does not seem to have realized how far democratic elections in the RSFR and other Soviet republics would undermine his authority. Since Gorbachev himself had not been elected to the presidency of the Soviet Union by popular vote, he would inevitably find it difficult to override the authority of genuinely elected representatives of the people.

Installed in charge of the RSFSR, Yeltsin made immediate moves to assert the Republic's sovereignty, giving its own laws priority over Soviet legislation and taking control of the economy. On July 12, at the Soviet Communist Party's 28th Congress, Yeltsin sensationally announced his resignation from the party. With this gesture, he shifted the whole focus of the political struggle in the Soviet Union. It was no longer a question of reforming Communism, but of seeing whether or not that system would survive.

THE IRAQI INVASION OF KUWAIT

In the early hours of August 2, 1990, Iraqi tanks rolled over the border into Kuwait. By midday, Kuwait City had fallen to the 100,000-strong Iraqi invasion force. Despite some sporadic resistance, which continued for a few days, the small oil-rich state was soon firmly in the grip of Iraq and its dictatorial leader Saddam Hussein. The only serious fighting had taken place outside the palace of the Kuwaiti Emir, Sheikh Jaber al-Ahmed al-Sabah, who subsequently managed to escape to Saudi Arabia.

Iraq justified its invasion on the basis of an ancient historical claim over Kuwait, but this was merely a pretext for Saddam's determination to impose his hegemony over the Gulf region, and to recoup some of the huge financial losses incurred during the recent war with Iraq. In addition, Saddam bitterly opposed OPEC's cheap-oil policy which had been championed by Kuwait.

News of the invasion caused an immediate international outcry. United Nations Resolution 660 was issued unanimously by the UN Security Council, condemning the invasion and demanding an immediate and unconditional Iraqi withdrawal. Fearful that the Iraqis might push on into Saudi Arabia and undermine the whole strategic balance in the Gulf, the United States was in the forefront of the condemnation.

US troops were despatched to the Gulf on August 7, following a Saudi request for military aid. Over the succeeding weeks they were joined by smaller contingents from 19 other countries. While the military build-up continued, economic sanctions were imposed upon Iraq. Iraq's isolation was completed in the political arena, too, when both the Soviet Union, Iraq's former Cold-War ally, and the Arab world criticised the invasion. Saddam's calls for a Jihad (holy war) against the West were ignored and 12 out of the 20 Arab League members went so far as to send troops to Saudi Arabia in support of Kuwait. By the end of the year, war in the Middle East seemed certain.

▶ **A refugee from Kuwait carries his belongings on his back, stranded in the no man's land between Jordan and Iraq.**

DISASTER AT MECCA

On July 2, 1990, one of the world's worst-ever crowd catastrophes took place in the Muslim holy city of Mecca, Saudi Arabia. Every year, at the start of the last month of the Muslim calendar, pilgrims from every corner of the globe gather in the city, which is the birthplace of the Prophet Mohammed. The numbers of pilgrims has expanded rapidly in recent times – a reflection both of the growth of world population and the relative ease of travel. The arrival of several million people every year posed mounting organizational problems with which the authorities struggled to cope.

The focus of the pilgrimage is the sanctuary of the Kaaba. Pilgrims have to walk around the Kaaba seven times and then proceed to Mount Arafat, outside the city. A walkway built to link the Kaaba to Mount Arafat passes through an air-conditioned tunnel. On July 2, in temperatures of around 43 degrees Centigrade, the air-conditioning failed. There were about 5,000 pilgrims packed into the tunnel and panic broke out. In the crush, some 1,400 people suffocated or were were trampled to death.

◀ **Holy shrine to Muslims the world over, the Kaaba was the site of one of the worst ever crowd disasters.**

TWO GERMANIES REUNITED

▲ The reunification of the state was widely welcomed by East Germans. The banner calls for "unification and freedom" and proudly proclaims: "We Dresdeners are German".

When the gates in the Berlin Wall were opened in November 1989, very few people expected the much-celebrated event to lead to German unification in the foreseeable future. An opinion poll conducted in East Germany two weeks after the Wall opened found that more than four out of five East Germans wanted their country to remain a separate, independent state. This was certainly the ambition of Neues Forum, the East German movement that had made the running in opposing the Communist regime during 1989. Its leaders wanted to create a democratic socialist state that would follow a "third way" between capitalism and Communism.

German unification was also not regarded as a desirable option abroad. The Soviet Union, which still had 300,000 troops stationed in East Germany, had traditionally regarded the idea of a united Germany within Nato as a totally unacceptable threat to its security. The Western powers rejected talk of unification as a dangerous provocation to the Soviets, who might respond by reversing their current tolerance to recent events in Eastern Europe. In any case, many in the West still remembered the two World Wars and were unhappy at the prospect of a resurgence of German power.

But West German Chancellor Helmut Kohl pursued the goal of a united Germany with single-minded determination from the day the Wall opened. Events quickly began to flow in his direction. Politically, the opening of the Wall was followed by a string of revelations about the Communist state that sickened and disillusioned the East German people. Those arguing for a reformed socialism soon found their audience drifting away as revelations of the prosperous lifestyles of Communist leaders and their corrupt currency dealings tore the last shreds of respectability from the old system. In January 1990, demonstrators who stormed the Berlin headquarters of the Stasi, the East German secret police,

◀ President Gorbachev and Chancellor Kohl formally bring an end to the states of East and West Germany.

discovered files on six million people. Around two million East Germans had informed on their friends, colleagues, and neighbours. It was hard to maintain pride in East Germany's "separate identity" faced with such facts.

Even more crucial was the growing momentum of economic collapse in the East. The flood of emigration that had precipitated the fall of Communism continued after the opening of the Wall. The Ostmark, East Germany's currency, went into free fall. Officially exchanged at three Ostmarks to one West German Deutschmark, it dropped to a street value of 20 to one. Even so, East Germans flocked to buy West German consumer goods, creating a disastrous outflow of currency. The interim government which took over from the Communists on December 6 hastily negotiated "economic cooperation" agreements with West Germany that effectively placed much of East Germany's industry and infrastructure in West German hands, in return for a vital injection of capital and expertise.

By mid-January 1990, with unemployment rising, the currency depreciating, emigration continuing, and the prospect of cuts in subsidies that would lead to a massive rise in rents and transport costs, the East German government and people had come to the conclusion that unification with the West was both necessary and unavoidable. It was the inevitable consequence of the disintegration of East Germany.

The first and last free elections in the short history of East Germany were held on March 18. Poorly organized, under-financed home-grown groups such as *Neues Forum* were swept aside as the major West German parties muscled in. Victory went

to the East German version of Helmut Kohl's Christian Democrats, with 48 per cent of the vote, ahead of the Social Democrats with 21 per cent. The only East German party to make a showing were the reformed Communists, now called the Democratic Socialist Party, which drew a respectable 16 per cent of the vote.

The election result provided a clear democratic mandate for German unification. Economic union was set for July 1. During the March elections, the Christian Democrats had promised that Ostmarks could be exchanged at parity with Deutschmarks when the currencies were unified. This overvaluation of the Ostmark offered an enormous windfall to East Germans with savings. The West German Bundesbank objected vigorously, but when the

idea of exchange at two-to-one was floated, protests in East Germany were so strong that Kohl backed down. On July 1, delighted East Germans queued to collect their Deutschmarks.

Political unification had to wait for the agreement of the four foreign powers still occupying Berlin. The 4 + 2 Talks – the United States, Britain, France, and the Soviet Union, plus the two Germanies – opened on March 15. It was impossible for the Western powers to oppose unification in the face of the clear, democratically expressed wishes of the German people. The Soviet Union tried at least to prevent the new Germany being part of Nato, but finally settled for cash. At a meeting with Soviet leader Mikhail Gorbachev in July, Kohl agreed to pay 12 billion Deutschmarks for the return of

Soviet troops to the Soviet Union – to be completed by 1994 – and to provide other forms of economic aid, including 350,000 tons of food that had been stockpiled in case of another Berlin blockade. Agreement was also reached between Germany and Poland, confirming Poland's postwar borders.

With no further obstacle to unification, on October 3, 1990, 327 days after the opening of the Wall, East and West Germany were united in a single state of over 77 million people. Even in the midst of the celebrations, it was impossible to hide the fact that East Germany was actually being taken over by the West.

▼ **Crowds celebrate around the Reichstag. The decision was taken to return the government to its traditional seat – Berlin.**

'90 END OF THE THATCHER ERA

On November 28, 1990, Margaret Thatcher resigned as the UK's Prime Minister after an extraordinary 11 years in office – the longest period served in Number 10 Downing Street by any Prime Minister this century. She had won three consecutive general elections, but had ultimately failed to convince her party that she could win a fourth.

Born in Grantham in 1925, the daughter of a grocer, Thatcher became Conservative MP for Finchley in 1959. She was

Secretary of State for Education and Science in Edward Heath's government from 1970 to 1974, earning the rhyming epithet "milk-snatcher" from her political opponents for her abolition of free school milk. In 1975 she defeated Heath in a contest for the Tory Party leadership, supported by the right of the party. Heath never forgave her.

The novelty of a woman party leader soon wore off, as Thatcher's abrasive style denied any link between the stereotypical qualities of her sex and her political persona. Her fervent anti-Communism soon saw her branded by Moscow as "the Iron Lady". In the run-up to the 1979 general election, her aggressive attitude towards the trade unions won her support from many voters appalled by the chaos of

◀ Margaret Thatcher dominated the government of Britain during the 1980s like no other politician of the twentieth century.

the "winter of discontent".

In her first speech as Prime Minister, on May 4, 1979, Thatcher said: "Where there is discord may we bring harmony". But this was not be the style of her rule. She embarked on a radical transformation of the British economy, making savage cuts in public spending and accepting mass unemployment as the price that had to be paid for financial stability and improved competitiveness. Her first term in office appeared a disaster, with rising unemployment matched by rampant inflation as whole sectors of British industry went under. But the Falklands War in 1982 gave her a chance to turn the political tide. Her Falklands triumph, plus the split in the Labour Party between old Labour and new Social Democrats, were the keys to her 1983 election victory.

The degree to which Thatcher achieved her political objectives was remarkable. She broke the power of the unions, especially through the brutal defeat of the miners' strike in 1984. She began a vast programme of "privatization" that dismantled the state sector of industry and introduced millions of people to share ownership. She radically reduced government borrowing and savaged much of the welfare state. She cut income tax, especially for high earners. Despite the persistence of mass unemployment, a permanent feature of the Thatcher years, enough people felt she had given them new opportunities and prosperity to bring her a third election victory in 1987.

Over time, Thatcher's overbearing style as Prime Minister alienated many of her most able Tory colleagues. Most spectacular was her clash with Defence Secretary Michael Heseltine in January 1986, when Heseltine stormed out of a cabinet meeting after being bluntly overruled by Thatcher in the Westland helicopter affair. The nub of the Westland affair, apart from a clash of personalities, was Heseltine's preference for closer links with Europe, opposed by Thatcher. In October 1989, Thatcher's anti-European views also led to a showdown with her Chancellor of the Exchequer, Nigel Lawson. The central issue was whether Britain should belong to the European Monetary System (EMS), a step towards a single European currency. Lawson was committed to the EMS, but found his policy undermined by Thatcher's personal economic adviser, Professor Sir Alan Walters. After a stand-up row with the Prime Minister, Lawson stormily resigned from office. He was replaced by John Major.

The Lawson affair led directly to the first formal challenge to Thatcher's leadership. A backbencher, Sir Anthony Meyer, stood against her as a token candidate to test the party's mood. Sixty Tory MPs failed to vote for her, a sufficient revolt to open up the prospect of a much more serious leadership challenge in the near future.

Thatcher's hold on power could hardly have been shaken, however, without the poll tax fiasco. The Prime Minister was one of the few people in Britain who felt the new Community Charge, introduced in April 1990, was a fair improvement on the old rates. The government's popularity plummeted. Local elections in May brought an 11 per cent swing to Labour. In October, the Liberal Democrats scored a shock by-election victory in Eastbourne, considered one of the safest Tory seats in the country. Ominously, the economy was also in trouble, with inflation heading above 10 per cent – higher than it had been when Thatcher came to power in 1979. This was a particular blow to a prime minister who had consistently made "beating inflation" a major plank of her policy platform.

At the start of November, the Deputy Prime Minister, Sir Geoffrey Howe, hitherto one of Thatcher's most loyal followers, resigned over European policy. His resignation speech in the House of Commons on November 13 was a sensational attack on the Prime Minister. The day after, Michael Heseltine announced that he was challenging for the party leadership.

In the first round of voting by Tory MPs on November 20, 152 backed Heseltine and 204 voted for Thatcher. Under the rules of the contest, this was four votes short of the total she needed for

outright victory. Thatcher's immediate response was to announce that she would fight on. Behind the scenes, however, it was made plain to her that if she stood in the second round of the ballot, she could expect to be comprehensively defeated. On November 22, commenting "It's a funny old world", she withdrew from the contest. Her favoured candidate, John Major, won the

leadership contest on the third ballot and duly took over as Prime Minister. He went on to lead the Conservatives to their fourth election victory in a row, albeit a narrow one, in 1992.

▼ "It's a funny old world" – still extremely popular among Tory voters, Margaret Thatcher was baffled by her demise.

MARY ROBINSON BECOMES IRISH PRESIDENT

On November 9, 1990, Mary Robinson, a 46-year-old lawyer, became the first woman President of the Irish Republic. Her victory, won on a liberal platform promising openness and change, was a shock to the two leading Irish political parties, Fianna Fail and Fine Gael. Standing as an independent, Robinson defeated her nearest rival, Fianna Fail's Brian Lenihan, by 86,566 votes. Her campaign slogan was: "You have a voice, I will make it heard."

Born Mary Bourke, a convent girl from County Mayo, she became a law professor at Trinity College, Dublin, at the age of 25. Her opposition to the oppressive narrowness of Irish life found expression in tireless campaigning on issues such as divorce, contraception, abortion, and homosexuality. She became leader of the Irish Labour Party, but resigned in 1985 because she felt the party was insensitive to the concerns of the Protestant population of Northern Ireland.

Robinson's election was partly

▲ **Mary Robinson, Ireland's first female President, meets veteran American politician Edward Kennedy.**

a protest against the corrupt shenanigans of traditional Dublin politics. Fianna Fail presidential candidate Brian Lenihan had been sacked from the government by Prime Minister Charles Haughey less than a fortnight before the election over allegations of dubious backroom manoeuvering for political advantage. Robinson promised to bring a new spirit to the corridors of power. After being elected, she declared: "I am of Ireland.

Come dance with me."

Robinson remained President for seven years, becoming a figure of international standing. By the time she resigned the presidency in 1997, to take up the post of UN Commissioner for Human Rights, she was without question the most popular political figure in the Irish Republic. Writer Roddy Doyle once said: "For God's sake, who'd want royals when you've got Mary Robinson?"

LECH WALESA TAKES OVER IN POLAND

In December 1990, Lech Walesa, the electrician from the Gdansk shipyards who had led a mass popular revolt against Communist rule in Poland ten years earlier, took his place as the country's first post-Communist President. It was a remarkable personal achievement and marked the completion of an extraordinary political upheaval.

General Wojciech Jaruzelski, effectively ruler of Poland since 1981, had invited Walesa's banned Solidarity movement to round-table talks in 1988, as the Polish economy was again running into difficulties, with strikes once more breaking out.

An agreement was thrashed out in April 1989. The ban on Solidarity was lifted and elections were called, in which Solidarity candidates would be allowed to contest one-third of the seats in the lower house of parliament and all the seats for the less powerful upper house, the Senate.

This arrangement was meant to guarantee that the Communists remained in power, but it did not. Solidarity swept the board in the seats it was allowed to contest, inflicting such a comprehensive defeat on the Communists that Jaruzelski was obliged to accept a Solidarity-dominated government in September 1989, with Tadeusz Mazowiecki, a staunch Catholic

and Solidarity intellectual, as Prime Minister.

The pace of change in the rest of Eastern Europe in late 1989 soon left Poland's political reform – with Jaruzelski still President and a Communist majority in the lower house of parliament – looking over-cautious and inadequate. The 1990 presidential election was the chance to make a clean break with the past. Lech Walesa was the obvious Solidarity candidate, but Mazowiecki also stood for President. Walesa's

◄ **Lech Walesa: in the space of a decade he went from shipyard electrician to leader of post-Communist Poland.**

nationalism, Catholic traditionalism, and allegedly anti-Semitic views were too much for many liberals who had backed the Solidarity movement.

In the event, Mazowiecki came only third in the first round of polling, behind Stanislaw Tyminski, a Polish émigré who returned from Canada to offer instant wealth to all Poles if they made him President. It was a measure of the immaturity of the Polish electorate that this extraordinary candidate won 23 per cent of the first-round vote. However, Walesa eventually carried off a landslide victory in the second round of voting, to take the place that he had surely earned.

YUGOSLAVIA FALLS APART

During 1989, the Communist Balkan state of Yugoslavia was caught up in the same pro-democracy upheaval that swept Communists from power in Poland, Czechoslovakia, Hungary, and East Germany. At the start of 1990, the Yugoslav Communists renounced the monopoly of political power that they had enjoyed since 1945. As in the Soviet Union, the advent of democracy led directly to the disintegration of the state.

A new nation risen from the ashes of the Hapsburg Empire after 1918, Yugoslavia combined an uneasy mixture of religions and ethnic backgrounds. It comprised six republics, of which Orthodox Christian Serbia was the most powerful. Two other republics provided a counter-balance to Serbia: Catholic Croatia and Bosnia-Herzegovina, which was predominantly Muslim but had substantial Serbian and Croatian minorities. The other, much smaller, republics were Slovenia, Montenegro and Macedonia.

Following the German invasion of Yugoslavia in 1941, ethnic rivalries had exploded. The Germans exploited these to the full by supporting the Croats against the Serbs. Massacres by both sides were commonplace – and were not forgotten when Marshal Tito imposed Communist rule over the country after 1945. For more than four decades, Communism put a stop to Yugoslavia's ethnic hatreds, but beneath the surface the divides remained deep.

Democratic elections in 1990 brought nationalists to power in the different republics. Most ominously, in Serbia the elections, held in December, were won by the Communist Slobodan Milosevic, who was an advocate of "Greater Serbia" – in effect, holding Yugoslavia together, but under exclusively Serbian control. In Croatia and Slovenia, on the other

hand, the most economically advanced areas of Yugoslavia, nationalists wanted self-rule. In the same month that Milosevic was elected, Slovenians voted for independence. The stage was set for a descent into civil war.

► **President Slobodan Milosevic's aim of creating a "Greater Serbia" would eventually invoke the wrath of Nato.**

'91

DESERT STORM

▲ **American airforce F-15 fighters demonstrate the strength of the United Nations in the skies above Kuwait. The oilfields below had been torched by retreating Iraqi troops.**

The Western allies' response to Iraq's invasion of Kuwait in August 1990, was to send large military forces to Saudi Arabia. By the start of 1991, the Allies were able to deploy nearly 500,000 ground troops, 3,600 tanks and 1,750 aircraft. The bulk of this force came from the United States, with sizeable contingents from Britain, France, Saudi Arabia, Syria and Egypt. Although the Iraqis had a numerical superiority in manpower, with nearly a million men divided evenly into regulars and reserves, they were of mixed quality and lacked the firepower and support services necessary to wage a modern war. Above all, the Iraqis were fatally deficient in air power.

During the Allied build-up, diplomats continued to shuttle across the globe in the hope of averting a conflict. UN Resolution 660, which demanded the immediate withdrawal of Iraq from Kuwait, was followed by other resolutions imposing sanctions on Iraq. Then, on November 29, 1990, came Resolution 678. This was the UN's final warning, demanding that Iraq withdraw from Kuwait by January 15, 1991 or accept the consequences of all-out war.

Despite this deadline on Iraq, final attempts were made to bring about a diplomatic resolution. On January 9, 1991, James Baker, the US Secretary of State and Iraqi Foreign Minister Tariq Aziz met in Geneva, but after six hours of talks the meeting was abandoned. For the United States and the Allied coalition, this was the signal for war. While Javier Perez de Cueller, the UN Secretary General, flew to Baghdad on January 10 in a last effort to head off hostilities, the Allied generals began to put their plans into effect.

◄ **A Kuwaiti citizen expresses his feelings of gratitude to the United States following the liberation of his country.**

The key to Allied strategy in the Gulf lay in their overwhelming air superiority. During the night of January 16–17, 1991, Iraq was subjected to a series of devastating air attacks. The initial Allied objective was to destroy Iraqi aviation units, anti-aircraft resources, ballistic missile batteries and command and communication systems. Unable to match the Allies, the Iraqi Air Force flew its aircraft to Iran, where they were impounded for the duration of the conflict. Iraqi anti-aircraft fire caused some casualties but the Allies had command of the air.

Through the use of "smart bomb" technology, the Allies hoped to take out military and industrial sites without hitting nearby civilian buildings. The value of smart bombs and cruise missiles in minimizing civilian casualties was emphasized to the world's media by the Allied commanders. In effect, however, smart weapons formed only a small percentage of the total bomb tonnage used, and even they could hit "wrong" targets, as when the Amiriya bunker in Baghdad was bombed on

February 13, causing the deaths of 300 civilians.

The second phase of the bombing campaign extended the target range to include military formations in Kuwait and Iraq. Allied aircraft, ranging from assault helicopters to B-52 bombers, rained down a heavy fire upon the Iraqi troops, with special attention being given to "degrading" Iraq's elite Republican Guard.

In an attempt to break-up the Allied coalition, Saddam launched seven modified Scud missiles against Israel on January 18. Further attacks followed, as did strikes against Saudi Arabia. Casualties were surprisingly light, however, and to the relief of the Israelis, the missiles carried no chemical or biological warheads. The United States prevailed upon Israel not to retaliate directly, fearful that such a response would alienate the Arab members of the coalition. Fortunately for coalition solidarity, Israel acceded to US demands; in return they were given US Patriot missiles to enable them to shoot down incoming Scuds.

By mid-February, Allied planners were preparing to initiate a land offensive. Under the command of the belligerent General Norman Schwarzkopf, Allied troops had moved up to the Saudi border with Kuwait and Iraq. Schwarzkopf's plan was for a strong force of US Marines, supported by Arab units, to cross into Kuwait and pin down the Iraqi forces around Kuwaiti City. Unknown to the Iraqis, who lacked aerial reconnaissance, the bulk of the Allied forces, spearheaded by US and British armoured formations, had secretly moved westward. They would swing round behind Kuwait, destroy the Republican Guard and cut off the remaining Iraqi forces.

In the early hours of February 24, Allied forces advanced into Iraq, meeting little resistance. So complete was Allied domination that the rate of advance was dictated by the speed of the Main Battle Tanks leading the attack. The only Iraqi response was to set fire to the oil fields in Kuwait. Thousands of Iraqis were killed by the Allied armour and aviation, and tens of thousands more soon began to surrender. Within three days, the Iraqi Army had ceased to exist as a fighting force. Their objectives achieved, the Allies called a halt to the conflict at 8 a.m. local time on February 28 – precisely 100 hours after the start of the land offensive.

The Allied combined air-land campaign had been a brilliant military success. Approximately 50,000 Iraqis had been killed and another 200,000 captured, against Allied casualties of 166 killed and 207 wounded. Yet, while Iraq had been expelled from Kuwait, now an environmental disaster area, Saddam remained in power. Two rebellions (irresponsibly encouraged by the Western powers) that immediately followed the war – by the Iraqi Kurds in the north and the Shi'ites in the south – were crushed by Saddam's forces. Despite the sanctions imposed upon Iraq, Saddam remained defiant and continued to do his utmost to frustrate the UN teams appointed to dismantle his "weapons of mass destruction".

▲ President George Bush greets "Stormin' Norman" Schwarzkopf, the commander of the Allied forces in Kuwait.

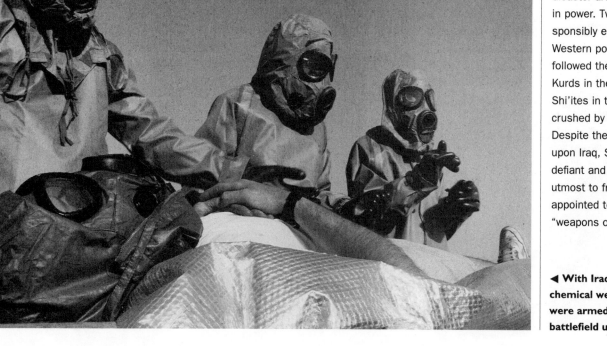

◄ With Iraq prepared to use chemical weapons, UN troops were armed with protective battlefield uniforms.

'91

WARSAW PACT DISSOLVED

On March 31, 1991, the military structure of the Warsaw Pact was dissolved, drawing a line under the Cold War era. Set up in 1955 as the Soviet Union's answer to Nato, the Warsaw Pact bound the countries of Eastern Europe together in a military alliance headed by the Soviet Union. It was the instrument used to suppress the attempt at liberal Communism in Czechoslovakia in 1968. The collapse of Communist regimes in Eastern Europe at the end of 1989 had rendered the Warsaw Pact obsolete.

The obvious question now arose: should Nato also cease to exist, having lost its rationale with the ending of the Cold War? But Nato leaders came to prefer the option of eventually extending Nato to include the former Communist countries of Eastern Europe, and possibly even the former Soviet Union itself. From the point of view of the former Communist bloc, a transfer from the Warsaw Pact to Nato could offer improved military hardware, funding for their armed forces, and improved security. Negotiations were soon under way.

▶ **A new beginning – leaders of the former Communist states of Eastern Europe attend the final meeting of the Warsaw Pact.**

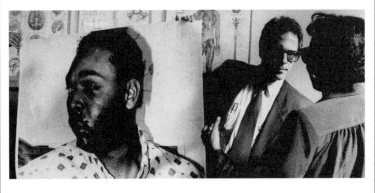

THE RODNEY KING AFFAIR

In March 1991 a young black motorist, Rodney King, was brutally beaten by four Los Angeles police officers. This not unusual case of police harassment became a public scandal because it was captured on video and shown on nationwide television. The police officers were put on trial, but on April 29, 1992 an all-white jury found them not guilty. This incomprehensible decision sparked the most destructive riots seen in the United States since the 1960s.

Poor blacks and Hispanics in Los Angeles' South Central district ran wild, attacking whites and Asians, looting, and setting fire to buildings. In one notorious incident that was also captured on video, a white truckdriver called Reginald Denny was pulled from the cab of his vehicle and savagely beaten in the street. The riots lasted for two days and nights, leaving more than 50 people dead and thousands injured.

The riots revealed the depth of the divisions in American society a quarter of a century after the apparent triumph of the civil rights movement. Black opinion was summed up by the *Los Angeles Sentinel*, the largest African American newspaper on the West coast, which stated: "The United States is on the verge of becoming a police state". Concerned liberal opinion was reflected in the *New York Times's* comment: "The acquittal of the policemen who clubbed Rodney King and the violent reaction in black communities showed us an American society that has lost its way".

King eventually won massive damages in a further court case, but the affair remained a powerful example of the racism prevalent in some American police forces and the anger stored up in the ghettos of America's major cities.

▲ **Rodney King following his unfortunate meeting with the LAPD. The acquittal of his attackers resulted in two days of rioting.**

GANDHI ASSASSINATED

On May 21, 1991, former Indian Prime Minster Rajiv Gandhi was assassinated by a suicide bomber at a Congress party election rally near Madras, in the southern Indian state of Tamil Nadu. The assassination was planned by Tamil extremists fighting for an independent state in neighbouring Sri Lanka.

Rajiv Gandhi was only three years old when his grandfather, Jawaharlal Nehru, became India's first Prime Minister at independence in 1947. The remarkable family dynasty continued to dominate Indian politics after Nehru's death in 1964 through Rajiv's mother, Indira Gandhi, who was Nehru's daughter. Rajiv's younger brother Sanjay was expected to inherit the leadership of the Congress Party, but his death in 1980 left Rajiv as the heir apparent. He duly became Prime Minister after his mother was assassinated by members of her Sikh guard in 1984. He resigned in 1989 after Congress was defeated in a general election.

At the time of Rajiv's death, no member of his family was old enough or of sufficient standing to inherit the family mantle: an era in the political life of independent India had come to an end.

▲ Although he was part of India's greatest ruling dynasty, Rajiv Gandhi had never actively sought a career in politics.

FAILED COUP ROCKS THE SOVIET UNION

By August 1991, the Soviet Union was careering down the path to disintegration. President Mikhail Gorbachev was struggling to maintain his liberal and democratic reforms while still upholding the territorial integrity of the Soviet state and the central role of the Communist party. As the Soviet Union's constituent republics began lining up to demand independence, a Union Treaty was brought forward which would turn the USSR into a looser association of sovereign republics. This treaty was due to come into force on August 20.

Most of the Soviet Union's Communist leadership felt that the time had come when the reforms must be stopped or the state that Lenin had created would disintegrate. On August 19, Vice-President Gennady Yanayev and a group of other leading Communists, including the Prime Minister, the minister of the interior, and the head of the KGB,

▲ Russian President Boris Yeltsin led the opposition to the failed Communist coup that signalled the end of the Soviet Union.

declared a state of emergency, banned all demonstrations, and sent tanks out on to the streets of Moscow.

President Gorbachev was on holiday in the Crimea. He was invited to back the coup but refused, and was put under house arrest. In Moscow, the Russian republic's President, Boris Yeltsin, led defiance of the crackdown, at one point climbing on top of a tank outside the Russian parliament to denounce the organizers of the state of emergency. Their's was, as it turned out, a thoroughly half-hearted attempt to turn the tide. Yanayev and his colleagues made no effort to suppress opposition on the streets or to arrest Yeltsin and other prominent reformers. On August 21, they quietly accepted defeat.

Flown back from the Crimea, Gorbachev was publicly humiliated by Yeltsin, who insisted that he read aloud a list of the people who had led the coup – all of them among his closest associates. Gorbachev resigned as First Secretary of the discredited Communist Party. The activities of the party were suspended and its assets were seized. The end of the Soviet Union was only a matter of time.

'91

YUGOSLAVIA GRIPPED BY CIVIL WAR

In 1991, the worsening political situation in post-Communist Yugoslavia slipped into outright civil war. Since 1980, the country had been ruled by a collective presidency made up of the leaders of each of the constituent republics and regions. The members of the collective presidency took it in turns to be chairman. In June 1991, however, Slobodan Milosevic, the ultra-nationalist Serbian President, blocked the Croatian leader Stipe Mesic from assuming the chairmanship. As a consequence, both Croatia and Slovenia ceded from Yugoslavia and declared themselves independent states. The Serb-dominated Yugoslav Army immediately went into action against both of the breakaway republics.

The attempt to intimidate Slovenia was swiftly abandoned, with the Yugoslav Army forced to withdraw in July. Croatia was another matter. The animosity between Serbs and Croats made this the bitterest of Yugoslavia's historic ethnic rivalries. The existence of a large Serbian minority inside Croatia gave a pretext and motive for a full-scale onslaught. The Yugoslav Army was joined by Croatian-Serb irregulars as heavy fighting escalated in September.

The Serbs launched major attacks on the towns of Osijek, Vukovar, and Vinkovici in northeast Croatia, near the border with Hungary, while in October the historic Adriatic port of Dubrovnik, a Croatian city considered one of the world's architectural treasures, was shelled by Yugoslav artillery.

A UN-brokered cease-fire came into effect in January 1992, by which time 30 per cent of Croatia was in Serbian hands. The cease-fire was only temporary, however, allowing the warring factions to reorganize their troops. The worst was still to come.

NEWS IN BRIEF

May
- President Mengistu of Ethiopia flees into exile; rebels capture the capital, Addis Ababa
- Free elections in Nepal
- Winnie Mandela convicted on kidnap and assault charges in South Africa
- Edith Cresson appointed France's first woman Prime Minister
- President of the Bundesbank resigns over policy dispute with the German government
- Zviad Gamsakhurdia elected President of Georgia

June
- Islamic fundamentalist agitation force resignation of Algerian Prime Minister Mouloud Hamrouche
- Strikes force resignation of Albanian government
- South African racist Population Registration Act repealed
- Colombian drug cartel leader Pablo Escobar Gavira surrenders to the government
- German Bundestag votes to move government from Bonn to Berlin
- Narasimha Rao becomes Prime Minister of India
- Deaths of British actors Dame Peggy Ashcroft and Lord Miles (Bernard Miles)

July
- EC imposes arms embargo on Yugoslavia
- START arms reduction treaty signed by the US and USSR

MYSTERIOUS DEATH OF NEWSPAPER TYCOON

On November 5, 1991, the flamboyant publishing tycoon Robert Maxwell was found dead in the Atlantic off the Canary Islands. He had been holidaying on board his yacht *Lady Ghislaine*. Since he disappeared from the deck in the early hours of the morning, he is suspected of having committed suicide, although the death may have been accidental.

Born in Czechoslovakia, Maxwell was a self-made millionaire who was often criticized for using sharp practices to expand his business empire. His response to criticism and revelations about his colourful life often involved a ruthless resort to libel lawyers, which made him much feared by investigative journalists. In politics he supported the Labour Party, and was a Labour MP from 1964 to 1970.

The revelation of the state of

▲ **Many still believe that Robert Maxwell committed suicide when he realized that his business empire was about to fall.**

Maxwell's business empire in the wake of his death certainly showed there was ample motive for him to have killed himself. Owner of newspapers such as the *Daily Mirror* and New York's *Daily News*, Maxwell had made labyrinthine business arrangements that concealed massive debts and heavy losses. In the months before he died, his creditors were closing in on him and he was engaged in a desperate struggle to prevent his empire going under. He had recently fraudulently taken £440 million from his employees' pension fund to stave off bankruptcy.

Within a month of his death, his companies were in receivership and his business affairs were under investigation by the serious fraud squad. His sons, Ian and Kevin, were cleared of fraud charges in 1996 after a long and expensive prosecution.

AIDS DEATHS CONTINUE

On November 24, 1991, singer Freddie Mercury, who made Queen one of the most successful rock bands of the 1970s, died of AIDS. The continuing menace of the disease was further highlighted by the revelation the same month that Earvin "Magic" Johnson, one of the most popular and successful American basketball players of all time, was infected with the HIV virus.

Both men showed, in different ways, how attitudes towards AIDS were evolving. Mercury, a flamboyant bisexual, had won widespread praise for publicly acknowledging that he had tested HIV positive. Far from alienating the public, his death from the disease provoked a wave of public sympathy and heavy sales of Queen back-list records.

The announcement by Magic Johnson that he was HIV positive challenged perceptions of the disease among the American public, especially because the basketball player credibly claimed that he had been infected through heterosexual sex. Most Americans had preferred to believe that AIDS was exclusively associated with homosexuals and drug abusers.

Johnson announced he was retiring from the sport so he could concentrate on raising AIDS awareness, but another prime motive for his retirement was the recognition that other players would hesitate to play against or share a dressing room with a man infected with HIV. A further step towards a rational attitude towards AIDS would be shown in 1996, when "Magic" Johnson briefly returned to professional basketball and was rapturously welcomed back.

▶ The highly publicized death of rock star Freddie Mercury raised public awareness and sympathy for AIDS sufferers.

HOSTAGES FREED

One of the most hopeful developments of 1991 was the freeing of almost all the hostages from Western countries being held by Islamic fundamentalist militants in Lebanon. The most prominent of these was Terry Waite, who had been kidnapped in Beirut in January 1987 while acting as a roving ambassador for the Archbishop of Canterbury – ironically, while on a mission to negotiate the release of other hostages.

In August 1991, journalist John McCarthy, who had been held in Beirut for more than five years, was released and reported that Waite was still alive and well. The release of the Archbishop of Canterbury's representative followed on November 18. The last American hostage, Terry Anderson, who had been held since March 1985, flew home in early December.

The hostages all had appalling stories to tell of how they had been treated, often kept for long periods in solitary confinement and darkness, under the constant threat of execution.

◀ After five years in captivity in the Lebanon, British journalist John McCarthy finally arrives back on home soil.

August
- Bangladesh reforms government system

September
- Incumbent government loses elections in Sweden
- Riots by miners demanding higher wages in Romania; government resigns
- Military coup in Haiti; President Jean-Bertrand Aristide flees
- Death of US jazz musician Miles Davis

October
- Anita Hill accuses US Supreme Court nominee Clarence Thomas of sexual harassment
- Incumbent Bulgarian government defeated in elections
- New coalition government under Carl Bildt formed in Sweden
- Dismissal of Prime Minister of Zaire by President Mobutu causes rioting
- Peace treaty agreed between Cambodian factions
- Free parliamentary elections in Poland produce no clear result
- President Kenneth Kaunda defeated in Zambian election

November
- Filip Dimitrov becomes non-Communist Prime Minister of Bulgaria
- Prince Sihanouk returns to Cambodia

December
- EEC sanctions on Yugoslavia lifted, apart from those on Serbia and Montenegro
- Kenyan general assembly votes to end one-party state
- Agreement on closer political union agreed by EC members at Maastricht in the Netherlands
- Paul Keating becomes Prime Minister of Australia
- Islamic National Front wins election in Algeria

NINETEEN·HUNDRED·AND·NINETY·ONE   **507**

'91 END OF THE SOVIET UNION

For most of its existence, the fact that the Soviet Union was a federal "Union of Soviet Socialist Republics" could be safely ignored, since all the republics were ruled by members of the Soviet Communist Party, under strict control from the Party centre in Moscow. When the authority of the Communist Party began to disintegrate amid the devastating economic collapse brought on by Soviet President Mikhail Gorbachev's *perestroika* policies, the republics offered an alternative power structure to fall back on as the centre fell apart.

The national groups that predominated in the different republics had diverse relationships with the Soviet Union, as they had had with the Russian Empire that had preceded it. Russia, Ukraine and Belorussia

▲ **Not a "Hammer and Sickle" in sight, the traditional Russian flag flies above the crowd heralding the final collapse of Soviet-style Communism.**

(White Russia) had long constituted the heartlands of what the outside world simply called "Russia". To the south and east were areas annexed during

Russia's imperial expansion in the eighteenth and nineteenth centuries, including Christian Georgia and Armenia, and predominantly Muslim republics such as Azerbaijan and Kazakhstan. The Baltic republics of Estonia, Latvia and Lithuania were special cases. They had enjoyed independence in the 1920s and 1930s, but were taken over by the Soviet Union at the start of World War Two.

Not surprisingly, it was in the Baltic states, where the legitimacy of Soviet rule had never been widely accepted, that the break up of the Soviet Union began. On March 11, 1990, Lithuania's President Vitautas Landsbergis unilaterally declared his republic independent of the Soviet Union. It had not been any part of Mikhail Gorbachev's plans to accept the disintegration of the Union over which he presided. The Soviet army was ordered on

to the streets of the Lithuanian capital, Vilnius. Undeterred, in May the other Baltic states, Latvia and Estonia, also declared their independence. But these were, for the time being, token gestures. The independence of the Baltic states was not recognized by the Soviet government nor by the rest of the world. In January 1991, unarmed demonstrators were gunned down by Soviet troops in Vilnius, as they tried to prevent the Soviet authorities taking over the local radio and television station. Soviet troops also seized key buildings in the Latvian capital, Riga. These brutal operations were proof that the will to preserve the Soviet Union still existed.

Another part of the Soviet Union where disintegration began early was in the Trans-Caucasian region, near the border with Turkey. In the small republics of

▲ **President Vitautas Landsbergis of Lithuania, one of the first Soviet states to declare independence.**

Armenia, Azerbaijan and Georgia national feelings ran high. By 1990, Armenia and Azerbaijan were at war over the disputed territory of Nagorno-Karabakh, while Azerbaijanis were simultaneously battling with the Soviet army to assert their independence. In Georgia, pro-independence demonstrators were attacked by security forces, stimulating rather than dampening demands for a break with Moscow. In April 1991, Georgia became the fourth Soviet republic formally to assert its independence.

The potential loss of the Baltic and Transcaucasian republics was not in itself a threat to the continued existence of the Soviet Union, since they were marginal territories with only a small percentage of the Soviet population. In the course of 1990, however, free elections in the larger republics consistently produced majority backing for at least an increased measure of autonomy, if not complete sovereignty. During the summer, both the Russian Federation, under its newly elected President, Boris Yeltsin, and the Ukraine opted for "sovereignty", remaining within the Soviet Union but asserting their right to pass their own legislation overriding Soviet law, and to conduct their own economic policy, including independently negotiating economic agreements with other republics.

In an attempt to accommodate these changes without causing the total break-up of the Moscow-ruled state, a Union Treaty was devised, replacing the Union of Soviet Socialist Republics with a looser federation. It was the prospect of this move that provoked most of the top Soviet Communist leadership, apart from Gorbachev, into imposing a state of emergency on August 19, 1991. The abject failure of this attempted coup sealed the fate of the Soviet Union. The Soviet Communist Party was closed down and on September 5 the Union of Soviet Socialist Republics was formally replaced by a Union of Sovereign States, still led by Gorbachev. The following day, Latvia, Lithuania, and Estonia were formally recognized as independent states.

The initiative now lay wholly with Boris Yeltsin, confirmed as President of the Russia Federation by popular vote in June 1991 and with his prestige immeasurably enhanced by his leadership of resistance to the August coup. He was soon in negotiations with the leaders of Ukraine and Belarus (formerly Belorussia) and on December 8 the three announced that they were forming a Commonwealth of Independent States (CIS). At a meeting in Alma Ata, capital of Kazakhstan, on December 21, eight other republics agreed to join the CIS. Only the three Baltic states and Georgia remained outside. Mikhail Gorbachev, now President of a country that no longer existed, announced his resignation on December 25.

The CIS turned out to be an almost entirely fictitious entity. The constituent republics of the former Soviet Union became fully independent, and in some cases mutually hostile, states. Ukraine and Russia, for example, were soon bickering over which of them should control the former Soviet Union's important Black Sea fleet. Far from solving the problems of the territory of the former Soviet Union, the break-up of the USSR ushered in a difficult period of local conflicts and continuing economic decline.

▼ **Boris Yeltsin, President of Russia, would soon emerge as one of the more colourful leaders on the world stage.**

'92 | WAR ESCALATES IN BOSNIA

The focus of the conflict in Yugoslavia moved away from Croatia to Bosnia-Herzegovina in 1992. That Bosnia should become a major battleground seemed inevitable, given its ethnic and religious diversity: 44 per cent of the population was Muslim, 31 per cent Serb and 17 per cent Croat. The various groups were scattered across Bosnia in a patchwork of small communities, making any division on ethnic lines virtually impossible. Because Bosnia lacked any overall ethnic majority, different minorities were encouraged to stake competing claims for overall territorial sovereignty.

Referendums supervised by the Bosnian government were held in February and March 1992 and produced a 63 per cent vote in favour of independence from Yugoslavia. In the face of strident Serb opposition, a new predominantly Muslim Republic of Bosnia was proclaimed, which in April was recognized by the European Community and the United States. The Serbs retaliated on March 27 by setting up their own Republic of Bosnia which, they insisted, was to be an integral part of Yugoslavia. During March and April the better armed and equipped Serbs began to grab as much territory as they could, causing thousands of refugees to flee their homes, seeking safety in their own ethnic strongholds.

The opening of hostilities in Bosnia produced a particularly brutal type of war, and a new phrase entered the language:

▲ **A Croatian Catholic refugee with the few possessions she has managed to salvage after the bombing of her home.**

"ethnic cleansing". A predominantly Serb tactic, ethnic cleansing entailed the removal of all non-Serbs from an area, either by driving them out or by simply killing them in their houses. Massacres of whole communities became a frequent event, as did the systematic rape of Muslim women by Serb troops. Internment camps were set up where prisoners were subjected to slow starvation and to the most horrifying tortures. Such Serb atrocities led to reprisal

massacres by Bosnian Croats and Muslim para-military units. By the end of 1992 more than a million people had been displaced from their homes, and tens of thousands had been killed. A level of barbarity not seen since World War Two had descended upon 1990s Europe.

The European Community, the United States and the United Nations all attempted to bring an end to the fighting, but with the refusal of all sides to accept their mediation the war continued.

Humanitarian agencies sent relief supplies into Bosnia and UN personnel monitored the rapidly deteriorating situation. A peace conference held in London in August came to nothing, while the despatch of substantial numbers of UN peacekeeping forces did little to reduce the intensity of the fighting.

Although Yugoslavia claimed to have no direct control over the activities of the Bosnian Serbs, the UN Security Council primarily blamed the Belgrade government of Slobodan Milosevic for the war in Bosnia. On May 30, 1992, the UN imposed economic sanctions against Serbia, including the freezing of international assets, and the refusal to recognize the new rump Yugoslavia as a continuation of the former state. In international terms, Yugoslavia was the "former Yugoslavia".

The UN's sanctions were undermined by the attitude of Russia and Greece, who both gave tacit support and aid to their co-religionists in Serbia. Oil supplies shipped along the Danube reached Belgrade with the collusion of the governments of Romania and Bulgaria. Despite these sanction-busting measures, the Serbian economy suffered and inflation soared.

Although the Bosnian Serbs were the main aggressors in Bosnia, the Croatian Serbs, supported by the new right-wing government of Franjo Tudjman in Croatia, began to consider ways of taking control of parts of Bosnia. Military clashes between Croats and Muslims became more common (although, at times, the two collaborated when fighting the Serbs). Muslim fears over Croat intentions were confirmed when, on July 3, the predominantly Croat area of western Herzegovina proclaimed itself an autonomous region, to be called Herceg-Bosna.

The intransigence of the leaders on all sides was the chief reason why peace efforts were doomed before they began. A former psychiatrist and poet, Radovan Karadzic became the leader of the new Serb Republic of Bosnia, and was supported by his hard-line Army commander in chief, General Ratko Mladic. Setting up their "capital" in the town of Pale, the Bosnian Serbs pursued an aggressive "Greater Serbia" policy. Their confidence in eventual victory was bolstered by the support given to them by President Milosevic.

Whereas the Serbs were openly contemptuous of international opinion, the Sarajevo-based Muslim government of Bosnia developed a highly successful policy of courting the world's media. No opportunity was lost to present the case of Serbian aggression against "poor little Bosnia", and, for the most part, the Muslims were successful in ascribing all blame for the conflict to the Serbs. Although this assertion was broadly true, it carefully

▲ **Members of the Croatian National Guard make a spirited defence of Kostajnica on the Bosnian border. The small town was eventually evacuated.**

concealed the facts that the Muslim government, headed by President Alija Izetbegovic, had its own concealed agenda of territorial and financial aggrandisement, and that it could be as ruthless as the governments of the Serbs or Croats in achieving its goals.

Although many people – especially in the media – attacked Western politicians for not taking a more decisive role in trying to end the conflict, it was difficult to know what, in fact, they could do. Few nations wanted to commit ground troops to a "peacemaking" rather than "peacekeeping" role; peacemaking would lead to heavy casualties which would be deemed unacceptable. The only other alternative was the use of air power, which would minimize casualties but would have only limited effect on preventing the fighting on the ground. Clearly, the Yugoslavia problem would continue to occupy the world's attention for years to come.

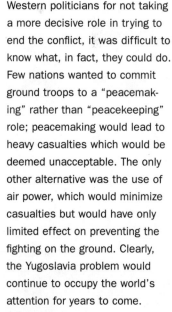

◀ **A group of young Bosnian Muslims bravely shelter from the Serb bombing of their capital city, Sarajevo.**

'92

THE MAASTRICHT TREATY

On February 7, 1992, representatives of the 12 member states of the European Community signed the Treaty of European Union, known as the Maastricht Treaty after the Dutch town in which the signing took place. The treaty committed the member states to European Monetary Union (EMU) and eventual political union. There was to be a single currency, the Ecu, a European Central Bank, and common foreign and defence policies. After a number of setbacks, including an initial defeat for the proposals in a referendum in Denmark, the treaty came into force in November 1993. The European Community duly became the European Union.

Implementation of the treaty was never going to be straightforward, especially given the many reservations about its content covertly held by the signatories. When Europe officially became a single market without frontiers on January 1, 1993, it was typical that four states, Britain, Ireland, Denmark and Greece, retained the

▲ **Even among the member states, support for wholesale European integration was not uniformly popular.**

right to demand that travellers show passports at entry. Even more difficult was the proposed route of progress towards a single currency. All 12 member were first to join an Exchange Rate Mechanism which would keep their national currencies broadly in line. They were then to fulfil a number of "convergence" criteria, including low inflation and the reduction of national debts.

Membership of the ERM soon proved too difficult for the UK. In September 1992, fierce

speculation against sterling on the international money markets threatened to force it below its ERM valuation. Despite panic measures, including a hike in base interest rates from 10 to 15 per cent and the spending of around £15 billion of the UK's reserves to support sterling, the British government was eventually forced to pull out of the ERM a nd to allow the pound to float downward. This crisis fundamentally undermined popular confidence in John Major's recently re-elected government, but paved the way for an export-led economic boom based on the drop in the value of the pound, which made the UK's exports more competitive.

From the time of its withdrawal from the ERM, the UK was placed at a distance from the mainstream of progress towards monetary union, an alienation that was increased by the hostility of some political groups, particularly on the right of the Conservative Party, to any further progress towards European integration.

TYSON ON RAPE CHARGE

In March 1992, 25-year-old world heavyweight boxing champion Mike Tyson was sentenced to 10 years in prison for rape and "criminal deviate conduct". Tyson had been found guilty of raping Desiree Washington, a contestant in the Miss Black America beauty pageant.

The trial and conviction raised questions of both racial and sexual politics. Although both Tyson and his accuser were black, there was a widespread feeling among black radicals that the case had been brought because the white authorities were "out to get" the champion. Other people

were disturbed by the specific grounds for the accusation. Washington had come willingly to Tyson's room, and had only complained about what had happened there much later.

Tyson was eventually released from detention in March 1995: four years of his sentence were suspended and another three years taken off for good behaviour. But he was soon in trouble again. His licence to box was revoked for

18 months after he bit a chunk out of his opponent Evander Holyfield's ear during a world championship bout in June 1997.

▶ **Mike Tyson's continual brushes with the law prevented him from living up to the potential of his early career.**

MAJOR WINS UK ELECTION

After the downfall of Margaret Thatcher in 1990, the Labour Party hoped and expected that its long period out of office would soon come to an end. Thatcher's replacement, John Major, was an uncharismatic figure who seemed ill-suited to rebuild the Conservative Party's popularity. The poll tax, the main cause of Thatcher's downfall, was hastily ditched, but many Tories entered the 1992 general election with a tacit conviction that the time had come for the other side to have a chance to bat.

Opinion polls during the run-up to the election consistently foretold a Labour win. Labour leader Neil Kinnock allowed himself to be the focus of a triumphalist campaign that doubtless irritated many voters with its complacency. More were alienated by the honesty of Labour's shadow chancellor of the exchequer, the prudent John Smith, who spelled out exactly what tax increases would be needed to finance Labour's programme.

In the election on April 9, the Conservatives polled almost 42 per cent of the votes cast to Labour's 34 per cent, giving the Tories an adequate Commons majority of 21. Shocked and humiliated by his second consecutive general election defeat, Neil Kinnock resigned as Labour party leader. John Smith was chosen to replace him.

▲ Running against the predictions of some pollsters, John Major won a fourth successive term in office for the Conservative Party.

NORIEGA LOCKED UP

In July 1992, a US court in Miami, Florida, sentenced General Manuel Noriega, former dictator of Panama, to 40 years in prison for drug trafficking. He had been a link in the supply chain from Colombian cocaine barons to the United States.

Noriega had risen to power in Panama as head of the feared National Guard. He enjoyed American support despite human rights abuses and gave assistance to the CIA in a number of undercover projects in Central America. The Americans distanced themselves from him in 1988, however, after a US grand jury indicted him on drugs and money-laundering charges.

In October 1989, an attempted coup against Noriega failed, and US President George Bush was criticized for not intervening to support Noriega's overthrow. The following December, taking as a pretext the need to protect American citizens in Panama, US forces invaded the country, forcing Noriega to take refuge in the papal nuncio's residence. When he eventually gave himself up, he was arrested.

▶ Panamanian leader General Manuel Noriega was also shown to be a central figure in the supply of drugs from Colombia.

'92

NEWS IN BRIEF
....

June
- Waldemar Pawlak becomes Polish Prime Minister
- Fidel Ramos wins presidential elections in the Philippines
- Over 30 people killed in alleged tribal violence in Boipatong in South Africa
- Israeli general election won by the Labour Party
- Algerian President Mohammed Boudiaf assassinated by Islamic extremists

July
- Ali Kafi becomes Algerian President
- Abdul Sabbur Fareed becomes Prime Minister of Afghanistan
- Czechoslovak President Vaclav Havel resigns following Slovak moves for independence
- Twenty-fifth Olympic games open in Barcelona
- Emergency economic legislation passed in Italy to prevent bankruptcy of government
- Former East German leader Erich Honecker forced to return to Germany to face manslaughter charges

August
- General elections in Bahamas: Lyndon Pindling stands down after 25-year rule
- Hurricane Andrew causes devastation in Florida and the Caribbean
- Air exclusion zones imposed by the USA and allies in southern Iraq
- Cease-fire in Afghan civil war

CLINTON ELECTED PRESIDENT

In November 1992, Democrat William Jefferson Clinton, the governor of Arkansas, was elected President of the United States, ending 12 years of Republican presidents in the White House. Clinton attracted 43.7 million votes, compared with 38.2 million for the incumbent George Bush, and 19.2 million for maverick independent Ross Perot.

On his way to this triumph, the 46-year-old Clinton had survived a number of damaging allegations about his past. In January 1992, an Arkansas state employee, Gennifer Flowers, had come forward to say that she and Bill Clinton had had intermittent adulterous sexual relations from 1977 to 1989. She produced tapes of phone conversations with Clinton which seemed to confirm her story. It was widely assumed that Clinton was finished. But he went on television, his wife Hillary beside him, and categorically denied having had sex with Flowers. He did not deny that he had been guilty of "wrongdoing" in his marriage, but said that such things were all in the past. His audience loved it.

Further revelations centered on Clinton's alleged evasion of the draft during the Vietnam War. Once again, extremely embarrassing evidence was produced, but "Slick Willie", as he was now being dubbed by his opponents, simply shrugged it off, as he did suggestions of corruption during his long period as Arkansas's governor.

Clinton's opponents made out a good case that he was an unsuitable man to be President of the United States, but the American people did not care. They liked the man and they liked his policies: a centre-of-the-road Democrat line combining balanced budgets and respect for business with concern for minorities and plans to improve health care. Bill Clinton was to prove a very popular President.

▲ In spite of an endless succession of scandals relating to his private life, President Bill Clinton (right) has remained a popular figure.

ANGLICANS APPROVE WOMEN PRIESTS

On November 11, 1992, the General Synod of the Church of England passed the Priests (Ordination of Women) Measure. After 20 years of debate within the Anglican church, women were at last to be allowed to join the priesthood.

The new measure was approved by around two-thirds of the clerical and lay members of the Synod, who had responded to an appeal by the Archbishop of Canterbury, Dr George Carey, to "take the risk of faith". But a large part of the minority opposed to women priests felt very deeply on the subject. Conservative politician Ann Widdecombe immediately announced she was quitting the Church of England, and her colleague, Minister of Agriculture John Gummer, resigned from his lay membership of the Synod, saying the decision was without "authority of scripture or tradition".

The Anglican leadership bent over backwards to accommodate

the discontented, agreeing that bishops could refuse the ordination of women within their own dioceses. "Episcopal visitors", dubbed "flying bishops" in the press, would be available for those who disagreed with their own bishop's line on women priests. Efforts to form a breakaway church came to nothing, though many Anglican priests, both married and unmarried, moved to the Catholic church, and the measure received royal assent in November 1993.

▶ **Dragging the church into the twentieth century – the decision to allow women priests was by no means universally popular.**

INTERVENTION IN SOMALIA

On December 9, 1992, the first contingents of a 28,000-strong US military force went ashore at Mogadishu, capital of Somalia. Dubbed Operation Restore Hope, the US mission was essentially humanitarian – to allow the distribution of food supplies to the starving.

Somalia had descended into chaotic civil war after the overthrow of President Mohammed Siyad Barre in January 1991. Such authority as existed was exercised by gunmen owing allegiance to local warlords, of whom the most powerful was General Mohammed Farah Aydid. The collapse of law and order and the disruption of communications rapidly brought the poverty-stricken east African nation to the verge of mass starvation. Relief agencies estimated that five million people were at risk, but the distribution of food aid was virtually impossible, as armed bands regularly looted relief supplies.

It was with the full backing of the United Nations that President George Bush sent in American troops in December 1992. Other countries agreed to contribute to the US initiative, under the UN banner, increasing the overall size of the intervention force to 35,000. These soldiers swiftly fanned out across Somalia, taking control of key areas and ensuring that aid convoys were able to reach the starving. Most Somalis broadly welcomed the humanitarian mission and there was almost no resistance.

In June 1993, however, the intervention in Somalia turned sour. The American forces saw it as part of their mission to disarm the warring factions, a goal they pursued with an aggressive determination that angered General Aydid. On June 5, 24 Pakistani UN soldiers were killed by Aydid's men in an ambush. The UN Security Council responded by issuing a warrant for Aydid's arrest. The Americans launched a full-scale assault on his Mogadishu headquarters, deploying helicopter gunships as well as ground forces in the middle of a densely populated area. Aydid escaped, but many civilians were killed. Henceforth, US forces were operating in an openly hostile city.

Over the following months, the death toll rapidly mounted as clashes with gunmen spread. In one incident in September, US helicopters fired on a Somali crowd including women and children which they believed was threatening American soldiers. More than 200 people were killed. On October 3, another botched attempt to capture Aydid resulted in gun battles in which 18 US soldiers died. For the American public, it was enough. President Bill Clinton announced that US troops would pull out as soon as they decently could.

Once again the Americans had learned how easily intervention in foreign countries, even with the best intentions, could go wrong. Unfortunately, the experience of Somalia helped discourage the United States from intervening in Rwanda in 1994, when genocide might have been stopped by timely action.

▲ **US peacekeeping troops confiscate arms from two Somali youths in an attempt to bring an end to the widespread looting.**

CZECHOSLOVAKIA SPLITS

When Czechoslovakia over-threw its Communist government in 1989, it was dubbed the "Velvet Revolution" because of the relatively non-violent and civilized way that the transition to democracy was managed. Within three years, however, the Velvet Revolution was followed by the "Velvet Divorce", as the newly established Czech and Slovak Federal Republic split in two, again without violence or bitter acrimony.

Czechoslovakia was founded in 1918, a union of two different Slav peoples, the Czechs and Slovaks, as its name made clear. After the takeover of the country by Nazi Germany in 1939, Slovak nationalists set up a nominally independent Slovak Republic, but it was little more than a Soviet puppet state, and Czechoslovakia was recreated in 1945. Nonetheless, many Slovaks remained discontented about domination by the Czechs, who outnumbered them two-to-one and were, in general, more prosperous.

The advent of democracy in 1990 allowed Slovak nationalism to resurface. The post-Communist constitution created a dual system, with a Federal Assembly and a government to rule the whole of Czechoslovakia, and with elected Czech and Slovak national councils and governments with considerable powers over their own regions. In elections in June 1992, however, Vladimir Meciar's Movement for a Democratic Slovakia, a party committed to independence for Slovakia, won the support of a majority of Slovak voters. At the same time, Czechs voted in Vaclav Klaus's Civic Democratic Party. Klaus was committed to thoroughgoing free market reforms, a policy opposed by Slovaks who wanted continued state support for industry. Klaus and his party decided that Slovakia, as a poor and backward region, was a drag on their plans for economic progress and actively supported "a reasonable and quiet separation".

Czechoslovakia's President and hero of the struggle against the Communists, Vaclav Havel, opposed the "divorce" and chose to resign rather than preside over it. A deal was soon struck between Klaus and Meciar. On January 1, 1993, Czechoslovakia became the separate Czech and Slovak Republics. There were scant popular rejoicings over the

▲ Although he was opposed to the division of Czechoslovakia, Vaclav Havel took the position of President of the Czech Republic.

event, with even the Slovak nationalists sobered by the obvious economic difficulties they faced. The government of the new Slovak Republic was soon coming under international criticism for the way it handled relations with minorities, especially the Roma people (gypsies). In Prague, Havel returned to take up the presidency of the new Czech Republic.

THE QUEEN PAYS HER TAXES

In February 1993, UK Prime Minister John Major announced that the Royal Family were renouncing many of their financial privileges. Henceforth, the Queen would pay income tax on her personal earnings and capital gains tax on income from her investments like any other individual. The Prince of Wales also agreed to pay full tax on his income from the Duchy of Cornwall, estimated at £3 million a year. At the same time, all the Royal Family except the Queen, Prince Philip, and the Queen Mother would cease to receive payments from the Civil List, the £7.9 million of public money received by the Queen every year for the fulfilment of her state duties. Instead, the costs of the public duties of junior members of the Royal Family would be met by the Queen.

The move was a response to a broad tide of criticism of the Royal Family that had gathered strength in the previous year, fuelled by sensational reporting, especially in the tabloids, of the private affairs of several members of the Royal Family. Most in the public eye were the Prince and Princess of Wales and the Duchess of York, all of whom had been shown to have had liaisons outside their marriages. Most sensational of all in 1992 was the publication of a "biography" of Princess Diana, *Diana: Her True Story* by Andrew Morton, which revealed the Princess's repeated suicide attempts and her alleged mistreatment by her husband and his family.

The Queen referred in public to 1992 as an *annus horribilis*, marked by the separations of the Prince and Princess of Wales and the Duke and Duchess of York and a fire that had destroyed part of Windsor Castle, though partly redeemed by her daughter, Anne's second marriage in December. For the first time in over a century, there seemed a chance that republicanism could take root again in Britain.

▲ The fire that devastated Windsor Castle was the result of an electrical fault in the private chapel.

TERROR AT THE TWIN TOWERS

On February 26, 1993, international terrorism arrived in the United States. A group of Islamic terrorists loaded a bomb on to a truck and drove it into a car park beneath the 381-metre (1,250-foot) twin towers of the World Trade Center in New York. The bomb exploded at lunchtime, starting a raging fire which sent smoke billowing up to the 96th floor of the 110-floor building, with its 55,000 workers. The explosion killed six people and injured thousands more, mostly with respiratory problems caused by breathing in fumes.

It was eventually established that the mastermind behind the bombing was a mysterious figure known as Ramzi Yousef, whose national origins were unclear. He left the United States on the night of the bombing but was arrested in Pakistan two years later and extradited. At his trial in New York in 1996, Yousef emerged as a figure whose

▲ Emergency vehicles surround the twin towers of the World Trade Center, the second tallest office complex in the world.

grandiose terrorist schemes were fortunately married to a great technical incompetence. The car park bomb had been intended to topple one of the World Trade Center towers against the other, an unlikely achievement, though Yousef believed it would kill tens of thousands of people. He had also planned to plant bombs in 12 American airliners, hoping to kill some 4,000 passengers simultaneously, although his only actual bombing of an airliner had killed one passenger but failed to down the plane.

Yousef's intention seems to have been to shock the United States into withdrawing its support for the state of Israel. The US federal court sentenced him to effective solitary confinement for life. Four other Muslims were also convicted for their roles in the bombing.

- Rupert Murdoch purchases Asian Star TV satellite television company
- Films released during the year include Jane Campion's *The Piano*, Steven Spielberg's *Schindler's List* and *Jurassic Park*, Andrew Davis's *The Fugitive*, Harold Ramis's *Groundhog Day* and Tran Anh Hung's *The Scent of Green Papaya*
- Andrew Lloyd Webber's musical version of *Sunset Boulevard* opens in London
- Books published this year include *A Suitable Boy* by Vikram Seth and *Paddy Clarke Ha Ha Ha* by Roddy Doyle
- Popular songs of the year include "Could it Be Magic" by Take That and "Boom! Shake the Room" by Jazzy Jeff and the Fresh Prince

January
- Single market of the European Community comes into force
- USA and Russia sign START 2 nuclear arms reduction treaty
- Government troops in Angola capture Huambo from UNITA forces
- Allied air strikes carried out on southern Iraq
- Elections in Haiti boycotted by population
- Hillary Clinton appointed to head task force on US health reform
- President Clinton orders military to lift ban on homosexual servicemen
- Deaths of US jazz trumpeter and be-bop pioneer Dizzy Gillespie, film actress Audrey Hepburn and Russian-born ballet dancer Rudolf Nureyev

February
- War crimes tribunal for crimes committed in the former Yugoslavia formed by the UN
- First direct elections to Cuban national assembly
- Deaths of British footballer Bobby Moore, US tennis star Arthur Ashe and actress Lillian Gish

'93

IRA BOMBINGS HIT HOME

In the spring of 1993, an IRA bombing campaign in mainland Britain was in full swing, as the terrorists continued their policy of trying to make the cost of staying in Northern Ireland unacceptably high for the British government and people. On March 20, two quite small devices were left in litter bins in a shopping centre in Warrington, Cheshire. Exploding in the middle of the day, they killed two children, Jonathan Ball, aged 3 and Timothy Parry, aged 12. About 50 other people were injured, some of them gravely.

The childrens' deaths aroused widespread condemnation. The IRA tried to distance itself from the consequences of its action, laying the blame for the deaths "squarely at the door of the British authorities who deliberately failed to act on precise and adequate warnings". This version of events was indignantly rejected by the police. A swiftly assembled group called "Peace Initiative 93" responded to the bombing by organizing peace rallies which were attended by thousands in London, Dublin and Belfast.

The IRA had no intention of calling off its campaign, however. On Saturday April 24, a huge bomb was left in a truck in Bishopsgate, in the heart of the City of London. When it exploded it not only killed a passer-by and injured 40 others, but also wrecked the prestigious office building of the Hong Kong and Shanghai Bank, the NatWest Tower and several other office blocks. Damage was estimated at around £1 billion.

The Bishopsgate bomb represented the first time that the IRA had managed to deliver a serious blow to the British economy. Large-scale security measures, including permanent police roadblocks at weekends, were put in place in the City in an effort to make a repetition of such an attack on one of the world's major financial centres impossible.

▲ **Members of the public lay wreaths to commemorate the deaths of two children, killed by an IRA bomb attack in Warrington, Cheshire.**

NEWS IN BRIEF

March
- UNITA retakes Huambo
- Doctor shot dead by anti-abortion extremists in USA
- Labour Party re-elected for fifth term in Australia
- Russian Congress votes to limit powers of Russian President and defeats constitutional reforms introduced by President Yeltsin
- North Korea retracts its agreement to nuclear Non-Proliferation Treaty
- Ezer Weizman elected President of Israel
- Edouard Balladur becomes Prime Minister of France, following general elections

April
- ANC leader Chris Hani assassinated in South Africa
- President Yeltsin wins vote of confidence in Russia
- Former President of Brazil, Fernando Collor de Mello, indicted on corruption charges
- Tennis champion Monica Seles is stabbed during a match in Germany

May
- President Ranasinghe Premadasa of Sri Lanka assassinated
- Denmark approves Maastricht Treaty in second referendum
- Eritrea gains independence from Ethiopia
- Uffizi Gallery and art works damaged in bomb explosion in Florence, Italy
- Five Turkish women killed in racially motivated attack by neo-Nazis in Germany

SIEGE AT WACO

On February 28, 1993, about 100 agents of the US Federal Bureau of Alcohol, Tobacco and Firearms (ATF) stormed the compound of the Branch Davidian sect in Waco, Texas, where alleged violations of firearms legislation had taken place. Under circumstances that are still controversial, a gun battle broke out in which ten people were killed, including four

◀ **The Waco headquarters of the Branch Davidians goes up in flames. 82 people died, leader David Koresh among them.**

ATF agents. The compound was put under siege by federal agents and a long stand-off began.

The Branch Davidians were a long-established offshoot of the far larger Seventh Day Adventist religious movement. They were famous for having wrongly predicted the Second Coming of Christ in 1959. Since 1986, the Branch Davidians had been led by David Koresh (born Vernon Howell), a controversial figure regarded by opponents as deeply disturbed and manipulative. He had allegedly declared himself the "sinful Messiah" after a visit to Jerusalem in 1985. Koresh had been particularly successful in recruiting British followers, with

the result that almost half of the 95 people besieged in the compound were from Britain.

The federal authorities used every form of psychological pressure in an effort to induce the heavily armed Branch Davidians to surrender. But on April 19, after the siege had lasted 51 days, an assault was launched to drive the sect's members out. Despite the fact that there were known to be at least 17 children inside, tanks were sent in to smash holes in the walls of the building where Koresh and his followers were hiding. CS gas was then pumped through the holes. According to the authorities, those inside suicidally set

fire to the gas-filled building. Other sources suggest that the gas was ignited when federal forces fired into the building. Either way, the building was soon an inferno. Only eight of those inside survived.

Eighty-two Branch Davidians died at Waco, 33 of them British. The massacre became an obsession with American right-wing extremists who regarded themselves as engaged in a life-or-death struggle against the oppressive force of the federal authorities. Two years to the day after the Waco inferno, a federal building in Oklahoma City was bombed in a revenge attack that killed a further 168 people.

PALESTINE DEAL
PROMISES PEACE

On September 13, 1993, at the White House, Israeli Foreign Minister Shimon Peres and Mahmoud Abbas of the Palestine Liberation Organization (PLO) signed an historic agreement providing for limited Palestinian self-government in the Occupied Territories of Gaza and the West Bank. When the two delegations emerged to confront the press, PLO leader Yasser Arafat extended his hand to Israeli Prime Minister Yitzhak Rabin. Hesitantly, seeing little alternative, Rabin shook the proffered hand, giving Arafat the image he had wanted for the world's media – an image far more powerful than words or treaties.

Leader of the PLO for more than 25 years, Arafat had proved a great political survivor, bouncing back time and again from apparently humiliating defeat, and avoiding assassination despite the intense desire of the Israelis and many of his Palestinian opponents

▲ **Yitzhak Rabin, flanked by President Clinton and Yasser Arafat, signs the agreement that it was hoped would bring peace to the Middle East.**

to see him dead. In 1974 he had managed to have the PLO recognized as the official representative of the Palestinian people by the United Nations, the basis for his ability in 1993 to negotiate on their behalf. Beginning as an out-and-out terrorist, he had trimmed his sails to the wind and ended up, in Palestinian terms, a moderate, persuading the PLO to accept recognition of the state of Israel

as the price to be paid for some form of Palestinian independence in the Occupied Territories.

Both Rabin and Arafat were aware that they had a difficult task ahead persuading hardliners in their respective constituencies to accept implementation of the step-by-step agreement – cautiously termed a "Declaration of Principles". Only time could tell where it would lead.

THE JAMES BULGER MURDER CASE

▲ **A final siting of two-year-old James Bulger taken by shopping mall security cameras shortly after his abduction.**

On February 12, 1993, two-year-old James Bulger disappeared from a busy shopping precinct in Bootle, Liverpool, where he had gone with his mother. Four days later his body was found alongside a railway line 5 km (3 miles) away. Security cameras in the precinct had captured the moment when he was abducted, showing him being led away by two older children. Ten days after the killing, two ten-year-old boys, Robert Thompson and Jon Venables, were charged with kidnapping and murder.

The case provoked a wave of moral outrage. When the two boys appeared at a local court they were assailed by a furious crowd, forcing the authorities to shift the hearings to a court in Preston. Politicians leapt forward to proclaim a breakdown in society. Home Secretary Kenneth Clarke spoke of "a loss of purpose and a loss of values" and introduced a new kind of custodial sentence for child offenders. Prime Minister John Major declared a "crusade against crime" and said society should "condemn a little more and understand a little less".

The boys, tried in an adult court, were found guilty in November and sentenced to be detained "during Her Majesty's pleasure". The trial judge suggested this should mean a minimum of eight years; the Lord Chief Justice upped this to 10 years; and the new Home Secretary, Michael Howard, intervened to order the boys to serve at least 15 years.

As emotions cooled, more rational voices made themselves heard suggesting that children who committed atrocious crimes were in a very real sense as much victims as those who suffered at their hands. In June 1997, the Law Lords upheld an appeal court ruling that Howard had exceeded his powers in raising the boys' minimum sentence to 15 years.

BOSNIA'S AGONY CONTINUES

The three-sided war in Bosnia, in which Serbs, Croats, and Muslims vied for advantage, was still on in 1993. But the year opened with at least the hope of more effective peace negotiations. As part of an initiative by the European Union and the United Nations, a peace plan was proposed by Lord Owen, a former

▶ **Towns and villages were reduced to rubble as warring factions in the former Yugoslavia continued to fight each other.**

British foreign secretary and US politician Cyrus Vance in February 1993. The Vance-Owen plan proposed dividing Bosnia into 10 autonomous provinces, based mainly on their ethnic affiliation, but with guarantees for balanced representation for the minorities in each area. In territorial terms, the Serbs would receive 46 per cent of the land, the Muslims would get 30 per cent, and the Croats 24 per cent.

Initially, the three factions in Bosnia reluctantly accepted the plan, but during meetings in Washington the talks collapsed, and in June Lord Owen despairingly announced that the plan had "been ripped up under our very eyes". As a holding measure, the UN Security Council announced on June 4 that six safe areas for the Muslims would be set up in eastern and central Bosnia, and that UN troops supervising these areas would have the right to retaliate if attacked.

While negotiations continued, the old Bosnian capital of Sarajevo was being progressively reduced to rubble. Most of the city, including the centre, was held by the Muslims but some of the suburbs and the high ground that surrounded Sarajevo was under Serbian control. This geographical division set the tone for the merciless siege of Sarajevo. The Serbs would rain down artillery and mortar shells on the city, while snipers on both sides would ruthlessly target the many civilians attempting to survive in the ruins. As ever, it was the civilians who suffered most: people lived like rats in cellars and battered apartments, subject to enemy fire at any time of the day or night, desperately short of food, medicine and fuel, and dependent on the arrival of relief-agency supplies.

NOBEL PRIZE FOR SOUTH AFRICAN PEACE BROKERS

The 1993 Nobel Peace Prize was awarded to ANC leader Nelson Mandela and President F W De Klerk. They were two very different South Africans: Mandela who had been prepared to face life in prison as part of the fight against the apartheid regime, and De Klerk, the apartheid hardliner

of the many problems that still lay ahead in South Africa, but also because of the many deep differences and mutual antipathies that divided them.

Since Mandela's release from prison in February 1990, his relations with De Klerk had often been rocky. For example, at the

▲ Nelson Mandela (left), leader of the African National Congress and President FW De Klerk (right) receive the Nobel Peace Prize.

who had finally decided that the need for change had to be faced. Between them they had found a peaceful path for the transition from racist apartheid to multiracial democracy. South Africa's first fully democratic elections were scheduled for April 1994.

The prize citation praised Mandela and De Klerk for their "personal integrity and great political courage" and their pursuit of a "constructive policy of peace and reconciliation". The response of the prize recipients, who travelled separately to Oslo for the ceremony, was muted. This was partly because of their awareness

opening of the Convention for a Democratic South Africa (Codesa) in December 1991, a gathering called to work out how to draw up a new constitution, Mandela had delivered a scathing attack on the President and his minority regime. In common with many whites, De Klerk felt offended that the "generous gift" of political rights he was offering South African blacks was not received with more gratitude. This was not a perspective that Mandela and his followers could be expected to take seriously after decades of oppression and struggle.

'94

UN INVOLVEMENT IN BOSNIA

Yet another soon-to-be-broken cease-fire was announced in Bosnia in February 1994 and, like its many predecessors, it was little more than a pause for breath to allow the warring sides to regroup prior to conducting new offensives. The human and material costs of the war were devastating: an estimated 200,000 had been killed by the spring of 1994, the vast majority of them civilians, with perhaps as many as four million people made homeless.

The United Nations continued to broker negotiations and organize humanitarian aid to the region. The number of peacekeeping troops in the former Yugoslavia was increased to 22,000, though they lacked the necessary military equipment and support services to take on any of the combatants in an effective manner. The designated six "safe areas" – Sarajevo, Tuzla, Srebrenica, Zepa, Gorazde, and Bihac – were continuously under attack and,

▲ **Bosnian children watch as British United Nations tanks set off to patrol frontline positions on the outskirts of Sarajevo.**

indeed, their names became part of the doleful litany of destruction and massacre relayed to the world by the news media.

The humiliation of the UN was completed by events in December 1994. Serb attacks on the Bihac enclave – defended by the brutal and charismatic General Atif Dudakovic of the Bosnian 5th Corps – led to a Nato air strike against a Serbian air base; the Serb response was to take UN troops hostage. The Serb leader Radovan Karadzic boasted "Bihac will become a safe area when Serbs occupy it".

By the end of the year, the Western powers had to accept the stark choice of either a phased withdrawal or of direct military action.

KURT COBAIN BURNS OUT

On April 5, 1994, Kurt Cobain, the lead singer of Seattle grunge band Nirvana, killed himself with a shotgun. His body was found by an electrician visiting his house three days later.

Kurt Donald Cobain was born in 1967 in a small town outside Seattle. His parents divorced when he was seven. The trauma of this event is credited with fuelling his angst-ridden music. A sickly youngster and a misfit,

◄ **The voice of "Generation X", Nirvana were one of the world's most popular bands when Kurt Cobain ended his life**

Cobain was fascinated by British punk bands, including the Sex Pistols. He formed Nirvana in 1986, but it was not until 1991 that their moody rough-edged grunge sound took the world by storm, with the album *Nevermind* selling around 10 million copies and making Cobain a millionaire virtually overnight.

A sensitive, sickly, and very private individual, Cobain was poorly-equipped to cope with rock stardom. He developed a heroin habit, which he shared with his wife, Hole's Courtney Love. he also seemingly found little cheer in the immense critical and popular success of the follow-up album, *In Utero*.

In his suicide note, Cobain described himself as a "miserable, self-destructive, death rocker" and said it was "better to burn out than to fade away". His death had a profound emotional impact on millions of young "Generation Xers", people whose anguish and passion Nirvana had deeply touched.

GENOCIDE IN RWANDA

In April and May 1994, at least half a million people were killed in the central African state of Rwanda in one of the worst genocidal massacres of recent times. The international community was fully aware of the killings but took no action to prevent them.

Rwanda and the neighbouring state of Burundi are both countries with a majority of Hutu people and a minority of Tutsi. Both have histories of inter-tribal bloodshed. In 1972, several hundred thousand Hutu were murdered by a Tutsi government in Burundi. In Rwanda, the Hutu held power and discriminated against the Tutsi minority. In 1990, Tutsi rebels, known as the Rwandan Patriotic Front, invaded Rwanda and a civil war began.

The Rwandan government of President Juvenal Habyarimana came under international pressure to enter peace talks with the rebels. In August 1993 a cease-fire was agreed and a United Nations observer force was sent into the country. But President Habyarimana began recruiting a youthful Hutu militia, the Interahamwe, which was trained as a killing machine for a future day of reckoning.

On April 6, President Habyarimana and his Burundian opposite number, Cyprien Ntaryamire, were flying into Rwanda from a regional peace

▲ **Hutu refugees queue for water in a makeshift camp at Goma, Zaire, following the bitter tribal warfare in Rwanda.**

meeting when their aircraft crashed, apparently shot down. Both men died. This unexplained event was followed immediately by the murder of thousands of political opponents of the Rwandan government, both Hutu and Tutsi, by the Presidential Guard in the capital, Kigali. The militia were then sent out into every part of the country under government control with orders to slaughter the Tutsi and anyone else who got in their way.

The massacres, mostly carried out in the most sadistic fashion with machetes, and sparing neither women nor children, occurred under the eyes of UN soldiers, who had no authority to intervene. When 11 Belgian UN soldiers were killed, Belgium

simply withdrew its contingent. US President Clinton refused to back intervention, saying in May "We cannot dispatch our troops to solve every problem where our values are offended by human misery, and we should not." France, which had close links with the Rwandan Hutu government, continued to support it during the massacres.

After the slaughter came military triumph for the Tutsi rebels, who took power in Kigali. Some four million Hutu fled to refugee camps in Zaire under the control of the bloodstained Interahamwe. Almost all returned home in 1996, while the clumsy process of allotting blame and punishing those deemed responsible for the killings got under way.

'94

BLAIR REPLACES SMITH AS LABOUR LEADER

On May 12, 1994, John Smith, the leader of the UK's Labour Party, died suddenly of a heart attack at the age of 55. He had been elected party leader in July 1992, after the resignation of Neil Kinnock in the wake of that year's Conservative election victory. Smith was a solid politician who had tackled his efforts to rebuild Labour with honesty, intelligence, and humour. Even his best friends, however, would not have described him as charismatic.

In the leadership contest which followed Smith's death, the main contenders appeared to be Gordon Brown and Tony Blair. Brown was persuaded to support Blair's candidacy, and the contest was eventually fought out between Blair and John Prescott, a bluff and hearty representative of the old Labour tradition. Young and smart, Blair presented himself as the advocate for a fundamental modernization of the party, involving abandoning many of the shibboleths of the past. He won the leadership election in July by a comfortable margin, becoming, at 41, Labour's youngest-ever leader. Prescott was elected deputy leader.

▶ **Widely respected by politicians of all persuasions, John Smith's death opened the way for the "New Labour" generation.**

Blair's promise to his followers was simple and straightforward: he would put Labour back where it belonged, "in government again". Twenty years after they had last won a general election, Labour members would prove themselves prepared to support any policy change that would achieve that desired end.

NELSON MANDELA BECOMES PRESIDENT OF SOUTH AFRICA

The first black President of South Africa, Nelson Mandela, was sworn in on May 10, 1994 at the Union Buildings in Pretoria under the blazing sunshine and before the largest gathering of international dignitaries ever assembled in South Africa.

In his speech after the ceremony, as thousands of South Africans danced and sang, he stated: "We pledge ourselves to liberate all our people from the continuing bondage of poverty, deprivation, suffering, gender and other discrimination. Never, never and never again shall it be that this beautiful land will again experience the oppression of one by another ... the sun shall never set on so glorious a human achievement." Then blacks and whites joined together to sing both the national anthems of South Africa, "Die Stem" and "Nkosi Sikelel' iAfrika", one after the other.

Nelson Mandela's inauguration took place 14 days after the first national elections in which every South African, whatever their colour, had a vote. The ANC had polled 62.6 per cent of the vote, giving them 252 of the 400 seats in the national assembly.

▲ **Prior to his presidency, Nelson Mandela casts his own vote in South Africa's first-ever democratic elections.**

THE CHANNEL TUNNEL

Britain effectively ceased to be an island on May 6, 1994, when Queen Elizabeth and French President Francois Mitterrand inaugurated the Channel Tunnel rail link between the south coast of England and the Continent. Running under the English Channel for 50 km (31 miles), it was one of the largest engineering projects ever carried out, and cost around £10 billion. The Queen travelled on a Eurostar train to Coquelles in France, where she met the President Mitterrand. She then travelled back to Britain with the President in the royal Rolls Royce on Le Shuttle.

An under-Channel tunnel link to the European mainland had frequently been proposed in the past, but had fallen foul of British insularity. In 1907, for example, a parliamentary bill to allow a rail tunnel to be built was withdrawn after military experts declared it a defence risk. This time round, the Continental invaders feared by Britons were mostly disease, especially in the form of rabid foxes, and illegal immigrants. Another main plank of opposition to the Tunnel was the issue of safety, particularly its vulnerability to terrorist attack.

Prime Minister Margaret Thatcher was not a person to allow objectors much scope, however. Construction of the Tunnel began in November 1987, and three years later workers from the two sides met in the middle. The project went massively over budget and there were some bitter disputes between the constructors and the Eurotunnel company that was footing the bill.

In the end, the only part of the project that comprehensively failed was the plan to build a high-speed rail link to a special terminal in London. A makeshift arrangement using existing track to Waterloo was still in place in 1999.

▲ **No longer an island – the two tunnels that link Great Britain to the mainland of Europe.**

OJ SIMPSON IN THE DOCK

In June 1994, Orenthal James "OJ" Simpson, one of the greatest players ever in American football and a leading black American media personality, was charged with the brutal murders of his white ex-wife Nicole Brown Simpson and her friend Ronald Goldman at Nicole's home. He failed to turn up for the arraignment proceedings on 17 June, and was identified driving a white Ford Bronco. In one of the most bizarre episodes in legal history, OJ's car was pursued by police and airborne TV news crews while thousands of people, alerted by TV, massed at the roadsides to watch him pass. When Simpson gave himself up, a passport, a disguise, and a large sum in cash were found in the car.

The trial, which opened in January 1995, proved an almost equally bizarre media circus. In front of a predominantly black jury, Simpson's defence played the race card for all it was worth. They were able to demonstrate that one of the police officers prominently involved in the murder investigation, Detective Mark Fuhrman, held racist views, and used this fact to undermine faith in the apparently overwhelming forensic evidence. After nine months in court, OJ was found not guilty, a verdict greeted with consternation and disbelief by most white Americans and jubilation by most blacks.

The families of the victims took their revenge by sueing Simpson for causing wrongful death. In February 1997, the predominantly white jury in the civil court found against O.J. and he was ordered to pay $8.5 million damages.

◄ **One of America's greatest sporting heroes, OJ Simpson's innocence still remains a subject for speculation.**

'94

FERRY DISASTER IN THE BALTIC

On the night of September 27–28, the *Estonia*, a car ferry heading across the Baltic Sea to Sweden, with 1,047 passengers and crew aboard, sank off Uto Island. Only 140 survived, making this Europe's worst ferry disaster since World War Two.

The accident occurred in heavy weather conditions, with winds gusting to 100 km (62 miles) an hour and waves 10 m (33 ft) high battering the ship. It is believed that the ferry's bow doors, used for embarking and disembarking its cargo of cars and lorries, were ripped off in the storm, causing the vessel rapidly to fill with water and sink stern first.

Recalling the *Herald of Free Enterprise* disaster in March 1987, in which 187 people died, the accident raised fresh doubts about the safety of roll-on, roll-off ferries. Ferry companies were criticized for being slow to implement recommendations to install watertight bulkheads that would prevent water filling the entire car deck even if the sea penetrated the vulnerable bow doors.

◀ **Mourners visit the monument on which is inscribed the names of the 907 victims of the *Estonia* ferry disaster.**

NEWS IN BRIEF

August
- UN establishes commission to investigate human rights abuses in Rwanda
- General strike in Nigeria by supporters of Chief Abiola, winner of annulled election in 1993
- Over 20,000 Cubans leave for America when Cuban government lifts restrictions on departure
- Terrorist Carlos the Jackal arrested in Sudan
- New coalition government formed in Sri Lanka after elections
- Bosnian government forces capture Bihac in Bosnia-Herzegovina
- Ernesto Zedillo becomes President of Mexico
- IRA in Northern Ireland announce end of "military operations"

September
- Labour Party under Owen Arthur win elections in Barbados
- Russian troops complete withdrawal from Poland
- US troops land in Haiti
- Deaths of author James Clavell and actress Jessica Tandy

SOLAR TEMPLE SUICIDES

Shortly after the northern hemisphere's autumn equinox, at the beginning of October 1994, mass suicides or murders took place within days of each other at two sites in Switzerland and one at Morin Heights near Montreal, Canada. In all, 53 bodies were found in burnt-out farmhouses: 15 had died by poisoning, the remainder had been shot or smothered. All were members of the apocalyptic quasi-Christian/New Age cult, the Order of the Solar Temple, founded by Luc Jouret in 1977.

Luc Jouret believed that he had been a member of the medieval Christian Order of the Knights Templar during a previous life, that he was Christ and that his daughter was "the cosmic child". He persuaded followers that the end of the world was imminent, because of an environmental catastrophe which would result in a completely destructive fire. He also convinced cult members that life continued after death on other planets.

In 1994, Jouret and other members of the inner circle, including Joseph Di Mambro, leader of an affiliated group, decided that some of the members of the Solar Temple should leave the Earth before its end and "transit" to a planet that revolved around the star Sirius. It was considered that in order to effect the transit successfully, they must die in fire. A few days before joining the others in the mass suicides, Di Mambro and 12 followers had a ritual last supper together.

Sporadic mass suicides by members of the Solar Temple group have continued every year since, always around the time of an equinox or solstice and always involving fire. By the end of 1997, 74 members of the cult had committed suicide. Today, the Order of the Solar Temple is thought to have up to 500 members worldwide, mainly in Canada, France and Switzerland.

▶ **The burnt-out remains of the Swiss farmhouse, formerly the headquarters of the Order of the Solar Temple cult.**

BRITAIN GAMBLES ON LOTTERY

▲ By the end of the decade, the British National Lottery was estimated to have created over a thousand new millionaires.

Britain's first National Lottery draw was held on November 19. Seven people shared the £15.8 million prize. An estimated 25 million people bought tickets, well over half the country's adult population. About one third of the £45 million take was allocated to a fund that would provide money for selected good causes.

The franchise to run the National Lottery had been won by Camelot, a consortium that intended to make a substantial profit out of the business.

This choice was severely criticized by Virgin boss Richard Branson, who had proposed a non-profit-making UK Lottery Foundation for the franchise.

Criticism of the lottery fever that swept the country came chiefly from religious leaders. Ordinary punters were more critical of the use to which their involuntary contributions to charity were put, such as the payment of £12 million to the Churchill family for Sir Winston Churchill's personal archives.

CONFLICT IN CHECHNYA

After the collapse of the Soviet Union in 1991, a rash of inter-ethnic disputes broke out in the former Soviet territory, some of them leading to open warfare. The most important conflict took place in the Russian Federation, where ethnic groups in the "autonomous regions" wanted the same right to independence that the republics had claimed.

One of the national groups in the Russian Federation that had most consistently opposed the rule of both the Russian Empire and the Soviet Union were the Muslim Chechens who lived in the wild and mountainous northern Caucasus. In November 1991, under the leadership of General Dzhokhar Dudaev, the Chechen autonomous region proclaimed itself the Republic of Chechnya. Russian President Boris Yeltsin responded by sending in units of the security forces. But in the face of resistance from Dudaev's national guard and Chechen volunteers, Yeltsin was forced to climb down.

Chechnya consolidated its independence over the next three years

▲ The bodies of five Russian soldiers, killed after their armoured personnel carrier had been hit by a Chechen anti-tank rocket.

with little interference from the Russian government, although Dudaev's rule became increasingly dictatorial. Chechen opposition politicians, driven out by force, appealed for Russian backing to oust Dudaev. On November 26, 1994 Russian tanks were sent on to the streets of the Chechen capital, Grozny, in an attempt at a coup that would have installed a new government. The operation went completely awry. The tanks were routed by Chechen fighters and Chechen national sentiment was greatly inflamed

Refusing to accept this humilia-

tion, the Russians embarked on a full-scale assault on Grozny, which they captured only after heavy fighting in January 1995. There followed a brutal guerrilla war that cost an estimated 30,000 lives. In August 1996, the Chechen rebels even briefly succeeded in retaking Grozny. This propaganda coup was quickly followed by a peace deal, aided by the fact that the extremist Dudaev had been killed in the conflict. Russian troops were to withdraw from the country, but recognition of Chechnyan independence was to be delayed at least until the new millennium.

EARTHQUAKE DEVASTATES JAPANESE CITY

▲ A giant crane pulls cars from the debris of Kobe's Hanshin Expressway following Japan's worst earthquake in half a century.

At 5.46 a.m. on January 17, a huge earthquake hit the city of Kobe in western Japan, causing massive damage and leaving a total of 3,842 dead and 14,679 injured. Measuring 7.2 on the Richter scale, the initial shock of the earthquake destroyed 54,949 buildings and damaged 31,783 more in this busy port, which lies at the centre of one of Japan's key industrial areas.

Trucks and cars were sent careering off overhead freeways as they folded and collapsed, while ruptured gas pipes fuelled raging fires across the shattered city. More than 114,500 people were immediately evacuated from the rubble-strewn streets, their homes either completely destroyed or left without electricity and heating as temperatures plummeted to near-freezing. Other towns and cities in the region, including Osaka, also suffered material damage, as fires broke out for miles around.

Stock markets in the Far East were sent reeling as the extent of the damage caused by the Kobe earthquake became known (contributing substantially to Nick Leeson's losses and the consequent demise of Barings Bank). Later renamed the Hyougo-ken Nanbu earthquake, Kobe's earthquake was the worst suffered in Japan since September 1, 1923 when the Tokyo/Yokohama earthquake killed 142,807 and devastated Tokyo.

LEESON BRINGS DOWN BARINGS BANK

On February 24, 1995, senior managers at Barings Bank in London realized that they were facing ruinous losses amounting to £860 million as a result of speculative and fraudulent trading by Nick Leeson, general manager of the bank's Singapore office. Deposits, including £1 million belonging to the Prince's Trust, were immediately frozen as chief executives sought a buyer for Britain's oldest merchant bank.

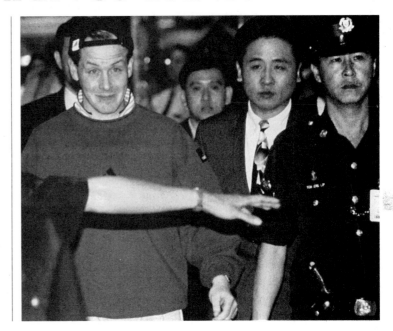

► Nick Leeson's speculation fraud might have gone noticed but for the Nikkei collapse that followed the Kobe earthquake.

Realizing that the writing was on the wall, the 28-year-old "boy wonder" from Watford had fled Singapore the previous evening, faxing his resignation and apologies from Kuala Lumpur, Malaysia, the next day. He and his wife Lisa then flew to Kota Kinabalu in Borneo, where they enjoyed a few days at a luxury "Shangri-La" resort before attempting to return to England on March 2 via Frankfurt, where German police were awaiting their arrival and arrested Leeson.

Appointed general manager and head trader of Barings Futures Singapore in late 1992, Leeson was a well-known figure on the trading floor of the Singapore futures exchange, where he was known as the man with the Midas touch. He reported unprecedented profits of £28.5 million in 1994, which Chairman, Peter Baring, described as "pleasantly surprising". But it was all an illusion. In fact, Leeson had accrued losses of £208 million by December 1994, which he was able to conceal in an account none of his bosses knew about because he controlled both the trading floor operations and the back-office settlements in Singapore.

On January 17, 1995 disaster struck in the form of the Kobe earthquake, which sent the Nikkei tumbling and Leeson's losses into freefall. He entered fictitious trades between the accounts in order to create fictitious profits, invented debts owed to Barings Futures, and borrowed money illegally to fund ever more desperate bets in an attempt to recover his soaring debts.

The Dutch bank, ING, bought Barings for £1 on March 5, but promised to inject £660 million new capital. Nick Leeson went on trial in Singapore on December 2, where he was sentenced to six and a half years' jail for fraud.

SINN FEIN BECOMES RESPECTABLE

In March 1995, Gerry Adams' bid to achieve respectability for Sinn Fein, the Republican party he led, received a marked boost from a triumphant visit to the United States. As Sinn Fein was generally recognized to be the political wing of the terrorist IRA, it had previously always been shunned by mainstream politicians. President Bill Clinton, however, not only invited Adams to lunch at the White House but treated him to a warm handshake that acknowledged his newfound role as a peacemaker.

Adams was widely credited with having persuaded the Republican movement that the way forward in Northern Ireland lay in a negotiated settlement. The announcement of a "complete cessation of military operations" by the IRA on August 31, 1994 had been greeted in many quarters as meaning peace after 25 years of war in Ulster. Irish Prime Minister Albert Reynolds said at the time, "As far as we are concerned, the long nightmare is over." Others were more cautious. British Prime Minister John Major continued to insist that the IRA had to disarm before they could be included in peace talks.

In February 1995, Major and the new Irish Prime Minister, John Bruton, came up with an agreed framework for peace in Northern Ireland. It included proposals for a legislative assembly in the Province and renunciation by the Irish Republic of its historic claim to Ulster. The framework was broadly welcomed by Sinn Fein, but the issue of the decommissioning of IRA arms blocked further progress towards all-party

▲ Presented as the new face of Irish republicanism, Sinn Fein leader Gerry Adams prepares for a US chat show appearance.

talks. The election of David Trimble as the new leader of the Ulster Unionists in September was, at the time, seen as another blow to the peace process, since Trimble was noted as a hardliner opposed to making concessions to the Republicans.

Despite numerous predictions to the contrary, however, the cease-fire held and in November 1995, after some prodding from the United States, a "two-track" approach was adopted to shift the stalled negotiations. The question of disarming terrorists was to be left to a commission under US Senator George Mitchell. Meanwhile, Sinn Fein would be included in preliminary peace talks. The deal allowed Clinton to pay a triumphant visit to Ulster at the end of the month and repeat his handshake with Adams on the Falls Road.

GAS ATTACK IN TOKYO

NEWS IN BRIEF

March
- UN troops complete withdrawal from Somalia
- Elections in Estonia won by coalition including former Communists
- Mexico announces austerity measures to curb financial crisis
- Ethnic violence breaks out in Burundi after murder of Hutu government minister
- Convicted Filipino maid in Singapore executed for murder
- Internal border controls between seven EU countries abandoned
- US troops withdraw from Haiti
- Deaths of British wartime commando leader Lord Lovat and SOE resistance worker Odette Hallowes

April
- Alberto Fujimori re-elected President of Peru
- State of emergency declared in Bolivia following strikes and civil unrest
- US special prosecutor interviews President and Mrs Clinton over involvement in Whitewater corruption investigation
- Thousands of Hutu refugees killed by Tutsi forces at Kibeho refugee camp in Rwanda
- Mahathir bin Mohamed wins elections in Malaysia
- Deaths of British disc jockey and comedian Kenny Everett and US actress and dancer Ginger Rogers

During Tokyo's morning rush hour on March 20, 1995, ten members of a Japanese cult, Aum Shinrikyo (Supreme Truth), dressed in business suits and carrying umbrellas, boarded five different underground trains bound for Kasumigaseki station in central Tokyo. They were carrying plastic bags containing the nerve gas sarin hidden inside rolled newspapers. When they punctured the bags with their umbrella tips, the deadly gas was released into the underground system, while the cult members fled at speed. There followed scenes of horror as blinded passengers struggled to find their way out of the underground and others lay collapsed on the platforms. In all, 12 people were killed and 5,500 injured, many of them seriously.

Aum Shinrikyo was a doomsday cult that had come to prominence in the 1980s. Its founder was the self-styled Shoko Asahara, born Chizuo Matsumoto in 1955 and half-blind from childhood glaucoma. Asahara, the author of a book modestly entitled *Declaring Myself the Christ*, had attracted a large following of young Japanese to a string of communes run by Aum. He also had a considerable following in Russia. An official investigation concluded that Aum had around 50,000 members worldwide and assets of almost $1 billion. Asahara had used this wealth to amass a considerable armoury in preparation for the armageddon that he predicted would soon usher in a new spiritual dawn.

Two days after the gas attack, Japanese police officers in gas masks stormed the cult's headquarters at Kamukuishiki, discovering large quantities of the chemicals needed to make the nerve gas. As arrests of cult members proceeded, evidence emerged of another sarin attack which had killed seven people in rural Matsumoto the previous year, as well as several murders and other crimes.

In the weeks after the underground gas attack there were further terrorist acts by Aum, including the shooting of a senior policeman, a letter bomb sent to the governor of Tokyo, and three further gas attacks on the underground, all of them fortunately unsuccessful. On May 16, Shoko Asahara was at last arrested. He was found concealed in a tiny hiding place at Kamukuishiki, where he had remained undiscovered by the police for almost eight weeks. He had with him cash to the value of $100,000.

▲ **Victims of the Aum Shinrikyo "doomsday" cult gas attack in which over 5,000 were injured.**

THE OKLAHOMA BOMBING

The most destructive domestic terrorist act in the history of the United States occurred at 9.02 on the morning of April 19, 1995. A bomb that had been left in a truck parked outside Oklahoma City's Alfred P Murrah federal building exploded, ripping a gaping hole in the nine-storey office block.

The full force of the explosion struck a first-floor day centre where working parents had just dropped off their children. The blast was so powerful it was felt 48 km (30 miles) away.

The escue operation was a horrifying experience. Rescuers aided by sniffer dogs crawled over bodies in the often futile search for survivors in the rubble – one firefighter commented that all he had found was "a baby's finger and an American flag". The death toll was eventually established at 168, with many more injured.

It was originally supposed that the bomb must have been planted by Middle East terrorists, but commentators soon noticed that the date was the second anniversary of the end of the Waco siege, regarded by many American right-wingers as a mass murder of members of the Branch Davidian sect committed by the federal authorities. The bombing was then correctly identified as a revenge attack on the federal offices.

Two individuals with connections to right-wing militias, Timothy McVeigh and Terry Nichols, were soon arrested and charged. They were eventually convicted without any wider conspiracy being proved.

► **The American flag flies before the tattered remnants of the Alfred P Murrah building in Oklahoma City.**

CROMWELL STREET: MURDER MOST FOUL

On New Year's Day 1995, Frederick West was found hanged in his cell in Winson Green prison, where he was awaiting trial in one of the most gruesome serial murder cases ever recorded in Britain. West had confessed to the killing of 12 named young women, mostly in the 1970s, but later told police that he had, in fact, murdered 20 more.

West was a builder who lived at 25 Cromwell Street, Gloucester. With his wife Rosemary, he ran a peculiar household, in which young drifters were often made welcome. West was obsessively interested in sex and engaged in multifarious sexual practices, from intercourse with his own off-spring to voyeuristic observation of his wife engaged in prostitution. He also often had sex with the young women who found a home in his house. The killings took place either in the course of sadistic sex sessions or in sudden explosions of violence against those who crossed or threatened him.

West was arrested in February 1994 when a body was found buried in his back garden. Further investigation of the house uncovered more remains around the house, mostly in the cellar. Later, bodies were uncovered in a field outside Gloucester and at the West's former home in another part of the city. The victims included Charmaine West, the eight-year-old illegitimate daughter of Fred West's first wife, Rena Costello; Shirley Robinson, murdered while pregnant with West's child; Lucy Partington, an Exeter University undergraduate, picked up by the Wests at a bus stop in 1973 and never seen alive again; a Swiss hitchhiker; and Heather West, Fred and Rosemary's daughter, murdered when she was 16.

After Fred West's suicide, Rosemary West was tried for ten of the murders. She was found guilty and sentenced to life imprisonment in November 1995.

▲ **Rosemary and Fred West, perpetrators of Britain's most gruesome serial killings. Although a dozen bodies were found, the true number of their victims will probably never be known.**

'95

LOUIS FARRAKHAN'S "MILLION MAN MARCH"

October 16, 1995 was the day that Louis Farrakhan, leader of the separatist Nation of Islam, one of the most controversial black movements in the United States, had designated for a "Million Man March" on Washington DC. It was in part a deliberate snook cocked at the memory of Martin Luther King and the celebrated 1963 March on Washington, which had attracted 250,000 people to hear the civil rights leader speak of his dream of a future of racial harmony.

Farrakhan's message is very different from King's: blacks must assert their own values and reject the white world. He is famous for his aggressive rhetoric, aimed in particular at Jews, which has seen him accused of the same racism he claims is the preserve of whites. His attitude towards women, consigned to a subordinate role, has also drawn sharp criticism.

Although falling well short of the million target, the October 16 gathering was an impressive one. Around 400,000 people, almost all black and male, filled the Mall below the US Capitol; prominent among them were members of the Nation of Islam in their distinctive suits and bow ties. They heard Farrakhan speak with unusual restraint of the need for black self-reliance, calling for the use of violence only in self-defence and the need for black self-discipline to avoid reliance on drugs or alcohol.

Despite the reassuring tone of Farrakhan's speech, there was widespread concern that a man known for his articulation of "black rage" and his aggressive denunciation of white oppression

▶ **Louis Farrakhan's "million" may only have numbered 400,000 but still managed to fill the Mall below the US Capitol.**

should have proved himself the most popular spokesman for African Americans in the 1990s. On the same day as the March on Washington, President Clinton, speaking in Austin, Texas, denounced the influence of "one man's message of malice and division". Yet even he could not deny the need for America "to clean its house of racism".

ISRAEL'S PEACEMAKER ASSASSINATED

▲ **Yitzhak Rabin (right), pictured alongside President Clinton and King Hussein of Jordan during the Middle East peace talks.**

On November 4, 1995, Israeli Prime Minister Yitzhak Rabin was shot dead as he left an evening peace rally at King of Israel Square in Tel Aviv. The assassin, 25-year-old student Yigal Amir, was arrested on the spot.

Amir was a right-wing Jewish fundamentalist opposed to the peace accord agreed between Rabin and Palestinian leader Yasser Arafat in 1993. Totally unrepentant, Amir told police "I acted alone on God's orders." He had intended also to kill the

Israeli foreign minister, Shimon Peres, but Peres left the peace rally separately and thus avoided the bullet meant for him.

Rabin had a distinguished record as a servant of Israel. He fought in the war of independence in 1948 and was Israeli chief of staff during the Six-Day War of 1967. Entering politics, he was Prime Minister for four years in the 1970s, and regained the post in 1992. It was precisely because of his record as an Israeli patriot and victorious military leader that he was able to persuade Israelis to back the ambitious peace deal with the Palestinians.

The assassination highlighted the deep divisions within Israeli society between those, particularly on the religious-fundamentalist right, implacably opposed to any concessions to the Palestinians, and those who believed that only a negotiated settlement could produce lasting peace and security. It was particularly shocking for many Israelis that the Palestinian representative in negotiations with their government should be PLO leader Yasser Arafat, a man widely seen as an unrepentant terrorist. Rabin's gesture in shaking hands with Arafat on the lawn of the White House in September 1993 probably cost him his life.

Rabin's assassination did not halt the peace process, which continued under the premiership of Peres. In January 1996, Arafat was elected head of the new Palestinian Authority exercising self-rule in the West Bank, Gaza, and East Jerusalem. But in Israeli elections the following May, Peres was defeated by Likud leader Benyamin Netanyahu, committed to taking a tougher line with the Palestinians.

BOSNIA AND THE DAYTON AGREEMENT

▲ **World leaders applaud as Presidents Milosevic, Tudjman and Izetbegovic put their names to the Dayton peace agreement.**

The stalemate that had characterized the Bosnia war during the previous two years was to be transformed in 1995. A key factor in this change was a hardening of attitudes in the West towards all sides, but especially the Serbs. The beleaguered UN peacekeepers began to receive the heavy weapons, mortars, artillery and armoured fighting vehicles that were essential if a credible threat was to be mounted against the warring factions. In addition, the UK, France and the United States all made a major commitment of high-quality ground forces capable of dealing with the Serb, Croat and Muslim fighters.

While the Nato-led build-up was taking place, the Serbs pressed harder against the Muslim enclaves. In July, Srebrenica fell to the Serbs, which led to a horrifying massacre of the Muslim defenders. When the neighbouring enclave of Goradze seemed likely to fall next, UN forces took decisive action: 3500 air sorties were flown against a variety of Serb targets, and British and French artillery shelled Serb positions around Sarajevo.

The Bosnian Serbs did not respond to the UN attacks, perhaps fearing a direct assault on their capital, Pale. At the same time, the Muslim and Croat forces were beginning to achieve some limited yet important local successes over the Serbs. Fearful of loosing all their gains, the Serbs began to look towards a negotiated settlement.

In November 1995, Presidents Milosevic, Tudjman and Izetbegovic met at Dayton, Ohio to discuss peace terms. Under the forceful leadership of the US negotiator, Richard Holbrooke, a compromise peace deal was finally hammered out. The peace agreement, signed in France in December, established a new state, the Union of Bosnia-Herzegovina, which consisted two self-governing parts, a Muslim-Croat federation and a Bosnian Serb republic. Increased numbers of UN troops were despatched to Bosnia to monitor the cease-fire, which – for the first time – held.

'96

NEWS IN BRIEF

- BSE crisis in Britain; safety of beef questioned by scientists
- Wave of arson attacks on churches in the USA
- Sexual harassment and assault scandal hits the US army
- The Globe Theatre opens in London; it is a reproduction of the original Shakespearean building
- Ancient cave art found near Vallont-Pont d'Arc in France
- US launches *Pathfinder* probe to explore Mars
- Fighting between Russian troops and rebels continues in Chechnya, with hostage-taking on both sides
- Films released during the year include Anthony Minghella's *The English Patient*, Roland Emmerich's *Independence Day*, Milos Forman's *The People vs Larry Flynt*, Scott Hicks's *Shine*, Nicholas Hytner's *The Madness of King George*, David Cronenberg's *Crash* and Eric Rohmer's *A Summer's Tale*
- The opera *Outis* by Luciano Berio premieres
- Books published this year include *The Last Thing He Wanted* by Joan Didion, *Ecstasy* by Irvine Welsh and *Last Orders* by Graham Swift
- Popular songs of the year include "Firestarter" by Prodigy, "Killing Me Softly" by the Fugees and "Wannabe" by the Spice Girls

IRA RESUMES BOMBING

On February 10, 1996, the IRA cease-fire that had held since August 1994 came spectacularly to an end with a devastating attack in east London. In the early evening, a massive bomb exploded outside South Quays station on the Isle of Dogs, in the heart of the Docklands redevelopment area. It caused damage over a wide area, killed two people and injured many more, most of them cut by flying glass from blown-out windows. As proof that this was not an isolated incident, a week later a bomb blew up on a bus in central London, killing the terrorist who had been using the bus to carry the bomb to its target.

The new IRA campaign on the British mainland was based chiefly on the use of large bombs to hit symbolic or economic targets. In April, two devices even larger than the Docklands bomb were positioned to blow up Hammersmith Bridge over the Thames in west London, but failed to explode. Next, it was the turn of Manchester. On June 15, a huge explosion devastated the city centre, injuring hundreds of people and causing damage to property on a scale not seen before from the IRA in Britain.

The renewal of the IRA bombing campaign led to the automatic exclusion of Sinn Fein, the IRA's political wing, from all-party talks on the future of Northern Ireland. The British government had made the cessation of violence an absolute precondition for Sinn Fein's involvement. In May, however, to the government's embarrassment, Gerry Adams's party won 17 seats in elections to the all-party forum where the talks were to take place.

The refusal to allow Sinn Fein representatives to take their seats in the forum, although understandable, rendered the talks largely futile, since it excluded a group without whose agreement peace could not be established. Eventually, the election of a new government in Britain in 1997 unjammed the peace process and brought about a renewed IRA cease-fire.

▲ Towering over London's Docklands, Canary Wharf was severely damaged by the bomb that signalled an end to the IRA cease-fire.

MASSACRE AT DUNBLANE

Just before 9.30 am on the morning of March 13, 1996, a former scout leader, Thomas Hamilton, walked into a primary school in the Scottish town of Dunblane, a bespectacled figure wearing a dark woolly hat and ear muffs. He was armed with four guns – two 9mm Browning self-loading pistols and two .357 Smith and Wesson revolvers – and 743 rounds of ammunition.

Hamilton entered the gymnasium, where a class of five- and six-year-olds were waiting to start their exercises. Also in the room was the class's teacher, Gwen Mayor, a part-time teacher, Eileen Harrild, and an assistant, Mary Blake. Using one of his Brownings, Hamilton first shot the adults, killing Mayor and wounding the others. He then opened fire on the children, walking around the room to pick them off as they attempted to take cover. After about four minutes he fired a volley into another classroom, then put a Smith and Wesson in his mouth and pulled the trigger. Hamilton had fired 105 rounds, killing 16 children and injuring 11 others. Only one of the class of 28 in the gymnasium escaped physically unscathed.

A 43-year-old bachelor, Hamilton's motivation for mass murder seems to have been his sense of grievance at frequent complaints about his behaviour around children. In 1973 he had been dismissed as a scout leader, a rebuff that rankled with him so bitterly more than 20 years later that he wrote a letter of complaint about it to the Queen only days before the massacre. He had also mentioned the Dunblane school specifically in complaints about what he claimed were unjustified slurs on his character.

The sense of shock and out-rage at the murders increased as more was revealed about the killer. It was asked why, for 20 years, he had been allowed to run boys' clubs despite so much evidence of his unsuitability. Even more extraordinary was his pos-session of a gun licence: the weapons he used in the attack were all fully legal. An inquiry chaired by Lord Cullen uncovered the fact that in November 1991, Detective Sergeant Paul Hughes had written a memo to Deputy Chief Constable Douglas McMurdo describing Hamilton as an "unsavoury character and unstable personality" who had an "extremely unhealthy interest" in young boys and should not have a firearms certificate. McMurdo took no action, and renewed Hamilton's licence in 1992 and again in 1995, when he was given approval for two more weapons. Criticized by the Cullen inquiry, McMurdo resigned from the police force.

A direct consequence of the Dunblane massacre was a ban on the personal ownership of handguns in the UK. Reacting to public opinion, MPs eventually passed a measure even stronger than the recommendations of Lord Cullen's report.

▲ **A community in shock – grief-stricken parents await news of the shooting at Dunblane Primary School.**

BRITISH BEEF SUCCUMBS TO "MAD COW" PANIC

On March 20, 1996, Health Secretary Stephen Dorrell admitted in parliament that there was a possible link between "mad cow disease" – bovine spongiform encephalopathy (BSE) – in cattle and a new strain of the potentially fatal Creutzfeld-Jakob disease (CJD) in humans. It was the end of a long battle by the government to deny any health risk to humans associated with BSE, which had developed in British herds in the 1980s, probably through the practice of feeding cows on offal from slaughtered animals.

Five days after Dorrell's sensa-tional statement, the European Commission imposed a worldwide ban on exports of British beef. The meat was also shunned by many British consumers and dropped by major outlets such as McDonald's. Prices fell to rock bottom, with cat-astrophic results for British beef farmers. The government belatedly attempted to restore confidence by a cull of millions of cattle considered to be most at risk, but this was too late as reports of individuals dying of CJD began to feature regularly in the press, and some experts refused to rule out a major epidemic.

▶ **Minister for Agriculture John Gummer places his faith firmly in British beef.**

'96

NEWS IN BRIEF
....

May
- Congress party defeated in elections in India
- UN deal allows Iraq to exchange oil for food and medicine
- Army mutiny in Central African Republic quelled by French troops
- Death of US counter-culture exponent Timothy Leary

June
- New coalition government with Deve Gowda as Prime Minister formed in India
- Anti government Freemen militia forced to surrender after 81 day siege in Montana
- Nineteen US army personnel killed by car bomb in Saudi Arabia
- Death of US jazz singer Ella Fitzgerald

July
- Boris Yeltsin wins Russian presidential elections
- Loyalist parade through Portadown in Northern Ireland blocked by army and RUC then allowed to proceed; rioting throughout Northern Ireland
- TWA airliner explodes off Coney Island in the US; all 228 on board killed
- Military coup in Burundi; ethnic violence between Tutsis and Hutus follows

UNABOMBER CAPTURED

On April 3, 1996 a former mathematics professor, Theodore Kaczynski, was arrested by the FBI and charged with being the Unabomber, America's most wanted terrorist. Kaczynski was living in the backwoods of Montana in a log cabin without running water or electricity. The FBI had been looking for the Unabomber for 18 years, but they only found him after a tip-off from his brother David.

The Unabomber was credited with 16 bombings in which three people died and 23 were wounded. The victims of his parcel bombs included the owner of a computer shop, a computer-science professor, a geneticist, an advertising executive, and the head of the pro-logging California Forestry Association. The Unabomber's declared motive was to alert the world to the necessity of abandoning industrial society and modern technology, which he saw as a threat to the true well-being of the human race and to the survival of the planet.

These sentiments were expressed in a 35,000-word manifesto, published by two leading American newspapers in 1995 in return for an offer by the Unabomber to end his terror campaign.

Going on trial in 1998, Kaczynski changed his plea to guilty at the last minute to avoid his lawyers' attributing his crimes to a decline in his mental state. He continued to insist on the rightness of his actions as a way of publicizing the ills of modern society – a stance that won him a surprisingly large number of admirers in the United States.

◄ **Theodore Kaczynski, known to Americans as the "Unabomber", is captured after eluding the FBI for 18 years.**

YELTSIN RE-ELECTED

In July 1996 Boris Yeltsin was re-elected as President of Russia, despite a background of spiralling economic breakdown, guerrilla warfare in Chechnya, and mounting evidence of his declining health. His victory was welcomed by the Western powers, who had feared a return to Communist government in Moscow.

In the first round of voting, Yeltsin came out only narrowly ahead of his main opponent, Communist candidate Gennadi Zyuganov, taking 35 per cent of the vote to Zyuganov's 32 per cent. With the ultra-nationalist Vladimir Zhirinovsky winning only 6 per cent of the vote and former Soviet President Mikhail Gorbachev taking a humiliating 0.5 per cent, the balance of power for the second round of the election lay with the charismatic General Alexander Lebed, who had attracted almost 15 per cent of the votes cast. Yeltsin's response was to appoint Lebed to a powerful post as secretary of the Russian security council, in return for his support. Yeltsin then duly won the absolute majority he needed, taking 53.7 percent of the second round vote to 40.4 per cent for Zyuganov.

It was hardly an enthusiastic confirmation of Yeltsin's authority, however. Only the deployment of substantial campaign funds and the exercise of control over the media had allowed him to fight off the Communist challenge. He had put on a remarkable display of energy and fitness during the campaign, but few people believed his health would survive another four-year term in office.

▲ **The narrow margin of Yeltsin's victory confirmed the fears of the West: that there was still hardcore support for Communism in Russia.**

THE ATLANTA OLYMPICS

The Centennial Olympic Games were held in Atlanta, Georgia, in July and August 1996. The nineteenth-century founders of the modern Games would have been astonished at the commercial razzmatazz now inseparable from what had once been a scrupulously amateur sporting event, but perhaps even more surprised by its sheer scale, with 11,000 athletes from 197 nations taking part.

The highlight of the Games' spectacular opening ceremony was a courageous appearance by former boxer Muhammad Ali, now crippled by Parkinson's Disease. Ali proudly overcame his disability to light the Olympic flame. Courage was also the hallmark of one of the other highlights of the Games, when US gymnast Kerri Strug carried on despite a sprained ankle to allow the US women's team to win a gold medal. The most impressive sporting achievements were by

sprinters – the Canadian Donovan Bailey, who won the 100 metres in a world record 9.84 seconds, and, above all, American Michael Johnson, who won both the 400 metres and 200 metres, the latter in a record-breaking 19.32 seconds.

The Games were marred, however, by a bomb explosion in the

Olympic Park on the night of July 26-27 which left two people dead and 111 injured. Suspicion at first focused on a security guard, Richard Jewell, but he proved to be completely innocent. In October 1998, Eric Rudolph, a fugitive on the FBI's "ten most wanted" list, was charged with the Atlanta bombing.

▲ **The great Muhammad Ali moved the world with his courageous appearance at the opening of the Atlanta Olympics.**

CHARLES AND DIANA DIVORCE

◄ **Tabloid revelations about the state of the Royal marriage resulted in widespread public sympathy for Princess Diana.**

On August 28, 1996, the 15-year marriage of the Prince and Princess of Wales was brought to an end with a decree absolute rubber-stamped at Somerset House in London.

The divorce was granted on the grounds that the couple had been officially separated since December 1992 – although adultery could have been cited, given that both parties had publicly admitted to it.

Charles and Diana's parting was the second royal divorce of the year, as the Duke and Duchess of York had received their decree absolute in May.

The Queen had suggested publicly in December 1995 that the Prince and Princess of Wales would do well to divorce, hoping that this would stem the seemingly endless tide of revelations about the couple's unhappy private life. There was immediate speculation that the Prince of Wales might plan to marry his long-term companion Camilla Parker-Bowles, herself divorced the previous year.

'96

BELGIAN PAEDOPHILE SCANDAL

▲ **Marc Dutroux had been at the centre of an international paedophile ring which some believed enjoyed protection from the Belgian police.**

In August 1996, the arrest of a 39-year-old Belgian paedophile, Marc Dutroux, opened up a horrifying story of abuse, murder, and scandalous official incompetence. Dutroux's arrest followed the discovery of the bodies of an adult and two eight-year-old girls, Melissa Russo and Julie Lejeune, buried in the garden of one of 11 properties he owned. Police also discovered two girls alive, chained up in an underground chamber.

It emerged that Dutroux had been convicted of serious paedophile offences in 1989, but had been released after serving only three years of a 13-year sentence. Police had twice visited his house while searching for the missing Russo and Lejeune, but had failed to find them in the underground hiding place. According to Dutroux, an accomplice had allowed the girls to die of starvation while he himself was in police custody on an unrelated charge.

It soon became apparent that Dutroux was a member of an international paedophile ring and suspicions surfaced that he might have enjoyed official protection. The case became a focus for widespread popular discontent in Belgium, with mass demonstrations and strikes demanding a full investigation.

Later, two more bodies of young girls were found in the garden of another of Dutroux's houses. Public confidence in the authorities was not increased when, in April 1998, Dutroux briefly escaped from a courtroom and was only recaptured after four hours on the loose.

THE USA ATTACKS IRAQ

In the aftermath of the 1991 Gulf War, the Western powers declared areas of northern Iraq "safe havens" for Kurds rebelling against Iraqi leader Saddam Hussein. In August 1996, however, Iraqi troops invaded the safe havens in support of the pro-Saddam Kurdish forces of the Kurdish Democratic Party. US President Bill Clinton responded by launching the first major strikes against Iraq since the 1991 cease-fire. Over a two-day period in the first week of September, US cruise missiles battered targets in the south of the country.

The attack had little effect on the fighting in the Kurdish areas, which continued to fluctuate. It was more an expression of American frustration at the survival of Saddam's regime – and of Clinton's need to boost his domestic popularity in the run-up to presidential elections in November. Britain was the only one of America's Nato allies fully to support the missile strikes.

▶ **The pariah of the West, Iraq's President Saddam Hussein once again falls foul of the international community.**

CLINTON STAYS IN THE WHITE HOUSE

In November 1996, US President Bill Clinton was comfortably re-elected for a second term, winning 49 per cent of the popular vote, as against 41 per cent for his Republican adversary, Bob Dole. Maverick millionaire Ross Perot, once seen as a serious threat to the major party candidates, ended up with only 8 per cent of the vote.

A second term for Clinton in the White House had seemed unlikely in 1994, when the Democrats were routed in Congressional

elections by an aggressively right-wing Republican party. But the hero of that hour, Republican Congressional leader Newt Gingrich, overplayed his hand and experienced a rapid waning of popular support. At the same time, Clinton swiftly adapted to the evident conservatism of American voters and took on board much of the "new right" agenda, slashing welfare spending to balance the budget, cracking down on crime, and embracing "family values".

Unable to contest policies stolen from their own portfolio, the Republicans rested their hopes on digging for scandal. The investigation of the Whitewater case, involving land deals in Clinton's native Arkansas during his time as governor there, smouldered but failed to ignite. A scandal that

◀ **Bill Clinton portrayed himself as the "Comeback Kid". Two years earlier, a Democrat victory would have seemed unlikely.**

brewed up at the last minute, concerning Clinton's alleged acceptance of illegal foreign contributions to his campaign fund, came too late to influence voters.

Dole, a Republican elder statesman, proved an unexciting candidate, his campaign enlivened only by mishaps such as falling off a platform during a rally in Chico, California. Clinton, on the other hand, once more demonstrated his exceptional ability to radiate charm and confidence on the campaign trail. It was significant that he won a far higher proportion of the female vote – 55 per cent – than of the male vote.

The most powerful impression left by the election, however, was of the high level of apathy about politics and politicians in the economically booming United States. Only 49 per cent of Americans turned out to vote, less than in any presidential election since 1924, and far below the levels regularly recorded in other democracies.

December

- Gerry Rawlings re-elected President in Ghana
- New coalition government under Jim Bulger formed in New Zealand
- New constitution signed by South African President, Nelson Mandela
- Kofi Annan appointed successor to Boutros Boutros Ghali as UN Secretary General
- Tupac Amaru guerrillas seize the Japanese embassy in Lima, Peru, taking many hostages; 200 hostages released 5 days later
- Six Red Cross workers murdered in Chechnya
- Two British nurses charged with the murder of a colleague in Saudi Arabia
- Strikes in South Korea
- Guerrillas and government sign peace accord in Guatemala

THE McLIBEL CASE

In December 1996, the longest libel trial in British legal history came to an end. Popularly known as the "McLibel case", it was brought by McDonald's, one of the world's largest multinational corporations, against two almost penniless ecology campaigners who had distributed leaflets critical of the fast-food chain. In 1990, McDonald's told Dave Morris, Helen Steel and three other campaigners that they must either apologize or face legal action. To the corporation's astonishment, Morris and Steel not only refused to retract the allegations made in their leaflet

but fought a two-and-a-half-year action in the High Court.

The case was heard without a jury, at McDonald's request. The judge delivered his detailed verdict in June 1997, when he predictably found in favour of the corporation. He allowed that the two campaigners had proved McDonald's was "culpably responsible" for cruelty to animals and exploited children, but they had not proved, on the other hand,

▶ **For many, the case of McDonald's versus Morris and Steel brought the words "sledgehammer" and "nut" to mind.**

allegations that the corporation was destroying rain forests, causing food poisoning, or creating starvation in the Third World.

McDonald's had spent an estimated £10 million on an action that had brought them nothing but ridicule.

'97

RISE OF THE ECO-WARRIORS

In 1990s Britain, no new motorway, by-pass, or airport extension could be planned and built without a prolonged battle between well-organized, dedicated environmental protesters – the "eco-warriors" – and the authorities. During 1996, the most attention-grabbing protest tactic, used especially on the proposed route of the Newbury by-pass in Berkshire, was to take to the trees. Protesters lived in tree houses connected by walkways, preventing roadbuilders clearing the route until a difficult and dangerous process of eviction had been completed.

In January 1997, a new obstructive tactic succeeded in winning extensive media coverage. Five protesters planning to block construction of a Honiton-to-Exeter link road at Fairmile in east Devon decided to dig a network of tunnels under the proposed route. They intended to live underground, day and night, defying bailiffs to find a way of evicting them. Attracted by the bravery and sheer oddity of the protest, the media quickly made the five into celebrities. With their jokey nicknames, such as "Animal", "Muppet Dave", and "Swampy", they provided newsmen with excellent copy.

The underground protest lasted seven days, before tunnelling experts brought in by the bailiffs reached most of the protesters. Swampy, whose real name was Daniel Hooper, was the last to emerge, coming out voluntarily. He became the main focus of later media interest as he proceeded to dig in again at the site of another protest, against the building of a second runway at Manchester airport.

Although in one sense the media exploited Swampy, feeding him into the celebrity machine – he even appeared on BBC2's

▲ A pair of young "eco-warriors" tie themselves to a tree during an attempt to stop the building of the Newbury by-pass.

satirical show "Have I Got News For You" – in another sense it was the eco-warriors who exploited the media. As Swampy said to journalists after the Fairmile eviction: "If I had just written a letter to my MP, would you lot be here? Think not."

HEAVEN'S GATE – SUICIDE ON THE NET

In the spring of 1997, the Hale-Bopp comet proved the most spectacular visitor in the night sky for many years, clearly visible to the naked eye. For one cult group in the United States, its advent signalled the moment for mass suicide.

Called Heaven's Gate, the cult was led by 66-year-old Marshall Herff Applewhite, known to his followers as Do. Applewhite's teachings were a bizarre blend of religion and UFOs – showing the influence both of Christianity and

◀ The "Higher Source" website discussed the aims of the bizarre Heaven's Gate science fiction cult.

Star Trek. He taught his followers that they were "angels" destined at some point to beam up to "a spacecraft from the Level Above Human" that would carry them off to eternal life. The cult wore black outfits, shaved their heads, and abstained from drink, drugs, and sex – some had themselves castrated. Many were computer experts, and the cult made a good living designing websites.

In March 1997, the cult was renting a mansion in Rancho Santa Fe, outside San Diego, California, when some startling news was revealed to Applewhite. He had for much of his life lived with a woman named Bonnie Lu Trusdale Nettles. She had died of liver cancer, but according to Applewhite she had ascended to the Level Above Human under the name Ti, or "the Older Member". Now she informed him that a spaceship was approaching Earth in the wake of the Hale-Bopp comet to pick up the chosen few.

On their website, Heaven's Gate, the cult posted a message saying they were going to leave Earth and rendezvous with the spaceship. Part of the message read: "The joy is that our Older Member has made it clear to us that Hale-Bopp's approach is the marker we've been waiting for. We are happily prepared to go with Ti's crew."

Over a three-day period, Applewhite and 38 cult members committed suicide, taking vodka and phenobarbital and putting plastic bags over their heads. In their "exit statements", they expressed the convictions that had driven them to this step. One member wrote: "We came from the Level Above Human in distant space and we have now exited the bodies that we were wearing for our earthly task, to return to the world from whence we came – task completed."

GUERRILLAS MASSACRED AFTER EMBASSY SIEGE

On April 22, 1997, a 126-day siege of the Japanese embassy in Lima, the capital of Peru, ended in a bloodbath when government special forces stormed the building, killing all 14 guerrillas who were holding hostages inside.

The guerrillas, belonging to the small left-wing Tupac Amaru Revolutionary Movement, had taken over the embassy on December 17, 1996, at a time when some 500 politicians, diplomats, officials, and Japanese businessmen were attending an embassy reception. All those present were taken hostage, including the brother of Peru's President, Alberto Fujimori, the President of the Peruvian supreme court, the heads of several major Japanese companies, and no less than 18 ambassadors. President Fujimori, himself of Japanese descent, refused the guerrillas' demand for the release of 400 left-wing prisoners who, they claimed, were being "mistreated and tortured" in Peruvian jails.

A long stand-off followed, with the guerrillas releasing batches of hostages at intervals, until only 72 key figures were left in their hands. While feigning to enter into negotiations, the government patiently preparing for an assault by anti-terrorist commandos. Tunnels were dug from outside the embassy compound into the embassy building, and surveillance devices were implanted to track the guerrillas' movements.

In the early afternoon of April 22, an explosive charge was set off in a tunnel under a room where many of the guerrillas were playing football. At the same time, commandos entered the building through a hole blown in the roof. Caught totally unprepared, the guerrillas were ruthlessly gunned down, without being offered the choice of surrender. One hostage also died in the operation.

▲ **Troops of the Peruvian special force survey a scale model of the area surrounding the Japanese embassy in Lima.**

'97

BLAIR AND NEW LABOUR WIN POWER

NEWS IN BRIEF

March
- Ohio River in the US floods, causing extensive damage
- Fire and explosion in Japanese nuclear waste processing plant
- Fighting between rebels and government forces in Albania, rebels having taken control in the south, reaches Tirana
- Kisangani in Zaire falls to rebel forces
- Controversy over Downey Report on cash-for-questions affair in Britain

April
- Bomb scare causes Grand National steeplechase in Britain to be abandoned; race is run two days later
- Rebels in Zaire take Lumumbashi
- Italian troops land in Albania
- Fire in Turin Cathedral in Italy
- General strike in Kinshasa, Zaire
- Death of US beat poet Allen Ginsberg

May
- New British government announces intention of joining Social Chapter EU agreement
- Rebel forces advance on Kinshasa in Zaire
- Earthquake in Iran kills over 4000 people
- Chess grandmaster Gary Kasparov defeated by Deep Blue computer
- Peace treaty between Russia and Chechnya
- Ban on unions in GCHQ in Britain lifted

The United Kingdom general election of May 1, 1997 was a political earthquake. Not only did a Labour government come to power after 18 years of Conservative rule, but it did so with the largest parliamentary majority for any party since World War Two. With 419 seats in the House of Commons to 165 for the Conservatives, Labour leader Tony Blair was almost certain to govern for the next five years.

Labour had captured 45 per cent of the votes cast to 31 per cent for the Conservatives. The scale of the Labour victory was magnified in terms of seats won both by the "first-past-the-post" electoral system and by tactical voting by Labour and Liberal-Democrat supporters, who generally backed whichever candidate was most likely to beat the Tories in a given constituency. The Lib-Dems won 17 per cent of the vote, which converted into an impressive 46 seats in the House of Commons. Liberal leader Paddy Ashdown was prepared to broadly support the new government, giving Labour an even more assured Commons majority.

The election victory was a personal triumph for Tony Blair who, at the age of 43, became Britain's youngest Prime Minister for 185 years. It was the culmination of his three-year drive to establish "New Labour" as an electoral force capable of defeating the Tories. In the process he had slaughtered Labour's sacred cows at an astonishing rate, embracing most aspects of the Thatcher revolution, from the privatization of nationalized industries to low direct taxation, tight limits on union power, and the culture of "enterprise". Yet he had done so without splitting the party – indeed, Labour had shown an impressively unified front during the election. Blair had been rewarded with the support of media mogul Rupert Murdoch and many other prominent business figures, including Virgin boss Richard Branson.

The election was a painful debacle for the Conservatives. John Major, a man far more popular than his party, resigned as Tory leader as soon as the result was known. Defeat was the logical conclusion to accumulating damage from splits and scandals over the previous two years. The party had become deeply divided on its policy towards Europe and over 70 "Eurosceptic" Tory MPs had been in more or less permanent revolt

▲ Tony Blair swept to power under the banner "New Labour, New Britain". In practice, this meant a sharp shift away from the party's traditional socialist policies.

against their own government on the issue. The government had also been weakened by setbacks such as the "arms to Iraq" affair, which had brought searing criticism of senior ministers from the Scott inquiry in February 1996, and the "mad cow" disease crisis which revealed powerful evidence of ministerial mishandling. Above all, the Conservative government had failed to distance itself from the misdeeds of a small number of Tory MPs, including Neil Hamilton, accused of accepting cash in return for asking parliamentary questions.

The defeat of Hamilton by an anti-sleaze candidate, journalist Martin Bell, was one of the highlights of a notably dramatic election night. Other prominent losers included the Defence Secretary Michael Portillo, beaten by a political beginner, Stephen Twigg, and former minister David Mellor, who lost his seat in Putney largely through the intervention of millionaire Sir James Goldsmith and his anti-European Referendum Party. In Northern Ireland, Sinn Fein leaders Gerry Adams and Martin McGuiness were elected to Westminster. Most notable of all, however, was the number of women elected – 119 in all, more than 100 of them Labour.

On winning the election, Blair told voters "You have put your trust in me and I intend to repay that trust." Gordon Brown, appointed chancellor of the exchequer, immediately stressed the new government's financial rectitude by handing over control of interest rates to the Bank of England. Remarkably, a Labour victory was followed by a rise in share prices. Only time would tell whether New Labour really stood for anything – if the earthquake was more apparent than real.

GIANNI VERSACE SHOT DEAD

▲ One of the great doyens of the fashion world, Gianni Versace. The true motive for his death remains unclear.

On July 15, 1997 Gianni Versace, the Italian fashion designer whose flamboyant creations clothed many of the rich and famous, was murdered outside his mansion, Casa Casuarina, in South Beach, Miami. He was returning home from buying a newspaper when a man shot him twice in the back of the head at point-blank range. He was 50 years old.

Rumours were soon circulating that Versace had been killed by a mafia hit-man. Frank Monte, a private investigator who claimed to have been hired by Versace, alleged that the fashion designer had been shot to prevent him going to the police with details of mafia money-laundering through his business empire. It was said that a dead bird had been found next to the body, a mafia warning to those who might be tempted to "sing" about the organization.

The FBI, however, were certain that Versace's death was connected with his homosexuality. As prime suspect they named Andrew Cunanan, a gay serial killer already on their "ten most wanted" list, who was known to be in Miami and who fitted the killer's description. It was suggested that Cunanan, who was believed to have murdered four gay men, might be HIV-positive, and that his killings might be a revenge on former lovers whom he thought had infected him.

On July 24, police located their suspect on a houseboat at Miami Beach. When they stormed the boat, they found Cunanan dead. He appeared to have committed suicide. Conspiracy buffs remained convinced that the mafia killed Versace and then disposed of Cunanan, thus conveniently closing down any further enquiry into the case.

- President Mobutu flees into exile from Kinshasa, Zaire
- Rebels take Kinshasa in Zaire; Laurent Kabila takes power
- Military coup in Liberia
- Prime Minister of France, Alain Juppé, resigns
- Death of British writer Laurie Lee

June
- Socialists win general elections in France; Lionel Jospin becomes Prime Minister
- Liberal Party wins elections in Canada
- Timothy McVeigh convicted of Oklahoma bombing and sentenced to death
- New coalition government formed in Ireland
- British government bans all handguns
- Amsterdam Treaty signed by EU leaders
- William Hague elected leader of British Conservative Party
- Verdict delivered in "McLibel" case, at 313 days the longest trial in British history
- Volcano erupts in Montserrat
- Bertie Ahern becomes Prime Minister of Ireland
- Death of French undersea explorer Jacques Cousteau

July
- China takes over Hong Kong from Britain
- Downey Report on cash-for-questions corruption affair in Britain finally published
- Protestant Orangemen parade in Drumcree, Northern Ireland; rioting and demonstrations ensue across Northern Ireland, including Belfast
- Slobodan Milosevic elected President in Serbia
- River Oder bursts its banks, causing flooding in Germany and Poland
- IRA declare cease-fire
- Deaths of US actors Robert Mitchum and James Stewart

'97

THE DEATH OF DIANA

▲ **During the grieving that followed her death, floral tributes to the "People's Princess" could be found in public places throughout Great Britain.**

In the early hours of the morning of August 31, 1997, a Mercedes carrying Diana, Princess of Wales, and her companion Dodi Fayed crashed into a concrete pillar in an underpass in Paris at high speed. Dodi Fayed and the driver of the car, Henri Paul, were killed instantly. The princess died at the hospital of La Pitié Salpetrière after a failed attempt to revive her. A bodyguard, Trevor Rees-Jones, survived the crash, though with very serious injuries.

At the time of her death, Diana was probably the most prominent celebrity in the world. Since her divorce from Prince Charles in 1996 she had never been out of the public eye, attracting attention equally for her support of humanitarian causes, such as AIDS charities and the campaign to ban landmines, and for

◄ **Happier times: the Prince and Princess of Wales enjoying a holiday in Spain with their young sons William and Harry.**

her glamour, enhanced by a dazzling succession of haute-couture frocks. Her relationship with Dodi Fayed, son of the owner of Harrods in London, Egyptian-born Mohamed Al Fayed, had been the talk of the tabloids throughout the summer.

None the less, few people were prepared for the astonishing wave of public grieving that swept Britain in the following week. Only Prime Minister Tony Blair immediately caught the appropriate tone. Speaking on the morning of the accident, he said: "She was the People's Princess and that is how she will stay ... in our hearts and our memories for ever." Millions of people clearly agreed. The area in front of the gates of Kensington Palace, the

Princess's London home, became a vast shrine to her memory – a sea of floral tributes interspersed with poems, personal mementos, candles, and cards. Mourners queued for hours to sign books of condolence in St James's Palace. Similar scenes were repeated on a smaller scale in many parts of the country.

With the sense of mourning came also a tide of anger. This was partly directed at the press. It was known that the Mercedes had been pursued by press photographers – the paparazzi – on motorbikes. Diana's brother, Earl Spencer, expressed a widely held view in his bitter statement immediately after the crash: "I always believed the press would kill her in the end, but not even I could believe they would take such a direct hand in her death."

Anger was also directed at the Royal Family, who were believed by Diana's admirers to have treated her shabbily, and whose

response to the tragedy was widely regarded as grudging and inadequate. Prince Charles flew to Paris to bring back Diana's body, which was taken to the Chapel Royal at St James's Palace. He then returned to Balmoral, where the Royal Family, including his sons, chose to grieve in private. The newspapers were soon expressing popular discontent at the lack of a public gesture from the Queen. The Royal Family were forced to issue a statement saying they were "hurt by suggestions that they are indifferent to the country's sorrow". On Friday, September 5 some of the damage was repaired, with a walkabout by the Queen and other Royals among mourners in London, and a televised address by the Queen in which she praised Diana as "a gifted human being".

Popular feeling dictated that there must be a state funeral for the Princess – by no means a foregone conclusion for the divorced wife of the heir to the throne. It took place in London on Saturday, September 6. A silent procession from Kensington Palace to Westminster Abbey was followed by a service of great drama and pathos. Earl Spencer delivered a stinging attack on the press and the Royal Family for their treatment of Diana, a speech that drew applause from part of the congregation and the huge crowd outside the Abbey. Singer Elton John, a friend of the Princess, sang a new version of his song "Candle in the Wind", dedicated to her and guaranteed to be one of the biggest-selling records of all time. When it was all over, the Princess's remains were carried off to the Spencer family home at Althorp, to be buried on an island in a lake.

Meanwhile, the story of the events of the fatal night had begun to emerge in more detail, without resolving the mysteries surrounding the crash. Princess Diana and Dodi Fayed had dined

▲ **A simple tribute from the Princes William and Harry. At her funeral, Princess Diana's brother, Earl Spencer, vowed to help raise the children in the way she would have wanted.**

at the Ritz hotel, owned by Dodi's father. The Mercedes' driver, Henri Paul, was not a trained chauffeur, but deputy head of security at the Ritz. Blood tests appeared to reveal that he had been drinking heavily before taking the wheel. Paparazzi on motorbikes had indeed buzzed around the vehicle, but the only evidence of a collision was with a mysterious white Fiat. The inevitable conspiracy theories began to circulate, with the open encouragement of Mohamed Al Fayed, attributing the death to a plot by the British secret service and the Royal Family. Evidence for this was totally lacking.

The extreme public mourning for Diana was such a striking phenomenon that many people saw in it evidence of some fundamental change in the emotions and attitudes of the British people. Tony Blair was far from alone in claiming that a more caring, compassionate society was emerging, evidenced by the reaction to Diana's death and encouraged by her example. Certainly, early contributions to her memorial fund were running at over £100,000 a day.

In the end, however, the most durable effect of the event seems to have been, rather surprisingly, a revival of respect and affection for the Royal Family. They had learned the lesson that a more popular image was needed. The Queen was soon to be seen visiting pubs and signing footballs, while Prince Charles jollied along with female pop stars. Opinion polls soon showed that their popularity was rising to the highest levels for many years.

◀ **The enduring image of Diana surrounded by a group of African children during her final campaign to ban the use of land-mines.**

PROGRESS TOWARDS PEACE IN IRELAND

In September 1997, all-party talks on the future of Northern Ireland got under way with the participation of both Sinn Fein, the political wing of the IRA, and the Ulster Unionists, the main Protestant party. This remarkable step forward for the peace process was due in large measure to the new British government elected the previous May.

One of Prime Minister Tony Blair's first speeches after taking office set the agenda, reassuring Unionists that a united Ireland was not a serious option, but offering to talk to all sides, despite the lack of a cease-fire by the IRA. The appointment of Mo Mowlam as Northern Ireland Secretary brought intelligence, directness, and evident goodwill to the process.

In the summer of 1997, it appeared that Northern Ireland was heading back into chaos. The

▲ Throughout the history of the "troubles" the vast majority of the people of Northern Ireland had declared their desire for peace.

decision to allow the annual Drumcree Orange Parade to pass through a Catholic area of Portadown on July 6 sparked Republican riots and bombings across the Province. A breakthrough, however, came almost immediately afterwards. First, Loyalists agreed to re-route marches to avoid Catholic districts, a major concession in the context of Northern Ireland sectarian tensions. Then, on July 19, the IRA announced a resumption of the 1994 cease-fire which they had abandoned 18 months earlier. The path to the peace talks was open.

DEVOLUTION UNDER WAY

▲ For many Scots voters the referendum victory was the first step along the path to complete independence.

During the 1997 election campaign, New Labour had promised major constitutional reforms, and once in power they proved true to their word. In September, referendums asked Scottish and Welsh voters to approve the setting up of national assemblies that would give them a considerable measure of control over their own affairs. The Scots were also asked whether they wanted their assembly to have the power to alter tax levels, a power not offered to the Welsh.

In Scotland, the prospect of devolution excited considerable enthusiasm. There had been deep resentment at the treatment of

Scotland by successive Conservative governments over the previous 18 years; as a result the Tories did not win a single seat north of the border in the general election. Scottish Secretary Donald Dewar led a high-profile campaign for a convincing "yes-yes" vote, with the active assistance of the Scottish Nationalists. On a reasonable turnout of electors, 73.4 per cent voted in favour of a Scottish assembly and 63.5 per cent approved that assembly having tax-varying powers. This scale of success could not be repeated in Wales, where the population was far more sceptical about devolution. In the event, the government managed to drum up a "yes" vote in Wales only by the narrowest of margins – a mere 6,721 votes.

It was generally agreed that the existence of a Welsh assembly would change little, but Scotland was another matter. The new parliament, which would meet in Edinburgh in 2000, marked the biggest change in Anglo-Scottish relations for 300 years. It was intended to have control of domestic matters such as health and education, while foreign policy and defence remained in the hands of Westminster. But once a democratically-elected parliament was in place clearly expressing the will of the Scottish people, what was to stop it extending its powers if it so wished – the same process that had recently led to the break-up of the Soviet Union and Yugoslavia? The Scottish Nationalist leader Alex Salmond was certain that devolution would prove to be the first step towards total independence for Scotland; Tony Blair asserted that it would strengthen the Union. The issue remained open.

THE TRIAL OF LOUISE WOODWARD

During the late autumn of 1997, the murder trial of British au pair Louise Woodward in a Massachusetts court attracted obsessive media attention and aroused a powerful emotional reaction from the British public. Woodward, a 19-year-old from the village of Elton in Cheshire, was alleged to have killed a nine-month-old baby, Matthew Eappen, who had been left in her care. The prosecution claimed she had hit the baby's head against a wall and then shaken him brutally. This Woodward vehemently denied.

Public interest focused partly on the treatment of au pairs in the United States. It emerged that they were expected to work excessively long hours and to take a large measure of responsibility for young children. Widespread sympathy was felt for Woodward, reinforced by her convincing performance on the witness stand. Emboldened by the way the case had gone, Woodward's lawyers rejected the option of a manslaughter verdict, insisting that the jury find her innocent or guilty of second-degree murder, which carried a statutory 15-year prison sentence. The jury duly found her guilty.

Much of the British press and public responded with outrage to the verdict. There was a wave of popular anti-American feeling and the US Embassy in London was picketed. Then, on November 9, the trial judge, Hiller Zobel, announced that he was overturning the jury's decision and substituting a verdict of guilty of manslaughter, citing Woodward's "confusion, inexperience, fright, and bad judgement" as the reasons for the baby's death. He sentenced her to 279 days, the time she had already spent in prison, so she was released immediately. She was not, however, free to return to Britain, since both sides decided to appeal – the defence wanting the guilty verdict overturned, the prosecution asking for the murder verdict to be reinstated.

Over the following months, some of Britain's tabloid newspapers completely reversed

▲ Is this the face of a murderer? British nanny Louise Woodward remains free but her name has never been cleared.

their stance on Woodward, becoming outspokenly hostile. In June 1998 the manslaughter verdict was upheld. Woodward's name was not cleared, but she was free to return home. There was no repeat of the jubilation that had greeted Judge Zobel's compassionate gesture the previous November. Mature and composed, Woodward set about the task of living with her notoriety.

November
- Iraq refuses access to installations by UN weapons inspectors, who are pulled out of Iran
- Jenny Shipley becomes Prime Minister of New Zealand
- World's first surviving septuplets born in the USA
- Japanese stockbrokers Yamaichi forced to stop trading
- Prime Minister of India resigns
- Death of former President of Malawi, Hastings Banda

December
- Beef on the bone banned by the British government
- EU bans tobacco advertising
- Kim Dae Jung wins South Korean presidential elections
- Terrorist Carlos the Jackal sentenced to life imprisonment in France
- Ex-President of Zambia Kenneth Kaunda arrested
- Loyalist terrorist prisoner Billy Wright assassinated in the Maze prison in Northern Ireland; IRA man Seamus Dillon killed in retaliation
- Violence breaks out during Kenyan elections
- Death of jazz violinist Stephane Grappelli

'98

THE GOOD FRIDAY PEACE AND THE OMAGH BOMB

On Good Friday, April 10, 1998, agreement was reached on a comprehensive peace settlement in Northern Ireland. Although rejected by some Unionists and derided by many political commentators, the Good Friday agreement was the best chance for an end to the Ulster Troubles since their escalation in the 1960s.

At the start of 1998, few people held out any great hopes for the all-party peace talks that had begun the previous September. But the British and Irish governments were unrelenting in their drive for an agreement. Prime Minister Blair had shown how far he was prepared to go in December 1997 when he had invited a Sinn Fein delegation, headed by Gerry Adams, to talks in Downing Street – the first time Irish

Republicans had set foot there since 1921. Northern Ireland Secretary Mo Mowlam went even further the following January by entering the Maze prison for talks with convicted Loyalist terrorists, who were threatening to veto the peace process. When the IRA were shown to have carried out a killing in breach of their cease-fire in February, Sinn Fein were banned from the talks for a paltry two weeks.

Only two days before Good Friday, which had been set as the deadline for agreement to be reached, it still seemed unlikely that all sides could strike an accord. The arrival of Tony Blair and his Irish opposite number, Bertie Ahern, at the talks, plus the intervention of President Bill Clinton by phone, eventually pushed the Northern Ireland parties into overcoming their

many doubts and reservations. The agreement provided for an Ulster parliament elected by proportional representation and a power-sharing executive committee. Various bodies would provide for co-operation with the Irish Republic. Terrorist prisoners were all to be released within two years. The key issue of the decommissioning of terrorist weapons was fudged.

After the agreement was reached, Blair said "I hope that the burden of history can at long last be lifted from our shoulders." It was an ambitious hope in a country so saturated in historic conflicts. Optimism rose, however, as successive hurdles were overcome. Ulster Unionist leader David Trimble and Sinn Fein's Gerry Adams both persuaded their own parties to back the agreement. Although other Unionist groups rejected the peace deal and the Protestant community was clearly deeply divided on the issue, in a referendum held in May the people of Northern Ireland overwhelmingly approved the agreement, with 71 per cent voting in favour. Mo Mowlam triumphantly proclaimed "They have voted to take the gun out of politics."

Elections for the new assembly were held in June and David Trimble became First Minister of the new Northern Ireland executive. But opposition from dissident Unionists remained fierce. As in the previous year, the annual Drumcree Orange march at Portadown in July was turned into a mass display of Protestant intransigence. As Orangemen confronted security forces ordered to stop the march

▲ **Deputy Prime Minister John Prescott surveys the damage caused by the Omagh bombing.**

passing through a Catholic area, a widespread breakdown of order in Ulster was predicted. But at the height of the confrontation, three young boys, Richard, Mark and Jason Quinn, were burned to death in a Loyalist petrol-bomb attack on their home. The horror was too great, and support for the Drumcree confrontation melted away.

The Quinn family massacre was soon dwarfed, however, by the Omagh bombing of August 15, the worst single outrage in the whole of the Northern Ireland conflict. A car bomb exploded in Market Street, Omagh's main thoroughfare, at 3.10 on a busy Saturday afternoon. Because of a confused telephone warning, police had cleared the wrong area. Twenty-eight people were killed and more than 200 injured. The dead included three generations of the same family – a grandmother, mother, and daughter. Yet the reaction to this massacre, caused by a Republican splinter group called the Real IRA, only proved how far the peace process had come. Gerry Adams denounced the attack, following up with a statement that violence must be "a thing of the past, over, done with and gone". Public revulsion was so great that the Real IRA were forced to announce the suspension of their terrorist campaign.

In October, it was announced that First Minister David Trimble and Social Democratic and Labour Party leader John Hume had been awarded the Nobel Peace Prize. Trimble cautiously commented, "There is an element of prematurity about this." The failure of terrorists to disarm remained a major obstacle to the full implementation of the peace agreement. But at least, for the first time in many years, there was hope in Northern Ireland.

GEORGE MICHAEL OUTED

▲ **In spite of the tabloid headlines, George Michael's "outing" has had little adverse impact on his popularity.**

On April 7, 1998, British pop singer George Michael was charged with performing a "lewd act" in a Beverly Hills public convenience, witnessed by an undercover police officer. A Los Angeles court later sentenced him to 81 days' community service and a fine of £500.

Shortly after he was charged, Michael announced on television that he was currently in a homosexual relationship. He told CNN, "I have not been in a relationship with a woman for almost 10 years." Michael had originally been marketed as a heterosexual heart throb with the pop duo Wham! and was at pains to state that, at that time, his relationships were with women.

Michael's discomfiture highlighted the continuing problems of gay life at the end of the twentieth century. Despite the generally liberated atmosphere prevailing in Western countries, many gays still preferred to remain in the closet. Their difficulties were emphasized again later in the year in the UK, when government ministers Peter Mandelson and Nick Brown were pursued by the tabloid press with allegations of homosexuality. Gay liberation still had a long way to go.

'98

NEWS IN BRIEF

....

May

- Over 100 die in border clashes between Eritrea and Ethiopia
- Border clashes between Chad and Nigeria
- Seven people killed when police open fire on pro-democracy demonstration in Nigeria
- Prime Minister of Benin, Adrien Houngbedji, resigns
- India detonates nuclear device
- Four Iranian diplomats expelled from Argentina following allegations of complicity in anti-Israel terrorist bomb attack which killed 86 in Argentina
- Civil unrest causes resignation of President Kemusu Suharto of Indonesia; B J Habibie succeeds
- Pakistan detonates nuclear device
- Joseph Estrada becomes President of the Philippines
- First round of presidential elections in Colombia

HURRICANE MITCH

In late October and early November 1998, Hurricane Mitch, the fourth strongest hurricane in the Caribbean this century, struck Central America. For five days there was a deluge, with up to 24 inches of rain falling daily. It was this rainfall, rather than the strength of the winds, that brought almost unprecedented destruction, especially to the republics of Honduras and Nicaragua.

Vast areas of countryside were under water as floods rose, and towns and villages were swept away in landslides of mud, trees, and rocks. In one well publicized case, more than 330 people were buried alive in a single mudslide on the slopes of the Casita volcano in Nicaragua. Estimates of the death toll fluctuated wildly as the authorities struggled to come to terms with the scale of the catastrophe, but it was soon reckoned that at least 10,000 had died in the two countries, and more than a million were homeless.

The tragedy was brought home to the British public through the story of one Honduran woman, Laura Isabella Arriola Batiz de

▲ The devastation that followed in the wake of Hurricane Mitch is estimated to have set the economy of Honduras back 20 years.

Guity. She was rescued by the British frigate *Sheffield* after being swept out to sea when her village was destroyed by the storm. She had survived for six days in the water, clinging to floating debris. Her husband, their three children, and all six members of her brother's family had died in the catastrophe.

It soon became apparent that the long-term economic impact of the disaster could be even more devastating than the short-term death toll. Roads and bridges had

been swept away and hundreds of thousands of homes had been destroyed. The banana industry, one of the main sources of income and employment in Honduras, had been wiped out. Honduran President Carlos Flores asserted that development in his country had been put back 50 years. After a slow start, the outside world rallied round to provide both immediate assistance and the promise of long-term aid, especially in the form of debt relief.

ASIAN FINANCIAL CRISIS

In late 1997 and early 1998, the boom that had transformed the economies and societies of the East Asian Pacific Rim since the 1980s came to a shattering halt. South Korea, one of the world's highest growth economies, held up as an inspiring example of youthful energy and enterprise, descended into financial chaos. As businesses went bust, the South Korean government sought massive aid from the International Monetary Fund (IMF), negotiating

a multi-billion dollar loan package. Thailand, Indonesia, and Malaysia also went into crisis, while the Hong Kong stock exchange struggled with the slump. Most important of all, Japan, the world's second-largest industrial economy, drifted into recession – its economy shrank by 5 per cent between mid-1997 and mid-1998 – with its political and business elite apparently incapable of adopting the measures needed to turn the tide.

The Asian crisis led to a sharp cutback in imports by those countries, plus a dumping of their excess production at bargain basement prices on the world market. This set alarm bells ringing in the West, where analysts were soon predicting the end of booming stock markets and a return to rising unemployment. Pessimism reached a new pitch in August 1998, when the Russian currency and financial markets went into free fall, revealing the bankruptcy of the free market reforms carried out since the break-up of the Soviet Union in 1991.

In October, President Bill Clinton told an IMF summit meeting that the world was facing its worst economic crisis for 50 years, and British Chancellor of the Exchequer Gordon Brown announced that "with Japan and one quarter of the world in recession, every country will be affected by the instability affecting the world economy". Yet the talk of "global financial meltdown" proved at the very least premature. By early 1999, Western stock markets had recovered most of the losses they suffered in the autumn panic. The Euro, the new European single currency, was launched successfully in January, giving an instant boost to confidence in the European Union.

The world financial system had proved to have far more stability than most people had believed.

▲ 1998 saw the "Tiger" economies of Asia losing their roar.

THUGS AND HEROES AT THE WORLD CUP

The football World Cup finals were held in France in June and July 1998, with both England and Scotland competing. Serious fears of hooliganism expressed in many quarters before the event were at least partly realised. There were serious disturbances involving drunken England supporters in Marseilles, followed by an even worse rampage by Germans in Lens. Despite the attention devoted to these incidents, to most people it was the football that mattered.

Football fever gripped both England and Scotland. On match days streets were empty and normal life came to a halt. Both home teams performed creditably.

Scotland gave the holders, Brazil, a close call in the opening match of the finals, before making their traditional exit at the end of the first round. England won through to a dramatic second-round tie against Argentina, illuminated by a spectacular individual goal from 18-year-old Michael Owen, the youngest player to appear for England this century. The match was marred by the sending off of midfielder David Beckham for petty retaliation, and England eventually lost on penalties.

Overall, the finals produced some attractive football but little of sensational quality. France ran out winners, beating a lacklustre Brazil 3-0 in the final. The fact that the French team was a racial mix, including exceptionally gifted black and Arab players, confounded France's buoyant right-wing National Front, who would have preferred the selection of an all-white squad.

▲ French World Cup hero Zinedine Zidane brandishes the trophy.

'98

NEWS IN BRIEF

August

- Hundreds killed in leftist guerrilla offensive in Colombia
- Rebellion against Laurent Kabila breaks out in Congo
- State of emergency declared in Sri Lanka
- Taliban forces capture Mazar-I-Sharif in Afghanistan to testify as defendant
- Canadian Supreme Court rules Quebec does not have right to secede unilaterally
- Cease-fire in civil war in Guinea-Bissau

September

- Deputy Prime Minister of Malaysia, arrested on trumped-up charges
- South Africa intervenes in conflict in Lesotho
- Chancellor Kohl defeated in elections in Germany
- Economic crisis engulfs Brazil

October

- British cabinet minister Ron Davies resigns following a "moment of madness" on London's Clapham Common
- John Glenn becomes the oldest person to go into space at the age of 77
- Winnie Mandela's gang, known as the Mandela United Football Club are implicated in the murders of 18 in Soweto

HEREDITARY PEERS TO GO

In October 1998, the Labour leader in the House of Lords, Baroness Jay of Paddington, announced that the government intended to abolish the right of hereditary peers to sit in the upper house of the UK parliament. She described the possession of political power by right of birth as "glaringly unfair and glaringly outdated".

The government faced a crucial difficulty in its effort to reform the Lords: the ability of peers to delay any legislation abolishing their powers. Of the 1,165 members of the House of Lords, 476 were committed Tory supporters, as against 175 for Labour. Among hereditary peers, 304 were committed Tories and 18 regularly supported Labour.

In an effort to smooth the path of reform legislation, in January 1999 the government accepted a compromise under which 91 hereditary peers would be allowed to remain in a "transition House" while a Royal Commission decided what exact formula a new Upper House should follow.

▲ The abolition of hereditary peers in House of Lords would benefit the Labour Party since 95% of them are committed Tories.

GENERAL PINOCHET ARRESTED

On October 17, 1998, the 82-year-old former Chilean dictator General Augusto Pinochet was arrested in a private London hospital, where he was recovering from back surgery. The arrest was at the official request of two

Spanish judges, Baltazar Garzon and Manuel Garcia Castellon, who had been investigating the disappearance or death of hundreds of Spanish nationals in Chile during the general's 17-year rule. They wanted Pinochet extradited to Spain to stand trial. The Swiss, Belgian, and French authorities subsequently filed their own requests for extradition.

Pinochet came to power in Chile in a military coup against the democratically elected left-wing government of Salvador Allende in 1973. The seizure of power was followed by thousands of well documented cases of human rights abuses, including the killing of at least 3,000

◄ Some may perceive him as an ailing old man, but many still seek General Pinochet's conviction for crimes against humanity.

people and the widespread use of torture. In 1990 Chile returned to democracy and Pinochet stepped down as President. However, he remained commander-in-chief of the Chilean armed forces, a post he held until March 1998, when he exchanged it for a life seat in the Chilean senate. An amnesty law guaranteed him freedom from prosecution in Chile for any offences committed while he was in power.

Ironically, Pinochet was an admirer of Britain, making annual visits to London to lunch at Fortnum and Mason and visit Madame Tussaud's. Former Prime Minister Margaret Thatcher was a great admirer of the general, who regularly sent her chocolates and flowers on her birthday, and had been to her house for tea. Along with other leading Conservatives, including the current party leader William Hague, Mrs Thatcher outspokenly attacked the proposed extradition, arguing variously that Pinochet had helped Britain during the Falklands War; that his arrest might damage Chile's fragile democracy; and that he was basically a good man who had prevented Chile falling under a Communist dictatorship. The British government stuck to the official line that the request for extradition was a purely legal matter, although individual ministers were more outspoken. Trade and Industry Secretary Peter Mandelson said that the idea of a brutal dictator claiming immunity from prosecution as a former head of state "would be pretty gut-wrenching stuff" for most people.

On October 28, the High Court upheld the view that Pinochet enjoyed immunity and declared his detention illegal. An appeal to the House of Lords produced a dramatic reversal of this decision, however, with the Law Lords voting 3-2 to allow extradition proceedings to continue. This decision, endorsed by Home Secretary Jack Straw, was subsequently undermined by the revelation that one of the Law Lords, Lord Hoffman, was associated with Amnesty International, an organization that had submitted evidence against Pinochet and campaigned in favour of his extradition.

Coming at a time when the first war crimes tribunal since the Nuremberg trials was attempting to bring to justice individuals guilty of "ethnic cleansing" in Bosnia, the Pinochet case, whatever its eventual outcome, clearly marked another step forward for those keen to see respect for human rights enforced by international law.

WAR AND THE PRESIDENT

On December 16, 1998, war flared once more in the Gulf. The United States and Britain launched Operation Desert Fox to punish Iraqi leader Saddam Hussein for his refusal to implement the cease-fire agreement that ended the 1991 Gulf War. Iraq had agreed to destroy all "weapons of mass destruction" and to allow UN inspectors access to any sites they might wish to visit to ensure the terms were being complied with. But Saddam had consistently obstructed the work of UN inspection teams and there was strong evidence that he was still developing the potential for chemical and biological warfare.

Between December 16 and 19, Iraq was hit by about 400 Cruise missiles fired from American warships or aircraft. RAF Tornado aircraft armed with "smart" weapons also carried out a large number of missions. Targets included secret bunkers, barracks of the elite Republican Guard, and communications centres.

The strikes were not authorized by the United Nations and were opposed by Russia and by most of America's allies. Britain once more stood out as Washington's closest friend. In the United States, many politicians and political commentators regarded the raids as a cynical ploy to distract attention from a vote in Congress on the impeachment of President Clinton in the Monica Lewinsky case, cynics dubbing it "the war of Monica's dress".

There were widespread doubts about the effectiveness of military action which was unlikely to topple Saddam or undermine his authority. In effect, the Western powers were in a trap: they could not allow Saddam to develop weapons of mass destruction with impunity, yet could not stop him without a full-scale invasion they were not prepared to undertake.

▲ The banishing of arms inspectors from Iraq once again brought a show of force from the United Nations.

'99

MIDDLE EAST LINCHPIN DIES

▲ **King Hussein of Jordan with his chosen successor, his eldest son Prince Abdullah, commander of Jordan's special forces.**

On February 8, 1999, King Hussein of Jordan, one of the key figures in the delicate political balance of the Middle East died. After a long fight against cancer at an American clinic, the King chose to return to Jordan for his final days. Hussein's death was accompanied by unprecedented scenes of national grieving; throughout the rest of the world, he was mourned in recognition of his central position in Middle East politics.

Hussein's education in England was interrupted in 1952 when his father, King Talal, was deposed. The 18-year-old prince took to the Jordanian throne a year later. Throughout the 1960s – as it was throughout his reign – Hussein steered a difficult course between his natural allegiance to neighbouring Arab states and the West on whom Jordan relied for financial aid.

He experienced a major set-back in June 1967 when his forces were heavily defeated in the Arab-Israeli War. This resulted in the loss of the West Bank to Israel and a heavy influx of Palestinian refugees into Jordan.

For the next three years Jordan became a base for the Palestinian Liberation Organization's (PLO) guerrilla war against Israel. Threatening to destabilize Jordan, in September 1970 a full-scale war broke out between the PLO and the Jordanian army in a struggle for control of the country. Hussein was victorious, expelling the PLO's forces from Jordan the following year.

The two decades that followed saw Hussein emerge as a world statesman as he refrained from a military confrontation with Israel, mended relations with the PLO and forged closer ties with Saudi Arabia and other moderate Arab states. He also worked hard to maintain good relations with the United States and Great Britain.

Following six months of cancer treatment in the US, the King returned to Jordan and immediately ordered the replacement of his brother, Prince Hassan. It was clear that the ailing King sought a more suitable successor, which he saw as his eldest son, Prince Abdullah, commander of the Jordanian Army's special Forces.

ZIPPERGATE RUNS OUT OF STEAM

February 12, 1999 saw the end of the most serious constitutional crisis to hit America since the days of Watergate. Having been found guilty of covering up the truth about his affair with former White House intern Monica Lewinsky, President Clinton was zealously pursued by Republican prosecutor Ken Starr who successfully campaigned to have the President impeached. Although the President was eventually acquitted, it had been a gruelling 13 months in which the government of the USA seemed to on hold while the private life of the most powerful man in the world came under scrutiny.

Throughout his two terms as President, Clinton's personal affairs had always been under question. As early as 1994 he was investigated about his involvement in an Arkansas real estate development known as Whitewater. Six months later, a lawsuit was filed alleging that Clinton sexually harassed a state clerk, Paula Jones, while he was

▲ Monica Lewinsky, pictured beyond President Clinton's left shoulder, the woman at the heart of the "Zippergate" scandal.

governor of Arkansas. Nevertheless, Clinton remained popular and was re-elected in 1996.

Clinton's troubles began in earnest in May 1997 when the Supreme Court ruled that Paula Jones would be allowed to pursue her lawsuit while Clinton was still in office. As a part of the investigation, former White House intern Monica Lewinsky, suspected of having an affair with the President, was served a subpoena to appear at a deposition for the Jones suit. Although she signed an affidavit claiming that no relationship had existed, one of her colleagues, Linda Tripp, gave the court copies of taped conversations with Lewinsky which proved the contrary.

On January 17 1998, President Clinton testified in the Jones lawsuit in which he denied a sexual relationship with Lewinsky or covering up the truth. Clinton then made his famous public declaration: "I did not have sexual relations with that woman … I never told anybody to lie." Events thereafter moved swiftly and farcically, peaking with the revelation that Monica Lewinsky still possessed a semen-stained dress that could prove the President's guilt.

Although the Paula Jones case was dismissed on April 1, 1998,

Kenneth Starr continued to pursue the President. On August 6, having agreed immunity from prosecution (having previously lied under oath), Monica Lewinsky testified to the Starr grand jury. Eleven days later, Clinton underwent more than four hours of questioning. Humiliated as the truth emerged, Clinton was forced to give a televised speech in which he admitted to the American public: "I did have a relationship with Miss Lewinsky that was not appropriate … it constituted a critical lapse in judgment and a personal failure on my part for which I am solely and completely responsible." When the Starr Report was published the author urged the Senate and House of Representatives to hold an impeachment inquiry.

Even after these damaging revelations, public opinion was still behind the President. In spite of his flaws, most Americans thought he had done a good job in office and fewer than a third believed he should be impeached. But despite growing public resentment, on December 19, 1998, the Republicans got

▶ Kenneth Starr, the Republican prosecutor who believed he could bring down President Clinton.

their way – President William Jefferson Clinton was impeached on counts of perjury and obstruction of justice.

The impeachment trial began on January 7 1999, and over the month that followed Clinton and Lewinsky were again called for questioning. By now the Republicans sensed that the most Americans now viewed the proceedings as a witch hunt and efforts were made to make the investigation brief. Finally, on February 12, the 100-strong Senate jury voted 55–45 against the perjury charge and 50–50 on obstruction – nowhere near the two-thirds majority required to remove Clinton from office.

In the aftermath of "Zippergate", Clinton's personal popularity was still high. He would be allowed to stay at the White House until the end of his presidency in January 2001. The behaviour of the Republicans was widely condemned and would most likely be used against them in the presidential elections during 1999. Meanwhile, Monica Lewinsky became a celebrity, earning millions of dollars from the media interest that surrounded the biggest sexual scandal ever to hit the political world.

MASSACRE AT COLUMBINE HIGH

▲ **Broadcast to the world live as it happened, students at Columbine High make their final dash to safety.**

" I'm a teacher at Columbine High School and there's a student here with a gun." This was the 911 call on April 20, 1999 that alerted the Colorado emergency services to the latest and most devastating schoolyard shooting to hit the United States.

Following on from similar attacks in Oregon, Mississippi, Pennsylvania, Kentucky and Arkansaw, two students carried out a carefully planned attack on their school which left 15 dead and many others injured. The siege ended when the two assailants turned their powerful Tec-9 sub-machine guns on themselves.

The Columbine tragedy highlighted a growing phenomenon that sees young self-styled "misfits" increasingly drawn to cult societies which often operate outside of conventional notions of social acceptability. The ringleader of the attack was 18-year-old Eric Harris. A young computer and Internet whiz-kid, Harris was so skilled in his field that teachers would often ask him for help. Harris and his colleague Dylan Klebold were part of a clique known as the Trenchcoat Mafia. They dressed similarly, in uniform duster trenchcoats, berets and shades, and greeted one another with Nazi salutes. Indeed, the attack was planned to coincide with the birthday of Adolf Hitler.

After the event, the media and authorities inevitably quizzed themselves for clues that might have enabled them to predict the tragic events of April 20. They needed to look no further than the Trenchcoat Mafia's internet site, the violent, racist content of which had evidently been reported to the Denver police on a number of occasions. Weeks before the attack, the web pages, which even had postings teaching how to make crude, home-built bombs, boasted of the intention to "shoot everyone at Columbine High". After the event, a search of Harris's home yielded a small stockpile of arms, which led many to question the degree to which he was monitored by his parents. And yet Harris and Klebold were not, as some might have expected, out-of-control "white trash", but products of a wealthy suburb – 17-year-old Klebold already owned his own BMW.

Once again, however, the subject of governmental gun control reared its head. It is here that some of the starkest differences between the cultures of Britain and America can be seen. The Dunblane massacre of 1994 brought about widespread public support for the banning of handguns and other firearms in Britain; in the USA, whatever the tragedy, the notion of taking steps to curb what is seen as an

▲ **America's Vice-President, Al Gore, and his wife Tipper pay the respects at Columbine High School.**

individual's basic freedom to own a weapon is invariably branded "unconstitutional" by the powerful National Rifle Association lobby. But the argument is undoubtedly a complex one. Indeed, barely a week after the Columbine massacre, Alberta in Canada was the scene of a "copycat" schoolyard shooting in which a student was killed and another wounded – this in a country with some of the world's strictest firearms legislation and virtually no "gun culture".

After Columbine some Americans were prepared to ask if these tragedies were a fair price to pay for "freedom". Professor Carl Raschke, a leading expert in twentieth-century cults, was brutally frank: "The problem with American democracy is that we just don't like setting limits to unacceptable behaviour – even when it's playing with political and spiritual nitro-glycerine."

THE MURDER OF A TELEVISION GOLDEN GIRL

Monday, April 26, 1999 saw Britain's television-viewing public reeling with shock as the news emerged that Jill Dando, one of the country's most popular presenters, had been murdered outside her home in West London.

Neighbours had heard a scream and found the 37-year-old star slumped on the doorsteps of her terraced house in Fulham. By the time she had been taken to nearby Charing Cross Hospital she was dead. Following an autopsy, it was established that Dando had been shot through the head at point-blank range.

Dando had started her career on a local newspaper in her home town of Weston-Super-Mare, on the west coast of England. She progressed through regional broadcasting to a regular place on the BBC's national news network. Her public fame, however, rested on her work with the "Holiday" and "Crimewatch", the latter a popular show in which members of the public were invited to help the police solve difficult, often violent, crimes.

Dando's murder brought tributes from colleagues who viewed her as both a consummate professional and someone whose character had been unchanged by celebrity. Deeply popular with the British viewing public, her baffling murder touched the public more

▲ The motive for television presenter Jill Dando's murder looks set to remain a mystery.

than any other figure since the death of Diana, Princess of Wales in August 1997.

A particularly sad irony was that in spite of an increasingly successful career her personal life had until recent times been less than settled. This seemed about to change with the announcement of a proposed autumn marriage to gynaecologist Alan Farthing.

The motives for Jill Dando's murder remain a mystery. Seemingly grasping at straws, some suggested that it may have been retribution for the Nato bombing of Serbian television buildings. Others considered that it may have been connected with her role on "Crimewatch". Indeed the calculated and professional manner in which she was murdered – a single silenced shot from a 9mm pistol – have all the hallmarks of a contract killing. But the baffling question remained – who on earth would want to kill Jill Dando?

▲ A police cordon surrounds Jill Dando's Fulham house: her killing took place in broad daylight on her own doorstep.

WAR IN EUROPE

It seemed somehow inevitable that should Europe once again find itself at war, the spark would be ignited in the Balkan region, a perpetual centre of conflict throughout the century. So it was that on March 24, 1999, the combined forces of Nato launched the first of many bombing raids on the Serbian capital of Belgrade following the refusal of President Slobodan Milosevic to end his program of "ethnic cleansing" in the Serbian province of Kosovo.

It was ethnic and religious differences that brought violent conflict to the tiny province of Kosovo. Over 90 percent of its population of two million were ethnic Albanians, the remainder were of Serb descent. A traditional hostility had always existed between the two groups, who pursued different religions, spoke different languages and even used different alphabets. However, in spite of its ethnic minority, Kosovo was a symbolically important to Serbia as the seat of the Serbian Orthodox Church. In one of the most important battles in Serbian history, Kosovo was seized by the Turks in 1389. It did not return to Serbian rule until 1913.

During the Tito administration that followed World War Two when the Balkan republics were united under Communism as the federation of Yugoslavia, Kosovo was largely self-governing. All of this changed with the revolution that swept through the Eastern Bloc at the end of the 1980s. Yugoslavia saw the secession of Bosnia, Croatia, Slovenia and Macedonia, leaving only Serbia and Montenegro in the federation. In 1989, former Communist Party leader Slobodan Milosevic came to power and immediately sought to restore full government control over the two Serb

▲ A mass grave inside Kosovo provides horrific evidence of Serbia's policy of ethnic cleansing.

provinces of Vojvodina and Kosovo. Appealing to a deep sense of nationalism among the Serbian people, Milosevic fought for the creation of a "Greater Serbia" during the chaos that ensued within neighbouring Bosnia and Croatia.

The new regime was hard-felt in Kosovo, where all Albanians in state employment immediately lost their jobs. Amid growing oppression, increasing numbers of ethnic Albanians called for total independence. Ex-government officials formed an "alternative" state, holding their own elections and levying their own taxes, at the same time appealing in vain to the West for support. Growing impatient, younger militant Kosovars took their own course

of action, forming the Kosovo Liberation Army (KLA). While the West ignored the troubles brewing in the province, the KLA grew in strength and by 1995 were engaged in regular sorties against the Serb authorities.

In 1998, international attention finally turned to Kosovo when President Milosevic sent in the Yugoslav army to deal with the KLA. However, his brutal tactics were not only aimed at the "terrorists" but at the Albanian population. Within months hundreds of thousands of ethnic Albanians had been forced to flee their homes. As towns and villages were razed, reports from the region began to suggest that an ethnic genocide was in progress.

With horrifying news of humani-

▲ Slobodan Molosevic asserting his position on one of his many broadcasts on Serb national televison.

▲ Reaching out for a peaceful end to a conflict that has destroyed many communities in Kosovo.

tarian disaster emerging daily, it was Nato rather than the United Nations that took the offensive against the Serbs. On October 18, 1998, Richard Holbrooke, the US envoy sent to broker peace in the region, gave President Milosevic an ultimatum to withdraw his forces from Kosovo at the threat of air strikes. Although the Serbs succumbed to the threats hours before the deadline, by the end of the year fighting between the two sides had resumed.

On January 16, 1999, the bodies of 45 ethnic Albanians were discovered at Racak in the south of Kosovo, evidently part of another massacre by Serbian troops. With growing outrage voiced from around the world, a six nation "contact group" met at Rambouillet near Paris bringing together Serb and ethnic Albanian leaders. A month of negotiations brought agreement on autonomy for Kosovo within the Serbian republic, but faltered on President Milosevic's refusal of a Nato peace-keeping force. Ultimately, Serbia would not sign up to the Rambouillet agreement.

With heavy fighting continuing to sweep through Kosovo, on March 22, Richard Holbrooke was once again despatched to Belgrade to present President Milosevic with a final ultimatum.

When on the following day he declared that the talks had failed, Nato announced their intention to launch a series of air strikes at military targets throughout Serbia. The first bombs fell on March 24.

Nato's strategy of debilitating Serbia's military machine through continuous air raids was widely criticized from outside of the Nato states. Unlike the campaign against Iraq, the bombing of Serbia did not have a United Nations mandate and some viewed it as an act of "Western Imperialism". Furthermore, military strategists declared that only the deployment of ground troops in the region would succeed in removing Serbian forces from Kosovo. However, America and Britain – the two strongest supporters of the air campaign – remained conscious of the need to avoid the casualties that would inevitably accompany a ground campaign. It was understood that war in the modern era could not be fought without public support. Although most Britons and Americans were broadly in favour of the air strikes, that support would soon diminish when presented with images of casualties returning home in body bags. With the air strikes alone costing an estimated £200 million each week, a growing vocal criticism

from within the Nato states was inevitable.

As the bombing campaign increased throughout April and May, so too did Serb military action in Kosovo, creating an unprecedented flow of refugees into neighbouring Albania, Macedonia and Montenegro. Over a million Kosovar Albanians were forced to flee their state – over half the population. Nato's competence was also brought into question with the accidental bombing of a refugee convoy and destruction of the Chinese embassy in Belgrade – the latter attributed to the use of an out-of-date map.

In the eyes of the world, Slobodan Milosevic had replaced Saddam Hussein as its newest *bête noire*. And like the Iraqi leader, Milosevic proved that he

was equally prepared to gamble with world opinion, provoking a reaction before pulling back from the brink of disaster. Most of all, however, the two leaders understood that an inevitable military defeat by the combined forces of Nato or the United Nations could be used effectively to strengthen their own positions at home.

At the end of the day, no matter how much damage Nato has inflicted on Serbia's infrastructure, President Milosevic would seem to have succeeded in ridding much of Kosovo of its ethnic Albanian population. Even when Serbia is forced to allow their return, most of the refugees will find that their homes, villages or even entire towns are now little more than bombed-out ruins. And so the question remains – what happens next?

▲ General Mike Jackson reads out the terms of the June 1999 peace agreement reached between Serbia and Nato.

INDEX

A

abdication crisis 143
Abdülhamid II, Sultan 32
Abel, Rudolf 286
Aberfan 324
Abyssinia 118–19, 141 *see also* Ethiopia
Adams, Gerry 529, 534
Aden 332-3
Adenauer, Konrad 216
Aehrenthal, Lexa von 33
Afghanistan 419, 478
African National Congress (ANC) 285, 309, 404, 466, 524
Afrikaner Resistance Movement 466
AIDS 460–1, 507
Akihoto, Crown Prince 278
Alabama 264–5
Alaska 280
Albania 48, 559
Alcock, John 77
Alexander, Harold 179
Alexander, King 137
Algeria 252–3, 272, 296–7
Ali, Muhammad 327, 537
Ali, Sherif Hussein ibn 62
Allende, Salvador 373
American Indian Movement (AIM) 372
Amiens, Battle of 72
Amin, Idi 369, 414–15
Amoco Cadiz 406
Amritsar 452–3
Amundsen, Roald 42–3
Anderson, William R 274
Andropov, Yuri 441, 456
Angola 388–9
anti-semitism 133, 140, 150, 184–5, 196–7
Anzio 188–9
apartheid 105, 143, 466, 492, 521, 524
Aquino, Cory 468
Arab Revolt 62, 66

Arabic 58
Arafat, Yasser 355, 438–9, 519
Aramburu, Pedro 254
Arbuckle, Roscoe "Fattie" 87
archaeology: Dead Sea Scrolls 206–7; Knossos 13; Lascaux Grotto 163; *Mary Rose* 440; Piltdown Man 243–4; Tutankhamen 89
Argentina 234, 254, 436–7
Armenia 481, 509
arms race 217, 226–7, 251, 252, 475
Armstrong, Louis 360
Armstrong, Neil 344–5
art: Andy Warhol 469; Edvard Munch 187; futurism 36; Henri Matisse 247; impressionism 19; Pablo Picasso 372; Paul Gauguin 19; Piet Mondrian 187; surrealism 101
Ashdown, Paddy 542
Asian financial crisis 550–1
Asquith, Herbert 28, 50, 63, 93
Astor, Nancy 77
Astor, William Waldorf 77
Aswan Dam 17, 275, 354
Atatürk 32, 46, 92
Atlanta 537
Atlantic Charter 171
atomic bomb 198–9
atomic physics 125, 198
Attlee, Clement 201, 226, 255
Aum sect 530
Aung San 182
Australia: and Gallipoli 59; Sydney Harbour Bridge 118
Austria 148, 463
Austria-Hungarian Empire: and Balkans 33, 39, 52, 53; World War One 52, 53, 55, 74
Avery, Oswald 186
Aydid, Mohammed Farah 515
Azerbaijan 200, 509

B

Ba Maw 182
Baader, Andreas 386
Baader-Meinhof Gang 386, 394
Bacall, Lauren 265
Baird, John Logie 102, 121
Bakker, Jim 477
Balaguer, Joaquin 316
Baldwin, Stanley 93, 102
Balfour, Arthur 66, 81
Balfour Declaration 66, 111, 212
Balkans: early conflicts 33, 39, 48; World War One 52; World War Two 167; 558–9
balloon flight 120, 147
Bangladesh 359, 363
Bannister, Roger 244–5
Bao Dai, Emperor 225
Baodouin I, King 228
Barings Bank 528–9
Barnard, Christiaan 333
Barnett, Ross 299
Barthou, Louis 137
Baryshnikov, Mikhail 380
Batista, Fulgencio 276
Battle of Britain 164–5
Bay of Pigs 292
Beatles 310–11, 330–1, 352
Becquerel, Henri 20, 21
Begin, Menachem 409
Belgium: Baudoin I 228; Brussels World Fair 272; and Congo 34–5, 286–7; Leopold III 228; paedophile scandal 538; and World War One 53, 54; and World War Two 158
Belgrano 437, 449
Ben Bella, Ahmed 297
Ben-Gurion, David 212
Benes, Eduard 211
Bennett, James Gordon 30

D

F

Pasha, Enver 46
Pasha, Kamil 46
Pauling, Linus 15, 246–7
Paulus, Freidrich 181
peace movements 252, 270–1, 450–1
Pearl Harbor 172–3
Pearse, Padraic 61
Peary, Robert 36–7, 42
Pele 273
penicillin 108–9
Perón, Eva 234
Perón, Juan 234, 254, 380–1
Pershing, John 60
Peru 308–9, 541
Pétain, Marshal 64, 160
Petrograd 68, 69
Petsamo 156
Phar Lap 124
Philby, Kim 229
Philippines 468–9
Picasso, Pablo 372
Piccard, Auguste 120
Piccard, Jacques 284
Piltdown Man 243–4
Pinochet, Augusto 373, 480, 552–3
Pius XII, Pope 254
Planck, Max 15
Pluto 116–17
Poindexter, John 474–5
Pol Pot 412
Poland 152–3, 184–5, 357, 410, 425, 440–1, 500–1
polio vaccine 244
poll tax riots 492–3
Ponting, Clive 449
Popular Front for the Liberation of Palestine (PFLP) 355, 368, 394
Port Arthur 24
Portugal 387
Potemkin 26
Potsdam Agreement 197, 232
Poulson, John 369
Powell, Enoch 335
Powers, Gary 286

Prague Spring 340
Preece, William 14
Presley, Elvis 258–9, 403
Pretoria 17
Princip, Gavril 53
Profumo, John 302–3
prohibition 80–1, 110, 131
Prudhomme, Sully 15
Pu–yi, Emperor 44
punk 401

R

Rabin, Yitzhak 519, 532–3
radar 138, 161, 165
radio 14, 41, 149
Rahman, Sheik Mujibir 359, 363
Rainbow Warrior 458–9
Rákosi, Matyas 260
Ranier II, Prince 261
Rawlinson, General 64, 72
Ray, James Earl 335
Reagan, Ronald 426–7, 429, 442, 444–5, 474–5
Red Brigade 406–7
Reichstag burning 136
Remagen 193
reparations 84, 121, 134
Republican Party 15, 44
revolutions: Cuba 276; Iranian 413; Portugese 387; Russia 26–7, 68–9, 94–5; Turkey 32
Reynolds, Albert 529
Reynaud, Paul 160, 162
Rhine 193
Rhodes, Cecil 16
Rhodesia 16, 318–19, 408–9
Rice, Donna 470
Rice-Davis, Mandy 302, 303
Riza, Ahmed 32
Robinson, Mary 500
rock and roll 258–9

Rockefeller, John D 51
Röhm, Ernst 137
Rolling Stones 311, 343
Roman Catholic Church: Argentina 254; France 20; Pope John Paul II 410
Romania 167, 489
Rommel, Erwin 166–7, 179, 190
Röntgen, Wilhelm 15
Roosevelt, Franklin: death 194–5; first Presidency 127; New Deal 127, 128, 130; World War Two 162, 170, 171, 173; Yalta Conference 192
Roosevelt, Theodore "Teddy" 15, 44
Rose, Alec 337
Rose, Ralph 33
Rosenberg, Ethel 239
Rosenberg, Julius 239
Rothstein, Arnold 83
Ruby, Jack 307
Ruhr occupation 84, 134
Rushdie, Salman 483
Rusk, Dean 301
Russell, Bertrand 252, 270
Russia: and Balkans 33, 48, 52–3; Bolsheviks 26–7, 68, 69, 72, 94, 95; Boris Yeltsin 494, 505, 509, 536; Chechnya 527; Constituent Assembly 68, 69; coup 505, 509; Duma 27; Mensheviks 26, 68, 69, 94; Provisional Government 68–9, 72, 94–5; revolution (1905) 26–7; revolution (1917) 68–9, 94–5; Russian–Japanese War (1904) 24; Social Revolutionaries 68, 69; Tibet 24–5; and Tsar Nicholas II 24, 26–7, 68, 72; and World War One 52, 53, 55, 68–9; *see also* Soviet Union
Russian–Japanese War (1904) 24
Rwanda 523

S

Sacco, Nicola 106
Sadat, Anwar 374, 409, 433
St. Elijah's Day Uprising 19
St. Petersburg 26
St. Valentine's Day Massacure 110, 123
Saipan 187
Salazar, Antonio 387
Salerno 183
Salk, Jonas 244
San Fransisco 28–9, 134–5
Sandanistas 416–17, 444–5
Sands, Bobby 431
Sanger, Margaret 63
Sarajevo 53
Saudi Arabia 375, 495
Savimbi, Jonas 388–9
Scargill, Arthur 454–5
Scheer, Reinhard 60
Schuschnigg, Kurt von 148
Schwarzkopf, Norman 503
science: Albert Einstein 27, 198, 249;
        atomic physics 125, 198;
        Darwinism 100; genetic 186;
        Marie Curie 20–1; Nobel
        Prize 15, 20–1, 125, 246–7,
        249; penicillin 108–9; Pluto
        116–17; polio vaccine 244;
        radar 138, 161, 165; Thomas
        Alva Edison 41, 46, 122–3
Scopes, John T 100
Scotland: devolution 546–7; Stone of
        Scone 225
Scott, Norman 392–3
Scott, Robert 42–3
sea exploration 284
Searle, Bobby 348
Sebastopol 178
Segovia, Andres 471
Selassie, Haile 118–19, 141, 382–3
Serbia: and Bosnia 510–11; early
        conflict 48; and Hapsburg

Empire 33, 39; Kosovo
558–9; World War One 53,
55; and Yugoslavia 501
Sex Pistols 401
Shanghai 98–9
Sharpeville Massacre 284–5
Shaw, Sir Walter 111
shipping: *Titanic* 45; transatlantic
        rivalry 31
Shipton, Eric 241
Shoda, Michiko 278
Sidi Barrani 162
Simpson O J 525
Simpson, Wallis 143, 232
Singh, Tara 208
Sinn Fein 77, 85, 431, 529, 534
Sirhan, Sirhan 337
Six Day War 328–9, 337
Slovakia 516
Slovenia 506
Smith, Edward J 45
Smith, Ian 318–19, 408–9
Smith, John 513, 524
Smuts, Jan 57
Social Democratic Federation 12
Social Democratic Party 428–9, 443
Social Revolutionaries 68, 69
Solar Temple suicides 526
Solidarity 425, 440–1, 446, 500–1
Solzhenitsyn, Alexander 378
Somalia 515
Somme, Battle of 64–5, 70–1
South Africa: African National
        Congress 285, 309, 404, 466,
        524; Afrikaner Resistance
        Movement 466; apartheid
        105, 143, 466, 492, 521, 524;
        Boer War 16–17; Cecil
        Rhodes 16; Hendrik Verwoerd
        323; Mohandas Gandhi 86,
        210; Nelson Mandela 309,
        492, 521, 524; Sharpeville
        Massacre 284–5; Steve Biko
        404; and World War One 57
South Korea 213, 222–3

South Pole 42–3
Soviet Union: and Afghanistan 419,
        478; Alexander Solzhenitsyn
        378; arms race 217, 251;
        atomic bombs 217; Berlin
        airlift 212; Chernobyl 464–5;
        collapse 508–9; creation 72,
        94–5; Cuban Missile Crisis
        300–1; and Czechoslovakia
        211, 340; Doctors Plot 238;
        and Finland 156; Five Year
        Plans 109; Gary Powers 286;
        and Germany 251, 497;
        glasnost 468; and Hungary
        260–1; and Iran 200; Joseph
        Stalin 98, 109, 238; Kulaks
        116; Leonid Brezhnev 441;
        Marshall Plan 207; Mikhail
        Gorbachev 456; Nikita
        Khrushchev 256, 279;
        perestroika 468; Potsdam
        Agreement 197; rise of Stalin
        98; Sebastopol 178; space
        exploration 268–9, 291, 315;
        Stalingrad 180–1; Vladimir
        Ilyich Lenin 26–7, 68, 69, 72,
        94, 162–3; Warsaw Pact
        248–9; women 177; World
        War Two 152–3, 168–9, 177,
        178, 180–1 *see also* Russia
space exploration 268–9, 291, 315,
        319, 326, 344–5, 353, 367
Space Shuttle 462
Spain: civil war 144–5, 150–1;
        democracy 389
Spanish-American War (1898) 15
Spartacist Uprising 76, 82
Spassky, Boris 371
Speer, Albert 194
sport: boxing 35, 215, 327; car racing
        30, 250; chess 371; Chicago
        White Sox 82–3; cricket 130;
        football 224, 270, 273, 321,
        551; horse racing 124; Le
        Mans 250; Olympics 32–3,

Y

Z

PICTURE CREDITS

The publishers would like to thank the following sources for their kind permission to reproduce the pictures in this book:

AKG London 31b, 133b, 220b, 267t/AP 208b, Tony Vaccaro 101t

Michael Coote 117b

Corbis 22, 23t, 56b, 107t, 169b, 187tr, 212, 245, 282–3, 298b, 311b339b, 344b, 345, 447t, 466b, 470b, 481b, 494, 498b, 515b, 516t, 517b, 532b/Jacques M. Chenet 474b, 532t, Bryn Colton/Assignment Photographers 436, Ric Ergenbright 448t, Kevin Fleming 459t, Owen Franken 463b, 496t, Bill Gentile 444b, Robert Maass 496b, Photo B.D.V. 545t, Reuters 476, 478, 487t, 489, 500t, 503b, 511, 517t, 519, 521t, 524b, 525b, 527, 529, 531t, 542b, Paul Seheult/Eye Ubiquitous 512t, S.I.N. 522b, Joseph Sohm; ChromoSohm Inc. 539t, Peter Turnley 461tr, 467t, 508t, 509b, Miroslav Zajic 504t

Corbis/Bettmann 20t, 26t, 35t, 37, 43br, 49t, 54–55, 59t, 60, 63t, 74, 83t, 86t, 88, 92, 107b, 131b, 133t, 152t, 179t,c, 187b, 220t, 254, 258t, 268t, 269t, 277c, 281b, 307t, 325t, 344t, 350–1, 352t, 435b, 442t, 444t, 464b, 466t, 495, 502b, 504b, 513b, 528t, 533t, 543b, **UPI** 23b, 31t, 75b, 98b, 111t, 112b, 113, 117b, 124, 127t, 131t, 133c, 135b, 145t, 150t, 153b, 154–5, 161tl, 163b, 175b, 179b, 181b, 185b, 186t, 191b, 202t, 208t, 209t, 213t, 221, 222b, 223, 240tl, 241t, 244t, 248, 250b, 253b, 258b, 259, 264, 271b, 273b, 277b, 279b, 280t, 285b, 303b, 307b, 308, 309t, 310, 311t, 312, 313b, 330b, 331t, 335t, 338, 339t, 346t, 348, 349b, 353b, 360b, 365, 371b, 372t, 377t, 384, 385b, 395t, 398t, 399b, 402b, 411, 413t, 414t, 422t, 426, 428t, 430t, 433b, 435t, 438, 446c,b, 453, 459b, 460b, 462, 465t, 467b, 470t, 474t, 475, 477, 482, 487b, 492, 503t,

Mary Evans Picture Library 25b, 29, 46t, 105b, 119t,

Courtesy Ford Motor Company Limited 34

Ronald Grant Archive 46b

Hulton Getty 10–18, 19b, 19c, 20b, 24, 25t, 26b, 27–28, 30, 32, 35b, 36, 38–9, 40–42, 43t, bl, 44–45, 47–48, 49b, 50, 51–53, 56t, 57, 58, 59b, 61, 62t, 63b, 64–73, 75t, 76–82, 83b, 84–85, 86b, 87, 89–91, 93–97, 98t, 99–100, 101b, 102–104, 106, 108–110, 112t, 114–5, 116, 117t, 118, 119b, 120–123, 125, 126, 127b, 128–130, 132, 134, 135, 136b, 137–144, 145b, 146–149, 150c, 151, 152b, 153t, 156–160, 161tr,b, 162, 163t, 164–168, 169t, 170–174, 175t,c, 176–178, 180, 181t, 182–184, 185t, 186b, 187l, 188–190,

191t, 192–201, 202b, 203–207, 209b, 210, 211, 213b, 214–219, 222t, 224–239, 240tr,b, 241b, 242, 243, 244b, 246, 247, 249, 250t, 251, 252, 253t, 255–257, 260–263, 265, 266, 267b, 268b, 269b, 270, 271t, 272, 273t, 274–276, 277t, 278, 280b, 281t, 284, 285t, 286–297, 298t, 299–302, 303t, 304–306, 309b, 313t, 314–324, 325b, 326–329, 330t, 331b, 332–334, 335b, 337, 340–343, 346b, 347, 349t, 352b, 353t, 354–356, 357t, 358, 359, 360t, 361–364, 366–370, 371t, 372b, 373–376, 377b, 378–383, 385t, 386–389, 390b, 391–394, 395b, 396, 397, 398b, 399t, 400, 401, 402t, 403–406, 408–410, 412, 413b, 414b, 415–419, 423–425, 427, 428b, 429, 430b, 431, 432, 433t, 434, 441, 442b, 443b, 446t, 448b, 449–452, 454–458, 460t, 461cl, 463t, 464t, 468t, 469, 471–473, 479t, 480, 481t, 483, 484, 486, 488, 493t, 502t, 505, 506, 507t, 510, 512b, 513t, 514, 520b, 522t, 523, 524t, 525t, 534, 542t, 544, /AFP 336

PA NEWS Ltd. 436b, 437, 440, 490–1, 498t, 499, 507b, 520t, 526, 540b, 553, 556t, 557, 559b, /AFP 537t, AFP/Frederic J. Brown 551t, AFP Photo/CNN 555t, AFP Photo/Orlando Sierra 550, EPA Photo 479b, 518b, 536t, EPA Photo/AFP 554, EPA Photo/AFP/Luke Frazza 555b, EPA Photo/AFP/INA 538b, EPA Photo/AFP/Mark Leffingwell 556b, EPA Photo/AFP/Eduardo Verdugo 541, EPA Photo ANSA/Danilo Schiavella 501t, EPA Photo/Mladen Antonov 559t, EPA/Belga 538t, EPA Photo/DPA/Achim Scheidemann 551b, EPA Photo/Louisa Gouliamaki 558t, EPA Photo/Serbian Television 558b, EPA Photo/Sergei Supinsky/MPC 465b, Fiona Hanson 543t, Jim James 535b, Peter McErlane 546t, John Stillwell 552t

Popperfoto 390t, 439,

Topham Picturepoint 19t, 21t, 33, 62b, 111b, 136t, 279t, 357b, 407, 422b, 443t, 445, 447b, 468b, 493b, 501b, 508b, 515t, 518t, 527t, 528b, 530, 531b, 535t, 536b, 537b, 539b, 540t, 546b, 547–549, 552b, /AP 420–1, 461b, 485,

Every effort has been made to acknowledge correctly and contact the source and/copyright holder of each picture, and Carlton Books Limited apologises for any unintentional errors or omissions which will be corrected in future editions of this book.

Carlton Books Ltd. would like to extend a special thank you to Colin Finlay Lorna Machray, Richard Philpott and Rebecca Wood for their help and co-operation with this project.